STOCHASTIC OPTIMIZATION - SEEING THE OPTIMAL FOR THE UNCERTAIN

Edited by **Ioannis Dritsas**

Stochastic Optimization - Seeing the Optimal for the Uncertain
Edited by Ioannis Dritsas

Published by InTech

Janeza Trdine 9, 51000 Rijeka, Croatia

Publishing Process Manager Ivana Lorkovic

Technical Editor Teodora Smiljanic

Cover Designer InTech Design Team

Additional hard copies can be obtained from orders@intechopen.com

Stochastic Optimization - Seeing the Optimal for the Uncertain, Edited by Ioannis Dritsas
p. cm.
ISBN 978-953-307-829-8

Meet the editor

Ioannis Dritsas completed his PhD at the City University London and is currently a visiting lecturer at the TEI of Chalkida (Greece). Dr Dritsas is also developing applications for mobile operating systems. His research interests include simulation based optimization, computational photonics, and stochastic programming.

Contents

Preface

The field of Stochastic Optimization produces intelligent algorithms that succeed in seeing the optimal for the uncertain. Such methods aim to insightfully search for global optima within probabilistic numerical environments, often highly multidimensional, nonlinear, and noisy.

In the context of stochastic optimization, the term "stochastic" is better described if approached via its classical meaning. From the Greek "stokhastikos" (στοχαστικός), it describes a meditative state of mind targeted to intuitively make sense of uncertain parameters that determine a future outcome. It is even attributed a flavor of a mind sharpening exercise requiring intense and deep thinking, far more perplexing than deterministic thinking.

Modern stochastic optimization algorithms, as a subset of artificial intelligence, strive to incorporate all aspects of optimal stochasticity and have found important applications in diverse fields. Their most pragmatic application is probably when incorporated within simulation based optimization frames. If virtual experiment grade simulations are performed then stochastic optimization algorithms can design spectacularly optimized systems at minimal cost.

Prior to presenting an overview of the material covered by each of the nineteen chapters, I believe it would be practical to present an algorithm and application field mapping of this book.

Firstly the plethora of algorithms presented:

- Genetic algorithm: Chapters 1-5, 15, 18
- Non dominated sorting genetic algorithm: Chapter 5
- Mesh adaptive direct search: Chapter 15
- Enhanced and stochastically perturbed Nelder-Mead method: Chapter 15
- Harmony search: Chapters 18, 19
- Stochastic processes and Monte Carlo instances: Chapters 6-8
- Shuffled complex evolution algorithm: Chapter 17
- Fast Monte Carlo algorithms: Chapter 16
- Artificial chemical process: Chapter 16
- Generalized pattern search: Chapter 15
- Particle swarm: Chapter 3

- Random search technique: Chapter 17
- Tribes: Chapter 3
- Differential evolution: Chapter 3
- Improved harmony search: Chapter 19
- Global harmony search: Chapter 19
- Least squares Monte Carlo: Chapter 6
- Markov chain Monte Carlo: Chapter 7
- Simultaneous perturbation stochastic approximation: Chapter 9
- Particle filtering: Chapter 9
- Integral analysis method: Chapter 10
- Simulated annealing: Chapters 11, 18
- Chance constrained programming: Chapter 13
- Lagrangian relaxation technique: Chapter 14

Secondly the diverse fields of application:

- Physics: Chapter 1
- Optics and photonics: Chapters 2, 15
- Electronics engineering: Chapters 4, 8
- Electrical engineering: Chapters 3, 5
- Investment management: Chapter 6
- Telecommunications: Chapter 7
- Merchandise transportation: Chapter 10
- Medical chemistry / drug discovery: Chapter 11
- Risk management: Chapter 12
- Energy management: Chapter 13
- Project management: Chapter 14
- Chemical kinetics: Chapter 16
- Hydrography: Chapter 17
- Industrial distillation: Chapter 18
- Thermodynamics: Chapter 19

Thirdly the comparative tests made:

- Generalized pattern search -versus- Mesh adaptive direct search -versus- Genetic algorithm -versus- Enhanced and stochastically perturbed Nelder&Mead method: Chapter 15
- Artificial chemical process -versus- Fast Monte Carlo algorithms: Chapter 16
- Random search technique -versus- Shuffled complex evolution algorithm: Chapter 17
- Genetic algorithm -versus- Harmony search -versus- Simulated annealing: Chapter 18
- Standard harmony search -versus- Global harmony search -versus- Improved harmony search: Chapter 19

And lastly a short description of the individual chapters:

- *Chapter 1*: Describes the application of a genetic algorithm in the field of experimental physics. More specifically, a genetic algorithm is placed in the closed loop between computer control and the analyses of ultra cold gases. The target is to optimize the various experimental tasks.

- *Chapter 2:* A genetic algorithm handles the optimization of the construction parameters of a multilayer optical system's theoretical model
- *Chapter 3:* The author summarizes some of his experience in the stochastic optimization of electromagnetic systems. Two algorithms are presented: the "differential evolution algorithm" and the "tribes", a particle swarm algorithm.
- *Chapter 4:* Proposes the optimization of a test pattern generator via a genetic algorithm
- *Chapter 5:* Employs the "non dominated sorting genetic algorithm" to solve a very practical problem: The reduction of noise in electrical machines
- *Chapter 6*: The decomposition and evaluation of real options based on stochastic chronological simulations via the "least square Monte Carlo" method is the essence of this chapter.
- *Chapter 7*: Elaborates on the subject of network tomography and brings forth the "Markov chain Monte Carlo" method to generate link performance parameters.
- *Chapter 8:* Applies a Monte Carlo method to optimize power networks in very large scale integrated circuits.
- *Chapter 9:* Adopts a theoretical view and proposing an adaptive estimation algorithm for non-linear dynamic systems. The effort combines the particle filtering and simultaneous perturbation stochastic approximation techniques.
- *Chapter 10*: Uses the "integral analysis method" to optimally load containers so to minimize wasted space.
- *Chapter 11*: Applies the "simulated annealing method" to the drug discovery field of medical chemistry
- *Chapter 12*: Approaches stochastically the problem of hedging against risks in electricity markets
- *Chapter 13*: Energy management is a crucial topic and this chapter attempts to apply "chance constrained programming" to stochastically optimize the field.
- *Chapter 14*: Develops a simulation based optimization technique based on the "Lagrangian relaxation technique" and applies that in the field of project evaluation.
- *Chapter 15*: Compares several direct search methods and proposes a stochastic simplex search approach in optimizing optical fiber structures. The global optimizers found are the outcome of simulation based optimization at very high dimensions.
- *Chapter 16*: Focuses on chemical kinetic problems and compares the "artificial chemical process method" with the "fast Monte Carlo" algorithm and hybrids.
- *Chapter 17*: Discusses hydrological modeling and compares the "random search technique" with the "shuffled complex evolution algorithm".
- *Chapter 18*: Compares the "genetic algorithm" with the "harmony search" and "simulated annealing" methods applied in the field of industrial distillation.
- *Chapter 19*: Presents a direct comparison of the "standard harmony search", "global harmony search", and "improved harmony search" techniques applied to phase equilibrium modeling for non-reactive systems.

I would like to thank all the authors for their excellent contributions to this book; a truly insightful reading.

Dr. Ioannis Dritsas
City University London
UK

Part 1

Natural Evolution at the Speed of Light

1

Stochastic Optimization of Bose-Einstein Condensation Using a Genetic Algorithm

W. Rohringer, D. Fischer, M. Trupke, J. Schmiedmayer, T. Schumm
Vienna Center for Quantum Science and Technology, Atominstitut,
TU Wien, 1020 Vienna
Austria

1. Introduction

In 1924/25, Satyendranath Bose and Albert Einstein predicted that particles of integer spin (today called bosons) should undergo a quantum statistical phase transition when cooled to temperatures very close to absolute zero (Bose, 1924; Einstein, 1925). This phenomenon, nowadays called Bose-Einstein condensation, has been experimentally observed seventy years later using ultracold (nanokelvin temperatures) gases of bosonic neutral atoms (Anderson et al., 1995; Bradley et al., 1995; Davis et al., 1995c). This spectacular experimental achievement was awarded the Nobel price in 1995 and has triggered a new research direction "ultracold quantum gases" with more than 200 groups worldwide today. [1]
Bose-Einstein condensates (BEC) of ultracold atomic gases represent a fascinating exotic state of matter with properties entirely determined by the laws of quantum mechanics. Although they consisting of several thousands up to millions of atoms, the quantum state can in most cases be described by a single collective wave function with a common quantum phase. This wave function usually has a spatial extent ranging between 1-100 microns, allowing us to observe quantum mechanics essentially by eye using basic magnification optics.
The Bose-Einstein condensate can be described as a coherent matter wave in close analogy to the optical field emitted by (or inside) a laser. This analogy has brought about the field of "quantum-atom-optics" which aims to implement standard elements and experiments known from laser optics using matter waves. As heavy rest mass particles, such as atoms, are very sensitive to gravity or acceleration/rotations, matter-wave interferometers promise orders of magnitude in sensitivity gain compared to their photonic counterparts (Berman, 1996).
Over the last decade, experimental tools for the creation and manipulation of ultracold quantum matter have reached an impressive degree of sophistication. This allows the construction of tailored Hamiltonians for the system and the "quantum simulation" of more general physical situations, not connected to atomic physics alone. Optical lattice potentials allow to mimic solid state physics with a high degree of control over essentially all experimental parameters. Particle interactions can be tuned via Feshbach resonances, allowing the study of superconductivity, superfluidity and the formation of ultracold

[1] (n.d.). see atom traps world wide: http://www.uibk.ac.at/exphys/ultracold/atomtraps.html and links therein.

molecules. One-dimensional and two-dimensional quantum systems have been realized with ultracold gases in constrained geometries. Experiments have also been extended to fermionic atoms which follow completely different quantum statistics at low temperatures and will one day allow to simulate electrons.
The creation of an ultracold gas of atoms is a complex and delicate procedure which involves many steps like laser cooling, conservative atom trapping, evaporative cooling etc. The fundamental steps common to most experimental approaches will briefly be outlined in section 2. Together with the actual experiment to be performed and the detection, a whole experimental sequence takes between several tens of seconds and a few minutes. Some operations within this sequence take place (and have to be timed) on a microsecond timescale, hence a computer based experimental control is inevitable. As the detection of the system is almost always destructive, the experimental cycle has to be repeated many times to accumulate statistics or vary experimental parameters. Complex optimizations or multi-parameter scans can require several days of continuous operation.
In most setups working with ultracold atoms the result of an experiment is an image of the atomic density distribution (see section 2.2 for details). These images are acquired using computer controlled CCD cameras, yielding a graphical file for immediate data processing. With modern computers and efficient algorithms, the analysis of a single result image takes a few seconds, usually much faster than the entire experimental cycle. Hence effectively real-time analysis for various feedback schemes is available, which is the basis for the stochastic optimization methods described herein.
In our work, we close the loop between computer-based experimental control and equally computer-based real-time analysis to automatically optimize various experimental tasks using a genetic algorithm (GA). These tasks range from optimizing specific parts of the experimental sequence for optimal result parameters (atom number, temperature, phase space density) to complex ramp shapes that produce quantum gases in specific external or internal states. To our knowledge, there are very few implementations of stochastic optimization to physical systems. Aside from our experiment (Rohringer et al., 2008; Wilzbach et al., 2009), some examples are the optimization of the temporal shape of laser pulses (Baumert et al., 1997), or the tailoring of pulse shapes to control chemical reactions (Assion et al., 1998).
We wish to underline that none of the methods described here is specific to our experimental setup or physical system. This approach is applicable in a large variety of fields of experimental and industrial research.
The following chapter will start with a brief and general introduction to experiments with ultracold atoms in section 2. In section 3 we describe the implementation and internal structure of the GA. Examples of stochastic optimizations on various levels are given in section 4. For comparison, a brief overview of purely computer-based optimization tasks is given in section 5. In section 6 we close with a summary and outlook on further developments.

2. Experiments with ultracold quantum gases

This section will give a brief introduction to experiments with ultracold atoms. Since the first realization of Bose-Einstein condensation in 1995, experimental techniques have evolved and diversified. We will focus on the major steps which are still common to most approaches and which are necessary to understand the optimizations performed and presented in section 4. For simplicity, we divide an experimental cycle into two main phases: first the preparation of the ultracold gas or Bose-Einstein condensate, which in itself consists of several stages. The second phase concerns the detection of the sample after manipulation, and the acquisition of significant physical quantities. These allow an evaluation of the experiment run and the chosen experimental parameters. This analysis is the starting point for the genetic optimization routines described in sections 3 and 4. For a more comprehensive review on the creation and characterization of ultracold Bose and Fermi gases see (Ketterle et al., 1998) and (Ketterle & Zwierlein, 2008) .

2.1 Preparation of ultracold atomic gases

In the following, we characterize a gas of neutral atoms by its temperature T, and by the corresponding de Broglie wavelength $\lambda_{dB} = (2\pi\hbar^2/mk_BT)^{1/2}$, where m is the mass of the atom and k_B is Boltzmanns constant.
The de Broglie wavelength can be regarded as the size of a quantum mechanical wave function of an individual atom of the gas. It increases as the gas gets colder. The gas density n is related to the average distance d between atoms through $n = d^{-1/3}$. The quantum phase transition to a Bose-Einstein condensate takes place when bosonic atoms are cooled to a point where the atomic wavepackets start to overlap, more precisely at a critical temperature T_c where the phase space density $n\lambda_{dB}^3 \approx 2.612$. This temperature T_c is typically between 100 nK and 1 μK, the atomic density is between 10^{13} cm^{-3} and 10^{14} cm^{-3} (compare figure 1).
The starting point for experiments with ultracold quantum gases is usually a thermally activated source of neutral atoms, providing particles at temperatures around 500 K and densities of 10^8 cm^{-3}. [2] Therefore to reach Bose-Einstein condensation the temperature has to be reduced by 9 orders of magnitude, while the atomic density needs to be increased by up to 6 orders of magnitude. This enourmous cooling power is attained by using a combination of extremely efficient techniques which will be briefly outlined in the following. A schematic trajectory through phase space on the path towards Bose-Einstein condensation is depicted in figure 1.

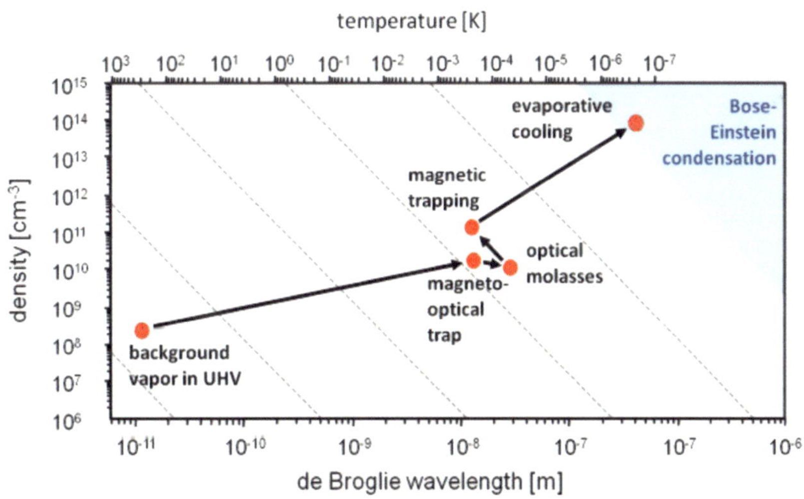

Fig. 1. Schematic representation of a typical trajectory through phase space in a Bose-Einstein condensation experiment. The various steps are explained in the text.

[2] The densities at the starting point of the experiment vary significantly depending on the specific approach, they may reach 10^{14} cm^{-3} in high flux Zeeman slowers.

2.1.1 Laser cooling

Laser cooling and trapping relies on light forces, emerging when a (near-) resonant laser interacts with atomic transitions (see (Metcalf, 1999) for a detailed description). When an atom absorbs a photon of energy $h\nu_{atom}$, its momentum changes by $\hbar k = 2\pi\nu_{atom}/c$ where k is the wave vector of the laser. When (spontaneously) emitting the photon again, the atom momentum changes again by $\hbar k$. While the momentum "kick" in emission is in random direction and averages out over many absorption-emission cycles, the momentum transfer in absorption is directive, pointing in the direction of the laser (light pressure). Hence, on average, one recoil momentum of $2\pi\nu_{atom}/c$ is transferred to the atom per cycle. The interaction with the laser changes the momentum of an atom, which is the action of a "light force". This force is only determined by the frequency ν_{atom} and the scattering rate R of the atom: $F = \dot{p} = \hbar k R$ with

$$R = \frac{\Gamma}{2} \frac{s_0}{1 + s_0 + (2\Delta/\Gamma)^2} \tag{1}$$

where $\Gamma = 1/\tau$ is the transition linewidth, $s_0 = I/I_{sat}$ is the saturation parameter, I_{sat} is the saturation intensity of the atomic transition and $\Delta = \nu_{atom} - \nu_{laser}$ the laser detuning with respect to the atomic transtion frequency ν_{atom}. The maximum light force amounts to $F_{max} = \Gamma\hbar k/2$ on resonance and is hence mainly determined by the linewidth of the used atomic transition. For the 780 nm D2 transition of ^{87}Rubidium used in the experiments presented here, the acceleration of an atom at rest by a resonant laser is $a \approx 10^5\,\mathrm{m/s^2}$, four orders of magnitudes higher than gravity!

Under the influence of the light force, the atom changes its velocity v quickly, giving rise to the Doppler effect. The laser now interacts with an effective detuning $\Delta_{eff} = \Delta + kv$. After a series of absorption-emission cycles, ($\approx$ 800 in the case of ^{87}Rubidium), the effective detuning is so large that no further interaction with the laser takes place. Turning this argument around, choosing the detuning of the laser allows to selectively address a specific velocity class of atoms, making the light force velocity-dependent. If the laser frequency is tuned below the atomic resonance frequency ν_{atom} ("red" detuning), the laser preferably interacts with atoms moving towards the laser, slowing them down. This method is routinely employed to slow down atomic beams coming from a hot thermal source (Metcalf, 1999).

If two counterpropagating laser beams of equal intensity and frequency are used on the atoms, the resulting light force has a dispersion-like shape. Around zero velocity, the force can be approximated to

$$F = \hbar k^2 \frac{8 s_0 \Delta/\Gamma}{(1 + (2\Delta/\Gamma)^2)^2} v. \tag{2}$$

The light force takes the form of a friction or "molasses" force (optical molasses, see below). The cooling strength can be adjusted again by adjusting the detuning Δ. A smaller (red) detuning leads to colder temperatures. However a more narrow velocity class is then addressed by the laser, leading to a lower number of cooled atoms. Therefore a compromise between number and temperature has to be found experimentally. An optimization of laser cooling parameters using a stochastic GA can be found in section 4.

The above description takes place entirely in momentum/velocity space, so far no spatial dependence and hence no trapping is introduced. To render the optical cooling force spatially dependent, the magnetic Zeemann effect is employed. Using a quadrupole magnetic field (e.g. generated by coils in anti-Helmholtz configuration) the atomic transition is shifted, depending on the position. With the right laser detuning (and polarization) and the right quadrupole field

the effective cooling force can be designed so that it points towards zero magnetic field, where the atoms will accumulate. The scheme can easily be extended to three dimensions, realizing a true 3d trapping of neutral atoms in free space.
The combination of optical and magnetic fields to at the same time cool and spatially trap atoms is called magneto-optical-trap (MOT) and has become a standard tool in atomic physics. Its development, together with a thorough theoretical explanation of the relevant effects, led to the award of a Nobel price in 1997 (Chu, 1998; Cohen-Tannoudji, 1998; Phillips, 1998).
A MOT usually catches atoms from the low-velocity tail ($\approx 10\,\mathrm{m/s}$) of the thermal distribution of a background gas at room temperature or from a slowed atomic beam. Typical total atom numbers (^{87}Rubidium) are $10^8 - 10^9$ with a density of $10^{11}\,\mathrm{cm}^{-3}$ and a temperature of $\approx 200\,\mu\mathrm{K}$. This constitutes a significant step towards Bose-Einstein condensation, as illustrated in figure 1. Almost all experiments with ultracold gases start with a phase of magneto-optical trapping.

2.1.2 Optical molasses

As described above, the experimental settings used in a magneto-optical trap are usually optimized for trapping high number of atoms, rather than for obtaining the lowest possible temperatures. Before loading atoms from a MOT into a conservative trapping scheme, a short phase of "optical molasses" (1-100 ms) is employed to further lower the temperature of the gas. Here, the magnetic fields are quickly switched off, extinguishing the spatial trapping. The lasers are adjusted to different detunings (usually significantly further from the atomic resonance) and amplitudes to provide an optimal optical molasses. Atoms hence expand in the laser field, but reduce their kinetic energy (and hence the temperature of the sample, once recaptured in a conservative trap). As the atoms fulfill a damped Brownian motion, they will ultimately diffuse out of the volume that can be captured by a conservative trap. Again a compromise has to be found between temperature (favoring long molasses times) and atom number (favoring short molasses times) to be transferred.
Several different processes contribute to the enhanced cooling in the optical molasses, such as Sisyphus cooling or dark state effects which go beyond the simple model of Doppler cooling described above. For a comprehensive overview see (Metcalf, 1999).

2.1.3 Conservative atom trapping

Even though laser cooling and optical molasses allow an enormous gain in phase space density, there are fundamental limits. As all optical forces rely on absorption and successive emission of photons, the random momentum transfer in spontaneous emission induces a heating mechanism which limits the temperatures that can be achieved. A lower bound, termed the recoil limit, can be obtained by calculating the energy associated with a single photon recoil:

$$E_{recoil} = k_B T_{recoil} = \frac{\hbar^2 k^2}{2m}. \tag{3}$$

For ^{87}Rubidium atoms and the standard 780 nm D2 transition, this corresponds to a temperature of $0.4\,\mu\mathrm{K}$.
Therefore to confine and further cool the gas, another trapping scheme has to be employed which does not rely on photon exchange. Such traps can be constructed using the interaction of an electric[3] or magnetic dipole moment with external electric or magnetic fields. These

[3] Note that most experiments with ultracold atoms are performed with alkali atoms, where the electric dipole moment is only induced in the presence of en external electric field.

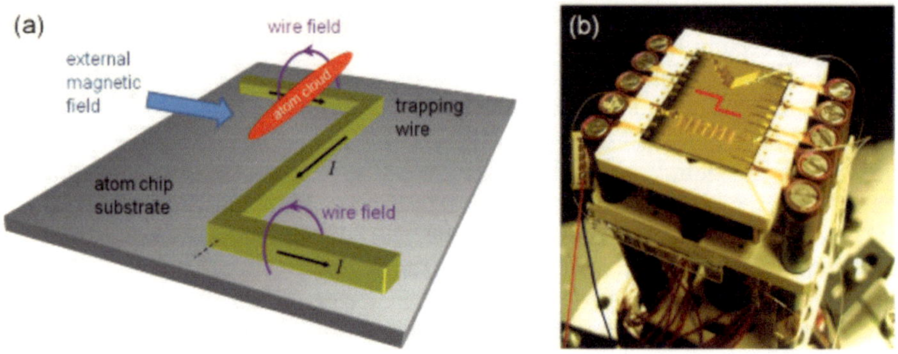

Fig. 2. (a) Schematic representation of a magnetic wire trap. The combination of a homogeneous external magnetic field and the magnetic field of a current carrying wire gives rise to a three-dimensional potential minimum above the wire, that can be used to trap and manipulate neutral atoms. (b) Experimental implementation of a wire trap using an atom chip. The position of the central trapping wire is indicated in red. Optical fibres used for on-chip fluorescence detection can also be seen.

fields give rise to a shift of the internal atomic energy via the Stark or Zeemann effect which acts as an effective potential for the atoms. As the experiments described in the following only employ magnetic interactions, we will concentrate on magnetic trapping. A comprehensive review on optical trapping relying on the electric interaction can be found in (Grimm et al., 2000).

The interaction of an atomic magnetic moment $\vec{\mu}$ with an external, inhomogeneous magnetic field $\vec{B}(\vec{r})$ gives rise to the potential $V(\vec{r}) = -\vec{\mu}\vec{B}(\vec{r})$. Solving the Zeeman Hamiltonian within an adiabatic approximation gives rise to the magnetic quantum numbers m_F and we can write the potential $V(\vec{r}) = m_F g_F \mu_B |B(\vec{r})|$, where g_F is the Landé factor and μ_B the Bohr magneton. For atomic states where $m_F g_F > 0$ atoms are attracted to a spatial minimum of the magnetic field ("low-field seekers") whereas for $m_F g_F < 0$ atoms are attracted to a magnetic field maximum ("high-field seekers")[4]. From Maxwell's equations, one can derive that only a minimum of magnetic field can be created in free space, hence only low-field seekers can be trapped magnetically (Wing, 1984). All experiments described in the following are in the $|F = 2, m_F = 2 >$ state of ^{87}Rubidium, where $g_F = 1/2$.

To give an order of magnitude: a magnetic field of 1 Gauss (10^{-4} Tesla) leads to a potential energy of $k_B \times 67\,\mu$K. As magnetic traps usually work with tens of Gauss, atomic clouds prepared by laser cooling and optical molasses ($\approx 50\,\mu$K) can easily be captured. However, directly catching from room temperature background gas would require hundreds of Tesla.

A plethora of magnetic field configurations has been developed over time to trap atoms and reviewing them here is beyond the scope of this chapter. An overview can be found in (Ketterle et al., 1998). A simple and elegant way to produce magnetic traps with strong spatial confinement are wire traps as used in the experiments described below (Folman et al., 2002; Fortagh & Zimmermann, 2007). In brief, combining the magnetic field of a current carrying wire and homogeneous fields produced by external coils creates a magnetic trap following the geometry of the wire (compare figure 2). Integrating these trapping wires by using techniques from electronic circuit lithography ("atom chips") allows the creation of potential landscapes and provides a high degree of spatial control over the atomic gas, with

[4] Obviously, atoms in the $m_F = 0$ state are insensitive to magnetic fields

high temporal resolution. Bose-Einstein condensation on a chip was first demonstrated in 2001 (Hänsel et al., 2001; Ott et al., 2001; Schneider et al., 2003), and atom chips have since then become a standard tool in ultracold atom research.

2.1.4 Evaporative cooling

Magnetic trapping as described above provides a means to confine neutral atoms of a specific temperature in free space. However, as magnetic (and also electric) potentials are conservative, no cooling takes place. The temperature of the gas can be changed by (adiabatically) changing the atomic confinement, however, phase space density is maintained and hence no progress towards Bose-Einstein condensation can be made.

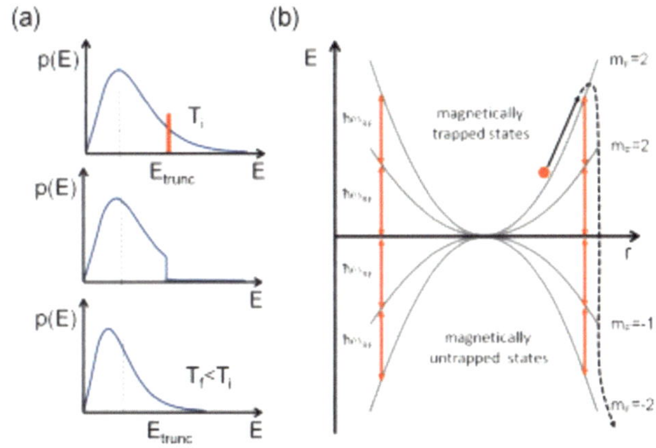

Fig. 3. (a) Principle of evaporative cooling. A thermal Maxwell-Boltzmann distribution characterized by a temperature T_i is truncated at energy E_{trunc} with $E_{trunc} > k_B T_i$. The truncated system relaxes to thermal equilibrium at a lower temperature T_f. (b) Selective removal of hot atoms by adjusting the frequency ω_{RF} driving spin flip transitions to untrapped states.

To gain in phase space density and decrease the gas temperature in a steady trap, an additional cooling mechanism termed "evaporative cooling" is employed. Similar to blowing onto a coffee cup, evaporative cooling relies on the selective removal of energetic (hot) particles. The system successively relaxes back to thermodynamic equilibrium (via particle collisions) at a lower temperature (see figure 3).
To selectively remove hot atoms from the magnetic trap, spin-flip transitions between trapped and untrapped Zeeman states are induced using radio frequency (RF) fields. By choosing the RF-field's frequency, the transitions occur at distinct regions in space (magnetic equipotential surfaces). The "hottest" atoms with highest kinetic energy explore the outwardmost regions of the magnetic trap, so these can be removed selectively ("RF knife"). As the system re-thermalizes at lower temperature, the frequency of the RF field has to be adjusted. This leads to dynamic forced evaporative cooling with time (Davis et al., 1995b; Luiten et al., 1996). As illustrated in figure 1, evaporative cooling allows to reduce the temperature of a gas by another two orders of magnitude and has enabled the creation of Bose-Einstein condensates (Davis et al., 1995a). However, the atom number is reduced by a similar factor. So far, no cooling method able to achieve such low temperatures while maintaining the initial atom number has been found. The details of the evaporative cooling process crucially depend on the details of the experimental implementation, in particular on the lifetime of

the magnetically trapped atoms and the collision and hence re-thermalization rate. The optimization of evaporative cooling using a stochastic GA is described in section 4.

2.2 Detection

Most information in ultracold atom experiments is gained through the interaction of atoms with light. Although several non-optical methods for specific applications or unique atom species (Santos et al., 2002) are in use, optical imaging is currently the main detection method for cold atomic gases. As far as imaging is concerned, atom-light interactions can be divided into three processes: absorption, re-emission and phase alteration of incident light, giving rise to three detection methods, two of which - absorption and fluorescence imaging - are used in our experiment[5]. Both methods result in a picture of the atom cloud, destroying it in the process. Quantities characterizing the state of the cloud can be extracted either from a single picture or from a series of images taken while varying one of the experimental parameters from shot to shot. The following section will describe these quantities and how to measure them. Suitable light sources for excitation of atoms are lasers tunable in the frequency range near an atomic transition, while CCD - cameras are ideal detectors for light (or lack thereof) whenever time resolution is not a critical factor.[6] In order to reach the resolutions needed for the examination of structures like interference fringes or vortices inside cold atomic clouds, it is neccessary to put special emphasis on the imaging optics, which usually has to be custom-built for each experiment.

2.2.1 Absorption imaging

This method consists in recording the shadow which an atom cloud casts onto a detector due to the absorption of a certain fraction of photons when irradiated with laser light. By comparison with the intensity of the beam in absence of the atomic cloud, the atoms' density distribution and a series of other parameters discussed in section 2.2.3 can be calculated. The detection beam can be absorbed almost completely if the density of the atom cloud becomes sufficiently high. These *optically dense* clouds make a quantitative analysis of an absorption image difficult. In order to compensate for this, it is possible to detune the laser light from resonance, lowering the absorption cross-section. The former introduces diffraction as well as a phase shift of the transmitted light, and going to high detunings as well as filtering out the unscattered transmitted light components leads to dispersive imaging. Absorption imaging introduces heating: Since each absorbed photon transfers a momentum $\hbar k$ to the atom, the cloud is literally blown away by the imaging light, making absorption imaging a destructive technique.

2.2.2 Fluorescence imaging

In fluorescence imaging, the atom cloud is also irradiated with a laser beam. However now it is not the transmitted intensity that is measured, but the number of photons scattered into the solid angle Ω covered by the detector. If Ω were equal to 4π, fluorescence imaging would just collect all the photons missing from an absorption picture. However, since the detector usually has a coverage factor $f_c = \frac{\Omega}{4\pi}$ of a few percent, in comparison the fluorescence signal is about a factor 100 weaker. Yet, fluorescence imaging has two advantages: In situations where the

[5] For a review of dispersive imaging methods, see for example (Ketterle et al., 1998) and references therein.

[6] For fast detection, photomultipliers or avalanche photodiodes are required, trading their advantages for lower detection efficiency and, in most cases, lower spatial resolution.

dissipative light force is used to trap the atoms - the MOT and optical molasses phase in our experiment - fluorescence photons come "for free" and allow non-destructive measurements. Additionally, fluorescence imaging has favourable properties for imaging dilute atom clouds. A comparison of the signal to noise ratio (SNR) - neglecting all noise sources except atomic shot noise - for absorption and fluorescence imaging yields:

$$\frac{SNR_f}{SNR_a} = \sqrt{\frac{f_c}{OD}}. \tag{4}$$

Thus, if the cloud's optical density OD drops below the coverage factor, fluorescence imaging becomes better in terms of SNR, at least as long as other noise sources deliver a comparable contribution for both methods. Hence, fluorescence imaging is the preferred technique for detecting extremely dilute clouds. In contrast to absorption imaging, fluorescence detectors need not be exposed to the high light intensities of the source laser illuminating the atoms. As a consequence, highly sensitive detectors like EMCCD cameras and avalanche photodiode - based single photon counting modules can be employed. Several techniques based on fluorescence, like lightsheet imaging (Bücker et al., 2009; Rottmann, 2006) or fiber-based detection methods allow to detect atomic clouds with single atom sensitivity.

2.2.3 Evaluating absorption images

The intensity of a monochromatic light beam travelling in y - direction through an opaque medium is attenuated with

$$\frac{dI}{dy} = -\sigma I n \tag{5}$$

where σ denotes the scattering cross-section and n the density of the atomic cloud. As long as the cross-section is a constant with respect to intensity, i.e. in the case of linear optics defined by low intensities[7], this equation can simply be integrated to yield *Lambert - Beer's law* as result:

$$I = I_0 e^{-\sigma n}. \tag{6}$$

If we allow a density distribution in the (x,z) direction, this gives $I(x,z) = I_0(x,z)e^{-\sigma n_c(x,z)}$, with column density $n_c(x,z) = \int dy\, n(x,y,z)$. The scattering cross-section depends on the detuning Δ, with $\sigma(\Delta) = \sigma_0 / \left(1 + (2\Delta/\Gamma)^2\right)$. The column density can then be expressed as:

$$n_c(x,z) = \sigma(\Delta) \ln\left(\frac{I_0(x,z)}{I_t(x,z)}\right). \tag{7}$$

This measured column density allows to deduce important basic properties of the dilute atomic cloud:

- **Total atom number**
  In the continuous case, the total atom number can be obtained by integrating the column density:

  $$N = \int n_c(x,z)\, dx\, dz. \tag{8}$$

  In the experiment, we have to consider that x and z are discrete, their step size defined by the area A imaged onto a single CCD pixel, with the magnification M. Therefore, for

[7] For high intensities, stimulated emission begins to play a role, leading to an enhanced forward scattering rate

a square region of interest containing p pixels, equation 8 becomes the discrete sum over these pixels:

$$N = A\sum_p n_p(x,y) = \frac{\Delta x_{Pixel}\Delta y_{Pixel}}{M^2}\sum_p n_p(x,y). \tag{9}$$

- **Thermal Atom Density in the Trap**

  In order to derive temperature or temperature-dependent quantities like phase space density, or to gain information about the trapping potential, we need a model which describes the density distribution of the atoms in the trap, as well as its evolution after releasing the cloud from the trap. Since thermal atom clouds and Bose - Einstein condensates represent different thermodynamic phases, where density is closely linked to the phase transition's order parameter, one expects different behaviour in the two regimes. Trapping potentials created by static magnetic fields are harmonic around the field minimum:

$$V(x,y,z) = \frac{m}{2}\left(\omega_x^2 x^2 + \omega_y^2 y^2 + \omega_z^2 z^2\right). \tag{10}$$

  For a thermal cloud of bosons, the density distribution for high temperatures can be expressed as (Ketterle et al., 1998; Reichl, 1998)

$$n(\mathbf{r}) = \left(\frac{2\pi\hbar^2}{mk_BT}\right)^{3/2} g_{3/2}\left(z\left(\mathbf{r}\right)\right) \tag{11}$$

  with $z = e^{(\mu - V(x,y,z))/k_BT}$. Here, $g_j(z) = \sum_i \frac{z^i}{i^j}$ is the *Bose function*, introducing *Bose enhancement*, which means increased density compared to the classical case, where the distribution would be Gaussian. For high temperatures or low densities, we can neglect Bose enhancement, and with the halfwidths $w_i = \sqrt{\frac{2k_BT}{m\omega_i^2}}, i = x,y,z$ and zero chemical potential, we recover a Gaussian distribution:

$$n(x,y,z) = n_0 e^{-\left(\frac{x^2}{w_x^2}+\frac{y^2}{w_y^2}+\frac{z^2}{w_z^2}\right)}. \tag{12}$$

  Experimentally, we only have access to column densities:

$$n_c(x,z) = \int dy\, n(x,y,z) = n_0\sqrt{\pi}w_y e^{-\left(\frac{x^2}{w_x^2}+\frac{z^2}{w_z^2}\right)} = \tilde{n}_0 e^{-\left(\frac{x^2}{w_x^2}+\frac{z^2}{w_z^2}\right)}. \tag{13}$$

  We can determine $\tilde{n}_0$ by normalization with respect to the atom number:

$$N = \int dx\, dz\, n_c(x,z) \Rightarrow \tilde{n}_0 = \frac{N}{\pi w_x w_z}. \tag{14}$$

  By comparison with equation 13 we can calculate the *peak density* of the thermal cloud:

$$n_0 = \frac{\tilde{n}_0}{\sqrt{\pi}w_y}. \tag{15}$$

Equivalently, n_0 can be determined directly from normalization of equation 12. Since the picture is integrated along y, we need an assumption about the density distribution on this axis. Our magnetic traps yield cigar-shaped atom clouds, therefore it usually holds that $w_y = w_z$.

- **Temperature**
  A thermal atom cloud released from a trap by suddenly (non-adiabatically) switching off the trapping potential expands isotropically, the intitial isotropic velocity distribution being conserved. The evolution of the cloud's half-width is given by

$$w_{r_i}(t)^2 = \frac{2k_B T}{m\omega_i^2} + \frac{2k_B T}{m} t^2. \tag{16}$$

  By repeatedly measuring $w_{r_i}^2$ at different times of flight t^2 and plotting the two quantities against each other, the temperature can be determined by the resulting line's slope $\frac{2k_B T^2}{m}$. For $t = 0$, an estimation of the trap frequency in direction r_i is possible.

- **Phase Space Density**
  The important quantity which has to reach a treshold value of 2.612 in order to achieve Bose–Einstein condensation is the phase space density of the atomic cloud:

$$D = n_0\, \lambda_{dB}^3 \tag{17}$$

  comprising the peak density n_0 and the thermal de Broglie wavelength $\lambda_{dB} = \sqrt{\frac{2\pi\hbar^2}{mk_B T}}$.

3. Stochastic optimization in an ultracold atom experiment

3.1 Setup of the feedback loop

The goal of our experiment is the investigation of ultracold ^{87}Rubidium clouds in chip - based magnetic traps, employing all steps involving preparation, manipulation and detection of the atoms described in the previous sections. The focus lies on the application of fiber optics integrated directly on the chip as a tool for the detection of ultracold atoms (Heine et al., 2010).

Figure 4 illustrates our hardware feedback loop. A real-time control system governs the behavior of the experimental apparatus via 30 output channels providing analog control voltage signals, as well as 28 digital TTL channels, with a time resolution of 25 μs. The control channels allow us to manipulate practically all aformentioned experimental quantities, including laser detunings and intensities, magnetic field strengths and radio frequency fields, both in timing and magnitude. User input is collected by an interface software written in MATLAB.

Our absorption images of atomic clouds are taken with a Pixelfly QE interline CCD camera, read out and evaluated by a MATLAB program on a dedicated computer. The algorithm providing feedback between acquisition and control software is also implemented in MATLAB as part of the acquisition software, and communication between acquisition and control hardware is established via a UDP interface provided by MATLAB.

Briefly, our experimental sequence consists of a magneto-optical trap followed by a molasses stage. The atoms are then loaded into a magnetic trap created using a macroscopic wire structure located behind the atom chip, and subsequently cooled using RF-induced evaporation. All data discussed in section 4 was obtained by absorption imaging of atomic clouds released from the magnetic trap at this experimental stage. This point in the sequence is crucial as it determines the atomic phase space density available for experiments using the chip structures, including condensation in the chip trap and transport to the fiber detector.

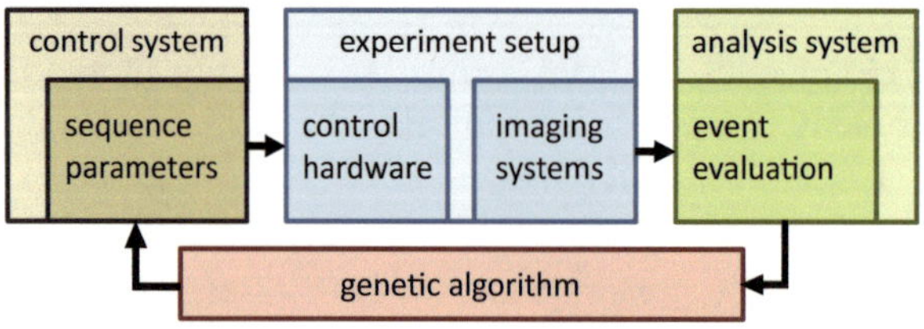

Fig. 4. Scheme of the hardware feedback loop.

In order to perform an experiment, the right set of input parameters for all the devices integrated within the experiment must be found. While for some devices optimal values can be directly calculated or gained through simulations, usually it is only possible to constrain the range of useful values to a certain extent. Within this value range, optimization is necessary. The typical approach is to scan one variable while fixing all others, and repeating this procedure for all variables, in some cases iteratively, until satisfactory conditions for the experiment are met. This is a time consuming task, and inefficient if subsets of these parameters are coupled.

Instead of performing this task manually, we implement an automatic optimization scheme. With the availability of a control system allowing relevant parameters to be set via a program running on a PC, evaluation software capable of automatically acquiring measurements as well as extracting all interesting information and with the possibility of communication between these two programs, the technical requirements for the implementation of an automated optimization scheme directly into a hardware feedback loop are met.

The big number of different optimization problems arising in our setup, depending on the choice of parameters to optimize, makes the implementation of a deterministic algorithm unfeasible. On the other hand, stochastic optimization algorithms have been successfully used in many applications.

3.2 Choice of algorithm

The question can be raised whether it is possible to build an optimal algorithm, outperforming all the others on all possible optimization problems. However, according to a 'No Free Lunch' - theorem for search and optimization (Wolpert & Macready, 1995; 1997) there is no such intrinsically optimal algorithm. This can be expressed as follows:

All algorithms that search for an extremum of an objective function perform exactly the same, when averaged over all possible objective functions. In particular, if algorithm A outperforms algorithm B on some objective functions, then loosely speaking there must exist exactly as many other functions where B outperforms A. (Wolpert & Macready, 1995)

In order to define a performance measure for an algorithm a, let $P(d_m|f,m,a)$ be the conditional probability of obtaining a particular sample d_m by iterating an algorithm a m times on an objective function f. For a finite problem space and a finite space of objective function values, it can be shown (Wolpert & Macready, 1997) that for any two algorithms a_1 and a_2 it applies that

$$\sum_f P(d_m|f,m,a_1) = \sum_f P(d_m|f,m,a_2). \quad (18)$$

Therefore in order to deliver optimal performance, optimization algorithms have to be matched or tailored to specific problems. The main point in this context is the balance between what is called 'exploration versus exploitation'. Any random search mechanisms within an algorithm contribute to exploration, while gradient search - based elements exploit the parameter space structure in order to find the optimum. As a consequence, picking an algorithm and choosing its parameters to fit the problem at hand is as valid an approach as choosing a specific algorithm.

Out of the many different methods available, we choose to implement a real coded genetic algorithm (RCGA). Belonging to the first stochastic optimization methods developed, the convergence behavior of genetic algorithms is well documented for different classes of problem spaces. They belong to the class of global optimization algorithms, exploiting information from different parts of the problem space in parallel as opposed to local algorithms like e.g. stochastic hill climbing or simulated annealing. This property reduces the probability of premature convergence towards local optima. RCGAs allow to define states directly from real valued optimization parameters, without any intermediate encoding, which is simple and intuitive. While early literature suggests that binary encoding is key to the convergence properties of genetic algorithms, more recent studies, backed up by an increasing number of applications, have shown that real coded algorithms suffer from no general disadvantages as compared to other encoding schemes, and even perform better for many applications.

3.3 Implementation

The basic concept of the algorithm, as depicted in figure 5, is the same as applies to the initial canonical genetic algorithm and most subsequent implementations. After generation of a random starting population of states, real valued parameter vectors, the experiment is performed and evaluated for each state with respect to a measured value representing the objective function of the optimization problem. Based on the measurement results, the states are ranked and fitness values are assigned accordingly. The fitness values determine the probability for each state to be selected as a parent for a recombination procedure providing the next generation of states. After recombination, each state undergoes mutation, a stochastic alteration of one of its parameter values, with a preset probability. Subsequently, the next iteration begins by evaluating the resulting parameter vectors by experiment.

The time consuming process in this setup is evaluating the objective function, which means performing the experiment, with a duration of 35 seconds. Even more so than in purely computational applications of GAs, it is crucial to minimize the number of iterations before finding the optimum. Since runtime crucially depends on the number of states within each generation, the population size, the design goal is to keep this number as low as possible while preventing premature convergence due to rapidly decreasing diversity of the states. Simulations, backed up by our experiments, indicate that with proper adjustment of the genetic operators, as described in the next section, a population size of 20 states can ensure reliable convergence behavior for realistic problem spaces.

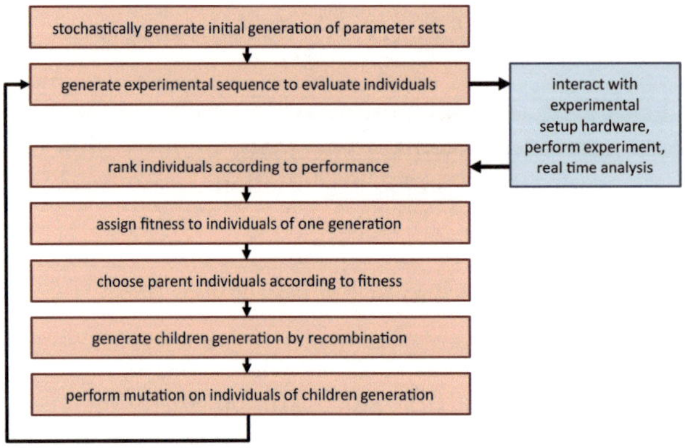

Fig. 5. Basic concept of the genetic algorithm.

3.3.1 Fitness assignment

Most fitness assignment schemes developed for genetic algorithms can be devided into two different classes: ranking based fitness assignment and proportional fitness assignment. The latter class has been shown to suffer from two problems, *premature convergence* and *stagnation* (Herrera et al., 1998; Pohlheim, 1999; Weicker, 2002, 2.Auflage 2007).

Ranking - based fitness assignment (Baker, 1985) avoids the two stated problems by distributing fitness values independently from the actual objective function values. A simple implementation chosen in our algorithm is linear ranking. Here, the sorted population members S_i, $i \in \{1...N_p\}$ are assigned a fitness given by

$$F(S_i) = \frac{2}{N_p}\left(1 - \frac{i-1}{N_p - 1}\right), \tag{19}$$

where N_p is the population size. This redistributes the fitness values linearly between 0 and 1. Several nonlinear ranking methods can be applied to shift recombination probability towards good or bad states.

3.3.2 Selection

Out of several available selection schemes, we chose *Stochastic Universal Sampling* (SUS), a variant of roulette selection. Given that each state has a fitness value $F(S_i)$ between 0 and 1 with a total fitness of 1, one can interprete the total fitness as the area of a roulette wheel devided into N_p sections with area $F(S_i)$. Creating a random number between 0 and 1 and selecting the state occupying the area including the random number is equivalent to spinning a roulette wheel and waiting for the pointer to stop in one of the sections. In this picture, SUS represents a roulette wheel which is spun once with n pointers equally partitioned between 0 and 1. SUS results in zero bias and minimum spread and is a widely used selection method. In order to speed up convergence, the best 20 percent of the parent states are taken over into the next generation, providing an *elitist* selection scheme.

3.3.3 Recombination

Generally, recombination is a genetic operator using two parent states to generate a new state. For binary strings, this means breaking each of the two strings at specific points and creating a new string by concatenating fragments stemming from different parents. The only option to

vary in this case is the number of fragments the parents are broken in, leading to *single-point*, *multi-point* or *uniform* crossover. The latter represents simply an extreme case of multi-point crossover, where the m - bit parent states are decomposed into n fragments.
For RCGAs, the state is represented by a string or vector of real numbers. Translating the idea of crossover to this situation gives what is called **discrete recombination**. One method to implement this is to decide for each vector component v_j of the child state $S_i^C(v_j)$ which parent (P_1 or P_2) contributes the variable value:

$$v_j^C = v_j^{P_1} a_j + v_j^{P_2} \left(1 - a_j\right). \tag{20}$$

Here, a_j is randomly chosen to be 0 or 1 for each v_j^C separately and $j \in \{1, ..., m\}$, where m denotes the total number of variables.
With discrete recombination, only variable values already realized in the starting population can be reached. In order to gain access to new value regions, real number represented states allow interpolation between two values. The most general recombination scheme to be derived this way is **intermediary recombination**. It can be implemented with equation 20, but an a_j picked from the interval $[-d, 1 + d]$ with uniformly distributed probability for each variable separately. This operator is also called BLX - α (*blend crossover*), where α equals $2d$.
The hypercuboid of possible new values has a volume of

$$V_{PS}^C = (1 + 2d) \prod_{j=1}^{m} l_j \tag{21}$$

with l_j as length of the value region spanned by the variables $v_j^{P1,P2}$ and a total of m variables.
For $d = 0$, the hypercuboid containing the possible children values is as big as the one spanned by the parent variables. Since the probability for a child value to lie inside the cuboid is higher than the probability to lie on its bounds, the cuboid volume will decrease with a growing number of iterations in this case, restricting the accessible part of the problem space without any influence of selection. By stretching the children's value space by the factor $(1 + 2d)$ one can compensate for this effect. Empirically, a value of $d = 0.25$ (BLX-0.5) has proven to conserve the cuboid volume in the limit of a large iteration number.
If a_j is not chosen for each variable separately, but rather once in the beginning of the recombination phase and kept the same for all variables, the **linear recombination** can be recovered as special case of intermediary recombination.
Since intermediary recombination with $d = 0.25$ (BLX-0.5) gives optimal convergence behaviour in many computer experiments Herrera et al. (1998); Pohlheim (1999), it has been chosen for our algorithm. Since it delivers real numbers as variable values while our stepsizes imposes a whole number representation, the routine's results are rounded to match the nearest allowed variable value.

3.3.4 Mutation

Mutation in an RGCA means randomly changing values in the state vector. A commonly used mutation routine has been presented in Mühlenbein & Schlierkamp-Voosen (1993) and Mühlenbein & Schlierkamp-Voosen (1995), and can be described as follows:

$$v_j^{mut} = v_j + s_j \cdot rD_j \cdot 2^{-u\kappa_m}. \tag{22}$$

Here, v_j^{mut} and v_j denote the mutated and source states respectively, while s_j randomly chooses the sign of the mutation step, r defines the *mutation range* as fraction of the variable *definition domain* D_j. The last term designates the used distribution characterized by the random number u which is uniformly distributed in the interval $[-1,1]$ and the *mutation precision* κ_m. The latter defines a lower limit of $\frac{1}{2}^{-\kappa_m}$ for the mutation step size. Favoring small mutation steps over big ones, nonuniform mutation operators like this have shown to be advantageous for RCGAs in computer experiments.
From runs on test problems, our algorithm with population sizes between 20 and 30 has given good results with $\kappa_m = 10$, $r = 0.2$ and an overall mutation rate of 10 percent. This is consistent with literature suggesting that optimal mutation rates are inversely proportional to population size Haupt (2000).

4. Examples of stochastic optimization

4.1 Optimization of an optical molasses

The measurement presented here allows a simple comparison of a grid scan to the genetic-algorithm approach. The optical molasses has already been briefly described in section 2.1.2. In this phase, it is possible to reduce the temperature of ^{87}Rubidium atoms from the magneto-optical trap by an order of magnitude to ensure that a large fraction of the cloud has low enough energy to be trapped in a conservative magnetic trapping potential. This phase relies purely on the interaction of atoms with laser light. In our measurement, the optimized quantity is the atom number within the magnetic trap after the molasses phase, and the optimized parameters are molasses duration and laser detuning. Variations in the experimental conditions due for example to environmental noise, lead to a statistical uncertainty in the measured value. We therefore average over multiple experimental runs to reduce this uncertainty. The successful optimization of this experimental stage is shown in figure 6. In the 2d grid scan, we changed the detuning in steps of 5 MHz and the molasses duration in steps of 0.2 ms, and computed the average of 4 atom-number measurements at each pair of values, resulting in a scan duration of approximately 17 hours. For the GA optimization, we used a population size of 20 states and recorded the convergence over 16 generations. In this case, we only averaged over 3 atom number measurements. This optimization approach led to a reduction of the runtime to approximately 9 hours. The set of surviving parameters has already clustered near the optimum after this time, demonstrating the efficiency of the approach.

4.2 Optimization of evaporative cooling in a magnetic trap

The goal of evaporative cooling in a magnetic trap is to increase phase space density (see sections 2.1.4 and 2.2) of the atomic cloud as efficiently as possible. Efficiency means maximizing the amount of removed energy per removed atom. Technically, evaporative cooling as described in 2.1.4 is implemented with the help of an RF source that is tunable in frequency and therefore can create *RF - cooling ramps* by lowering the frequency of the applied field on timescales ranging from milliseconds to seconds. Frequencies from 10 MHz down to the 100 kHz range with sub - kHz stability and corresponding resolution have to be provided. In an ideal system, efficiency grows with ramp duration. The slower the ramp, the more time the system has to stochastically produce atoms with high energy that are removed by the RF field, while fast cooling means removing more atoms with lower energy. In reality, constraints for the steepness of these ramps are imposed mainly by two mechanisms: On the one hand,

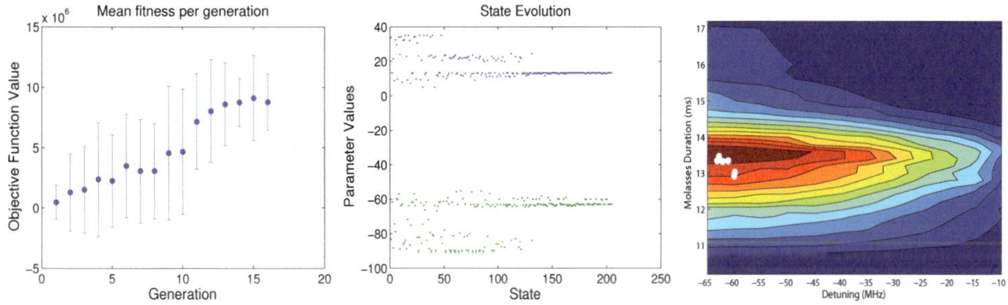

(a) (b) (c)

Fig. 6. Results of the optical molasses optimization. (a) Plot of the mean fitness per generation. (b) State Evolution. Blue points correspond to times given in milliseconds, whereas green points represent laser detunings, in MHz. (c) The plot depicts atom number as a function of duration and laser detuning. The points indicate the set of surviving parameters found by the algorithm.

evaporative cooling competes with different loss or heating mechanisms leading to decreasing phase space density by removal of cold atoms, providing an upper limit for the duration of useful cooling ramps. On the other hand, it is necessary to ensure that the atomic cloud has sufficient time to thermalize by interatomic collisions, which provides a lower bound for ramp duration. The optimum depends critically on technical details and usually has to be found empirically.

We optimize our RF-cooling ramp to yield a maximum in a dimensionless parameter $PSD \propto N^{1/3}/T$, which therefore requires a simultaneous measurement of the atom number N and the cloud temperature T. The temperature is determined from the expansion of the atom cloud as it is released from the trap 2. Ours is a cloud with a normal density distribution in the x-direction, described by

$$n_x \propto Exp\left[-\left(\frac{x}{\sigma_N(x)}\right)^2\right]. \tag{23}$$

Here σ is the $1/e-$radius of the cloud. The temporal evolution of its spatial extent is given by

$$\sigma_N(x,t) = \sqrt{\sigma_N^2(x,0) + (\sigma(v_x) \times t)^2}. \tag{24}$$

The velocity distribution is related to the temperature with $\sigma^2(v_x) = 2k_B\overline{T}_x/m$. The same relationships hold for expansion along the other directions. However, because of the anisotropy of the trap, the initial cloud size as well as the velocity distribution will be different along each axis. The trap shape is near-identical along the x- and z-directions, but rather more elongated along the y-axis. To measure the expansion, we record four absorption images of the cloud at 4, 8, 12 and 16 ms after release from the trap. These two-dimensional images allow us to extract the expansion rate for the x- and $y-$ axes, and give us four measurements of the atom number for a particular set of GA parameters. The fitness of a given parameter set is determined by averaging over the measured temperatures in the x- and $y-$ axes, as well as averaging over the atom numbers from the four images.

The cooling ramp under consideration consists of two linear segments determined by three RF - frequencies and two times (see fig. 7 a). We present two measurements:

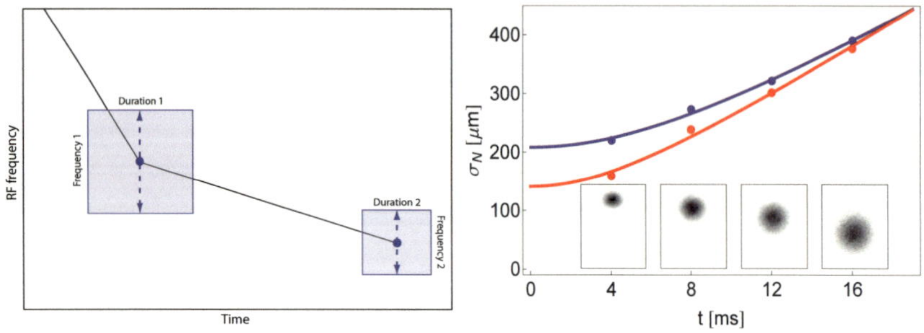

(a) (b)

Fig. 7. Example of data for one population member. a) Schematic of an RF - ramp, depicting the used optimization parameters. Arrows indicate the RF frequencies modified in the 2d - optimization run. In the 4d scan, the cooling ramp was optimized over the rectangular areas spanning duration and frequency of the two stages. b) Fits to equation (24) for the x- and $y-$ axes in red and blue, respectively. The inset panels show absorption images of the atom cloud as it falls and expands after release from the magnetic trap, at the corresponding times. Each panel shows a region of approximately 1.5 mm $\times$ 1.8 mm.

- A **2d** measurement, where the algorithm adjusts the intermediate and final value of the RF frequency. The values ranges from 0 to 10 and 0 to 1 MHz, respectively.
- A **4d** measurement, where the algorithm adjusts both field values from the 2d measurement as well as both times. RF values range from 2 to 6 and 0.3 to 0.6 MHz respectively, in steps of 0.01 MHz. The times for the first and second ramp segment can take values each from 500 to 2000 ms (duration 1) and 500 to 3500 ms (duration 2), in steps of 1 ms.

The results are summarized in figure 8. Unlike the molasses optimization described above, we have not compared this measurement to a grid scan. In the case of the 4d-optimization this is simply not feasible, given that the explored parameter space contains of over 10^{11} individual points corresponding to over 10000 years of experiment runtime. Even by reducing the time resolution to 10 ms as well and changing the frequency steps to 0.05 MHz, the measurement duration remains large, at roughly 50 years. Unless an optimization approach like ours is implemented, only physical arguments and a certain degree of parameter separability can be used to find useful working points for ramp parameters for this and similar problems, leading to a labor-intensive manual search.

For the 2d measurement, the algorithm finds values of 3 MHz and 0.65 MHz for the RF - ramp frequencies. Although we cannot make a quantitative statement about the quality of this solution without knowledge of the parameter space, these values are similar to the cooling ramp values which have been successfully used before GA - optimization as well as the corresponding phase space densities. Note that the algorithm has not fully converged for the intermediate RF value; a competing subpopulation with 2 MHz RF - value is still present in the last generation.

For the 4d measurement, the algorithm also finds an intermediate value of 3 MHz, but a lower end frequency of 0.47 MHz. Objective function values, especially those of the best performing states within the run, are only slightly inferior to those in the last generations of the 2d measurement. It is interesting to see however that performance increases towards the end of the run, at the same time when the competing subpopulation for short times of duration 1

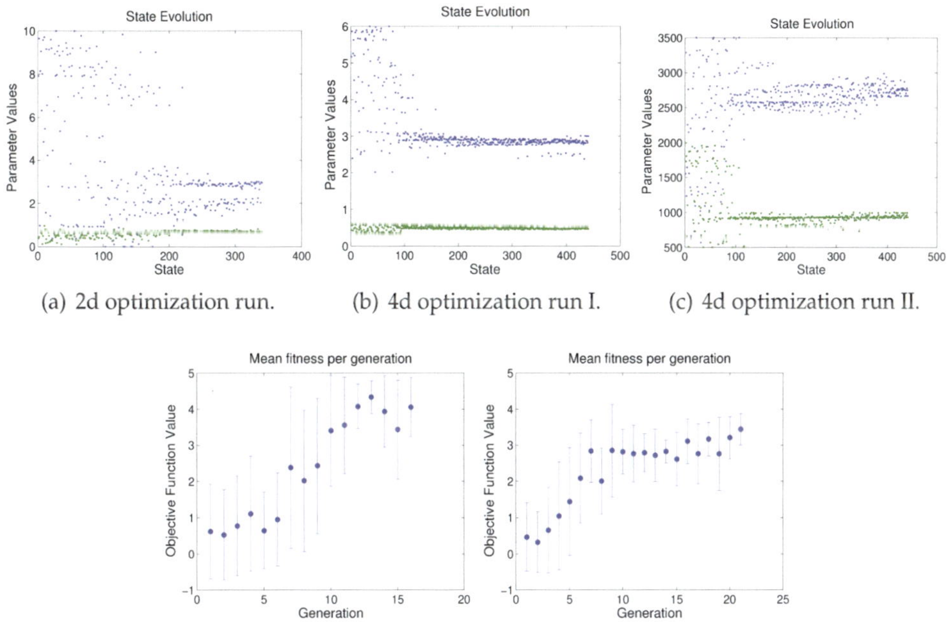

(a) 2d optimization run. (b) 4d optimization run I. (c) 4d optimization run II.

(d) 2d optimization run. (e) 4d optimization run.

Fig. 8. Results of the RF - cooling ramp optimization. The parameters in (a) and (b) are frequencies of the RF field during the ramp, given in MHz. In (c), parameters are times in milliseconds. The parameters represented in (b) and (c) belong to states consisting of two times and two frequencies, but are presented in distinct graphs due to the different unit scales. (e), (f). Mean fitness per generation for the 2d and 4d optimization runs.

(green points) vanishes and duration 2 (blue points) begins to develop a trend towards bigger values. A noteworthy point, however, is that overall ramp duration for these results with 3.7 seconds is significantly shorter than the preset 4.5 seconds, with only marginally worse phase space densities.

In summary the algorithm has found useful working points in both optimization runs, reproducing optimal values found with the help of other experiments in one case, and significantly shortening the cooling ramp with only a small tradeoff in phase space density in the second measurement.

5. Computer experiments

As stated above, algorithm runtime as part of the hardware feedback loop is on the order of a few hours due to the duration of an experimental sequence of 35 seconds. As a consequence, in order to characterize the algorithms performance and for parameter tuning, computer experiments on several test problems have been carried out, with runtimes of seconds to minutes and full knowledge of the parameter space.

The tests go from simple, unimodal problems in two dimensions to complicated, multidimensional functions commonly used as test functions for stochastic optimization problems. In each case, the algorithms task was to find the global maximum or minimum of the respective test function.

Representative for all optimization problems, figure 9 illustrates the algorithm's walk through the parameter space of the 2d Rastrigin function (see section 5.2) through a subset of stages out of a total of 48 generations.

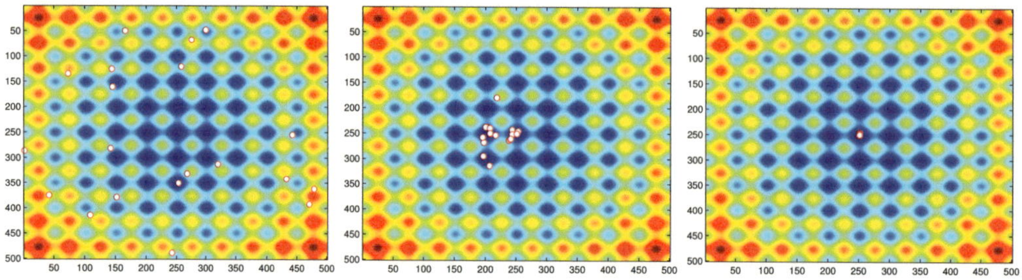

Fig. 9. Population in parameter space in generations 1, 32 and 48.

5.1 Unimodal test functions

A first, very simple function is

$$f(x_i) = \sum_{i=1}^{n} x_i^2 \tag{25}$$

which is known as *De Jong's first function* as benchmark for optimization algorithms. It is continuous, convex and unimodal. As second problem, we used a bivariate normal distribution, creating a peaked structure in an otherwise flat parameter space as depicted in figure 10. This problem is slightly more difficult since the algorithm can find an exploitable gradient only in the vicinity of the optimum.

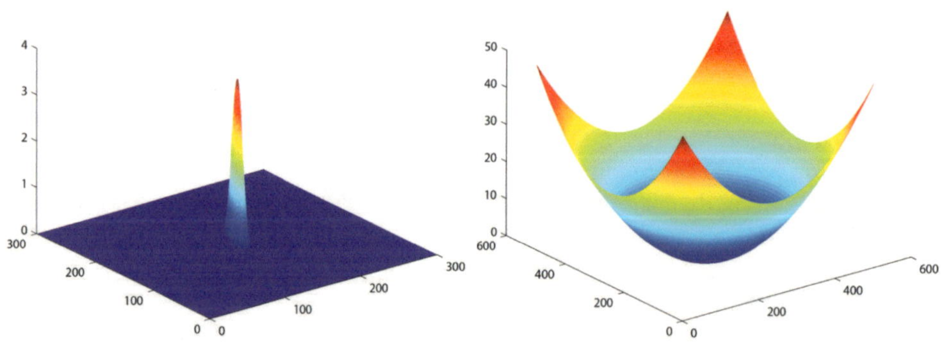

(a) Peaked 2d distribution

(b) De Jong F1 - Function

Fig. 10. 2d representations of the used unimodal test functions.

5.1.1 Results

In this benchmark, the algorithm was supposed to minimize De Jong's function in three and five dimensions as well as the bivariate Gaussian distribution. Each task was repeated 50 times in order to gain statistics about the convergence behavior.

As an example, the first two panels in figure 11 show the properties of one typical optimization run.
In the different fitness graphs, the value of the objective function is plotted as fitness measure. With exception of the bivariate normal distribution, all functions had to be minimized, thus smaller values correspond to better states.

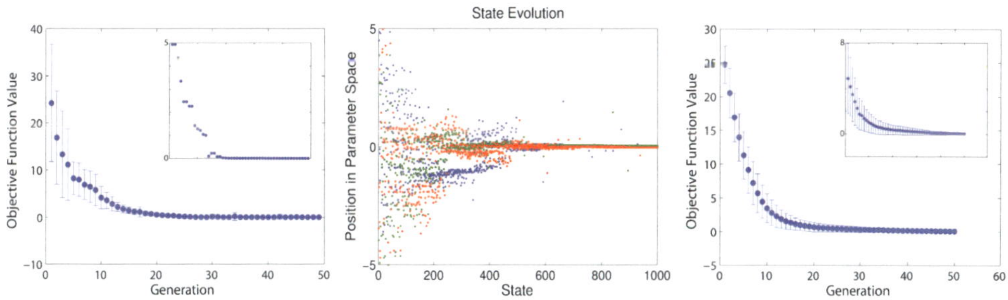

Fig. 11. Results for De Jong's function in three dimensions. Panel 1 contains the mean fitness of each generation within one typical optimization run. Error bars show the standard deviation, corresponding to the spread of different states within the generation, with the fitness of each generation's best state depicted in the inset. The evolution of states is given in Panel 3. Different colors correspond to different variables, i. e. components of the state vectors. Panel 3 contain the fitness of each generation averaged over the total number of 50 runs and the fitness of each generation's best state averaged over the total number of 50 runs in the inset. The spread in expected convergence time is related to the fitness variance expressed through the bars.

The results demonstrate the algorithm's ability to converge towards the global optimum located at the center of the parameter space on a scale of 20 to 30 generations, while finding the optimum takes 10 - 20 generations.
Figure 12 summarizes convergence behavior for the same function, but in 5 dimensions. For the data presented in figure 12 a), the population size was set to 20 states per generation, as opposed to 30 states per generation for b). The additional degrees of freedom cause bigger fitness spreads and hence slower convergence for both settings, although the effect is not as pronounced for the runs with larger population size. The results underline the tradeoff between population size and convergence time in terms of generations one is confronted with in large parameter spaces.
To conclude, the results on the bivariate Gaussian distribution are presented in figure 12 c). For this problem, the algorithm had to find a sharp maximum with an objective function value of 3.5. The peaked structure also represents itself in a fitness spread, since even states close to the minimum achieve a significantly lower objective function value than maximally possible.

5.2 Multimodal test functions

The first multimodal benchmark used is known as *Rastrigin's function*:

$$f(x_i) = 10 \cdot n + \sum_{i=1}^{n} \left[x_i^2 - 10 \cdot cos(2\pi x_i) \right]. \tag{26}$$

Both this form and the 2d representation given in figure 13 show that this is an overall convex function with a sinusoidal modulation, creating a large number of local optima.

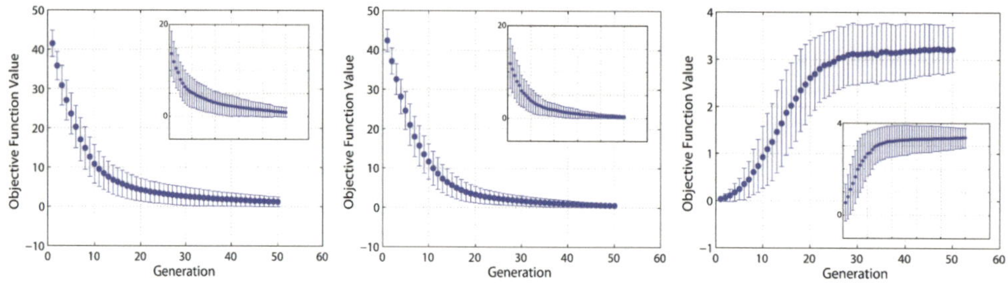

(a) (b) (c)

Fig. 12. Results for De Jong's function in five dimensions. Figures (a) and (b) represent results gained with a population size of 20 states and 30 states respectively. (c) Results for the optimization of a 2d bivariate Gaussian function.

As a second benchmark, we use the function

$$f(x_i) = \sum_{i=1}^{n} \left[-x_i \cdot sin\left(\sqrt{|x_i|}\right) \right], \tag{27}$$

also known as *Schwefel's function*. It does not feature as many local extrema as Rastrigin's function within the search space under consideration, however it is a *deceptive function* in that the global minimum is distant in parameter space from the next best local minima.

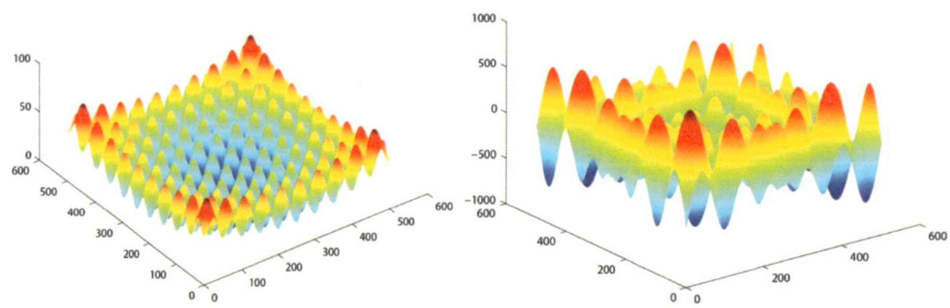

(a) Rastrigin's function (b) Schwefel's F6 function

Fig. 13. 2d representations of the used multimodal test functions.

5.2.1 Results

Results on the 2d and 5d Rastrigin function are summarized in figure 14. While the algorithm can locate the global optimum of this complicated test problem in 2d, for the 5d problem with a population size of 20 states in most of the cases the optimization gets stuck in a local minimum. Raising population size to 50 states shows a clear improvement. Evolution of the fitness per generation as well as each generation's best state's fitness for these cases are shown in figure 14 a, b and c and the insets, respectively.

The last test problem presented here is optimization of Schwefel's function. The global minimum has a function value of $-418 \cdot d$, where d represents the number of dimensions.

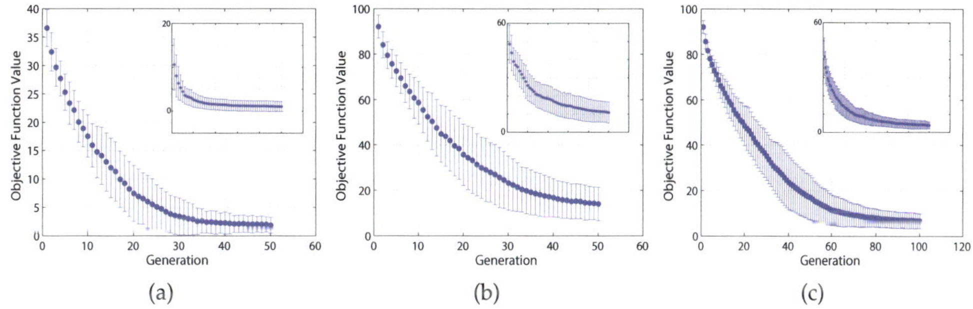

Fig. 14. Convergence behavior for Rastrigin's function (see text).

Similarly to the case of Rastrigin's function, a population of 20 states per generation still locates the global minimum in 60 % of runs for 2d (figure 15 a), while in five dimensions (figure 15 b), the algorithm usually converges towards a local optimum.

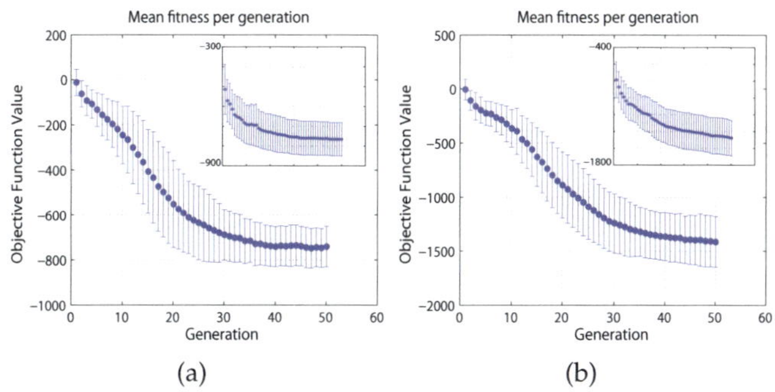

Fig. 15. Evolution of the fitness per generation as well as each generation's best state's fitness in 2d (a), and 5d (b).

In summary, the computer experiments suggest that for moderately complex optimization problems, our simple RCGA can perform optimization tasks even with comparatively small population sizes. In complicated problems with many local optima, bigger population sizes cannot be avoided.

6. Summary and outlook

In this chapter, we have described the implementation of shot-to-shot real-time stochastic optimization of a physics experiment. Our approach is broadly applicable and can be implemented for all computer-controlled parameters of any given physical apparatus. As with most implementations of GA optimization, the approach is particularly useful for multidimensional parameter spaces with multiple local optima and little or no quantitative predictions of their coordinates. This is a situation which arises often in atomic physics as well as in other branches of experimental research, and is usually tackled by making use of intuition, physical arguments and a certain degree of parameter separability to restrict the initial parameter space. This approach often amounts to a human-controlled, semi-stochastic search which is usually time-consuming and has no guarantee of yielding a global optimum.

Using the genetic-algorithm approach, we have seen rapid convergence to optimal parameters in 2- and 4-dimensional parameter spaces, and that the approach is robust even in the presence of local optima and experimental noise. We envisage a number of possible augmentations for future implementations. Among these are the weighting of the fitness of a population member according to its experimental uncertainty, and the inclusion of qualitative physical predictions in some implementations. These predictions can then be progressively quantified with each generation and used to steer mutations to speed up the search convergence. In future implementations, this method may also be extended to perform "optimal experimental control" that automatically finds the best experimental sequence to produce a defined target quantum state. In conclusion, optimization using a genetic algorithm can be an efficient tool to improve the performance of a 'real-life' apparatus.

7. References

(n.d.). see atom traps world wide: http://www.uibk.ac.at/exphys/ultracold/atomtraps.html and links therein.

Anderson, M. H., Ensher, J. R., Matthews, M. R., Wieman, C. E. & Cornell, E. A. (1995). Observation of Bose-Einstein condensation in a dilute atomic vapor, *Science* 269: 198.

Assion, A., Baumert, T., Bergt, M., Brixner, T., Kiefer, B., Seyfried, V., Strehle, M. & Gerber, G. (1998). Control of Chemical Reactions by Feedback-Optimized Phase-Shaped Femtosecond Laser Pulses, *Science* 282(5390): 919–922.
URL: *http://www.sciencemag.org/cgi/content/abstract/282/5390/919*

Baker, J. E. (1985). Adaptive selection methods for genetic algorithms, *Proceedings of the 1st International Conference on Genetic Algorithms*, Lawrence Erlbaum Associates, Inc., Mahwah, NJ, USA, pp. 101–111.

Baumert, T., Brixner, T., Seyfried, V., Strehle, M. & Gerber, G. (1997). Femtosecond pulse shaping by an evolutionary algorithm with feedback, *Applied Physics B: Lasers and Optics* 65: 779–782. 10.1007/s003400050346.
URL: *http://dx.doi.org/10.1007/s003400050346*

Berman, P. R. (1996). *Atom Interferometry*, Academic Press, New York.

Bose, S. N. (1924). Plancks gesetz und lichtquantenhypothese tex, *Z. Phys.* 26: 178.

Bradley, C. C., Sackett, C. A., Tollett, J. J. & Hulet, R. G. (1995). Evidence of Bose-Einstein condensation in an atomic gas with attractive interactions, *Phys. Rev. Lett.* 75: 1687.

Bücker, R., Perrin, A., Manz, S., Betz, T., Koller, C., Plisson, T. , Rottmann, J., Schumm, T. & Schmiedmayer, J. (2009). *Single-particle-sensitive imaging of freely propagating ultracold atoms*, New J. Phys. 11, 103039 (2009).

Chu, S. (1998). The manipulation of neutral particles, *Rev. Mod. Phys.* 70: 685.

Cohen-Tannoudji, C. N. (1998). Manipulating atoms with photons, *Rev. Mod. Phys.* 70: 707.

Davis, K. B., Mewes, M.-O., Andrews, M. R., van Druten, N. J., Durfee, D. S., Kurn, D. M. & Ketterle, W. (1995). Bose einstein condensation in a gas of sodium atoms, *Phys. Rev. Lett.* 75: 3969.

Davis, K. B., Mewes, M.-O., Ioffe, M. A., Andrews, M. R. & Ketterle, W. (1995). Evaporative cooling of sodium atoms, *Phys. Rev. Lett.* 74: 5202.

Davis, K., Mewes, M.-O. & Ketterle, W. (1995). An analytical model for evaporative cooling of atoms, *Appl. Phys. B* 60: 155.

Einstein, A. (1925). Quantentheorie des einatomigen idealen gases. ii, *Sitzungsber. Preuss. Akad. Wiss.* Bericht 1: 3–14.

Folman, R., Krüger, P., Schmiedmayer, J., Denschlag, J. & Henkel, C. (2002). Microscopic atom optics: from wires to an atom chip, *Adv. At. Mol. Opt. Phys.* 48: 263–356.

Fortagh, J. & Zimmermann, C. (2007). Magnetic microtraps for ultracold atoms, *Rev. Mod. Phys.* 79: 235.

Grimm, R., Weidemüller, M. & Ovchinnikov, Y. B. (2000). Optical dipole traps for neutral atoms, *Adv. At. Mol. Opt. Phys.* 42: 95.

Hänsel, W., Hommelhoff, P., Hänsch, T. W. & Reichel, J. (2001). Bose-Einstein condensation on a microelectronic chip, *Nature* 413: 498.

Haupt, R. (2000). Optimum population size and mutation rate for a simple real genetic algorithm that optimizes array factors, *Antennas and Propagation Society International Symposium, 2000. IEEE* 2: 1034–1037 vol.2.

Heine, D., Rohringer, W., Fischer, D., Wilzbach, M., Raub, T., Loziczky, S., Liu, X., Groth, S., Hessmo, B. & Schmiedmayer, J. (2010). A single-atom detector integrated on an atom chip: fabrication, characterization and application, *New Journal of Physics* 12(9): 095005.
URL: *http://stacks.iop.org/1367-2630/12/i=9/a=095005*

Herrera, F., Lozano, M. & Verdegay, J. L. (1998). Tackling real-coded genetic algorithms operators and tools for behavioural analysis, *Artificial Intelligence Review* 12(4): 265–319.
URL: *citeseer.ist.psu.eduherrera98tackling.html*

Ketterle, W., Durfree, D. S. & Stamper-Kurn, D. M. (1998). Making, probing and understanding bose-einstein condensates, Contribution to the proceedings of the 1998 Enrico Fermi summer school on Bose-Einstein condensation in Varenna, Italy, Academic Press, p. 1. and references therein.

Ketterle, W. & Zwierlein, M. W. (2008). Making, probing and understanding ultracold fermi gases, Contribution to the proceedings of the 1998 Enrico Fermi summer school on ultracold Fermi gases condensation in Varenna, Italy, IOS Press, p. 1. and references therein.

Luiten, O. J., Reynolds, M. W. & Walraven, J. T. M. (1996). Kinetic theory of the evaporative cooling of a trapped gas, *Phys. Rev. A* 53: 381.

Metcalf, H. J. (1999). *Laser Cooling and Trapping*, Springer Verlag, Heidelberg Berlin New York.

Mühlenbein, H. & Schlierkamp-Voosen, D. (1993). Predictive models for the breeder genetic algorithm, i.: continuous parameter optimization, *Evol. Comput.* 1(1): 25–49.

Mühlenbein, H. & Schlierkamp-Voosen, D. (1995). Analysis of selection, mutation and recombination in genetic algorithms, *Evolution and Biocomputation, Computational Models of Evolution*, Springer-Verlag, London, UK, pp. 142–168.

Ott, H., Fortagh, J., Schlotterbeck, G., Grossmann, A. & Zimmermann, C. (2001). Bose-Einstein condensation in a surface microtrap, *Phys. Rev. Lett.* 87: 230401.

Phillips, W. D. (1998). Laser cooling and trapping of neutral atoms, *Rev. Mod. Phys.* 70: 721.

Pohlheim, H. (1999). *Evolutionï£¡re Algorithmen: Verfahren, Operatoren und Hinweise fï£¡r die Praxis*, Springer Verlag. ISBN 3-540-66413-0.

Reichl, L. E. (1998). *A Modern Course In Statistical Physics*, John Wiley & Sons.

Rohringer, W., Bücker, R., Manz, S., Betz, T., Koller, C., Göbel, M., Perrin, A., Schmiedmayer, J. & Schumm, T. (2008). Stochastic optimization of a cold atom experiment using a genetic algorithm, *Applied Physics Letters* 93(26): 264101.
URL: *http://link.aip.org/link/?APL/93/264101/1*

Rottmann, J. (2006). *Towards a Single Atom Camera*, Diploma thesis, University of Heidelberg.

Santos, F. P. D., Leonard, J., Wang, J., Barrelet, C., Perales, F., Rasel, E., Unnikrishnan, C., Leduc, M. & Cohen-Tannoudji, C. (2002). Production of a bose einstein condensate of metastable helium atoms, *Eur. Phys. J. D* 19: 103–109.

Schneider, S., Kasper, A., Hagen, C. V., Bartenstein, M., Engeser, B., Schumm, T., Bar-Joseph, I., Folman, R., Feenstra, L. & Schmiedmayer, J. (2003). Bose-Einstein condensation in a simple microtrap, *Phys. Rev. A* 67: 023612.

Weicker, K. (2002, 2.Auflage 2007). *Evolutionï£¡re Algorithmen*, B.G. Teubner Verlag / GWV Fachverlage GmbH.

Wilzbach, M., Heine, D., Groth, S., Liu, X., Raub, T., Hessmo, B. & Schmiedmayer, J. (2009). Simple integrated single-atom detector, *Opt. Lett.* 34(3): 259–261.
URL: *http://ol.osa.org/abstract.cfm?URI=ol-34-3-259*

Wing, W. H. (1984). On neutral particle trapping in quasistatic electromagnetic fields, *Prog. Quant. Electr.* 8: 181.

Wolpert, D. H. & Macready, W. G. (1995). No free lunch theorems for search, *Technical report*, Santa Fe Institute.

Wolpert, D. H. & Macready, W. G. (1997). No free lunch theorems for optimization, *IEEE Transactions on Evolutionary Computation* 1: 67.

2

Theoretical Model of the Physical System: Optimization by the Genetic Algorithm

Stanislav Jurečka
University of Žilina
Slovakia

1. Introduction

Present state in investigation of complicated physical systems is connected in many cases with the numerical analysis of studied phenomena. Equations used for the description of given system are often complicated and have to be modified very often to reach adequate coincidence with observed behaviour of modeled system. Constructed theoretical model contains a lot of assumptions, it tries to describe various influences connected with his own structure as well as with interactions of given system with his environment. In consequence of this model complexity the searching for reliable and comfortable techniques for studying these systems is important. In our approach a theoretical model of physical system is constructed in two steps. Initial estimation of model parameters is performed in graphical user interface and obtained theoretical model is then refined by the genetic algorithm. This enables comfortable realization of changes in theoretical model, implementation of subjective decisions and restrictions as well as controlled refinement of searched model parameters. In this chapter we use this approach for study of optical properties of multilayer system.

2. Optical properties of solids

Detailed knowledge of the optical properties of materials and structures are important for a number of industrial and research applications, especially for optoelectronics, photovoltaics, optical communications, senzorics, laser technology and so on. Optical properties are studied by analysis of light and matter interactions. The phenomena that occur while light propagates through an optical medium can be classified into several groups. The simplest are reflection, propagation and transmission. Some of the light beam incident on an front surface of the medium is reflected, while the rest enters the medium, propagates through it and can reach the back surface of the media. Here it can be reflected again, or it can be transmitted through to the next medium. When a light propagates through the optical medium several other phenomena occur: refraction, luminiscence, scattering and if the intensity of the beam is very high other nonlinear phenomena can occur.
Refraction causes the light waves propagate with a smaller velocity than in free space. Refraction does not affect the intensity of the light wave.
Absorption occurs if the frequency of the light is resonant with the transition frequencies of the atoms in the medium. The light beam is attenuated as it progresses in this case. The

transmission of the medium is therefore related to the absorption, selective absorption is responsible for the colouration of material.

Luminiscence denotes all processes connected to the spontaneous emission of light by excited atoms in a solid state material. It can accompany the propagation of light in an absorbing medium, light is emitted in all directions and contains the different frequencies.

During *scattering* the light changes direction and possibly also its frequency after interacting with the medium. The total number of photons is unchanged but the light is redirected in other directions.

2.1 The complex refractive index

The optical phenomena described above can be quantified by several parameters that determine the properties of the medium at the macroscopic level. The reflection at the surface is described by the reflectivity R and is defined as the ratio of the reflected power to the power incident on the surface. The propagation of the light through the medium is described by the refractive index n, defined as the ratio of the velocity of light in free space to the velocity of light in the medium. The refraction index depends on the frequency of the light. This is called *dispersion*. The absorption of light by an optical medium is described by its *absorption coefficient* α. According to the Beer's law the intensity of light (optical power per unit area) at position z in the propagation direction is given by the equation

$$I(z) = I(0)e^{-\alpha z} \tag{1}$$

The absorption coefficient strongly depends on frequency. The absorption and the refraction can be incorporated into a single quantity called complex refractive index $\tilde{n}$

$$\tilde{n} = n + i\kappa \tag{2}$$

The real part of complex refractive index is refractive index n and the imaginary part κ, called the extinction coefficient, is directly proportional to the absorption coefficient α of the medium

$$\alpha = \frac{4\pi\kappa}{\lambda_0} \tag{3}$$

where λ_0 is the free space wavelength of the light. We can relate the complex refractive index to the complex relative dielectric constant $\tilde{\varepsilon}_r = \varepsilon_1 + i\varepsilon_2$

$$\begin{aligned} n &= \sqrt{\varepsilon_1} \\ \kappa &= \frac{\varepsilon_2}{2n} \end{aligned} \tag{4}$$

The microscopic models usually enable calculation of complex dielectric function. The measurable optical parameters are then determined by converting ε_1 and ε_2 to n and κ. The reflectivity R of given surface depends on both n and κ. Reflectivity between the medium and the vacuum at normal direction is given by

$$R = \left| \frac{\tilde{n} - 1}{\tilde{n} + 1} \right|^2 = \frac{(n-1)^2 + \kappa^2}{(n+1)^2 + \kappa^2}. \tag{5}$$

In a transparent material in the visible region of the spectrum, the absorption coefficient is very small, ε_2 and κ values are neligible. If there is significant absorption, then we need to know both the real and imaginary parts of $\tilde{n}$ and $\tilde{\varepsilon}$.

2.2 Thin film system

Thin film systems are widely used in various branches of applied research and industry. Analytical expressions describing the spectral dependencies of the optical parameters of the thin film have important applications in semiconductor devices development. Such analytical expressions can be used to analyse optical data and extract material parameters. The values of parameters deduced from the optical experiment include the atomic oscillator properties and provide information on composition and microstructure of the sample. To be able to determine the optical properties of the thin film system in a wide spectral region an adequate microstructural and physical model of this system have to be created. Spectral dependencies of the optical quantities depend on the electronic structure and existing bonds and thus provide information useful for the material structure and its properties understanding. A lot of consideration was devoted to the gap and interface states and methods developed for their passivation are studied to increase quality of the thin film systems in the semiconductor devices.

Properties of the amorphous hydrogenated silicon (a-Si:H) samples prepared for the solar cell and TFT applications by various techniques were analysed in our laboratory. The main goals of these studies are the defect states in the thin film structure determination and improvement of the structural, electrical and optical material properties for the device construction. In this chapter a mathematical background and implementation of a new method of the optical properties of the thin film system analysis is presented. Optical properties of the thin film system are determined by computer modeling of the optical transitions connected with the electronic states. The properties of the developed method as well as experimental results obtained by analysis of the experimental spectral reflectance of the a-Si:H samples will be described.

The interaction of photons and matter is explained by quantum electrodynamics. Adequate description of this interaction for the purposes of the optical properties analysis can be also obtained by using the classical theory of electricity and magnetism. The wavelength of light wave λ in material is determined by

$$\lambda = \frac{2}{\sqrt{\mu\varepsilon}\,\omega}, \tag{6}$$

where ω is the angular frequency, μ is the permeability and ε is the permitivity of the material. Both μ and ε depend on the medium properties and therefore the wavelength depends on the material the light is propagating through.

Electron can be considered as harmonic oscillator coupled to a fixed nucleus. The electron - nucleus interaction is modeled by a spring force that implies a harmonic oscillator frequency ω_0. A physical motivation of the spring force model is the coulombic force that binds the electron to the nucleus. There is also a damping force that is proportional to the velocity of the electron movement. The frequency that the electron moves depends on the distance from the nucleus. The distance of the electron from the nucleus is related to the energy of the electron state. The nucleus is assumed to be fixed and motionless and does not interact with photons. Each electron in an atom has a resonating frequency ω_0 that is associated with the energy of the electron state.

The interaction of photon with frequency ω and a single electron with an oscillating frequency ω_0 can be described by Maxwell's equations. The displacement of the electron by the electric field component of the light creates a dipole moment in the atom. The time-dependent dipole moment $\tilde{p}(t)$ created by the movement of the electron is

$$\tilde{p}(t) = \frac{e^2}{m_e\left(\omega_0^2 - \omega^2 - i\gamma_j\omega\right)}\vec{E}_0\, e^{-i\omega t} \tag{7}$$

where m_e is the mass of an electron, e is the charge of an electron, γ_j is a damping factor, and $\vec{E}_0$ is the amplitude of the electric field. In real material electrons may oscillate at one of several different oscillating frequencies that are material specific. If there are N atoms per unit volume, and there is a fraction f_j of the electrons with frequency ω_j and damping factor γ_j, the complex permitivity of material takes the form

$$\tilde{\varepsilon} = \varepsilon_0\left[1 + \frac{Ne^2}{m_e\varepsilon_0}\sum_j \frac{f_j}{\omega_0^2 - \omega^2 - i\gamma_j\omega}\right]. \tag{8}$$

The term f_j is called the oscillator strength. It is the measure of how one electron contributes to the overall response of the material to the incident light wave at given frequency. The electronic structure of a material determines the energies with which the electrons are bound to the nuclei and the bonds with the surrounding atoms. The optical properties of materials in the UV region of the spectrum depend primarily on the core electrons. The bonded valence electrons do not significantly affect the inner electrons. The bonding of the valence electrons to the surrounding atoms does not significantly change the optical constants at energies above 100 eV. In the visible and infrared region the interaction of light depends on the energies of the valence electrons. The bonds of the valence electrons with valence electrons in the neighbor atoms determine the energy of valence electrons in a bulk material. The oscillator properties of the core electrons do not play significant role in this case. In the visible and IR region the optical properties are determined mainly by the states of the valence electrons in bonding orbitals. Important role play also vibrational and rotational movements of molecules. Interaction of incident electromagnetic wave with molecules leads to rotational and vibrational spectra in infrared and microwave regions.

The refractive index and the extinction coefficient are experimentally accessible by reflective and absorptive spectroscopies. Theoretical formulations of the refractive index n and the extinction coefficient κ for the semiconductor materials can be obtained from the energy-dependent dielectric function. *Jellison and Modine* derived the analytical expression for the $\varepsilon_2(E)$ function in the form

$$\varepsilon_2(E) = \frac{AE_0\Gamma E}{E^2 - E_0^2 + \Gamma^2 E^2}\frac{\left(E - E_g\right)^2}{E^2} = L(E)G(E), \tag{9}$$

where A, Γ, E_0 are amplitude, broadening and resonance energy. E_g denotes the semiconductor band gap, E is the photon energy. The function $L(E)$ is a lineshape function and the $G(E)$ function describes $\varepsilon_2(E)$ for $E \approx E_g$. The real part of the dielectric function $\varepsilon_1(E)$ can be expressed by

$$\varepsilon_1(E) = \varepsilon_{1\infty} + K\{\varepsilon_2(E)\} = \varepsilon_{1\infty} + \frac{2}{\pi}\int_0^\infty \frac{s\varepsilon_2(s)ds}{s^2 - E^2} \tag{10}$$

where $\varepsilon_{1\infty}$ accounts for possible high-energy transitions and K is the Kramers-Kronig integral. Within the Jellison-Modine dispersion model the absorption connected with the localized states in the band gap of the semiconductor material is not accounted. The band-to-band transitions are only respected. To obtain better expression for the dielectric function applicable to various types of semiconductors the $G(E)$ function was modified. In the *Urbach-Tauc-Lorentz model* the imaginary part of the dielectric function $\varepsilon_2(E)$ was changed

$$G(E) = \frac{(E - E_g)^2}{E_P^2 + (E - E_g)^2} \tag{11}$$

where $E_P \approx E_g$ is a variable parameter. Function $G(E)$ in this dispersion model improves the theoretical dielectric function values for the photon energies above the band gap. The real part of the dielectric function $\varepsilon_1(E)$ is given by the Kramers-Kronig integral too.
Forouhi and Bloomer derived a formula for the extinction coefficient and the refractive index in the forms

$$n(E) = n_b + \frac{B_0 E + C_0}{E^2 - BE + C} \tag{12}$$

$$\kappa(E) = \frac{A(E - E_g)^2}{E^2 - BE + C} \tag{13}$$

where A, B, B_0, C, C_0 are model parameters. The extinction coefficient in the Forouhi-Bloomer dispersion model does not comply with *f*-sum rules. *f*-sum rules are important constraints for the analysis of optical quantities and involve all absorption processes including valence-band excitations and inner-shell ionizations over the entire energy interval. The Forouhi-Bloomer dispersion model cannot be therefore applied to photon energies above the resonant values.
Typical spectrum of the optical quantity of semiconductor material usually reveals separated peaks due to different absorption processes. For example the spectral dependency of the refractive index of crystalline silicon is in Fig. 1.
Theoretical derivations of the optical parameters dispersion relations assume zero energy breadth in the interband transitions. This assumption leads to the Dirac δ-function dependence of the extinction coefficient on photon energy

$$\kappa(\omega) = \frac{\pi f_0}{4\omega_0}\left[\delta(\omega - \omega_0) - \delta(\omega + \omega_0)\right] \tag{14}$$

where f_0 is the dipole oscillator strength and ω_0 is the transition frequency. The refractive index is given by the Kramers - Kronig integral of $\kappa(\omega)$. In reality, the spontaneous emission produces the damping of excited states in agreement with the Heisenberg relations. To accommodate the damping effect, the $\delta-$ functions can be replaced by the Cauchy functions.

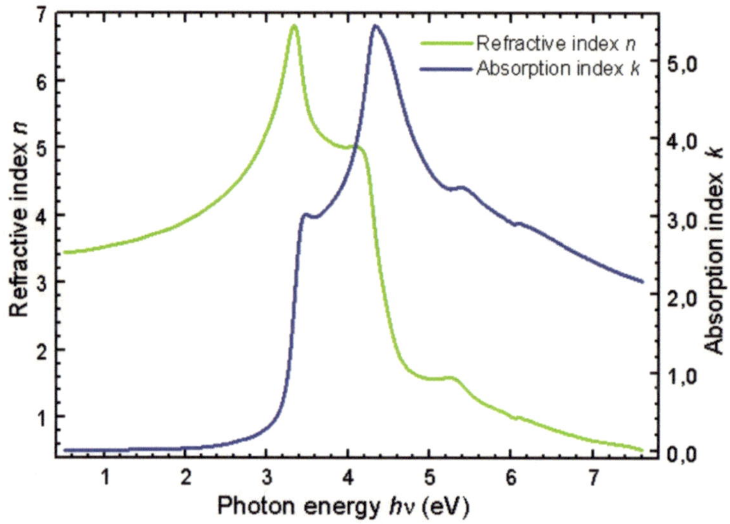

Fig. 1. Refractive index and absorption coefficient of crystalline silicon (www.ioffe.ru).

Theoretical expressions for the refractive index and the extinction coefficient after incorporating the damping effect then take the form

$$\kappa(\omega) = \sum_{i=1}^{s} \frac{f_i \Gamma_i \omega}{\left((\omega - \omega_i)^2 + \Gamma_i^2\right)\left((\omega + \omega_i)^2 + \Gamma_i^2\right)}, \tag{15}$$

$$n(\omega) = n_b - \frac{1}{2}\sum_{i=1}^{s} \frac{f_i \left(\omega^2 - \omega_i^2 - \Gamma_i^2\right)}{\left((\omega - \omega_i)^2 + \Gamma_i^2\right)\left((\omega + \omega_i)^2 + \Gamma_i^2\right)}. \tag{16}$$

In these equations s denotes the total number of transitions from the valence to the conduction bands, n_b is the background refractive index due to the contribution from core electrons in inner shells

$$n_b \approx 1 + \frac{1}{2}\sum_{i=1}^{s} \frac{f_i}{\omega_i^2 + \Gamma_i^2}. \tag{17}$$

The broadening of the spectral line describing the optical transition is in this dispersion model expressed by the Cauchy function (Chen et al., 1993).
A computation of the spectral reflectance for a plane electromagnetic wave incident upon a multilayer structure can be described by Fig. 2. In a case of a finite number of homogeneous and isotropic layers the determination of the theoretical spectral reflectance is efficient for

the experimental reflectance interpretation and enables spectral dependencies of the optical parameters calculations. For the optical field of the layered media calculations the matrix method is usually applied (Abeles, 1950; Lekner, 1987).

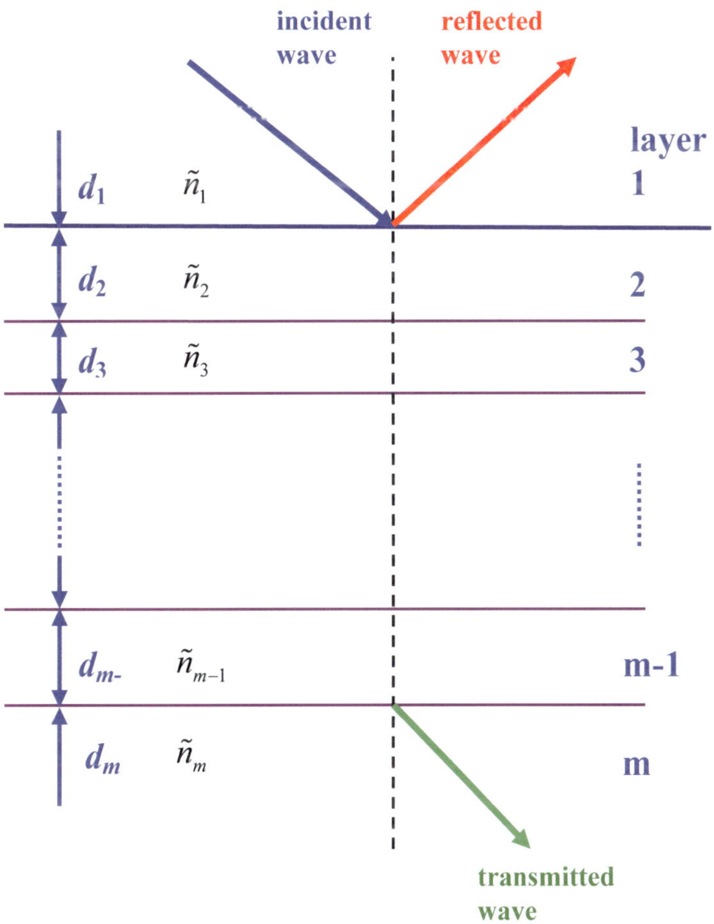

Fig. 2. Waves reflected and transmitted by a multilayer system.

The matrix procedure for calculating the reflectance from multilayers in transverse electric (TE) mode uses convention shown in Fig. 3.
Similar convention is used for the transverse magnetic TM mode. The TE reflection coefficient is given by

$$r_{TE} = \frac{E_R}{E_i} = \frac{(m_{00} + m_{01}p_m)p_1 - (m_{10} + m_{11}p_m)}{(m_{00} + m_{01}p_m)p_1 + (m_{10} + m_{11}p_m)} \tag{18}$$

where m_{xx} are the elements of the matrix M

$$M = \begin{pmatrix} m_{00} & m_{01} \\ m_{10} & m_{11} \end{pmatrix} = \prod_{i=0}^{m-1} M_i \tag{19}$$

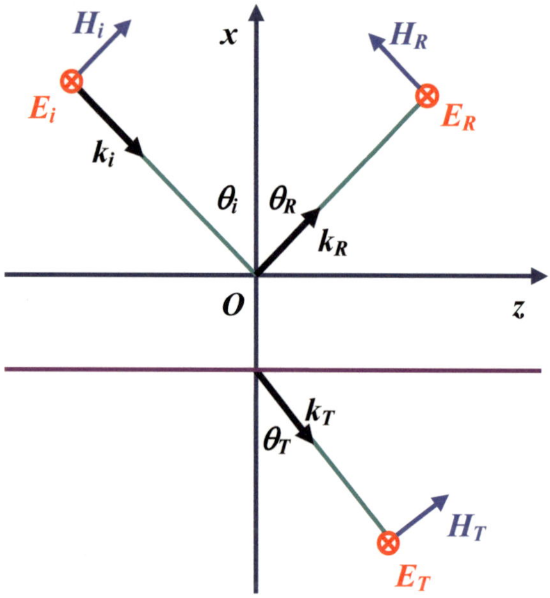

Fig. 3. Description of TE mode. *I-incident wave, R reflected wave, T- transmitted wave.*

where

$$M_k = \begin{pmatrix} \cos\beta_k & -\frac{i}{p_k}\sin\beta_k \\ -i p_k \sin\beta_k & \cos\beta_k \end{pmatrix} \tag{20}$$

$$\beta_k = \frac{2\pi}{\lambda} n_k d_k \sqrt{\mu}\cos\theta_k \tag{21}$$

$$p_k = \begin{cases} \sqrt{\frac{\varepsilon_0}{\mu}}\, n_k \cos\theta_k, & \text{TE mode} \\ \\ \sqrt{\frac{\varepsilon_0}{\mu}}\, n_k \cos\theta_k, & \text{TM mode} \end{cases} \tag{22}$$

and the subscript k denotes the layer number (Hecht, 2002; Born & Wolf, 2002; Furman & Tikhonravov, 1992). The spectral reflectance is then defined by

$$R = |r_{TE}|^2 = r_{TE}\, r_{TE}^* \tag{23}$$

for TE mode or

$$R = |r_{TM}|^2 = r_{TM}\, r_{TM}^* \tag{24}$$

for TM mode. The spectral transmittance can be derived by the similar way.

2.3 The inhomogeneity of the layer material

Optical properties of inhomogeneous material can differ from the homogeneous media. In a multilayer structure we can observe inhomogeneous overlayers or transition layers consisting of the mix of materials of adjacent layers. A powerful way to handle the optical properties of such composite materials is the effective medium approximation (EMA) theory. Three famous EMA models can be jointly expressed by

$$\frac{\langle\varepsilon\rangle - \varepsilon_h}{\langle\varepsilon\rangle + \gamma\varepsilon_h} = \sum_j f_j \frac{\varepsilon_j - \varepsilon_h}{\varepsilon_j + \gamma\varepsilon_h} \tag{25}$$

where $\langle\varepsilon\rangle$ is the permitivity of the effective medium, ε_h is the permitivity of the host medium, ε_j and f_j is the permitivity of the jth constituent and its fraction, and γ is a factor related to the screening and shape of the inclusions (for example, $\gamma = 2$ for 3-dimensional spheres) (Tompkins & Irene, 2005). Within the structure of this equation the three EMA models are:

- Lorentz-Lorentz: $\varepsilon_h = 1$, where the host material is air. This EMA model assumes that the individual constituents are mixed on the atomic scale. Real materials tend to be mixed on a larger scale and therefore this model is of limited usefulness.
- Maxwell-Garnett (MG): $\varepsilon_h = \varepsilon_l$, where the host material is the material that has the largest constituent fraction. MG EMA is the most realistic model when the fraction of inclusions is significantly less than the fraction of host material (Sihvola, 1993; Weiglhofer & Lakhtakia, 2003).
- Bruggemann: $\varepsilon_h = \langle\varepsilon\rangle$, where the host material is just the effective dielectric function. The Bruggemann EMA makes no assumption concerning the material that has the highest constituent fraction. It is very useful when no constituent forms a majority of the material. It can be used for modeling the surface roughness by using a mix of approximately 50% voids and 50% host material.

When applying the EMA model for computation of optical properties one has to pay attention to the limitations of individual EMA model. More sophisticated models take into account the multiple scattering theories, statistical distributions of densities of scatterers as well as the finite-size effects of the scatterers. For most of these expressions the MG EMA is found to be the limiting case as the size of the inclusions goes to zero. The Monte Carlo simulations for configurations that correspond to random defects in periodic composite materials and investigate the role of multiple scattering and the influence of the statistical distribution of scatterers show that the MG EMA model remains accurate also at very high density of scatterers (Mallet et al., 2006).

The complications with the multivalued inversion of a complex functions in the EMA models can be avoided by re-parametrization of Eq. (25) due to (Roussel et al., 1993). The effective value of the permitivity is in this EMA model given by

$$\langle\varepsilon\rangle = z\sqrt{\varepsilon_1\varepsilon_2} \tag{26}$$

where

$$z = b + \sqrt{b^2 + 0.5}$$
$$b = \frac{1}{4}\left[(3f_2 - 1)\left(\frac{1}{p} - p\right) + p\right]. \qquad (27)$$
$$p = \sqrt{\frac{\varepsilon_1}{\varepsilon_2}}$$

2.4 Visual modelling and stochastic optimization (VIMSO) method

Determination of the optical properties of multilayer structure consists, in our approach, of constructing of appropriate structural and physical model and of fitting this model to the experimental data. The theoretical model of the spectral reflectance SR is estimated and refined in steps depicted in Fig. 4.

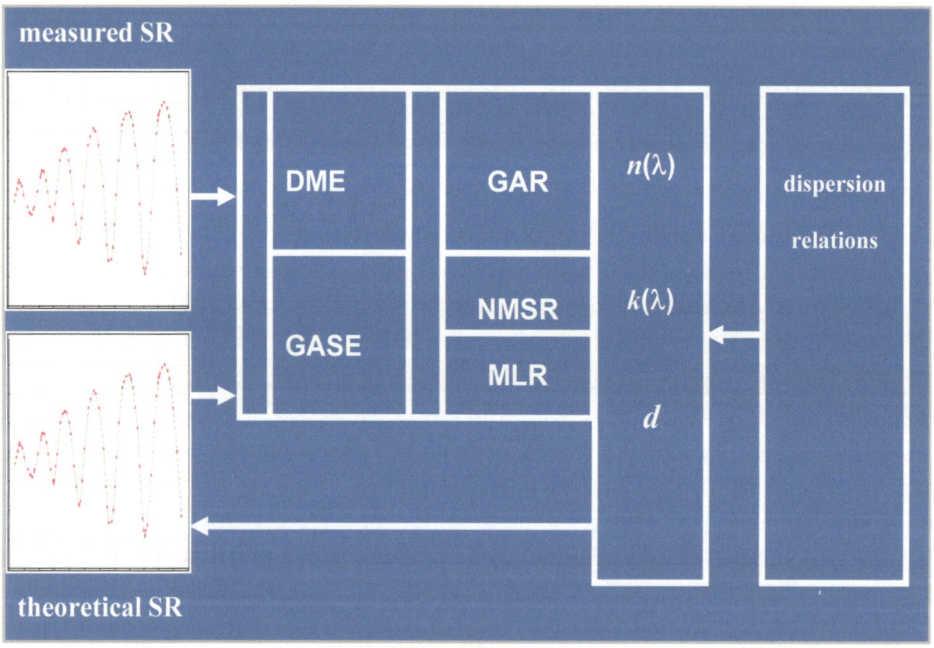

Fig. 4. Construction of theoretical model of spectral reflectance.

In this scheme DME is the visual modeling step used for the dynamic estimation of initial values of the theoretical model parameters, GASE is genetic algorithm search of these initial values, GAR is the genetic algorithm refinement step, NMSR and MLR are Nelder-Mead simplex method and Marquard-Levenberg optimization method used for the refinement of initial estimation. Implementation details of NMSR and MLR methods are not involved in this chapter. In the dispersion relations part the number of layers is fixed, and basic structure concerning the contents of each layer is set - material, thickness and homogeneity model. The dispersion relations describing the spectral behaviour of optical quantities for individual layers are defined. Here existing experimental data sets or suitable parametrization of the dispersion model are used. The last step consists of the optimization process. Here we need to estimate the values of model parameters, estimate the errors and obtain a suitable measure of goodness of fit. Resulting theoretical model describing the spectral reflectance of multilayer structure contains a lot of unknown parameters. We divided the process of determination of the optical properties into two procedures. The first step consists of visual estimation of the structural model, dispersion relations of the optical parameters and the initial estimation of values of constructed theoretical model parameters. In the following step the values of parameters of theoretical model estimated in previous procedure are refined by the genetic algorithm. We used this approach also for solving problems in x-ray diffraction analysis (Jurečka et al., 2004), in analysis of the ion transport processes in glassy electrolytes (Bury et al., 2004) and in other applications. We use an abbreviation VIMSO for this visual modeling and stochastic optimization method.

In order to make this approach to the optical properties determination more comfortable, the graphical user interface (GUI) was built. This GUI contains:

- a table with the structure of layers,
- a list of dispersion models,
- a list of EMA models,
- a list of roughness model,
- a table of fixed parameters,
- a table of values of parameters of the theoretical model,
- a table describing the environment of the GA optimization process,
- control elements for setting the values of parameters of theoretical model,
- graphs with the experimental and theoretical data,
- a goodness of fit value.

GUI layout built in the NetBeans IDE 6.7 (SUN) is in shown Fig. 5.

Fig. 5. GUI for determination of optical properties of multilayer structure.

In the first step of determination of the optical properties of multilayer system a suitable dispersion model is selected in a list of dispersion models. GUI structures with the dispersion models, layer homogeneity and surface roughness models are shown in Fig. 6. By selecting some cell in a column of dispersion models in a table of structure layers (see Fig. 7) the dispersion model selected in a list of dispersion models is assigned to the given layer. The same dispersion model can be assigned to several other layers in the structure.

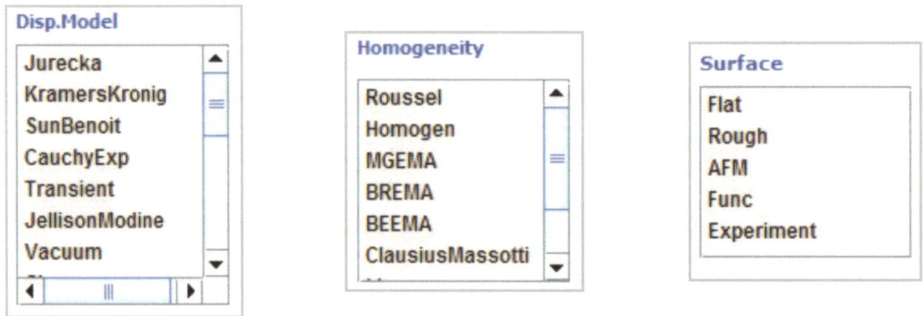

(a) (b) ©

Fig. 6. GUI structures with a) layers dispersion models, b) homogeneity models, c) surface roughness models.

Similar way of the definition of layer structure properties is used for the description of homogeneity and other structure parameters.

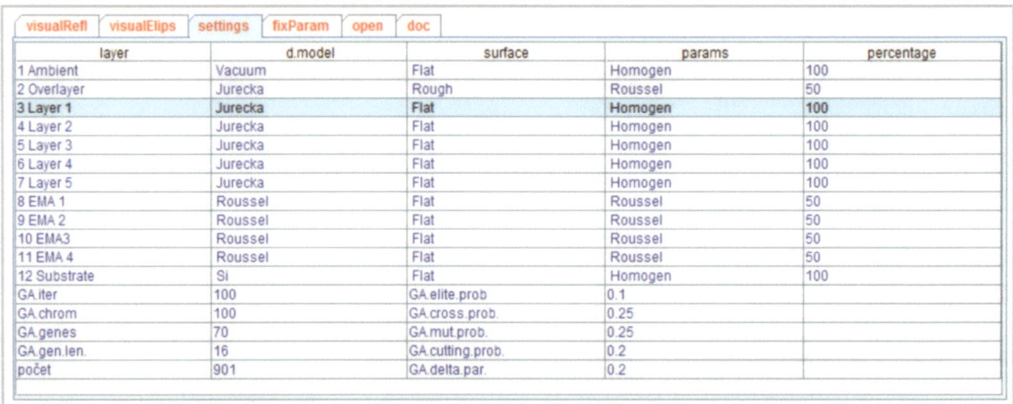

layer	d.model	surface	params	percentage
1 Ambient	Vacuum	Flat	Homogen	100
2 Overlayer	Jurecka	Rough	Roussel	50
3 Layer 1	Jurecka	Flat	Homogen	100
4 Layer 2	Jurecka	Flat	Homogen	100
5 Layer 3	Jurecka	Flat	Homogen	100
6 Layer 4	Jurecka	Flat	Homogen	100
7 Layer 5	Jurecka	Flat	Homogen	100
8 EMA 1	Roussel	Flat	Roussel	50
9 EMA 2	Roussel	Flat	Roussel	50
10 EMA3	Roussel	Flat	Roussel	50
11 EMA 4	Roussel	Flat	Roussel	50
12 Substrate	Si	Flat	Homogen	100
GA.iter	100	GA.elite.prob	0.1	
GA.chrom	100	GA.cross.prob.	0.25	
GA.genes	70	GA.mut.prob.	0.25	
GA.gen.len.	16	GA.cutting.prob.	0.2	
počet	901	GA.delta.par.	0.2	

Fig. 7. GUI structure with a table defining the layer structure.

In this first step the dispersion relations for individual layers are defined. According the selected layer the columns with the variables of corresponding dispersion relation are set in a table of parameters (see Fig. 8).

The value of selected parameter p can be directly written into the table cell or modified by clicking on corresponding cell of the parameters table. Parameter table mouse event listener triggers modification of clicked parameter by adding a value, defined in the control panel. Control panel contains two spinners, spinner_1 and spinner_2. Value added to the modified model parameter p' is computed by equation $p' = \pm spinner\_1(value)E(\pm spinner\_2(value))$.

We can study the influence of chosen theoretical model parameter onto the model behaviour visualRefl | visualElips | settings | fixParam | open | doc

Omega	L.Gama	F	d.nm	Nb	ParamStruct	Disp.CE	Params1	Params2	Params3	x
3.43	1.51	0.6	40	1.33	1.1	5	1	1	0.5	1
3.48	0.71	5.9	500	1.33	1.1	5	1	1	0.5	2
3.72	0.476	7.2	10	1.33	1.1	5	1	1	0.08	3
4.35	0.9	1.5	20	1.33	1.1	5	1	1	0.05	4
4.75	0.88	5.5	30	1.33	1.1	5	1	1	1.8	5
5.75	3.36	21	40	1.33	1.1	5	1	1	0.8	6
6.4	8.9	23	50	1.33	1.1	5	1	1	0.5	7
7.8	25	70	60	1.33	7	5	0.6	0.04	0.5	8
10.6	3.7	70	70	1.33	1.5	5	0.3	1.8	0.08	9
23.55	9.8	0.9	0	1.33	1	5	0.3	0.8	0.05	10

Fig. 8. Table with dispersion model parameters

in a wide range of values very comfortable by this way. Alternatively we can modify selected parameter smoothly by using spinner_3. The value of this spinner defines new correction value by the equation $p'' = spinner\_3 * p'$. Control panel with these spinners is shown in Fig. 5 under the structure settings table. By this way we estimate the composition of multilayer structure and initial values of theoretical model variables. When developing the structure model and estimate the parameter value the theoretical model curve and experimental data are compared graphically at a GUI panel with plots (see Fig. 5). The figure of merit of the instant theoretical model is characterized by the χ^2 value defined by the equation

$$\chi^2 = \frac{1}{N-m-1} \sum_{j=1}^{N} \left[\frac{\left(R_{\exp}(\lambda_j) - R_{theor}(\lambda_j, \vec{p}) \right)}{\sigma(\lambda_j)} \right]^2 \tag{28}$$

where N is the total number of data points, m is the number of model parameters, $R_{\exp}$ is the experimental reflectance, R_{theor} is theoretical spectral reflectance, and σ^2 is the variance of experimental data. The χ^2 value is shown at the control panel after modification of specified model parameter value. The variance limits obtained by an optimization procedure using χ^2 value is related to the actual variance limits of the fitted parameters.

3. GA optimization of theoretical model: chromosomes and fitness function

The optimization of theoretical model is complicated by the variability of suggested structure models and models of suitable dispersion relations. The number of parameters assigned for optimization is determined by the complexity of theoretical model. For optimization of theoretical model constructed and initialised in a visual modeling step of VIMSO method the genetic algorithm (Koza, 1992; Coley, 1999) is very useful. Individual parameters of theoretical model are represented by genes of the chromosome in the GA algorithm. We represented chromosome genes by the binary strings of 16 bits in our first GA implementation. The chromosome was then constructed by a concatenation of these binary strings. The number of binary strings in a chromosome was modified in accordance to proposed theoretical model. Reprogramming of the genetic operators and computation of the chromosome fitness after changing the chromosome length is necessary too. This progress of work is laborious and requires detailed checkout. To make the procedure of the theoretical model estimation more comfortable the program packages designed for implementation of genetic algorithms enabling the object-oriented programming (Hawlitzek, 2000) are suitable. We decided to implement JGAP - a genetic algorithms and genetic programming component provided as a JAVA framework (JGAP). JGAP is designed to be flexible and modular. It is possible to create specific chromosome, genetic operators, random number generator, natural selection and other. To support these possibilities JGAP uses a Configuration object. Setting the Configuration object with all these new definitions prior running the genetic search is the first task. It is necessary to provide three extra pieces of information here: what fitness function will be used, how the Chromosomes are set and how many Chromosomes creates a population. These steps are implemented in void solveGa(.), shown in Listing 1.

Listing 1.

```
//========================================================= solveGA
 public static void solveGa(double[] parametreModelu, double[] wavelengths, double[]
experimentalData, double[] sigma, boolean[] fixedParams) throws Exception
  {
    double[] Rexp = new double[wavelengths.length]; //experimental reflectance Rexp
    double[] tempE = new double[wavelengths.length]; //theoretical reflectance Rtheor
    double[] initParametre = new double[parametreModelu.length]; //model parameters
    double[] thick = new double[10]; //layer thicknesses
    int generations = (int) parametreModelu[60];
    int numchroms = (int) parametreModelu[61];
    double delta = parametreModelu[68];

   //configuration of GA environment:
    Configuration conf = new DefaultConfiguration();

   //elitism:
    conf.setPreservFittestIndividual(true);

   //instantiate & register fitness function:
    FitnessFunction fitnesFunkcia = new modelFitness(parametreModelu, wavelengths,
    experimentalData, sigma, fixedParams);
    conf.setFitnessFunction(fitnesFunkcia);

   //set number of genes:
    int geneCount = (int) fixedParams.length;
    for(int r=0; r<fixedParams.length; r++){
      if (fixedParams[r]) {geneCount--;}
    }
    //genecount = the number of genes, representing released parameters, max
    fixedParams.length
```

```
    //allocate genes:
  Gene[] mGene = new Gene[geneCount];
  int geneIndx = 0;
  for(int r=0; r< parametreModelu.length; r++){
    if (!fixedParams[r]) {
      //use structure DoubleGene(configuration, minBound, maxBound), double precision
      //delta = permitted interval for modification of suggested variable, percent
      try {
                mGene[geneIndx] = new DoubleGene(conf, parametreModelu[r]-
                delta*parametreModelu[r]/100,
                parametreModelu[r]+delta*parametreModelu[r]/100);
                geneIndx++;
      }
      catch (InvalidConfigurationException iex) {
                System.out.println("Invalid configuration: gene creation");}
    }
  }

 //instantiate model Chromosome mChromosome:
  IChromosome mChromosome;
  try {
    mChromosome = new Chromosome(conf, mGene);
   }
  catch (InvalidConfigurationException iex)
   {System.out.println("Invalid configuration: Instantiate mChromosome");}

 //register chromosome structure -> configuration
  try {
   conf.setSampleChromosome(mChromosome);
  }
  catch (InvalidConfigurationException iex)
   {System.out.println("Invalid configuration: register Chromosome");}

 //set number of Chromosomes/population
  try {
   conf.setPopulationSize(numchroms); // user defined
  }
  catch (InvalidConfigurationException iex)
   {System.out.println("Invalid configuration: Population size");}

 //seed zero population:
  Genotype population;
  population = Genotype.randomInitialGenotype(conf);//random seed

 //timing:
  long startTime = System.currentTimeMillis();
```

```
  //run GA process:
  for( int i = 0; i < generations; i++ ) {
    population.evolve();
  }

  long endTime = System.currentTimeMillis();
  System.out.println("\n"+"Total optimization time: " + (endTime - startTime)+ " ms");
  ...
}
```

3.1 Construction of GA chromosome

For the GA optimization process some of defined parameters of theoretical model can be fixed (by selection in a table of fixed parameters) and parameters released for optimization are then assigned to genes of constructed chromosome. In previous listing void solveGA(.) receives information about fixed parameters in boolean[] fixedParams. Then array fixedParams is used for the determination of number of genes and construction of chromosomes:

```
  //set number of genes:
  int geneCount = (int) fixedParams.length;
  for(int r=0; r<fixedParams.length; r++){
    if (fixedParams[r]) {geneCount--;}
  }
  //genecount = the number of genes, representing released parameters, max
fixedParams.length

  //allocate genes:
  Gene[] mGene = new Gene[geneCount];
  int geneIndx = 0;
  for(int r=0; r< parametreModelu.length; r++){
    if (!fixedParams[r]) {
     //use structure DoubleGene(configuration, minBound, maxBound), double precision
     //delta = permitted interval for modification of suggested variable, percent
     try {
              mGene[geneIndx] = new DoubleGene(conf, parametreModelu[r]-
              delta*parametreModelu[r]/100,
              parametreModelu[r]+delta*parametreModelu[r]/100);
              geneIndx++;
     }
     ...
```

In this definition a genes of chromosome are defined as double precision data type and are created only for parameters released for GA optimization. The size of the chromosome is therefore defined according to the number of released parameters. Parameter of theoretical model parametreModelu[r] represented by given gene is used also for determination of bound interval (minBound, maxBound) defining the interval of acceptable change of parametreModelu[r] value. We use special parameter *delta* defined in range (0,100) for determination of the bound interval as percentage of the parametreModelu[r] value. Value delta is taken from an array parametreModelu[68]. User defined parameters for the GA optimization are taken from parametreModelu[60] (number of evolution steps) and parametreModelu[61] (number of chromosomes in a population). Information about inserting of the fittest chromosome into new population (elitism) is provided to the JGAP Configuration object by conf.setPreservFittestIndividual(true) statement.

3.2 Computation of fitness

The name of the fitness function (*fitnesFunkcia*) is provided to the Configuration object in a statement conf.setFitnessFunction(fitnesFunkcia). In our JGAP implementation fitnesFunkcia is defined in a public class *modelFitness.java*. This class extends FitnessFunction class of JGAP. From given chromosome it reconstructs (in public double evaluate(.)) the values of parameters coded in genes of proposed chromosome and calls getActualFitness(.). This is illustrated in Listing 2.

Listing 2.

```
public double evaluate(IChromosome chromParametre, double[] parametre, double[]
wavelength, double[] experimentalData, double[] sigma, boolean[] fixedParams){

    for(int r=0; r<this.fixedParams.length; r++){
      if (!this.fixedParams[r])
      {this.parametre[r]=((Double)
chromParametre.getGene(g).getAllele()).doubleValue();}
      }
fitnessE=getActualFitness(

this.parametre,this.wavelength,this.experimentalData,this.sigma,this.fixedParams);

return fitnessE;
}
```

Public double getActualFitness(this.parametre, this.wavelength, this.experimentalData, this.sigma, this.fixedParams) receives in *this.parametre* a set of parameters for reconstruction of theoretical model of spectral reflectance. These values are proposed by the GA for testing of improvement of theoretical model. In getActualFitness(.) the value of proposed model fitness is computed by using Eq. (28), with passed experimental spectral reflectance in *experimentalData* at wavelengths passed in *wavelength* with dispersion *sigma*.

4. VIMSO method application: study of optical properties of amorphous silicon thin films

Undoped amorphous silicon thin films passivated by hydrogen are important for the applications in photovoltaics and optoelectronics. Plasma-enhanced chemical vapour deposition (PECVD) and hot-wire assisted chemical vapour deposition are techniques often used to deposit amorphous silicon thin films (a-Si). Amorphous a-Si thin films suffer from light-induced metastability of the microscopic origin. In optical applications based on hydrogenated amorphous silicon, control of the optical properties is crucial to obtain well functioning devices.

Thin films deposited from hydrogen diluted silane plasma (a-Si:H) have improved stability against prolonged light soaking when compared with films deposited from pure silane (SiH_4). Hydrogen plays a central role in modifying the electrical and optical properties of amorphous Si for the photovoltaic and optical sensor applications. It is important to have a-Si:H with high optical absorption and with high content of hydrogen in the material to get sufficient electrical quality. The introduction of hydrogen modifies the silicon layer structure by changes in short and intermediate-range order (network bond-length and angle distributions). The presence of Si-H bonds also results in the creation of new states in the electron and phonon densities of states and in modifications of densities of electronic and vibrational states of Si. We have examined a series of a-Si:H films grown under varying PECVD deposition conditions with different hydrogen dilution, the film thickness or the substrate material. Material properties are strongly dependent on the deposition conditions and therefore a systematic investigation of sample properties connected with these deposition and passivation procedures is necessary. In this part we shall describe results, obtained by implementation of VIMSO method for determination of optical properties of the a-Si:H thin films deposited on glass from hydrogen diluted silane plasma.

4.1 Experiment

Hydrogenated amorphous silicon (a-Si:H) films have been deposited under a wide range of deposition conditions on a Corning 1737 glass substrates by 13.5 MHz rf excited parallel plate PECVD deposition system (Müllerová, 2005). The rf power was 13.5 W, the substrate temperature 194 °C and the total chamber pressure 200 Pa. The samples were deposited from the hydrogen (H_2) diluted silane (SiH_4) plasma under varied H_2/SiH_4 gas flows (the dilution D). The sample series deposited under varying dilution is described in a Table 1. All the samples were prepared with approximately the same thickness (~ 400 nm) to avoid the film thickness influence on the sample properties.

sample	dilution D	thickness [nm]	rms roughness [nm]
s1	0	390	-
s2	10	394	0.756
s3	20	385	1.013
s4	30	388	3.629
s5	40	402	5.476
s6	50	397	5.021

Table 1. Samples under study.

UV-VIS spectral reflectance measurements were performed with Pye Unicam/Philips PU 8800 spectrophotometer in the single beam mode with 2 nm slit at nearly normal incidence and at room temperature. The spectral region was set to (300 – 800) nm The probed sample areas were ~ 0.2 cm^2. A freshly evaporated aluminium sample was used for the reference reflectance data collection. Surface roughness was measured by the atomic force microscope NT - MDT SPM Solver P7 LS operating in the contact repulsive mode using a silicon tip cantilever. The lateral resolution of AFM measurements was ~ (1 – 2) nm, the vertical resolution 0.01 nm. Standard rms roughness values were determined from the measured surface height function at area (2 x 2) μm^2 . Experimental spectral reflectances of a-Si:H thin films are shown in Fig. 9.

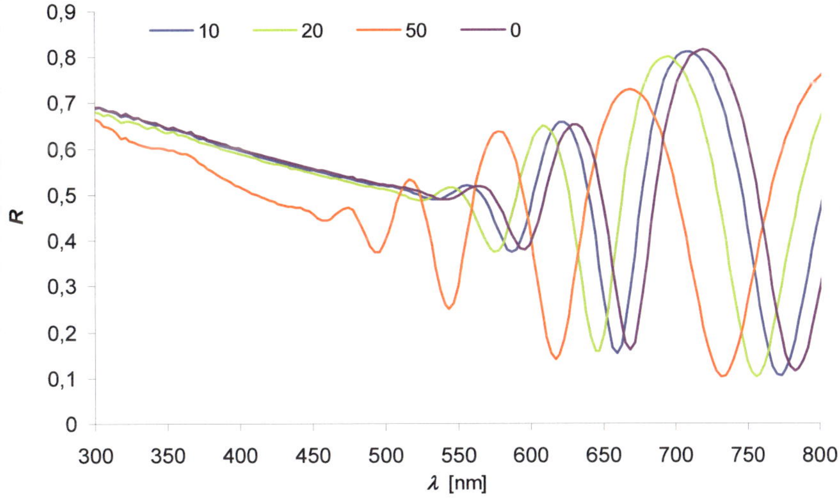

Fig. 9. Experimental spectral reflectances *R* of a-Si:H thin films prepared with hydrogen dilution D = 0, 10, 20, 50.

4.2 Theoretical model of a-Si:H thin film reflectance

The VIMSO method is based on two step optimization procedure, used for the construction and refinement of theoretical model of the spectral reflectance or trasmittance of the analysed structure. In the first step the microstructural model of the layered system is constructed in graphical interface. Here the materials, thickness and homogeneity of individual layers are defined and the initial estimation of theoretical model variables is obtained. In our approach a set of dispersion relations commonly used for the determination of optical properties of semiconductor and dielectric materials is implemented. The values of the theoretical model variables are modified interactively and temporary defined theoretical model is graphically compared to the experimental data. Simultaneously the numerical value of the χ^2 value defined by Eq.(28) is used as a goodness of fit measure. Proposed structural model describing the optical and structural properties of investigated samples is shown in Fig. 10. It consists of the overlayer, a-Si:H and transition layer on a glass substrate.

In the following step the values of theoretical model parameters are numerically refined by the genetic algorithm. In our implementation the environment for the GA optimization is interactively modified (the probabilities of the genetic operators, number of chromosomes in population, number of populations, maximal interval for changing selected value, and other). It is possible to fix some selected parameters and not allow the GA to change these fixed values. This enables avoiding the influence of the mutual correlation of theoretical model variables onto the convergence properties of the optimization process and

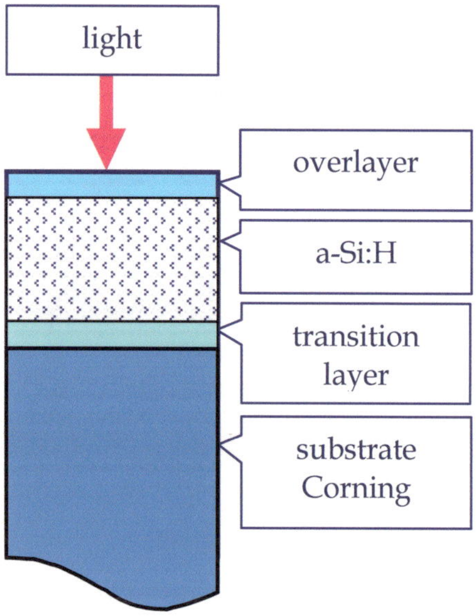

Fig. 10. Structural model proposed for analysis of optical properties of a-Si:H thin films.

implementation of the subjective decisions concerning the importance of individual variables for the problem solution. This combination of visual modeling followed by the stochastic optimization of theoretical model speeds up the solution of the structure theoretical model. The set of possible dispersion relations contains analytical models, derived by the quantum theory of interaction of light and matter as well as phenomenological equations and experimentally obtained data were implemented.

For the description of the spectral dependency of the refractive index n and the extinction coefficient κ of amorphous a-Si:H layer we proposed a simple polynomial model

$$n(\lambda)=\sum_{i=0}^{6}a_i\lambda^i,\ \kappa(\lambda)=\sum_{j=0}^{6}b_j\lambda^j,\ a_i,b_j\in R. \tag{29}$$

The optical properties of overlayer and transition layer are described by a Bruggeman model of the effective media approximation with the fraction f of the embedded phase

$$f\frac{\varepsilon_1-\varepsilon_{eff}}{\varepsilon_1+2\varepsilon_{eff}}+(1-f)\frac{\varepsilon_2-\varepsilon_{eff}}{\varepsilon_2+2\varepsilon_{eff}}=0, \tag{30}$$

where $\varepsilon_1,\varepsilon_2,\varepsilon_{eff}$ are permitivities of the embedded phase, of a matrix material and resulting effective permitivity of the a-Si:H layer respectively. The overlayer is used to account for the natural oxide layer influence and the transition layer describes local changes of the optical properties at the a-Si:H/glass substrate interface. The ambient is air and the substrate is Corning 1737 glass. Theoretical spectral reflectance R_{theor} of proposed structural model is computed from multilayer reflection coefficients by equation Eq.(23-24).

The theoretical spectral reflectance of the whole structure is corrected for the surface roughness by the equation

$$R_{corr}(\lambda) = R_{theor}(\lambda)\frac{c_1}{1+\frac{c_2}{\lambda}}, \tag{31}$$

where c_1 and c_2 are real constants. Theoretical model of spectral reflectance $R_{corr}(\lambda)$ contains in this approach 20 unknown parameters: $a_0,\ldots,a_6,b_0,\ldots,b_6,c_1,c_2,f,d_1,d_2,d_3$.

4.3 Results

Resulting theoretical model of spectral reflectance for sample s3 obtained by the VIMSO method is in Fig. 11. Similar results were obtained also for other analysed samples. Refractive indices and extinction coefficients reconstructed from $R_{corr}(\lambda)$ models are in Fig. 12 and Fig. 13.

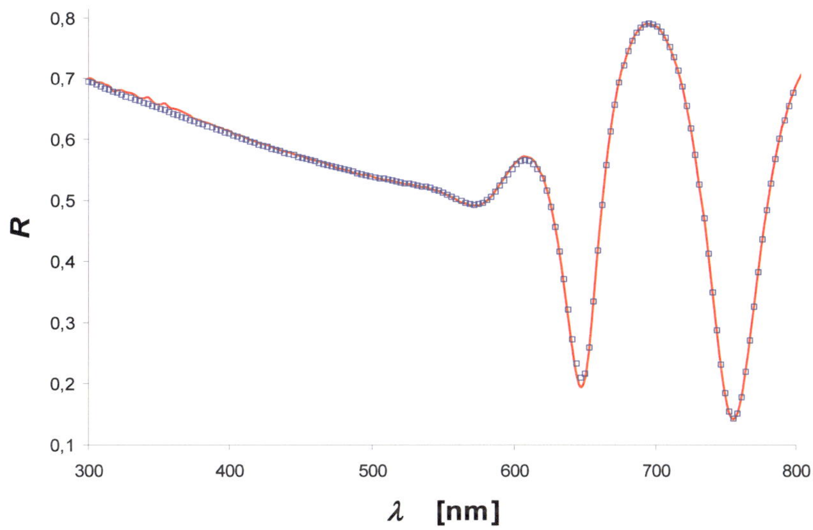

Fig. 11. Fit of theoretical model of spectral reflectance of sample s3 (blue squares), and experimental reflectance function (red line).

By using of proposed theoretical model the spectral reflectance function can be modeled in agreement with the experimental data.

The size of the surface structural objects measured by the AFM increases with increasing dilution. We suppose that with increasing dilution D the a-Si:H structure becomes polycrystalline. The samples prepared at the dilution under 20 remain amorphous. The films prepared at D ≥ 30 show polycrystalline features. The protocrystalline regime occurs between the dilutions 20 and 30. Reduction of the refractive index and extinction coefficient of a-Si:H layers with increasing dilution can be explained by the development of a void fraction in the structure. These voids are created under hydrogenation and creation of the polycrystalline phase. Remarkable changes of the optical properties connected with these processes can be observed under dilution D ≥ 30 as can be seen in Fig. 12 and Fig. 13.

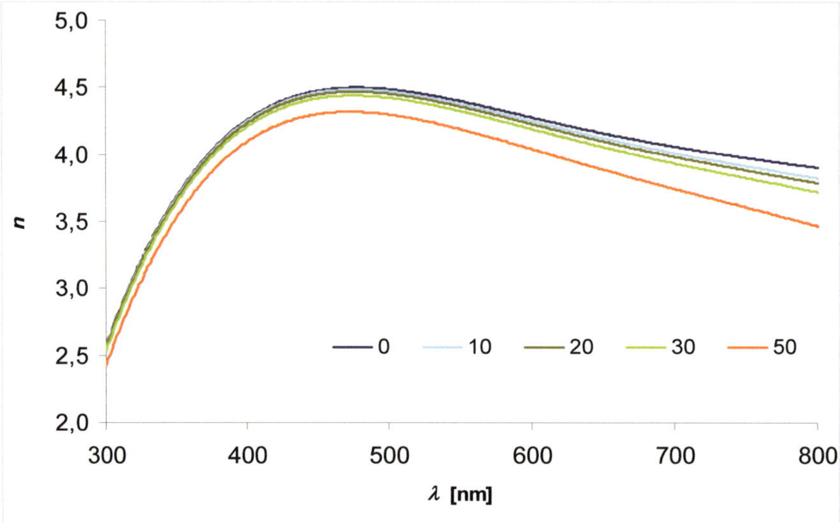

Fig. 12. Reconstructed spectral refractive indices of a-Si:H thin films.

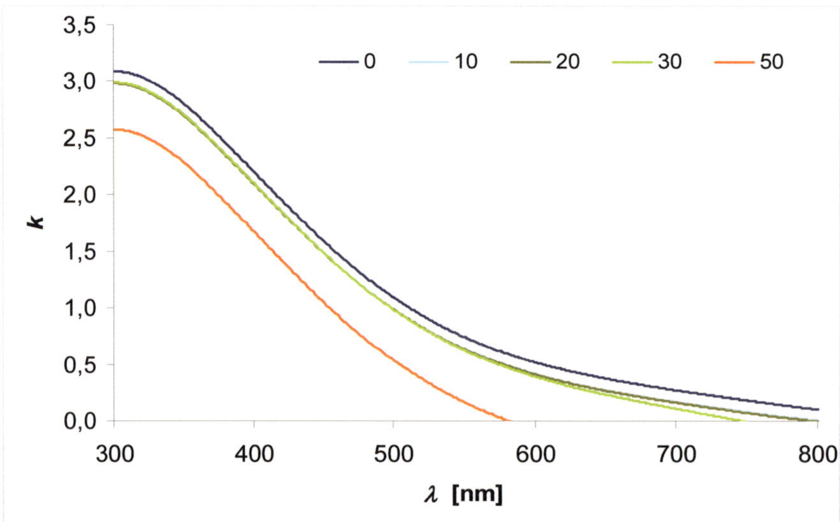

Fig. 13. Reconstructed spectral extinction coefficients of a-Si:H thin films.

5. Conclusion

Theoretical model of physical system is constructed in our approach in two steps. Microstructural and optical properties of multilayer system are proposed in visual environment and then the initial estimation of model parameters is refined by the genetic algorithm. It enables comfortable modification of proposed theoretical model, incorporating of subjective criteria, testing of mutual correlation of model parameters and control of convergence abilities of resulting numerical model. The VIMSO method is implemented in

JAVA language in NET Beans IDE. For the GA optimization of estimated numerical model the JAVA JGAP package is used. It is based on object-oriented programming and provides all benefit from this property - implementation of data abstraction, modularity, encapsulation and inheritance. It is possible to define special chromosomes and fitness function suitable for solving of specified problem. By using of the VIMSO method adequate description of experimental spectral reflectance of semiconductor thin film samples was reached. It is supported by implementation of several dispersion models for semiconductors and dielectrics, suitable effective media approximation models, surface roughness correction, and by the "user friendly" philosophy applied to building of the layer structure and modification of model variables.
Changes in optical properties of real a-Si:H thin films due to the increasing hydrogen dilution were analysed by optimising of the spectral reflectance theoretical model. Proposed microstructural and dispersion theoretical model was successfully optimised by comparison to the experimental data. Development of the spectral index of refraction and extinction coefficient with change of the deposition conditions was obtained. Changes in optical properties of a-Si:H samples determined by using the VIMSO method provide reliable tool for making conclusions about development of the material structure and about interaction of light and prepared optical media.
Beside of the refractive index and extinction coefficient a set of other important parameters describing the structure and optical properties can be extracted from fitted theoretical model. Very useful is information about the thicknesses of individual layers, influence of the effective media approximation, connection of surface roughness and spectral reflectance and other parameters extracted from the resulting fit. The combination of visual estimation of initial theoretical model and refinement of this estimation by the genetic algorithm is suitable tool for modeling of complex physical systems. It enables reliable incorporation of new phenomena into theoretical model in order to explain the experimental data. When solving this task correlated parameters can be easily fixed and suitable restrictions of remaining parameters can be effectively implemented.

6. References

Abeles, F. (1950). *Recherches sur la propagation des ondes electromagnetiques sinusoidales dans les milieux stratifies. Application aux couches minces.* Annales de Physique. Paris.

Born, M. & Wolf, E. (1975). *Principles of Optics.* Pergamon Press, London.

Bury, P.; Hockicko, P.; Jurečka, S. & Jamnický, J. (2004). Analysis of Acoustic Attenuation Spectra Due to Ion Transport Processes in Glassy Electrolytes. *Physica Status Solidi.* No. 11, 2004, pp. 2888-2891.

Coley, D., A. (1999). *An introduction to genetic algorithms for scientists and engineers.* World Scientific Publishing Co., Singapore.

Furman, S., A. & Tikhonravov, A., V. (1992). *Basics of optics of multilayer systems.* Edition Frontieres, Gif-sur-Yvette, Paris.

Hawlitzek, F. (2000). *Java 2.* Adsdison-Wesley Verlag, München, Germany.

Hecht, E. (2002). *Optics*, Addison Wesley, San Fransisco.

Chen, Y., F.; Kwei, C., M. & Tung, C., J. (1993). Optical-constants model for semiconductors and insulators. *Physical Review B.* Vol. 48, No. 7, 1993, pp. 4373-4379.

JGAP http://jgap.sourceforge.net/index.html

Jurečka S.; Havlík M. & Jurečková M. (2004). Genetická syntéza difrakčného profilu. *Advances in Electrical and Electronic Engineering,* Vol. 3, No. 1, 2004, p. 27-30.

Koza, J. R. (1992). *Genetic Programming: On the Programming of Computers by Means of Natural Selection.* Massachusetts Institute of Technology, USA.

Lekner, J. (1987). *Theory of reflection.* Martinus Nijhoff Publishers, Dordrecht, The Netherlands.

Mallet, P.; Guérin, C., A. & Sentenac, A. (2005). Maxwell-Garnett mixing rule in the presence of multiple scattering: Derivation and accuracy. *Physical Review* B 72, 014205, 2005.

Müllerová, J.; Jurečka, S., Šutta, P. & Mikula, M. (2005). Structural and optical studies of a-Si:H thin films: from amorphous to nanocrystalline silicon. *Acta Physica Slovaca,* Vol. 55, No. 3, 2005, pp. 351-359.

Roussel, P., H.; Vanhellemont, J. & Maes, H., E. (1993). Numerical aspects of the implementation of effective-medium approximation models in spectroscopic ellipsometry regression software. *Thin Solid Films,* Vol. 234, 1993, pp. 423-427.

Sihvola, A. (1999). *Electromagnetic Mixing Formulas and Applications.* The Institution of Electrical Engineers, New York.

SUN http://www.oracle.com/us/sun/index.html

Tompkins, H., G. & Irene, E., A. (2005). *Handbook of ellipsometry.* Springer Verlag, ISBN 3-540-22293-6, Heidelberg.

Weiglhofer, W. S. & Lakhtakia, A. (2003). *Introduction to complex mediums for optics and electromagnetics.* SPIE, Bellingham, USA.

3

Electromagnetic Device Optimization with Stochastic Methods

P. Alotto
Dipartimento di Ingegneria Elettrica, Università di Padova, Padova, Italy

1. Introduction

Device optimization using metaheuristic methods has been successfully applied to electromagnetic devices since their development in the early 1980s. Some recent examples of the application of metaheuristics in electromagnetic device design include, among others, genetic algorithms [Zaoui2007], evolution strategies [Coelho2007], Tabu search [Cogotti2000], artificial immune systems [Campelo2006], particle swarm optimization (PSO) [Ciuprina2002].

In this chapter the author summarizes some of his experiences in the use of two stochastic optimization techniques which are very suitable to typical electromagnetic devices and systems. First the algorithms are briefly introduced and then their application to typical challenging problems, including Polymer Exchange Membrane Fuel Cells (PEMFC), high-field-uniformity solenoids and Superconducting Magnetic Energy Storage (SMES) systems, is presented.

2. Algorithm 1: differential evolution

Evolutionary algorithms (EAs) are a class of nonlinear optimization approaches which somehow mimic features of biological systems and Darwin's principle of the survival of the fittest. EAs have some particular advantages such as robustness, parallelism, and global search capability, which make them applicable and attractive within a wide range of engineering problems including electromagnetic optimization.

DE is a powerful and simple EA which improves a population of individuals over several generations through the operators of mutation, crossover and selection. DE presents good convergence characteristics and requires few control parameters. The most important operation in DE is its offspring-generating scheme, namely, each offspring is generated by differential mutation and probabilistic crossover from the current population.

In the context of EAs, an attractive and repulsive (AR) approach was introduced in [Ursem2002], [Ursem2003] within the framework of particle swarm optimization. AR uses a diversity measure to control the population and the result is a powerful algorithm which alternates between phases of attraction (exploitation) and repulsion (exploration).

Such a diversity measure can be applied within the framework of Differential Evolution (DE) in order to improve both the global convergence as well as the local search performance. The DE approach showed here uses an attractive-repulsive, diversity-guided operator (ARDGDE) prevents the fluctuation of the estimated parameters during the evolution procedure. ARDGDE will be applied on the well-known TEAM workshop problem 22 which has been solved with a number of different techniques in the past [Magele1993], [Alotto1998], [Saldanha1999], [Magele 2007]. The benchmark consists in determining the optimal design of a superconducting magnetic energy storage (SMES) device in order to store a significant amount of energy in the magnetic field with a fairly simple and economical coil arrangement which can be rather easily scaled up in size.

2.1 Classical DE

The fundamental idea behind DE is the scheme which generates the trial parameter vectors. DE, at each time step, mutates vectors by adding weighted, random difference vectors to them. If the cost (objective function value) of the trial vector is better than that of the target, the target vector is replaced by trial vector in the next generation. This greedy behavior lies at the heart of the efficiency of DE.
In 1995 Storn and Price [Storn1995] proposed several variants of the basic DE which are identified by the notation DE/*ind*/*num*/*mode*, where *vec* indicates the individual to be mutated (i.e. either a randomly chosen individual, *rand*, or the best individual of the current generation, *best*), *num* is the number of difference vectors used in the mutation (i.e. either 1 or 2) and *mode* is the method of crossover used. For independent binomial experiments of the degrees of freedom, this is set to *bin*, whereas independent exponential experiments are indicated by *exp*.
Studies have shown that for general problems two of the most effective strategies are DE/*rand*/1/*bin* and DE/*best*/2/*bin*. The variant implemented here is the DE/*rand*/1/*bin* given by the following steps:

i. Initialize a population of M individuals (real-valued solution vectors) $x_i(t)$, $i=1,\dots,M$, with random values generated according to a uniform probability distribution in the n dimensional problem space. In this step, $t = 0$.
ii. For each individual, evaluate its fitness (objective function value), F.
iii. Mutate individuals according to following equation:

$$\mathbf{z}_i(t+1) = \mathbf{x}_{r_1}(t) + f_m \cdot [\mathbf{x}_{r_2}(t) - \mathbf{x}_{r_3}(t)] \tag{I.1}$$

where r_1, r_2 and r_3 are three mutually different random integers in [1,M], and $f_m > 0$ is a real parameter, called *mutation factor*, which controls the amplification of the difference between two individuals and is usually taken in the range [0.1, 1]. Practically, each mutant individual irradiates from a current individual by addition of a vector depending on the weighted difference between randomly chosen population members (Fig. I.1).

iv. Following the mutation operation, crossover is applied to the population. For each mutant vector, $z_i(t+1)$, an index $r_i \in [1, M]$ is randomly chosen using a uniform distribution, and a *trial vector*, $\mathbf{u}_i(t+1)$, is generated (component by component) by

$$u_{i_j}(t+1) = \begin{cases} z_{i_j}(t+1), & \text{if } (r_j \le CR) \text{ or } (j = r_i), \\ x_{i_j}(t), & \text{otherwise} \end{cases} \tag{I.2}$$

where r_j is the j-th evaluation of a uniform random number generation within [0, 1] and CR is a *recombination* or *crossover rate* in the range [0, 1]. It has been shown that the

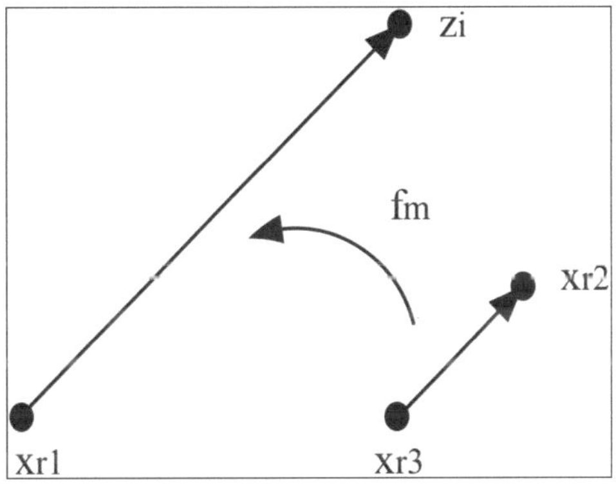

Fig. I.1. Generation of mutants according to the DE/best/1/exp approach.

performance of DE does not depend very critically upon the choice of *CR*. To decide whether or not the vector $\boldsymbol{u}_i(t+1)$ should be a member of the population comprising the next generation, it is compared to the corresponding vector $x_i(t)$. In this context, if F is the objective function subject to minimization, then

$$\mathbf{x}_i(t+1) = \begin{cases} \mathbf{u}_i(t+1), \text{ if } F(\mathbf{u}_i(t+1)) < F(\mathbf{x}_i(t)), \\ \mathbf{x}_i(t), \text{ otherwise} \end{cases} \tag{I.3}$$

v. Update $t = t + 1$. Loop to step (ii) until a stopping criterion is met, usually a maximum number of iterations (generations), t_{max}.

Usually, the performance of a DE algorithm depends on the population size M, the mutation factor f_m, and the crossover rate *CR*. Various studies have shown that the mutation factor is the parameter which most critically influences the performance and robustness of DE.

2.2 DE using diversity-guided operator

Population diversity is a key issue in the performance of evolutionary algorithms. A common hypothesis is that high diversity is important to avoid premature convergence and to escape local optima. Various diversity measures have been used to analyze algorithms, but so far few algorithms have used a measure to *guide the search.*

To improve the control over the population diversity, Ursem introduced a diversity guided evolutionary algorithm (DGEA) [Ursem2002], [Ursem2003]. The idea behind DGEA is simple. Unlike most other evolutionary algorithms DGEA uses a diversity measure to alternate between exploiting and exploring behaviors. These behaviors are also called attraction and repulsion, hence the acronym AR. To use a measure for this purpose it has to be robust with respect to the population size, the dimensionality of the problem, and the search range of each of the variables. An immediate measure for N-dimensional numerical problems is the "distance-to-midpoint" measure, which is defined as:

$$diversity(P) = \frac{1}{|D| \cdot M} \cdot \sum_{i=1}^{M} \sqrt{\sum_{j=1}^{n} \left(x_{ij} - \bar{x}_j \right)^2} \tag{I.4}$$

where $|D|$ is the length of the diagonal (assuming that each design variable is in a finite range) in the search space $X \in \Re^n$, P is the population, M is the population size, n is the dimensionality of the problem, x_{ij} is the j-th component of the i-th individual, and $\bar{x}_j$ is the j-th component of the midpoint $\bar{x}$.
Based on this diversity concept, a modified attractive-repulsive diversity guided DE (ARDGDE) is used here. The pseudocode for ARDGDE based on DE/*rand*/1/*bin* is listed in Fig. I.2. The diversity measure is given by

$$diversity(P_i) = \frac{1}{D_i \cdot M} \cdot \sum_{i=1}^{M} \sqrt{\sum_{j=1}^{n} \left(x_{ij} - \bar{x}_j\right)^2} \tag{I.5}$$

where

$$D_i = \max\left\{\sum_{j=1}^{n} \left(x_{ij} - \bar{x}_j\right)^2\right\} \tag{I.6}$$

The ARDGDE algorithm has an adaptive mutation factor which alternates between phases of attraction and repulsion. The diversity analysis of $x_{i,r_2}(t)$ and $x_{i,r_3}(t)$ determines which phase ARDGDE is currently in, simply by setting sign-variables, d_1 and d_2, either to 1 or -1 depending on the diversity. Here the lower and higher bounds of diversity measure, d_{low} and d_{high}, are set to 0.05 and 0.25, respectively.

3. Algorithm 2: Tribes

3.1 Motivation

As will be shown in the sections devoted to typical electromagnetic applications, most realistic problems have a rather high number of parameters and highly non-linear objective functions. In some cases appropriate models of modest computational cost can be built and in these cases robust and possibly parameter free (self-adapting) stochastic optimizers can be used.
The *Tribes* algorithm, proposed in [Clerc2006][Cooren2006], and which has attracted attention from researchers in different application areas such as the optimization of milling operations [Onwubolu2005], flow shop scheduling [Onwubolu2005], and molecular docking [Chen2006], seems to be the particularly suitable for solving this kind of problems.

3.2 Particles

The population in *Tribes* is called *swarm* and each individual is called *particle*. Each particle flies around in a multi-dimensional problem search space. In other words, a swarm consists of N particles moving around in a D-dimensional search space.

3.3 Informers

An informer for a given particle P is a particle Q that can pass some information to P. Typically this information includes the best position ever found by Q and the function value at this best position. The informer Q, therefore, influences the behavior of P.

```
ARDGDE main
{
  Generation t = 0;
  Initialize the direction variables d1=1 and d2=1;
  Initialize the population P(t) of individuals;
  While (stopping criterion is not met),
     Evaluate the fitness of population,
     Update the generation number, t = t + 1;
     Apply mutation operator given by:
     Select the indices r1, r2 and r3
     Update the adaptive mutation factor using f_m(t) = 0.5·(t / t_max) + 0.3
     If rand > 0.5   (where rand is a random number generated using uniform probability
     distribution function)
       If diversity ( P_{i,r2}(t) ) < d_low
         d1 = 1;
       Else if diversity( P_{i,r2}(t) ) > d_high
         d1 = -1;
           Endif
         z_i(t+1) = x_{i,r1}(t) + d1 · f_m(t) · |x_{i,r2}(t) − x_{i,r3}(t)|
    Else if
       If diversity ( P_{i,r3}(t) ) < d_low
         d2 = 1;
       Else if diversity( P_{i,r3}(t) ) > d_high
         d2 = -1;
           End if
         z_i(t+1) = x_{i,r1}(t) + d2 · f_m(t) · |x_{i,r2}(t) − x_{i,r3}(t)|
    End if
    Apply crossover operator
  End while
}
```

Fig. I.2. Pseudocode of ARDGDE with adaptive mutation factor.

3.4 Tribes

A tribe is a sub-swarm formed by particles which have the property that all particles inform all others belonging to the tribe (a symmetrical clique in graph theoretical language). The concept is therefore related to the "cultural vicinity" (information neighborhood) and not on "spatial vicinity" (parameter-space neighborhood). It should be noted that, due to the above definition, the set of informers of a particle (its so-called *i-group*) contains the whole of its tribe but is not limited to it. This is shown in Fig. II.1 where the *i-group* of particle B1 contains all particles of its tribe (black) and particle W1 belonging to the white tribe.

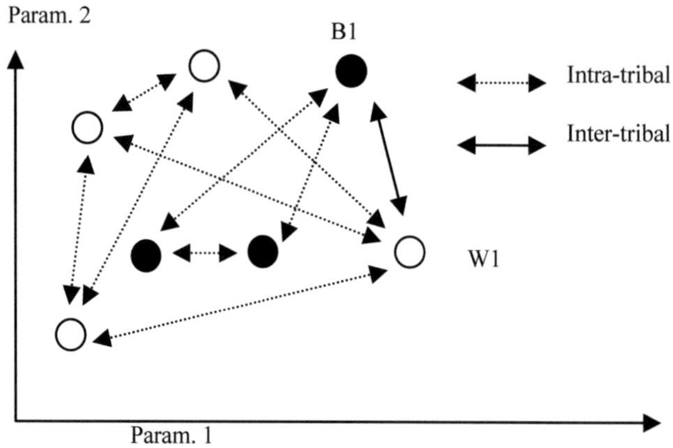

Fig. II.1. Tribal relationships

3.5 Optimization procedure

The Tribes mechanism is auto-parametrising. The principles of Tribes are: i) the swarm is divided in tribes; ii) at the beginning, the swarm is composed of only one particle; iii) according to tribes' behaviors, particles are added or removed; and iv) according to the performances of the particles, their displacement strategies are adapted. The so-called structural adaptation rules describe when a particle is created or removed and when a particle becomes the informer of another, whereas so-called moving strategies indicate how particles modify their positions.

3.6 Structural adaption rules

The most important structural adaption rule is that "good" tribes may benefit from the removal of their weakest member, since they already possess good problem solutions and thus may afford to reduce their population; "bad" tribes, on the other hand, may benefit from the addition of a new member, increasing the possibility of improvement. In Tribes, for each "bad" tribe, the best particle generates a new particle using uniform probability distribution and becomes its informer. Particles generated in one iteration step are interconnected into a tribe and provide inter-tribe exchange of information.
Crucial for the above steps is the definition of "good" and "bad" tribes: the more "good" particles a tribe has, the more "good" the tribe is. This behavior is obtained by generating a random number between 1 and N_{tribe}–the number of particles in a tribe–, and checking if it is less than or equal to G_{tribe}–the number of "good" particles in the tribe.
In contrast to most standard PSO approaches, particles keep memory of their last two previous cost function values. The particle is said to be "good" if the last movement produces an improvement of the objective function, "excellent" if both the last two movements produce an improvement, otherwise the particle is "neutral".
Structural adaptation should not take place after each iteration since some time (iterations) are necessary for information to propagate throughout the swarm.
In his original algorithm Clerc proposes to reevaluate and modify the population structure every $L/2$ iterations, where L is the dynamically changing number of links in the population. In fact, a more sophisticated approach would be to compute the length of all shortest paths between all couples of particles and the longest of such paths would indicate the number of

iterations it would take to propagate information through the whole swarm. Since such algorithm could quickly become expensive in the case of large swarms the above heuristic, which has been tested to give similar results to the more complex one, is implemented instead.
As a result, Fig. II.2 shows the dynamics of tribe and particle creation/deletion for the μ-DMFC optimization problem described later.

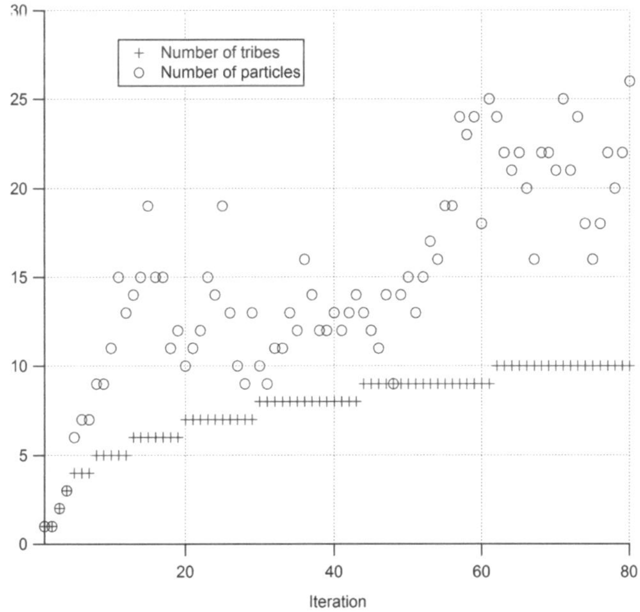

Fig. II.2. Tribe and particle creation/deletions vs. number of iterations.

3.7 Moving strategies

In contrast with standard PSO algorithms particles do not have explicit associated velocities: their position is updated according to history only. "Excellent" particles are updated according to the "simple pivot" strategy [Serra1997], whereas "good" and "neutral" particles evolve according to the "noisy pivot" method.
In the "simple pivot" method two positions are used: the best position p of a given particle P and the best position q of its informer Q. Then two hyperspheres of radius $|p\text{-}q|$ are created around p and q and the new position is generated inside the intersection of the two hyperspheres in such a way that the newly generated point is most likely to be nearer to the best between p and q. In order to obtain such behavior two weights w_1 and w_2 proportional to the relative fatnesses of P and Q are generated and the new position is obtained by $w_1h_p+w_2h_q$., where h_p and h_e are two randomly generated points in the hyperspheres surrounding p and q respectively.
In the "noisy pivot" method the same procedure is applied but random noise is added to the obtained position in such a way that exploration beyond the hyperspheres becomes possible.
The combined use of these strategies has a twofold effect: very good particles search in their close neighborhood (exploitation) whereas all other sample wider regions of parameter space (exploration).

3.8 Brief description of the algorithm

Summarizing, the Tribes algorithm consists of following steps:

Initialization of swarm

Set iteration t=1. Initialize a population of 1 particle (real-valued D-dimensional vector) and 1 tribe with random values generated according to a uniform probability distribution within given upper and lower bounds.

Evaluation of each particle in the swarm

Evaluate the fitness (objective function) value of each particle.

Swarm moves

Apply the moving strategies ("simple pivot" or "noisy pivot") according to the quality of particles ("excellent", "good" or "bad").

Adaptation scheme

After every $L/2$ iterations, where L is the number of links in the population, adapt the structure of the swarm by applying the above described structural adaptation rules.

Stopping criterion

Set the generation number for $t = t + 1$. Proceed to step *Evaluation of each particle in the swarm* until a stopping criterion is met, usually a maximum number of iterations or a maximum number of objective function evaluations.

4. Application 1: fuel cells

Recently, small-scale direct methanol fuel cells (μ-DMFCs) have gained considerable attention as power sources with potentially higher energy density compared to traditional Li-ion batteries [Larminie2003]. This feature, together with the low operating temperature and low weight, makes μ-DMFCs particularly suited for supplying low-power portable devices such as laptops, PDAs, or mobile phones.

Several factors contribute to the overall cell performance, e.g., methanol concentration, load current, room humidity and temperature, membrane conductivity and permeability, catalyst loadings. Modeling and optimizing the cell performance becomes particularly complex since electro-chemical coupled problems are fully non-linear.

To date design procedures have been developed mainly for polymer electrolyte fuel cells (PEMFC) [Katykatoglu2007][Cheng2006]. Here a one-dimensional analytical model of a μ-DMFC that accounts for current generation, mass transport, electronic and protonic electrical conduction, and electrochemical reactions is shown.

4.1 Direct methanol fuel cell modeling

A small-scale direct methanol fuel cell consists of a proton exchange membrane (PEM) sandwiched between the anode and cathode electrodes (Fig. III.1). In passive fuel cells methanol is stored in a tank, while oxygen is taken from the atmosphere. Reactants are distributed through diffusion layers to catalyst layers, where the electro-chemical energy conversion occurs. Electrons generated at the anode catalyst layer flow to the external circuit by means of a current collector.

The model takes into account the following physical phenomena: electrochemical reactions, electronic and protonic conduction, methanol crossover through the PEM, diffusion of reactants inside the substrates, and electric current generation.
In the following sections the static and dynamic modeling of the μ-DMFC are treated separately.

4.2 Static modeling of a μ-DMFC

The electric steady-state external characteristic of the fuel cell is obtained from mass transport and electro-chemical relations under the assumption of a one-dimensional geometry.

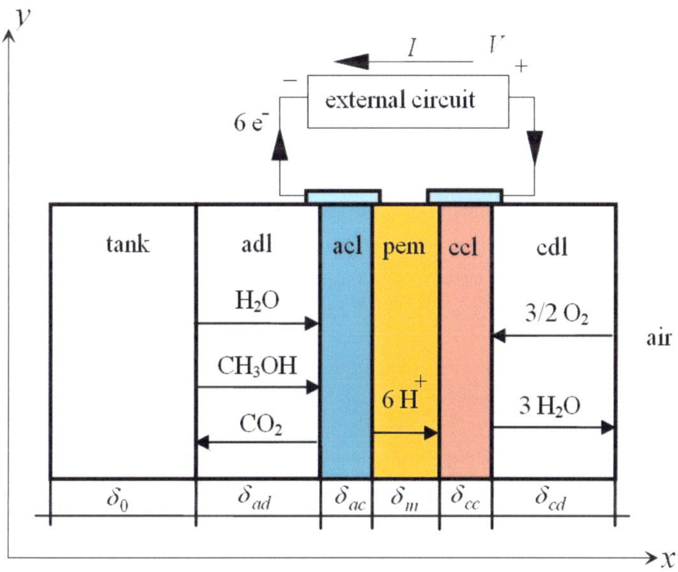

Fig. III.1. DMFC schematic (a=anode, c=cathode, pem=proton exchange membrane, dl=diffusion layer, cl=catalyst layer).

The external circuit is coupled to the cell by the following generalized continuity equations that apply at catalyst layers:

$$\nabla \cdot \mathbf{J}^{+} + \partial_t \rho^{+} = \partial_t \rho_g^{+}$$
$$\nabla \cdot \mathbf{J}^{-} + \partial_t \rho^{-} = \partial_t \rho_g^{-} \qquad \text{(III.1)}$$

where superscripts indicate protons and electrons, ρ, ρ_g the stored/ generated charge densities, and $\mathbf{J}$ the current density.
Current densities at the anode and cathode are computed by Butler-Volmer's equation, neglecting the concentrations of reduced (anode) and oxidized species (cathode), as [Bard2001]:

$$J_a = J_a^* (C_a / C_a^*)^{\gamma} \exp(\alpha_a f v_a)$$
$$J_c = J_c^* (C_c / C_c^*)^{\gamma} \exp(\alpha_c f v_c) \qquad \text{(III.2)}$$

where concentrations C_a, C_c and over-voltages v_a, v_c are independent variables, and the other quantities are constant.
Reactant concentrations at both catalyst layers depend on the diffusion rate across diffusion layers by Fick's law:

$$\mathbf{N} = -D\nabla C \tag{III.3}$$

where $\mathbf{N}$ is the reactant molar flow, and D is the diffusivity. Using (3) methanol flow from the tank can be expressed as:

$$N_{ad} = K_a(C_{0,a} - C_{ac}) \tag{III.4}$$

assuming very thin layers and a one-dimensional mass flow. In the same way, oxygen flow at the cathode can be expressed as:

$$N_{cd} = K_c(C_{0,c} - C_{cc}) \tag{III.5}$$

where K_a, K_c are the mass transfer coefficients, $C_{0,a}$ and $C_{0,c}$ the methanol and oxygen concentrations in the tank and in the ambient, and C_{ac}, C_{cc} those at catalyst layers.
Due to electro-osmosis and concentration gradient effects, part of the methanol does not react completely at the anode and flows through the membrane. This effect is the so-called *crossover*, causing significant voltage loss and waste of fuel. The anode current density J_a is related to crossover N_m, as:

$$J_a = 6F(N_{ad} - N_m) \tag{III.6}$$

where F is the Faraday's constant (96.485 C mol^{-1}). At the cathode side, current density J_c can be derived as:

$$J_c = 4F(N_{ad} - \tfrac{3}{2}N_m) \tag{III.7}$$

The methanol crossover in (III.6) and (III.7) can be computed by means of the following mass balance equation:

$$\mathbf{N}_m = -D_m\nabla C + n_d\,\mathbf{J}_a / F \tag{III.8}$$

where D_m is the methanol diffusivity on the membrane, and n_d the electro-osmotic drag coefficient.
The anode activation over-voltage is obtained by combining (III.4) and (III.6) with (III.2), as:

$$v_a(J) = \frac{1}{f\alpha_a}\log\frac{C_a^* J_a / J_a^*}{C_{eq,a}(1 - J / J_{\lim,a})} \tag{III.9}$$

where the anode equivalent concentration and limiting current values are:

$$C_{eq,a} = \frac{K_a\delta_m}{K_a\delta_m + D_m}C_{0,a}, \quad J_{\lim,a} = \frac{K_a C_{0,a}}{\frac{1}{6F} + \frac{n_d}{F}}$$

where thickness δ_m is defined in Fig. III.1.

Similarly, the cathode over-voltage can be computed by combining (III.5) and (III.7) as:

$$v_c(J) = \frac{1}{f\alpha_c}\log\frac{C_c^* J_c / J_c^*}{C_{eq,c}(1 - J / J_{\lim,c})} \tag{III.10}$$

where the equivalent cathode concentration and limiting current values are:

$$C_{eq,c} = C_{0,c} - \frac{3}{2}\frac{D_m}{K_a\delta_m + D_m}\frac{K_a}{K_c}C_{0,a}, \; J_{\lim,c} = \frac{K_c(C_{eq,c}/C_{eq,a})C_{0,a}}{\frac{1}{4F} + \frac{3}{2F}n_d}$$

Anode and cathode current densities in (III.9) and (III.10) can be related to load current density J on the external circuit, as:

$$\begin{aligned} J_a &= J \\ J_c &= J + 6FN_m \end{aligned} \tag{III.11}$$

which states that the electron flow at the anode equates the proton flow, while at the cathode the electron flow from methanol crossover oxidation must be considered as well.
Finally, the fuel cell voltage at the collector is obtained from anode and cathode over-voltages in (III.9) and (III.10), as

$$V(J) = E_{eq}(J) - R_{eq}J \tag{III.12}$$

where $E_{eq}(J) = E^0 - v_a(J) - v_c(J)$ is the equivalent fem, E^0 the standard cell voltage, $R_{eq} = \delta_m / \sigma_m + R_c$ the equivalent resistance, σ_m the PEM non-linear conductivity, and R_c the contact resistance between collectors and diffusion layers.

4.3 Dynamic modeling of a μ-DMFC

The fuel cell dynamics on the long time scale is dominated by the consumption of the methanol in the reservoir, which can be computed by using the mass conservation law [Bard2001]:

$$\nabla \cdot \mathbf{N} + \partial_t C = 0 \tag{III.13}$$

where ∂_t is the time derivative. The voltage discharge of the DMFC is evaluated for a constant load current density.
The state variable model is obtained by assembling (III.4), (III.6) and (III.13) into the following ODE system:

$$\mathbf{M}_1\mathbf{x} + \mathbf{M}_2\dot{\mathbf{x}} = \mathbf{g} \tag{III.14}$$

where:

$$\mathbf{M}_1 = \begin{pmatrix} K_a & -K_a - D_m/\delta_m \\ K_a & -K_a \end{pmatrix} \quad \mathbf{M}_2 = \begin{pmatrix} 0 & 0 \\ \delta_0 & 0 \end{pmatrix}$$

$$\mathbf{g} = \begin{pmatrix} J/6F + n_d J/F \\ 0 \end{pmatrix} \qquad \mathbf{x} = \begin{pmatrix} C_{0,a} \\ C_{ac} \end{pmatrix}$$

and δ_0 is the tank thickness indicated in Fig. III.1. This system is solved numerically by the so-called *θ-method*, which consists in the following iterative scheme:

$$\left(\theta \mathbf{M}_1 + \frac{\mathbf{M}_2}{\tau}\right)\mathbf{x}_{k+1} = \left[(\theta - 1)\mathbf{M}_1 + \frac{\mathbf{M}_2}{\tau}\right]\mathbf{x}_k + \mathbf{g} \qquad \text{(III.15)}$$

where τ is the time integration step, and the parameter θ is set to 2/3 in order to ensure unconditional stability.

As an example, Fig. III.2 shows the voltage discharge profiles computed at different load current densities and for an initial methanol concentration in the reservoir of 3 M.

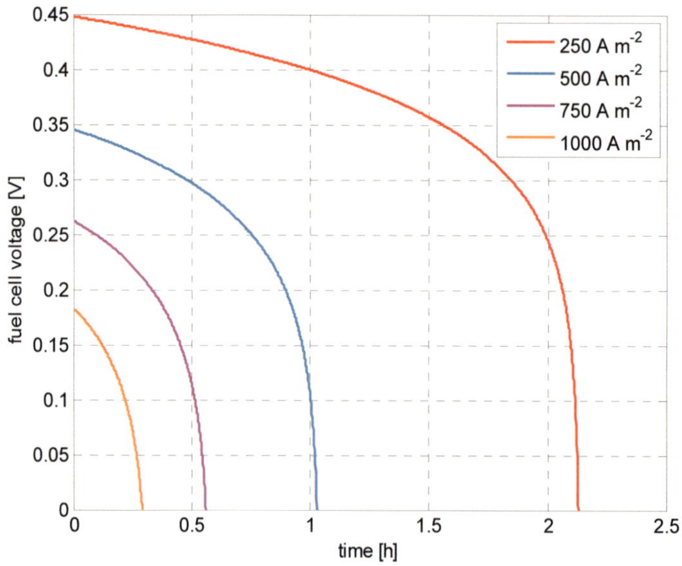

Fig. III.2. Voltage discharge profiles at constant current densities.

4.4 Particle swarm optimization

In order to optimize the cell performance two conflicting objectives were considered, i.e., the maximization of the cell duration between two consecutive fuel recharges - obtained from (15) - and the minimization of the methanol crossover. The importance of the second objective is twofold: on one hand crossover is obviously a waste of (limited) fuel, on the other hand fuel cell life-time is shortened by catalyst poisoning due to the carbon monoxide produced at the cathode from crossover methanol oxidation.

Both the objectives depend on the following parameters: methanol concentration in the tank, diffusion/catalyst layer thicknesses, membrane thickness, current density, and room temperature.

The above-described Tribes algorithm was applied to the μ-DMFC model with a maximum number of 5000 objective function evaluations as a stopping criterion.

It was observed that the optimization procedure identifies quite rapidly the shape of the Pareto front, and then further refines it. Fig. III.3 shows that the Pareto front is coarsely identified when number of individuals on the front first reaches one hundred (triangular markers). This happens after roughly 300 function evaluations. In the remaining iterations the algorithm spreads out individuals along the front.

Fig. III.4 shows that particles are very well distributed on the front. The corresponding positions in parameter space, i.e., the *Pareto set*, show that the solutions forming the Pareto front lie in completely different positions. These correspond to really different design solutions. For instance, Fig. III.5 shows the Pareto set in the three-dimensional subspace $(C_{0,a}, \delta_{ad}, \delta_{ac})$.

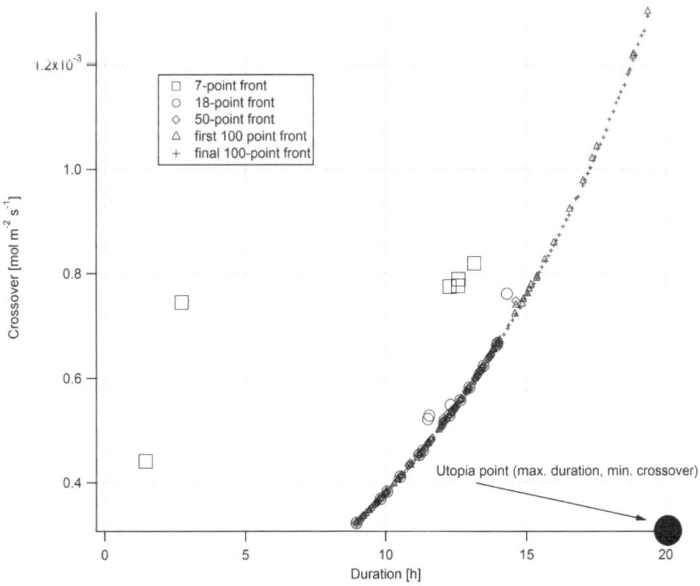

Fig. III.3. Evolution of the Pareto front during iteration.

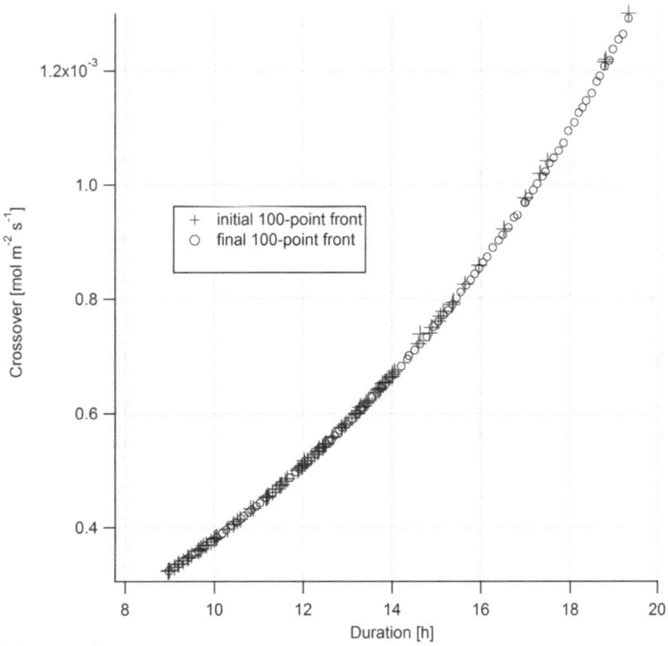

Fig. III.4. Final Pareto front.

Once the front has been identified it is the responsibility of a decision-maker to choose one or more particular designs which emphasize one of the two objectives with respect to the other depending on the specific application field of the DMFC.

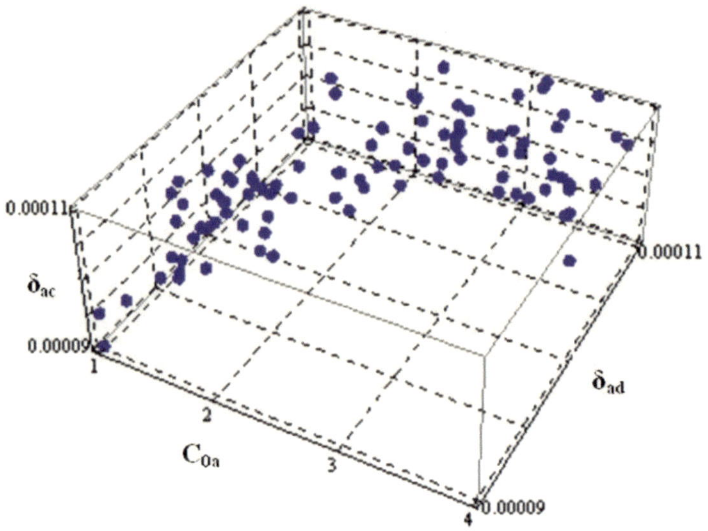

Fig. III.5. Pareto set (three parameters only)

5. Application 2: solenoid design

The electrical engineering literature has several references to optimization approaches which have been used to solve Loney's solenoid design problem [Cogotti2000], [Ciuprina2000].

Appropriately stated, Loney's solenoid design problem consists in determining the position and size of two correcting coils in order to generate a uniform magnetic flux density *B* within a given interval on the axis of a main solenoid.

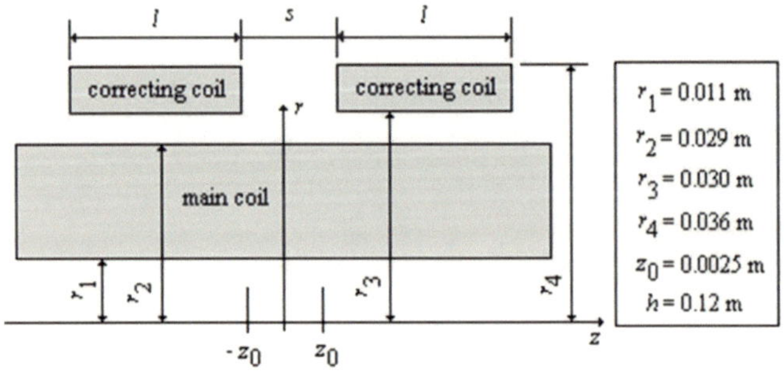

Fig. IV.1. Axial cross-section of Loney's solenoid

The upper half plane of the axial cross-section of the system is presented in Fig. IV.1. The interval of the axis, where the magnetic flux density *B* must be as uniform as possible is ($-z_o$, z_o). The separation s and the length *l* of the correcting coils are to be determined while all other dimensions are given. Both s and l are bounded in [*0,0.2*] according to the problem definition.

The field behavior along the axis can in principle be computed by several means, but in order to allow for a fair comparison between different methods we chose to follow the same route followed by other research groups, namely to represent each coil by four coaxial current sheets.
The optimization problem to be solved is:

$$\min F(s,l) \tag{IV.1}$$

where the objective function F is given by:

$$F = \frac{B_{max} - B_{min}}{B_0} \tag{IV.2}$$

where B_{max} and B_{min} are the maximum and minimum values of the magnetic flux density in the interval $(-z_o, z_o)$ and B_0 is the flux density at $z=0$.
Due to the peculiar way in which the field is computed (coils are represented by four current sheets) and due to the way B_{max} and B_{min} are evaluated (five uniformly spaced points in $[-z_0, 0]$) the objective function is very noisy.
Three different basins of attraction of local minima can be recognized in the domain of F with values of $F > 4 \cdot 10^{-8}$ (high level region: HL), $3 \cdot 10^{-8} < F < 4 \cdot 10^{-8}$ (low level region: LL), and $F < 3 \cdot 10^{-8}$ (very low level region - global minimum region: VL). The very low level region is a small ellipsoidally shaped area within the thin low-level valley. In both VL and LL small changes in one of the parameters can give rise to changes in objective function values of several orders of magnitude.
Tribes was run with a stopping criterion of either 1000 or 2000 objective function evaluations. Table IV.1 summarizes the behavior of the swarm size and number of tribes at convergence. It is interesting to note that the adaptive mechanism practically always generates the same number of tribes for a given number of function calls. The overall swarm size is also quite stable.

F calls	*S=Swarm Size, T=Number of tribes*							
	S_{min}	S_{avg}	S_{max}	S_{stdev}	T_{min}	T_{avg}	T_{max}	T_{stdev}
2000	22	34,9	56	6,2	9	9,7	10	0,48
1000	13	27,8	43	5,8	8	8,1	9	0,29

Table IV.1 Simulation Results of *F* in 100 runs

Table IV.2 summarizes the behavior of the algorithm in terms of the best objective function value found in 100 independent runs of the algorithm. The last three columns show the number of optima lying in the above-defined basins of attraction.
Results are very good also in the case of just 1000 function evaluations. A more detailed representation of the distribution of optima for both convergence criteria can be seen in Fig. IV.1, while Fig. IV.2 shows the location of the 100 optima for the case of 2000 function evaluations.
Tribes, like all stochastic optimizers, can be successfully coupled to a deterministic optimizer, like the derivative-free SolvOpt [Kappel2000] method which is based on Shor's method and is very well suited to noisy objective functions. Furthermore, SolvoOpt was chosen because lack of derivative information was hypothesizes also for the stochastic optimizer.

F calls	HL=High Level, LL=Low Level, VL=Very Low Level						
	F_{min} 10^{-8}	F_{avg} 10^{-8}	F_{max} 10^{-8}	F_{stdev} 10^{-9}	N_{VL}	N_{LL}	N_{HL}
2000	2,0574	3,4870	3,9526	5,23	18	82	0
1000	2,2732	3,6450	4,5052	4,18	9	88	3

Table IV.2 Simulation Results of *F* in 100 runs

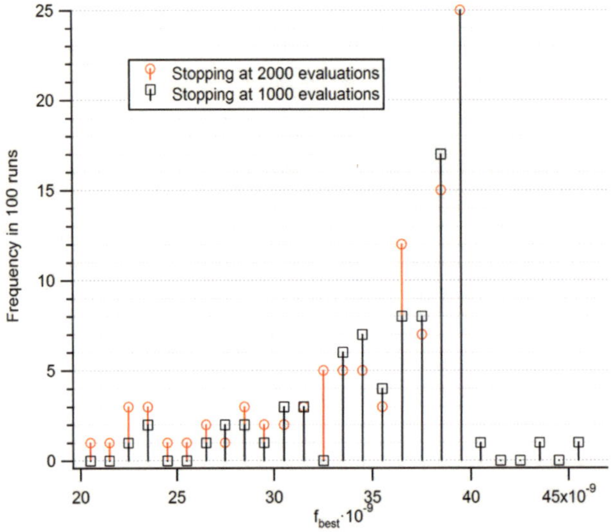

Fig. IV.1. Distribution of optima in 100 runs

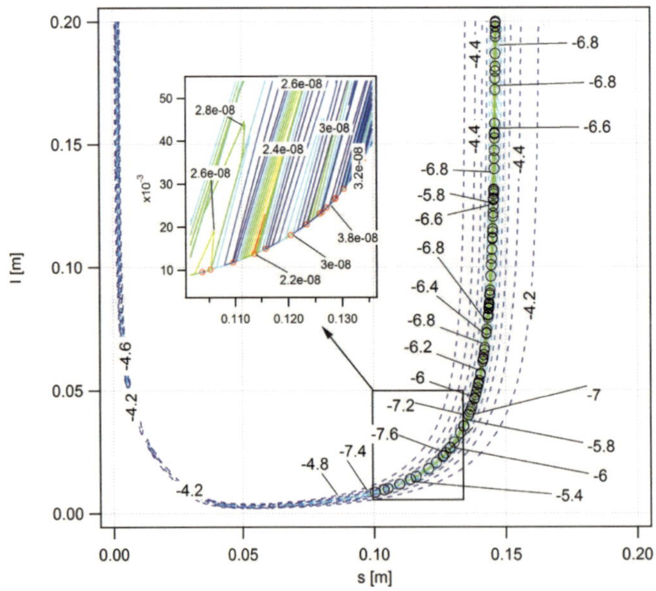

Fig. IV.2. Location of optimal solutions in 100 runs

Results of this coupling are shown in Fig. 5. Tribes was run with increasingly high numbers of function evaluations as stopping criterion (20, 40, 80, 160, 320, 640, 1200, 2400) and the best, average and worst optimal solutions are shown in Fig. IV.3. The algorithm improves only minimally after about 1200 function evaluations.

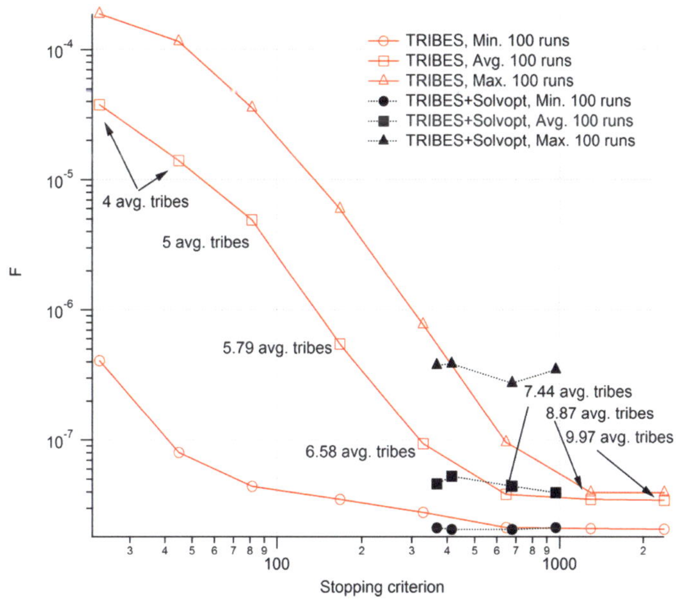

Fig. IV.3. Convergence of TRIBES and TRIBES+Solvopt

Tribes was then coupled to Solvopt and the deterministic optimizer was executed after the convergence of Tribes with stopping criteria of 20, 40, 320, 640 evaluations, respectively.
It can be seen that, for a given number of evaluations, the coupling of the two optimizers gives improvements for the first three cases but becomes practically useless afterwards (in fact the coupled optimizer becomes worse since it increases evaluations without improving the objective). It should also be noted that while the best and average optimal values improve, the worst values are almost always much worse, indicating misconvergence (remaining trapped in a local minimum) of the deterministic optimizer in some cases.

6. Application 3: superconducting magnetic energy storage

TEAM workshop problem 22 is a continuous, eight-parameter benchmark. Mathematically, this optimization problem has an objective function consisting of the weighted average of two conflicting goals (energy and stray field requirements). The optimization problem to be solved is the following:

$$\min\ OF = \frac{B_{stray}^2}{B_{normal}^2} + w \cdot \frac{\left| Energy - E_{ref} \right|}{E_{ref}} \tag{V.1}$$

where OF is the objective function to be minimized; the reference stored energy and stray field are E_{ref}= 180 MJ, B_{normal} = 200 μT, and w is a penalty factor with value equals to 100. The introduction of the penalty factor w is a deviation from the problem definition in which w=1.0. The penalty factor was introduced to make the stray field and energy error terms of roughly the same magnitude in order to achieve better convergence of the algorithm (failure to introduce w slightly worsen the average results). It should be noted, however, that results reported in Table 3 include reference to the original problem definition for ease of comparison with other approaches.

B_{stray}^2 is defined as

$$B_{stray}^2 = \frac{\sum_{i=1}^{22} \left| B_{stray,i} \right|^2}{22} \qquad \text{(V.2)}$$

where $B_{stray,i}$ is evaluated along 22 equidistant points along *line a* and *line b* in Fig V.1. Both the energy and the stray field are calculated using an integral formulation for the solution of the forward problem (*Biot-Savart law*). The bounds of the optimization parameters are shown in Table V.1.

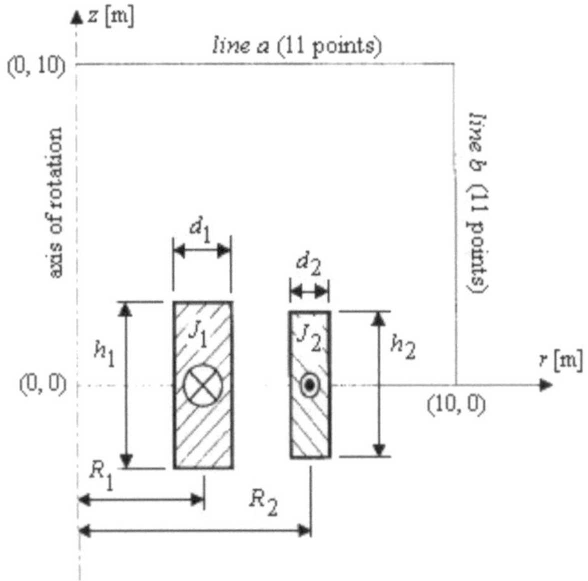

Fig. V.1. Setup of the SMES device (TEAM workshop problem 22).

Variables	R_1 [m]	R_2 [m]	$h_1/2$ [m]	$h_2/2$ [m]
Minimum	1.00	1.80	0.10	0.10
Maximum	4.00	5.00	1.80	1.80
Variables	d_1 [m]	d_2 [m]	J_1 [A/mm^2]	J_2 [A/mm^2]
Minimum	0.10	0.10	10.0	-30.0
Maximum	0.80	0.80	30.0	10.0

Table V.1. Limits of the optimization Parameters for the SMES Device.

Finding the optimal design is not an easy task because, besides usual geometrical constraints, there is a material related constraint: the given current density and the maximum magnetic flux density value on the coil must not violate the superconducting quench condition which can be well represented by a linear relationship shown in Fig. V.2. In the TEAM 22 workshop study used to investigate the performance of the classical DE and ARDGDE approaches, the population size *M* was 15 and the stopping criterion t_{max} was 100.

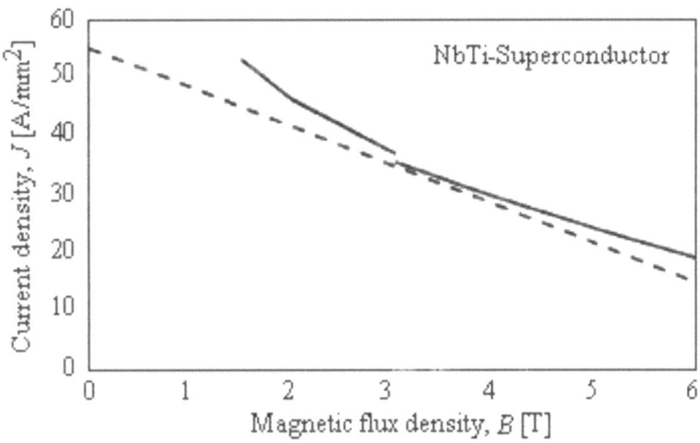

Fig. V.2. Critical curve of the superconductor.

Table V.2 reveals that ARDGDE2 provides better solutions than the DE1, DE2, and ARDGDE1 for the TEAM 22 workshop problem, particularly in terms of mean and best *OF* values. In Table 3 the best results of each tested approach (mentioned with statistical details in Table V.2) are shown (OF_{std} refers to OF with w=1).
It should also be noted that the "2" variants (adaptive f_m) always beat the respective "1" variants (constant f_m) and that the ARDG variants (attractive/repulsive diversity guided) always beat the respective standard non-ARDG variants.

DE approach	Description	Objective Function *OF* in 30 Runs			
		Max (Worst)	Mean	Min (Best)	Standard Deviation
DE1	classical DE with $f_m = 0.4$	69.4793	38.7011	2.9292	24.5652
DE2	classical DE with adaptive mutation factor	19.5515	5.4716	0.3967	6.4238
ARDGDE1	ARDGDE with $f_m = 0.4$	105.1539	46.0814	2.2359	35.1500
ARDGDE2	ARDGDE with adaptive mutation factor	**8.1377**	**2.2967**	**0.2296**	**2.5668**

Table V.2. Best Results (30 runs) for TEAM Workshop Problem 22.

Parameter	DE1	DE2	ARDGDE1	ARDGDE2
R_1 [m]	3.1339	1.2387	1.3248	1.2173
R_2 [m]	3.5174	1.8000	1.8080	1.8424
$h_1/2$[m]	0.4174	0.9366	0.3185	0.4367
$h_2/2$ [m]	1.1600	1.1986	1.7944	0.9577
d_1 [m]	0.5912	0.4303	0.7919	0.7999
d_2 [m]	0.2627	0.3801	0.1377	0.4184
J_1 (A/mm^2)	20.8337	23.8491	29.9255	24.5171
J_2 (A/mm^2)	-13.461	-10.079	-16.4139	-9.6477
Energy [MJ]	180.017	179.831	180.012	179.847
B_{Stray} [mT]	341.762	110.069	298.607	76.107
OF	2.9292	0.3967	2.2359	0.2296
OFstd	2.9201	0.3038	2.2292	0.1457

Table V.3. Best Results (30 runs) for TEAM Workshop Problem 22.

7. Acknowledgements

The author whishes to express his gratitude to his colleagues and friends F. Moro, Massimo Guarnieri and A. Stella from the Dipartimento di Ingegneria Elettrica, Università di Padova, Padova, Italy for sharing their expertise in the joint work on fuel cell modeling and to L. dos Santos Coelho from the Industrial and Systems Engineering Graduate Program, Pontifical Catholic University of Paraná, Curitiba, Paraná, Brazil for the cooperation on the development of optimization algorithms over the years.

8. References

[Alotto1998] Alotto, P. G., Eranda, C., Brandstätter, B., Fürntratt, G., Magele, C., Molinari, G., Nervi, M., Repetto, M., Richter, K. R., Stochastic algorithms in electromagnetic optimization, IEEE Transactions on Magnetics, vol. 34, no. 5, pp. 3674-3684, 1998.

[Bard2001] A.J. Bard and L. R. Faulkner, *Electrochemical methods: fundamentals and* applications. New York: J. Wiley & Sons Inc., 2001.

[Borghi1999] C. A. Borghi and M. Fabbri, "Loney's solenoid multi-objective optimization problem," *IEEE Trans. on Magn.*, vol. 35, no. 3, pp. 1706-1709, 1999.

[Campelo2006] F. Campelo, F. G. Guimarães, H. Igarashi, J. A. Ramírez and S. Noguchi, "A modified immune network algorithm for multimodal electromagnetic problems," *IEEE Trans. on Magn.*, vol. 42, no. 4, pp. 1111-1114, 2006

[Chen2005] R. Chen, T.S. Zhao, "Mathematical modeling of a passive-feed DMFC with heat transfer effect", *Journal of Power Sources*, vol. 152, pp. 122-130, 2005

[Chen2006] K. Chen, T. Li and T. Cao, "Tribe-PSO: a novel global optimization algorithm and its application in molecular docking," *Chemometrics and Intelligent Laboratory Systems*, vol. 82, no. 1-2, pp. 248-259, 2006

[Cheng2006] C. H. Cheng and H.H. Lin, G.J. Lai, "Design for geometric parameters of PEM fuel cell by integrating computational fluid dynamics code with optimization method," *Journal of Power Sources*, vol. 165, pp. 803-813, December 2006.

[Ciuprina2002] G. Ciuprina, D. Ioan and I. Munteanu, "Use of intelligent-particle swarm optimization in electromagnetics," *IEEE Trans. on Magn.*, vol. 38, no. 2, pp. 1037-1040, 2002

[Clerc2006] M. Clerc, "Stagnation analysis in particle swarm optimization or what happens when nothing happens," *Technical Report CSM-460,* Department of Computer Science, University of Essex, August 2006.

[Coelho2007] L. S. Coelho and P. Alotto, "Electromagnetic device optimization by hybrid evolution strategy approaches," *COMPEL*, vol. 26, no. 2, pp. 269 279, 2007.

[Cogotti2000] E. Cogotti, A. Fanni and F. Pilo, "A comparison of optimization techniques for Loney's solenoids design: an alternative tabu search algorithm," *IEEE Trans. on Magn.*, vol. 36, no. 4, pp. 1153-1157, 2000.

[Cooren2006] Y. Cooren, M. Clerc, and P. Siarry, "Tribes - a parameter-free particle swarm optimization," *Proc. 7th EU/Meeting on Adaptive, Self-Adaptive, Multi-level Metaheuristics*, Paris, France, 2006.

[DiBarba1995] P. Di Barba, A. Gottvald and A. Savini, "Global optimization of Loney's solenoid: a benchmark problem," *Int. J. of Appl. Electromagnetics and Mech.*, vol. 6, no. 4, pp. 273-276, 1995.

[Kappel2000] F. Kappel and A. Kuntsevich, "An Implementation of Shor's r-Algorithm", *Comput. Optim. Appl.* 15, no. 2, pp. 193-205, 2000.

[Katykatoglu2007] S. Katytakoglu and L. Akylun, "Optimization of the parametric performance of a PEMFC," *Int. Journal of Hydrogen* Energy, vol. 32, pp. 4418-4423, August 2007.

[Larminie2003] J. Larminie and A. Dicks, *Fuel cell systems explained,* Chichester: J. Wiley & Sons Inc., 2003.

[Magele1993] Magele, C. A., Preis, K., Renhart, W., Dyczij-Edlinger, R., Richter, K. R., "Higher order evolution strategies for the global optimization of electromagnetic devices", IEEE Transactions on Magnetics, vol. 29, no. 2, pp. 1775-1778, 1993.

[Magele2007] Magele, Ch., TEAM Benchmark Problem 22. [Online]. Available: http://www-igte.tu-graz.ac.at/team, 2007.

[Onwubolu2004] G. C. Onwubolu, "Tribes application to the flow shop scheduling," in *New Optimization Techniques in Engineering*, Springer-Verlag, Germany, G. C. Onwubolu and B. V. Babu (eds.), pp. 515-535, 2004.

[Onwubolu2005] G. C. Onwubolu, "Optimization of milling operations for the selection of cutting conditions using Tribes," *Proc. IMechE - Part B: J. Engineering Manufacture*, vol. 219, pp. 761-771, 2005.

[Saldanha1999] Saldanha, R. R., Takahashi, R. H. C., Vasconcelos, J. A., Ramirez, J. A., "Adaptive deep-cut method in ellipsoidal optimization for electromagnetic design", IEEE Transactions on Magnetics, vol. 35, no. 3, pp. 1746-1749, 1999.

[Serra1997] P. Serra, A. F. Stanton, and S. Kais, "Pivot method for global optimization", *Phys. Rev. E*, vol. 55(b), pp. 1162 - 1165, 1997.

[Storn1995] Storn, R., Price, K., "Differential evolution: a simple and efficient adaptive scheme for global optimization over continuous spaces," Technical Report TR-95-012, International Computer Science Institute, Berkeley, USA, 1995.

[Ursem2002] Ursem, R. K., "Diversity-guided evolutionary algorithms", Proceedings of Parallel Problem Solving form Nature Conference - PPSN VII, Granada, Spain, pp. 462-471, 2002.

[Ursem2003] Ursem, R. K., "Models for evolutionary algorithms and their applications in system identification and control optimization", PhD thesis, Department of Computer Science, University of Aarhus, Aarhus, Denmark, 2003.

[Zaoui2007] F. Zaoui and C. Marchand, "Using genetic algorithm for the optimization of electromagnetic devices," *COMPEL,* vol. 17, no. 1-3, pp. 181-185, 2007.

4

Stochastic Approach to Test Pattern Generator Design

Gregor Papa[1] and Tomasz Garbolino[2]
[1]*Computer Systems Department, Jožef Stefan Institute, Ljubljana*
[2]*Institute of Electronics, Silesian University of Technology, Gliwice*
[1]*Slovenia*
[2]*Poland*

1. Introduction

The fast growing complexity of modern integrated circuits and rapid changes in technology pose a number of challenges in testing of electronic products. With the introduction of surface mounted devices, small pitch packaging becomes prevalent, which makes the access to the test points on a board either impossible or at least very costly. Traditional in-circuit test techniques that utilize a bed-of-nails to make contact to individual leads on a printed circuit board have become inadequate. This forced the development of a boundary-scan approach that is already widely adopted in practice (Khalil et al., 2002; Parker, 2003). But, a limited number of input/output pins represents a bottleneck in testing of complex embedded cores where transfers of large amounts of test patterns and test results between the automatic test equipment (ATE) and the unit-under-test (UUT) are required. However, the implementation of a built-in self-test (BIST) (Garvie & Thompson, 2003) of the UUT with on-chip test pattern generation (TPG) and on-chip output response analysis logic presents an efficient solution. Then the communication with external ATE is reduced to test initiation and transfer of test results. This approach has the drawback, while BIST implementation leads to the area overhead, causing longer signal routing paths. Therefore, we need to minimize this BIST logic.

Different TPG structures have been proposed in the past. In general, they can be classified as ROM-based deterministic, algorithmic, exhaustive and pseudo-random. In the first approach, deterministic patterns are stored in a ROM and a counter is used for their addressing, (Edirisooriya & Robinson, 1992). The approach is limited to small test pattern sets. Algorithmic TPG are mostly used for testing regular structures such as RAMs (van de Goor, 1991). Exhaustive TPG is counter-based approach that is not able to generate specific sequence of test vectors. With some modifications, however, counter-based solutions are able to generate deterministic test patterns, (Chakrabarty et al., 2000). Pseudo-random TPG is most commonly applied technique in practice; here Linear Feedback Shift Register (LFSR) or Cellular Automata (CA) are employed to generate pseudo-random test patterns. In order to decrease the complexity of a TPG, designers usually try to embed deterministic test patterns into the vector sequence generated by some linear register. Such embedding can be done either by re-seeding a TPG or modifying its feedback function (Hellebrand et al., 1995). Some solutions also modify or transform the vector sequence produced by a LFSR in such a way that it contains deterministic test patterns (Bellos et al., 2002; Fiser, 2007; Hakmi et al., 2007; Touba & McCluskey, 2001).

Regarding the way the test patterns are delivered to the UUT, there are also different approaches. In the test-per-scan approach each test pattern first needs to be shifted in a scan path during several clock cycles before it is applied to the inputs of the UUT (Hakmi et al., 2007; Touba & McCluskey, 2001). This usually leads to long testing times. If a shorter test duration is required, test-per-clock method has to be adopted (Chakrabarty et al., 2000; Fiser, 2007; Garbolino & Papa, 2008), so that each test pattern is produced and stimulates the UUT inputs in a single clock cycle.

Some types of non-concurrent on-line BIST (Aktouf et al., 1999) may require TPG structures that are capable to generate the set of precomputed deterministic test patterns in the minimum number of clock cycles. In one of the first approaches the set of predefined test vectors is encoded into an appropriately designed network of the OR gates (Dufaza et al., 1993). In turn, the solution proposed in (Bellos et al., 2002) uses a network of XOR gates to transform a sequence of consecutive vectors produced by a LFSR into a sequence of deterministic test patterns. In (Garbolino & Papa, 2008; 2010) a Multi-Input Signature Register (MISR) is combined with a combinational logic which modifies its state diagram in such a way that the MISR generates a sequence of expected deterministic test patterns. A method of designing a deterministic TPG based on non-uniform CA was proposed in (Cao et al., 2008), while another solution employs a group of small Finite State Machines (FSMs) to generate a relatively short vector sequence that contains all deterministic test patterns (Sudireddy et al., 2008).

The proposed LFSR structures are based on D-type flip-flops, while in recent years LFSR composed of D-type and T-type flip-flops or even of T-type flip-flops only, has been gaining popularity. The main reason is its low area overhead and high operating speed (Garbolino & Hlawiczka, 1999; Garbolino et al., 2000). Some applications of such a type of LFSRs can be found in (Garbolino & Hlawiczka, 2002; Garbolino & Papa, 2008; Novák et al., 2004). In particular, works (Garbolino & Hlawiczka, 2002) and (Garbolino & Papa, 2008) present some concepts of optimizing the LFSR structure containing D-type and T-type flip-flops for generation of deterministic test pattern sets.

Evolutionary stochastic techniques for the optimization of hardware are widely used (Bolzani et al., 2007; Drechsler & Drechsler, 2002; Guo et al., 2007; Mazumder & Rudnick, 1999). In (Sanchez & Squillero, 2007) a software-based methodology that automatically generates test programs is described. The methodology is based on an evolutionary algorithm able to generate test programs for different microprocessor cores. In (Corno et al., 2000) an automatic approach, based on genetic algorithm (GA), targeting processor cores is described that computes a test program able to attain high fault coverage figures.

GA has also been used for the derivation of test pattern sets for target UUTs (Corno, Prinetto, Rebaudengo & Sonza Reorda, 1996), and for optimization of test sequence for weighted pseudo-random test generation to achieve the best test efficiency (Favalli & Dalpasso, 2002). As regards the synthesis of the TPG logic for actual generation of the derived test patters, GA approach has also been used for the solutions based on CA (Corno, Prinetto & Sonza Reorda, 1996). A detailed summary and analysis of various test pattern generation techniques based on GA is presented in (Fin & Fummi, 2003).

The work presents a design approach of a deterministic TPG logic based on a LFSR, that is composed of D-type and T-type flip-flops. The use of LFSR for TPG eliminates the need of a ROM for storing the seeds since a LFSR itself jumps from a state to the next required state (seed) by inverting the logic value of some of the bits of its next state. In contrast to (Garbolino & Papa, 2010) here the counter is connected to the inputs of the modification function. The search for the proper LFSR employs a GA to find an acceptable practical solution in a large space of possible LFSR implementations, where the goal is to develop a TPG that would generate only the required test vectors. Here, we concurrently optimize the TPG structure (type of flip-flops, presence of inverters), the order of patterns in test sequence, and the bit-order of a test pattern.

The rest of the chapter is organized as follows: in Section 2 we describe the TPG structure, and give an example of area minimization through the modification of the TPG structure and its test vectors; in Section 3 we describe the GA and the work of its operators; in Section 4 we describe the optimization process and evaluate it; and in Section 5 we draw the conclusion.

2. TPG structure

A TPG is initialized with a given deterministic seed and run until the desired fault coverage is achieved. The test application time using an LFSR is significantly larger than what is required for applying the test set generated using a deterministic TPG; vector set generated by a LFSR includes not only useful vectors but also many other vectors that do not contribute to the fault coverage. In our approach, the goal is to develop a TPG that would generate only the required test vectors (i.e., with no intermittent non-useful vectors).

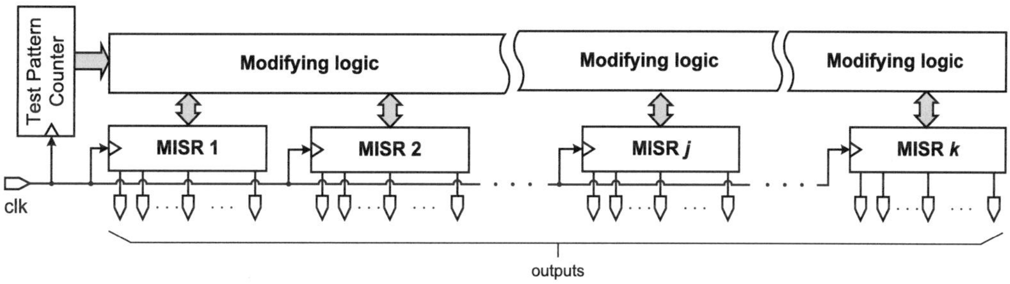

Fig. 1. Block diagram of the n-bit TPG.

A general block diagram of the proposed n bit test pattern generator is shown in Figure 1. A TPG contains k MSIRs which operation is synchronized by a common clock signal clk. A MISR is a variant of a LFSR that is additionally equipped with parallel inputs. A bit vector applied to the parallel inputs of a MISR influences the sequence of vectors produced at the outputs of the register. The k' MISRs have width N while the width of k'' remaining registers is $N + 1$, where $N = n/k$, $k'' = (n \ MOD \ k)$ and $k' = k - k''$. Parallel inputs of all MISRs are connected to the outputs of the common block of a combinational logic, which is called a modifying logic because its aim is to modify the MISRs' state diagrams. Outputs of all registers are in turn fed back to the inputs of the modifying logic block. Moreover, the modifying logic may be optionally fed by the outputs of a test pattern counter (TPC), which anyway has to be present in any BIST structure. We expect that the latter property should simplify optimization of the modifying logic and enable its further reduction by a synthesis tool. In this study we take into account two types of TPCs, namely binary and one-hot counter.

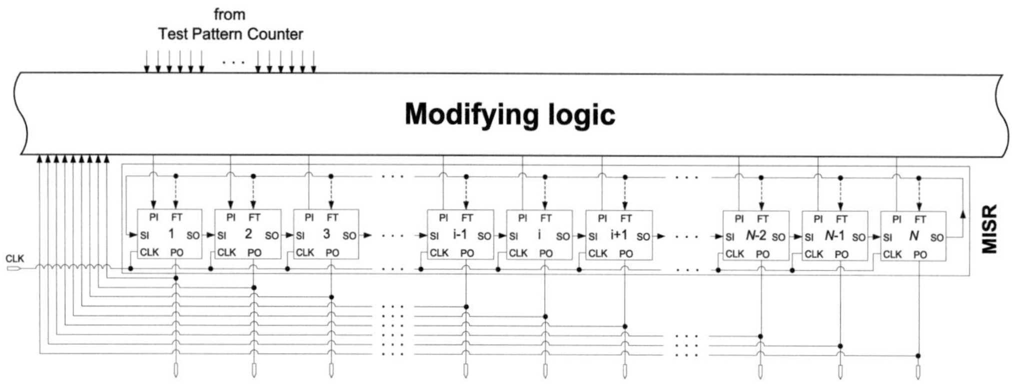

Fig. 2. Scheme of the j-th N-bit MISR.

A scheme in Figure 2 shows an internal structure of the MSIR and interconnections between the register and the modifying logic. The MISR is composed of N cells connected in series and always has a global feedback path connecting the serial output (SO) of the last stage to the serial input (SI) of the first stage. Some other cells, depending on their internal structure, may also have their feedback tap (FT) inputs connected to the global feedback path (connections marked by a dotted line). The parallel input (PI) of each cell is controlled by an output of the modifying logic. Parallel outputs (PO) of the cells constitute the actual outputs of a TPG and at the same time they are fed back to the inputs of the modifying logic module.
A general scheme of the i-th cell of the MISR is presented in Figure 3. The cell contains a D- or T-type flip-flop. The input of the flip-flop is fed by the logic implementing a XOR or XNOR function of the cell's inputs: serial input SI, parallel input PI and - in a case of some cell structures - feedback tap input FT. The output Q of the flip-flop is connected to the parallel output PO of the cell either directly or via an inverter. It is also connected to the serial output SO of the cell. All elements of the cell that are optional and may or may not be present in its particular configuration are marked grey in Figure 3. Thus, a single cell may have 16 different structures. An exception are the first and the last cell of a MISR, which have only 8 different structures. In consequence, the number α of different structures of a N-bit MISR is $\alpha = 16^{N-2} + 8^2 = 2^{4N-2}$.

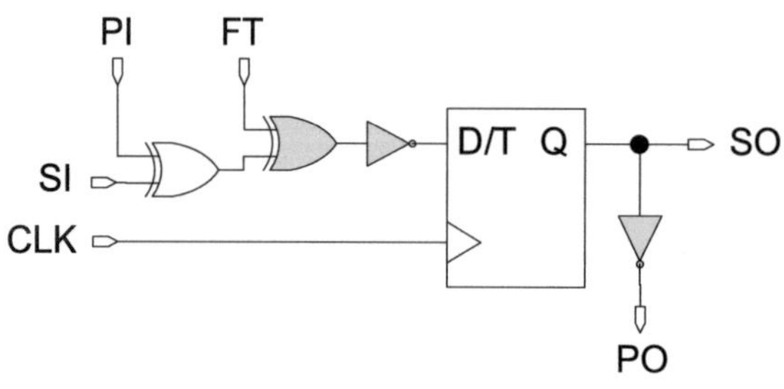

Fig. 3. A general scheme of an i-th cell of a MISR.

The modifying logic - which is a simple combinational logic and acts as a decoder - allows that in the subsequent clock cycles the contents of the MISR assumes the values specified by the target test pattern set. Hence the MISR and the modifying logic are application specific: they are synthesized according to the required test pattern set.

Particularly important parameter in the case of deterministic test pattern generators is the area overhead, which is influenced by:

- a structure of each stage in each MISR,
- an order of the test patterns in a test sequence,
- a bit-order of the test patterns,
- a number of MISRs in a TPG.

The first factor influences the complexity of both the MISR and the modifying logic, only. The relationships are illustrated below with the use of a simple TPG designed for TSMC 0.35 μm technology.

Initial structure and test vectors

Having the set of seven 5-bit vectors the resulting structure of a TPG is shown in Figure 4. It is assumed that all flip-flops in the scheme are scannable. A T-type flip-flops comprise a scannable D-type flip-flop and a XOR gate. The total complexity of the initial structure of a TPG is 55 equivalent gates.

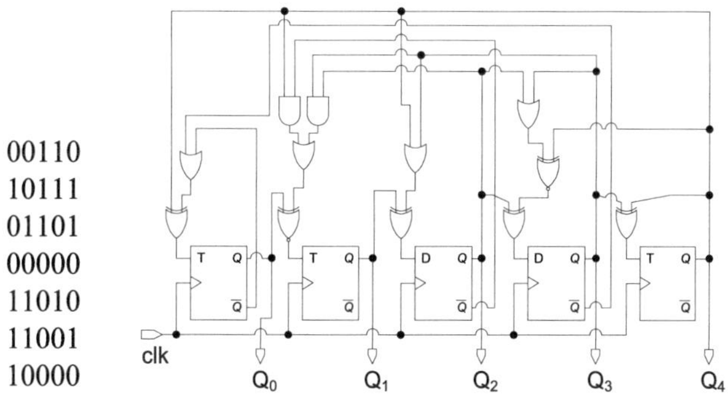

Fig. 4. TPG structure modification: initial solution.

Flip-flop type replacement

Replacing the T-type flip-flop with the D-type one in the stage No. 4 of a TPG, the new configuration of a TPG is presented in Figure 5. The replacement of the type of the flip-flop has lead to reduction of the total complexity of a TPG structure to 51 equivalent gates.

Column permutation

Permutation of columns of the test pattern sequence further decreases the area of a TPG. If we permute columns in the test sequence as illustrated in Figure 6, a TPG is simplified to the structure with the area of 49 equivalent gates.

Vectors permutation

Further we can permute test patterns in the test sequence. Exchanging the order of test patterns in the test sequence, like shown in Figure 7, simplifies a TPG structure to the area of 38 equivalent gates.

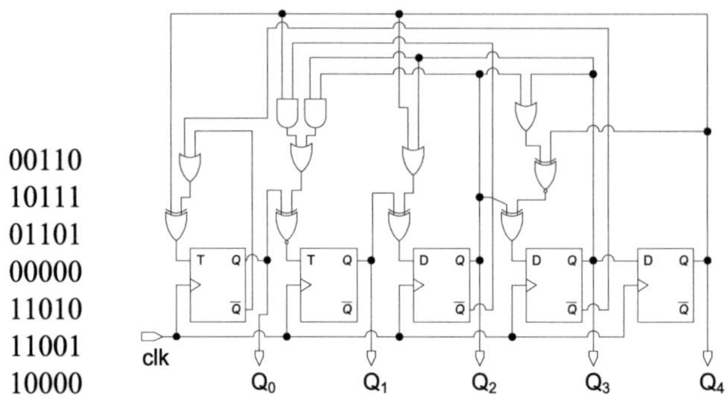

Fig. 5. TPG structure modification: after replacing the flip-flop type.

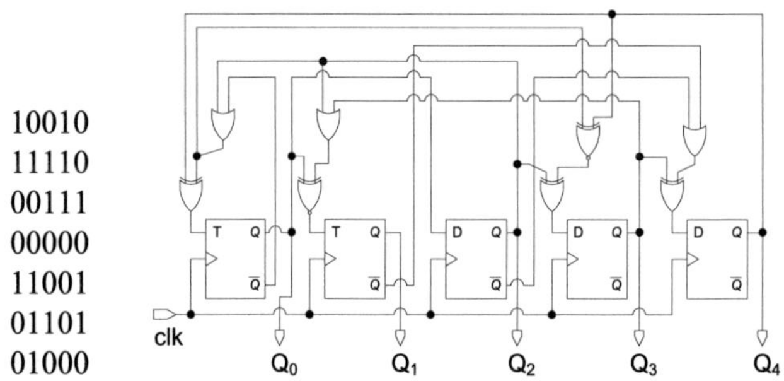

Fig. 6. TPG structure modification: after permutating columns.

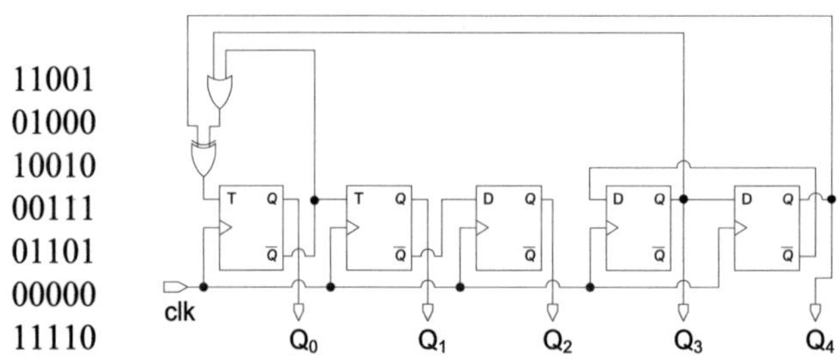

Fig. 7. TPG structure modification: after permutating vectors.

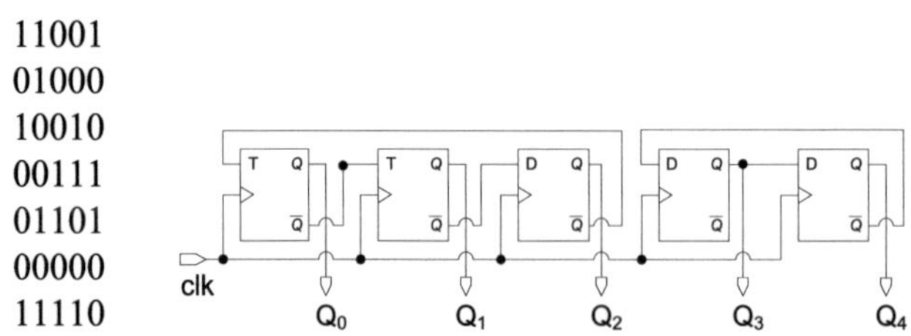

Fig. 8. TPG structure modification: after MSIR structure splitting.

Structure splitting

Splitting a MISR structure into several parts (Figure 8) may potentially lead to the further reduction of its area. Implementing the exemplar TPG in the form of two independent MISRs results in the structure whose complexity is only 35 equivalent gates.
A change of the MISR structure, the order of the test patterns in a test sequence, the bit-order of the test patterns and the number of parts a MISR is split to may result in a substantial reduction of the TPG area. The solution space is very broad: for an n-bit TPG producing the sequence of m test patterns there are about $2^{4n-2k}m!n!n$ possible solutions; therefore, effective optimization procedure is required to find an acceptable practical solution.

3. Genetic algorithm

The intelligent stochastic optimization is implemented through genetic algorithm (GA) (Goldberg, 1989). The GA's intrinsic parallelism allows searching within a broad database of solutions in the search space simultaneously. There is some risk of converging to a local optimum, but efficient results in other optimization problem areas (Korošec & Šilc, 2008; Papa & Koroušić-Seljak, 2005; Papa & Šilc, 2002) encouraged us to use GA approach in TPG synthesis optimization. Our version of the GA, which was already presented in (Garbolino & Papa, 2010), is adapted to the problem to be able to optimize multiple design aspects, i.e., type of flip-flops, presence of inverters, order of patterns in test sequence, and bit-order of a test pattern.

3.1 TPG encoding

In the initialization phase of the GA the structure of a TPG, order of test patterns, and their bit order are encoded with three different chromosomes. These three chromosomes do not interact with each other, but are used to concurrently optimize the structure of a TPG, the order of the test patterns, and the bit order of test patterns. They have to be optimized concurrently since their influence on the final solution is interdependent.
The first chromosome, which encodes the structure of n-bit TPG, looks like

$$C_1 = i_{11}i_{12}i_{13}i_{14}\dots i_{n1}i_{n2}i_{n3}i_{n4}, \tag{1}$$

where i_{jx} represents a binary value; j ($j = 1, 2, \dots, n$) determines each flip-flop and x determines the properties of a flip-flop (see Table 1).

position	property	value 0	value 1
1	flip-flop type	D-type	T-type
2	inverted input	no inverter	inverter
3	feedback input	no feedback	feedback
4	inverted output	no inverter	inverter

Table 1. Flip-flop properties

The second and third chromosome, which encode the order of the test patterns, and the bit order of test patterns, look like

$$C_2 = a_1a_2\dots a_m, \tag{2}$$

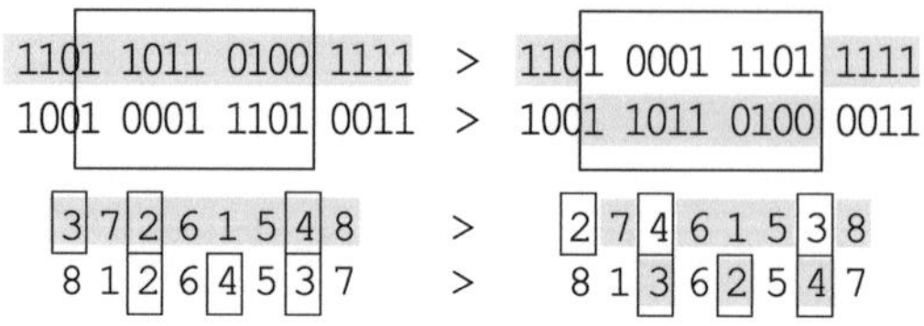

Fig. 9. Crossover: TPG configuration (top), pattern and bit orders (bottom).

where m is the number of test vectors and a_j $(j = 1, 2, \ldots, m)$ is the label number of the test vector from the initial vector list, and

$$C_3 = b_1 b_2 \ldots b_n, \tag{3}$$

where n is the number of flip-flops in the structure and b_j $(j = 1, 2, \ldots, n)$ is the label number of the bit order of the initial test patterns.

3.2 Population initialization

The population consists of N chromosomes, of each type. Depending on requirements and input settings, the initial chromosome of the configuration can be set as (i) random values on all positions, (ii) with values 0 on all positions, (iii) with values 1 on all positions, (iv) based on some input configuration. For the last three possibilities the values are permutated with some given probability to avoid identical chromosomes.
The initial chromosomes for orders are set as (i) random distribution of order values or (ii) consecutive order of numbers. In the latest case some chromosomes are permutated to ensure versatile chromosomes. While the numbers in these two chromosomes represent the order of patterns or bits in patterns, their values cannot be duplicated and also consecutive values cannot be missed; both conditions must be considered during the initialization.

3.3 Genetic operators

The elitism strategy prevents losing the best found solution by memorizing it. Better solutions have more influence on the new generation due to the substitution of the least-fit chromosomes with the equal number of the best-ranked chromosomes. The ratio of all chromosomes in the population to be replaced is set by r.
In a two-point crossover scheme, chromosome mates are chosen randomly and, with a probability p_c, all values between two randomly chosen positions are swapped. This leads to the two new solutions that replace the original solutions. Figure 9(top) shows the example of crossover with crossover points on positions 3 and 12.
The crossover in case of test patterns order and bit-order of the test patterns is performed with the interchange of positions that store the ordered numbers within the range (order-based crossover); for an example within the range [2, 4], see Figure 9(bottom).
In the mutation process each value of the chromosome mutates with a probability p_m. Since a high mutation rate results in a random walk through GA search space, p_m has to be low enough. Two different types of mutation are applied (see Figure 10 for details): bit inversion that changes the configuration for the first chromosome and position-based mutation for the other two chromosomes, where pattern order and bit order are changed.

1101 1011 0100 1111 > 1111 1011 0100 0111

3 7 2 6 1 5 4 8 > 3 7 5 6 1 2 4 8

Fig. 10. Mutation: TPG configuration (top), pattern and bit orders (bottom).

3.4 Fitness evaluation

After modifying the solutions, the whole new population is ready to be evaluated. The external evaluation tool is used to evaluate each new chromosome created by GA, and TPG cost approximation is obtained for each solution. The obtained cost approximation does not exactly represent an area overhead of the given solution. It rather reflects in quantitative form some set of properties of TPG that make its structure either more or less susceptible for effective area reduction during actual synthesis process.

On the basis of the equations for the register's next-state, values of the outputs of the modifying logic for each vector but last in the test sequence can be derived. In (Garbolino & Papa, 2008) an Espresso (UC Berkeley, 1988) boolean optimization software was used for approximate cost estimation of the modifying logic. On the one hand, the cost approximation provided by the Espresso software was quite accurate in majority of cases. On the other hand, however, its use led to long computation times of a GA what limited the applicability of the complete tool to small and medium size circuits only. Moreover, the approach proposed in (Garbolino & Papa, 2008) was focused on reducing an area of the modifying logic only, neglecting the complexity of MISR at all.

In this work the authors used a new function f_c for cost evaluation of the TPG, which was already proposed in (Garbolino & Papa, 2010). The detailed formula of the function is provided below:

$$f_c(TPG_i) = C_{MISR}\frac{x_i}{X} + C_{MF}\frac{b_i}{B}\frac{1-l_i}{n}\frac{1-e_i}{n}, \tag{4}$$

where

- n is the width of test patterns, the number of stages of the TPG, the maximum number of outputs of the module implementing modification function;
- m is the number of patterns in a test sequence;
- i is the index of the given individual in the population, i.e. the index for the TPG structure and its parameters;
- TPG_i is the structure of the TPG corresponding to the i-th individual in the population;
- C_{MF} and C_{MISR} are the coefficients that enable a user to control whether to put more stress on minimizing the complexity of modifying logic or a MISR, respectively;
- x_i is the number of XOR gates required to implement the MISR for the TPG_i structure;
- X is the maximum number of XOR gates that may be used to built up the n-bit MISR composed of D- and T-type flip-flops ($X = 3n - 1$ in the case where there is a T-type flip-flop, feedback tap and parallel input in every stage of the MISR);
- b_i is the total number of bit flips at the outputs of the module implementing modification function for the TPG_i structure, produced during the generation of deterministic test patterns in consecutive m clock cycles;

- B is the maximum possible number of bit flips at the outputs of the module implementing modification function during m consecutive clock cycles ($B = n(m-2)$);
- l_i is the number of the outputs of the module implementing modification function for the TPG_i structure that keep constant value during generating deterministic test patterns in consecutive m clock cycles;
- e_i is the total number of MISR inputs that can be fed from the same output of the module implementing modification function for the TPG_i structure.

The cost evaluation function aims at reducing the size of the modifying logic module by minimizing the number of bit flips b_i at the outputs of the module. In addition, it favors such structures of the TPG in which some number (l_i) of parallel inputs of the MISR can be driven by a constant value or where several (e_i) parallel inputs of the MISR can be driven by the same output of the modifying logic module. At the same time the function promotes the less complex structures of the MISR by reducing the number x_i of XOR gates that are necessary to construct the register. Through appropriately setting the values of C_{MF} and C_{MISR} coefficients, the user may decide whether the function will put more stress on minimizing the complexity of modifying logic or a MISR.
Note that the functionality of the inverter at the input of the flip-flop can be implemented by substituting the XOR gate with the XNOR one, or vice versa. Similarly, instead of adding the NOT gate at the Q output of the flip-flop, the complemented output $\overline{Q}$ can be used. Therefore, an employment of the inverted inputs or outputs of the MISR does not influence the cost of the register and that is why the number of inverters has not been involved in the TPG cost evaluation function f_c.
It turned out that the TPG structures with lower value of the cost evaluation function tend to have lower area overhead than those with higher value of the function. Moreover, although the function delivers less accurate cost approximation than Espresso software, it is much faster and it tries to reduce the area overhead of the whole TPG instead of modifying logic only.

4. Results

The initial TPG structure is based on the desired sequence of test patterns. The GA operators try to make new configuration while checking the allowed TPG structure and using the external evaluation tool. The evaluation tool calculates the cost of a given structure. The best structure, found during the optimization, is chosen and implemented.
Considering the chromosome length and short pre-experimental tests we set GA parameters to give the results in an acceptable computing time. Population size for each circuit was in the range from 60 to 300 (depending on circuit complexity), while the number of generations was about 5 times the population size. Crossover and mutation probabilities did not change with circuits and were 0.8 and 0.01, respectively.
The results are presented for all ISCAS'85 and some ISCAS'89 test benchmark circuits. These circuits are used to benchmark various test pattern generation systems. ISCAS benchmark suite has been introduced in simple netlist format at the International Symposium of Circuits and Systems in 1985 (ISCAS'85), and was expanded with additional circuits at 1989 Symposium. ISCAS'85 benchmarks are purely combinational circuits while these belonging to the ISCAS'89 set are sequential structures equipped with a scan path.
The compact sets of deterministic test patterns for ISCAS'85 and ISCAS'89 circuits were obtained from MINTEST ATPG tool (Hamzaoglu & Patel, 1998). For each benchmark, the

Circuit	Test pattern width	Number of test patterns
c432	36	27
c499	41	52
c880	60	16
c1355	41	84
c1908	33	106
c2670	233	44
c3540	50	84
c5315	178	37
c6288	32	12
c7552	207	73
s349	24	13
s382	24	25
s386	13	63
s400	24	24
s444	24	24
s510	25	54
s526	24	49
s1196	32	113
s1238	32	121
s1494	14	100
s5378	214	97
s9234	247	105

Table 2. Benchmark properties.

test pattern width (number of inputs of the circuit under test) and the number of test patterns (number of test vectors that are mutually different and together provide 100% fault coverage of stuck-at faults in the circuit) are given in the second and third column of Table 2, respectively.

Table 3 presents the results of the approach used in (Garbolino & Papa, 2010). Here, the total cost - in terms of equivalent gates - for the optimized TPG structure is presented. It is common assumption that TPG shares D-type flip-flops with the circuit under test. The cost of the combinational logic part of a TPG only was taken into account, while it represents a real area overhead for the given TPG (excluding area of the output D-type flip-flops, multiplexers and the binary pattern counter, since these elements need to be in any TPG). An initial solution was derived by randomly choosing a structure of the MISR as well as order of vectors in a test sequence and order of bits in test vectors. Synthesis of TPGs was carried out using a commercial synthesis tool and a standard cell library for a 0.35 μm technology. The last column of Table 3 shows the achieved improvement. Note that each of the last two columns of the table contains several numbers (subcolumns) for each benchmark circuit. These numbers correspond to the best, the worst and the average solution, respectively, obtained during 10 independent runs of the genetic algorithm.

Tables 4-6 show the synthesis results for the TPG structure proposed in this study. The first, second and third column of the table contain, respectively, the name of the benchmark, the number of parts a MISR is split to (1, 2 or 4) and the type of the TPG structure (NC or OHC).

Circuit	Optimized TPG			Improvement in %		
	best	worst	average	best	worst	average
c432	329.3	358.9	347.5	12.2	4.3	7.4
c499	448.7	517.9	485.7	20.9	8.7	14.4
c880	345.6	402.2	367.9	11.4	-3.1	5.7
c1355	698.9	789.4	747.8	2.1	-10.6	-4.8
c1908	1078.8	1165.2	1127.8	12.0	5.0	8.0
c2670	2669.4	2777.5	2727.9	-0.8	-4.9	-3.0
c3540	1353.8	1437.3	1395.5	4.5	-1.4	1.5
c5315	1744.7	1845.2	1807.4	8.7	3.4	5.4
c6288	128.7	173.0	146.0	30.9	7.1	21.6
c7552	3876.6	4048.6	3948.9	0.3	-4.1	-1.6
s349	85.2	175.3	103.5	47.9	-7.3	36.6
s382	180.3	207.6	196.6	28.7	17.9	22.2
s386	280.7	310.0	295.2	15.5	6.7	11.2
s400	173.6	199.3	184.6	32.8	22.9	28.6
s444	176.6	194.6	188.0	29.1	21.9	24.5
s510	438.1	473.3	458.0	16.0	9.2	12.1
s526	362.6	400.2	380.3	17.2	8.7	13.2
s1196	1195.5	1279.7	1244.9	5.8	-0.8	1.9
s1238	1271.0	1314.9	1292.0	7.3	4.1	5.7
s1494	487.3	537.9	515.5	8.3	-1.2	3.0
s5378	4909.4	5107.7	4963.6	7.0	3.3	6.0
s9234	5994.8	6405.6	6150.4	7.1	0.8	4.7

Table 3. Results of TPG area based on the approach in (Garbolino & Papa, 2010).

The label NC denotes the TPG which modifying logic is fed solely by the outputs of a MISR or MISRs while the label OHC is a symbol of the TPG that contains the one-hot counter. For the sake of clarity the TPG structure discussed in (Garbolino & Papa, 2010) as well as the two proposed in this study are henceforth denoted as TPG+BC, TPG+NC and TPG+OHC, respectively.

Columns 4 and 5 of Tables 4-6 include the cost - in terms of equivalent gates - of the initial and optimized TPG structure, respectively. An initial solution was derived in the same way like in (Garbolino & Papa, 2010). The same synthesis tool and target technology were also used to carry out synthesis of TPGs. The achieved improvement is shown in the last column of each of the tables. Similarly to Table 3 each of the last two columns of Tables 4-6 contains several numbers (subcolumns) for each benchmark circuit. These numbers correspond to the best, the worst and the average solution, respectively, obtained during 10 independent runs of the genetic algorithm. In the case of the TPG+NC structure the cost of the combinational logic part of a TPG only is taken into account, excluding area of the output D-type flip-flops, multiplexers and binary pattern counter, since these elements need to be in any TPG. The cost of the TPG+OHC structure is calculated in a similar way but it also includes the area of the one-hot counter. The obtained value is further diminished by the area of the binary counter. The last step results from the fact that in the TPG+OHC structure the one-hot counter replaces the binary counter in a role of a test pattern counter. Since the area of a test pattern counter

Circuit			Initial TPG	Optimized TPG			Improvement in %		
				best	worst	average	best	worst	average
c432	1	NC	389.9	261.8	288.7	270.1	32.8	25.9	30.7
		OHC	486.7	358.6	385.5	366.9	26.3	20.8	24.6
	2	NC	381.2	255.5	281.1	266.0	33.0	26.3	30.2
		OHC	478.0	352.3	377.9	362.8	26.3	20.9	24.1
	4	NC	372.9	243.8	294.1	259.5	34.6	21.1	30.4
		OHC	469.7	340.6	390.9	356.3	27.5	16.8	24.2
c499	1	NC	564.8	361.6	404.8	384.1	36.0	28.3	32.0
		OHC	784.7	581.4	624.7	604.0	25.9	20.4	23.0
	2	NC	569.8	364.9	403.5	387.8	36.0	29.2	31.9
		OHC	789.7	584.8	623.3	607.6	25.9	21.1	23.1
	4	NC	525.6	363.9	399.5	386.4	30.8	24.0	26.5
		OHC	745.4	583.8	619.4	606.3	21.7	16.9	18.7
c880	1	NC	392.2	188.9	204.2	198.1	51.8	47.9	49.5
		OHC	440.4	237.2	252.5	246.3	46.1	42.7	44.1
	2	NC	398.8	185.6	207.2	197.9	53.5	48.0	50.4
		OHC	447.1	233.9	255.5	246.2	47.7	42.9	44.9
	4	NC	388.5	190.6	224.2	201.6	50.9	42.3	48.1
		OHC	436.8	238.9	272.5	249.9	45.3	37.6	42.8
c1355	1	NC	761.1	514.3	549.2	535.6	32.4	27.8	29.6
		OHC	1141.2	894.4	929.4	915.8	21.6	18.6	19.8
	2	NC	739.1	513.9	554.2	536.9	30.5	25.0	27.4
		OHC	1119.3	894.1	933.0	916.9	20.1	16.6	18.1
	4	NC	772.7	518.6	560.5	542.8	32.9	27.5	29.8
		OHC	1152.9	898.8	940.7	923.0	22.0	18.4	19.9
c1908	1	NC	1206.8	1048.1	1110.0	1071.7	13.1	8.0	11.2
		OHC	1704.1	1545.4	1607.3	1568.9	9.3	5.7	7.9
	2	NC	1235.1	971.0	1103.4	1051.7	21.4	10.7	14.9
		OHC	1732.3	1468.2	1600.6	1548.9	15.2	7.6	10.6
	4	NC	1189.2	1005.2	1134.3	1040.6	15.5	4.6	12.5
		OHC	1686.4	1502.5	1631.6	1537.8	10.9	3.3	8.8
c2670	1	NC	2772.2	2040.4	2079.3	2049.2	26.4	25.0	26.1
		OHC	2949.5	2217.7	2256.6	2226.5	24.8	23.5	24.5
	2	NC	2668.4	2030.4	2092.6	2051.3	23.9	21.6	23.1
		OHC	2845.7	2207.7	2269.9	2228.5	22.4	20.2	21.7
c3540	1	NC	1422.7	1204.5	1292.3	1261.4	15.3	9.2	11.3
		OHC	1802.9	1584.7	1672.5	1641.6	12.1	7.2	8.9
	2	NC	1439.0	1240.4	1306.3	1267.1	13.8	9.2	11.9
		OHC	1819.2	1620.6	1686.4	1647.2	10.9	7.3	9.5
	4	NC	1405.1	1242.4	1314.3	1271.4	11.6	6.5	9.5
		OHC	1785.2	1622.6	1694.4	1651.6	9.1	5.1	7.5

Table 4. Results of TPG area (part 1).

Circuit			Initial TPG	Optimized TPG			Improvement in %		
				best	worst	average	best	worst	average
c5315	1	NC	1884.7	1384.8	1424.4	1401.9	26.5	24.4	25.6
		OHC	2024.8	1524.8	1564.4	1541.9	24.7	22.7	23.8
	2	NC	1849.1	1374.5	1408.7	1394.5	25.7	23.8	24.6
		OHC	1989.2	1514.5	1548.8	1534.5	23.9	22.1	22.9
	4	NC	1909.4	1390.8	1418.4	1403.0	27.2	25.7	26.5
		OHC	2049.4	1530.8	1558.4	1543.0	25.3	24.0	24.7
c6288	1	NC	186.6	80.2	90.1	84.5	57.0	51.7	54.7
		OHC	213.6	107.1	117.1	111.5	49.8	45.2	47.8
	2	NC	192.6	77.5	91.5	84.5	59.8	52.5	56.1
		OHC	219.6	104.5	118.4	111.3	52.4	46.1	49.3
	4	NC	182.0	73.2	91.1	82.1	59.8	49.9	54.9
		OHC	208.9	100.1	118.1	108.7	52.1	43.5	48.0
c7552	1	NC	3857.3	3218.6	3225.6	3219.3	16.6	16.4	16.5
		OHC	4178.9	3540.2	3547.2	3540.9	15.3	15.1	15.3
	2	NC	3861.3	3183.0	3218.3	3214.8	17.6	16.7	16.7
		OHC	4182.9	3504.7	3539.9	3536.4	16.2	15.4	15.5
s349	1	NC	153.3	72.8	94.1	84.2	52.5	38.6	45.1
		OHC	185.6	105.1	126.4	116.5	43.4	31.9	37.2
	2	NC	153.3	73.8	90.1	81.9	51.8	41.2	46.6
		OHC	185.6	106.1	122.4	114.2	42.8	34.0	38.5
	4	NC	159.7	76.8	92.8	83.5	51.9	41.9	47.7
		OHC	192.0	109.1	125.1	115.8	43.1	34.8	39.7
s382	1	NC	249.1	170.6	186.3	178.2	31.5	25.2	28.5
		OHC	335.3	256.8	272.4	264.3	23.4	18.7	21.2
	2	NC	262.8	172.3	192.9	181.2	34.4	26.6	31.0
		OHC	348.9	258.5	279.1	267.4	25.9	20.0	23.4
	4	NC	257.1	164.7	191.3	176.5	36.0	25.6	31.3
		OHC	343.3	250.8	277.4	262.7	26.9	19.2	23.5
s386	1	NC	332.0	268.8	287.7	278.9	19.0	13.3	16.0
		OHC	610.4	547.2	566.1	557.3	10.4	7.2	8.7
	2	NC	324.3	253.5	288.7	269.1	21.8	11.0	17.0
		OHC	602.7	531.9	567.1	547.5	11.8	5.9	9.2
s400	1	NC	243.2	152.0	193.3	172.5	37.5	20.5	29.1
		OHC	324.0	232.9	274.1	253.3	28.1	15.4	21.8
	2	NC	233.5	154.7	181.3	169.6	33.8	22.4	27.4
		OHC	314.3	235.5	262.1	250.4	25.1	16.6	20.3
	4	NC	225.2	154.7	184.9	171.8	31.3	17.9	23.7
		OHC	306.0	235.5	265.8	252.7	23.0	13.2	17.4

Table 5. Results of TPG area (part 2).

Circuit			Initial TPG	Optimized TPG			Improvement in %		
				best	worst	average	best	worst	average
s444	1	NC	223.5	151.4	185.9	168.0	32.3	16.8	24.8
		OHC	304.4	232.2	266.8	248.9	23.7	12.3	18.2
	2	NC	226.5	156.0	182.0	171.1	31.1	19.7	24.4
		OHC	307.4	236.8	264.5	252.3	22.9	14.0	17.9
	4	NC	234.2	158.7	176.3	169.5	32.2	24.7	27.6
		OHC	315.0	239.5	257.1	250.3	24.0	18.4	20.5
s510	1	NC	508.6	406.2	452.4	436.6	20.1	11.1	14.2
		OHC	739.1	636.7	682.9	667.1	13.9	7.6	9.7
	2	NC	546.9	409.8	453.7	433.3	25.1	17.0	20.8
		OHC	777.4	640.3	684.2	663.8	17.6	12.0	14.6
	4	NC	513.9	417.5	460.4	439.6	18.8	10.4	14.5
		OHC	744.4	648.0	690.9	670.1	13.0	7.2	10.0
s526	1	NC	471.4	341.3	384.2	360.4	27.6	18.5	23.5
		OHC	675.2	545.2	588.1	564.3	19.3	12.9	16.4
	2	NC	433.8	343.6	385.5	361.3	20.8	11.1	16.7
		OHC	637.7	547.5	589.4	565.2	14.1	7.6	11.4
	4	NC	455.1	340.6	378.5	357.3	25.1	16.8	21.5
		OHC	658.9	544.5	582.4	561.2	17.4	11.6	14.8
s1196	1	NC	1266.0	1113.7	1175.9	1141.5	12.0	7.1	9.8
		OHC	1800.5	1648.2	1710.4	1676.0	8.5	5.0	6.9
	2	NC	1259.0	1108.7	1184.9	1143.8	11.9	5.9	9.1
		OHC	1793.6	1643.2	1719.4	1678.4	8.4	4.1	6.4
	4	NC	1266.0	1117.3	1178.5	1154.9	11.7	6.9	8.8
		OHC	1800.5	1651.9	1713.1	1689.4	8.3	4.9	6.2
s1238	1	NC	1367.2	1213.1	1286.3	1236.6	11.3	5.9	9.5
		OHC	1944.2	1790.2	1863.4	1813.7	7.9	4.2	6.7
	2	NC	1333.6	1202.8	1285.3	1251.9	9.8	3.6	6.1
		OHC	1910.6	1779.9	1862.4	1829.0	6.8	2.5	4.3
	4	NC	1376.1	1209.8	1259.7	1230.3	12.1	8.5	10.6
		OHC	1953.2	1786.9	1836.8	1807.4	8.5	6.0	7.5
s1494	1	NC	546.9	448.1	488.6	466.9	18.1	10.6	14.6
		OHC	1012.2	913.4	954.0	932.2	9.8	5.8	7.9
	2	NC	535.9	448.7	494.0	470.3	16.3	7.8	12.2
		OHC	1001.2	914.1	959.3	935.6	8.7	4.2	6.6
s5378	1	NC	5344.9	4741.1	4741.1	4741.1	11.3	11.3	11.3
		OHC	5794.2	5190.5	5190.5	5190.5	10.4	10.4	10.4
s9234	1	NC	6374.0	5738.4	5749.7	5740.4	10.0	9.8	9.9
		OHC	6866.0	6230.3	6241.6	6232.3	9.3	9.1	9.2
	2	NC	6444.2	5761.0	5761.0	5761.0	10.6	10.6	10.6
		OHC	6936.2	6252.9	6252.9	6252.9	9.9	9.9	9.9

Table 6. Results of TPG area (part 3).

is excluded from the cost calculation for the TPG+BC and TPG+NC structures, it seems to be justified to subtract its area from the total cost of the TPG+OHC structure as well.
Analysis of the contents of Tables 3-6 leads to the following observations.

- Average improvement values are positive for all benchmarks except three in the case of the TPG+BC structure and for all benchmarks in the case of the TPG+NC and TPG+OHC structures. Therefore, an application of the proposed optimization algorithm leads to reduction in area overhead of the TPG in majority of cases. Moreover, if the result is negative (increase in area overhead in comparison with an initial solution) there is high probability that running GA tool again will provide improvement in results.
- The TPG+NC is the structure that is the most susceptible for a significant area reduction by an application of the proposed optimization algorithm while the TPG+BC structure seems to be the most resistive for optimization.
- The degree of TPG area optimization is much better in the case of small and medium size test patterns sets (e.g. more than 50% improvement). This may partially result from the fact that in the case of large pattern sets the population size and the number of generations were limited so that the runtime of GA tool was acceptable.
- A huge reduction of TPG area is possible for particular test sets - like in the case of c880, c6288 and s349 benchmarks. A closer examination of these cases revealed that GA tool found TPG structures where some parallel inputs of the MISR can be tied either to the power supply or to the ground while several other PIs of the MISR are fed from the same output of the modifying logic.
- Dividing the MISR into several shorter registers may lead to a further reduction of the TPG area. However, an improvement is rather insignificant.

In the framework of this study all experiments were carried out on a PC equipped with the quad-core Intel 2.66 GHz microprocessor and 4 GB of RAM. Computation time, that varies from several seconds up to several hours for different circuits, is proportional to the number of patterns in a test set and the number of bits in test patterns as well as the size of population and the number of generations of GA. However, in order to obtain satisfactory results of GA execution the population size and the number of generations need to be proportionally increased with the growth of the size of a test pattern set. Thus, the size of a test pattern set influences computation time both directly and indirectly through the parameters of GA.
On the other hand, since TPG design is off-line and one-time optimization process, optimization effectiveness is considered more important than reducing the computation time. Therefore execution times that are less than one day are still acceptable. Moreover, according to the observations for large test pattern sets containing more than several vectors some time consuming procedures of the evaluation software can be turned off (it was actually done in (Garbolino & Papa, 2010)) without a significant influence on the final result. In consequence, this will lead to essential reduction of computation time.
In order to evaluate the TPG+NC structure optimized by the GA algorithm, which has been proposed in this study, the authors compared it with some other state-of-the-art solutions (Bellos et al., 2002) and (Cao et al., 2008) as well as with TPGs presented in some of their previous works (Garbolino & Papa, 2008) and (Garbolino & Papa, 2010). Table 7 reports the area overhead of all the above-mentioned TPG structures for several benchmarks. Because test pattern sets that were used in (Bellos et al., 2002) and (Cao et al., 2008) differ from those

	a)	b)	c)	d)	e)
c432	0.47	N/A	0.11	0.34	0.25
c499	0.47	0.23	0.10	0.21	0.17
c880	0.44	N/A	0.29	0.36	0.19
c1355	0.44	0.25	0.09	0.20	0.15
c1908	0.44	0.38	0.32	0.31	0.28
c2670	0.36	0.17	N/A	0.26	0.20
c3540	0.46	N/A	N/A	0.32	0.29
c5315	0.40	N/A	N/A	0.26	0.21
c6288	0.48	0.67	0.54	0.34	0.19
c7552	0.37	0.28	N/A	0.26	0.21

Table 7. A comparison of different approaches through *area_per_bit*: a) (Bellos et al., 2002), b) (Cao et al., 2008), c) (Garbolino & Papa, 2008), d) (Garbolino & Papa, 2010), and e) this study.

exploited in (Garbolino & Papa, 2008) and (Garbolino & Papa, 2010), the area is expressed in terms of equivalent gates per bit of a test pattern set. The calculation for *area_per_bit* is performed with the following equation, as already defined and used in (Garbolino & Papa, 2008) and (Garbolino & Papa, 2010):

$$area\_per\_bit = \frac{area}{test\_pattern\_width \times number\_of\_test\_patterns}. \tag{5}$$

The TPG+NC structure outperforms TPGs worked out in (Bellos et al., 2002) and (Garbolino & Papa, 2010) for all considered benchmarks. It has also lower area overhead than solutions presented in (Cao et al., 2008) and (Garbolino & Papa, 2008) for all benchmarks but one (c2670 and c1355, respectively).

Thus, a MISR combined with combinational logic that modifies the state diagram of the register proves to be an effective TPG solution, particularly after its structure has been optimized by the GA algorithm proposed by the authors. On the other hand, feeding the inputs of the modifying logic block from the outputs of a counter in addition to the outputs of the MISR seems to be a wrong approach because it leads to deterioration of the results.

5. Conclusion

Whenever a TPG fails to provide the desired fault coverage within the given test length, application specific deterministic TPGs are employed. Deterministic TPGs are more complex than pseudo random TPGs since they employ additional logic to prevent generation of non-useful test patterns. Area overhead is one of the important issues in the design of deterministic TPGs. In this work, a deterministic TPG is presented that is based on a single MISR or several MISRs composed of D and T-type flip-flops, XOR and XNOR two input gates and inverters.

Artificial intelligence structure optimization of a TPG is performed by a genetic algorithm combined with a relatively fast but simple cost approximation function. Instead of performing actual boolean optimization or synthesis of a TPG the function only examines some properties of the components of a TPG (i.e. a MISR and a modifying logic) that influence their area and expresses these properties in a numerical form.

Among a few TPG structures that have been considered in this study and which are all based on the above-mentioned concept, one turns out to be particularly susceptible to reduction of its area by the use of the proposed GA-based tool. Experimental results prove that this TPG structure outperforms - with respect to the area overhead - several other state-of-the art solutions.

6. References

Aktouf, C., Robach, C., Kač, U. & Novak, F. (1999). On-line testing of embedded architectures using idle computations and clock cycles, *5th IEEE International On-line Testing Workshop*, pp. 28–32.

Bellos, M., Kagaris, D. & Nikolos, D. (2002). Test set embedding based on phase shifters, *EDCC-4: Proceedings of the 4th European Dependable Computing Conference on Dependable Computing*, Springer-Verlag, London, UK, pp. 90–101.

Bolzani, L., Sanchez, E., Schillaci, M. & Squillero, G. (2007). Co-evolution of test programs and stimuli vectors for testing of embedded peripheral cores, pp. 3474 –3481.

Cao, B., Xiao, L. & Wang, Y. (2008). A low power deterministic test pattern generator for bist based on cellular automata, *Electronic Design, Test and Applications, IEEE International Workshop on* 0: 266–269.

Chakrabarty, K., Iyengar, V. & Murray, B. T. (2000). Deterministic built-in test pattern generation for high-performance circuits using twisted-ring counters, *IEEE Trans. Very Large Scale Integr. Syst.* 8(5): 633–636.

Corno, F., Prinetto, P., Rebaudengo, M. & Sonza Reorda, M. (1996). Gatto: a genetic algorithm for automatic test pattern generation for large synchronous sequential circuits, *Computer-Aided Design of Integrated Circuits and Systems, IEEE Transactions on* 15(8): 991 –1000.

Corno, F., Prinetto, P. & Sonza Reorda, M. (1996). A genetic algorithm for automatic generation of test logic for digital circuits, *Tools with Artificial Intelligence, 1996., Proceedings Eighth IEEE International Conference on*, pp. 10 – 16.

Corno, F., Sonza Reorda, M., Squillero, G. & Violante, M. (2000). A genetic algorithm-based system for generating test programs for microprocessor ip cores, pp. 195 –198.

Drechsler, R. & Drechsler, N. (2002). *Evolutionary Algorithms for Embedded System Design*, Kluwer Academic Publishers, Norwell, MA, USA.

Dufaza, C., Chevalier, C. & L.F.C., L. Y. V. (1993). Lfsrom - a hardware test pattern generator for deterministic iscas85 test sets, *Proc. 2nd IEEE Asian Test Symposium*, Bejing, China, pp. 160–165.

Edirisooriya, G. & Robinson, J. (1992). Design of low cost rom based test generators, *Proceedings IEEE VLSI Test Symposium*, pp. 61–66.

Favalli, M. & Dalpasso, M. (2002). An evolutionary approach to the design of on-chip pseudorandom test pattern generators, *DATE '02: Proceedings of the conference on Design, automation and test in Europe*, IEEE Computer Society, Washington, DC, USA, p. 1122.

Fin, A. & Fummi, F. (2003). Genetic algorithms: the philosopher's stone or an effective solution for high-level tpg?, *HLDVT '03: Proceedings of the Eighth IEEE International Workshop on High-Level Design Validation and Test Workshop*, IEEE Computer Society, Washington, DC, USA, p. 163.

Fiser, P. (2007). Pseudo-random pattern generator design for column-matching bist, *DSD '07: Proceedings of the 10th Euromicro Conference on Digital System Design Architectures, Methods and Tools*, IEEE Computer Society, Washington, DC, USA, pp. 657–663.

Garbolino, T. & Hlawiczka, A. (1999). A new lfsr with d and t flip-flops as an effective test pattern generator for vlsi circuits, *EDCC-3: Proceedings of the Third European Dependable Computing Conference on Dependable Computing*, Springer-Verlag, London, UK, pp. 321–338.

Garbolino, T. & Hlawiczka, A. (2002). Efficient test pattern generators based on specific cellular automata structures, *Microelectronics Reliability* 42(6): 975 – 983.

Garbolino, T., Hlawiczka, A. & Kristof, A. (2000). Fast and low-area tpgs based on t-type flip-flops can be easily integrated to the scan path, *ETW '00: Proceedings of the IEEE European Test Workshop*, IEEE Computer Society, Washington, DC, USA, p. 161.

Garbolino, T. & Papa, G. (2008). Test pattern generator design optimization based on genetic algorithm, *IEA/AIE '08: Proceedings of the 21st international conference on Industrial, Engineering and Other Applications of Applied Intelligent Systems*, Springer-Verlag, Berlin, Heidelberg, pp. 580–589.

Garbolino, T. & Papa, G. (2010). Genetic algorithm for test pattern generator design, *Applied Intelligence* 32(2): 193–204.

Garvie, M. & Thompson, A. (2003). Evolution of self-diagnosing hardware, *ICES'03: Proceedings of the 5th international conference on Evolvable systems*, Springer-Verlag, Berlin, Heidelberg, pp. 238–248.

Goldberg, D. E. (1989). *Genetic Algorithms in Search, Optimization and Machine Learning*, Addison-Wesley Longman Publishing Co., Inc., Boston, MA, USA.

Guo, R., Li, B., Zou, Y. & Zhuang, Z. (2007). Hybrid quantum probabilistic coding genetic algorithm for large scale hardware-software co-synthesis of embedded systems, pp. 3454 –3458.

Hakmi, A.-W., Wunderlich, H.-J., Zoellin, C., Glowatz, A., Hapke, F., Schloeffel, J. & Souef, L. (2007). Programmable deterministic built-in self-test, pp. 1 –9.

Hamzaoglu, I. & Patel, J. H. (1998). Test set compaction algorithms for combinational circuits, *ICCAD '98: Proceedings of the 1998 IEEE/ACM international conference on Computer-aided design*, ACM, New York, NY, USA, pp. 283–289.

Hellebrand, S., Rajski, J., Tarnick, S., Venkataraman, S. & Courtois, B. (1995). Built-in test for circuits with scan based on reseeding of multiple-polynomial linear feedback shift registers, *IEEE Trans. Comput.* 44(2): 223–233.

Khalil, M., Robach, C. & Novak, F. (2002). Diagnosis strategies for hardware or software systems, *J. Electron. Test.* 18(2): 241–251.

Korošec, P. & Šilc, J. (2008). Using stigmergy to solve numerical optimization problems, *Computing and Informatics* 27(3): 377–402.

Mazumder, P. & Rudnick, E. M. (1999). *Genetic algorithms for VLSI design, layout & test automation*, Prentice Hall PTR, Upper Saddle River, NJ, USA.

Novák, O., Plíva, Z., Nosek, J., Hlawiczka, A., Garbolino, T. & Gucwa, K. (2004). Test-per-clock logic bist with semi-deterministic test patterns and zero-aliasing compactor, *J. Electron. Test.* 20(1): 109–122.

Papa, G. & Koroušić-Seljak, B. (2005). An artificial intelligence approach to the efficiency improvement of a universal motor, *Eng. Appl. Artif. Intell.* 18(1): 47–55.

Papa, G. & Šilc, J. (2002). Automatic large-scale integrated circuit synthesis using allocation-based scheduling algorithm, *Microprocessors and Microsystems* 26(3): 139–147.

Parker, K. (2003). *The boundary-scan handbook, Third edition*, Kluwer Academic Publishers.

Sanchez, E. & Squillero, G. (2007). Evolutionary techniques applied to hardware optimization problems: Test and verification of advanced processors, *in* L. Jain, V. Palade & D. Srinivasan (eds), *Advances in Evolutionary Computing for System Design*, Vol. 66 of *Studies in Computational Intelligence*, Springer Berlin / Heidelberg, pp. 303–326.

Sudireddy, S., Kakade, J. & Kagaris, D. (2008). Deterministic built-in tpg with segmented fsms, pp. 261 –266.

Touba, N. & McCluskey, E. (2001). Bit-fixing in pseudorandom sequences for scan bist, *IEEE Transactions on Computer-Aided Design of Integrated Circuits And Systems* 20(4): 545–555.

UC Berkeley (1988). Espresso, `http://www-cad.eecs.berkeley.edu:80/software/software.html`.

van de Goor, A. J. (1991). *Testing semiconductor memories: theory and practice*, John Wiley & Sons, Inc., New York, NY, USA.

5

Optimal Design and Placement of Piezoelectric Actuators using Genetic Algorithm: Application to Switched Reluctance Machine Noise Reduction

Ojeda Javier[1,3], Mininger Xavier[2], Gabsi Mohamed[1] and Li Yongdong[3]
[1]*SATIE, ENS Cachan, Paris XI, CNRS, UniverSud, 61, av President Wilson, F-94230 Cachan,*
[2]*LGEP, CNRS UMR 8507; SUPELEC; UPMC Univ Paris 06; Univ Paris-Sud; 11 rue Joliot-Curie, Plateau de Moulon, F-91192 Gif-sur-Yvette Cedex,*
[3]*IPEMC, Dept. Electrical Engineering, Tsinghua University, 100084 Beijing,*
[1,2]*France*
[3]*China*

1. Introduction

Thanks to a good robustness, an easy production and high performances, switched reluctance machine (SRM) is an interesting drive for electro vehicular applications (Rahman et al., 2000) (Wang et al., 2005) or high speed applications (Kub et al., 2007). However, noise and vibrations generated by the SRM limit its integration. Previous studies on vibration reduction have considered SRM supplied by a pulsed current source. In this context, many solutions have been successfully applied to this problem such as adapted control schemes (Hong, 2002) and optimized stator design (Blaabjerg et al., 1994). However, these methods are less efficient in high speed operation zones. This chapter deals with the optimal placement and design of piezoelectric actuators used to reduce the noise and vibration generated by a SRM. Piezoelectric actuators are stuck on the SRM stator and controlled in order to reduce the generated vibrations. The design and placement are achieved by a genetic algorithm, NSGA II (Deb et al, 2002), with multi contradictory objectives in order to obtain a set of optimal solutions. Considering the number of actuators and the minimization of final displacement energy as contradictory objectives, a set of optima is found and a solution is chosen in order to be experimentally tested on a SRM.
In electrical machines, noise and vibrations are mainly due to aerodynamic (Fiedler et al., 2005), mechanical and magnetic issues. Aerodynamic vibrations are due to air displacement along rotating rotor (laminar flow) and vortices (turbulent flow) on SRM air gaps. These vibrations are located on inner surface of SRM stator. Mechanical vibrations are generated by relative movement between machine part and shock inside ball bearing. These vibrations are un-located on SRM. At last, magnetic vibrations are due to permeability gradient and generated on stator air-gap interface. Such sources can excite mechanical resonances of the structure and then generate vibratory displacement on the structure. Each source of noise

contributes to the measured vibratory displacement with two different ways. On the one hand, forces generated by one part of sources such as magnetic forces or rotating flow on the SRM excite the mechanical behavior by a deterministic excitation depending on the rotational speed. On the other hand, these sources excite the mechanical behavior by a random excitation, like shocks inside ball bearing or the turbulent flow. In both cases, the vibratory displacement can be described by modal superposition theory as follow (Mininger et al., 2007), figure 1:

$$d^{ext}(t,\theta) = \sum_{i\,modes} \left\{D_i^{aero} + D_i^{mec} + D_i^{mag}\right\} \cos i\theta \cos \omega_i t \tag{1}$$

where d^{ext} is the measured vibratory displacement, θ the angular position of measurement on SRM stator, i the considered vibration mode, ω_i the resonance frequency associated with the mode i and D^x_i the amplitude of excitation sources for each mode i.

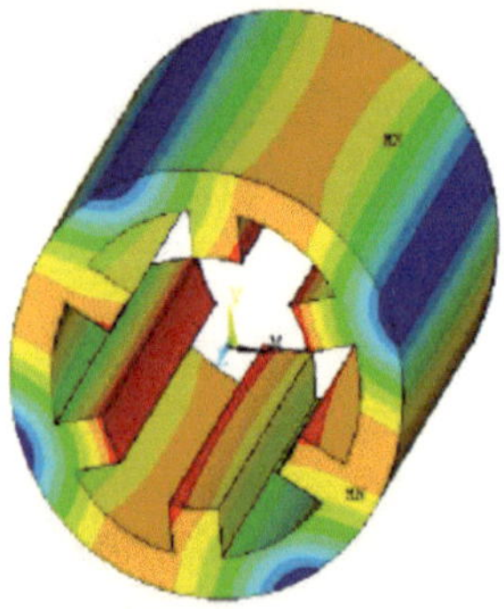

Fig. 1. Mode 2 resonance of SRM

This chapter is organized as follows: The first part deals with the optimization of dimensions and placement of piezoelectric actuators in the aim of reducing the generated vibrations. In this paragraph, the purpose and formulation used for the stochastic optimization is detailed. The second part deals with the validation of the optimization results by the mean of finite element simulations and experimental tests on a switched reluctance machine with piezoelectric actuators.

2. Optimal design and placement by genetic algorithm

2.1 Purpose of the optimization

The non dominated sorting genetic algorithm (NSGA-II) is an efficient multiobjective evolutionary algorithm based on both genetic laws and Darwin evolution (Deb and al, 2002). From an initial population composed of individuals and with crossover, mutation, and selection sequences for these individuals, a final optimal population is created. This final population constitutes a set of optimal solutions of the initial problem that respect the constraints and minimize objectives. NSGA-II algorithm includes the selection of individuals in the objective functions. In order to determine this function, one approach is suggested. This approach, based on final displacement minimization, corresponds to an electrical engineering approach and takes into account modeling both the electrical feed and the rotational speed.

Genetic algorithm, NSGA-II, has been efficiently applied on other applications (Besnerais et al., 2007) (Qiu et al, 2007) due to its performances and its implementation on non linear problems. From a random initial population corresponding to a set of configurations (placement and design), an optimal set of solutions is found by best individual selections, crossovers and mutations. The main topic of this chapter is the design and placement of PZT actuators in order to reduce the SRM vibrations and, consequently, the level of noise generated. These design and placement steps are performed in the presence of constraints (no overlap of actuators, maximum actuator number) and opposite objectives: minimizing the number of actuators, while maximizing vibration damping. Thus, not only one single optimal solution exists, but also a set of optimal solutions (Pareto front). The simulation scheme is given in figure 2.

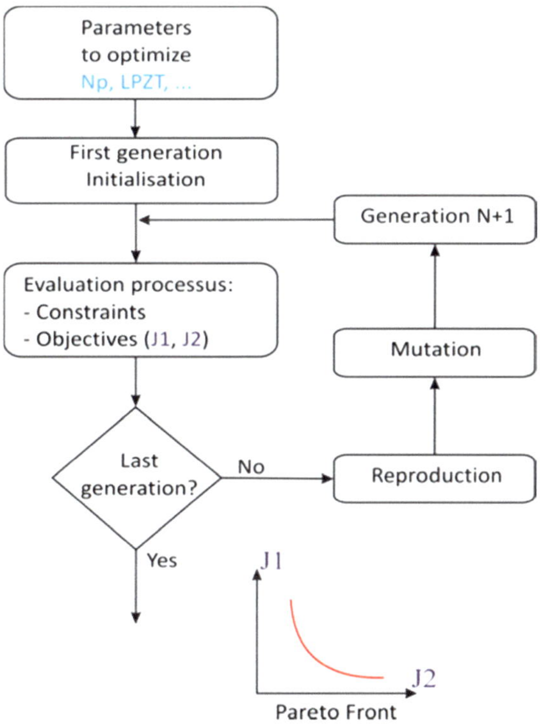

Fig. 2. NSGA II optimization scheme (Np: Number of actuators, Lpzt: length of an actuator)

Under these conditions, a genetic algorithm is more suitable than a determinist one.

2.2 Optimization formulation for active damping

Optimization is achieved with two opposite objectives used for individual selection: the number of PZT actuators (J_1) and the resulting RMS global displacement (J_2) after active damping. The minimization of the two objectives J_1 and J_2 allows the selection of the actuators optimal configuration.

$$J_2 = \sum_{i\,modes} \frac{\omega_i^2}{4\pi^2} \int_0^{2\pi} \int_0^{2\pi/\omega_i} \left\{ d_i^{ext}(t,\theta) + \sum_{actuators} d_i^{PZT}(t,\theta) \right\}^2 d\theta\, dt \qquad (2)$$

d_i^{ext} is the modal displacement due to disturbance external forces (aerodynamic, mechanical and magnetic) on the SRM stator for a vibration mode i. d_i^{PZT} is the controlled modal displacement due to designed and placed PZT actuators for a mode *i*. According to linear modeling of piezoelectric actuators, the vibratory displacement generated is expressed with the expression (1) (Young et al., 2003):

$$d_i^{PZT}(\mathrm{t},\theta) = \sum_{i\,modes} \{\mathrm{K}_\mathrm{i}^{\mathrm{PZT}}\mathrm{V}_\mathrm{i}^{\mathrm{PZT}}\} \cos i(\theta - \theta_i) \cos(\omega_i t - \varphi_i) \tag{3}$$

K_i^{PZT} is the PZT conversion coefficient which depends on the geometry and material properties (Young's modulus, piezoelectric coefficient d_{31}…) for the considered mode. V_i^{PZT} is the voltage applied to the piezoelectric actuator for the considered mode. θ_i and φ_i are mechanical angle (angular placement of the actuator) and the electrical phase applied to the actuator for the considered mode, respectively.

Each individual is composed by the number of actuators and corresponding dimensions (length, thickness and angular position). The associated population size (1000 individuals) and the number of generation (1000 generations) are designed in order to have good constitution heterogeneity of individuals and enough iterations for convergence. The optimization result is a set of best individuals minimizing the two objectives and represented by a Pareto front.

The minimization problem is realized with constraints. First, overlap between two actuators is not allowed (same angular position) and second, geometrical parameters (actuators thickness, length and height) have limited range. The experimental actuator control is realized by a Matlab Simulink platform. Thus, the actuator voltage is also limited to ±10V.

Figure 3 represents the Pareto front of optima individuals according to selection functions J_1 and J_2 considering 4 modes: mode 2 at 5000 Hz, mode 3 at 12600Hz, mode 4 at 21400 Hz and mode 5 at 29700 Hz.

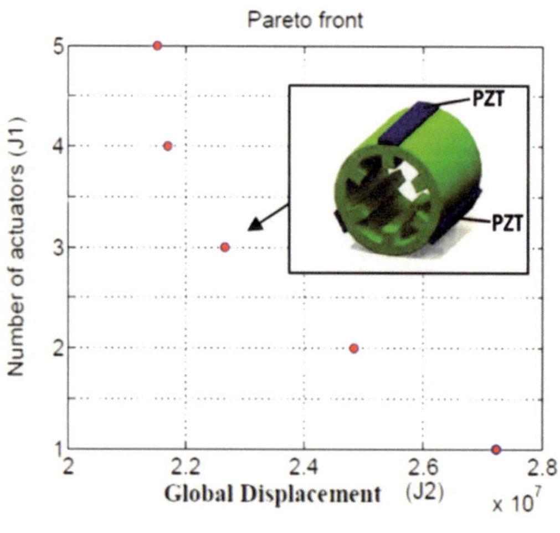

Fig. 3. Pareto configuration optima for actuator placement with an example of optimal individuals

After optimization, all dimensions for each configuration of actuators are the same: length, 40mm; thickness, 2.4 mm; height, 12 mm and correspond to analytical optima. As the optimum placement, for the control of mode 2, does not correspond to optimum placement considering the other modes, thus, the angular placement is a compromise between the damping of each mode. It is the main reason to use the genetic algorithm (compared to determinist algorithm) because many optima exist. Considering one actuator the best placement is obtained on modes anti-nodes. However, only few positions correspond to antinodes for several modes. Thus, in the Pareto front the number of actuators increasing from one to two actuators decreases strongly the vibratory displacement reduction. However, when the number of actuators increases from four to five actuators, the displacement energy decreasing is less efficient. The final decision for one configuration of actuators depends on designer criterions, as the price or the manufacturing ease. In our application, the optimal solution with 3 actuators has been chosen. In order to keep the 180° symmetry of the structure, 3 more actuators have been placed at 180° with the same dimension of the others. The final SRM with PZT actuators is represented on the following figure 4.

Fig. 4. Final design and placement of PZT actuators

3. Finite element and experimental validation

3.1 Finite element active damping results

For this configuration of actuators, finite element simulations allow the validation of the placement and the design of piezoelectric actuators for several vibration excitations. Forces exciting one or multiple modes are imposed on the stator and adequate voltages are applied to the actuators in order to reduce the resulting vibratory acceleration. Different voltage amplitudes are tested so as to conclude on the efficiency of this active damping method.

On Figure 5, a sinusoidal force corresponding to the mode 2 resonance of stator is applied on stator teeth. For the first phase, the associated vibratory displacement can be described by:

$$d_2^{ext}(\mathrm{t}, \theta) \propto \cos 2\theta \cos \omega_{mode\ 2} t \tag{4}$$

Displacements associated with the two phases are deduced from the first phase applying a mechanical and electrical phase of ±120°. These forces generate a vibratory displacement on the stator (curve V_{PZT}=0V). Voltages, which temporal phases opposite to the ones of the forces on the teeth, are applied on PZT actuators (V_{PZT}=5V and V_{PZT}=10V). The electrical phase between two pairs of actuators is equal to 120°. For the first pair of actuators, the vibratory displacement generated is:

$$d_2^{PZT}(\mathrm{t}, \theta) \propto \mathrm{V}_2^{\mathrm{PZT}} \cos 2\theta \cos(\omega_{mode\ 2} t - \varphi_i) \tag{5}$$

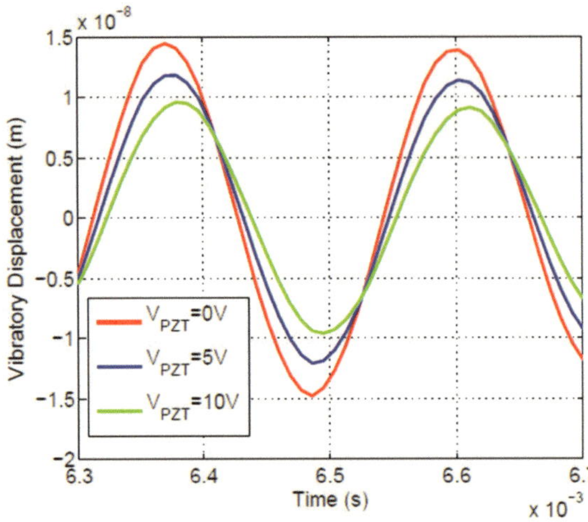

Fig. 5. Mode 2 active damping on SRM stator (4.6 KHz)

The vibratory displacement is reduced due to actuator interactions on structure (Mininger et al., 2007). The more the PZT voltage is increased, the more the vibratory displacement is reduced until the vibratory displacement is cancelled. In order to validate the superposition hypothesis, a multimodal configuration is considered. Figure 6 presents two sinusoidal forces corresponding to mode 2 and mode 4 resonances, which are applied on stator teeth of each phase:

$$d_{2,4}^{extPZT}(\mathrm{t}, \theta) \propto \mathrm{A}\cos 2\theta \cos \omega_{mode\ 2} t + \mathrm{B}\cos 4\theta \cos \omega_{mode\ 4} t \tag{6}$$

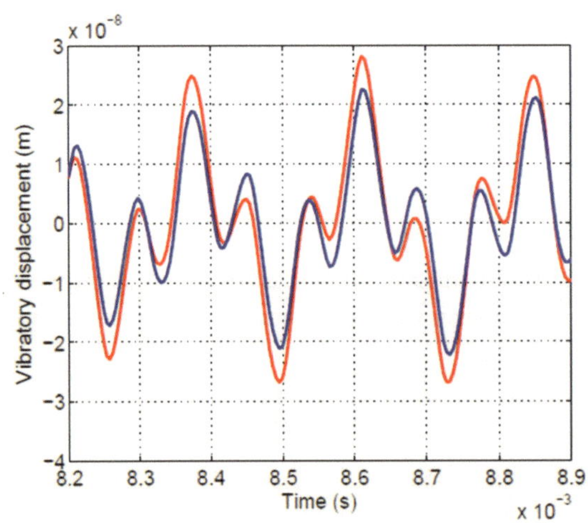

Fig. 6. Mode 2 and Mode 4 active damping on SRM stator (red: open loop, blue: closed loop)

Figure 7 is a Fast Fourier Transformation of the previous result. Without PZT voltage, the spectrum is composed by two excitations corresponding to mode 2 and mode 4. With a mode 2 excitation of PZT actuators, only the mode 2 resonance is reduced. Thus, each mode can be treated separately. It is the starting point so as to design a controller for active damping so as to separately control the different modes.

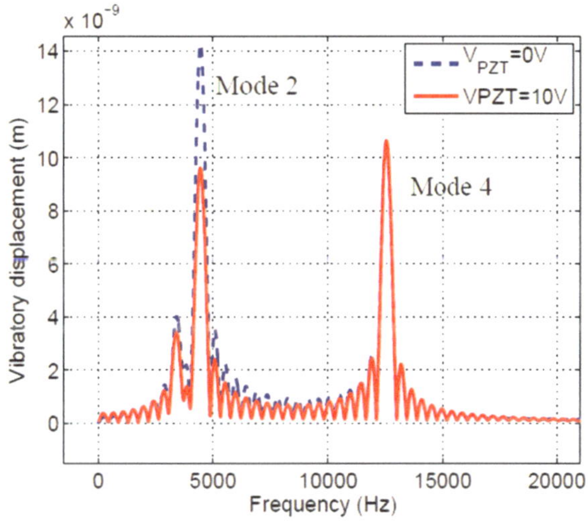

Fig. 7. Vibratory displacement FFT

3.2 Experimental results with MIMO controller

The experimental test bench, figure 8, is composed by two motors sharing the same shaft: a Permanent Magnet (PM) one and the SRM. Using the PM motor, it is possible to obtain the rotation of the SRM without magnetic excitation of this one. In this case, only mechanical and aerodynamic disturbances are considered. The frame has been designed in order to minimize the vibration exchange between the two motors. Holes and slops on the frame are equivalent to multiple springs and are use to filter the vibration between the two motors.

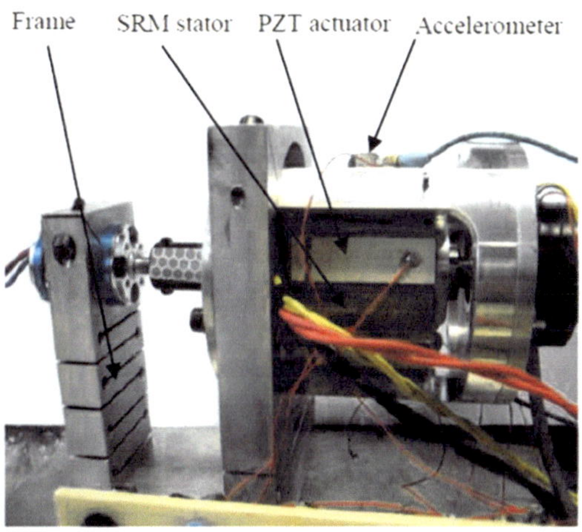

Fig. 8. Experimental test bench (left motor: PM motor, right motor: SRM)

The PZT voltage control is a multi-input multi-output system, figure 9.

On figure 9, the inputs of the control system are the vibratory displacements deduced from the vibratory acceleration measured on two stator points. The system outputs are the 3 PZT voltages applied to PZT phase 1, 2 and 3. Each PZT phase is composed by two PZT actuators controlled by the same voltage.

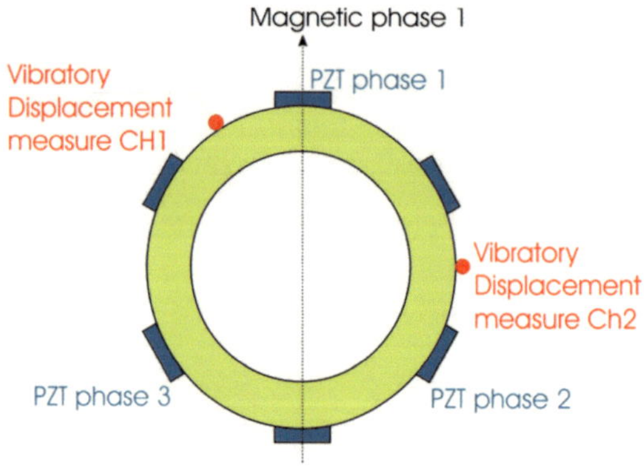

Fig. 9. Scheme representation of actuators and sensors placement

Considering only the piezoelectric excitation, the vibratory measurements in CH1 and CH2 depend on the voltage applied to the PZT phase 1, 2 and 3. In this case, the mode 2 vibratory displacement measurements in CH1 and CH2 can be expressed by:

$$\begin{pmatrix} d_2^{CH1} \\ d_2^{CH2} \end{pmatrix} = \begin{pmatrix} 0.5 & 0.5 & -1 \\ -1 & 0.5 & 0.5 \end{pmatrix} \begin{pmatrix} d_2^{PZT,1} \\ d_2^{PZT,2} \\ d_2^{PZT,3} \end{pmatrix} \tag{7}$$

One can see that one pair of actuators is more efficient than the two others to act on the displacement associated to one d_2^{CH} (e.g. PZT 3 for d_2^{CH1}). Indeed, it is placed on the corresponding antinode for mode 2, the controller is then realized so as to un-correlate each PZT with each measurement point and on the same time maximizes the influence of the measured vibratory displacement to the corresponding PZT phase.

Often used on active damping problem and resonant system, the Positive Position Feedback (PPF), is an efficient controller for one input one output system (Preumont, 2002). The controller described in this paper is based on three PPF controllers (Moheimani et al., 2005), and each PPF controller controls only one PZT phase. The uncoupling between each phase (e.g. PZT 3 acting only on d_2^{CH1}) on measurement points is realized by a matrix gain (G).

$$(G) = \begin{pmatrix} 1 & -0.5 & -0.5 \\ -0.5 & 1 & -0.5 \\ -0.5 & -0.5 & 1 \end{pmatrix} \tag{8}$$

Assuming, a third virtual measurement point CH3 exists defined by the relation $d_2^{CH1} + d_2^{CH2} + d_2^{CH3} = 0$, the system can be defined by:

$$\begin{pmatrix} V_2^{PZT,1} \\ V_2^{PZT,2} \\ V_2^{PZT,3} \end{pmatrix} = \begin{pmatrix} H_{PPF}(s) & 0 & 0 \\ 0 & H_{PPF}(s) & 0 \\ 0 & 0 & H_{PPF}(s) \end{pmatrix} (G) \begin{pmatrix} d_2^{CH1} \\ d_2^{CH2} \\ d_2^{CH3} \end{pmatrix} \tag{9}$$

The filter $H_{PPF}(s)$ is design by Mac Ever method (McEver, 1999) and is defined as:

$$H_{PPF}(s) = \frac{H_O}{1 + 2m_{PPF}\frac{s}{\omega_{PPF}} + \frac{s^2}{\omega_{PPF}{}^2}} \tag{10}$$

The PPF filter has an only significant action on vibratory problem around a central frequency, increasing the equivalent damping ratio around this frequency. Thus, it has been designed in order to reduce the vibratory acceleration, and consequently the vibratory displacement, around the mode 2 resonance frequency (5000 Hz). The controller scheme is given in figure 10.

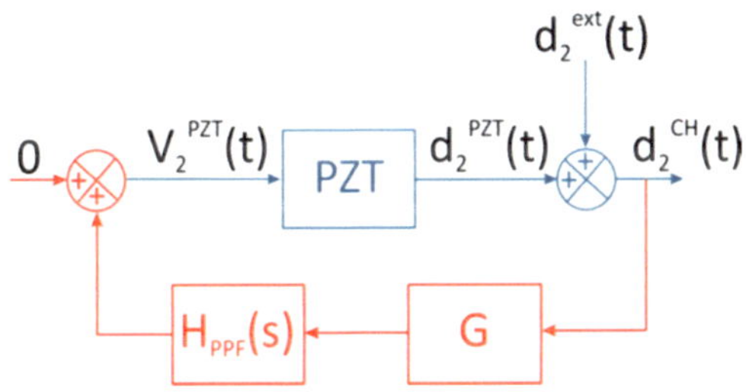

Fig. 10. PPF controller scheme for active damping

So as to test the active damping robustness, an experimental test has been realized on the more disadvantageous case. In this case, the vibration generated on the SRM stator is generated by aerodynamic and mechanical excitations. On figure 11, the active damping has been tested at 10 000 rpm.

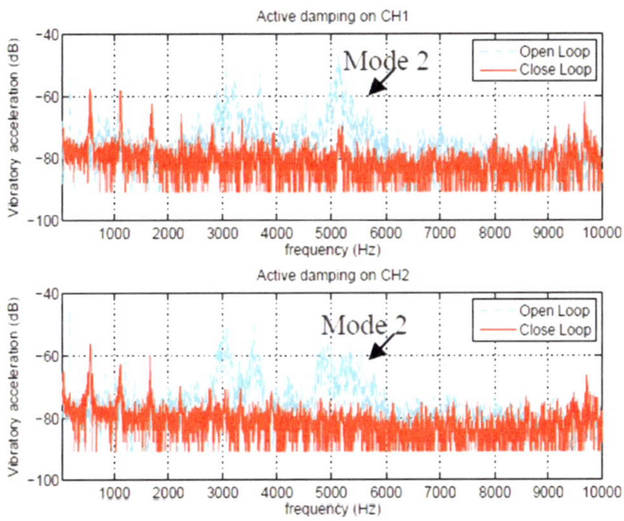

Fig. 11. Experimental active damping at 10 000 rpm

A significant reduction of the vibratory acceleration has been measured. With this principle, a vibratory reduction from 15 dB is obtained around the PPF filter frequency from a large range of rotational speed from 1 rpm to 15 000 rpm. This method is efficient on both low and high speed operation range. Moreover, the method has been successfully applied with all kind of excitations (Ojeda et al., 2007).

4. Conclusion

In this chapter, design and placement of piezoelectric actuators by genetic algorithm have been presented in the aim of SRM noise damping. A formulation based on the vibratory displacement energy reduction has been successfully applied so as to select optimal configuration of actuators. Piezoelectric actuators have been used in order to reduce the noise generated by SRM functioning in a large operation range. Optimal placement and design allow the reduction of all vibration sources by the actuator voltage control. This compensation method with optimized design and placement allows a 15dB noise reduction in audible frequencies. It could be efficiently applied on all low vibration applications using electrical machines, like compressors or flight direction.

5. References

Besnerais, J. L.; Hequet, M.; Lanfranchi, V. & Brochet, P. Multi-objectives optimization of the induction machine with minimization of audible electromagnetic noise, *European Physical Journal*, 2007.

Blaabjerg, F.; Pedersen, J.; P. Nielsen, Andersen, L. & Kjaer P. Investigation and reduction of acoustical noise from switched reluctance drives in current and voltage control, *in Proc. 1994 International Conference on Electrical Machines*, pp. 589-594, 1994.

Deb, K.; Amrit, P.; Sameer, A. & Meyarivan T. A fast and elitist multi- objective genetic algorithm: NSGA-II, *IEEE Trans. Evol. Comput.*, vol. 6, no. 2, pp. 182–197, Apr. 2002.

Fiedler, J.O.; Kasper, K. A. & De Doncker, R. W. Acoustic noise in switched reluctance drives: an aerodynamic problem?, *IEEE IEMDC conference*, 2005.

Hong, J. Stator pole and Yoke design for vibration reduction of switched reluctance motor, *IEEE Transactions on Magnetics*, 38(2):929-932, Mars 2002.

Kub, H.; Wichert, BT. & Szymanski, B. Design of a high speed switched reluctance motor for spindle drive, *Compatibility in power electronics, CPED'07*, pp. 1-5, 2007

Rahman, K. M.; Fahimi, R.; Suresh, G.; Rajarathnam, A. V. & Ehsani, M. Advantages of switched reluctances motor, applications to EV and HEV: Design and control issues, *IEEE transactions on industry applications*, Vol.36 N.1, 2000.

Mininger, X.; Gabsi, M.; Lécrivain, M.; Lefeuvre, E.; Richard, C.; Guyomar, D. & Bouillault, F. Vibration damping with piezoelectric actuators for electrical motors, *COMPEL*, Vol. 26, N.1, 2007.

Moheimani, SOR.; Vautier, BJG. & Bhikkaji, B. Experimental implementation of extended multivariable PPF control on an active structure, *Control Systems Technology, IEEE Transactions on*, Vol. 14, pp. 443-45, 2006.

Preumont, A. *Vibration control of active structures an introduction*, 2nd ed., Kluwer academic publishers, 2002.

McEver, M. Optimal vibration suppression using on-line pole/zero identification, *PHD Thesis, Faculty of Virginia Polytechnic Institute and State University*, 1999.

Ojeda, X.; Mininger, X.; Gabsi M. & Lécrivain, M. Noise reduction using piezoelectric active control on high speeds switched reluctance drives, *IAS conference*, 2007.

Qiu, Z.; Zhang, X.; Wu, H. & Zhang H. Optimal placement and active vibration control for piezoelectric smart flexible cantilever plate, *Journal of sound and Vibration*, Vol. 301, pp. 521-543, 2007

Wang, S.; Zhan, Q.; Ma, Z. & Zhou, L. Implementation of a 50-kW four-phase switched reluctance motor drive system for hybrid electric vehicle, *Magnetics, IEEE transactions on*, Vol. 41, pp. 501-504, 2005.

Young, WC.; Budynas RG. & Roark RJ. *Roark's formulas for stress and strain*, Tsinghua University Press, 2003

Part 2

Monte Carlo: The Stochastic Experiments

6

Optimal Decision-Making under Uncertainty - Application to Power Transmission Investments

Gerardo Blanco[1] and Fernando Olsina[2]
[1]*Facultad Politécnica, Universidad Nacional de Asunción,*
[2]*Institute of Electrical Energy, National University of San Juan,*
[1]*Paraguay*
[2]*Argentina*

1. Introduction

Investment could be defined as the act of incurring immediate costs with the expectation of future returns. An investment project, as every asset has a value. Thus, for successfully investing in and managing these assets is crucial not only recognizing what the value is but also the sources of this value (Damodaran, 2002).

Most investment decisions share three important characteristics in different degrees. First, investments are partially or totally irreversible. Roughly speaking, the initial investment cost is at least partially sunk; i.e. it is impossible to recover all the expenditures if the decision-maker changes her mind. Second, there is uncertainty in the revenues from the investment, and therefore, risk associated with this. Third, all decision-making has some leeway about the timing of the investment. It is possible to defer the decision making to get more information about the future. These three features interact to determine the optimal decisions of investors on a given investment project (Dixit & Pindick, 1994).

Transmission utilities are faced with investments, which hold these three characteristics significantly: irreversibility, uncertainty and the choice of timing. In this context, an efficient decision making process is, therefore, based on managing the uncertainties and understanding the relationships between risks and opportunities in order to achieve a well-timed investment execution.

Therefore, strategic flexibility for seizing opportunities and cutting losses contingent upon the market evolution is of huge value. Strategic flexibility is a risk management method that is gaining ongoing research attention as it enables properly coping major uncertainties, which are unsolved at the time of making decisions. Hence, valuing added flexibility in transmission investment portfolios, for instance, by investing in power electronic-based controller meanwhile transmission line projects are deferred, is necessary to make optimal upgrading.

However, expressing the value of flexibility in economic terms is not a trivial task and requires new, sophisticated valuing tools, since the traditional investment theory has not recognized the implications of the interaction between the three aforementioned investment features. Any attempt to quantify investment flexibility almost naturally leads to the concept of Real Options (RO). The RO technique provides a well-founded framework -based on the theory of financial options, and consequently, stochastic dynamic programming- to assess strategic investments under uncertainty (Trigeorgis, 1996).

In the first RO applications (Myers, 1977), valuation was normally confined to the investment options that can be easily assimilated to financial options, for which solutions are well-known and readily available (Rodriguez & Rocha, 2006). Nevertheless, an investor confront with a diverse set of opportunities. From this point of view, investment projects can be seen as a portfolio of options, where its value is driven by several stochastic variables. The introduction of multiple interacting options into real options models highly increases the problem complexity, making the utilization of traditional analytical approaches unfeasible. However recently, simulation procedures for solving multiple American options have been successfully proposed. One of the most promising approaches is the Least Square Monte Carlo (LSM) method proposed by Longstaff and Schwartz (2001). LSM method is based on stochastic chronological simulation and uses least squares linear regression to determine the optimal stopping time (optimal path) in the decision making process.
This chapter lays out a general background about key concepts -uncertainty and risk- and the most usual risk management techniques in transmission investment are provided. Then, the concept of strategic flexibility is introduced in order to set its ability for dealing with the uncertainties involved in the investment problem. In addition, new criteria and advantages of the ROV approach compared with classical probabilistic choice are presented. A LSM-based method for decomposing and evaluating the complex real option problem involved in flexible transmission investments under uncertainties is developed.
The proposed methodology is applied to a study case, based on (Blanco *et al.*, 2010a), which evaluates an interconnection reinforcement on the European interconnected power system, showing how the valuation of flexibility is a key task for making efficient and well-timed investments in the transmission network. The impact of two network upgrades on the system-wide welfare is analyzed within the proposed framework. These upgrades are the development of a new transmission line and the installation of a power electronic-based controller. Both upgrades represent measures to strengthen the German transmission network due to the fact that these are among the most important corridors within the Central Western European (CWE) region. Hence, a transmission project, which is currently under study, is compared to flexible investment in order to shed some light on the influence of the strategic flexibility on the optimal decision-making process. The research is focused on assessing the impact of the uncertainty of the demand growth, generation cost evolution and the evolution of the installed wind capacity on the decision-making process.

2. Risks and uncertainties in the investment decision-making process

According to Webster's dictionary, the word risk is defined as "possibility of loss or injury, someone or something that creates or suggests a hazard". Accordingly, risk is normally perceived in negative terms. In finance, the definition of risk is different and broader. Thus, risk refers to the probability of receiving a return on an investment different from expected return. Therefore, risk includes not only negative results, i.e. results that are lower than expected, but also positive results, i.e. returns that are higher than expected. In fact, it may refer to the former as downside risk and upside risk to the latter, but are considered both in the measurement of risk (Damodaran, 2002).
Thus, risk management procedures aim to develop a model to quantify the investment risk and then try to turn it into an opportunity that is necessary to compensate for the hazards.
On the other hand, uncertainty is the randomness of the external environment. Investors cannot change their level. Uncertainty is an input into the valuation of investments.

Exposure of an investment to uncertainty -the sensitivity of returns and the value of the investment against a source of uncertainty- is determined by a number of factors, including business line, the structure cost and nature of the markets of the investment. Through investment, the managers are able to change the level exposure of assets, with a resulting economic impact, the risk.

Thus, although in the literature uncertainty and risk are often used interchangeably, it is relevant to note the difference between them. Uncertainty refers to an unstructured collection of randomness and risk to the situation in which a result can be specified and may be assigned a probability of occurrence.

In general terms, there are variables involved in the valuation investment process whose evolution is gravitating to the generation of worth of the investment project. If these variables have uncertainties on their unfolding, it is generated a certain level of risk associated with the project value.

The identification and quantification of the project´s risk must be obtained within the evaluation process. This risk assessment is fundamental for making optimal decisions as well as providing the needed inputs that properly replicate the uncertain behavior of the driving variables for conducting an active risk management throughout the project development.

2.1 Implication of risk and uncertainty within the traditional decision tool

Nowadays, markets require strategic decisions to invest in highly uncertain environments, characterized by the unknown of relevant aspects such as: market size, development costs or movements of the competing players. Therefore, there is currently a broad gap between what managers want to do and the capabilities of the available information and the decision tools (Olafsson, 2003).

In current decision tools, there are two main features that stand out as significant problems. The first one is that most of the tools require a forecast of future returns. Since the analysis often uses a single or point forecast, this is very subjective. Is this an overly optimistic projection of the defender of a project? , what are the growth rate and profit margin foreseen in the projection? In this context, managers consider often the forecast as reality, creating the illusion of certainty in relation to the results. To improve this, some practitioners try to extend the analysis to a set of projections or scenarios. These efforts seem sound knowledge to the authors, however, arbitrary to everybody else. Both, single stage or in the various scenarios, forecasting cash flow, under these conditions, becomes a subjective input (Damadaran, 2002).

The second problem of decision-making tools -most commonly used- is that future investment decisions are determined from the outset. Managers update and revise the investment plans, but the analysis, according to the structure of most of the tools, only includes the initial plan. Therefore, the world changes, but its model does not. As the gap between the tools and reality becomes bigger, the instruments are discarded, and important decisions are made in terms of strategic considerations and management expertise (Amran & Kulatilaka, 1998).

Accordingly, alternative actions in response to changed conditions or new information, which emerge in the lifetime of the project are not accounted for. Commonly, the only decision made at the beginning is to go ahead with the project, or not. Thereafter management remains passive to a fixed operating strategy. Clearly, this approach is unsuitable in a competitive world, characterized by continuous change and uncertainty.

Consequently, an efficient decision tool needs to take account of the volatility in project profits and remain flexible in response to unforeseen events (Olafsson, 2003).

2.2 Risk and uncertainties in the worth creation

Once the uncertainty and flexibility are explicitly included in the valuation of investments, there is a complete change of paradigms within the decision making process. From an active and strategic management of the uncertainties, one of the most important transformations in the way of visualizing a decision on an uncertain environment is derived: uncertainty creates worth. Consequently, by rethinking strategic investments, decision-makers must try to consider their markets taking into account the origin, history and evolution of the uncertainty, to determine the degree of exposure of their investments (how external events are reflected in profit and loss), then respond by positioning their investments, so that they can take full advantage of uncertainty.

From the traditional point of view, the higher the uncertainty level the lower value of the project. However, under an approach which manages the uncertainties actively and strategically, greater uncertainties may lead to higher asset value. For doing this, decision-makers strive to identify and using their strategic options to flexibly respond to uncertainty developments.

An intuitive way to analyze this interaction between uncertainty and risk within the investment problem is by the see-saw investment metaphor. By visualizing the performance of an investment as a weighing-scale (Fig. 1), where the externalities are weighted according to the threats and opportunities of an investment, it could reveal the interaction between its final return range and the uncertainties. If it contemplates the uncertainty as the base of this scale, the level of risk -i.e. fluctuations around the expected return- clearly is constrained by the magnitude of the uncertainties that the investment is exposed to (Blanco, 2010b).

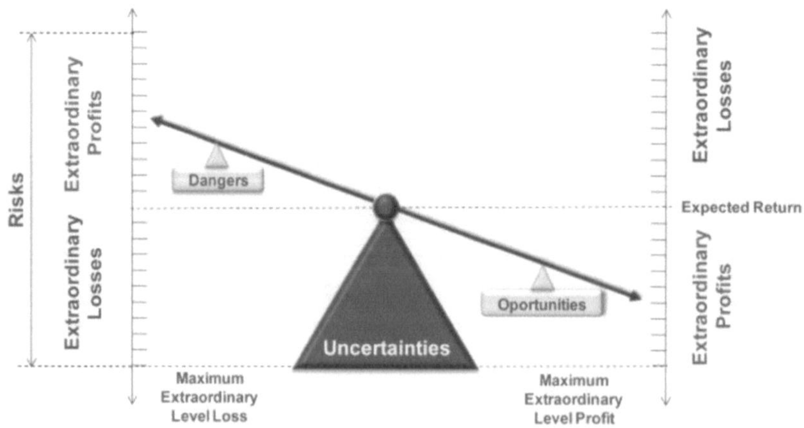

Fig. 1. Interaction between uncertainty and risk in investment performance

Therefore, if the investment is exposed to lower uncertainty, it would be exposed to lower extraordinary losses, but also, at the same time, would be less likely to seize extraordinary profits (Fig. 2).

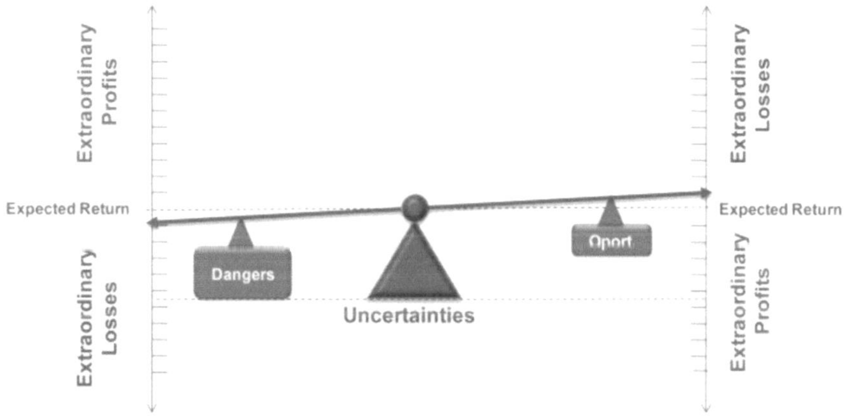

Fig. 2. Sensitivity of risk related to the uncertainties

However, the use of contingent claims (strategic flexibility of the investment) may limit the level of extraordinary losses, but remaining open a significant likelihood of extraordinary profits (Fig. 3).

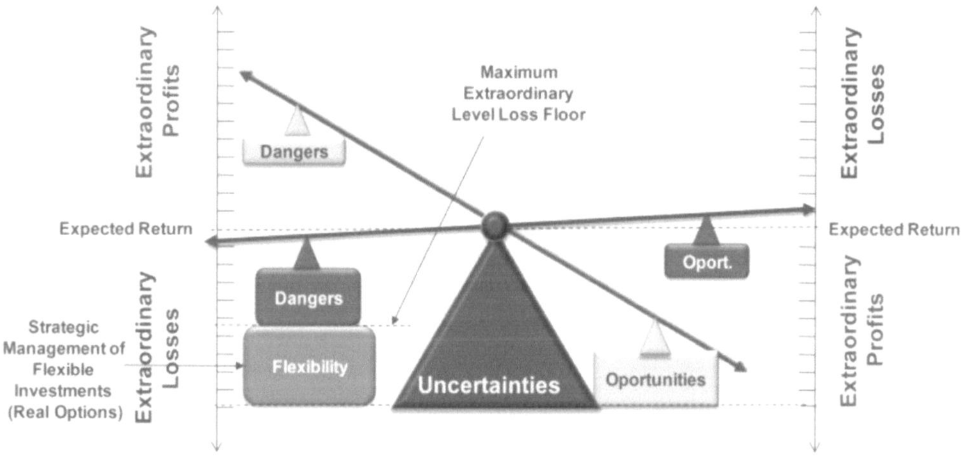

Fig. 3. Effect of Flexibility in the value of investments under uncertainty

Thus, through the optimal use of the flexibility of investments, it is possible to increase the value of the investment project with increasing uncertainties. Therefore, the key is flexibility in dealing with the uncertainties by having various options in place that can be exercised as new information emerges. The options derive their value from the fact that they establish a floor under possible project losses.

2.3 Risk and uncertainties in the electric power system

Nowadays, the risk analysis theory is widely used by decision-makers who face investment decision problems under uncertainty, since it provides a systematic and logical approach for the decision making process (Vásquez, 2009). In the context of restructuring the electricity supply business, the problem of valuing transmission system expansions could be addressed as a risk management problem (Blumsack, 2006), seeking to formulate a transmission expansion plan that led the planner to make adjustments in an easy, economic way for seizing opportunities or cutting losses according to the evolution of the uncertain variables.

Therefore, the uncertainties variables play a key role in the valuation of transmission investments, and consequently, their behavior should be properly replicated within the assessment models[1]. In what follows, the main uncertainties of transmission system expansion are briefly analyzed:

- *Evolution of demand.* The evolution of the electricity demand is a key variable heavily influencing the performance of transmission investments[2]. The uncertainty over its future evolution is often represented according to a growth rate of demand in each period of the analysis horizon.
- *Generation costs.* Most of the electricity generated worldwide is produced from one of the following primary energy carriers: coal, oil, gas, nuclear and renewable (hydro, wind, solar, etc.). No public markets or trading platforms exist for renewable, nuclear and hydro. On the other hand, there are market prices for coal, oil and gas, which could be subject to considerable fluctuations over the long-run[3]. Therefore, the main uncertainty over generation cost could be related to thermal-units. Many of these plants use fossil fuels as primary energy sources. Thus, generation costs can be closely correlated with the fuel prices. The significant volatility present in the fuel market makes this uncertainty relevant exerting a profound influence on investment decisions in the transport system.
- *Discount rates.* The discount rates usually allow transferring temporal cash flow to the present or future. From a financial point of view, these rates represent the returns expected by the investor, and are strongly related to their risk perception over a given project. Uncertainty over the discount rate can have two effects on an investment decision. First, random fluctuation in interest rates can enhance the expected value of a future payoff from investing. However, uncertainty over future interest rates can also lead to a postponement of investment. The reason is that uncertainty over futures discount rates creates a value to waiting for new information (to see whether interest rates rise or fall) (Dixit & Pindick, 1994). Hence, there are two opposite effects of uncertainties over the discount rates, which should be carefully analyzed in order to make optimal investment decisions.
- *Investment costs of transmission projects.* The uncertainty in the evolution of prices of the raw material of the transmission equipment such as: steel, aluminium, copper and insulation has a considerable impact on investment costs in transmission projects and

---

1 The stochastic model of the uncertain variables of the transmission investment problem -taken into account in this chapter- is discussed in detail later.

2 Over the last years, electricity demand has grown only slowly in most developed countries. However, this growth has been far from certain and subject to stochastic fluctuations. Especially in the longer run, uncertainty on electricity demand growth has therefore also to be taken into consideration (Weber, 2004).

3 For example, crude oil prices have risen by a factor of two between the beginning of 2007 and the middle of 2008, and have again dropped by factor of three at the beginning of 2009. The price of coal has not been more stable in comparison; it has varied by about a factor of three between 2008 and 2009. The factor for the same time-window for the natural gas is two (http://tinyurl.com/27ns7ut).

therefore affects decisions on expansion. It also was mentioned earlier that the costs of FACTS devices have a tendency to decrease, which must also be considered.

- *Availability of system components.* States of operation with unavailability of some components is frequent in the large-scale power systems. Therefore, they are relevant within the transmission investment assessment. The reason of this is that the price spikes, which appear in energy markets under perfect competition during deficit conditions, would provide, in theoretical terms, substantial revenues to attract the investment needed to ensure the optimal level of adequacy over the long-term. Notwithstanding, although these profits under deficit conditions are very significant, they occur infrequently and are very difficult to predict. This situation often encourages the investors, usually risk-averse, to postpone or discard investments that are needed for ensuring the adequacy of the system (Olsina *et al.*, 2007). Therefore, these variables are relevant to investment analysis and should be considered.

Several approaches for assessing transmission investment have been proposed (Latorre *et al.*, 2003), defining the evolution of the variables of the problem with certainty. These models are known as deterministic and represent the variables aforementioned by their expected values. These assumptions often make these models unsuitable for evaluating investment strategies in practice (Garver, 1970; Seifu *et al.*, 1989; Romero & Monticelli, 1994). There are also stochastic models that consider the random behavior of some input parameters (Yu *et al.*, 1999). However, there are only a few antecedents regarding the management of risk associated with financial performance, despite, its profound influence on the new market structures (Vásquez & Olsina, 2007). Thus, the theory and tools for assessing transmission investments (TI) are still below the practical requirements of the new power markets. This is particularly true in aspects such as the transmission investment flexibility and the introduction of transmission controllers.

3. Basic Net Present Value (NPV) calculations

A classic NPV analysis works as follows. Let consider an immediate investment of I_0 today will generate cash flow C_j for the next n years. As cash flow obtained in the future does not have the same value as cash flow received today, then future cash flow requires discounting. The discount rate represents the opportunity cost of capital, k (Brealey, 2001).

$$NPV_0 = \sum_{j=1}^{4} \left(\frac{C_j}{\prod_{i=1}^{j}(1+k_i)} \right) - I_0 = PV_0 - I_0 \tag{1}$$

Generalizing;

$$NPV = \sum_{j=0}^{N} \left(\frac{FF_j}{\prod_{i=0}^{j}(1+k_i)} \right) \tag{2}$$

where FF_j is the cash flow of the year j and N is the investment horizon. Note that in general, the discount rate may differ from year to year. This is considered by the subscripts in discount rates. As was aforementioned this rate equals the opportunity cost or the cost of capital of the company making the investment. Therefore, it should reflect the level of project risk. This rate is also known as hurdle rate, that is, a minimum acceptable rate of return for investing resources in a project.

3.1 Flaws & drawbacks of the NPV approach under uncertainties

The net present value rule is implicitly based on some assumptions that are often overlooked. The most important is that either investment are entirely reversible[4], that is, it can be undone and the capital outlays invested fully recovered if market conditions unfold unfavorably; or if it is irreversible, this is a proposition of a now-or-never opportunity, i.e. if the decision-maker does not execute the investment now, he will not be able to execute it in the future (Dixit & Pindick, 1994).

Even though some investments fulfill these hypotheses, not all do. In practice, decision-makers have the ability to adapt their investment strategies in response to undesired events, and therefore, limit the downside effects of the uncertainties. However, under the NPV framework, the only decision made at the beginning is to execute the investment, or not. Thereafter the decision-maker remains immovable to a fixed operating strategy.

Consequently, a major shortcoming the NPV approach is that these strategic options, which are often embedded into the project, are disregarded. Hence, contingent measures in response to changed conditions or new information, which emerge in the lifespan of the project, are simply overlooked.

The inevitable uncertainties associated with the transmission investments are better managed with investments that provide flexibility. As new information arrives, investors need the flexibility to alter operating strategies to seize favorable opportunities or to cut losses in the case of adverse scenarios. This flexibility may include various actions at different stages of the planning horizon, such as the options to defer, expand, reduce or even abandon the project. This flexibility to adapt to changing market conditions has a substantial value, which has to be considered when an investment implementation is being decided. It is thus essential that flexibility be properly quantified. Any attempt to quantify investment flexibility almost naturally leads to the notion of Real Options (Olafsson, 2003).

The ROV technique provides a well-founded framework–based on the theory of financial options- to assess strategic investments under uncertainty. It quantitatively takes into account investment risks and the value of the open options for planners. The next sections provide a detailed background about the option theory and its applications into the capital investment evaluations.

4. Option valuations applied to flexible investments

The paradigm behind the real option concept is simple and straightforward. On one hand, it is simple because there is a strong analogy between the options on financial assets and the opportunities to acquire real assets. On the other hand, straightforward, because the theory of valuing derivative assets in financial markets, option pricing theory, offers powerful tools

[4] Investment expenditures are sunk costs when they are firm or industry specific (Dixit & Pindick, 1994)

that can be applied to value real options accurately. The sense of real options lies on quantifying the worth generated by the intrinsic flexibility embedded into an investment project, thereby providing a correct basis for making strategic investment decisions (Brosch, 2001).

Strategic flexibility emphasizes the inherent asymmetry between gains and losses in the structure of a project. The real option concept extends the conventional (static) NPV approach by including the value associated with the flexibility inherent in a project. Therefore, the static NPV is augmented to become flexible NPV (Olafsson, 2003):

$$\textit{Flexible NPV} = \textit{Static NPV} + \textit{Value of flexibility}$$

Since the value of flexibility always is positive, it adds value to the project; its value is the key concept in the real options approach. Therefore, the availability of these options will generally impact on the actual decision-making process, and consequently, must be fairly quantified.

4.1 Financial options[5]

An option is the right but not the obligation, to make a particular decision in the future. In general, one can say that the options are bilateral contracts by which a party pays a sum of money to another to acquire the right (option) to conduct a transaction (purchase and sale) or claim a specific sum of money in the future.

In this context, a financial option entitles the holder the right to buy or sell an asset at a specified price on or before a certain date. The set price is called the strike or exercise price and the date on or before which the right can be exercised is called maturity.

Financial options are a particular type of financial assets called derivative securities. The value of the derivative depends on the value of another asset on which is based on it, called the underlying asset. This means, the value of a derivative security derives from the value of another elemental asset.

There are essentially two different types of financial options. An option to buy -call option- entitles the holder to acquire an asset at a specified price on or before a certain date and the option to sell -put option- gives the holder the right to sell an asset at a specified price on or before a certain date.

In addition, financial options can be classified as *American* or *European*. When the option holder can exercise the option on a certain future date, it is implying that he can only use his right at that moment (on the date of expiry or maturity), and neither before nor after that, the derivative security is an *European* option.

Moreover, when the holder can exercise his contract until a specified future date, it means that the option holder can use his right until the expiration date; in this case, the financial option is an *American* option.

The holder of the right to exercise an option is said to have a long position (long position) in an option contract. The issuer (seller) of an option takes a short position (short position), and the obligation to buy or sell the asset (underlying) at the exercise price to or from the holder of the right (the long position), who should wish to take advantage of his rights.

Instead of buying the assets directly (i.e. take long position in the underlying), the investor can defer the investment by purchasing a call option to buy the asset at a later stage a certain

---

5 This section closely follows (Olafsson, 2003).

strike price. The holder of the option pays a premium to the call issuer for this entitlement. This premium is the price for the risk assumed by the issuer to take a short position (Olafsson, 2003).
A long position in an asset has a return (profit) profile, which is limited below by the price of the asset but has no upper limit. The profile of return for a long position in a call option, on the other hand, has a limit to the loss equal to the premium paid for the option. As long as the asset price rises above the purchase price there is gain, which increases linearly with the asset price. Similarly, when the price falls below the purchase price there is loss, which increases linearly with the dropping price. This is simply because the investor retains the asset.
The return profile for a long position in a call is quite different. When the asset price increases and exceeds the exercise price, it is said that the call option is in-the-money. If a call in-the-money is exercised, the gain (ignoring the premium) is given by the expression:

$$IV_{LC} = \max(S - X, 0) \tag{3}$$

where S is the underlying asset price, X the exercise price. The difference between both values is called the intrinsic value of the purchase option. Any increase in the asset price also leads to an increase in the intrinsic value of the option. However, before an option is exercised, the market value is generally higher than its intrinsic value. For this reason it is usually more profitable to sell the option instead of exercising it. This is an important point to be discussed in more detail later. If the underlying price falls below the strike price, out-the-money, the intrinsic value of the call also falls, but only to the floor set by the premium paid for the long position. In other words, the premium is the maximum loss that a long position in a call may suffer.

4.2 Real options

Real options are based on the concepts of financial options discussed in the previous section. The real option approach applies financial option theory to theories of decision making for investment in capital projects.
The traditional NPV approach does not seize the intangible aspect of these high-risk investments with potential extraordinary returns. Hence, the key issue is the use of the available options, to set a lower limit to potential losses while the possibility of these profit remaining open. In fact, a firm may have a portfolio of options which defines its performance profile. The real options approach can therefore be extended to a portfolio management of the underlying project together with all available flexibility options. Some examples of the possible options are presented below.
According to Copeland *et al.* (2003), real options can be classified into:
Postponement option: It represents the right of an owner to postpone an investment for a period of time while waiting for new information that arrives to the market. In exchange for this, the decision-maker rejects the cash flow that would generate the project on the future, if it is executed immediately. From a financial point of view, it can be interpreted as an American call option.
Abandonment Option: It allows ending activities and selling off assets that originally composed the capital investment (plant and equipment). This option is analogous to an American put option with a strike price equal to the scrap value of the project.

Expansion or growth option: It allows expanding production capacity and/or accelerating the use of available resources, if the market conditions that occur after one has performed some initial investment, are more favourable than expected. This option is equivalent to an American call option.
Reduction or contraction option: This option provides the holder the right to reduce the size of operations if conditions are unfavourable; a project which can be reduced is more worth than the same project without that opportunity. Financially, it is equivalent to an American put option.
Extension or pre-cancellation option: It is the possibility to extend (reduce) the lifespan of an asset or the term of a contract by the payment of some monetary amount. The extension option is equivalent to an American call option while the possibility of shortening is analogous to a put American type.
Switch option: It offers the possibility of using the same assets and inputs to produce different products. Furthermore, it is available when an alternative is to change the primary inputs without altering the final product. These options are equivalent to a portfolio of financial options with both call and put American options.
Closing and reopening option: It provides the ability to stop and restart the operation of a project according to market conditions. Restart operations that previously have been turned off is equivalent to an American call option. Cancelling initiated operations previously, it is equivalent to an American put option.

5. Real options valuation

Different methods were developed to value financial options but their applications in the real options setting are conditioned to the particular characteristics of each problem. In practice, the underlying assumptions of traditional option valuation methods often do not hold when assessing capital investment projects. There are three general solution methods:
Stochastic differential equations: This method solves a partial differential equation (PDE). It mathematically expresses the dynamics of the option value for specific conditions. The analytic solution of the PDE provides the option value as a direct function of the inputs. The Black-Scholes's equation is the best known analytic formulation (Black & Scholes, 1973).
A major advantage of this analytical solutions is that there are many available tools and algorithms are quite fast.
A disadvantage is that computational complexity increases as more sources of uncertainty are incorporated. Furthermore, it usually works as a black-box, making it difficult to interpret the consequence and effects of the contingent decisions.
Stochastic dynamic programming: As it shown by Dixit & Pindick (1994), dynamic programming is a very useful approach for dynamic optimization problems under uncertainties. It decomposes a whole decision sequence into two components: the immediate decision and a valuation function that encapsulates the consequences of all subsequent decisions, starting with the position that results from the immediate decision.
The more popular method is the binomial lattice, introduced by Cox *et al.* (1979).
The advantages of the binomial lattice are: it can analyze a large number of applications of real options; it is practical because it retains the appearance of the analysis of discounted cash flow; uncertainty and contingent consequences of decisions are described in a natural way; therefore, the model binomial generates a good picture of the problem and the decision can be easily traced.

The disadvantages of binomial trees are: the method is developed based on a number of assumptions and these should be fulfilled by the options discussed. The most important assumptions are: perfect financial market; possibility of buying or selling short; constant short-term risk-free interest rate throughout the period under analysis; perfectly divisible assets; changes in the underlying asset price according to a multiplicative binomial process that follows a GBM (probability distribution of the underlying lognormal and the volatility grows linearly with time).

Stochastic simulation models: In this case the model takes several possible paths of the underlying asset evolution into account from current date to the moment of decision. The commonly used method is Monte Carlo simulation. At the end of each path, the optimal investment sequence for this particular realization can be obtained, and the income of the project can be calculated.

As it was aforementioned, the advantages of Monte Carlo simulation method are: it can handle various aspects of real world applications, allows direct processing of all types of assets, whatever the number and kind of stochastic behavior of the sources of uncertainties. In addition, including new source of uncertainty is much simpler than in the case of other numerical models. The disadvantage inherent in the implementation of this method is that it requires a large amount of calculations, which involves extensive computing resources and is quite expensive in computation time. However, this disadvantage is being overcome daily with the progress of software and hardware.

5.1 Least Square Monte Carlo (LSM) method

In the early stages of the ROV, valuation was normally confined to the options for which solutions of the financial could directly be applied. This was done mainly using few underlying assets and simple options with European features or American perpetual options (Rodriguez & Rocha, 2006). However, an investor is normally confronted with a vast opportunity set. Hence investment projects are a portfolio of options; frequently depending on several stochastic variables.

The introduction of multiple interacting options into the real options models substantially increases the difficulty of solving them, making traditional numerical approaches inadequate. Nevertheless, simulation procedures for successfully solving multiple American options have been proposed. One of the most promising approaches is the Least Square Monte Carlo (LSM) method proposed by Longstaff and Schwartz (2001).

LSM method is based on Monte Carlo simulation and uses least squares linear regression to determine the optimal stopping time in the decision making process. Moreover, this approach has proven to be a very intuitive and flexible tool.

The value of an American option, with a state variable X_τ, payoff $\Pi(\tau, X_\tau)$ where Π is a known function[6], and that can be exercised from t until maturity T, is equal to:

$$F(t, X_\tau) = \max_{\tau \in T} \left\{ \mathbb{E}_t^* \left[\Pi(\tau, X_\tau) \cdot (1+\rho)^{-(\tau-t)} \right] \right\} \tag{4}$$

---

[6] In formal mathematical terms, $\Pi \in \mathcal{L}^2(\Xi, \mathcal{F}, \mathbb{Q})$ is the space of square-integrable functions with respect to $\mathbb{Q}$, where Ξ represents the space of all feasible states of the economy, $\mathcal{F}$ is the filtration generated by the state variables and $\mathbb{Q}$ is the equilibrium probability measure on $\mathcal{F}$.

where τ is the optimal stopping time ($\tau \in [t,T]$) and the operator $\mathbb{E}_t^*$ [.] represents the risk neutral expectation conditional on the information set available at t. The discount factor between any two periods is $df = (1+\rho)^{-1}$, where ρ is the risk adjusted discount rate.

As is exposed in (Rodriguez & Rocha, 2006), the LSM approach proposed a Monte Carlo simulation algorithm to estimate the option value stated in (Cortazar *et al.*, 2006). Eq. (4) can be expressed in a discrete time splitting the maturity time T in N discrete intervals. Then, sample paths of the underlying asset stochastic evolution are generated by means of Monte Carlo simulation techniques.

It is assumed that the option can only be exercised in discrete times into a restricted set of dates: $[t_0 = 0, t_1 = \Delta t, \cdots, t_N = N.\Delta t = T]$. The optimal stopping policy -along the path ω - can be derived by applying the Bellman`s principle of optimality: "*An optimal policy has the property that, whatever the initial action, the remaining choices constitute an optimal policy with respect to the sub-problem starting at the state that results from the initial action*" (Dixit & Pindick, 1994). This statement can mathematically be expressed as follows:

$$F(t_n, X_{t_n}) = \max\left\{\Pi\left(t_n, X_{t_n}\right), \mathbb{E}_{t_n}^*\left[F\left(t_{n+1}, X_{t_{n+1}}\right)\right].df\right\} \tag{6}$$

By using this equation, we can determine the path-wise optimal policy, restricted to the given dates, by comparing the continuation value,

$$\Phi\left(t_n, X_{t_n}\right) = \mathbb{E}_{t_n}^*\left[F\left(t_{n+1}, X_{t_{n+1}}\right)\right].df \tag{7}$$

with the payoff $\Pi(t_n, X_{t_n})$. Hence, the optimal stopping time for the ω-th realization, is found, beginning at T and working backwards, applying the following condition:

$$\text{if} \quad \Phi\left(t_n, X_{t_n}(\omega)\right) \le \Pi\left(t_n, X_{t_n}(\omega)\right) \quad \text{then} \quad \tau(\omega) = t_n \tag{8}$$

At the maturity time, the options are no longer available, therefore, the continuation value equals zero $(\Phi(T, X_T) = 0)$, consequently (8) holds as long as the payoff value is positive. Prior to T at t_n, the option holder must compare the payoff obtained from the immediate exercise $(\Pi(t_n, X_{t_n}(\omega)))$ with the continuation value $(\Phi(t_n, X_{t_n}(\omega)))$. When the decision rule (8) holds the stopping time is updated. Finally, $(\tau(\omega) = t_n)$ the value of the American option is then calculated as the average of the values over all realizations (Longstaff & Schwartz, 2001):

$$F(0,x) = \frac{1}{\Omega}\sum_{w=1}^{\Omega}\Pi\left(\tau(\omega), X_{\tau(\omega)}\right).(1+r)^{-(\tau(\omega))} \tag{9}$$

Then, the problem reduces to one of finding the expected continuation value at (t, X_t), in order to apply the rule (8). Here is where the LSM method makes its main contribution. This method estimate the continuation for all previous time-stages by regressing from the discounted future option values on a linear combination of functional forms of current state variables. Considering that the functional forms are not evident, the most common implementation of the method is simple powers of the state variable (monomial) (Longstaff & Schwartz, 2001).

As exposed in (Cortazar *et al.*, 2006), let define L_j, with j=1,2,…,J as the orthonormal basis of the state variable X_t used as regressors to explain the occurred present value in the ω-th realization, then the least square regression is equivalent to solve the following optimization problem:

$$\min_{\varphi} \sum_{w=1}^{\Omega} \left[\Pi\left(t+1, X_{t+1}(\omega)\right).df - \sum_{j=1}^{J} \varphi_j L_j(X_t(\omega)) \right]^2 \tag{10}$$

Then the resulting optimal coefficients φ^* from solving (10) are utilized to estimate the expected continuation value $\Phi^*(t, X_t(\omega))$ applying the following expression:

$$\Phi^*\left(t, X_t(\omega)\right) = \sum_{j=1}^{J} \varphi_j^* L_j\left(X_t(\omega)\right) \tag{11}$$

Working backwards until t =0, the optimal decision policy on each sample path -choosing the largest between the immediate exercise and the expected continuation value- can be determined. Finally, by applying (9) the value of the American option can be computed.
Fig. 4 represents the process described for an individual deferral option for two periods.
Recently, Gamba (2003) proposed a model which extending the LSM approach decomposes complex multiple real options (with interacting options) into simple hierarchical sets of individual options. The decomposition principle can be used by applying any kind of methodology based on dynamic programming and Bellman equation (Cortazar *et al.*, 2006).

5.2 Multi-option investment problems

As mentioned before, Gamba(2003) has presented an extension of the LSM method to value independent, compound and mutually exclusive options. According to that approach, options can be classified as (Rodriguez & Rocha, 2006):

Independent options: The value of a portfolio comprising only independent options is equal to the sum of each individual option value, computed by the LSM method. Only in this situation, the additivity property holds, even when the underlying assets might not be independent.

Compound options: Let a portfolio of H compounded options, where the execution of h-th option creates the right to exercise the subsequent (h+1)-th option. A typical example of this kind of sequential options is the right to expand capacity, which is just originated when the initial investment option is exercised. The payoff $\Pi_h(t, X_t)$ of the h-th option, must take into account the value of the option (h+1)-th. These options can be valued by applying the LSM approach. Consequently, the value of the h-th option is calculated according to:

$$F_h(t, X_t) = \max_{\tau \in [t, T_h]} \left\{ \mathbb{E}_{t_n}^* \left[\Pi_h(\tau, X_\tau) + F_{h+1}(\tau, X_\tau) \right].df \right\} \tag{12}$$

The Bellman equation for a set of sequential real options can be formulated as following:

$$F_h(t_n, X_{t_n}) = \max \left\{ \begin{matrix} \Pi_h\left(t_n, X_{t_n}\right) + F_{h+1}(t_n, X_{t_n}), \ldots \\ \mathbb{E}_{t_n}^* \left[F_h\left(t_{n+1}, X_{t_{n+1}}\right) \right].df \end{matrix} \right\} \tag{13}$$

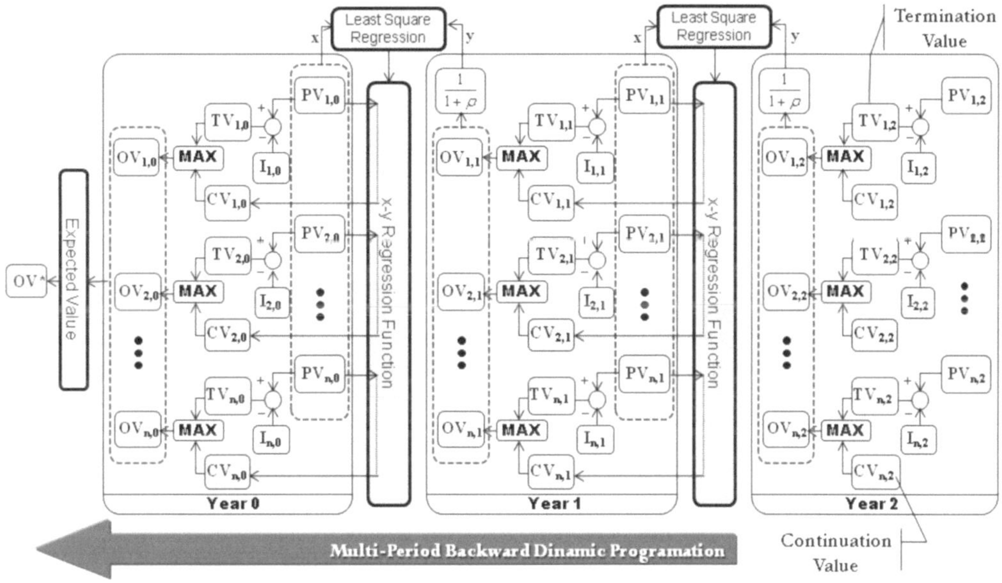

Fig. 4. Optimization of exercising time of an option to defer investment using LSM

Mutually exclusive options: A set of options are mutually exclusive when the exercise of one of them eliminates the opportunity of execution of the remainder. The expansion and abandon options are common examples of mutually exclusive options. Thus, the problem is extended to find both the optimal stopping time and optimal option to be exercised. Therefore, the control variable is a bi-dimensional variable (τ ,ζ), where τ is a exercising time in [t, T_h] and $\zeta \in \{1, 2,\ldots, H\}$. The value of the option, choosing the best among H mutually exclusive options, is:

$$G(t,X_t) = \max_{(\tau,\zeta)} \left\{ \mathbb{E}^*_{t_n} \left[F_\zeta(\tau, X_\tau) \right] .df \right\} \tag{14}$$

Thus, the Bellman equation of a portfolio of mutually exclusive options is given by:

$$G_h(t_n, X_{t_n}) = \max \begin{Bmatrix} F_1(t_n, X_{t_n}), \cdots, F_H(t_n, X_{t_n}), \cdots \\ \mathbb{E}^*_{t_n} \left[G_{h+1}(t_{n+1}, X_{t_{n+1}}) \right] .df \end{Bmatrix} \tag{15}$$

Each $F_h(t_n, X_{t_n})$ and the continuation value (Φ_n) is estimated by the LSM approach as explained before.

6. Decision making of flexible investment portfolios in transmission system

This section addresses the problem of assessing flexible transmission investment portfolios under uncertainty on the basis of the social welfare of the electricity market. It proposes a methodology based on the real options approach for valuing the flexibility of strategic investments in the transmission network and finding the optimal timing of the execution of the investment alternatives.

Within this model, the research work develops a suitable approach for assessment of Transmission Investment Portfolios (TIPs) considering Flexible Alternative Current Transmission Systems (FACTS) devices. FACTS are power electronics–based devices for the control of voltages and/or currents, enhancing controllability and increasing power transfer capability (Zhang *et al.,* 2006). In addition, FACTS could add flexibility to the investment portfolio through new strategic options such as relocation and abandon.

The evolution of fundamental uncertain variables is modelled through appropriate stochastic processes. Some of these are:

- power demand growth,
- power generation costs,
- penetration level of renewable generation.

The reduction of the system costs incurred for serving the load demand over the optimization horizon is used as the measure to evaluate the economic performance of the proposed network upgrades.

Under this framework, the value of a TIP is defined by the increase (or decrease) of the social welfare resulting from executing the investments considered in the portfolio. Taking into account an inelastic demand, the incremental social welfare should be quantified through the generation cost savings between the base scenario (BS, without investment) and the investment scenario (IS, with the investment executed).

6.1 Stochastic simulation of the transmission investment in power market

The study case analyzes aims to present a method for assessing flexible investments in a reduced European interconnected transmission system model under uncertain scenarios.

This section takes FACTS devices into account again, which add flexibility to the investment portfolio through new strategic options such as relocation and abandonment. These investment alternatives are evaluated according to the Real Option method by applying the LSM approach.

The proposed methodology is applied in a study case which evaluates a reinforcement at the German transmission network, by showing how the valuation of flexibility is a key task for making efficient and well-timed investment in the transmission network.

This study case is an extension of the paper (Blanco *et al.,* 2010a), incorporating the model of an uncertain cumulative growth of the installed wind capacity according to a stochastic logistic growth law.

Moreover, the stochastic behaviour of system components, demand growth and generation cost evolution is simulated through the Monte Carlo method. In order to determine the operation cost for each hour of the investment horizon under the BS and the IS, an Direct Current Optimal Power Flow (DC-OPF) model is applied. The cost difference between both scenarios defines the underlying asset.

The OPF model has been widely used in many pool-based deregulated electricity markets to calculate the generation dispatch based on the bids submitted by generators and loads, also taking into account the network constraints.

Normally, the objective is to maximize the social welfare or to minimize the generation cost if loads are inelastic. Evidently, the OPF calculation often neglects some characteristics of the real market behaviour within the regarded system. For instance, national borders and the respective cross-border trading cannot be regarded explicitly but is incorporated by the capacity limits of the lines.

The advantage of the OPF calculation is that the results represent the true value of network upgrades irrespective of the actual market behaviour (Blanco *et al.*, 2010a).
Thus, the optimization problem can be mathematically formulated as follows:

$$\min\left[\sum_i \sum_g C_g\left(P_g^i\right)\right]$$
$$s.t.\begin{cases} a)\ \sum_g P_g^i \quad \sum_d P_d^i \quad \sum_l \Gamma_l^i = 0 \\ b)\ P_g^{i,\min} \le P_g^i \le P_g^{i,\max};\ F_l^{\min} \le F_l \le F_l^{\max} \\ c)\ P_{F,i} + \dfrac{X_{TCSC}^{\max}}{X_{ij}.(X_{ij} - X_{TCSC}^{\max})} \ge 0; \\ d)\ P_{F,i} + \dfrac{X_{TCSC}^{\min}}{X_{ij}.(X_{ij} - X_{TCSC}^{\min})} \le 0 \end{cases} \tag{16}$$

where C_g is the supplier bid curve as well as P_g^i and P_d^i are the power generated and demanded by unit *g* and load *d*, respectively at node *i*. The power flow through all transmission lines connected to node *i* is denoted by F_l. The operation limits of each generator unit are stated by $P_g^{i,\min,\max}$ and the network restrictions are set by $F_l^{\min,\max}$.
This research analyses the FACTS devices called Thyristor Controlled Series Compensator (TCSC) under steady state operation For static implementations, these FACTS devices can be modelled by power injection models (PIM) (Wang *et al.*, 2002). The PIM model depicts FACTS as devices that inject a certain amount of active and reactive power into its nodal connections; meaning that this controller operation is replicated by these injection flows. Constrains c) and d) are related to this model of operation of the FACTS devices connected between the nodes *i* and *j*.
The stochastic behaviour of the power market model contemplated in this chapter can be defined as a fundamental or bottom-up model, since annual generation costs are directly influenced by the long-term stochastic movements of the uncertain variables. Hence, a several realizations are necessary to conduct Monte Carlo simulations with accurate statistical estimations.
From the economical point of view, the stochastic cash flow, defined by the annual generation cost saving for each realization, is applied in order to evaluate the performance of the transmission investment. Setting the investment cost and discount rate, stochastic discounted cash flow calculations are performed. Finally, real option techniques are applied for adding the flexibility value of each investment alternative, and the optimal investment decision is pointed out.

Load growth modelling

The growth of the electricity demand is a key variable largely influencing the performance of transmission investments. This growth of electricity demand is stochastic by nature. Certainly, climate changes, acceleration and downturns of the economic cycle as well as population dynamics turn random deviations out around the long-run expected value of the growth rate (Olsina *et al.*, 2006).

These random deviations of the growth rate around the expected values of the annual drift, interpreted as an error of forecasted growth, are commonly assumed to be Gaussian - according to the Central Limit Theorem- by following a generalized Wiener process. This process might be formulated as shown below:

$$dw = \varepsilon\sqrt{dt} \tag{16}$$

where the variation in the variable w during a short period Δt is defined by the product of a random variable and the square root of the period length. ε is so-called white noise, i.e. a random variable which has a Gaussian distribution with an expected value equal to 0 and a variance of 1. A Wiener process can be classified as a particular form of a Markov-process, i.e. it is a stochastic process, where the current value contains all the information retrievable from the random variable wander (Weber, 2004).
Then, the stochastic model of the demand growth rate can be represented by a generalized Brownian Motion (BM) according to the following expression:

$$dR_j(t,n) = \mu_R(t,n)\cdot dt + \sigma_R(n)\cdot dw \tag{17}$$

Thereby the estimated unconditional mean load growth rate at the n–th node, at the instant t is $\mu_R(t,n)$; $\sigma_R(n)$ is the estimated unconditional standard deviation for this period and dw is the Wiener process.
Within this work, the demand growth of the German power system is taken as an uncertain variable. The demand growth within the other regarded countries are taken as covered by new local generation, this is due to the lack of information about the generation capacity expansion in those countries. Nevertheless, a stochastic fluctuation around this null growth is taken into account, representing the possible inability of new generation entrance. The parameters used into the stochastic process are exposed in (Blanco *et al.*, 2010a).

Country	$\mu_{L_i}^{peak}(0)$ [%]	$\sigma_{L_i}^{peak}$	$\mu_{L_i}^{base}(0)$ [%]	$\sigma_{L_i}^{base}$
Germany	1.5	0.15	1.5	0.1
Benelux countries	0	0.1	0	0.1

Table I. Demand Growth Parameters (ENTSO, 2009).

Generation cost modelling

The main impact of a transmission investment on the social welfare is reflected as generation cost savings by bringing down the network-related system operational costs such as out-of-merit generation costs caused by network bottlenecks. Fluctuations of the transmission investment performance, according to this benchmark, are mainly related to generation cost fluctuations of the thermal units, which are strongly correlated with their own fuel prices. Commonly, the average marginal cost of generation of the unit generator g at each instant t, denoted as $\overline{MC_g}(t)$, can be derived from the average thermal efficiency $\overline{\eta}_g(t)$ and the prevailing fuel prices p_g^F at that moment:

$$\overline{MC}_g(t) = \frac{p_g^F(t)}{\eta_g(t)} \tag{18}$$

Therefore, the uncertainty over the generation cost savings are strongly linked with fuel price uncertainties. A reasonable and realistic way to replicate the uncertain evolution of the fuel prices is through a mean-reverting stochastic process. A mean-reverting process is one where the stochastic paths evolve fluctuating around a known long-run mean. The simplest mean-reverting process, called Ornstein-Uhlenbeck stochastic process, is expressed below:

$$d\left(\ln p_g^F(t)\right) = \alpha\left(\ln \overline{p_g^F} - \ln p_g^F(t)\right) + \sigma^{\ln p_g^F(t)} dW \tag{19}$$

where α is the speed of reversion to the mean, $\sigma^{\ln p_g^F(t)}$ is the volatility of natural logarithmic of fuel prices, and $\overline{p_g^F}$ is the normal level of the natural logarithmic of fuel price $p_g^F(t)$, i.e. the level to which p_g^F tends to revert.
Within this work, the stochastic paths of fossil fuel prices are simulated according to the exposed process. The historical as well as the forecast data (IER, 2009) on costs and prices have been used to estimate the numerical parameters of Eq. 19. These parameters are listed in Table II. In the simulations, nuclear fuel cost prices are assumed constant over the time horizon. The main fundamental of this assumption is based on the fact that the uranium cost is only a small fraction of the total variable cost (around 5 %) in nuclear plants and the deviations around the expected value are quite narrow in comparison to the fuel price fluctuations (Webber, 2005). Furthermore, nuclear power stations seldom are the marginal units setting the market clearing price.

Fuel Type	$p_g^F(0)$ €/MW	$\overline{p_g^F}$ €/MW	$\sigma^{\ln p_g^F(t)}$ %
Gas	12.46	17.94	0.129
Oil	20.99	28.21	0.3
Coal	5.51	6.64	0.14

Table II. Mean Reversion Process Parameters

Network model

The optimal power flow calculations are performed on the reduced network model presented in (Blanco *et al.*, 2010a), which is built in order to replicate realistic scenarios of the transmission system in the Central Western European (CWE) region (Belgium, France, Germany, Luxembourg, and the Netherlands). Nodes are also modelled in Austria, the Czech Republic, Poland, and Switzerland in order to taking possible loop-flows into account. The detailed characteristics of the network model and the data which have been used are presented in (Waniek *et al.*, 2009). Figure 5 gives a general view of the configuration of the network model. Within Germany, 31 nodes are allocated to the 16 federal states. This data is useful as relevant statistical informations are often divided up into the federal states. These statistics include current and expected values of installed capacity in renewable energies like wind energy, photovoltaics, biomass, etc. as well as the use of combined heat and power. The large conventional power plants are explicitly allocated to the network nodes utilizing a detailed data base.

The model accuracy of the other regarded regions and markets is nearly the same as for Germany although the focus of the entire model is the implications for the German market and the transmission system. The numbers of nodes of the other regions are the following: *Belgium:* 4 nodes, *France:* 13 nodes and, *The Netherlands:* 9 nodes.

In addition, the feed-in from conventional power plants and its future development is crucial in order to replicate possible future congestions. A detailed dataset of the power plants in the modelled regions presented in (Blanco *et al.*, 2010a) is utilized for the present situation. The included units can be differentiated by installed capacity, fuel type, and age. These units are assigned to the nodes of the sample network using geographical information.

The net generating capacity of the conventional power plants in Germany is almost constant until 2020 by raising capacities of hard coal and natural gas-fired plants. This is mainly due to the closure of nuclear plants which is currently under discussion and could end up being postponed. In addition, the use of renewable energies, especially wind energy, is expected to increase further. The intermittent in-feed is modelled with different situations which are explained later on.

Regarding the pumping storage plants, the complexity in the modelling of these units results from the interdependency of the pumping and generating process. Units without any natural inflow can only generate that amount of electricity that was stored before, taking into account the limited process efficiency. Within the presented approach, this problem is solved by a sequential simulation of the base load situation first, followed by the peak load situation. During the different base load situations, the pumping storage units are considered as dispatchable loads in the OPF. Depending on the price, a certain amount of electricity is stored in the reservoir. The assumed size of the reservoir results from the assumption that every unit is able to generate maximum power during all peak load hours. The formal formulation of this approach can be founded in (Blanco *et al.*, 2010a).

	2007	2010	2015	2020
Nuclear	20.5	16.5	13.0	1.3
Lignite	20.5	22.6	22.0	22.0
Hard Coal	30.5	33.0	34.6	32.8
Natural Gas	25.3	27.8	33.6	42.8
Total	96.8	99.9	103.4	98.9

Table III. Development of the power plant mix in Germany (in GW)

Wind scenarios

Two demand scenarios (base load and peak load) and three wind situations are regarded, in order to reduce the number of calculated situations for each realization and each year. The probability of each wind situation occurring is determined according to the empirical histogram shown in Fig. 6.

The underlying data are actual values of the wind feed-in in Germany during 2006 in a 15 minute resolution.. The histogram is split into three sections. The first region on the left-hand side, low wind, covers 50% of all values. The next 30% of the values are in the second region, medium wind, and the third 20% correspond to a high wind condition.

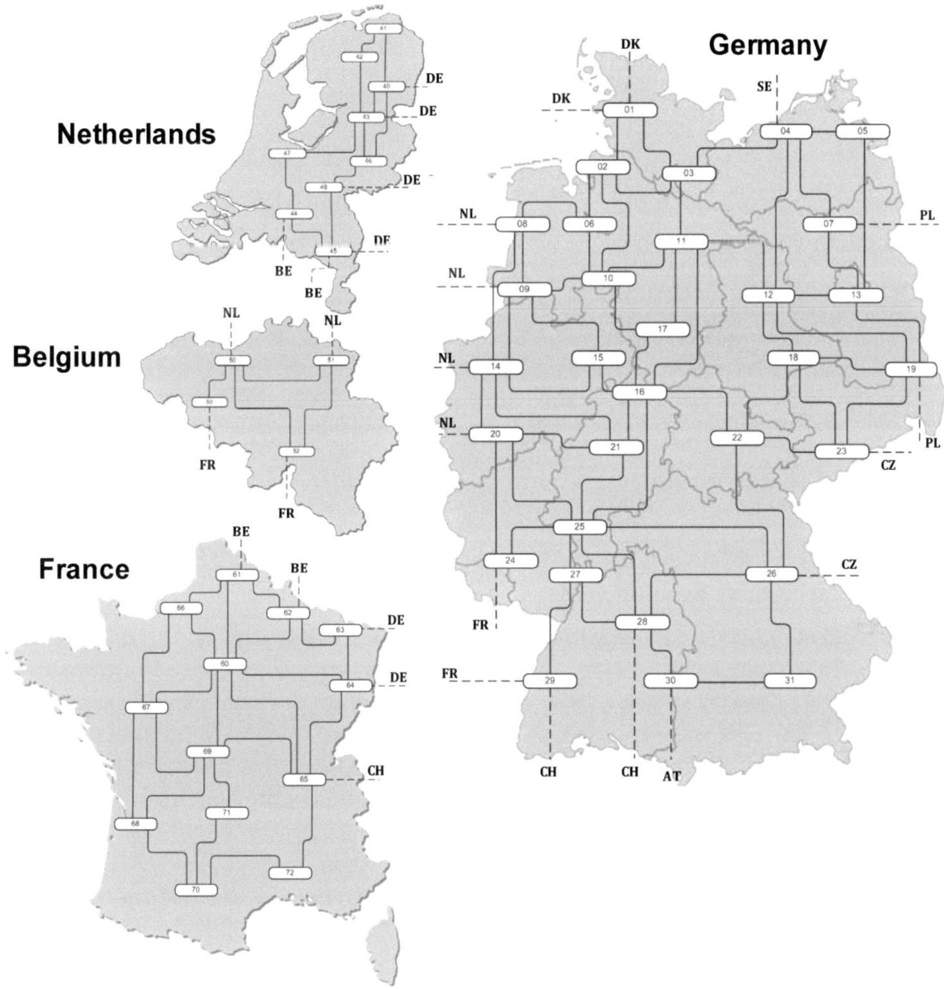

Fig. 5. Structure of the network ENTSO-E model (Waniek *et al.*, 2009)

Hence, the wind feed-in that is used in the calculations is defined as the median in these three sections. The matrix shown in Table IV of the six possible combinations is obtained under the assumption that 70% of the year can be represented by a base load situation. Consequently, for each realization and each year, six situations are calculated and weighted according to their probability of occurrence in order to get representative results of one year.

	low wind	**medium wind**	**high wind**	
peak load	15 %	9 %	6 %	30 %
base load	35 %	21 %	14 %	70 %
	50 %	30 %	20 %	100 %
→ feed-in	6 %	19 %	46 %	

Table IV. Weighting of the Wind feed-in Scenarios

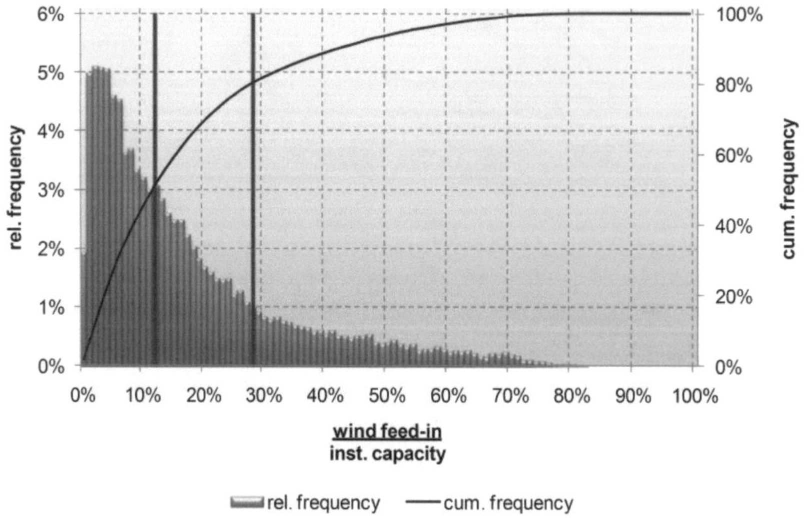

Fig. 6. Weighting of the calculations based on the frequency distribution of the wind feed-in

Modeling wind capacity development

The future development of wind capacity installations in Germany is possibly the single most important uncertain factor affecting investment decisions in transmission infrastructure. At the end of year 2009, a total of 21164 wind turbines with a cumulated rated power of 25.7 GW were installed in Germany (Ender, 2010). Although onshore wind development already shows some symptoms of stagnation, the focus of further wind capacity additions is now on offshore wind farm installations in the North Sea and the Baltic Sea. Specialized agencies predict that installed wind power capacity could reach to about 65 GW in Germany by 2030 (DEWI, 2008).

The massive addition of wind power registered in Germany in the last decade and the foreseen huge offshore wind capacity integration to the existing networks make necessary major reinforcements of the transmission network. However, actual offshore wind development depends on a number of complex factors (technology advancements, cost development, regulatory framework, etc.) that make long-term forecasts highly uncertain. Given the high irreversibility and costs involved in major network upgrades, transmission expansion strategies that retain flexibility in order to adapt to unexpected or unlikely wind scenarios are particularly attractive. In order to properly assess the various investment alternatives, a wind capacity model that account for the ongoing uncertainties is required.

This section presents a novel stochastic model for simulating possible paths of the aggregate wind capacity development in Germany up to year 2030. The model specifically takes into consideration the different stages of maturity and development of onshore and offshore wind technology. Whereas onshore wind capacity growth is slowing down since peaked in 2002 and some constraints to further development are already evident (e.g. permits, land use, network restrictions, etc.), offshore wind development in Germany is in the very early stage and some rapid adoption rate it is expected for the coming years.

In order to model the penetration rates of wind energy technology, a stochastic logistic diffusion model is proposed for both, the onshore and the offshore capacity development processes. Besides population dynamics modeling, logistic curves have been widely used for modeling adoption rates and market penetration of many energy technologies (Lund, 2006, Lund, 2008; Usha Rao & Kishore, 2010). Recently, S-shaped logistic growth have been extensively applied for modeling wind development trends in India and China (Carolin Mabel & Fernandez, 2008; Changliang & Zhanfeng, 2009; Pillai & Banerjee , 2009; Usha Rao & Kishore, 2009).

The logistic diffusion (Verhulst-Pearl) process is mathematically represented by the following first-order non-linear ordinary differential equation:

$$\frac{dP(t)}{dt} = \beta P\left(1-\frac{P}{K}\right) \text{ whose solution is given by } P(t) = \frac{KP_0 e^{\beta t}}{K + P_0(e^{\beta t}-1)} \tag{20}$$

where $P(t)$ is the wind power capacity installed at time t, P_0 is the capacity already installed at initial time t_0, β is the mean adoption rate and K the saturation level or maximum carrying capacity that the system can support.

Most of these mentioned logistic models assume a maximum capacity K given by the wind potential of the relevant geographic region. While wind conditions play an important role, this maximum capacity should actually be regarded as an extreme upper bound to the wind development. In fact, in most circumstances, the maximum achievable capacity is significantly lower than this level and it is instead determined by other factors, such as site permits, regulatory framework, subsidizing mechanisms and grid and operational constraints, etc. The saturation level depends on the context and it might not be well correlated to the geographical wind potential. Unlike models establishing an exogenous maximum capacity, we use a rather different approach to establish the saturation level K. For onshore wind capacity, we estimate the adoption rate and the saturation level from the observed wind development itself and for offshore wind capacity installations from available forecast data.

By expressing the logistic differential equation in terms of its finite difference approximation we obtain:

$$\frac{\Delta P_t}{\Delta t} = \frac{P_{t+1}-P_t}{\Delta t} = \beta P_t\left(1-\frac{P_t}{K}\right); \text{ solving for } P_{t+1} \text{ we get } P_{t+1} = \beta P_t\left(1-\frac{P_t}{K}\right)\Delta t + P_t \tag{21}$$

what forms the basis for implementing a numerical simulation model of the wind capacity development. We can estimate parameters β and K by expressing the observed fractional growth rate $\Delta P_t/(P_t\Delta t)$ in terms of the linear regression model where ε_t is a zero-mean independent normally distributed error residual term with finite variance σ^2:

$$\frac{\Delta P_t}{P_t}\frac{1}{\Delta t} = \hat{\beta} - \hat{\lambda} P_t + \varepsilon_t \quad \varepsilon_t \sim N(0,\sigma) \text{ where } \hat{\lambda} = \frac{\hat{\beta}}{\hat{K}} \tag{22}$$

Fig. 7 illustrates the observations, the regressed line and the estimated parameters as well as the obtained regression residuum. Analysis of residuals shown in Fig. 8 conforms to the hypothesis of Gaussianity and independence required by the linear regression model.

Based on the linear regression model stated above, we can numerically generate sample development paths for the installed wind capacity by adding the stochastic error term $\varepsilon_t \sim N(0,\sigma)$ to the logistic difference equation. Fig. 9 depicts the observed and expected

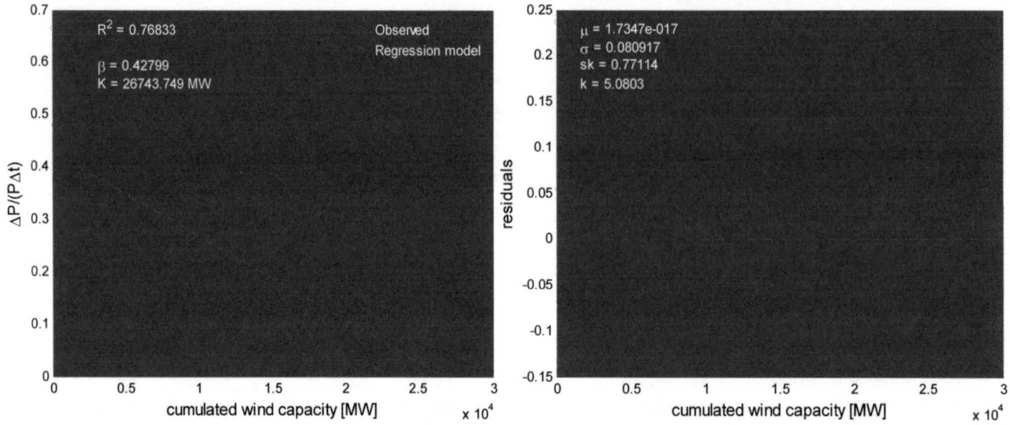

Fig. 7. Estimated logistic model of wind power capacity in Germany and resulting regression residuals

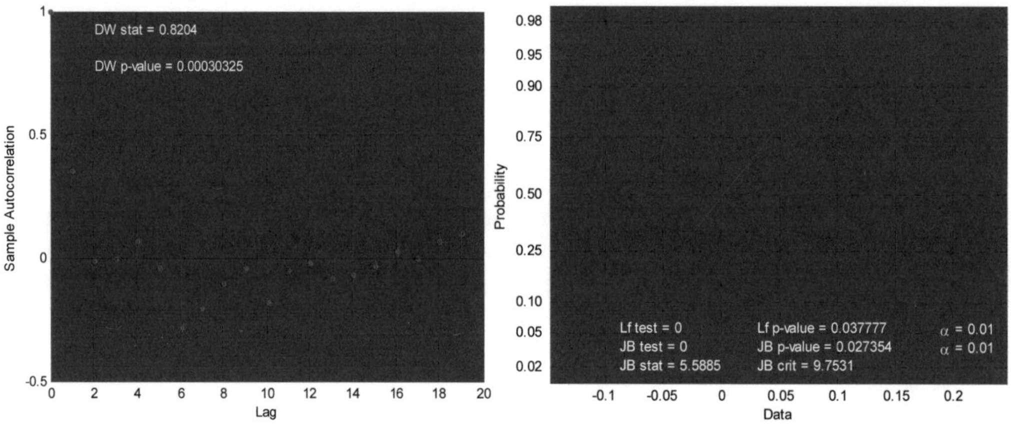

Fig. 8. Normal probability plot, Jarque-Bera/Lilliefors test statistics and autocorrelation of residuals

onshore wind capacity development in the future along with the 95% confidence bounds. It should be noticed that for the current conditions, the logistic growth model suggests that onshore wind development in Germany is already near saturation. Furthermore, uncertainty on future evolution of onshore capacity is not a severe issue as the logistic process is almost complete.

The diffusion process of the offshore wind technology in Germany is right in its beginning and therefore the ongoing uncertainties on the future development are huge. The substantial involved uncertainties are evident from the large spread shown by wind capacity forecasts for Germany collected from a number of agencies and institutions (Nitsch, 2005), as illustrated in Fig. 10 (left). The logistic regression model is applied to the prediction ensemble data in order to estimate the adoption rate and the capacity saturation level implied by forecasts (see Fig. 10 right). As it can be noticed from the scatter plot and residuals, predictions on the future offshore wind capacity development are subjected to high uncertainties.

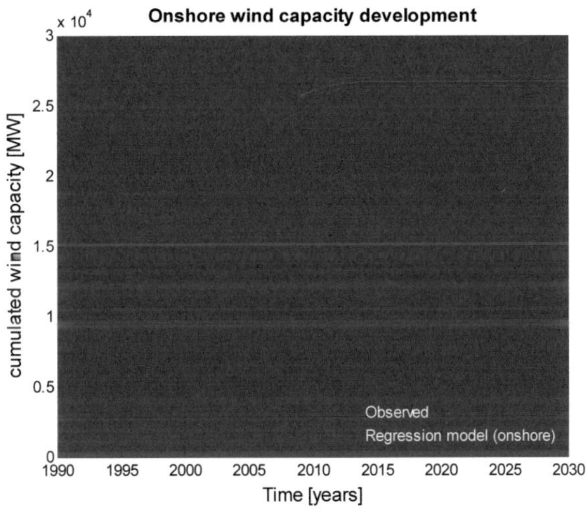

Fig. 9. Uncertainty on the future development of onshore wind power

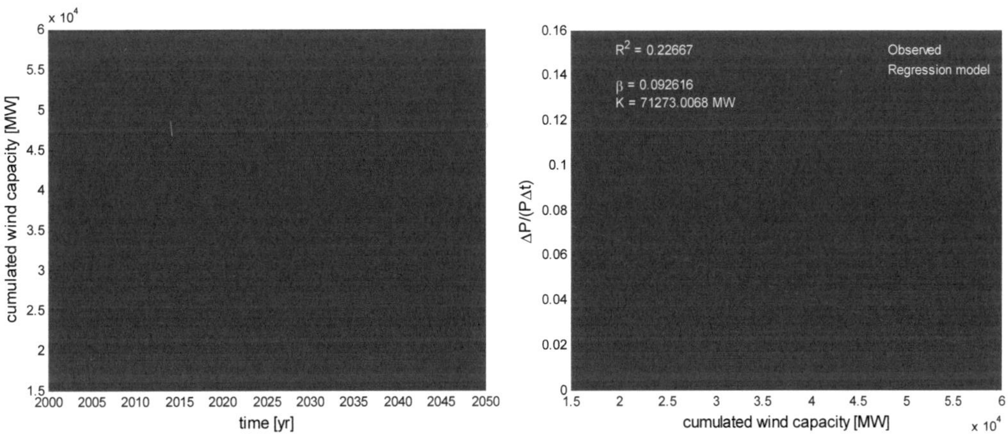

Fig. 10. Wind capacity forecast ensemble and estimated logistic model to forecast data

As there are still no available observations, the describe approach unfortunately does not apply to the stochastic simulation of the possible scenarios of offshore wind power capacity. However, the estimated parameters $\hat{\beta}$ and $\hat{\lambda}$ in the offshore logistic model are actually independent random variables normally distributed, for which confidence intervals can be computed from the Student's T-distribution. This confidence bounds allows estimating the standard deviation of each estimated parameter, $\hat{\sigma}_\beta$ and $\hat{\sigma}_\lambda$ respectively. These confidence intervals represent the uncertainty implied by the currently available forecasts. We can generate different logistic development paths for the offshore wind capacity by properly sampling model parameters values for their corresponding normal distributions, $N(\hat{\beta},\sigma_\beta)$ and $N(\hat{\lambda},\hat{\sigma}_\lambda)$.

After computing a large number of sample paths, Fig. 11 shows the resulting expected development of the total (onshore + offshore) wind power capacity in Germany up to year 2030 along with the rather wide 95% confidence bound, which in turns reflect the substantial current uncertainties on offshore wind installations. It is worth to mention, that the logistic offshore model suggest a much slow adoption of the offshore wind technology as conventionally reported.

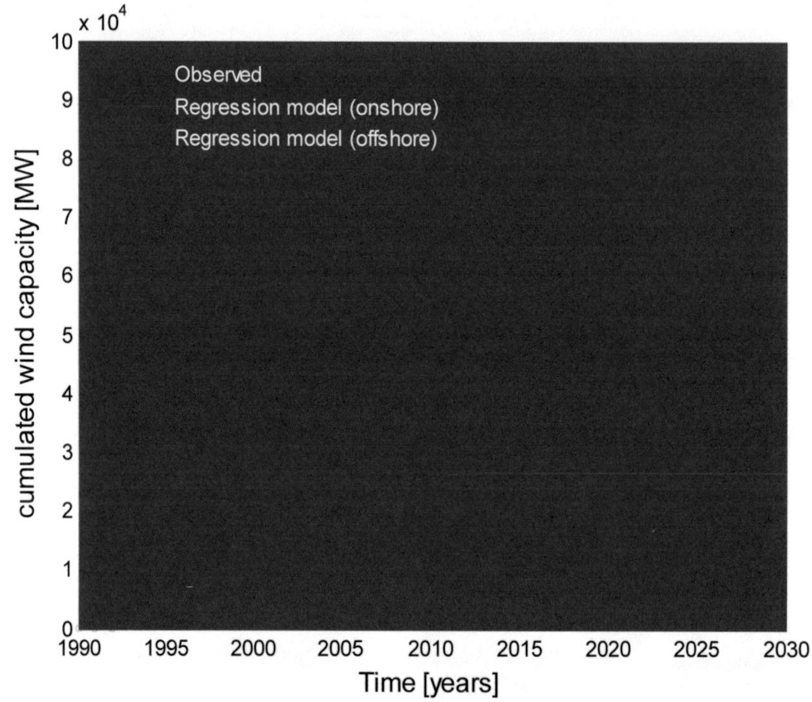

Fig. 11. Stochastic logistic simulations of the total wind power capacity development in Germany

6.2 Valuing flexible investment portfolios in the transmission system

The cost savings (*CS*) are estimated for each realization on the investment horizon by means of the Monte Carlo simulation. A stochastic cash flow for the investment projects can be numerically simulated. The resulting cash flow of each Monte Carlo realization is composed of the annual cost saving $CS^{s}_{i,\omega}$, investments costs (I_{s,t_n}) and operation cost (OC_{s,t_n}).
Later on, this cash flow is discounted by the hurdle rate of the investment (ρ) in order to obtain the present value of the Incremental Social Welfare (*ISW*), which can be stated as following:

$$PV\left(ISW\right)_{s,\omega,t_n} = \sum_{i=t_n}^{M}\left(\frac{CS^{s}_{i,\omega}}{(1+\rho)^{i}}\right); \quad (23)$$

$$NPV\left(ISW\right)_{s,\omega,t_n} = \sum_{i=t_n}^{M}\left(\frac{CS^{s}_{i,\omega} - I_{s,i} - OC_{s,i}}{(1+\rho)^{i}}\right); \quad (24)$$

$$E\left[NPV\left(ISW\right)_{s,\omega,t_n}\right] = \sum_{\omega=1}^{\Omega}\frac{1}{\Omega}\left(NPV\left(ISW\right)_{s,\omega,t_n}\right) \quad (25)$$

where $CS_{i,\omega}^{s}$ and $I_{s,i}$ are the generation cost savings and the investment cost respectively in the ω realization, $PV\left(ISW_{s,k}^{j}\right)$ and $NPV\left(ISW_{s,k}^{j}\right)$ are the Present Value (PV) and Net Present Value (NPV) of the ISW by executing the investment strategy s in the year t_n and by M the investment horizon, finally, $E\left[NPV\left(ISW\right)_{s,\omega,t_n}\right]$ is its expected value for Ω Monte Carlo realizations. In each case, the subscripts correspond to the h-th hour, i-th year, ω-th realization of the Monte Carlo power system simulation.

Within this chapter, the following have been considered as investment alternatives: firstly, a FACTS device and afterwards, a transmission line (TL). Therefore, the available investment options either invest in the FACTS first, in the line first or both in the FACTS and the line. The strategic flexibility of postponing both investments as well as abandoning or relocating the FACTS device are compounded options. Hence, these available options are valued by means of the LSM method, by applying the following Bellman's equations (Blanco, 2010):

1. Option to invest in the FACTS first:

$$F_F(t_n,X_{t_n})=\max\left\{\begin{matrix}\Pi_F\left(t_n,X_{t_n}\right)+\max\left(F_R\left(t_{n+1},X_{t_{n+1}}\right);F_A\left(t_{n+1},X_{t_{n+1}}\right);F_{TL}^{F}\left(t_{n+1},X_{t_{n+1}}\right)\right)\cdot df;\\ \cdots\mathbb{E}_{t_n}^{*}\left[F_F\left(t_{n+1},X_{t_{n+1}}\right)\right]\cdot df\end{matrix}\right\} \qquad (26)$$

2. Option to invest in the line first:

$$F_{TL}(t_n,X_{t_n})=\max\left\{\Pi_{TL}\left(t_n,X_{t_n}\right)+F_F^{TL}(t_{n+1},X_{t_{n+1}})\cdot df;\mathbb{E}_{t_n}^{*}\left[F_{TL}\left(t_{n+1},X_{t_{n+1}}\right)\right]\cdot df\right\} \qquad (27)$$

3. Option to invest both in the FACTS and the line:

$$F_{TL\&F}(t_n,X_{t_n})=\max\left\{\begin{matrix}\Pi_{TL\&F}\left(t_n,X_{t_n}\right)+\max\left(F_R^{TL\&F}(t_{n+1},X_{t_{n+1}});F_A^{TL\&F}(t_{n+1},X_{t_{n+1}})\right)\cdot df;\\ \cdots\mathbb{E}_{t_n}^{*}\left[F_{TL\&F}\left(t_{n+1},X_{t_{n+1}}\right)\right]\cdot df\end{matrix}\right\} \qquad (28)$$

where $F_m^{n}(t_n,X_{t_n})$ is the option value and $\Pi_m^{n}(t_n,X_{t_n})$ the profit value, both for the option m (F: FACTS, TL: transmission line, R: FACTS relocation, A: FACTS abandon) in the state n (F: FACTS investment done, TL: line investment done, Ab: FACTS abandon done. Expanding the equation (26):

$$F_R(t_n,X_{t_n})=\max\left\{\begin{matrix}\Pi_R\left(t_n,X_{t_n}\right)+\max\left(F_{TL}^{R}(t_n,X_{t_n});F_A(t_{n+1},X_{t_{n+1}})\cdot df\right);\cdots\\ \mathbb{E}_{t_n}^{*}\left[F_R\left(t_{n+1},X_{t_{n+1}}\right)\right]\cdot df\end{matrix}\right\} \qquad (29)$$

$$F_A(t_n,X_{t_n})=\max\left\{\Pi_A\left(t_n,X_{t_n}\right)+F_{TL}^{A}(t_n,X_{t_n});\mathbb{E}_{t_n}^{*}\left[F_A\left(t_{n+1},X_{t_{n+1}}\right)\right]\cdot df\right\} \qquad (30)$$

$$F_{TL}^{F}(t_n,X_{t_n})=\max\left\{\begin{matrix}\Pi_{TL}^{F}\left(t_n,X_{t_n}\right)+\max\left(F_R^{TL\&F}(t_{n+1},X_{t_{n+1}});F_{Ab}^{TL\&F}(t_{n+1},X_{t_{n+1}})\right)\cdot df;\\ \cdots\mathbb{E}_{t_n}^{*}\left[F_{TL}^{F}\left(t_{n+1},X_{t_{n+1}}\right)\right]\cdot df\end{matrix}\right\} \qquad (31)$$

Likewise, expanding the equations (29) and (30):

$$F_F^{TL}(t_n,X_{t_n})=\max\left\{\begin{array}{l}\Pi_F^{TL}\left(t_n,X_{t_n}\right)+\max\left(F_R^{TL\&F}\left(t_{n+1},X_{t_{n+1}}\right);F_{Ab}^{TL\&F}\left(t_{n+1},X_{t_{n+1}}\right)\right)\cdot df;\\ \cdots\mathbb{E}_{t_n}^{*}\left[F_F^{TL}\left(t_n,X_{t_{n+1}}\right)\right]\cdot df\end{array}\right\} \quad (32)$$

$$F_R^{TL\&F}(t_n,X_{t_n})=\max\left\{\Pi_R^{TL\&F}\left(t_n,X_{t_n}\right)+F_{Ab}^{TL\&F,R}\left(t_{n+1},X_{t_{n+1}}\right)\cdot df;\mathbb{E}_{t_n}^{*}\left[F_R^{TL\&F}\left(t_{n+1},X_{t_{n+1}}\right)\right]\cdot df\right\} \quad (33)$$

$$F_A^{TL\&F}(t_n,X_{t_{n+1}})=\max\left\{\Pi_A^{TL\&F}\left(t_n,X_{t_n}\right);\mathbb{E}_{t_n}^{*}\left[F_A^{TL\&F}\left(t_{n+1},X_{t_{n+1}}\right)\right]\cdot df\right\} \quad (34)$$

For the investment option exercising:

$$\Pi_m^n\left(t_n,X_{t_n}(\omega)\right)=PV\left(ISW\right)_{s,\omega,t_n}-I_{s,t_n,\omega} \quad (35)$$

where $I_{s,t_n,\omega}$ is the investment cost of the *s*-th investment strategy at the t_n-th year. On the other hand, in the relocation and abandon cases:

$$\Pi_R^n\left(t_n,X_{t_n}(\omega)\right)=PV\left(ISW_{R,t_n,\omega}\right)-CR_{t_n,\omega} \quad (36)$$

$$\Pi_A^n\left(t_n,X_{t_n}(\omega)\right)=SV_{t_n,\omega}-PV\left(ISW\right)_{s,\omega,t_n} \quad (37)$$

where $CR_{t_n,\omega}$ is the relocation cost and $SV_{t_n,\omega}$ is the scrap value of the FACTS devices by the t_n-th year.

The resulting cash flow is estimated according to each available investment strategy. It is relevant to remark that all possible investment strategies and their intrinsic real options are evaluated exhaustively, so that all possible combinations among the available flexibility options are assessed.

The option values for each strategy are calculated by applying this procedure. Hence, the optimal investment strategy is the one with the highest value. It is important to note that the optimal decision policy obtained by the LSM approach is not a deterministic one. In fact, there is an optimal policy for each simulated path. Consequently, a probability density function of option values can be determined.

The precision of the estimation value of the options might be improved by increasing the number of time steps N and the number of simulated path Ω. In this sense, the Monte Carlo stop criterion applied is the control of the relative error (Fishman, 2005). Setting $\delta=10\%$ entails demanding a confidence level in the attributes assessment of 95%.

$$\varepsilon_S\left(F_n^m(0),\sigma_{F_n^m(0)}\right)=\frac{\phi^{-1}\left(1-\dfrac{\delta}{2}\right)\cdot\sigma_{F_n^m(0)}}{F_n^m(0)\cdot\sqrt{\Omega}} \quad (38)$$

where ϕ^{-1} is the inverse of the Standard Normal Distribution (SND), $(1-\delta/2)$ the confidence level specified, $\phi^{-1}(1-\delta/2)$ the critical value of a SND with mean 0 and standard deviation 1 and $\sigma_{F_n^m(0)}$ the volatility of the expected option value. In this chapter it is assumed as maximum relative error 1%.

7. Study cases

The influence of two network upgrades on the out-of-merit cost is evaluated based on the approach presented in the previous section. These reinforcements projects are the development of a new 380-kV-double circuit and/or the installation of a FACTS controller. Both upgrades represent measures to strengthen the German network. Hence, a static and inflexible expansion project, which is currently under study, is compared to flexible investment in order to shed some light on the impact of the strategic flexibility on the optimal decision making process. The reinforcement alternatives have the following characteristics:

- **Reinforcement 1:** Development of a new 380-kV- double circuit on a length of 167 km between nodes 20 and 25, leading to investment costs of about 117 M€.
- **Reinforcement 2:** Installation of a TCSC devices of 286/-80 MVar between nodes 21 and 25, with the option to further relocate it between the nodes 20 and 25, leading to investment costs of about 47,63 M€ (Schaffner, 2004). Moreover, the relocation cost of the FACTS controller and its residual value are taken equal to 40% and 20% of the total FACTS cost respectively.

Thus, as starting point, there are three mutually exclusive alternatives (options) to be assessed, namely:

- Investing in the FACTS device first (S_1),
- investing in the transmission line first (S_2) or,
- investing in the FACTS and line jointly (S_3).

Maturity is set for all investments options equal to three years and 15 years as the investment horizon. Lead construction time is assumed to be one year and discount rate is considered to 8% per year, for all considered investment alternatives.

The network and data described in the previous sections is applied to compute 1000 sample realizations for ensuring the maximum relative error established before. Hence, several OPF calculations are performed for each scenario (base and investment). By this means, the stochastic annual generation cost savings are estimated.

The results of the investment evaluations are depicted in Table V. The traditional NPV appraisal suggests S_3 as the optimal investment choice. Conversely, the real option valuation determines S_1 as the optimal decision by taking into account the strategic flexibility provided on each strategy. Since the option value can be calculated according to (9), the economic value of the flexibility of each investment strategy is given by subtracting the expected NPV of the expected option value.

It should be highlighted that the investment alternative with the higher flexibility value is S_1, investing in FACTS first. This can be explained by noting that the flexibility of FACTS remains after the investment option has been exercising allowing a better adaption to possible adverse scenarios in the long-term.

Strategy	𝔼 [Option Value] (M€)	𝔼[NPV value] (M€)	Flexibility (M€)
S_1	140.14 (1st)	48.26 (3rd)	91.882 (1st)
S_2	91.03 (2nd)	57.347 (2nd)	33.782 (2nd)
S_3	90.447 (3rd)	90.441 (1nd)	0.006 (3rd)

Table V. Ranking of expansion strategies by applying the proposed evaluation approach and the traditional appraisal

Table VI portrays the feasible structure of the RO portfolios and its respective value. Thus, for instance, the structure TL-F-R-A implies that the option to invest in the TL, FACTS, relocation and abandon are available. It is important to notice that in all the RO portfolios, the deferral option is considered available.

As can be also seen, the S_1 value decreases when are unavailable the abandon and relocation options. This means that these options are worth and its valuation is relevant. Thus, in the situation where the relocation option is unavailable, the optimal decision is to invest in the TL first.

In a portfolio which includes FACTS, an important option is the option to defer the new TL. This can be observed by comparing the option values with (TL-F-R-A) and without (F-R-A) in their set of options. By comparing this value with the flexibility value of S_1 is easy to note that the largest flexibility of the strategic to invest in FACTS first is the TL deferral option.

On the other hand, the value of the deferral option of the TL can be obtained from the option by subtracting the S_2 (TL) portfolio value minus the static NPV(S_2) of Table V. In this particular study case, this value is low. Therefore, it possible to conclude that if the FACTS device is not regarded as an investment strategy the execution of the TL is probably going to be executed.

Strategy	Available Options Value [M€]								
	TL-F-R-A	TL-F-R	TL-F-A	TL-F	F-R-A	F-R	F-A	F	TL
S_1	140.14	96.18	88.807	88.44	70.52	70.51	48.27	48.26	
S_2	91.03	90.742	91.02	90.74					58.6
S_3	90.45	89.04	90.45	89.04					

Table VI. Option Value and the composition of the option portfolio.

The probability density function (PDF) of the option value is illustrated in Fig. 12. By mean of this figure, it can be observed that both S_2 and S_3 have a relevant downside risk in comparison with S_1. This risk acquires more relevance due to the facts that the TL expansions are irreversible investments. For that reason, the inclusion of flexibility in the TI problem is needed. In this sense, FACTS devices allow making expansions, retaining flexibility for properly managing uncertainties of the TI problem.

8. Conclusion

In this chapter, the application of a new approach has been developed for assessing flexible options embedded in investments projects. The option values have their roots in the fact that they put a floor against possible project losses. It has been shown that static NPV methods may be inappropriate for assessing flexible investments, since the existence of uncertainties

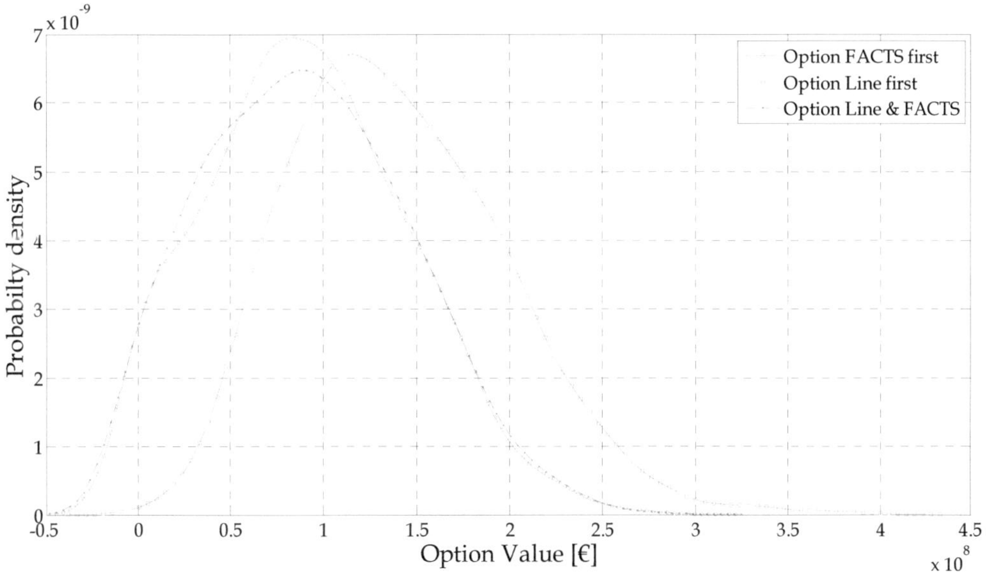

Fig. 12. Probability density function (PDF) of the analyzed strategies.

significantly increment the value of the strategic flexibility embedded in the decision-making process. In this sense, a RO framework has been developed, using the novel LSM simulation approach for solving the stochastic optimization problem.

The proposed appraisal framework was focused on the economic quantification of the main flexibility options in transmission investments projects. Particularly, flexible options of FACTS devices, i.e. postponement of large transmission project execution, relocation and abandonment of the controller was analyzed. The main uncertain variables and risks to which transmission projects are exposed, have been modelled. Long-term uncertainties have properly been handled by incorporating flexible expansion projects aiming at improving investment risk profiles. Particularly, this chapter included a novel modeling approach based on logistic diffusion process to the generation of future wind capacity scenarios. Finally, the flexibility value has been quantified for the postponement, relocation or abandonment of an investment project.

In a study case, it has been shown that more flexible investment strategies can be obtained and the adaptability to uncertain future scenarios is considerably improved by suitably combining FACTS controllers and conventional investments in transmission lines over the considered time horizon. In addition, it has been illustrated how the optimal decision could be misleaded under the traditional NPV investment rule. Hence, by applying the proposed RO valuation approach an important but yet uninvestigated feature of FACTS devices has been remarked: inducing investment execution in stages and postponing large and irreversible transmission line projects.

9. References

Amram, M., & Kulatilaka N. (1998). *Real Options: Managing Strategic Investment in an Uncertain World*. Oxford University Press, ISBN-10: 0875848451, USA.

Black, F., and M. S Scholes. 1973. The Pricing of Options and Corporate Liabilities. *Journal of Political Economy* 81, no. 3. Journal of Political Economy: 637-54.

Blanco, G., Waniek D., Olsina F., Garcés F., & Rehtanz, C. (2010a). Flexible Investment Decisions in the European Interconnected Transmission System, *Electric Power System Research,* EPSR-D-10-00390, doi: 10.1016/j.epsr.2010.12.001 (accepted for publication).

Blanco, G. (2010b). *Evaluación de portafolios de inversiones flexibles en el sistema de transmisión incluyendo dispositivos FACTS.* Ph.D. Dissertation. Editorial Fundación de la Universidad Nacional de San Juan, ISBN: 978-987-05-8411-7Argentina.

Blumsack, S., Apt, J. & Lave, L. B. (2006). Lessons from the Failure of U.S. Electricity Restructuring. *The Electricity Journal,* 19, no. 2 (March): 15-32.

Brealey, R. A., Myers, S. C. &. Allen, F. (1996). *Principles of Corporate Finance.* 9th ed. McGraw-Hill Companies, ISBN-10: 0071266755, USA.

Brosch, R. (2001). *Portfolio-aspects in real options management.* Department of Finance, Goethe University Frankfurt am Main, February. RePEc.

Carolin Mabel, M. & Fernandez, E. (2008). Growth and future trends of wind energy in India, *Renewable and Sustainable Energy Reviews,* Vol. 12 (6), pp. 1745-1757.

Changliang, X. & Zhanfeng, S. (2009) . Wind energy in China: Current scenario and future perspectives, *Renewable and Sustainable Energy Reviews,* Vol. 13 (8), pp. 1966-1974.

Copeland, T. & Antikarov V. (2003). *Real Options, Revised Edition: A Practitioner's Guide.* 1st ed. Texere, *ISBN*: 1587991705, USA.

Cortazar, G., Gravet, M., & Urzua J. (2008). The valuation of multidimensional American real options using the LSM simulation method. *Computers & Operations Research* 35, no. 1 (January): 113-129.

Cox, J. C., Ross, S. & Rubinstein, M. (1979). Option pricing: A simplified approach. *Journal of Financial Economics* 7, no. 3. Journal of Financial Economics: 229-263.

Damodaran, A. (2002). *Investment Valuation. 2nd Edition University with Investment Set.* 2nd ed. Wiley, ISBN-13: 978-0471280811, USA.

DEWI, Deutsches Windenergie-Institut (2008). WindEnergy Study 2008, Husum WindEnergy, 9-13 September 2008, Husum, Germany.

Dixit, A. K., & Pindyck, R.(1994). *Investment under Uncertainty.* Princeton University Press, ISBN-10: 0691034109, USA.

Ender, C. (2010). Wind Energy Use in Germany - Status 31.12.2009, *DEWI Magazine,* Vol. 36, pp. 28-41.

ENTSOE. (2009). *Online Database [Online].* Available: www.entsoe.eu

Fishman, G. (1995). *Monte Carlo: Concepts, Algorithms, and Applications,* New York: Springer, ISBN 038794527X, USA.

Gamba, A. (2003). Real Options Valuation: A Monte Carlo Approach. *SSRN eLibrary* (December).

Garver, L.L. (1970). Transmission Network Estimation Using Linear Programming. *Power Apparatus and Systems, IEEE Transactions on* PAS-89, no. 7: 1688-1697.

IER. (2007). Energy System Development in Germany, Europe and Woldwide.

Latorre, G., Cruz, R.D.,.Areiza, J.M, & Villegas A. (2003). Classification of publications and models on transmission expansion planning. *Power Systems, IEEE Transactions on* 18, no. 2: 938-946.

Longstaff, F. A. & Schwartz E.. 2001. Valuing American Options by Simulation: A Simple Least-Squares Approach. *Review of Financial Studies* 14, no. 1. Review of Financial Studies: 113-47.

Lund, P. (2006). Market penetration rates of new energy technologies, *Energy Policy*, Vol. 34 (17), pp. 3317-3326.

Lund, P. (2010). Exploring past energy changes and their implications for the pace of penetration of new energy technologies, *Energy*, Vol. 35 (2), pp. 647-656.

Myers, S. (1977). Determinants of corporate borrowing. *Journal of Financial Economics* 5, no. 2 (November): 147-175.

Nitsch, J., Staiß, F., Wenzel, B. & Fischedick, M. (2005). *Ausbau Erneuerbarer Energien im Stromsektor bis zum Jahr 2020*, Bundesministeriums für Umwelt, Naturschutz und Reaktorforschung, Germany.

Olafsson, S. (2003). Making Decisions Under Uncertainty - Implications for High Technology Investments. *BT Technology Journal* 21, no. 2: 170-183.

Olsina, F., Garcés F. & Haubrich H-J. (2006). Modeling long-term dynamics of electricity markets. *Energy Policy* 34, no. 12 (August): 1411-1433.

Olsina, F., Röscher, M, Larisson C. & F. Garcés. (2007). Short-term optimal wind power generation capacity in liberalized electricity markets. *Energy Policy* 35, no. 2 (February): 1257-1273.

Pillai, I. & Banerjee, R. (2009). Renewable energy in India: Status and potential, *Energy*, Vol. 34 (8), pp. 970-980.

Rodrigues, A. & Rocha, M. (2006). The Valuation of Real Options with the Least Squares Monte Carlo Simulation Method. *Working Paper. SSRN eLibrary* (February).

Romero, R. & Monticelli, A. (1994). A hierarchical decomposition approach for transmission network expansion planning. *Power Systems, IEEE Transactions on* 9, no. 1: 373-380.

Seifu, A., Salon, S. & List, G. (1989). Optimization of transmission line planning including security constraints. *Power Systems, IEEE Transactions on* 4, no. 4: 1507-1513.

Trigeorgis, L. (1996). *Real Options: Managerial Flexibility and Strategy in Resource Allocation.* The MIT Press, ISBN-13: 978-0262201025, USA.

Usha Rao & K., Kishore, V. (2010). A review of technology diffusion models with special reference to renewable energy technologies, *Renewable and Sustainable Energy Reviews*, Vol. 14 (3), pp. 1070-1078.

Usha Rao, K. & Kishore, V. (2009). Wind power technology diffusion analysis in selected states of India, *Renewable Energy*, Vol. 34 (4), pp. 983-988.

Vásquez, P. & Olsina, F. (2007). Valuing Flexibility of DG Investments in Transmission Expansion Planning, *Proceeding of Power Tech, 2007 IEEE Lausanne*, 695-700, July 2007, IEEE-PES, Lausanne.

Vásquez, P. 2009. *Flexibility-based decision-making for facing the current transmission expansion planning problem.* PhD Thesis, Instituto de Energía Eléctrica, UNSJ San Juan, ISBN: 978-987-05-6401-0.

Wang, X., Song, Y.H., Lu, Q. & Sun Y. (2002). Optimal allocation of transmission rights in systems with FACTS devices. *Generation, Transmission and Distribution, IEE Proceedings-* 149, no. 3: 359-366.

Waniek, D., Rehtanz C. & Handschin E. (2009). Analysis of market coupling based on a combined network and market model. *Proceeding of PowerTech, 2009 IEEE Bucharest,* 1-6, July 2009, IEEE-PES, *Bucharest.*

Weber, C. (2004). *Uncertainty in the Electric Power Industry: Methods and Models for Decision Support.* 1st ed. Springer, ISBN-10: 0387230475, Germany.

Yu, C., Leotard, J. & Ilić M. (1999). Dynamic Transmission Provision in Competitive Electric Power Industry. *Discrete Event Dynamic Systems: Theory and Applications*, 9, Kluwer Academic Publishers, Boston, MA.

Zhang, X., C. Rehtanz, and B. Pal. 2006. *Flexible AC Transmission Systems: Modelling and Control.* 1st ed. Springer, ISBN-*10*: 3540306064, Germany.

7

Research on Network Tomography Measurement Technique

Cai Wandong, Yao Ye and Li Yongjun
School of Computer Science, Northwestern Polytechnical University, Xi'an City, 710072, China

1. Introduction

Network measurement depends on certain measurement method, technique and standard to obtain measurement sample based on measurement devices or tools, which applies the network performance analysis model to identify network topology architecture, and to infer performance parameter and traffic characteristics that provides the scientific decision for network resources optimization deployment, network management, failure point position, and so on[1~3]. For the wired network with solid infrastructures, such as Internet, it often adopts a interior direct measurement method that is also defined as traditional measurement technique in the chapter.
During the middle period of 90 years in last century, NT measurement technique was brought forward by Y. Vardi[4],which used the end-to-end measurement sample to infer network link performance parameters. Traditional network measurement technique is often applied in Internet with solid infrastructure, which does not need the interior nodes to collaborate with each other in the same autonomous area, but requires some IP network standard protocols to help, such as SNMP, ICMP, and so on. NT measurement technique could adopt the active or passive measurement method, and analyzes statistically the end-to-end network performance sample to infer link performance parameters, topology architecture or traffic characteristics. The objective of NT measurement technique mainly focuses on link delay or loss rate inference, link bandwidth and throughput inference, network topology architecture identification and traffic matrix estimate[6~13].
The measurement process in NT technique consists of three steps[14,15]. At first, measurement system model must be built on, including measurement topology model and performance analysis model, which generally adopts logic tree network topology model, and makes use of the relationship between nodes in measurement topology model and packet transmission behavior to build on performance analysis model. Secondly, active or passive measurement method is used to obtain the end-to-end measurement sample, then to evaluate the temporal and spacial independence of measurement sample. At last, the mathematics and statistics theory are used to analyze and evaluate the measurement sample based on performance analysis model to infer link performance or to identify topology architecture, etc.

1.1 NT measurement topolgy model

Measurement topology model is the basis on NT measurement technique. If the number of source node which has the chance to send measurement probes, is only one in measurement process, that of leaf nodes collecting measurement sample is more than one, where exists one-to-many relationship between source node and leaf nodes, this measurement style is often called as single-source measurement model, and often uses tree topology measurement model to descript as the figure 1(a). Otherwise, if the source nodes and leaf nodes exit many-to-many relationship, this measurement style is generally called as multi-source measurement and often uses the non-loop graph topology measurement model to descipt as the figure 1(b).

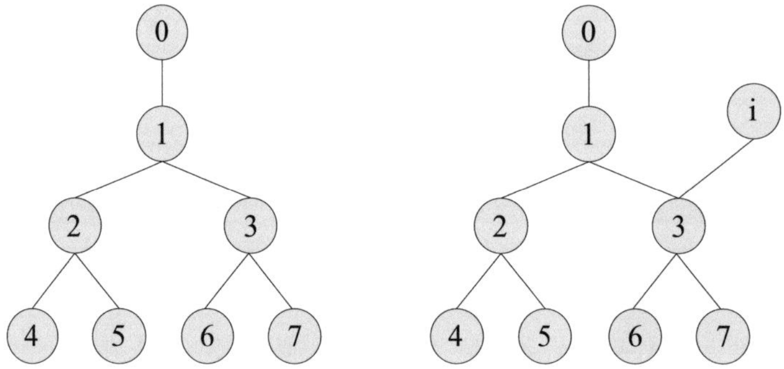

(a) single-source measurement system model (b) multi-source measurement system model

Fig. 1. NT measurement topology model

In the tree topology measurement model, Let T=(V, L) denotes a reverse tree with the node set V and link set L. V could be finely classified as $V=\{S,M,R\}$, where S denotes the set of source nodes, M the set of interior forwarding nodes and R the set of leaf nodes(or receiver nodes). As in figure 1(a), $S=\{0\}$, Because there is only one source node to send the probes. However, leaf nodes 4,5,6,7 has the chance to collect the measurement sample. The link set contains ordered pairs (i, j) such that node i sends its data to node j directly, destined for the leaf node r($r \in R$). The link (i, j) is simply denoted by $l_{i,j}$ ($l_{i,j} \in L$). Howerver, the path from the node i to j is denoted by $P_{i,j}$, Let f(i) denote the father set of the node i. The ancestor set of node i could be denoted as: $F(i)=\{f^1(i),f^2(i),...,f^n(i) \mid f^n(i) \in S\}$, noted that there exists the following rules: $f^0(i)=i$, $f^1(i)=f(i)$ and $f^n(i)=f(f^{n-1}(i))(n \geq 1)$. In the multi-source measurement model as in figure 1(b), there are more than one source nodes which has the chance to send probes, such as $S=\{0,i\}$. If the number of source nodes and leaf nodes are M and N respectively, the network architecture in multi-source measurement is called as M-by-N topology architecture[16].

1.2 NT measurement analysis model

NT measurement analysis model mainly consists of performance analysis model and network topology architecture identification model, the former focuses on link loss rate and delay inference, and the latter on topology architecture identification.

1.2.1 Link loss rate analysis model

It is to use the mathematical method to describe the relationship between the link and path performance. For example, Bernoulli model[17,18] and Gilbert model[19,20] are often used in link loss rate inference. The former supposes that the loss of packets in one mobile node is independent of each other, which actually is a Bernoulli stochastic process. Stochastic process $X = (x_r)$ ($r \in R$) is used to describe state of the leaf node r receiving probes, $x_r = 1$ denotes node r receiving a probe, otherwise $x_r = 0$. For the N probes, the receiving state of leaf node r could be denoted as $X_r = \{x_r^{(n)}\}$ ($1 \le n \le N$). If the link loss rate parameter is presented as $\alpha = (\alpha_{l_r})(l_r \in L)$, where α_r is the loss rate of link l_r, the aim of Bernoulli model is to obtain the maximum pre estimate: $\alpha^* = \arg Max_\alpha P(X_{r \subset R} \mid \alpha, T)$. However, the latter considers that there exits time dependence correlation between the consecutive probes. For instance, if the probe with sequence one is lost in one mobile node, the probability of probe with sequence two in the same mobile node being lost is higher. Gilbert model uses two states Markov process to describe this temporal dependence, 1 denotes probe loss and 0 not loss. In Gilbert model as in figure 2, p denotes that the probability of current probe is not lost where the one after which is lost, while q denotes that the probability of current probe is lost where the one after which is not lost. If $p + q = 1$ is satisfied, Gilbert model could be changed into Bernoulli model.

1.2.2 Link delay analysis model

In link delay anlysis model, we often suppose that the system clocks in each nodes are synchronous, and discrete delay mode and continuous delay one are often used. In general, the discrete delay model adopts the discrete time method to study the probability distribution of link delay based on NT. However, the continuous delay time model often uses the cumulate generating function (abbreviated as CGF) to infer link delay parameters. Owing to using the logarithmic operation in CGF for its un-linear correlation, there exists some variances in the inference result, and even sometimes the variance is high. In order to reduce and correct the variance, Yolanda et al. [21] adopts a linear optimization method to correct the variance estimation of inference results. Network delay includes the fixed delay time and variational one, the sending delay(T_t)and transmission one (T_g) composes the former, and the process delay(Tp) and queuing delay (Tq)the latter. Link delay analysis model could be presented as the formula 1, where m is the number of link, $T_{t,0}, T_{g,0}$ denotes the sending delay of source node and transmission delay of the first link respectively.

$$Delay = T_{t,0} + T_{g,0} + \sum_{n=1}^{m} (T_{t,n} + T_{g,n} + T_{p,n} + T_{q,n}) + T_{q,d} \tag{1}$$

1.2.3 Network topology inference analysis model

Network topology inference analysis model is founded on the basis of the following hypothesis, that the correlative degree between brother nodes is stronger than that between non- brother nodes. [22,23] bring forth a bias relationship of probe receiving to infer network topology architecture, which defined a hamming distance of probes receiving between node i and j as the formula 2. where n is the number of measurement.

$$d(i,j) = \sum_{m=1}^{n} (x_i^m \oplus x_j^m), i, j \in V \tag{2}$$

If $d(i,j) < \varepsilon$ is satisfied, node i and j are deemed to brother node, and ε is a liminal value. Therefore, network topology architecture could be inferred through computing the $d(i,j)$ between nodes, which is a bin-tree architecture. However, a tree topology architecture could be inferred by expanding the method above.

1.3 NT measurement probes

unicast probe Unicast probe is transmitted by the source node to the leaf nodes according to a certain sample rule as in figure 2(a). Link loss rate and delay could be inferred on the basis of the number of unicast probes and that the leaf node receiving, end-to-end delay, and so on. Owing to unicast communication is supported by many networks, the merit of unicast probe is its broad application scope. Although the interval between unicast probes accords with a certain sample rule, which could reduce the influence brought by active measurement in a certain extent, it will destroy the correlation of the two conterminous unicast probes and reduce the precision of measurement. As in figure 2(a), the source node 0 sends unicast probe, since the leaf node 3 and 4 receive unicast probe dependently, if the node 3 receive a unicast probe, but node 4 not, it is difficult to judge where the unicast probe is lost.

multi-cast probe In order to settle the limitation of unicast probe, the multicast probe is put forward in network measurement. As in figure 2(b), the source node 0 transmits the multicast probe to a group of leaf nodes, such as node 4,5,6 and 7. Since the multicast probes have the same communication characteristic in the shared path, it will resolve the problem the correlation of probes and improve the precision of measurement. If node 3 receives the multicast probe, but node 4 not, it is easy to infer that the probe is lost in the link l_4. Of course, there are much limitation on municast probes, one is that some network devices,

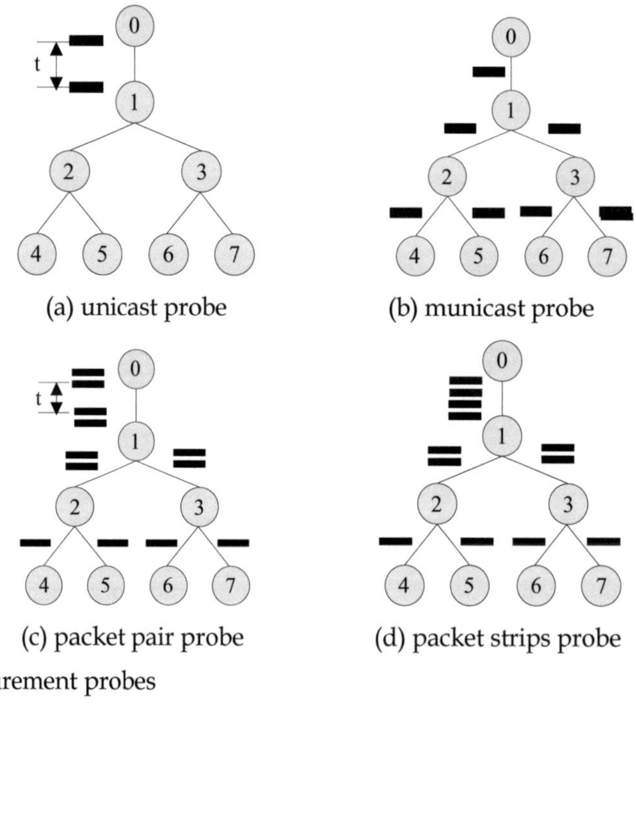

Fig. 2. NT measurement probes

such as switcher and router, do not support or configure multicast communication protocols, which will influent its application scope, another is some network devices adopt difference process method on unicast and multicast, which will also affect the measurement precison in some extent.

packet pair probe Nowak Robert et al. brings forth to using packet pair to measurement network performance as in figure 2(c). Packet pair comprised of two unicast probes with small interval, which is smaller than that between different packet pairs. In figure 2(c), source node 0 sends one packet pair to node 3 and 4, if the first unicast probe arrives at node 3 successfully, the we could safely guess that the probability of node 4 receiving the second unicast probe is near to 100%. Therefore, packet pair not only has the properties of multicast probe, but also extends the application scope of unicast probe. However, packet pair only takes into account the correlation between unicast probe, it is just used for bin-tree measurement analysis model.

packet stripes probe In order to resolve the limitation of packet pair, N.G. Duffield introduce the packet strips into network measurement, which extends the number of unicast probes from two to many as in figure 2(d). From the other point of view, the packet strip could be considered as many packet pairs, which supports the different packet pairs with correlation in the shared path. However, when the number of unicast probes is more enough, packet strip could be changed as unicast probes.

1.4 NT measurement inference method

NT measurement inference method is to use end-to-end network performance measurement sample to infer the probability distribution of link performance based on measurement analysis model and performance analysis model, which mainly composed of Maximum Likelihood Estimate(MLE), Expectation Maximization method(EM) and Bayesian estimate.

Maximum Likelihood Estimate Method MLE[24] is one of the elementary method on parameter estimate, which supposes that link performance parameter accords with distribution $f(X;\Theta)$, where $\Theta=(\theta_1,\theta_2,\cdots,\theta_n)$ is the estimated parameter. If end-to-end measurement sample is denoted as $\{y_1,y_2,\cdots,y_n\}$, supposing that they follows the same distribution rule independently, the distribution function of path performance parameter Y could be expressed as $Y=p(Y;\Theta)$, then the pseudo function follows the formula 3

$$L(Y;\Theta)=\prod_{i=1}^{n}p(y_i;\Theta) \tag{3}$$

The objective of MLE is to find the value of the parameter Θ when $L(Y;\Theta)$ obtains its maximum value, which could be denoted as $\hat{\Theta}=\arg MaxL(Y;\Theta)$. Nevertheless, it is difficult to find the transcendent distribution function $f(X;\Theta)$ of network link performance parameter X. Even though it was founded, there are high computing complexity degree of pseudo parameter estimate for the complexity of pseudo function with large network scale.

Expectation Maximization method EM algorithm[25,26] is to use partial measurement sample to infer maximum pseudo value of link performance distribution function, including two procedures, that is, E-step and M-step. The main problem about EM algorithm is that it could obtain the partially optimized solution, not the unitary optimized one. For the sake of computing complexity increasing by the scale of network, Pseudo-EM Algorithm[4] decomposes a large scale problem to several small scale ones. The maximum likelihood of these small scale problems could be expressed as formula 4, where S is set of all small scale problems.

$$L\,(Y_1,Y_2,...,Y_n;X)=\prod_{i=1}^{n}\prod_{s\in S}P^s(Y_i^s;X^s) \quad (4)$$

Bayesian estimate method It uses the transcendent probability distribution of link performance to infer the posterior one. However, how to get the former probability distribution is a difficult work. It is also difficult for Bayesian estimate method to obtain the link performance parameter with large network scale for its computing complexity. In order to solve this problem, Markov Chain Monte Carlo method is brought forth to infer link performance parameters by using Gibbs and Metropolis-Hasting sample rule based on Bernoulli and Gilbert probability model[27].

In short, MLE and Bayesian estimate methods needs to know the transcendent distribution, but it is very difficult to obtain in practice. EM resolves the problem of computing the estimated parameter of network link performance in math, but it is easy to converge on a partially optimized solution.

2. NT measurement technique in WSNs

Recent technological advances have made the development of low cost sensor nodes possible, and this allows the deployment of the large-scale sensor network to be feasible. The accurate network performance plays an important role in the successful design, deployment and management of sensor networks. However, the inherent stringent bandwidth and energy constraints of sensors create challenging problems in the network performance measurement. Motivated by the needs of accurate sensor network performance measurement and the inherent constraint of sensor network, in this section, we concentrate on: (1) the problem of efficiently estimating the internal link loss Cumulant Generating Function (CGF); (2) the problem of efficiently estimating the internal link loss rate from the passive end-to-end measurement.

There has been much research in the field of network tomography for the wireless sensor network .In [28], Li et al. proposed a simple method based on the hamming distance of sequences on receipt/loss of aggregated data between each pair of parent-child node to identify the lossy nodes. Under the assumptions that the link losses are mutually independent, Li et al. [29] formulated the problem of link loss estimation as a Bayesian inference problem and propose a Markov Chain Monte Carlo algorithm to inferring the internal link loss characteristics from passive end-to-end measurement. In [30] this problem was formulated as a Maximum-Likelihood Estimation problem and used the Expectation-Maximization algorithm to solve it. Almost existed methods used the iterative approximating approach to estimate the loss rate that requires a long execution time. In addition, iterative approach may trap into a local maximum. To overcome this problem, a simple up-bottom approach [31] and a bottom-up [32] to estimate loss rate in wireless sensor network were proposed, which identifies parameters of loss probability model based on the observations collected in the sink node. Knowledge of sensor network topology is a crucial component of sensor network tomography techniques. Based on the partial ordering relation on the packet receipt/loss between a node and its descendant nodes in the data aggregation process, Li et al. [33][34] formulated the problem of sensor network topology identification as a topological sorting problem and proposed a topological sorting algorithm to solve it. In [35], an algorithm that named hamming distance and hop count based classification algorithm (HHC), to infer network topology by using end-to-end data in sensor network.

2.1 Loss cumulate generating function inference method

Each link loss CGF preserves all the statistical information of the loss since it is the log of the Fourier transform of the link loss probability density function. We can accurately infer many features of the link loss distribution from loss CGF[36].

2.1.1 Cumulate generating function

We suppose the link losses X_i are mutually independent, $i = 1,\cdots,n$. Define the end-to-end loss cumulate generating function (CGF) of the path i $K_{Y_i} = \log E\left[e^{tY_i}\right]$ and the link loss CGF $K_{X_i} = \log E\left[e^{tX_i}\right]$, with CGF parameter t, $t \in (-\infty,\infty)$. The CGF of $\boldsymbol{Y}$ can therefore be expressed as

$$\begin{aligned} K_{Y_i}(t) &= \log E\left[e^{tY_i}\right] = \log E\left[e^{t(\Sigma j\in M_i X_j)}\right] = \log\left\{\prod_{j\in M_i} E\left[e^{tX_j}\right]\right\} \\ &= \sum_{j\in M_i} \log E\left[e^{tX_j}\right] = \sum_{j=1}^{m} a_{ij}\cdot K_{X_j}(t) = A_{(i)}\cdot K_X(t) \end{aligned} \tag{5}$$

where $A_{(i)}$ denotes the ith row of the matrix A and $K_X(t) = \left[K_{X_1}(t),\cdots,K_{X_n}(t)\right]^T$ (^{T} denotes transpose). Thus the vector of end-to-end CGF's $K_Y(t) = \left[K_{Y_1}(t),\cdots,K_{Y_n}(t)\right]^T$ can be expressed by the following linear relation

$$K_Y(t) = A\cdot K_X(t) \tag{6}$$

There are n links and n paths in the sensor network, so the matrix A is full rank. The relation (2) is invertible and the link loss CGF $K_X(t)$ can be determined from the end-to-end loss CGF $K_Y(t)$ as the following equation

$$K_X(t) = \left(A^T A\right)^{1} A^T K_Y(t). \tag{7}$$

Let $B = \left(A^T A\right)^{-1} A^T$, then we have

$$K_{X_j}(t) = \sum_{i=1}^{n} b_{ji}\cdot K_{Y_i}(t). \tag{8}$$

Define the end-to-end loss moment generating function (MGF) of path i $M_{Y_i} = E\left[e^{tY_i}\right]$, and the loss MCF of link i $M_{X_i} = E\left[e^{tX_i}\right]$. Similarly, we can get the relationship between M_{X_i} and M_{Y_i} $M_{X_j}(t) = \sum_{i=1}^{n} b_{ji}\cdot M_{Y_i}(t)$.

2.1.2 Loss CGF inference

Let N be the number of data collection trial, then the estimated value of M_{Y_i} can be obtained using the following equation

$$\hat{M}_{Y_i}(t) = \frac{1}{N}\sum_{k=1}^{N} e^{tY_i^k} \tag{9}$$

where Y_i^k is the end-to-end loss of path i in the kth data collection trial. We obtain estimates of the vector $K_X(t)$ from $\hat{M}_Y(t) = \left[\hat{M}_{Y_1}(t), \cdots, \hat{M}_{Y_n}(t)\right]^T$. Note that $\hat{M}_{Y_i}$ is an unbiased estimate of the MGF M_{Y_i}. According to equation (8), we have

$$\hat{K}'_{X_j} = \sum_{i=1}^{n} b_{ji} \cdot \log\left(\hat{M}_{Y_i}(t)\right). \tag{10}$$

As mention in [37], $\hat{K}'_{X_j}$ is biased estimate of K_{X_i} due to non-linearity of the log. We apply the technique adopted in [37] to obtain a bias corrected estimator for K_{X_i}.

$$\begin{aligned}
\hat{K}'_{X_j} &= \sum_{i=1}^{n} b_{ji} \cdot \log\left(\hat{M}_{Y_i}(t)\right) \\
&= \log\left\{\Pi_{i=1}^{n}\left(\hat{M}_{Y_i}(t)\right)^{b_{ji}}\right\} \\
&= \log\left\{\Pi_{i=1}^{n} E^{b_{ji}}\left[\hat{M}_{Y_i}(t)\right] - \left(\Pi_{i=1}^{n} E^{b_{ji}}\left[\hat{M}_{Y_i}(t)\right] - \Pi_{i=1}^{n}\left(\hat{M}_{Y_i}(t)\right)^{b_{ji}}\right)\right\} \\
&= \log\left\{\Pi_{i=1}^{n} E^{b_{ji}}\left[\hat{M}_{Y_i}(t)\right]\left(1 - \left(1 - \frac{\Pi_{i=1}^{n}\left(\hat{M}_{Y_i}(t)\right)^{b_{ji}}}{\Pi_{i=1}^{n} E^{b_{ji}}\left[\hat{M}_{Y_i}(t)\right]}\right)\right)\right\} \\
&= \log \Pi_{i=1}^{n} E^{b_{ji}}\left[\hat{M}_{Y_i}(t)\right] + \log\left(1 - \left(1 - \frac{\Pi_{i=1}^{n}\left(\hat{M}_{Y_i}(t)\right)^{b_{ji}}}{\Pi_{i=1}^{n} E^{b_{ji}}\left[\hat{M}_{Y_i}(t)\right]}\right)\right) \\
&= \log \Pi_{i=1}^{n} E^{b_{ji}}\left[\hat{M}_{Y_i}(t)\right] + \log\left(1 - \omega_j\right) \\
&= K_{X_j}(t) - \omega_j - \frac{1}{2}\omega_j + H.O.T. \\
&\approx K_{X_j}(t) - \omega_j - \frac{1}{2}\omega_j
\end{aligned} \tag{11}$$

where $\omega_j = 1 - \dfrac{\Pi_{i=1}^{n}\left(\hat{M}_{Y_i}(t)\right)^{b_{ji}}}{\Pi_{i=1}^{n} E^{b_{ji}}\left[\hat{M}_{Y_i}(t)\right]}$. This suggests that we can correct the bias using the following equation:

$$\hat{K}_{X_j} = \sum_{i=1}^{n} b_{ji} \cdot \log\left(\hat{M}_{Y_i}(t)\right) + \hat{E}\left[\omega_j\right] + \frac{1}{2}\hat{E}\left[\omega_j^{\,2}\right] \tag{12}$$

where $\hat{E}(\cdot)$ denotes empirical average,

$$\hat{E}\left[\omega_j\right] = 1 - \frac{\Pi_{i=1}^{n} \hat{E}\left[\left(\hat{M}_{Y_i}(t)\right)^{b_{ji}}\right]}{\hat{M}_{X_j}(t)} \tag{13}$$

$$\hat{E}\left[\omega_j^2\right] = 1 - \frac{2 \cdot \Pi_{i=1}^{n} \hat{E}\left[\left(\hat{M}_{Y_i}(t)\right)^{b_{ji}}\right]}{\hat{M}_{X_j}(t)} + \frac{\Pi_{i=1}^{n} \hat{E}\left[\left(\hat{M}_{Y_i}(t)\right)^{2b_{ji}}\right]}{\hat{M}_{X_j}^2(t)} \tag{14}$$

$\hat{M}_{X_j}(t)$ is an estimate of the loss moment generating function of link j, which can be obtained from

$$\hat{M}_{X_j}(t) = \prod_{i=1}^{n}\left(\hat{M}_{Y_i}(t)^{b_{ji}}\right). \tag{15}$$

The empirical average $\hat{E}\left[\left(\hat{M}_{Y_i}(t)\right)^{b_{ji}}\right]$ can be obtained by implementing a sliding window method with window size W and step size S [9]. Define the number $N_w = \left\lfloor \frac{N - W}{S} \right\rfloor$ of windows increments

$$\hat{E}\left[\left(\hat{M}_{Y_i}(t)\right)^{b_{ji}}\right] = \frac{1}{N_w}\sum_{l=1}^{N_w}\left(\frac{1}{W}\sum_{k=(l-1)S+1}^{(l-1)S+W} e^{tY_i^k}\right)^{b_{ji}}. \tag{16}$$

We obtain the empirical average $\hat{E}\left[\left(\hat{M}_{Y_i}(t)\right)^{2b_{ji}}\right]$ in a similar manner,

$$\hat{E}\left[\left(\hat{M}_{Y_i}(t)\right)^{2b_{ji}}\right] = \frac{1}{N_w}\sum_{l=1}^{N_w}\left(\frac{1}{W}\sum_{k=(l-1)S+1}^{(l-1)S+W} e^{tY_i^k}\right)^{2b_{ji}}. \tag{17}$$

2.1.3 Simulation study and application

The ns2 simulator was extended to perform the simulation of the sensor network.and simulate the data flow through sensor network. For each data collection round, whether a node successfully received data sent to it by its child nodes was determined randomly but with a specified intended loss rate for each link. That is, as the number of data collection rounds increases the actual loss rate of each link should converge to the intended loss rate. Two networks were used in the simulations. One consisted of 120 nodes while the other contained 9 nodes. Figure 3 shows the topology of the 9-node network. An intended success rate of 0.9 was chosen for all normally links in the simulation network. Each simulation consisted of 1200 data collection trials. Once all of the data was collected, each link loss CGF was inferred using the approach presented in Section 4. To estimate the loss CGF, we set the window size W to be 400, and the window shift step size S to be 10.

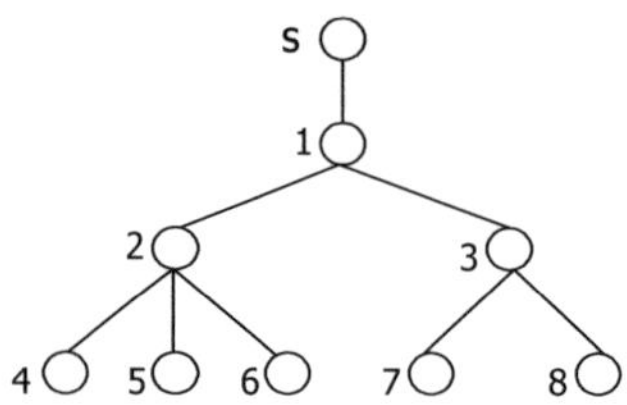

Fig. 3. A 9-node data aggregation tree

Two possible scenarios were simulated that may occur in a real sensor network. These scenarios were: (1) Equal losses throughout the network; (2) Cascaded losses. i.e., Heavy losses at links on the same path to the sink. The cascaded losses scenario was simulated by setting the intended success rates of links 2 and 5 to be 0.7.
Because each internal link loss CGF preserves all the statistical information of the link loss, we can accurately estimate many features of the link loss distribution from the link loss CGF. Here we give an example of lossy link detection. We define a lossy link in sensor network as the link whose loss rate exceeds a predefined threshold δ. In practical application, we can infer a link as the lossy link when the probability of a link loss rate exceeding δ exceeds a predefined threshold P. By the Chernoff Bound [38],

$$P\left(X_i \geq \delta\right) \leq e^{-t\delta} E\left[e^{tX_j}\right] = P_j$$

By appropriately selecting the threshold δ and threshold P close to 1, we can detect a lossy link by testing whether $P_j > P$. In Table 3, we show the Chernoff Bounds for $P(\boldsymbol{X}_j \geq 0.3)$ which were estimated from the simulation in Cascaded losses scenario. By setting the threshold P to 0.95, we can identify link 2 and 5 as the lossy link. This accord with the simulation configures.

Link	1	2	3	4	5	6	7	8
P(Xj ≥ 0.3)	0.66952	0.99671	0.67041	0.66942	0.99918	0.67060	0.66826	0.66684

Table 1. Chernoff Bound for each link in Cascaded losses scenario

2.2 Loss temporal dependency characteristic inference method

Here we concentrate on the problem of efficiently estimating the internal link loss rate from the passive end-to-end measurement. We use the Bayesian inference problem to formulate the sensor network loss inference problem and use the Metropolis-Hastings Sampling to find out link-level characteristics.

2.2.1 Loss inference based on gilbert model

In our proposed approach, firstly the unobservable data is inferred based on the link relationship and the observable data collected at the sink node. Once the unobservable data has been identified, for every link this proposed approach uses Metropolis-Hastings algorithm to generate a sequence of samples of Gilbert model parameter. We iterate the unobservable data inference process and the sampling process until it reaches the given number of the samples. The following two subsections are used to detail the proposed algorithm for unobservable data and sampling algorithm, respectively. Without loss of generality, we also take the figure 1 for instance in this subsection.

2.2.2 Unobservable data inference

We employ the up-down approach to infer the unobservable data. Firstly, we infer the unobservable data of the node 1, the reception or loss of the packets sent from the children node of the node 1 to node 1, and then we move one level down to estimate the unobservable data of the lower level nodes that are children node of node 1. The process is continued until it reaches the leaf nodes.

Assume that one of children nodes of node i is node j. Using the similar method as presented above, we have the conditional posterior distribution of $y^m_{j,i}$,

$$p(y^m_{j,i}=0\mid \boldsymbol{X},\boldsymbol{Y}^{[-m]}_{j,i},\boldsymbol{\Theta})=\begin{cases} 0 & \text{if } x^m_j=1 \\ p(y^m_{j,i}=0\mid y^{m-1}_{j,i})\cdot p(y^{m+1}_{j,i}\mid y^m_{j,i}=0) & \\ =[y^{m-1}_{j,i}\cdot p_j+(1-y^{m-1}_{j,i})(1-q_j)]\cdot[y^{m+1}_{j,i}\cdot q_j+(1-y^{m+1}_{j,i})(1-p_j)] & \text{if } x^m_j=0 \end{cases} \tag{18}$$

$$p(y^m_{j,i}=1\mid \boldsymbol{X},\boldsymbol{Y}^{[-m]}_{j,i},\boldsymbol{Y}\setminus\boldsymbol{Y}_{j,i},\boldsymbol{\Theta})=\begin{cases} 1 & \text{if } x^m_j=1 \\ p(x^m_j=0\mid\{y^m_{k,f(k)},k\in a(i)\},y^m_{j,i}=1)\cdot p(y^m_{j,i}=1\mid y^{m-1}_{j,i})\cdot p(y^{m+1}_{j,i}\mid y^m_{j,i}=1) & \\ =[(1-\prod_{k\in a(i)}\frac{q_k}{p_k+q_k}]\cdot[y^{m-1}_{j,i}\cdot(1-p_j)+(1-y^{m-1}_{j,i})q_j]\cdot[y^{m+1}_{j,i}(1-p_j)+(1-y^{m+1}_{j,i})\cdot p_j] & \text{if } x^m_j=0 \end{cases} \tag{19}$$

According to the conditional posterior distribution of $y^m_{j,i}$ as described above, we can draw a sequence of samples of $y^m_{j,i}$.

2.2.3 Loss performance parameter inference

We infer the Gilbert model parameters Θ according to the samples of $y^m_{j,i}$ and the observable data X. As the problem formulation describes, the estimated value $\hat{\Theta}$ should agree with the posterior distribution $p(\Theta \mid X,Y)$. However, the posterior distribution $p(\Theta \mid X,Y)$ is not a closed-form expression. That is, the value of $\hat{\Theta}$ can't be calculated from the data X and Y directly. In this paper, we consider the Metropolis-Hastings algorithm for sampling the parameters $\{(p_k,q_k),k\in V\}$. Here we do not pay much attention on choosing the proposal distribution and the initial value of parameters, but concern that how to sample the parameters using Metropolis-Hastings algorithm. In [39], it is discussed in detail that choosing the proposal distribution and the initial value of parameters

We can choose a random walk proposal distribution for the proposed sampler, e.g.

$$g(p_k^{(j-1)},p_k^{(j)})\sim U(p_k^{(j-1)}-\sigma,p_k^{(j-1)}+\sigma) \tag{20}$$

That is, we draw a sample $p_k^{(j)}$ based on the above proposal distribution and accept it with probability

$$\alpha(p_k^{(j)},p_k^{(j-1)})=\min\left\{1,\frac{p(p_k^{(j)}\mid \boldsymbol{X},\boldsymbol{Y}^{(j)},\Theta\setminus p_k^{(j)})}{g(p_k^{(j)},p_k^{(j-1)})}\cdot\frac{g(p_k^{(j-1)},p_k^{(j)})}{p(p_k^{(j-1)}\mid \boldsymbol{X},\boldsymbol{Y}^{(j-1)},\Theta\setminus p_k^{(j-1)})}\right\} \quad (21)$$

where by assuming uniform prior on p_k, we have

$$p(p_k\mid \boldsymbol{X},\boldsymbol{Y}^{(j)},\boldsymbol{\Theta}\setminus p_k)\propto p(\boldsymbol{X},\boldsymbol{Y}^{(j)}\mid\boldsymbol{\Theta})\propto p(y_{k,f(k)}^{0})\cdot p_k^{n_{1,0}}\cdot(1-p_k)^{n_{1,1}} \quad (22)$$

where n_{uv} is the number of occurrences of the adjacent pair (u, v) in the sequence $\boldsymbol{Z}_{k,f(k)}$, $u, v \in\{0,1\}$. As the loss model describes, each node tries to send data in each round. Thus the marginal distribution on $y_{k,f(k)}^{0}$ can be given by $p(y_{k,f(k)}^{0}=0)=\frac{p_k}{p_k+q_k}$ and $p(y_{k,f(k)}^{0}=1)=\frac{q_k}{p_k+q_k}$.

Using the formula (21)(22)(23), we can draw the random samples of p_k based on the samples of the unobservable data $\boldsymbol{Y}$ and observable data $\boldsymbol{X}$. Similarly, we can also draw the random samples of q_k where

$$p(q_k\mid \boldsymbol{X},\boldsymbol{Y}^{(j)},\boldsymbol{\Theta}\setminus q_k)\propto p(\boldsymbol{X},\boldsymbol{Y}^{(j)}\mid\boldsymbol{\Theta})\propto p(y_{k,f(k)}^{0})\cdot q_k^{n_{0,1}}\cdot(1-q_k)^{n_{0,0}} \quad (23)$$

The proposed sampler iterates between sampling $y_{j,i}^{m}$ from the observable data $\boldsymbol{X}$ and sampling the Gilbert model parameters (p_k,q_k) based on the above sampler. After the sample procedure is finished, we can calculate the estimated value of $\hat{\Theta}=\{(p_k,q_k),k\in \boldsymbol{V}\}$. For a general sensor network, we can similarly infer link loss rate as in this simple example described above, and expand the sampling strategy as an up-bottom approach where we start from the child node of the sink node, followed by their child nodes, and so on, until we reach the leaf nodes.

2.2.4 Algorithm description

Suppose the total number of samples is $J=J_0+J_1$, where J_0 is the number of samples as 'burn-in' period and J_1 is the number of samples used to infer link loss parameters. Denote $\boldsymbol{\Theta}^{(i)}$ and $\boldsymbol{Y}^{(i)}$ as the ith round sample value.

Initialization : Draw random samples $\boldsymbol{\Theta}^{(0)}$ and $\boldsymbol{Y}^{(0)}$ from their perior.

Sample: for $j=1,2,\cdots J$ do

- Given $\boldsymbol{\Theta}^{(j-1)}$, for each $k\in V\setminus\{\{s\}\cup d(s)\}$, and $m=1,2,\cdots,N$, draw a sample $(y_{k,f(k)}^{m})^{(j)}\sim p(y_{k,f(k)}^{m}\mid x_{k,f(k)}^{m},\{(y_{k,f(k)}^{i})^{(j-1)},i=m-1,m+1\},\{(p_n^{(j-1)},q_n^{(j-1)}),n\in\{k\}\cup a(k)\})$.
- Given $\boldsymbol{Y}^{(j)}$, for each $k\in V\setminus\{s\}$, draw a random sample of $p_k^{(j)}$ based on $p_k^{(j-1)}$

$$g(p_k^{(j-1)}, p_k^{(j)}) \sim U(p_k^{(j-1)} - \sigma, p_k^{(j-1)} + \sigma)$$

and accept it with probability $\alpha(p_k^{(j)}, p_k^{(j-1)})$.

Inference : Calculate $\hat{\Theta}$ from $\left\{\Theta^{(J_1)}, \Theta^{(J_1+1)}, \cdots, \Theta^{(J)}\right\}$

Output : $\hat{\Theta}$

Denote the size of sensor network as $|V|$. From the algorithm described as above, we can get the time complexity of this proposed algorithm is $O(J \times N \times |V|)$.

2.2.5 Simulation study

NS2 was used to perform the simulation of the sensor network. The ns2 was extended to simulate the data flow through sensor network. For each data collection round, whether a node successfully received data sent to it by its child nodes was determined randomly but with a specified intended loss performance for each link. The inference algorithm is implemented in MATLAB.

Two networks were used in the simulations. One consisted of 120 nodes while the other contained 9 nodes. Figure 3 shows the topology of the 9-node network. We used the Gilbert error model to model the link loss performance with parameters (p, q) as (0.1, 0.85) for all normally links in the simulation network. Each simulation consisted of 1000 data collection trials.

In the 9-node simulation network, we simulated two possible scenarios that may occur in a real sensor network. These scenarios were: 1) Equal losses throughout the network; 2) Heavy losses at some links. The second scenario was simulated by setting the loss parameters of links 2, 5 and 7 to be (0.15, 0.80).

Four plots of the inferred and sampled internal link loss performance parameters for all links are shown in Fig.4-Fig.7, respectively. The inferred link loss performance value is very close to the sampled link loss performance value. In the second scenario the error was significant since some of the losses that should have been attributed to link 2 were instead attributed evenly amongst link 2's child links. However, it is still possible to infer that these lossy links is in fact experiencing the heavy losses.

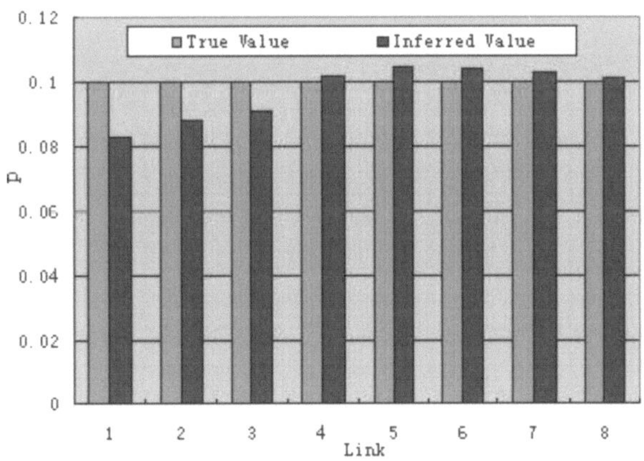

Fig. 4. True Value vs. Inferred Value in the equal loss scenarios for p

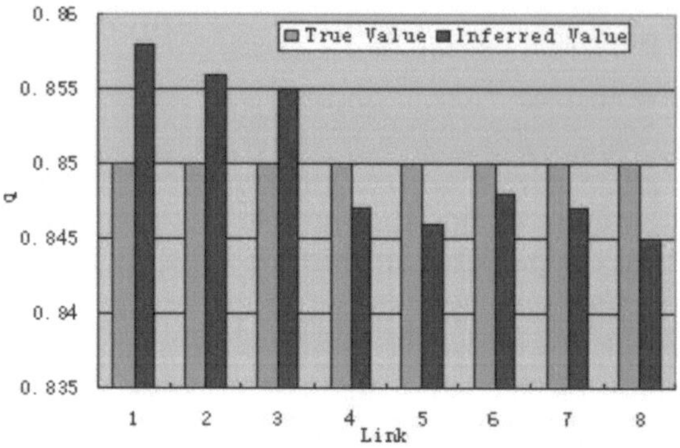

Fig. 5. True Value vs. Inferred Value in the equal loss scenarios for q

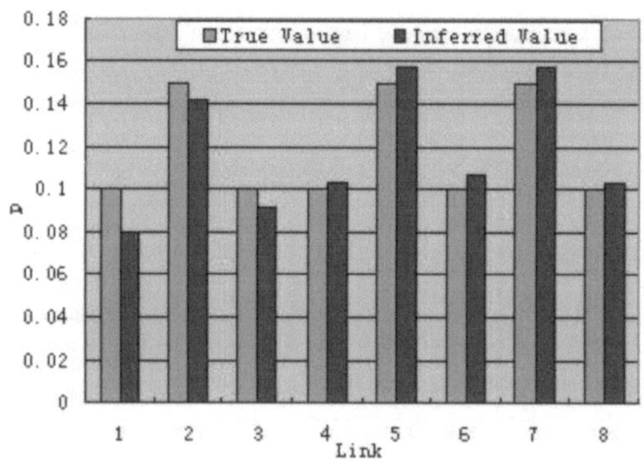

Fig. 6. True Value vs. Inferred Value in the heavy loss scenarios for p

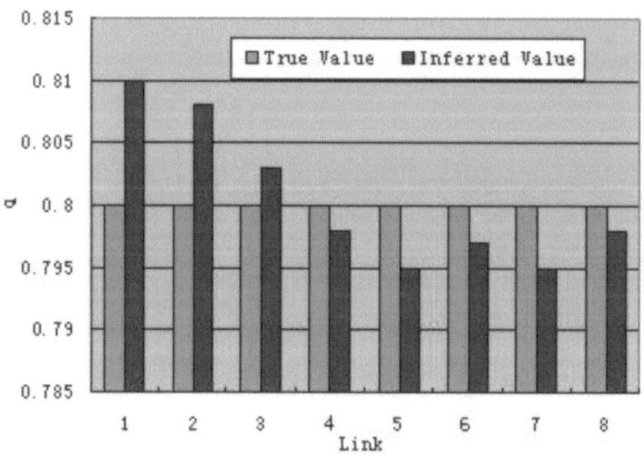

Fig. 7. True Value vs. Inferred Value in the heavy loss scenarios for q

Take the link 2 for instance. Figure 8 shows the relationship between the convergence speeds of the estimated loss performance value and the number of samples. Before the burn-in period was over, the error between the estimated value and the true value is significant. With the sample number increases, the estimated value is approaching to the true value.

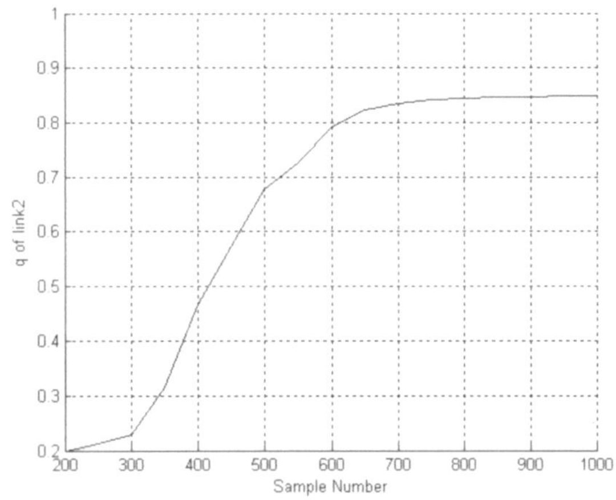

Fig. 8. Inferred Value vs. Sample Number in equal loss scenarios for q of link 2

Table1 provides the simulation result in 120-node network. It shows that the inferred link loss performance value is close to its true value. In the two simulation scenarios, the maximum error of link loss estimation is only 0.027 and 0.0312, respectively. These results show that our loss rate inference algorithm scales well.

Equal losses	Mean Error	*p*	0.043
		q	0.021
	Max Error	*p*	0.070
		q	0.052
Heavy losses on some links	Mean Error	*p*	0.058
		q	0.027
	Max Error	*p*	0.089
		q	0.061

Table 2. Absolute errors: 120-node network

3. NT measurement technique in ad hoc network

NT measurement technique adopts Edge nodes not only as the source sender to send the measurement packets, but also as the receivers to receive the measurement data sample used for inferring link performance parameters in Ad Hoc network. Since it is independent of network infrastructure and protocols, NT measurement outweighs internal network measurement in Ad Hoc network. Of course, there will appear new problems for introducing the NT technique to Ad Hoc network measurement.

The dynamic characteristic of Ad Hoc network topology is the main obstacle to use NT technique in Ad Hoc network measurement, because it effects the correctness not only of the measurement results, but also of the link performance parameters inference results. Therefore, the following problems must be resolved at first: (1) to put forward a feasible analysis method on dynamic characteristic of Ad Hoc network so as to meet the requirement of NT technique. (2) to found the Ad Hoc network measurement topology architecture and link performance inference model. (3) to chose the proper measurement method so as to obtain measurement sample of performance parameters based on End-to-End. (4) to bring forth a link performance inference method so as to infer the link performance parameters by using measurement data sample, link performance inference model , mathematical and statistical theory.

3.1 Ad hoc network topology dynamic characteristics

Although researches have focused on the dynamic characteristics of mobility models in Ad Hoc network and taken much achievements recently[40], little attention was paid on the link topology dynamic characteristics of mobile models. Narayannan Sadagopan et al. [41]puts forward a statistical method to obtain the dynamic characteristic of MM, which includes how to obtain the probability density distribution of link and path connection time. Nevertheless, the research mainly focus on the viewpoint of the influence of dynamic characteristic on the performance of active network protocols, not on that of the Ad Hoc network measurement. At the same time, statistical analysis method is only applicable for the certain mobility models with one time to change its' velocity or direction in one second, such as RPGM, Freeway and Manhattan mobility model, not for the other mobility models in NS-2 tool, such as RW and RWP. Although Tian et al. [42]brings forward a link connection time model which could be used to compute the link connection minimum time, and further to obtain the minimum value of network topology lifetime. However, the computing model is too complicated for not being simplified. Besides, it is only adaptable for the RWP mobility model, not for the other mobility models in Ad Hoc networks. Wang et al. [43] brings forth a circle mobility model, in which when the initialization position of mobile nodes is known, the network topology architecture of Ad Hoc network could be computed according to the rules of nodes' movement. Specially, the minimum of network topology lifetime could also be obtained statistically. However, this research on NT measurement technique in Ad Hoc network mainly focus on circle mobility model, it fails to be useful for other mobility models. Therefore, How to put forward a analysis technique on the dynamic characteristic of Ad Hoc network topology , which could be used for all the mobility model as are supported in NS-2 tool, is an interesting issue to be solved.

In order to resolve the above problem, Yao et al.[44] presents a network topology snapshots capture method to obtain the Ad Hoc network topology architecture at any moment on the basis of analysis on the scene files of mobility models in Ad Hoc network. Through analyzing on the Ad Hoc network topology snapshots, the times of network topology in steady state or unsteady state during a certain time t could be obtained statistically, as well as the durative time of network topology in steady state or unsteady state during the whole simulation time. Furthermore, Yao et al.[45] adopts the discrete time and continuous time Markov stochastic process theory to predict the probability of the network topology invariability event happening and that of the network topology variability event happening, and the experiential formula of the probability of the network topology invariability and variability was deduced. The simulation result shows that the statistical analysis technique on Ad Hoc network topology dynamic characteristic not only is effective, but also has the general attribute, which could be used in the statistical analysis technique on Ad Hoc network topology dynamic characteristic under any mobility model.

3.1.1 Formalized description on mobility model

All the mobility models supported by NS-2 [46]have the same format of scene files produced by setdest tool. Through analysis on the scene files we could arrive at the conclusion that there is a certain spatial relativity among mobile nodes. That is, the destination position of node *j* at time *i* is its current position at time *i* + 1 on condition that V_i^j equals zero, where V_i^j denotes the velocity of node *j* from time *i* to *i* + 1. Furthermore, during the period from time *i* to *i* + 1, node *j* moves along a line at the velocity of V_i^j from $C_i^j = (c_{x,i}^j, c_{y,i}^j)$ to $D_i^j = (d_{x,i}^j, d_{y,i}^j)$, where C_i^j denotes current position of node *j* at time *i*, $c_{x,i}^j$ and $c_{y,i}^j$ the x position and y position respectively of node *j* at time *i*, D_i^j the destination position of node *j* at time *i*. Then the spatial relativity of mobile nodes could be expressed as formula (24).

$$\begin{cases} C_{i+1}^j = D_i^j, & \text{if } C_i^j \neq D_i^j \ \& \ v_i^j != 0 \\ C_{i+1}^j = C_i^j, & \text{if } v_i^j = 0 \end{cases} \tag{24}$$

If let γ denote the snapshot time slot, the relativity between velocity and spatial position could be expressed as formula (25).

$$\begin{cases} c_{x,i+1}^j = c_{x,i}^j + v_{x,i}^j \times \gamma \\ c_{y,i+1}^j = c_{y,i}^j + v_{y,i}^j \times \gamma \end{cases} \tag{25}$$

where $v_{i,x}^j$ and $v_{i,y}^j$ denote the x-axis and y-axis value of speed v_i^j at time *i*, which could be obtained by using position C_i^j, D_i^j and v_i^j. Thus it can be seen, the state information of node *j* at time *i* could be expressed as a three tuple $\langle C_i^j, D_i^j, V_i^j \rangle$. Furthermore, position snapshots of mobile nodes at any moment could be derived from formula (25). The method how to get physical topology snapshot is to compute the Euclid distance *R* between node *j* and $l(l \in V \setminus \{j\})$ at each time, where *V* denotes the node set of Ad Hoc network. If *R* is smaller than the transmission range of mobile node denoted as *r*, illuminating that there is a chance for the node *j* and *l* to build up a wireless connection at link layer, the state of link between node *j* and *l* could be set as 1, otherwise, as 0. If the same operation is implemented between any mobile nodes at each snapshot time, we could achieve the physical topology snapshot. At last, the steady and un-steady period of Ad Hoc network topology can be obtained by computing all the physically topology snapshots statistically.

3.1.2 Simulation study

Through analyzing on the Ad Hoc network topology snapshots with RW and RWP mobility model, the relation of the link topology in steady or un-steady state and link topology varying ratio varying with time are shown as in Fig. 9(a~d). Next, we will explain the three concepts used in Fig. 9. Link connection ratio is the ratio of the links having a wireless connection with each other to all links in Ad Hoc networks in each one topology snapshot. Topology varying ratio is the ratio of the number of links that the state of which has varied

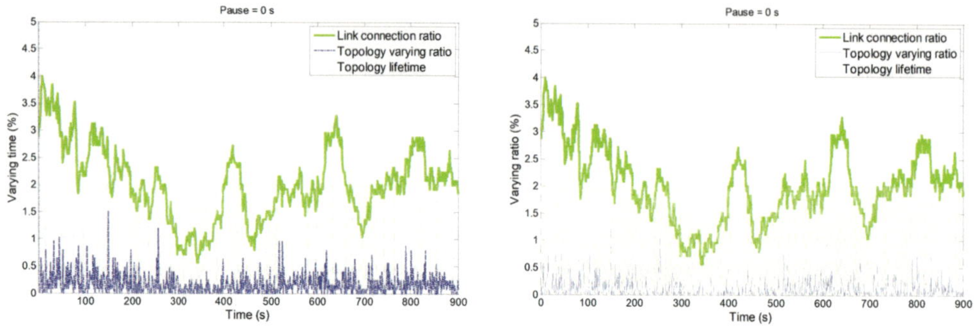

(a) snapshot time = 1.0s in RW (b) snapshot time = 0.5s in RW

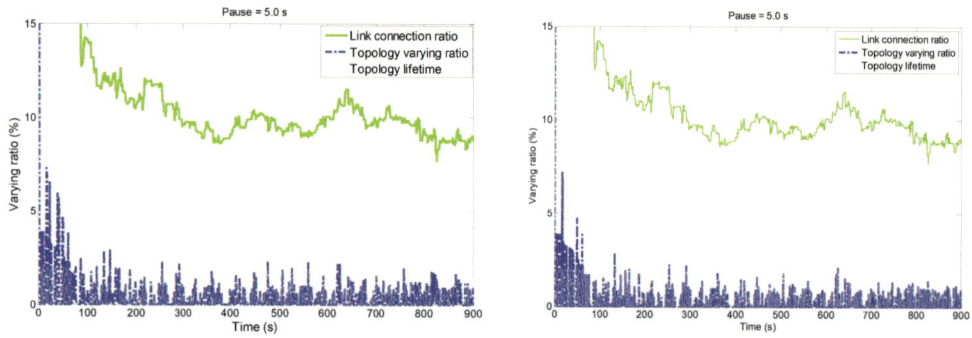

(c) snapshot time =1.0s in RWP (d) snapshot time = 0.5s in RWP

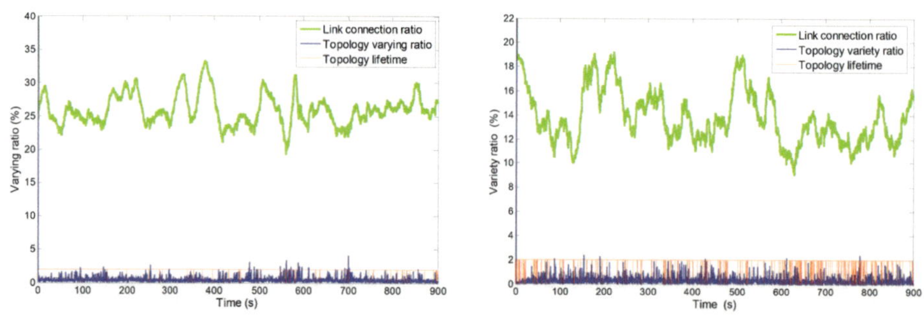

(e) snapshot time = 0.25 in Freeway (f) snapshot time = 0.25 in Manhattan

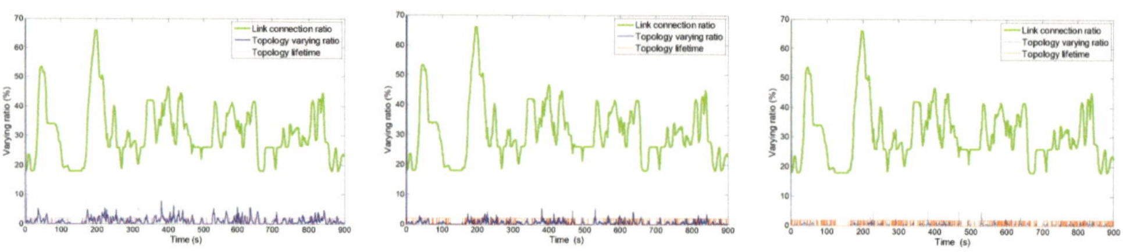

(g) snapshot time =1.0s in RPGM (h) snapshot time =0.5s in RPGM (i) snapshot time =0.25s in RPGM

Fig. 9. Topology dynamic characteristic

to all links between the two consecutive topology snapshots. Topology lifetime is the time during which the Ad Hoc network topology does not vary. Actually the curve of topology lifetime is equivalent to that of the topology varying ratio in Fig.9, since when the value of topology varying ratio between the two consecutive topology snapshots is not equal to zero, the topology lifetime is set as two, otherwise set as zero to denote that the Ad Hoc network topology does not vary between the two consecutive topology snapshots. The mobile scene is set as the following parameters in NS-2: There are all 50 mobile nodes, and the stop time is 0s in RW and 5s in RWP respectively. The maximum velocity of mobile nodes is 20m/s, simulation being 900s, and the scene covers a square area with 1200m*1200m. The wireless communication coverage range is set as a circle with radius being 250m.

According to the result of analysis on the RW, RWP mobility model as in Fig. 9(a~d)[47], and that on the Freeway, Manhattan and RPGM mobility model in Fig.9(e~i)[48], we could safely arrive at the conclusion: The steady and un-steady period appear in turn during all simulation time, and the number of the steady and un-steady state, and the duration time in each state vary with different mobility models and the parameters of movement scenes.

3.1.3 Statistical characteristic of the steady period number

In a certain time t, the number of steady period (or un-steady period) is a discrete stochastic variable X. Through analyzing on the stochastic variable X, we could obtain the frequency of the steady period (or un-steady period) appearing in a certain time. We used the data in Fig. 9(d) as an example to obtain the probability distribution chart of the number of steady period appearing in $t = 10$ s, $t = 15$ s and $t = 20$ s as in the Fig. (a), (b) and (c) respectively.

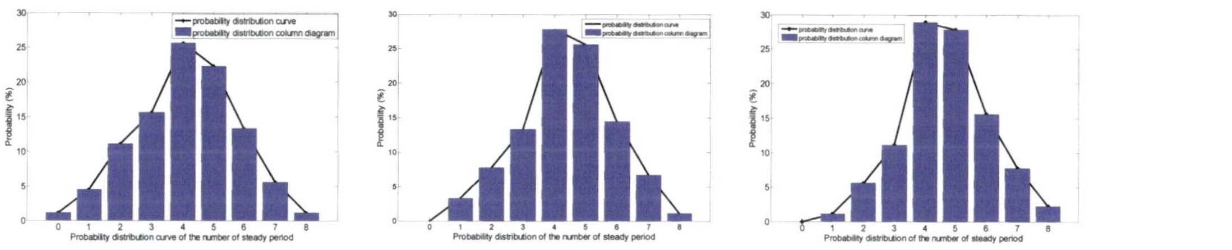

(a) $t = 10$ s (b) $t = 15$ s (c) $t = 20$ s

Fig. 10. Probability distribution chart of the number of steady period

From the Fig. 10, we could likely arrive at the inconclusive hypothesis that the number of steady period appearing in a certain time approximately follows the poison distribution, and for different time there exists different parameter λ. Next, we will use χ^2 Fit hypothesis testing method to verify this hypothesis. At first, we put forward the following hypothesis test problem:

H_0 : The number of steady period follows the poison distribution,

H_1 : The number of steady period does not follow the poison distribution.

If the statistical time is set as $t = 10$ s, that is, we will count the number of steady period once per 10 seconds. Through processing the data in Fig. 10(a), about 90 statistical data is obtained as in the table 3.

i	0	1	2	3	4	5	6	7	8
$\widehat{np_i}$	1.43	5.93	12.28	16.95	17.54	14.52	10.02	5.93	3.07
m_i	1	4	10	14	23	20	12	5	1
$\lvert m_i-\widehat{np_i}\rvert$	0.44	1.93	2.28	2.95	5.46	5.48	1.98	0.93	2.07
$\frac{(m_i-\widehat{np_i})^2}{\widehat{np_i}}$	0.13	0.63	0.42	0.51	1.70	2.07	0.39	0.15	1.40

Table 3. χ^2 fit hypothesis testing table about the number of steady period

And then, we discuss how to verify the hypothesis test problem in the following three steps.

Step 1. To compute parameter λ in poison distribution by using the maximum likelihood estimate under the condition that hypothesis H_0 is true.

If the sample of stochastic variable X is denoted as $x_i, i=0,1,...,n(n=89)$, the maximum likelihood function about parameter λ could be expressed as formula (26).

$$L(\lambda)=\prod_{i=1}^{n}(\frac{\lambda^{x_i}}{x_i!}e^{-\lambda})=e^{-n\lambda}\frac{\lambda^{\sum_{i=1}^{n}x_i}}{\prod_{i=1}^{n}(x_i!)} \tag{26}$$

Though implementing the logarithmic operation on both sides of the formula (26), the logarithmic maximum likelihood function could be expressed as formula (27).

$$\ln L(\lambda)=-n\lambda+\ln\lambda\sum_{i=1}^{n}x_i-\sum_{i=1}^{n}\ln(x_i!) \tag{27}$$

In order to let the formula (27) equal to its maximum, we implement the differential coefficient operation for parameter λ on both sides of formula (27), and let it equal to zero as the formula (28).

$$\frac{d\ln L(\lambda)}{d\lambda}=-n+\frac{1}{\lambda}\sum_{i=1}^{n}x_i=0 \tag{28}$$

Through computing the formula (28), the maximum likelihood estimate of parameter λ in poison distribution could be expressed as the following:

$$\hat{\lambda}=\frac{1}{n}\sum_{i=1}^{n}x_i.$$

Noted that the maximum likelihood estimator of parameter λ has the attributes, such as, an un-bias and effective estimate. According to the data in table 1, we could easily obtain the estimate value of parameter λ as $\hat{\lambda}$:

$$\hat{\lambda}=\frac{1}{n}\sum_{i=1}^{n}iv_i=4.14.$$

Step 2. To compute the test statistic variable V as is expressed in formula (29).
According to analysis on the data in table 1, we could obtain the value of the test statistic variable: $v = 7.40$.

$$V = \sum_{i=1}^{n} \frac{(m_i - np_i)^2}{np_i} \tag{29}$$

Step 3. Under the condition that significance level α equal to 0.05, we could get the in-equation relation between the theoretical value and statistical one as the following:

$$\chi_{\alpha}^2(r-1) = \chi_{0.05}^2(9-1) = 15.507 > 7.40$$

This in-equation relation means that the test statistic variable v does not belong to the reject range, therefore, we have to accept the hypothesis H_0, and to refuse another hypothesis H_1. It is reasonable for us to believe that the number of steady period appearing in 10 seconds follows the poison distribution with $\lambda = 4.21$, when we choose RWP mobility model in a certain mobile scene as our research object.

At the same time, that the number of un-steady period appearing in 10 seconds follows the poison distribution with $\lambda = 4.21$ could also be verified as the method above. When the statistical time is equal to different values, such as 15s, 20s, and so on, or when we choose other different mobility models, such as RW, Freeway, Manhattan and RPGM, we could also safely arrive at the conclusion that the number of steady or un-steady period appearing in a certain time also follows the poison distribution with different parameter λ. The paper does not discuss these for the limit to its length.

3.1.4 Statistical characteristic of the steady or un-steady duration time

When Ad Hoc network topology is in the steady state, the duration of which is called as steady duration time, otherwise, called as un-steady duration time. Because the steady duration time is a continuous stochastic variable, the statistical analysis method on the data about steady duration time in Fig. 9(d) is different from that on the number of steady period appearing in a certain time. Therefore, we divide the analysis method into three steps as the followings.

Step 1. To coordinate the data.
At first, we should coordinate the data about steady duration time, such as $x_1, x_2, \ldots, x_n$, in the sort ascending order as $x_{(1)} \le x_{(2)} \le \ldots \le x_{(n)}$, where n is the scale size of data sample about steady duration time, $x_{(1)}$ is the minimal value of the steady duration time, and $x_{(n)}$ the maximal one.

Step 2. To discrete the zone $[x_{(1)}, x_{(n)}]$.

Secondly, the zone $[x_{(1)}, x_{(n)}]$ is discrete to l smaller zones or groups as $I_i (1 \le i \le l)$ according to the scale size of data sample about steady duration time n. In general, if $n \ge 100$, the value of l belongs to the zone $[10,20]$; when n is equal to 50 or so, l usually is set as 5 or 6. Since in Fig.1(d), $n = 332 \ge 100$ comes into existence, we set the value of l as 10. The case of small zones about the data in Fig.1(d) is processed and analyzed as in table 4.

Zone number: i	1	2	3	4	5	6	7	8	9	10
Zones	(0.0, 1.0]	(1.0, 2.0]	(2.0, 3.0]	(3.0, 4.0]	(4.0, 5.0]	(5.0, 6.0]	(6.0, 7.0]	(7.0, 8.0]	(8.0, 9.0]	(9.0, ∞]
$n\widehat{p_i}$	157.0	87.6	48.8	27.2	15.2	8.5	4.7	2.6	1.5	1.9
m_i	172	77	35	18	13	6	5	2	2	2
$\lvert m_i - n\widehat{p_i}\rvert$	15.0	10.6	13.8	9.2	2.2	2.5	0.3	0.6	0.5	0.1
$\frac{(m_i-n\widehat{p_i})^2}{n\widehat{p_i}}$	1.43	1.28	3.90	3.11	0.32	0.74	0.02	0.14	0.17	0.01

Table 4. χ^2 fit hypothesis testing table about steady duration time

Step 3. To analyze on the steady duration time

According to the data in the anterior three lines in table 4, the probability distribution of steady and un-steady duration time in Fig. 9(d) is shown as the Fig. 11 and Fig. 12 respectively. If we connect the middle points in the upper side line of the each rectangle to construct a fold line, when n and l are big enough, the fold line is approximate to the PDF curve of the stochastic variable, the steady or un-steady duration time, according to the probability statistic theory as in Fig. 11 and 12.

The larger is the scale size of data sample, the steady duration time, the smaller is the each zone, and PDF curve of the steady duration time of Ad Hoc network topology is more precise. According to the curve in Fig. 11, we could also likely arrive at the inconclusive hypothesis that the steady duration time approximately follows the exponential distribution. Next, we will use χ^2 fit hypothesis testing method to verify this hypothesis. At first, we put forward the following hypothesis test problem.

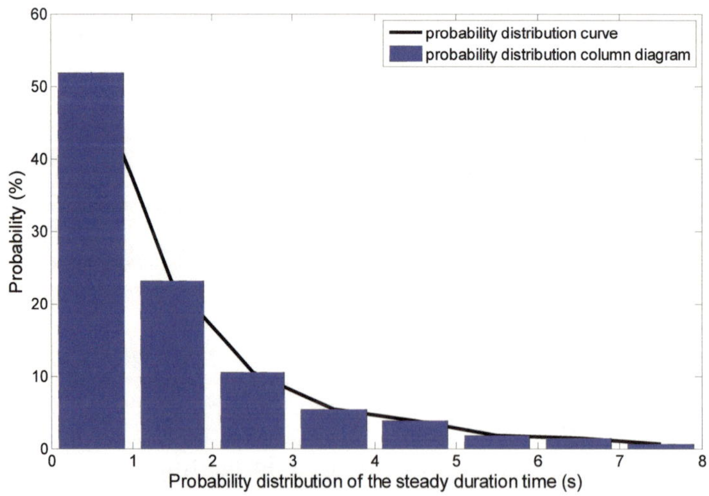

Fig. 11. PDF of steady duration time

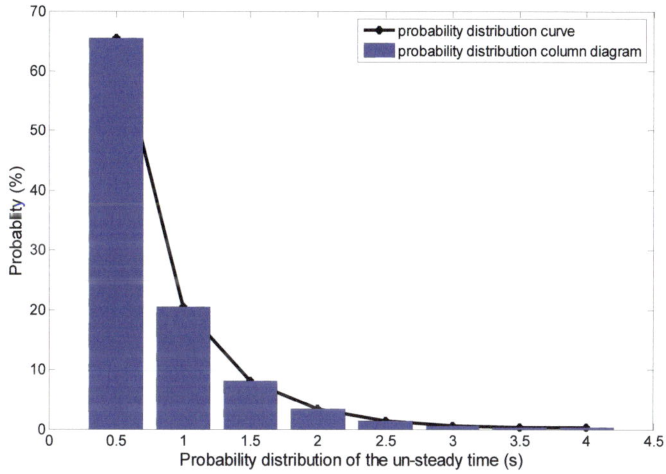

Fig. 12. PDF of un-steady duration time

H_0: The steady duration time follows the exponential distribution,

H_1: The steady duration time does not follow the exponential distribution.

According to analysis on the data in Fig. 9(d), we could obtain 332 data sample about the steady duration time. The analysis result about the 332 data sample is shown as in the table 2. Next, we will discuss the hypothesis test problem in the following three steps as the similar to that in section 3.1.

Step 1. To compute parameter λ in exponential distribution by using the maximum likelihood estimate under the condition that hypothesis H_0 is true.

If the sample of stochastic variable X , the steady duration time, is denoted as $x_i, i=0,1,...,n(n=331)$, the maximum likelihood function about parameter λ could be expressed as formula (30).

$$L(\lambda)=\lambda^n \exp(-\lambda \sum_{i=1}^{n} x_i) \tag{30}$$

Though implementing the logarithmic operation on both sides of formula (30), the logarithmic maximum likelihood function could be expressed as formula (31).

$$\ln L(\lambda)=n\ln\lambda-\lambda\sum_{i=1}^{n} x_i \tag{31}$$

In order to let the formula (31) equal to its maximum, we implement the differential coefficient operation for parameter λ on both sides of formula (31), and let it equal to zero as the formula (32).

$$\frac{d\ln L(\lambda)}{d(\lambda)}=\frac{n}{\lambda}-\sum_{i=1}^{n} x_i=0 \tag{32}$$

Through computing the formula (32), the maximum likelihood estimator of parameter λ in exponential distribution could be expressed as formula (33).

$$\hat{\lambda} = \frac{1}{\sum_{i=1}^{n} x_i} = 1 \Big/ X_n \tag{33}$$

Noted that the maximum likelihood estimate of parameter λ also has two attributes, such as, an un-bias and effective estimate. To the limit of this paper, we ignore its proof. According to analysis on data in table 4, we could easily obtain the estimate value of parameter λ as $\hat{\lambda}$:

$$\hat{\lambda} = \frac{1}{\frac{1}{n}\sum_{i=1}^{n} i v_i} = 1 \Big/ 1.713$$

Step 2. To compute the test statistic variable: $V = \sum_{i=1}^{n} \frac{(m_i - np_i)^2}{np_i}$. According to analysis on the data in table 4, the value of the test statistic variable could be obtained as $v = 11.12$.

Step 3. Under the condition that significance level α is equal to 0.05, there exists the inequation relation between the theoretical value and the statistical one as $\chi^2_{\alpha}(r-1) = \chi^2_{0.05}(9-1) = 15.507 > v$.

This in-equation relation means that the test statistic variable v does not belong to the reject range, therefore, we have to refuse the hypothesis H_1, and accept another hypothesis H_0. It is reasonable for us to believe that the steady duration time follows the exponential distribution with the $\hat{\lambda} = 1/1.713$ =0.584, when we choose RWP mobility model in a certain mobile scene as our research object. At the same time, we could also prove that the un-steady duration time in the whole simulation time follows the exponential distribution with $\hat{\lambda} = 1.276$. In the same way, when the statistical time is equal to different values, such as 15s, 20s, and so on, or when we choose other different mobility models, such as RW, Freeway, Manhattan and RPGM, we could also safely arrive at the conclusion that the steady or un-steady duration time follows the exponential distribution with different parameter λ. The paper does not discuss these for the limit to its length.

3.1.5 Markov stochastic process analysis method

According to the analysis result above, the dynamic characteristic of Ad Hoc network topology mainly embodies the following two points: one is that there is two states about Ad Hoc network topology, that is, the steady state and the un-steady state. Specially, the number of steady state or un-steady state appearing in a certain time follows the poison distribution with parameter λ. Another is that the steady or un-steady duration time follows the exponential distribution with parameter λ'. Therefore, we could easily arrive at the theorem 1.

Theorem 1 The dynamic varying process of Ad Hoc network topology is actually a continuous time and discrete state Markov stochastic one.

Proof:

When the data of Ad Hoc network topology snapshots with the snapshot time set as 0.25s is compared with that snapshot time set as 0.125s about RWP, RW, RPGM, Freeway and Manhattan mobility models, we find that the absolute error between them is less than 1%. Therefore, it is reasonable for us to consider that when the snapshot time is small enough, the states of the two consecutive Ad Hoc network topology snapshots does not vary except of the skip varying of state. This shows that time of MM is comprised of a serial of the steady and un-steady duration time periodically as in Fig. 13, where t1~t4 represent each different steady duration time, and s1~s4 the different un-steady ones , which could be achieved by counting the states of all the Ad Hoc network topology snapshots with small snapshot time.

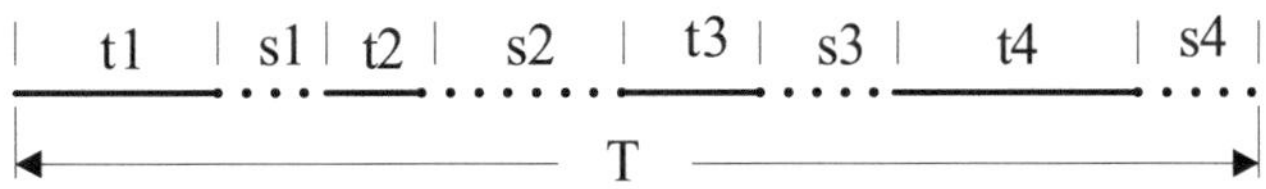

T: time, t1~t4: the steady duration time, s1~s4: the un-steady duration time

Fig. 13. Time sequence

If the state space is set as $I = \{i_n, n \geq 0\}(i_n \in \{0,1\})$, where "0" denotes the steady state and "1" the un-steady state, for any time $0 \leq t_1 < t_2 < ... < t_n < t_{n+1}$ and the its corresponding states $i_1, i_2, ..., i_n, i_{n+1} \in I$, there exists the following formula:

$$P\{X(t_{n+1}) = i_{n+1} \mid X(t_1) = i_1, X(t_2) = i_2, ..., X(t_n) = i_n\}$$

$$= P\{X(t_{n+1}) = i_{n+1} \mid X(t_n) = i_n\} \tag{34}$$

According to formula (34), the state of Ad Hoc network topology snapshot is not only correlative merely to that of its former one, but also a discrete stochastic variable. Further more, the duration time of each state, that is, the steady or un-steady duration time is a continuous ones. Therefore, the theorem 1 is proved.

According to the analysis results in above section, if the Ad Hoc network topology is in steady state (denoted as "0")now, after a steady duration time in this state, it transfers to the un-steady state (denoted as "1"), and the un-steady duration time keeps to the exponential distribution with parameter λ_1. However, the steady duration time follows the same distribution with parameter λ_2. Therefore, the density matrix of this Markov stochastic process could be denoted as the following Q.

$$\begin{pmatrix} -\lambda_1 & \lambda_1 \\ \lambda_2 & -\lambda_2 \end{pmatrix}$$

According to the forward differential equation of continuous time Markov stochastic process[19,20], $P'(t) = P(t)Q$, the following differential equations (35) could be obtained.

$$\begin{cases} p_{00}'(t) = -\lambda_1 p_{00}(t) + \lambda_2 p_{01}(t) \\ p_{01}'(t) = \lambda_1 p_{00}(t) - \lambda_2 p_{01}(t) \\ p_{10}'(t) = -\lambda_1 p_{10}(t) + \lambda_2 p_{11}(t) \\ p_{11}'(t) = \lambda_1 p_{10}(t) - \lambda_2 p_{11}(t) \end{cases} \tag{35}$$

According to the probability theory, there exists the following restriction condition.

$$\begin{cases} p_{00}(t) = 1 - p_{01}(t) \\ p_{11}(t) = 1 - p_{10}(t) \end{cases}$$

If we use the equation $p_{01}(t) = 1 - p_{00}(t)$ to replace the $p_{01}(t)$ in the first differential equation of formula (35), then the following equation could be obtained.

$$p_{00}'(t) = \lambda_2 - (\lambda_1 + \lambda_2) p_{00}(t)$$

Let $Q_{00}(t)$ be equal to $e^{(\lambda_1+\lambda_2)t} p_{00}(t)$, that is, $Q_{00}(t) = e^{(\lambda_1+\lambda_2)t} p_{00}(t)$,Then to implement the differential coefficient operation on both sides of this equation for the parameter t, we could get the formula (36).

$$Q_{00}'(t) = (\lambda_1 + \lambda_2) e^{(\lambda_1+\lambda_2)t} p_{00}(t) + e^{(\lambda_1+\lambda_2)t} p_{00}'(t) \tag{36}$$

To multiply the first equation of the formula (35) by $e^{(\lambda_1+\lambda_2)t}$ on its both sides, the formula (36) could be simplified as the following formula (37).

$$Q_{00}'(t) = \lambda_2 e^{(\lambda_1+\lambda_2)t} \tag{37}$$

Through implementing the integral operation on the both sides of the formula (37) and adopting the initial condition: $p_{00}(0) = 1$, we could finally obtain the following forecast experimental formula (38) and (39).

$$p_{00}(t) = \frac{\lambda_2}{\lambda_1+\lambda_2} (1 + e^{-(\lambda_1+\lambda_2)t}) \tag{38}$$

$$p_{11}(t) = \frac{1}{\lambda_1+\lambda_2} (\lambda_1 + \lambda_2 e^{-(\lambda_1+\lambda_2)t}) \tag{39}$$

Formula (38) means that if the Ad Hoc network topology is in the steady state now, after time t, the probability that it is still in steady state is $p_{00}(t)$. Formula (39) means that if the Ad Hoc network topology is in the un-steady state now, after time t, the probability that it is still in un-steady state is $p_{11}(t)$. Therefore, formula (38) and (39) are called as the Ad Hoc network topology steady and un-steady duration time forecast experimental formula respectively. Next, we use the concept of opposite events in probability theory to obtain warning experimental formal (40) and (41).

$$p_{01}(t)=1-p_{00}(t)=\frac{\lambda_1}{\lambda_1+\lambda_2}(1-e^{-(\lambda_1+\lambda_2)t}) \tag{40}$$

$$p_{10}(t)=1-p_{11}(t)=\frac{\lambda_2}{\lambda_1+\lambda_2}(1-e^{-(\lambda_1+\lambda_2)t}) \tag{41}$$

Formula (40) means that if the Ad Hoc network topology is in the steady state now, after time t, the probability that its state varies as un-steady one is $p_{01}(t)$. While formula (41) means that if the Ad Hoc network topology is in the un-steady state now, after time t, the probability that its state varies as steady one is $p_{10}(t)$. When time is set as 4s and 10s respectively, the experimental probability about state keeping invariable and varying is shown as the Fig. 14,15and 16 according to the forecast formula (38),(39)and the warning formula (40),(41), where x axis denotes the parameter of exponential distribution λ_1, y axis the parameter λ_2, and z axis denotes the probability value.

In order to understand the rule that the parameter of exponential distribution , λ_1 and λ_2, varies with time , we set λ_2 as 1.276 and λ_1 as 0.584 which are the same values as the analysis results in section 3.2, the experimental probability about state keeping invariable and varying with λ_1 or λ_2 and time could also be obtained according to the forecast formula (38),(39), and the warning formula (40),(41), but they are not shown for the limited length of paper.

As shown in Fig 14~16, we could safely arrive at the following conclusion: (1) P01 and P11 increases, while P00 and P10 decrease with the increment of parameter λ_1. (2) P00 and P10 increase, while P01 and P11 decrease with the increment of parameter λ_2. (3) P01 and P10 increases, while P00 and P11 decrease with the increment of time t.

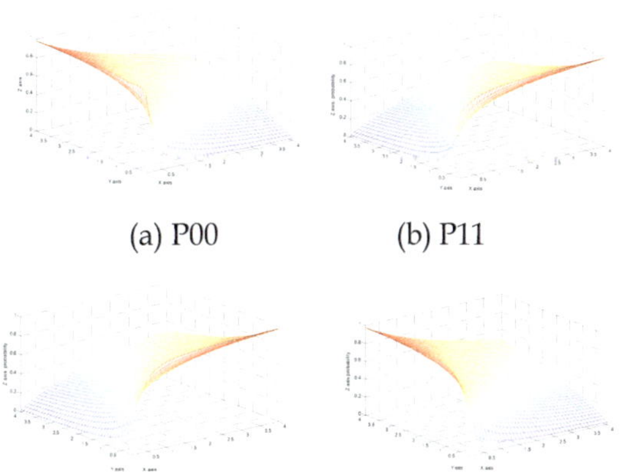

(a) P00 (b) P11

(c) P01 (d) P10

Fig. 14. Experimental probability about forecast and warning formula with t=4s

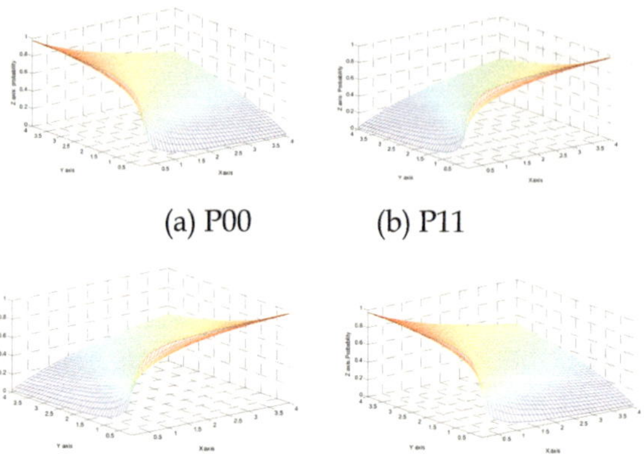

(a) P00 (b) P11

(c) P01 (d) P10

Fig. 15. Experimental probability about forecast and warning formula with t=8s

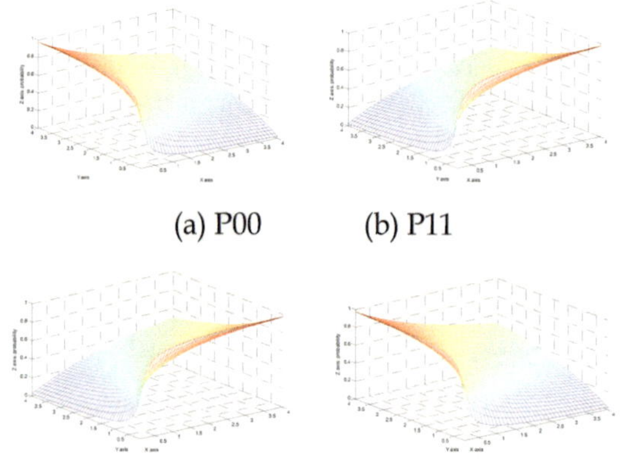

(a) P00 (b) P11

(c) P01 (d) P10

Fig. 16. Experimental probability about forecast and warning formula with t=10s

If the number of steady period appearing in a certain time is larger than 2, with the increment of parameter λ_1 in passion distribution, the number of steady period appearing will becomes smaller according to the progression theory, that is, the probability of Ad Hoc network topology keeping steady period will decrease. Therefore, P01 and P11 increases, while P00 and P10 decrease with the increment of λ_1 in a certain time. If steady duration time is lager than 1.0s, with the increment of parameter λ_2 in exponential distribution, the steady duration time will become larger according to the progression theory, that is, the probability of Ad Hoc network topology keeping steady period will increase. Therefore, P01 and P11 decreases, while P00 and P10 increase with the increment of parameter λ_2 in a certain time. With the increment of time t, the probability of Ad Hoc network topology keeping its former state(i.e., steady state or un-steady state) will become smaller. Therefore, P01 and P10 increase, while P00 and P11 decrease with the increment of time t with a certain parameters λ_1 and λ_2.

In a practical Ad Hoc network application system, we could use GPS or other position location technology to obtain the position of mobile nodes in any moment, instead of analyzing on the scene file. Next we could use the computing and analysis method in the paper to obtain the dynamic characteristic of Ad Hoc network topology, which could be used for performance evaluation and optimization of Ad Hoc network.

3.2 Performance inference method in ad hoc network

At present, Ad Hoc network performance measurement mainly focus on traditional network intra-measurement technique. [49][50] bring forth to use active probing in Ad Hoc network to measure available bandwidth. [51] puts forward a DEAN (Delay Estimation in Ad Hoc Networks) protocol, in which neighbor nodes uses Hello message to exchange delay time between each other, that is, to measuring delay time needs the collaboration of intra-nodes. All the research above actually is traditional intra-measurement, which has many faults as described above. Above all, there are many theory problems to be solved in Ad Hoc network measurement. At fist, how to deal with the influence of dynamic characteristic of network topology on performance measurement is a key issue. Second, measurement model and inference method is another key issue to be dealt with in NT measurement of Ad Hoc network.

3.3 Performance inference based on linear analysis model

In the process of the performance measurement on Ad Hoc network based on End-to-End measurement technology, the dynamic characteristic of link topology directly influences the measurement results. Yao et al. [52] consider that if the measurement could be completed under the condition that link topology remains relatively invariable, which maybe improve the veracity and precision of performance measurement. In his pervious works, the positions of mobile nodes in Ad Hoc networks at any moment could be obtained through link topology snapshots capturing algorithms according to analyzing on the scenario files of mobility models, and then the serials of snapshots of physical topology could be archived. The different periods during which physical topology is invariable can be gained by analyzing on the snapshots statistically, which is called as measurement window time in this paper. According to the results of analysis on the scenario files of RW, RWP, RGMP, and Manhattan mobility models, we could safely arrive at the conclusion: measurement window time will appear periodically in the whole simulation time.

During measurement window time, since the state of link in Ad Hoc network could not vary, the inference results of link performance based on the samples of End-to-End measurement could reflect the interior link characteristics effectively. Yao et al.[52] call this phenomenon as time validity in the measurement of Ad Hoc network. The next section presents a interior link delay reference algorithm of Ad Hoc network on the basis of End-to-End measurement method[53]. The main content of this algorithm is as followings: First to obtain the measurement time window through a link topology snapshot algorithm, Second to build up a measurement model and linear delay analysis model for Ad Hoc networks, Third to complete End-to-End measurement, Forth to refer interior link delay of Ad Hoc network according to measurement data sample, correlation among mobile nodes in Ad Hoc network topology, linear delay analysis model and mathematical statistics theory.

3.3.1 Link delay linear analysis model

On the assumption that we have done the measurement experiments m rounds. Each round we could get the End-to-End delay vector of receiver i denoted as $Y_i=\{y_{i,1}, y_{i,2},\ldots,y_{i,m}\}$

($1 \le i \le n$), where n is the number of leaf node, and $y_{i,j}(1 \le j \le m)$ is the sample of stochastic variable $Y_i(i \in [1,n], Y_i \in [0,\infty])$. After the m times experiments have finished, the delay probability distribution of the End-to-End measurement could be obtained as: $P(Y) = \{P(Y_1), P(Y_2), \ldots, P(Y_n)\}$. If the estimated link delay probability distribution is denoted as $P(X) = \{P(X_1), P(X_2), \ldots, P(X_v)\}$, then the maximum likelihood function could be expressed as formula (42):

$$L(Y;X) = P(Y_1, Y_2, \ldots, Y_n; X_1, X_2, \ldots, X_v) = \prod_{i=1}^{n} P(Y_i;X) \tag{42}$$

When Formula (42) equals to the maximum, we use $\widehat{X} = \arg_X \max \prod_{i=1}^{n} p(Y_i;X)$, where $\widehat{X} = (\widehat{X}_1, \widehat{X}_2, \ldots, \widehat{X}_n)$, as the estimated value of link delay X. However, the maximum likelihood estimation algorithm is very difficult to obtain the estimated value of link delay X for computing complexity. In order to obtain the link delay X, [25] adopts the expectation maximum (EM) algorithm including two procedures: E-step and M-step. The main problem about EM algorithm is that it could obtain the partially optimized solution, not the unitary optimized one. For the sake of computing complexity increasing by the scale of network, Pseudo-EM Algorithm[26]decomposes a large scale problem to several small scale ones. The maximum likelihood of these small scale problems could be expressed as:

$$L\,(Y_1, Y_2, \ldots, Y_n; X) = \prod_{i=1}^{n} \prod_{s \in S} P^s(Y_i^s; X^s) \tag{43}$$

where S is set of all small scale problems. The method to get the solution for Formula (43) is similar to that for Formula (42). The Bayesian estimation method uses the former probability distribution of link delay to infer the posterior one, however, how to get the former probability distribution is a difficult work.

The linear analysis model of delay will be presented next. As we all know, the delay of $path(i \to j)$, denoted as $d(i,j)$, is the sum of all link delay along this path, denoted as $d(k)$ ($k \in F(j) \cup \{j\}$), that is,

$$d(i,j) = \sum d(k)(k \in F(j) \cup \{j\}) \tag{44}$$

In the End-to-End measurement of Ad Hoc networks, the node i belongs to the set of S, and node j to the set of R. The task of link delay inference is to infer $d(k)$ according to the measurement samples of $d(i,j)$. If we only utilize one formula, it is impossible to infer $d(k)$. In order to obtain the link delay, we must use multi-formula and constitute simultaneous equations to resolve the link delay. The simultaneous equations could be expressed as formula (45).

$$Y = AX + \varepsilon \tag{45}$$

Formula (45) is referred to as interior link delay linear analysis model of Ad Hoc network in this paper. In Formula (45), Y is the delay of path which could be obtained or observed in End-to-End measurement procedure. cis the traffic matrix, and ε is the noisy which is ignored in this paper. X is the interior link delay of Ad Hoc network. Our task is that on the condition of Y and A known, ε ignored, how to resolve X. The solution of X is concerned with the types of A. In the next section, we will present the algorithm of link delay inference on the condition of A being square traffic matrix and non-square traffic matrix.

3.3.2 Algorithm of link delay inference

To compute the formula (45) is equivalent to resolve a non-homogeneous linear equations according to linear algebra theory. According to different type of traffic matrix A, we will divide two types(i.e., square traffic matrix and non-square traffic matrix) to discuss how to resolve the solution space for the formula (45) in this section.

Square Traffic Matrix When the traffic matrix is a square one, the solution for the non-homogeneous linear equations as formula (45) is concerned with the rank of the traffic matrix A. If the rank of traffic matrix A is full, there is a unique solution for the non-homogeneous linear equations, otherwise, the question of solution for the equation in section 3.1 is translated to that of a non-square traffic matrix problem. Now we only consider the A as a full rank traffic matrix. At first we could obtain the reverse matrix of A denoted as A^{-1}, the interior link delay can be expressed as formula (46).

$$X = A^{-1} \times Y \tag{46}$$

If the sender node sends N probes to every leaf nodes in Fig. 1(a) respectively, then every link delay in Ad Hoc networks could be achieved according to Formula (46) at different N time. However, we do not care about the link delay at different time, but are concerned about the link delay probability distribution during measurement window time, which could be obtained through analyzing on the link delay statistically during measurement window time based on the discrete link delay time. In practice, it is not possible to construct a square traffic matrix A in Ad Hoc networks. There is only one case that if there are N mobile nodes in Ad Hoc network, only one node is the sender, the other N-1 nodes are all leaf nodes. Under this condition, it is not necessary to use End-to-End measurement technology to infer the link delay, since there is only one step between the sender and leaf nodes, we could obtain the link delay directly through measurement.

Non-square Traffic Matrix When the rank of traffic matrix A is not full, or the traffic matrix A is a non-square matrix, the problem in section A is translated to how to resolve a non-homogenous linear equations. We will discuss this problem from the following two sides. (1) When the rank of the traffic matrix A is not equal to that of its augmentation matrix(i.e., $A \mid Y$), there is no solution for the non-homogenous linear equations. (2) When the rank of the traffic matrix A is equal to that of its augmentation matrix, there is a solution space for the non-homogenous linear equations. If the traffic matrix A is denoted as $A = (a_{i,j})_{m \times n}$, and rank(A)=rank($A \mid Y$)=r($r < n$), then the solution space is composed of n-r characteristic solutions (i.e., $\{\eta_i\}(1 \le i \le n-r)$) for the homogenous linear equations and one special solution(i.e., β) for the non- homogenous linear equations. Therefore, the solution space of the non-homogeneous linear equations could be denoted as the following formula (47).

$$S = \sum_{i=1}^{n-r} k_i \times \eta_i + \beta \tag{47}$$

Since the solution space S comprised of infinite solutions, it is necessary to limit the scale of solution space. The link l ($l \in L$) delay inference result is as formula (47), which is shared by χ paths. If the End-to-End delay of the χ paths is denoted as $T_j(1 \le j \le \chi)$, the minimum delay of the χ paths Γ could be expressed as the following formula (48).

$$\Gamma = \min\{T_j(1 \le j \le \chi)\} \tag{48}$$

Then the solution space S could be reduced to Ω: $\Omega = \sum k_j \times \eta_j + \beta(\Omega \subset S, 0 \le k_j \times \eta_j + \beta \le \Gamma)$. Next it is similar to the section A that we could obtain any link delay probability distribution through analyzing on the N times of solution space based on the discrete delay time. The unique difference between the square traffic matrix and non-square traffic matrix is that the lessen solution space maybe belongs to many discrete bins, but unique solution only to one bin. The algorithm of interior link delay probability distribution is as the following Algorithm

Step 1. To discrete the link delay time.
Step 2. $Count = 0$, and to compute the rank of traffic matrix A and augmentation matrix $A \mid Y$. If
$rank(A) \ne rank(A \mid Y)$ is true, Goto step10.
Step 3. To compute the characteristic solution for the homogenous linear equations as $\{\eta_i\}(1 \le i \le n-r)$
Step 4. To compute the special solution for the non-homogenous linear equations as β
Step 5. To construct the solution space for the non-
Homogenous linear equations as $S = \sum_{i=1}^{n-r} k_i \times \eta_i + \beta$
Step 6. To reduce the scale of S to Ω.
Step 7. $Count++$.
Step 8. If $Count < N$ (N is the times of End-to-End measurement), Go to Step3.
Step 9. To compute the link delay probability distribution through analyzing on the link delay in all N times statistically based on discrete delay time.
Step 10. Finish.

Delay time discrete method Let Θ be a set of finite delay, and link delay time $\theta_j(1 \le j \le 15)$ is discretized to Θ, then θ_j takes a value in Θ. If we suppose that discrete parameter is α, then bin size of delay time is $1/\alpha$, and the set Θ could be defined as following formula (49) based on the fixed bin size delay time discrete model.

$$\Theta = \{0, 1/\alpha, 2/\alpha, \dots i/\alpha \dots, 1\}(i \in [0, \alpha]) \tag{49}$$

Then discrete function of delay time could be defined as the following formula (50)

$$Discrete-Function(\theta_j) = \begin{cases} 0 & \theta_j \in [0, \frac{1}{2\alpha}] \\ \frac{i}{\alpha} & \theta_j \in (\frac{i}{\alpha}-\frac{1}{2\alpha}, \frac{i}{\alpha}+\frac{1}{2\alpha}] \\ 1 & \theta_j \in (\frac{2\alpha-1}{2\alpha}, 1] \end{cases} \quad (i \in [0,\alpha], j \in [1,\infty]) \tag{50}$$

The value of α is an important factor to influence the reference accuracy and computing complexity. If α is small, although more discrete delay time zone and reference accuracy could be obtained, the computing complexity will increase quickly. Otherwise, in despite of computing complexity being reduced, discrete delay time zone and reference accuracy will be reduced. Therefore, it is necessary to make a compromise between computing complexity and reference accuracy according to difference application requirement.

3.4 Link performance inference based on multi-sources measurement

Yao et al.[54] presented a interior link loss rate reference algorithm of Ad Hoc network on the basis of End-to-End and multi-sources & multi-destinations measurement method. The main content of this algorithm is as followings: First to obtain the measurement time window through a link topology snapshot algorithm, Second to build up a measurement model and link loss analysis model for Ad Hoc networks, Third to complete End-to-End and multi-sources & multi-destinations measurement, Forth to refer interior link loss rate of Ad Hoc network according to measurement data sample, correlation among mobile nodes in Ad Hoc network topology, link loss analysis model and mathematical statistics theory. Results of simulation indicate that the loss rate reference algorithm based on multi-sources & multi-destinations measurement is not only better than on one-source & multi-destinations measurement, but also the former has short computing time, which is very adaptable to interior link performance reference for Ad Hoc networks.

3.4.1 Methodology and measurement framework

We make the following assumption on routing behavior[55], (1) The routes from the sources to the destinations are fixed during the measurement period. (2) There is a unique path from each source to each destination. (3) Two paths from the same source to different receivers take the same route until they branch. Two paths from different sources to the same receiver use exactly the same set of links after they join. (4) The routers and switches in the topology obey a first-in first-out policy for packets of the same class. In order to make the assumption A1 more reasonable, we seek to limit probing and keep the measurement period as short as possible. The assumptions A1 and A2 are motivated by the shortest-path nature of routing in the Internet and the situations of the load balancing and multiple-paths are not considered in the paper. The assumption A4 is reasonable as the measurement probes is steady flow from one source to one destination.

Let $P[a,b]$ devotes the path from a to b; $H(p)$ devotes the hop count of the path of p; $SP[s;i,j]$ devotes the shared path of paths from the source s to the destinations i and j; $SP[i,j;d]$ devotes the shared path of paths from the sources i and j to the destination d; $P^{\lceil h \rceil}[a,b]$ devotes the portion path of $P[a,b]$ with hop count is h and the path begins from a;

$P^{\lfloor k \rfloor}[a,b]$ devotes the portion path of $P[a,b]$ with hop count is h and the path ends with a; $\ell^{\lceil h \rceil}[a,b]$ devotes the hth link in the path $P[a,b]$. Let $\psi(p)$ ($\varphi(p)$) devotes the minimal delay of the large packets (the small packet) which probe the path p. The minimal delay (also called stable delay) includes the propagation delay, transmission delay and the stable processing delay and does not include the queuing delay. In this paper, the probe with the minimal delay is called the valid probe, and the size of the small packet is set 56 bytes (the minimum packet size in IP) and the size of the large packet is set 1500 bytes (the maximum packet size in IP). Let $\lambda(p)$ devotes the minimal delay difference of the path p measured by the large packet and the small packet, so $\lambda(p) = \psi(p) - \varphi(p)$. Then $\lambda(p)$ is a path metric and has monotonicity and separability properties.

The main process of the new methodology to identify the routing topology includes four steps. Firstly, we calculate the hop count of the path from the each source to each destination. Secondly, we infer the hop count of the share path for every 1-by-2 component. Thirdly, we infer the hop count of the share path for every 2-by-1 component. Fourthly, the routing topology is constructed by the topology construction algorithm based on hop count information

Hop count of a path In this step, we calculate the hop count of the path from the source i to the destination j by subtracting the left TTL value of a packet received by destination j (devoted by ttl_j) from the initial TTL value (devoted by ttl_0).

$$H(P[i,j]) = ttl_0 - ttl_j$$

One source to two destinations In this step, which contains two sub steps, we consider a single source (devoted by s_0, $s_0 \in S$) transmitting probes to two destinations (devoted by i and j, $i,j \in R$). In first step, as depicted in Figure 3(a), s_0 sends back-to-back packet pairs with the large packet destined for j and the small packet destined for i, in which the large packet is followed closely by the small packet. As the large packet and the small packet will be separate at the branching node, the share path of the large packet and the small packets is $SP[s_0;i,j]$. If the packet pair do not suffer the queuing delay, then

$$d_{s_0;i,j} = \psi(SP[s_0;i,j]) + \varphi(P^{\lfloor H(P[s_0,i]-H(SP[s_0;i,j])\rfloor}[s_0,i])),$$

where $d_{s_0;i,j}$ devotes end-to-end stable delay of the small packet.

In second step, we measure the delay difference of very physical link in the path from the source to the destination using a serial of the back-to-back packet pair, in which the large packet with the initial TTL value ttl_0 from 0 to $H(P[S,i])$ (specially , when the ttl_0 is set 0 the source does not send the large packet)is followed closely by the small packet with the initial TTL value larger than $H(P[S,i])$. As the large packet will be discarded by the internal node when the TTL number is reduced to zero, the share path of the large packet and the small packets is $P^{\lceil ttl_0 \rceil}[s_0,i]$. If the packet pair do not suffer the queuing delay, we get the relationship of hop count and the delay difference,

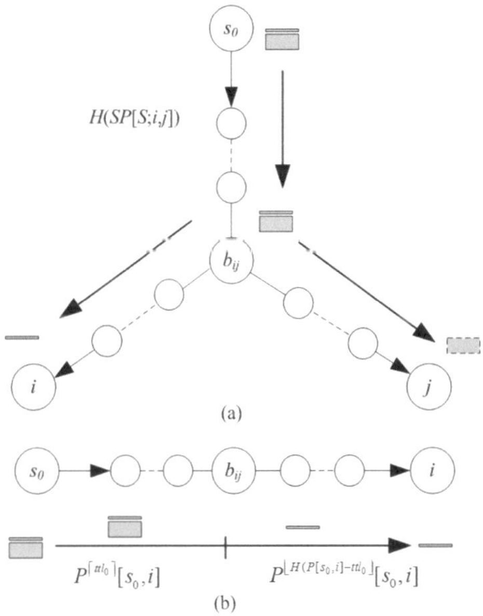

Fig. 17. Packet pair probes for every 1-by-2 component. (a) The meathead of probing the delay difference of the share path $SP[s_0;i,j]$ of each 1-by-2 component in the first sub step. (b) The meathead of probing the delay difference of every physical link in the path from s_0 to i in the second sub step.

$$d_{s_0,i}^{ttl_0} = (\psi(P^{\lceil ttl_0 \rceil}[s_0,i]) + \varphi(P^{\lfloor H(P[s_0,i]-ttl_0 \rfloor}[s_0,i]))\ ,$$

$$\begin{aligned}\lambda(\ell^{\lceil h \rceil}[s_0,i]) &= \psi(\ell^{\lceil h \rceil}[s_0,i]) - \varphi(\ell^{\lceil h \rceil}[s_0,i]) \\ &= (\psi(P^{\lceil h \rceil}[s_0,i]) + \varphi(P^{\lfloor H(P[s_0,i]-h \rfloor}[s_0,i])) \\ &\quad - (\psi(P^{\lceil h-1 \rceil}[s_0,i]) + \varphi(P^{\lfloor H(P[s_0,i]-(h-1) \rfloor}[s_0,i])) \\ &= d_{s_0,i}^{ttl_0} - d_{s_0,i}^{ttl_0 - 1}\end{aligned}$$

where $d_{s_0,i}^{ttl_0}$ devotes end-to-end stable delay of the small packet with the TTL value of the large packet is ttl_0. Meanwhile, as depicted in Figure 4, we can get the follow formula:

$$d_{s_0;i,j} = d_{s_0,i}^{H(SP[s_0;i,j])}\ .$$

So we can infer the hop count of the share path by

$$H(SP[s_0;i,j]) = \arg_{ttl_0 \in [0, H(P[s_0,i])]} \min\{\left|d_{s_0;i,j} - d_{s_0,i}^{ttl_0}\right|\}\ .$$

Let $M(i, ttl_0, K)$ devotes the *digging* measurements process, in which s_0 sends packet pair destined to i and large packets with initial TTL value ttl_0 and K measurements are collected in total. For each measurement $k = 1,2,...,K$, let $x_{s_0,i}^{ttl_0}(k)$ denotes measured delay time, then

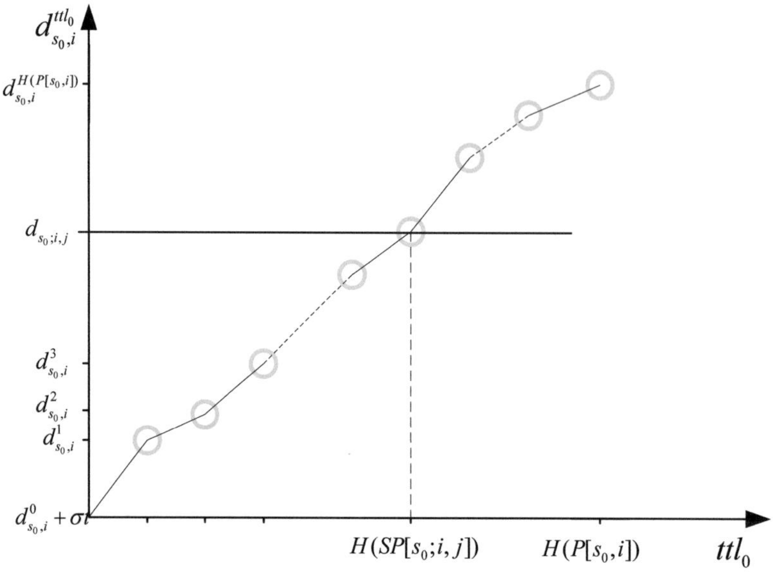

Fig. 18. The relationship of the ttl_0 and the delay difference. As the internal nodes may have different bandwidth, the increase values of delay difference produced at internal nodes may be not equal. So the points corresponding to delay differences are not placed on a straight line.

$$x_{s_0,i}^{ttl_0}(k) = d_{s_0,i}^{ttl_0} + q_{s_0,i}^{ttl_0}(k) + \sigma t_{s_0,i},$$

Where $q_{s_0,i}^{ttl_0}(k)$ devotes the queuing time, $\sigma t_{s_0,i}$ devotes the clock difference between the nodes s_0 and i. Similarly, let $x_{s0;i,j}(k)$ denotes measured delay time of the share path in the first sub step, then

$$x_{s_0;i,j}(k) = d_{s_0;i,j} + q_{s_0;i,j}(k) + \sigma t_{s_0,i}.$$

For each type measurement we assume that these measurement results are independent and identically distributed; this assumption is reasonable if the probes are sufficiently separated in time. Then the hop count of the share path can be inferred by ttl_0 which makes the difference of minimal delay of packets (meathead 1) or the difference of the mean delay (meathead 2) reach the minimum value.

•
•
•

$$\hat{H}(SP[s_0;i,j]) = \arg_{ttl_0 \in [0, H(P[s_0,i])]} \min\{\left|\min_{k'=1,2,\dots,K'}\{x_{s_0;i,j}(k')\} - \min_{k=1,2,\dots,K}\{x_{s_0,i}^{ttl_0}(k)\}\right|\}$$

$$\hat{H}(SP[s_0;i,j]) = \arg_{ttl_0 \in [0, H(P[s_0,i])]} \min\{\left|\frac{1}{K'}\sum_{k'=1}^{K'} x_{s_0;i,j}(k') - \frac{1}{K}\sum_{k=1}^{K} x_{s_0,i}^{ttl_0}(k)\right|\}$$

To simply the inference process and reduce the probing traffic load, we use the binary search algorithm to search $\hat{H}(SP[s_0;i,j])$ as the $\min_{k=1,2,...,K}\{x_{s_0,i}^{ttl_0}(k)\}$ and $\frac{1}{K}\sum_{k=1}^{K} x_{s_0,i}^{ttl_0}(k)$ have monotonicity property when K is large enough.

Two sources to one destination For two sources (devoted by i and j $i,j \in S$), the main process of measurement in our new methodology to infer the hop count of the share path to one destination (devoted by d_0, $d_0 \in R$) also includes two sub steps and the first sub step is the same to the second sub step in second step above to measure $d_{i,d_0}^{ttl_0}$.

In the second sub step, we measure the stable delay difference of the share path $SP[i,j;d_0]$. As depicted in Figure 5, the sources i and j send small packet and the large packet destined for d_0 periodically.

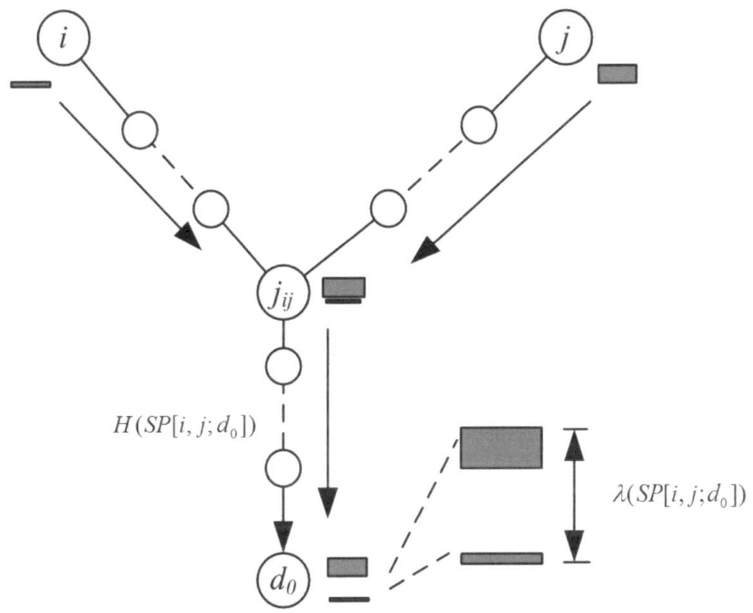

Fig. 19. The meathead of probing the delay difference of the share path of each 2-by-1 component. The sources i and j send small packet and the large packet destined d_0. If the large packet reach the joining node just after the small packet, then the interval equals the delay difference when they reach d_0.

Let sm_i and sm_j devotes the sending moment of the packet by the node i and the node j in the measurement periods; rm_{is} (rm_{il}) and rm_{js} (rm_{jl})devotes the receiving moment of the small packet (the large packet) sent by the node i and the node j; $x_s(k)$ ($x_l(k)$) devotes the measured delay time of the small packet (the large packet).

If the small valid packet and the large valid packet reach the joining node almost synchronously (this mean the interval time between and two packet is smaller than the minimal link delay difference in the path from the source to destination.), then difference of the received moment equals the stable delay difference on the share path.

$$\lambda(SP[i,j;d_0]) = rm_{is} - rm_{jl}$$

$$H(SP[i,j;d_0]) = \arg_{ttl_0 \in [0,H(P[s_0,j])]} \min\{\left|(rm_{is} - rm_{jl}) - (d_{j,d_0}^{H(P[s_0,j]} - d_{j,d_0}^{ttl_0})\right|\}.$$

Then we can infer the hop count of the share path by

$$\hat{H}(SP[i,j;d_0]) = \arg_{ttl_0 \in [0,H(P[s_0,j])]} \min\{\left|(rm_{is} - rm_{jl}) - (\min\{x_{j,d_0}^{H(P[s_0,j]}(k)\} - \min\{x_{j,d_0}^{ttl_0}(k)\})\right|\}.$$

or

$$\hat{H}(SP[i,j;d_0]) = \arg_{ttl_0 \in [0,H(P[s_0,j])]} \min\{\left|(rm_{is} - rm_{jl}) - (\frac{1}{K}\sum_{k=1}^{K} x_{j,d_0}^{H(P[s_0,j]}(k) - \frac{1}{K}\sum_{k=1}^{K} x_{j,d_0}^{ttl_0}(k))\right|\}$$

To synchronize the valid packets of the same size from the two sources to the destination to reach the joining node synchronously, one source only need to adjust the sending time forwards (or backwards) by the difference of the received moment of the two packets, because if packets reach the destination synchronously, they must have reached the join node synchronously.

To synchronize the valid packet of different size, we use the *synchronization measurement process* to adjust the sending moment. As the order of the valid packets reaching the joining node will remain to the destination, the destination can tell which valid packet reached the joining node firstly (secondly), and then inform the source to adjust the sending time backwards (forwards). In the synchronization measurement process, we keep the same sm_i and change sm_j using binary search algorithm to make the small valid packet and the large valid packet reach the joining node closely enough. To accelerate search process and to reduce the probing traffic load, we make *advance measurements* and use the measurement result to set the appropriate upper bound and the lower bound of sm_j.

In the advance measurements, as depicted in Figure 20, *j* sends small packets and large packets alternately, and *i* sends only small packets with the same period.

If we change the sending moment of *j* from sm_j to $sm_j + rm_{is} - rm_{js}$, the small valid packets from the two sources will reach the joining node at the same. Meanwhile in another period the small packet from *i* will reach the joining first than the large packet from *j*. So the upper bound of sm_j can be set $sm_j' + rm_{is} - rm_{js}$. In the same way, if we the change sending moment of node j to $sm_j' + rm_{is} - rm_{jl}$, then the small packet from *i* and the large packet from *j* will reach the destination at the same time, that means the large packet reaches the joining packet firstly. So the lower bound of sm_j can be set $sm_j' + rm_{is} - rm_{jl}$. After the advance measurements , the range of the sm_j is limited to $\lambda(P[j,d_0])$.

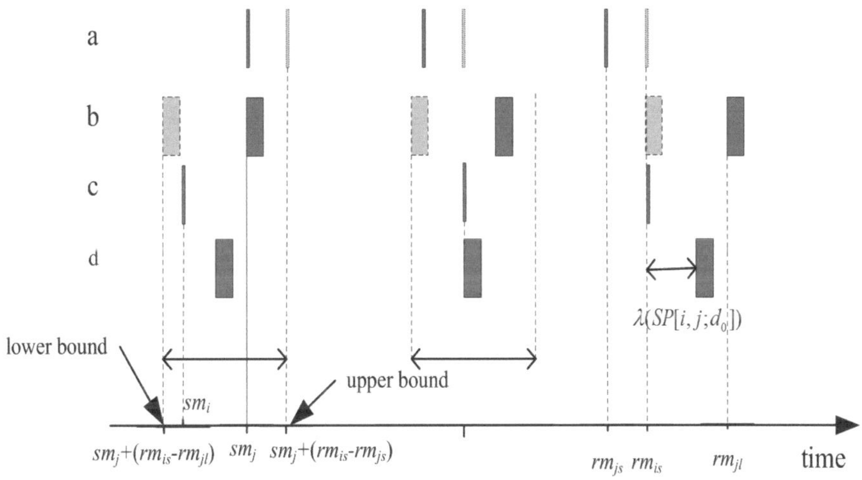

Fig. 20. The sending moment at the *i* and *j*, reaching moment at the joining node and the receiving moment at the d_0 of valid probes in the advance measurements. The packets in lines a, b and c are the small packet sent by *j*, the large packet sent by j and the small packet sent by *i*. The packet in line d is the synchronized large packet sent by *j*.

Algorithm computer the $\hat{\lambda}(SP[i,j;d_0])$

Input: the sources *i*, *j* and the destination d_0 .

Output: $\hat{\lambda}(SP[i,j;d_0])$

Precess:

1. Set the initial sending moment sm_i and sm_j, and let *j* sends small packets and large packets alternately, and *i* sends only small packets with the same period. Make measurements for K times.
2. Set $high = sm_j' + \min_{k\in[1,K]}\{rm_{is}(k)\} - \min_{k\in[1,K]}\{rm_{js}(k)\}$,

   $low = sm_j' + \min_{k\in[1,K]}\{rm_{is}(k)\} - \min_{k\in[1,K]}\{rm_{jl}(k)\}$, $sm_i = sm_i'$,.

   While ($high - low < \min_{h\in[1,H(P[j,d_0])]} \hat{\lambda}(\ell^{\lceil h \rceil}(j,d_0))$) Do

   $mid = \lceil (low + high)/2 \rceil$;

   $sm_j = mid$;

   Let *j* sends small packets and *i* sends small packets periodically for K times;

   If ($\min_{k\in[1,K]}\{rm_{is}(k)\} < \min_{k\in[1,K]}\{rm_{jl}(k)\}$)

   Then $high = mid$;

   Else $low = mid$

   End If

   End While

   $sm_j = low$;

Let *j* sends small packets and *i* sends small packets periodically for K times;

Return $\min_{k\in[1,K]}\{rm_{jl}(k)\} - \min_{k\in[1,K]}\{rm_{is}(k)\}$;

Algorithm topology Identification

Input: the source set S and the destination set D; $\hat{H}(P[i,j])$, $i \in S$, $j \in D$; $\hat{H}(SP[i,j;d])$, $i,j \in S, i \neq j$, $d \in D$; $\hat{H}(SP[s;i,j])$, $s \in S$, $i,j \in D, i \neq j$; topology $G = < S \cup D, \varnothing >$.

Output: identified topology G

Precess:

1. For (each node i in S)
    For (each node j in D) Do
      Inset $\hat{H}(P[i,j]) - 1$ nodes and $\hat{H}(P[i,j])$ links in the path from i to j;
   End For
   End For
2. For (each node s in S)
    For (each two nodes i and j in D) Do
      Merge $P^{\lceil \hat{H}(SP[s;i,j]) \rceil}[s,i]$ and $P^{\lceil \hat{H}(SP[s;i,j]) \rceil}[s,j]$;
   End For
   End For
3. For (each node d in D)
    For (each two nodes i and j in S) Do
      Merge $P^{\lfloor \hat{H}(SP[i,j;d]) \rfloor}[i,d]$ and $P^{\lfloor \hat{H}(SP[i,j;d]) \rfloor}[j,d]$;
   End For
   End For
   Return G

Delay Measurement and Clock Synchronization The methodology above need the condition that the clock of the measurement node have higher timing precision than the size of table delay difference of one-hop in the path from the source to destination. Furthermore, the system errors (such as the location errors) will be eliminated we computer the table delay difference, so only the random error influence the methodology accuracy. If the maximal bandwidth of link in the path is 1Gb/s, the timing precision should be higher than 10us which can be realized based on general PC[17]. So our methodology can be applied widely and has lower measurement cost than the meathead that need the assumption that the source and the destination have the strict clock synchronization, as to satisfy the assumption need deploy costly GPS receivers for every measurement node.

Probing Traffic Load For the M-by-N network, the probe number of the probe packet can be computed by the follow formula approximately:

$$\begin{aligned} \text{probing number} &= MN + 2KM\binom{N}{2} + 2KMNE(h) \\ &+ 2KN\binom{M}{2}\log_2(E(h)E(\frac{\max wd(\ell)}{\min wd(\ell)})) \end{aligned}$$

where $E(h)$ devotes the average hop count of the paths from the sources to the destinations and $E(\frac{\max wd(\ell)}{\min wd(\ell)})$ devotes the average ratio of the maximal bandwidth and minimal bandwidth of the links in the path the sources to the destinations. As usually during several seconds measurement time we can get the stable delay with a high probability [18, 19, 20], the value of K can be set from 50 to 100. In many case, the value of $E(h)$ ranges from 5 to 20 and the value of $\log_2(E(h)E(\frac{\max wd(\ell)}{\min wd(\ell)}))$ ranges from 5 to 10.

3.4.2 Simulation study

Firstly, we make simulations for the 1-by-2 component and 2-by-1 component, using the simulation tool *ns-2*. The hop count of every logical link ranges from 3 to 10. The physical link bandwidths range from 100Mb/s to 1000Mb/s. The background traffic added to every physical link is poisson traffic or self-similar traffic generated by three pareto traffics with $\alpha = 1.9$. Simulations were conducted in a low utilization scenario, a medium utilization scenario and a higher utilization scenario (by varying background traffic). In the first scenario, the average utilization over every physical link and runs was 10%, with a range of 5-15%; in the second scenario the average was 30 %, with a range of 10-50%; in the last scenario, the average was 50 %, with a range of 30-70%. As there are many physical links between the source and the destination, the average utilization of every logical link in three scenario are 45%, 90%, 99%.

The packet size in background ranges from 56byte to 1500byte; the small packet size of probe is 56 bytes and the large packet size of probe is 1500bytes. For every scenario, the simulation runs 200 times. The correctness of identification is depicted in Figure 8, Figure 9, and Figure 10. Generally speaking, the correctness increases quickly with the number of the probe packet and tend to 100%. The correctness of 1-by-2 component identification is higher than the correctness of 2-by-1 component identification, which can be improved by increasing the synchronization measurement process in the binary search algorithm. The background traffic become more unstable, the meathead1 adapt it better than meathead2.

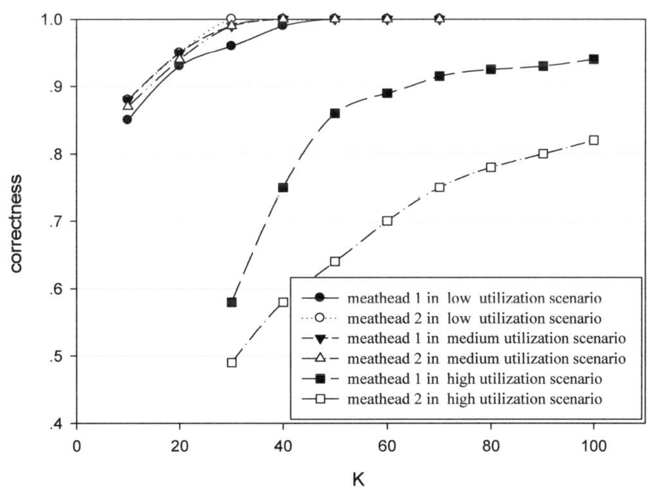

Fig. 21. The correctness of the identification vs. the number of the probes for 1-by-2 component with poisson background traffic.

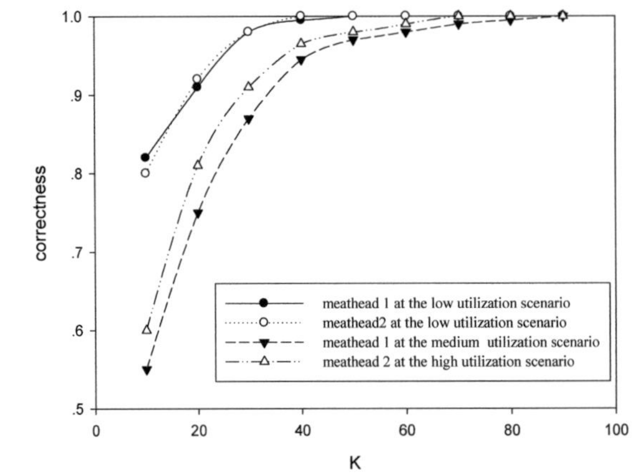

Fig. 22. The correctness of the identification vs. the number of the probes for 2-by-1 component with poisson background traffic.

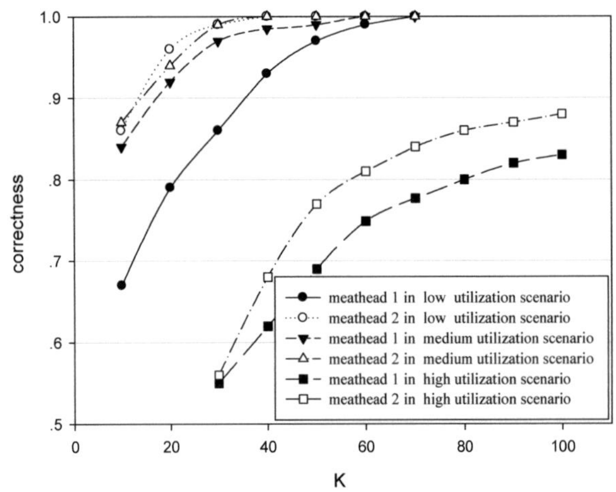

Fig. 23. The correctness of the identification vs. the number of the probes for 2-by-1 component with self-similar background traffic.

Secondly, we make simulations for a 3-by-4 network depicted in the Fig. 1(a) with the medium utilization poisson background traffic. We using meathead1 and set K=50. The simulation runs 200 times and the correctness of identification is 98%.

3.5 Ad hoc network delay tomography based on circle mobility model

The circle mobility model (CMM) is proposed by Wang[56], which is suited to patrolling periodically for gathering information in the military area or forest fireproofing. The assumptions are as follows. First, the location of SN is known to other nodes. Second, the MN knows the direction and how far it will move to next destination. This is true in real situations where nodes know their destinations. The process, representing the movement of a node within a circular area A with radius R, can be described as follows. A SN (n_0) is placed at the point O, the centre of the circle. Initially, MN (n_i, n_j and n_k) are placed at points over A, see Fig.1-a. Without losing the generality，n_i is in initial position P_{i0} with radius r_i. Then a destination point P_{i1} is chosen from the circle with radius r_i and the node moves along arc L_i with constant velocity v_i and central angle θ_i. Once n_i reaches P_{i1}, n_i stays a pause time t_i and a new destination point P_{i2} is drawn, ...$P_{i(n-1)}$,P_{in}.... Obviously, the step time $ST_i = \theta_i / v_i + t_i$ and the step length $L_i = \theta_i r_i$. The nodes (n_i and n_j) with same radius have identical mobile properties, such as $\theta_i = \theta_j$, $v_i = v_j$, $t_i = t_j$, $ST_i = ST_j$ and $L_i = L_j$, otherwise they might have different mobile properties.

3.5.1 Circle mobility model

The MANET with CMM could be denoted as a dynamic logical tree $\Psi = (V, L(T))$ with the node set V and link set $L(T)$ at time T [2]. A source node to probe is called the root. A set of receivers, which called leaves, is denoted as $RCE \subset V$. The nodes between the source and receivers represent internal nodes. The tree model is defined by the set of paths. Each path, which is from the root to an end receiver denoted by $rce \in RCE$, comprises one or more links (direct connections with no intermediate nodes). A logical link is referred to as a subpath in which every internal node has only one child. In Ψ, the interal links are the logical links that link these branch nodes at T. Each node k, apart from the root, has a parent $f(k)$ such that link $(f(k), k) \in L(T)$ could be denoted as link k. The physical topology and the logical topology are depiced in Fig. 24(c) and Fig.24(d) respectively. The Fig.24(d) shows a typical binary tree in which the root and the receivers are 1, 3 and 4.

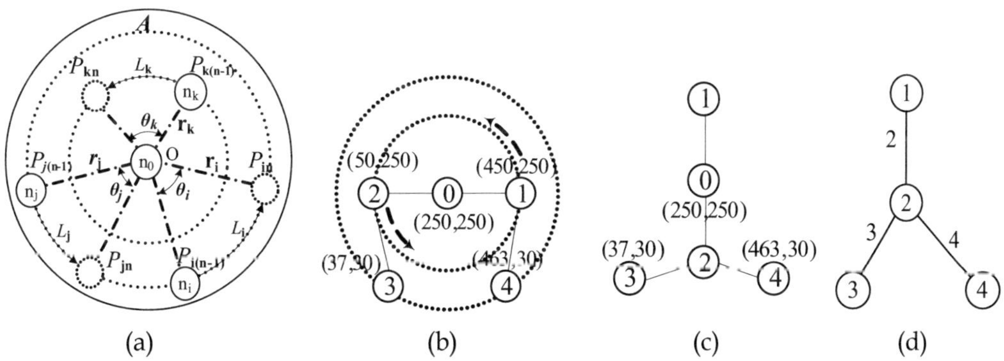

Fig. 24. The CMM mobility model and the topology used for the NS2 measurements (a) CMM mobility model. (b)Initial topology and nodes coordinates. (c) Physical topology within IT_1 and IT_2. (d) Logical topology inferred within IT_1 and IT_2.

There are many random components determining link delay, such as propagation delay, queuing at the node, node packet servicing delay and dropped event due to the overload of finite output buffer of the node or link breakage. The key assumption of our delay model is that the individual delays between different links and packets should be considered independently within IT. IT means the period of time during which the topology is relatively stable under CMM, to overcome the stubborn topology changes. A series of *ITs* can be calculated during the simulation period due to the breakage and comebacke along the paths. The internal link delay could be inferred which is associated with the corresponding *IT* by probing two closely time-spaced packets (back-to-back packet pair) from the source to two different receivers. This is the difference between our delay model and previous works [4]. Each members of a packet pair passes through a common set of links in their paths, but diverge at some branch node to arrive to the respective destination. Apparently, if the gap between the two members is on the order of the machine's smallest unit of time, the difference between the delay experienced by the first and the second member of pair crossing same link can be ignored. Approximatively, the two packets experience identical network conditions along the shared links and any delay experienced will be identical for both probes.

During the *i*-th *IT* denoted by $IT_i = t_{end}^{(i)} - t_{start}^{(i)} > 0$ ($t_{start}^{(i)}, t_{end}^{(i)} \in T$), two members of the packet pair (i,j) are sent to destination rce_i and rce_j, respectively. Since the round trip paths of the probe are unsymmetrical, a measurement represents the E2E one way delay (OWD) of the couple of packets, denoted by $X_{ij}^{IT_i} = (X_i^{IT_i}(1), X_j^{IT_i}(2))$. Where $X_i^{IT_i}(1)$ and $X_j^{IT_i}(2)$ are the delays from source to the two end receives, respectively. The sending time is stamped on every packet by the sender, and the OWD is calculated at the receiver. An experiment consists in sending n packets pairs (i,j) for each pair of rce_i and rce_j. The set of measurements, the cumulated delay along the respective paths are associated with $X^{IT_i} = (X_{rec_i}^{IT_i(m)}(1), X_{rec_j}^{IT_i(m)}(2))_{m=1,\dots,n; rec_i \neq rec_j \in RCE}$ for each couple of end receivers. The complete set of measurement X^{IT_i} is obtained by combining all possible pair of distinct rce_i and rce_j in Ψ winthin IT_i.

3.5.2 Link dealy probability distribution inference method

Let $D_{1k}^{IT_i}$ and $D_{2k}^{IT_i}$ represent the estimated value of delay over link *k* in MANET for the first member and for the second one of the packet pair during the IT_i. Since the distribution of a link delay is unknown, the characterization of the variable delay is obtained by non-parametric discrete distributions. The delay could be quantified as a finite set of possible delay $Q = \{0, q, 2q, \dots\dots, Mq, \infty\}$, where q, M and ∞ denote the width bin, a positive integer and the lost, respectively. The bin associated to $iq \in Q$ is the interval $[iq - q/2, iq + q/2]$, where $i = 0,1,2\dots,M$. Many similar delays are grouped in a unique interval. The estimation of $D_k^{IT_i}$ is the probability of these intervals, denoted by $\alpha_k^{IT_i} = (P[D_k^{IT_i} = d])_{d \in Q}$. Our goal is to estimate $\alpha^{IT_i} = (\alpha_k^{IT_i})_{k \in V}$. Let D^{IT_i} be the set of delays experienced by the packet pairs along each link. It is possible to define the log-likelihood function for the pair (X^{IT_i}, D^{IT_i}) of the measurement X^{IT_i}, which is the complete data for inference problem:

$$L(X^{IT_i}, D^{IT_i}, \alpha^{IT_i}) = \log P_\alpha[X^{IT_i}, D^{IT_i}] = \sum_{k \in V} \sum_{d \in Q} n_k(d) \log \alpha_k^{IT_i}(d) \tag{51}$$

Where $n_k(d)$ is the number of packet pairs with delay d over link *k*. We estimate $\hat{\alpha}_k^{IT_i}(d) = n_k(d) / \sum n_k(d) = n_k(d)/n$ could be estimated by formula (51) with Maximum

Likelihood Estimate. Although $n_k(d)$ is an unknown value, the maximum of formula (51) could be estimated by using the Expectation Maximum algorithm.

① ***Initialization***. Calculate the IT_i to infer Ψ according to CMM and select the initial delay distribution $\hat{\alpha}^{IT_i(0)}$. First, the positions of the end nodes (source and receivers) are calculated by movement parameters along respective circles at time $t \in T$. At the same time *t*, the coordinates of the other MN between source and recivers can be obtained. Second, comparing the distance between nodes and the radio link range, the topology whose life time is from $t_{start}^{(i)}$ to $t_{end}^{(i)}$ could be inferred. The distribution of $\hat{\alpha}^{IT_i(0)} = P[D_k^{IT_i} = d]$ is the initial distribution for the iterative EM algorithm.

② ***Expectation.*** Let X^{IT_i} be discretized to the set Q. The measurement $x_{rce_i,rce_j}^{IT_i}$ depends on rce_i and rce_j, simply $x_{rec}^{IT_i}$. Using theorem of Bayes, $\hat{n}_k(d)$ could be derived as the following:

$$\begin{aligned}\hat{n}_k(d) &= \sum_{h=1}^{n} P_{\hat{\alpha}^{(l)}}[D_k^{IT_i} = d \mid X^{IT_i} = x_{rec}^{IT_i(h)}] \\ &= \sum n(x_{rec}^{IT_i})(P_{\hat{\alpha}^{(s)}}[X^{IT_i} = x_{rec}^{IT_i} \mid D_k^{IT_i} = d] / P_{\hat{\alpha}^{(s)}}[X^{IT_i} = x_{rec}^{IT_i}])\hat{\alpha}_k^{IT_i(s)}(d)\end{aligned} \tag{52}$$

Where $n(x_{rec}^{IT_i})$ is the number of times of the same discretized measurement in $x_{rec}^{IT_i}$. The count $\hat{n}_k(iq)$ for each $iq \in Q$ can be calculated in the formula (2). The iterative algorithm is expressed by the distribution $\alpha_k^{IT_i}$ computed at step *s*.

③ ***Maximization.*** The conditional expectation calculation of $\hat{\alpha}^{IT_i(s+1)}$ maximizes the function $L(X^{IT_i}, D^{IT_i}, \alpha^{IT_i})$, given X^{IT_i} and $\hat{\alpha}^{IT_i(s)}$. It is possible to obtain the new estimate at *(s+1)*-th step, using the $\hat{n}_k(d)$ in ②.

④ ***Iteration***. The joint application ② and ③ gives the stationary solution of the maximization, and $|\hat{\alpha}^{IT_i(s+1)} - \hat{\alpha}^{IT_i(s)}| < threshold$, where *threshold* allows the algorithm to know if the maximum is reached. Although the smaller *threshold* means the estimations are more precise, complicated calculations will be produced. In our simulations (Section 4), $threshold = 0.01$.

3.5.3 Simulation study

The NS2 simulator could be extended to simulate the traffic through CMM model with simulation time of 150s. MANET with two-receiver (3 and 4) is depicted in the Fig. 1-b. We simulate 2 scenarios by the CMM in a rectangular field (500m × 500m) with 5 nodes and *R*=250m. We let 3 and 4 be static ($v_3=v_4=0$) for simplification, but these nodes is mobile for scalability and inferences algorithm. The MN (1 and 2) with $r = 200$, $\theta = 10^{\circ}$, $v = 12m/s$ and $t = 1s$. Radio propagation range for each node is 250 meters and channel capacity is 1.5 *Mb/s*. We can easily infer Ψ throughout $IT_1 = 8s$ ($t_{start}^{(1)} \approx 32s$, $t_{end}^{(1)} \approx 40s$) and $IT_2 = 8s$ ($t_{start}^{(2)} \approx 136s$, $t_{end}^{(2)} \approx 144s$), see Fig.1-d. A link between two nodes shows that the two nodes can hear each other within IT_1 and IT_2. The probes comprise packet pairs with a 0.15*s* inter-pair time. The packet pairs were CBR with an inter-packet time of 0.1 microseconds by periodically sent to 3 and 4.

In scenario 1, background traffic consists of 2 TCP connections (2 to 1, 4 to 3) and the source is 0 and *q=0.1s*. In scenario 2, the source is 1, *q=0.05s*, and background traffic consists of 2 TCP connections (0 to 3, 4 to 1). The typical initial delay probability of every link can be chosen by the uniform distribution from 0 to *M*.

Fig.25 shows the simulation results plotted by Matlab6.5 along links (2,3 and 4). From left to right show results for link 2, link 3 and link 4. The estimated delay and actual delay are indicated with white and black, respectively. Obviously, internal links' actual average delays with high probability (>0.1) accord with estimated average delay. Since the complexity of the analysis is a function of the numbers of bins, a small *q* to ensure a desired level of accuracy results in excessive computational costs.

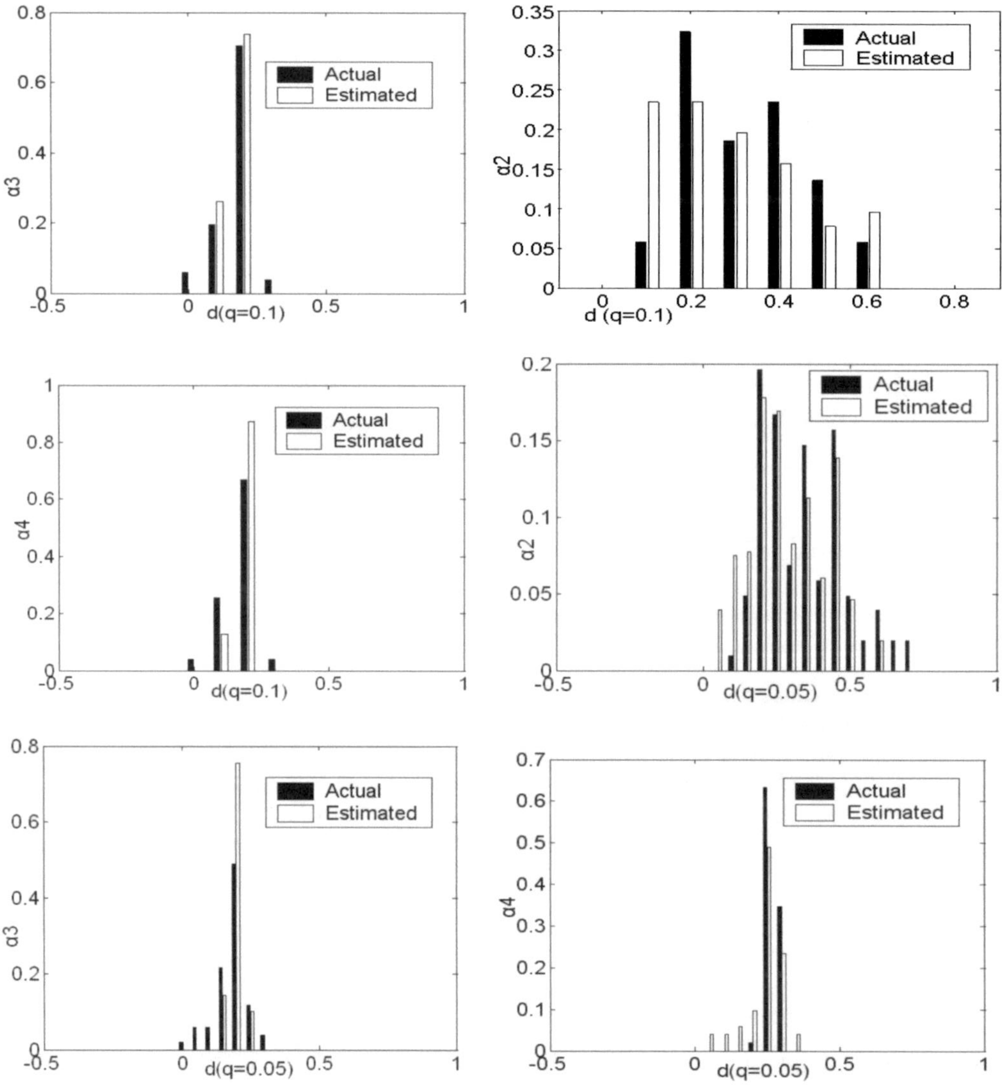

Fig. 25. Estimated vs. actual delay probability distributions from each scenario.

4. Acknowledgment

The research is supported in part by the National high technology research development plan (863 plan) of china (Grant No. 2009AA01Z424), and the Ph.D. Programs Foundation of Ministry of Education of China (Grant No. 200806990030), and the Innovative Foundation of Northwestern Polytechnical university in P.R.China(2008KJ02028).

5. References

[1] Duan Qi, Cai Wanddong. BC_EM: A Link Loss Inference Algorithm for Wireless Sensor Network. 5th International Conference on Wireless Communications, Networking and Mobile Computing(WiCom '09), p1-5, 2009.9,Beijing

[2] Duan Qi, Cai Wanddong. A Simple Graph-structure Network Tomography Topology Identification Method. 2009 International Joint Conference on Artificial Intelligence(JCAI '09), p 337-340, 2009.4,Haikou

[3] Li Guishan, Cai Wandong et al. Link Delay Estimation in Network with Stochastic Routing. 2009 WRI World Congress on Computer Science and Information Engineering, v2, p 110-114,2009.3, Los Angeles USA.

[4] Y. Vardi. Network tomography: Estimating source-destination traffic intensities from link data.J. Amer. Stat. Assoc., 91(433): 365-377, 1996.

[5] Yongjun Li, Wandong Cai et al. Wireless Sensor Network Topology Identification based on Data Aggregation. Journal of Computational Information Systems, 3(6), p2359-2365, 2007

[6] LI Yong-jun CAI Wan-dong WANG Wei TIAN Guang-li, Research on network topology identification algorithm based on end-to-end loss performance, JOURNAL ON COMMUNICATIONS, 28(10), 2007

[7] Zhao tao, Cai wandong, Li huixian, Sensor network level-topology inference based on Hamming distance, Journal of Huazhong University of Science and Technology(Nature Science) , 36(10): 71-74, 2008

[8] Tao Zhao, Wandong Cai et al. Topology control for wireless sensor network. 2007 IFIP International Conference on Network and Parallel Computing(NPC 2007),p343-348,2007.9, Dalian

[9] Li Yongjun, Cai Wandong, Wang Wei, Tian Guangli, Topology Identification Based on End-to-End Link Utilization, Journal of System Simulation, 18(22)

[10] Yongjun Li, Wandong Cai et al. A Fast Multicast-based Approach to Inferring Loss Performance. Journal of Communication and Computer, 2006.3

[11] Yongjun Li, Wandong Cai et al. Loss Temporal Dependency Tomography in Wireless Sensor Network. 2007 IEEE International Conference on Wireless Communications, Networking and Mobile Computing, p2352-2355, 2007.9, Shanghai

[12] Zhao tao, Cai wandong, Li Yongjun, A Method for Link Loss Inference Based on End-to-End Measurement, Journal of northwestern polytechnical university, 26(02): 158-161, 2008

[13] TIAN Guang-li,CAI Wan-dong,YAO Ye,ZHAO Zuo, Research on Topology Duration of Ad Hoc Networks and Limit Time of End-to-end Measurement, Journal of System Simulation,Vol 16, 2009.

[14] Guangli Tian , Wandong Cai et al. Routing Topology Identification Based on End-to-end measurements. 2008 IEEE International Conference on Information and Automation (ICIA 2008), p 1595-1598, 2008.6, Zhang JiaJie
[15] Wei Wang, Wandong Cai et al. The factor graph approach for inferring link loss in MANET. 2008 International Conference on Internet Computing in Science and Engineering (ICICSE 2008), 2008.1, Harbin
[16] Duan Qi, Cai Wanddong. Topology Identification Based on Multiple Source Network Tomography. IIS'2009, p125-128, 2009
[17] Duffield Nicholas G., orowitz Joseph, Lo Presti Francesco, et al.. Explicit loss inference in multicast tomography. IEEE Transactions on Information Theory, August, 2006, 52(8): 3852-3855.
[18] Nick Duffield. Network Tomography of Binary Network Performance Characteristics. IEEE Transactions on Information Theory, 2006, 52(12): 5373-5388.
[19] Guo Dong, Wang Xiaodong. Bayesian inference of network loss and delay characteristics with
applications to TCP performance prediction. IEEE Transactions on Signal Processing, 2003, 51(8): 2205-2218.
[20] Arya Vijay, Duffield N.G., Veitch Darry. Multicast inference of temporal loss characteristics. Performance Evaluation, 2007,vol (64): 9-12.
[21] Yolanda Tsang, Coates M., Nowak R.D. Network delay tomography, IEEE Transactions on Signal Processing, Aug. 2003, 51(8): 2125 – 2136
[22] Bestavros Azer, Byers John. Harfoush Khaled. Inference and labeling of metric-induced network topologies. IEEE Transactions on Parallel and Distributed Systems, November, 2005, 16(11): 1053-1065.
[23] Tian Hui, Shen Hong. Multicast-based inference for topology and network-internal loss performance from end-to-end measurements. Computer Communications, 2006, 29(11): 1936-1947.
[24] N.G. Duffield, F. Lo Presti, V. Paxson, et al.. Inferring link loss using striped unicast probes.IEEE INFOCOM 2001, Anchorage, Alaska, 2001, vol 2: 915-923.
[25] Liang, B. Yu. Maximum pseudo likelihood estimation in network tomography. IEEE Transactions on Signal Processing, 2003, 51(8): 2043-2053.
[26] Wang Wei, Cai Wandong, Wang Beizhan, et al.. Mobile Ad hoc Network Delay Tomography. Proceedings of 2007 IEEE International Workshop on Anti-counterfeiting Security, Identification. Xiamen University, Xiamen, Chian, April, 2007, pp: 365-370.
[27] Jianzhong Zhang. Origin-Destination Network Tomography with Bayesian Inversion Approach. Proceedings of the 2006 IEEE/WIC/ACM International Conference on Web Intelligence, 2006, pp: 38-44
[28] Yongjun Li Wandong Cai Wei Wang Guangli Tian, Lossy Node Identification in Wireless Sensor Network, Proceeding of Fifth IEEE International Symposium on Network Computing and Applications, Cambridge, Massachusetts, USA, NCA 2006, v 2006, p 255-258, July 2006
[29] Yongjun Li Wandong Cai Guangli Tian Wei Wang, Loss Tomography in Wireless Sensor Network Using Gibbs Sampling, Proceeding of EWSN 2007, LNCS 4373, p 150–162, Delft, Netherlands, Jan 29-31 2007.

[30] Tao Zhao, Wandong Cai, Yongjun Li. Sensor network loss inference using end-to-end measurement. Journal of Computational Information Systems, 3(6):2383-2388, 2007

[31] Yongjun LI Wandong CAI Wenli JI Tao Zhao, A Fast Inference of Loss Rate in Wireless Sensor Network, Journal of Computational Information Systems, 3(1):125-132, 2007

[32] Tao Zhao, Wandong Cai, Yongjun Li. Bottom-up inference of loss rate in sensor network, Journal of Computational Information Systems, 4(4):1429-1434, 2008

[33] Yongjun LI Wandong CAI Wenli JI Tao Zhao, Wireless Sensor Network Topology Identification based on Data Aggregation, Journal of Computational Information Systems, 3(6):2359-2365, 2007

[34] Tao Zhao, Wandong Cai, Yongjun Li. MPIDA: A sensor network topology inference algorithm, International Conference on Computational Intelligence and Security, Harbin, Heilongjiang, China, 451-455, Dec, 2007

[35] Tao Zhao, Wandong Cai, Yongjun Li. Using End-to-End Data to Infer Sensor Network Topology, The 7th IEEE International Symposium on Signal Processing and Information Technology, Cairo, Egypt, 99-103, Dec, 2007

[36] Yongjun Li, Wandong Cai et al. Loss Cumulate Generating Function Inference in Wireless Sensor Network. 2006 IEEE International Conference on Wireless Communications, Networking and Mobile Computing, p1-4, 2006.9, Wuhan

[37] Meng-fu Shih, Alfred Hero, "Unicast inference of network link delay distributions from edge measurements," Proceedings of 2001 IEEE International Conference on Acoustics, Speech, and Signal Processing (ICASSP '01), p3421-3424, 2001

[38] "The chernoff bound explained", available: http://people.deas.harvard.edu/~ho/ DEDS/OO/Idea/ Slide03.html

[39] B. Walsh. Markov Chain Monte Carlo and Gibbs Sampling, http://nitro.biosci.arizona.edu/ workshops/Aarhus2006/ pdfs/ Gibbs.pdf

[40] Yao Ye, Cai Wanddong, Koukam Abder, Hilaire Vincent. A Multi-hierarchical Group Mobility Model for Tactical Mobile Wireless Networks. Journal of Computational Information Systems, 5(1):275-282, February 2009

[41] N Sadagopan, F Bai, B Krishnamachari, A. Helmy. Paths：Analysis of path duration statistics and their impact on reactive MANET Routing Protocols. Proceedings of the 4th ACM International Symposium on Mobile Ad Hoc Networking and Computing(MobiHoc'03), Annapolis, p245~256,2003.

[42] Guangli Tian , Wandong Cai et al. Topology Variety Model for Mobile Ad Hoc Networks. Mobilware'08, 2008.2, Innsbruck, Austria

[43] Wang Wei, Cai Wandong, Wang Beizhan, et al., Research on a Mobility Model Based on Circle Movement in Ad Hoc Network. Journal of Computer Research and Development , 44(6), p 932-938, June 2007

[44] Yao Ye, Cai Wandong, Tian Guangli, A Method of Snatching Ad Hoc network Link Topology Snapshot, Science paper Online of China, http://www.paper.edu.cn/index.php/default /releasepaper/content/200903-3, 2009.03

[45] Yao Ye, Ad Hoc Networks Measurement Model and Methods Based on Network Tomography[Ph.D], Northwestern Polytechnical University, 2010.

[46] Information Sciences Institute of University of Southern California. "The Network Simulator 2," available:www.isi.edu/nsnam/ns2.

[47] Yao Ye, Cai Wanddong, Hilaire Vincent, Koukam Abder. Research on Physical Topology Steady Degree of RWP Mobility Model on Ad Hoc Network. Journal of Computational Information Systems, 5(4): p1203-1211, August 2009

[48] Yao Ye, Cai Wanddong et al. Research on the Link Topology Lifetime Of Mobility Model in Ad Hoc Network. 2009 International Conference on Networks Security, Wireless Communications and Trusted Computing(NSWCTC' 2009), v 1, p103-107, 2009.4, Wuhan

[49] Andreas Johnsson, Mats Björkman, Bob Melander. A Study of Dispersion-based Measurement Methods in IEEE 802.11 Ad-hoc Networks. The International Conference on Communication in Computing, Las Vegas, June, pp.227-230, 2004

[50] L. J. Chen, T. Sun, G. Yang, M. Y. Sanadidi and M. Gerla. Ad Hoc Probe: Path Capacity Probing in Wireless Ad Hoc Networks. The first IEEE International Conference on Wireless Internet (WICON 2005), Budapest, Hungary, 2005.

[51] Cheikh Sarr and Isabelle Guerin Lassous. Estimating Average End-to-End Delays in IEEE 802.11 Multihop Wireless Networks. Technical Report 1, INRIA, July 2007.

[52] Yao Ye, Cai Wanddong. Ad Hoc Network Measurement Based on Network Tomography: Theory, Technique, and Application. Journal of Networks, 5(6): 666-674, June 2010

[53] Yao Ye, Cai Wanddong. Interior Link Delay Reference of Ad Hoc Networks Based on End-to-End Measurement: Linear Analysis Model of Delay. Journal of Networks, 4(4), p 244-253, June 2009

[54] Yao Ye, Cai wandong, Tian guangli , A Link Loss Rate Inference Method for Ad Hoc Networks Based on End-to-End Measurement, Journal of northwestern polytechnical university, 28(1), p82-86, February 2010

[55] Guangli Tian, Cai Wanddong. Routing Topology Identification Based on Multiple Sources End-to-end Measurements. APWCS'2010, p322-325, 2010

[56] Wei Wang, Wandong Cai et al. Mobile ad hoc network delay tomography. 2007 IEEE International Workshop on Anti-counterfeiting, Security and Identification (ASID), p365-370 2007.4, Xiamen

8

Stochastic Optimization Over Correlated Data Set: A Case Study on VLSI Decoupling Capacitance Budgeting

Yiyu Shi[1], Jinjun Xiong[2] and Lei He[3]
[1]ECE Dept., Missouri University of Science and Technology, Rolla, MO, 65409
[2]IBM Thomas J. Watson Research Center, Yorktown Heights, NY, 10598
[3]EE Dept., University of California, Los Angeles, LA, 90095
U.S.A

1. Introduction

It is very common in engineering society to optimize certain objective functions under the worst scenario among a set of possible scenarios, i.e.,

$$\begin{aligned} &\min_{\mathbf{x}} \max_i f(\mathbf{x}) \\ &s.t. \quad \mathbf{x} \in S(\mathbf{p_i}), \\ &\qquad i = 1, 2, \ldots, \end{aligned} \tag{1}$$

where $\mathbf{p_i}$ are the parameters that control the feasible region S of x. For example, in the contingency analysis of power systems, $\mathbf{p_i}$ is a vector of 0-1 variables, indicating which of the branches are open. Each $\mathbf{p_i}$ corresponds to one contingency situation. Another example is the decoupling capacitance budgeting for very large scale integrated (VLSI) circuits and systems, where $\mathbf{p_i}$ can be different load current profile.

When the number of possible scenarios are small, we can use enumeration to find out the worst case. But when it is large or even infinite, enumeration becomes computationally expensive, sometimes even infeasible, and accordingly, we need some elegant algorithms that can efficiently solve the problem. In this chapter, we will use the decoupling capacitance budgeting problem in very large scale integrated (VLSI) circuits and systems to illustrate one recently developed algorithm when the Pi's are correlated.

The continuous semiconductor technology scaling leads to growing process variations (Agarwal & Nassif, 2007), and statistical optimization has been actively researched to cope with process variations. Recent examples include stochastic gate sizing for power reduction (Bhardwaj & Vrudhula, 2005; Mani et al., 2005) and for yield optimization (Davoodi & Srivastava, 2006; Sinha et al., 2005), stochastic buffer insertion to minimize clock delay (He et al., 2007), and adaptive body biasing with post-silicon tuning (Mani et al., 2006). However, all these papers ignore *operation variation* such as crosstalk difference over input vectors, power supply noise fluctuation over time, and processor temperature variation over workload. We argue that a better design could be achieved by considering both operation and process variations.

The P/G network has to provide large currents within a short period of time but without causing considerable IR-drop and *Ldi/dt* noises. The noises on the P/G network can degrade signal integrity of the whole design, causing longer path delay, reduced noise margin, and even logic failures. In the presence of process variation, a fraction of chips after manufacturing may fail to meet the given power noise constraints, even though they were predicted to do so by the deterministic techniques, thus causing unnecessary yield loss. This observation has also been confirmed in recent studies on both statistical timing analysis (Chang & Sapatnekar, 2003; Visweswariah et al., 2004) statistical power network analysis (Ghanta et al., 2005; Kouroussis et al., 2005; Pant, Blaauw, Zolotov, Sundareswaran & Panda, 2004).

Decap budgeting is one of the most effective techniques to reduce the noise in P/G network. Assuming the netlist and the initial placement is given, decap budgeting assigns the right amount of decap to the right location. To solve the decap budgeting problem, most work employs a sensitivity-based optimization technique, such as those solved by either linear programming (Zhao et al., 2006), quadratic programming (Su et al., 2003), or conjugate gradient method (Fu et al., 2004; Li et al., 2005). At each iteration step during optimization, sensitivities of the objective function with respect to various decaps are obtained by running circuit simulations on the adjoint network followed by time-domain convolution (Li et al., 2005; Su et al., 2003). Because both simulation and convolution are time-consuming operations, the overall runtime is high and suffers from the scalability problem for large P/G networks. To mitigate this runtime issue, different techniques have been proposed. For example, (Su et al., 2003) employed piecewise-linear approximation for the time-domain waveforms so that convolution can be carried out faster with bounded accuracy loss. (Fu et al., 2004) exploited regular structures of P/G networks, and reduced circuit sizes by equivalent circuit transformation (such as Y-Δ transformation). Because of the reliance on special P/G structures, the applicability of this technique to large P/G networks is limited and the reduction ratio is not high in general. (Li et al., 2005) employed a divide-and-conquer approach that partitioned a P/G network into a number of sub-circuits so that decap budgeting can be solved efficiently for each sub-circuit. But to consider the inter-dependence between different sub-circuits, an artificial boundary condition has to be imposed, hence the accuracy of the solution cannot be guaranteed. Recently, (Zhao et al., 2006) used macromodeling and linear programming based approaches to solve the decap problem. However, same as the previous studies (Fu et al., 2004; Li et al., 2005; Su et al., 2003), it assumed a maximum current load at every port to guarantee the worst-case design scenario.

The maximum current model is over pessimistic as it ignores operation variation. Specifically, current loads at different ports are correlated and cannot reach the maximum at the same time due to the inherent logic dependency for a given design, hence exhibiting *logic-induced correlation*; and the current at a port also exhibits *temporal correlation*, i.e., the current cannot attain maximum all the time, and depending on the functionality being performed, the current variations for certain periods of clock cycles are correlated.

Unfortunately, few research has been conducted on how to extract these operation correlations. The stochastic modeling of IR drop with respect to given correlated current loads for a P/G network was studied in (Pant, D.Blaauw, Zolotov, S.Sundareswaran & Panda, 2004). However, the paper did not discuss how to extract the correlation of those current loads.

Moreover, it is still not clear how to use the correlation to guide the P/G network design and optimization such as decap budgeting.

In addition, the current loads are affected by process variations. (Ferzli & Najm, 2003) has considered process variation induced leakage variation for power grid analysis. While the leakage power is comparable to the dynamic power because not all components are active simultaneously in a large system-on-chip, we believe that the dynamic peak current is still dominant compared with the leakage current. However, how to design a reliable P/G network in the presence of process variation (particularly L_{eff} variation) has not been explicitly studied in existing work (Fu et al., 2004; Li et al., 2005; Su et al., 2003).

In this chapter, we develop a novel stochastic model for current loads, taking into account operation variation such as temporal and logic-induced correlations and process variations such as systematic and random L_{eff} variation. We propose a formal method to extract operation variation and formulate a new decap budgeting problem using the stochastic current model. We develop an effective yet efficient iterative alternative programming algorithm and conduct experiments using industrial designs. We show that under the same decap area and compared with the baseline model assuming maximum current peaks at all ports, the model considering temporal correlation reduces the noise by up to 5×, and the model considering both temporal and logic-induced correlations reduces the noise by up to 17×. Compared with using deterministic process parameters, considering L_{eff} variation reduces the mean noise by up to 4× and the 3σ noise by up to 13× when both applying the current model with temporal and logic-induced correlations. Therefore, we convincingly demonstrate the significance of considering both operation and process variations and open a new research direction for optimizing signal, power and thermal integrity with consideration of operation variation.

The remaining of the chapter is organized as follows. We introduce the decap budgeting problem in Section 2, and develop the stochastic current model and parameterized MNA formulation in Section 3. We discuss the algorithms to solve the variation-aware decap budgeting problem in Section 4, and present experiments in Section 5. We conclude in Section 6. An extended abstract of this chapter with less details and no sequential quadratic programming (in Sections 4 and 5.3) was published by the 2007 International Conference on Computer-Aided Design (Shi et al., 2007).

2. Problem formulation

The P/G network can be modeled as a linear RLC network with each segment and pad modeled as a lumped RLC element from extraction. The behavior of any linear RLC network with p ports of interests is fully described by its state representation following the modified nodal analysis (MNA)

$$Gx + C\frac{dx}{dt} = Bu(t), \tag{2}$$

$$y = L_0^T x, \tag{3}$$

where x is a vector of nodal voltages and inductor currents, u is a vector of current sources at all ports, G is the conductance matrix, C is a matrix that includes both inductance and capacitance elements, B and L_0 are port incident matrices, and y is the output voltages of interests at the p ports.

We model the P/G network noise based upon the response $y(t)$ from (3). Because of the duality between power and ground networks, in the following, we will focus our explanation on the power network design. But it is understood that the same formulation applies to the ground network design as well. Same as (Fu et al., 2004; Li et al., 2005; Su et al., 2003; Visweswariah et al., 2000), we model the power network induced noise at a node as the integral of the voltage drop below a user specified noise ceiling $\overline{U}$ over a certain period of time:

$$z_i = \int_{\Omega_i} (\overline{U} - y_i(t))dt, \tag{4}$$

where Ω_i is the time duration when voltage at port i, y_i, drops below the noise ceiling $\overline{U}$, i.e.,

$$\Omega_i = \{t | y_i(t) \leq \overline{U}\}. \tag{5}$$

The figure of merit that measures the qualify of the whole power network design is defined as the sum of noise at all ports of interest, i.e.,

$$f = \sum_{i=1}^{p} \int_{\Omega_i} (\overline{U} - y_i(t))dt. \tag{6}$$

We will call the noise measurement in (6) simply as noise in the rest of the chapter.

Based upon the noise modeling above, we can formulate the decap budgeting problem as the following optimization problem:

Formulation: **Decap Budgeting**: Given a power network modeled as an RLC network with specified power pads, time-varying current at different ports, and total available white space $\overline{W}$ for decoupling capacitance, the DecapOpt problem determines the places to insert decoupling capacitance and the sizes of each decoupling capacitance, such that the noise defined in (6) is minimized, considering the time-varying current $u(t)$ in (2) caused by logic-induced variation, temporal variation and process variation.

3. Stochastic modeling

In this section, we first propose our stochastic current model for the current loads of the P/G network in Section 3.1, where we extract the correlation from the extensive simulation of the circuit and then apply ICA to get the parameterized model of the load current. Then in Section 3.2, based on the load current model, we propose the parameterized MNA formulation and mathematically represent the variation-aware decap budgeting problem.

3.1 Stochastic current modeling

In this section, we propose our stochastic current modeling for current loads of the P/G network, i.e., $u(t)$ in (2). Similar to the vectorless P/G analysis in (Kouroussis et al., 2005), we assume that the circuit is partitioned into blocks such that different blocks are relatively independent. For each block, there are multiple ports connected to the power network, and each port is modeled as a time-varying current load for the power network. We apply extensive simulation to each block *independently* to get the current signatures. Because we ignore the interdependence between blocks, the obtained current signatures are still conservative compared with the real current profiles.

For simplicity of presentation and similar to (Su et al., 2003) [1], we represent the current in one clock cycle as a triangular waveform with rising time, falling time, and peak value $\hat{I}$. The peak values vary in different clock cycles and over different ports. The correlation between currents for different ports is called *logic-induced correlation*. In addition, the currents of the same port in different clock cycles are also correlated. We call this type of correlation as *temporal correlation*. For example, it might take a block several clock cycles to execute certain functions and the current profile inside those clock cycles are dependent to each other. We denote L, the *correlation length*, as the maximum number of clock cycles in which the peak currents might be correlated and can be decided from the simulation results.

In the following, we devise a stochastic model which can efficiently capture the correlation from both the logic-induced variation and temporal variation, as well as from process variation.

3.1.1 Stochastic model to consider current interdependence

We record the peak currents at port k ($1 \leq k \leq p$ with p as the total port number) at different clock cycles, and put them into vectors, i.e.,

$$b_k^j = [\hat{I}_k^j, \hat{I}_k^{1+j}, \ldots], \quad 1 \leq k \leq p, 1 \leq j \leq L \tag{7}$$

where $\hat{I}_k^i$ is the peak currents at port k in clock cycle i, and b_k^j is the set of peak currents sampled every clock cycles starting from cycle j. Properly truncation from the end of b_k^j is necessary to make them of the same length for further processing. In other words, the corresponding samples in vectors $b_k^{j_1}$ and $b_k^{j_2}$ are $|j_1 - j_2|$ clock cycles apart. If the peak current at port k in the first clock cycle is selected from the r-th element of b_k^1, then the peak current in the second clock cycle should be the r-th element of b_k^2. As an example, if the peak values in each clock cycle for port 1 are $[0.1, 0.2, 0.3, 0.4]$, and for port 2 are $[0.01, 0.02, 0.03, 0.04]$, and we choose $L = 2$, then

$$\begin{aligned} b_1^1 &= [0.1, 0.2, 0.3], \quad b_2^1 = [0.01, 0.02, 0.03], \\ b_1^2 &= [0.2, 0.3, 0.4], \quad b_2^2 = [0.02, 0.03, 0.04]. \end{aligned} \tag{8}$$

We model the peak current at each port as a stochastic process. Then all the elements of b_k^j are the samples for the stochastic variable $\mathcal{B}_k^j$ with its mean $\mu(\mathcal{B}_k^j)$ and standard deviation $\sigma(\mathcal{B}_k^j)$. We call the correlation between $b_k^{j_1}$ and $b_k^{j_2}$ as temporal correlation, and the one between $b_{k_1}^j$ and $b_{k_2}^j$ as logic-induced correlation.

With those stochastic variables B_k^j's and their corresponding samples b_k^j's, we can compute the logic-induced correlation matrix $\rho(j; k_1, k_2)$ which describes the correlation between the peak

[1] Our noise verification in the experiment part does not depend on this assumption.

currents at any two ports k_1 and k_2 in clock cycle j as

$$\rho(j;k_1,k_2) = \frac{cov(\mathcal{B}^j_{k_i}, \mathcal{B}^j_{k_2})}{\sigma(\mathcal{B}^j_{k_1})\sigma(\mathcal{B}^j_{k_2})}, \quad (1 \le k_1, k_2 \le p), \tag{9}$$

where $cov(\mathcal{B}^j_{k_1}, \mathcal{B}^j_{k_2})$ are the covariance between $\mathcal{B}^j_{k_1}$ and $\mathcal{B}^j_{k_2}$, and $\sigma(\mathcal{B}^j_{k_1})$ and $\sigma(\mathcal{B}^j_{k_2})$ are their standard deviations, respectively. Similarly, the temporal correlation matrix $\rho(j_1, j_2; k)$ which describes the correlation between the peak currents between clock cycles j_1 and j_2 of a same port k can be computed as

$$\rho(j_1,j_2;k) = \frac{cov(\mathcal{B}^{j_1}_{k}, \mathcal{B}^{j_2}_{k})}{\sigma(\mathcal{B}^{j_1}_{k})\sigma(\mathcal{B}^{j_2}_{k})}, \quad (1 \le j_1, j_2 \le L). \tag{10}$$

3.1.2 Extension to process variation with spatial correlation

(Orshansky et al., 2002) relates the current to the process parameters L_{eff}, t_{ox} and V_t as

$$\hat{I}^i_k \sim L_{eff}^{-0.5} t_{ox}^{-0.8} (V_{dd} - V_t). \tag{11}$$

As pointed out in (Cao & Clark, 2005), in 90nm regime the most significant variation source is the effective channel length (L_{eff}), and L_{eff} variation can be more than 30%. Furthermore, L_{eff} variation is mostly spatially correlated but not random (Orshansky et al., 2002). Therefore, we will use L_{eff} variation as an example to show how process variation can be embedded into our stochastic modeling. It is understood that the process variation of other parameters can be dealt with in a similar way.

We use the variation model for L_{eff} based on (Orshansky et al., 2002):

$$L_{eff} = L_0 + L^{prox} + L^{spat} + \epsilon, \tag{12}$$

where L_0 is the overall mean, L^{prox} is a discrete stochastic variable with a distribution determined by the frequency of each gate, L^{spat} corresponds to the spatial variation, and ϵ is the local random variation.

From (11), with L_{eff} variation, the sample $\hat{I}^j_k$ becomes a set of samples

$$\left[\hat{I}^j_k \sqrt{\frac{\bar{L}_{eff,k}}{L^1_{eff,k}}}, \hat{I}^j_k \sqrt{\frac{\bar{L}_{eff,k}}{L^2_{eff,k}}}, \dots \right], \tag{13}$$

where $L^i_{eff,k}$ with different i are the samples of $L_{eff,k}$ for the circuit block corresponding to port k with the nominal value $\bar{L}_{eff,k}$, and $\hat{I}^j_k$ are the peak current sample for $\mathcal{B}^j_k$ in the deterministic case without L_{eff} variation in (7). In other words, if we have n samples for $L_{eff,k}$ $(L^1_{eff,k}, L^2_{eff,k}, \dots, L^n_{eff,k})$, then every current sample I^j_k becomes n samples. Therefore, the sample vector b^j_k becomes n times longer in the presence of L_{eff} variation, and we denote this new vector as $\tilde{b}^j_k$. In addition, we denote the stochastic variable representing the set of $\tilde{b}^j_k$

as $\tilde{\mathcal{B}}_k^j$. In this case, the temporal correlation (9) becomes

$$\tilde{\rho}(j;k_1,k_2) = \frac{cov(\tilde{\mathcal{B}}_{k_i}^j, \tilde{\mathcal{B}}_{k_2}^j)}{\sigma(\tilde{\mathcal{B}}_{k_1}^j)\sigma(\tilde{\mathcal{B}}_{k_2}^j)}, \quad (1 \le k_1, k_2 \le p), \tag{14}$$

and the logic-induced correlation (10) becomes

$$\tilde{\rho}(j_1,j_2;k) = \frac{cov(\tilde{\mathcal{B}}_k^{j_1}, \tilde{\mathcal{B}}_k^{j_2})}{\sigma(\tilde{\mathcal{B}}_k^{j_1})\sigma(\tilde{\mathcal{B}}_k^{j_2})}, \quad (1 \le j_1, j_2 \le L). \tag{15}$$

3.2 Parameterized problem formulation

3.2.1 Parameterized current via ICA

Directly considering the temporal and logic-induced correlation including process variation as formulated in (14) and (15) is difficult for optimization. Therefore, we propose to remove the correlation between $\tilde{B}_k^j$'s and build a parameterized current model in the following.

If all those variable $\tilde{B}_k^j$'s are Gaussian, we can apply principal component analysis (PCA) to remove the interdependence between the stochastic variables $\tilde{\mathcal{B}}_k^j$'s. However, this is not the case for our stochastic current model. Therefore, we use independent component analysis (ICA) that is applicable to non-Gaussian distribution (Hyvarinen et al., 2001). The input to ICA is the samples $\tilde{b}_k^j$ as well as their correlation matrices (14) and (15), and the output are a set of independent stochastic variables r_i and their corresponding coefficients $a_i(j,k)$ to reconstruct each $\tilde{\mathcal{B}}_k^j$, i.e.

$$\tilde{\mathcal{B}}_k^j \approx \sum_{i=1}^{q} a_i(j,k) r_i. \tag{16}$$

The order q is determined for each design such that the relative error between the original currents and model predicted currents is less than 5%. The probability density function (PDF) for each r_i is also given in the output of ICA as a one-dimensional lookup table, based on which we can bound the range of r_i as

$$\underline{r_i} \le r_i \le \overline{r_i}, \tag{17}$$

where $\underline{r_i}$ and r_i can be related to r_i's mean (μ) and variance (σ^2). For example, we can take $\underline{r_i}$ as $\mu - 4\sigma$ and $\overline{r_i}$ as $\mu + 4\sigma$.

Therefore, assuming uniform rising and falling times across the chip for the triangular current waveform within a clock cycle [2], together with $a_i(j,k)$ which represents the i-th component of the peak current at port k in clock cycle j, we have all the necessary information to obtain the i-th time-varying current waveform component $u_i(t;j,k)$. If we denote T as the clock period,

[2] This uniform assumption does not affect the results in our experiments.

then $jT \leq t \leq (j+1)T$. Put those $u_i(t;j,k)$ at all ports in clock cycle j together as

$$u_i(t;j) = \begin{pmatrix} u_i(t;j,1) \\ u_i(t;j,2) \\ \vdots \\ u_i(t;j,p) \end{pmatrix}, \quad jT \leq t \leq (j+1)T, \tag{18}$$

and then combine all the $u_i(t;j)$ in different clock cycles, we can get $u_i(t)$ with $0 \leq t \leq LT$. Finally, according to superposition theorem, we have

$$u(t) = \sum_{i=1}^{q} u_i(t) r_i, \quad 0 \leq t \leq LT. \tag{19}$$

We call (19) as parameterized current load model.

3.2.2 Parameterized MNA for decap budgeting

Considering the inherent parasitics, we model the decap similarly to (Zheng et al., 2003) as an equivalent series capacitor (ESC), and equivalent series resistor (ESR) and an equivalent series inductor (ESL). When a decap with size w_i is inserted into the power network at a given location, its impact can be considered by adjusting matrices G and C in (2) based on the location at the network and the size of the decap. Mathematically, it can be represented as

$$G = G_0 + \sum_{i=1}^{M} w_i \cdot G_{w,i}, \tag{20}$$

$$C = C_0 + \sum_{i=1}^{M} w_i \cdot C_{w,i}, \tag{21}$$

where G_0 and C_0 are the original matrices for the power network without decap, M is the total number of decaps, and $G_{w,i}$ and $C_{w,i}$ provide the stamping of a unit width decap at the i-th location. Due to the placement constraint, each w_i has an upper bound, i.e., we have the local constraints

$$0 \leq w_i \leq \overline{w_i}. \tag{22}$$

If only noise minimization is considered, then we can simply choose $w_i = \overline{w_i}$ ($\forall i$), i.e., use up all the white space from the physical placement constraints. However, there are two other important issues we need to take into consideration: the leakage and the area overhead. With those two constraints, we cannot add too much decap, and therefore we have the global decap area constraint

$$\sum_{i=1}^{M} w_i \leq \overline{W}. \tag{23}$$

In practice we always have the following relationship between the local constraints (22) and the global constraint (23)

$$\sum_{i=1}^{M} \overline{w_i} \geq \overline{W}, \tag{24}$$

which implies that (23) is always tight for the optimization problem, and (22) is not tight for all i. In other words, we are given the total amount of decaps, and we want to allocate those decaps to the proper locations, so that the noise is minimized while there is no violation to (22).

The MNA equation of (2) with G given by (20), C given by (21), and u given by (19) can be written as follows

$$(G_0 + \sum_{i=1}^{M} w_i \cdot G_{w,i})x + (C_0 + \sum_{i=1}^{M} w_i \cdot C_{w,i})\frac{dx}{dt}$$
$$= B\sum_{i=1}^{q} u_i(t)r_i, \tag{25}$$

where $0 \le t \le LT$ and r_i is a stochastic variable with $\underline{r_i} \le r_i \le \overline{r_i}$. We call this MNA equation as *parameterized MNA formulation* for decap budgeting. One of the major advantages in using this parameterized MNA formulation is that it enables us to implicitly compute sensitivities efficiently and accurately, which will become clearer in the later part of this chapter.

With the parameterized MNA, the variation-aware decap budgeting problem can be mathematically represented as follows:

$$(\mathbf{P1}) \quad \min_{w_i} \ \sup_{r_k} f = \sum_{i=1}^{p} \int_{\Omega_i} (\overline{U} - y_i(w_i, r_k; t))dt \tag{26}$$
$$s.t. \ \ \underline{r_k} \le r_k \le \overline{r_k} \quad 1 \le k \le q, \tag{27}$$
$$0 \le w_i \le \overline{w_i}, \quad 1 \le i \le M \tag{28}$$
$$\sum_{i=1}^{M} w_i \le \overline{W}, \tag{29}$$

where voltage y_i is a function of w_i, r_k, and time t and can be solved from (25) and (3).

Problem (**P1**) is a constrained min-max optimization problem. The *sup* operation over all random variables r_k is to find the worst-case noise violation measures for a given power network design. This operation guarantees that all P/G network designs satisfy the given design constrains while considering the temporal and logic-induced correlations as well as L_{eff} variation among ports. This is of particular use for ASIC-style designs, where the worst-case design performance has to be ensured for sign-off. The *min* operation over all decap sizes w_i is to find the optimal decap budgeting solution so that the worst-case noise violation is minimized.

4. Algorithms

In this section ,we present our iterative alternative programming approach to solve the problem (**P1**) stated in Section 3. In Section 4.1, we decompose the original min-max problem into two alternative optimization sub-problems, which are solved in Section 4.2 by an efficient sequential programming approach based. The detailed algorithm to compute sensitivities from parameterized MNA for such sequential programming is zoomed into detail in Section 4.3.

4.1 Iterative alternative programming with guaranteed convergence

Because there exists no general technique to solve the constrained min-max problem (**P1**) optimally, we resort to an effective iterative optimization strategy, which we call *iterative alternative programming* (IAP). That is, instead of solving the min-max problem (**P1**) directly, we solve it by iteratively solving the following two sub-problems alternatively.

The first sub-problem assumes that all decaps' sizes w_i are known, hence the worst-case noise can be obtained by solving the following optimization problem

$$(\mathbf{P2}) \quad \max_{r_k} \; f = \sum_{i=1}^{p} \int_{\Omega_i} (\overline{U} - y_i(w_i, r_k; t))dt \tag{30}$$

$$s.t. \; \underline{r_k} \leq r_k \leq \overline{r_k}, \quad 1 \leq k \leq q \tag{31}$$

The second sub-problem assumes that all random variables r_k have fixed values, hence the decap sizes to achieve the minimum noise can be obtained by solving the following optimization problem

$$(\mathbf{P3}) \quad \min_{w_i} \; f = \sum_{i=1}^{p} \int_{\Omega_i} (\overline{U} - y_i(w_i, r_k; t))dt \tag{32}$$

$$s.t. \; 0 \leq w_i \leq \overline{w_i}, \quad 1 \leq i \leq M \tag{33}$$

$$\sum_{i=1}^{M} w_i \leq W, \tag{34}$$

where W is the total white space available. Problem (**P3**) is exactly the deterministic version of the original problem formulation (**P1**).

We illustrate our idea in Fig. 1 and the overall algorithm can be described in Algorithm 1, where *iter* is the current iteration number and ϵ determines the stop criteria of the optimization procedure. For each iteration, we increase the total available white space by ΔW until $\bar{W}$.

The algorithm terminates when the change of objective function $|\Delta f|$ is sufficiently small indicating the convergence of the solution, or we have reached the global decap constraint (29). The first case corresponding to the situation where we have reduced noise below the bound before all the white space are used up, while the second case indicates that we have reached the global decap area constraint. In either case, the algorithm will terminates and the convergence of our algorithm is guaranteed as long as the algorithms for solving (**P2**) and (**P3**) converge, which will be discussed shortly. As shown in Fig. 2, the choice of ΔW reflects a tradeoff between the runtime and the solution quality. Smaller ΔW can result in smaller noise under the same decap area but the runtime is increased as well. Setting $\Delta W = 0.004W$ gives a good balance in our experiment.

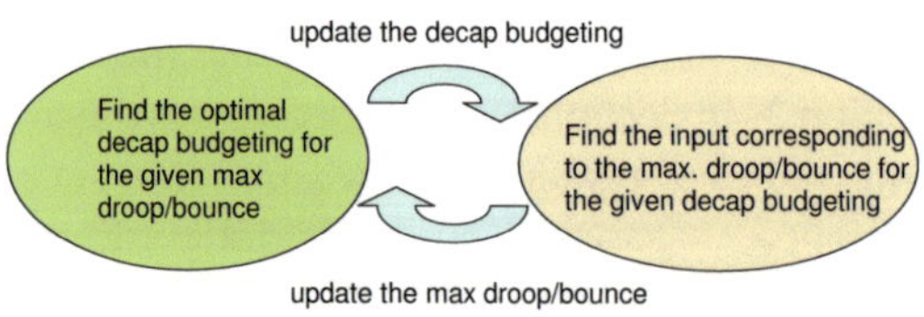

Fig. 1. Solve the min-max problem by iteratively solving two sub-problems.

Algorithm 1 Iterative alternative programming.

INPUT: initial guess w_i, r_k, current white space $\bar{W}$;
OUTPUT: final solution w_i to problem (**P1**);
Initialize: The current white space available $W = 0$;
for $iter = 0$; $|\Delta f| \leq \epsilon$ and $W \leq \bar{W}$; $iter++$ **do**
  $W = W + \Delta W$;
  w_i = solve-P3($iter$, w_i, r_k, W);
  r_k = solve-P2($iter$, w_i, r_k, W);
  Compute objective function with new r_k and w_i;
end for

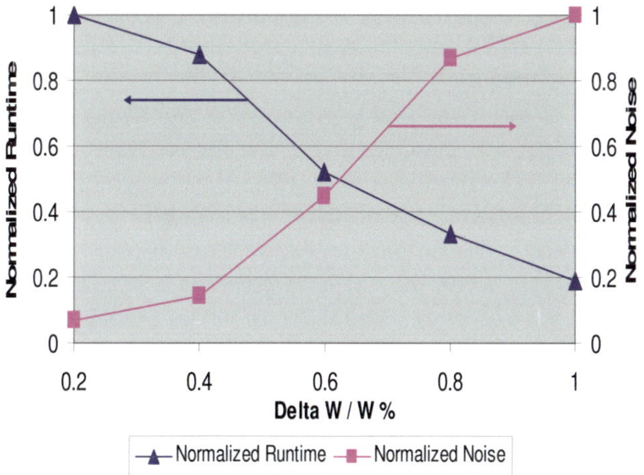

Fig. 2. The normalized runtime and noise w.r.t different $\frac{\Delta W}{\bar{W}}$.

4.2 Efficient sequential programming

Both problems (**P2**) or (**P3**) are constrained nonlinear optimization problems, and there exits no general technique to solve them efficiently. Because the constraints in both problems are linear, if we can approximate the objective function f by a first-order linear function, the original problems would become linear programming (LP). Or if we can approximate the objective function f by a second-order quadratic function, they would become a quadratic programming (QP) problem. Because efficient solvers exist for both LP and QP problems, we can solve the approximated problems more efficiently than solving the original problems directly. Therefore, we propose to solve the original (**P2**) or (**P3**) problem via sequential programming, either through LP or QP in the following.

For now, let us assume that we know how to compute the first- and second-order sensitivities of the objective function f with respect to changing variables, which will be discussed in Section 4.3. Therefore, we can easily obtain the linear and quadratic approximations of the objective function. For example, for the objective function in problem (**P3**), the changing variables are all Δw_i. Therefore, we have the following linear and quadratic approximations for the objective function

$$f_{lp} \approx f_0 + \sum_{i=1}^{M} \frac{\partial f}{\partial w_i} \Delta w_i, \tag{35}$$

$$f_{qp} \approx f_0 + \sum_{i=1}^{M} \frac{\partial f}{\partial w_i} \Delta w_i + \sum_{k=1}^{M} \sum_{j=1}^{M} \frac{\partial^2 f}{\partial w_i \partial w_j} \Delta w_i \Delta w_j, \tag{36}$$

where f_0 is the current value of the objective function, and $\frac{\partial f}{\partial w_i}$ and $\frac{\partial^2 f}{\partial w_i \partial w_j}$ are the first- and second-order sensitivities of f, respectively.

Apparently, (35) is a linear function of Δw_i, while (36) is a quadratic function of changing variables Δw_i. By replacing (30) with (35), we obtain an approximated LP formulation for (**P3**). Or by replacing (30) with (36), we obtain an approximated QP formulation for (**P3**). Both LP and QP can be solved efficiently.

A high-level description of the sequential programming algorithm to solve either problem (**P2**) or (**P3**) is shown in Algorithm 2, where *iter2* is the current iteration number, *ITER2* is the maximum iteration bound. The iterations stop when the change of objective function $|\Delta f|$ is smaller than ϵ_2, which is dynamically adjusted according to the iteration number *iter* in the outer-loop of Algorithm 1. We employ an exponential decreasing function to adjust ϵ_2 in this work. The idea is that when the out-loop iteration is small (or we are far from the optimal solution), we can have an early termination of the inner-loop optimization procedure as shown in Algorithm 2 early. But when the outer-loop iteration becomes large enough (or we are close to the optimal solution), we should spend more time in each inner-loop optimization to find a better global optimal solution. Parameter η is used to control the efforts that we should spend in the inner-loop's optimization.

The convergence for Algorithm 2 is guaranteed by noting that though the iterations the objective function is monotonically decreasing, and thus the loop must exit when a local or global minimum/maximum is obtained.

Algorithm 2 Sequential programming (sLP or sQP) for solving (**P2**) and (**P3**).

INPUT: *iter*, w_i, r_i, W;
OUTPUT: updated w_i for (**P3**) or r_i for (**P2**);
ϵ_2 = exp(-η·iter);
for *iter*2=0; $|\Delta f| \leq \epsilon_2$ or *iter*2 $\leq$ $ITER2$; *iter*2++ **do**
  Compute the first- (and second-order) sensitivities of f;
  Formulate (**P2**) or (**P3**) as an LP (or QP) problem;
  Call LP (or QP) solver to solve the above problem;
  Compute objective function with new w_i (**P2**) or r_i (**P3**);
end for

Even though we can solve problem (**P2**) and (**P3**) via either sequential LP or QP programming (sLP or sQP) as shown in Algorithm 2, there are several differences between these two approaches. If we approximate the problem as an sLP, at each optimization iteration we can find a guaranteed local optimal solution because of the convexity of LP formulation. But because of the relatively poor first-order approximation quality, we may not find a good final solution at the end. In contrast, if we approximate the problem as an sQP, the approximation quality is improved because of the use of higher-order sensitivity information. And each optimization iteration works more like a Newton step for solving convex optimization problems. Thus we may find a better final solution compared to the first-order LP approximation. Our experimental results will show that, in practice, sQP solutions are indeed better than sLP's for large test cases. Of course we notice that the QP formulation at each iteration is not necessarily convex, as we cannot prove that the Hessian of (36) is always positive semidefinite. In practice, however, we find that the solution quality from sQP is high.

For practical use, the number of variables for the sLP or sQP can be huge. Luckily, promising research results have been presented which show that by fully utilizing partitioning, parallel computing and efficient data compression, problems with millions of variables and thousands of constraints can be solved within several hundred seconds (Andersen & Anderson, 1998; Karypis et al., 1994).

4.3 Sensitivity computation

To solve (**P2**) and (**P3**) via sLP or sQP, we need to compute the sensitivities of the objective function f with respect to the design variables, i.e., either w_i or r_i. Because this computation is similar for both (**P2**) and (**P3**), we will focus our discussion on (**P3**) in the following.

The first- and second-order sensitivities of the objective function f of problem (**P3**) are defined as

$$\frac{\partial f}{\partial w_i} = -\sum_{i=1}^{p} \int_{\Omega_i} \frac{\partial y_i}{\partial w_i} dt = -\sum_{i=1}^{p} \int_{\Omega_i} L_{0i}^{T} \frac{\partial x}{\partial w_i} dt, \tag{37}$$

$$\frac{\partial^2 f}{\partial w_i \partial w_j} = -\sum_{i=1}^{p} \int_{\Omega_i} \frac{\partial^2 y_i}{\partial w_i \partial w_j} dt = -\sum_{i=1}^{p} \int_{\Omega_i} L_{0i}^{T} \frac{\partial^2 x}{\partial w_i \partial w_j} dt. \tag{38}$$

For simplicity of presentation, we have loosely applied the derivative notation on a vector for component-wise derivative.

To compute the sensitivity of f w.r.t. w_i, all we need to know is the sensitivity of the state vector x with respect to w_i. We use Taylor expansion to express x as follows

$$x = x_0 + \sum_{i=1}^{M} \alpha_i \Delta w_i + \sum_{i=1}^{M} \sum_{j=i}^{M} \beta_{ij} \cdot \Delta w_i \Delta w_j + \ldots, \tag{39}$$

where α_i is the first-order sensitivity of x w.r.t. random variable w_i, and β_{ij} is the second-order sensitivity of x with respect to random variable w_i and w_j. In other words, we have

$$\frac{\partial x}{\partial w_i} = \alpha_i, \quad \frac{\partial^2 x}{\partial w_i \partial w_j} = \beta_{ij}. \tag{40}$$

To compute these sensitivities, we recognize that x also satisfies the differential equation given by the parameterized MNA formulation (25). By Laplace transformation, we re-write (2) as follows

$$(G + \sum_{i=1}^{M} \Delta w_i \cdot G_{w,i})x + s(C + \sum_{i=1}^{M} \Delta w_i \cdot C_{w,i})x = Bu. \tag{41}$$

By plugging (39) into (41), we obtain terms of Δw_i with different orders. By equating the zero-order terms of Δw_i from both left and right hand sides in (41), we obtain a set of equations as follows

$$(G + sC)x_0 = Bu. \tag{42}$$

By equating the first-order terms of Δw_i, we obtain sets of equations as follows for all $1 \leq i \leq M$

$$(G + sC)\alpha_i = -(G_{w,i} + sC_{w,i})x_0. \tag{43}$$

Similarly, by equating the second-order terms of $\Delta w_i \Delta w_j$, we obtain another sets of equations as follows for all $1 \leq i \leq M$

$$(G + sC)\beta_{ij} = -(G_{w,i} + sC_{w,i})\alpha_j - (G_{w,j} + sC_{w,j})\alpha_i \tag{44}$$

By applying the Backward Euler integration formula and assuming the time step as h, we can re-write (42) and (43) as follows

$$(G + \frac{C}{h})x_0(t+h) = Bu(t+h) + x_0(t)\frac{C}{h}, \tag{45}$$

$$\begin{aligned}(G + \frac{C}{h})\alpha_i(t+h) &= -(G_{w,i} + \frac{C_{w,i}}{h})x_0(t+h) \\ &+ \frac{x_0(t)C_{w,i} + \alpha_i(t)C}{h},\end{aligned} \tag{46}$$

$$\begin{aligned}(G + \frac{C}{h})\beta_{ij}(t+h) &= -(G_{w,i} + \frac{C_{w,i}}{h})\alpha_j(t+h) \\ &-(G_{w,j} + \frac{C_{w,j}}{h})\alpha_i(t+h) \\ &+ \frac{\alpha_j(t)C_{w,i} + \alpha_i(t)C_{w,j} + \beta_{ij}(t)C}{h}.\end{aligned} \tag{47}$$

Because all equations in (45) and (46) share the same left-hand side matrix, $(G + C/h)$, we only need to perform LU-factorization once, and then reuse the same factorization to solve for x_0, α_i and β_{ij} sequentially at each time step. This computation is efficient because it only involves some matrix-vector multiplications, and backward and forward substitutions.
The integral interval Ω_i for port i is decided by x_0. Once x_0 is solved, we have $y = L_0^T x_0$, and then the corresponding interval can be decided from (5). By doing so we have assumed that the incremental δw_i is relatively small in each step and will not significantly influence the integral interval. In summary, we can compute the first and second-order sensitivities of the objective function f of problem (**P3**) by following the Algorithm 3.

5. Experimental results

In this section, we present experiments using four industrial P/G network designs. For each benchmark, we randomly select 20% of total nodes as candidate nodes for decap insertion, i.e., $M = 20\%N$. For fair comparison, when comparing the runtime and noise, the same white space is used up for different methods. We run experiments on a LINUX workstation with Pentium IV 2.66G CPU and 1G RAM. We partition the circuits according to the method in (Kouroussis et al., 2005). We use the package FASTICA (Hyvarinen & Oja,

Algorithm 3 Sensitivity computation for (**P3**).

```
INPUT: w_i, r_k, h, T;
OUTPUT: f, α_i and β_ij;
factorization: LU factorize G + C/h;
for t = 0; t + h ≤ T; t = t + h do
  Solve (45) for x_0(t + h);
end for
for i = 1; i ≤ p; i + + do
  Use (5) to compute Ω_i from y(t) = L_0^T x_0(t);
end for
for t = 0; t + h ≤ T; t = t + h do
  Solve (46) for α_i(t + h);
  Solve ∂f/∂w_i from (37);
end for
for t = 0; t + h ≤ T; t = t + h do
  for 1 ≤ i ≤ K do
    for 1 ≤ j ≤ K do
      Solve (47) for β_ij(t + h);
      Solve ∂²f/(∂w_i ∂w_j) from (38);
    end for
  end for
end for
```

1997) to perform ICA. Finally, we use MOSEK as the linear/quadratic programming solver (http://www.mosek.com, n.d.) and random walk based simulator (Qian et al., 2005) with detailed (not triangular) input current waveform to obtain the noise reported in this section.

5.1 Decap budgeting with operation variation

We compare three current models as shown in Table 1: maximum current peaks at all ports[3] (model 1), stochastic model (model 2) with logic-induced correlation only ($L = 1$), and stochastic model (model 3) with both logic-induced and temporal correlation. For temporal correlation, we always use $L = 4$ since all circuits tested take at most four clock cycles to complete any one instruction. Table 1 reports the noise and runtime for the four benchmarks with different number of nodes at the same decap area. Compared with the baseline model with maximum current peaks at all ports [4], the model considering temporal correlation reduces noise by up to 5×; and the model considering both temporal and logic-induced correlations reduces noise by up to 17× (see bold in Table 1). This is because the first two models cannot model the currents effectively and lead to inserting unnecessarily large decaps in some regions. As for the runtime, model 2 needs about 1.5× more time than model 1, while model 3 needs about 2.3× more. The runtime overhead is the price we have to pay in order to achieve better designs.

In Fig. 3, we plot the time-domain responses at one randomly selected port for two optimization iterations by alternatively solving the problem (**P3**) and (**P2**). The benchmark has 1284 nodes. The initial waveform is denoted by "A0:initial". After performing decap sizing once by solving problem (**P3**) with a fixed choice of random variables r_k, we obtain the

[3] We still use the detailed waveforms for the currents, except that the maximum values of those waveforms are always set to be the worst case values.

[4] We solve it by iteratively solving (**P3**) without altering to (**P2**).

Model 1	maximum current peaks at all ports
Model 2	stochastic model with logic-induced correlation
Model 3	Model 2 + temporal correlation

Node #	Port #	noise (V*s)			runtime (s)		
		model 1	model 2	model 3	model 1	model 2	model 3
1284	**426**	**6.33e-7**	**1.28e-7**	**4.10e-8**	**104.2**	**161.2**	**282.3**
10490	3398	5.21e-5	1.09e-5	4.80e-6	973.2	1430	2199
42280	13327	7.92e-4	5.38e-4	9.13e-5	2732	3823	5238
166380	42146	1.34e-2	5.37e-3	2.28e-3	3625	5798	7821
avg		1	1/3×	1/9×	1	1.50×	2.26×

Table 1. Noise, runtime and area comparison between the three models.

new waveform as denoted by "A1:(**P3**)". We then switch to solve problem (**P2**) by varying the values of those random variables r_k, but with fixed decap sizes w_i. We see that the waveform of the final worst-case voltage drop becomes worse compared to the deterministic solution; hence we obtain a new voltage drop waveform as denoted by "A2:(**P2**)". We then switch back to solve the decap sizing problem (**P3**) with fixed but newly updated choice of random variables r_k. At the end of this optimization, we arrive at a new voltage waveform as denoted by "A3:(**P3**)". Apparently, compared to "A1:(**P3**)", the new solution has smaller voltage drop. If we continue the same procedures by following the IAP algorithm given in Fig. 1, similar sequences of time domain voltage drop waveforms would repeat as we have shown in Fig. (3) until we converge to an optimal solution. Also, The voltage drop is reduced mostly in the first optimization iteration denoted as "A1:(**P3**)". Afterward, the voltage drop reduction is relatively small. This observation is in agreement with the common knowledge about any sensitivity-based optimization techniques. In this particular example, we find that the first two iterations reduces the noise by 51.4%.

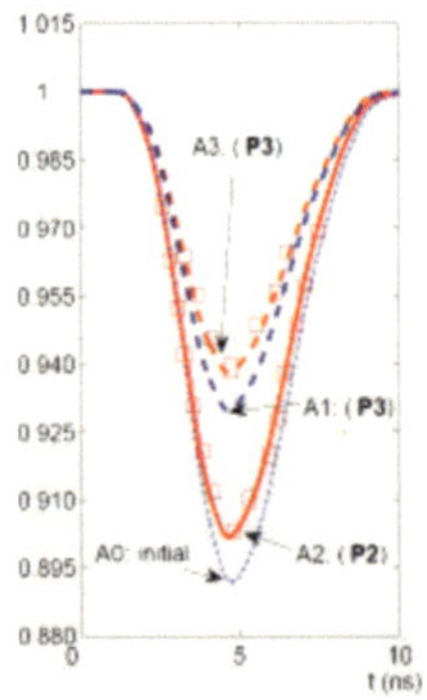

Fig. 3. Time domain waveforms at one port after sLP for different iterations.

5.2 L_{eff} variation aware decap budgeting

In the presence of process variation, we want to minimize the worst-case noise for L_{eff} variation. We solve this via the proposed IAP technique in Algorithm 1. We denote our L_{eff} variation aware approach as $sLP + L_{eff}$ and the counterpart as sLP. Before we quantitatively compare the two methods, we first use Fig. 4 to demonstrate the effectiveness of L_{eff} variation aware decap budgeting. We use the same circuit with 15% L_{eff} variation and perform Monte Carlo simulations with 14000 samples to obtain the noise histogram of the design from the sLP

Node #	Port #	sLP			$sLP + L_{eff}$		
		μ (V*s)	3σ (V*s)	RT (s)	μ (V*s)	3σ (V*s)	RT (s)
1284	426	9.28e-7	3.97e-7	184.2	6.14e-7	1.38e-7	332.8 (1.81×)
10490	3398	1.03e-4	4.79e-5	1121	7.22e-5	1.23e-5	3429 (3.06×)
42280	13327	2.29e-3	9.72e-4	2236	8.23e-4	1.01e-4	6924 (3.10×)
166380	**42146**	**2.06e-2**	**9.91e-3**	**3824**	**5.31e-3**	**8.32e-4**	**11224** (2.93×)
avg		1	1	1	0.50×	0.20×	2.73×

Table 2. The mean value μ, 3σ variance of the noise and runtime (RT) comparison between $sLP + L_{eff}$ and sLP with 10% intra-die L_{eff} variation.

and $sLP + L_{eff}$, respectively. From the figure we can see that the noise from $sLP + L_{eff}$ (mean value 8.4×10^{-9} V*s, 3σ value 0.4×10^{-9} V*s) is much smaller than that from sLP (mean value 9.7×10^{-9} V*s, 3σ value 1.9×10^{-9} V*s), although both have the same decap area constraints.

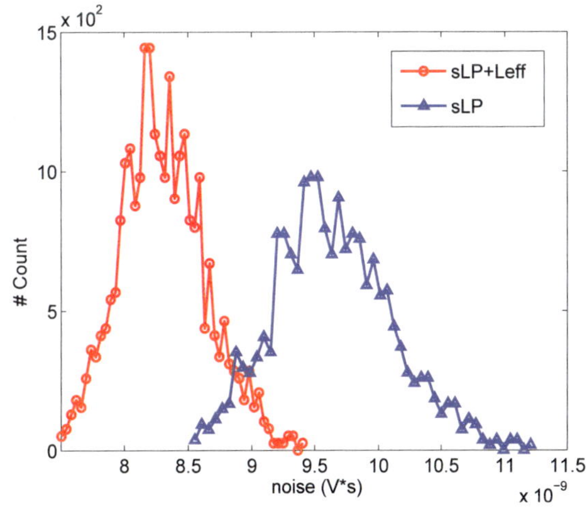

Fig. 4. The noise distribution for the an industry power mesh with decap budgeting using sLP and $sLP + Leff$.

Next we compare the mean value μ and 3σ value of the noise distribution with 10% L_{eff} variation based on Monte Carlo simulation with 10,000 runs, and the results are reported in Table 2. Compared with using deterministic L_{eff}, considering L_{eff} variation reduces the mean noise by up to 4× and 3σ noise by up to 13× (see bold in Table 2), when both applying the current model with temporal and logic-induced correlations. As for the runtime between sLP and $sLP + L_{eff}$, the latter needs about 2.7× more time than the former on average.

5.3 Comparison between sLP and sQP

We study the difference between our sLP and sQP approaches in terms of noise and runtime for five benchmarks with different number of nodes in Table 3 for deterministic case. The same white space are used up for both methods. An interesting observation from Table3 is that sQP almost always obtain smaller noise than sLP, particularly for those large test cases, with longer runtime. This is expected, as higher-order sensitivities are used in sQP to guide the optimization. In terms of noise, sQP is much better than sLP for large test cases and slightly worse for the small test case. In terms of runtime, however, sLP is on average 3.25× faster than sQP. Similar experimental results are presented in Table 4 in the presence of Leff variation. We can see that not only the mean noise is reduced by 19%, the 3σ valude is also

Node	Port	sLP		sQP	
#	#	noise (V*s)	time (s)	noise (V*s)	time (s)
128	41	1.83e-9	2.4	1.85e-9 (1.01×)	8.3 (3.46×)
512	174	1.83e-9	23.8	1.81e-9 (0.99×)	66.0 (2.77×)
1280	477	1.85e-9	151	1.79e-9 (0.97×)	497 (3.29×)
5120	1731	1.91e-8	982	1.30e-8 (0.68×)	3779 (3.85×)
12800	3324	1.94e-4	1960	0.81e-4 (0.42×)	5658 (2.89×)
Avg		1	1	0.81×	3.25×

Table 3. Noise and runtime comparison between sLP and sQP.

Node #	Port #	$sLP + L_{eff}$			$sQP + L_{eff}$		
		μ (V*s)	3σ (V*s)	RT (s)	μ (V*s)	3σ (V*s)	RT (s)
1284	426	6.14e-7	1.38e-7	332.8)	4.98e-7	7.70e-8	985.0 (2.96×)
10490	3398	7.22e-5	1.23e-5	3429)	5.91e-5	5.28e-5	11932.9 (3.48×)
42280	13327	8.23e-4	1.01e-4	6924)	6.77e-4	5.93e-5	18348.6 (2.65×)
166380	**42146**	**5.31e-3**	**8.32e-4**	**11224**	**4.11e-3**	**4.71e-4**	**36365.8** (3.24×)
avg		1	1	1	0.81×	0.54×	3.08×

Table 4. The mean value μ, 3σ variance of the noise and runtime (RT) comparison between $sLP + L_{eff}$ and $sQP + L_{eff}$ with 10% intra-die L_{eff} variation.

reduced by 46%. We believe both sLP and sQP are of practical value, and they provide good trade-off between runtime efficiency and design quality. Note that no existing approach in the literature leverages them for decap budgeting. Our sLP/sQP solution is the first of the kind.

6. Conclusions and discussions

This chapter studied a variation-aware decoupling capacitance (decap) budgeting problem for reliable power network design. The major contributions of this work are two-fold: (1) a novel method to solve the the deterministic decap budgeting problem efficiently; and (2) a new variation-aware decap budgeting problem that takes into account process variation effects. Experimental results show that compared to existing industrial quality decap budgeting techniques as proposed in the literature, we achieve 13× speed-up while achieving similar design quality. It also serves as an example for general stochastic optimization.

7. References

Agarwal, K. & Nassif, S. (2007). Characterizing Process Variation in Nanometer CMOS, *IEEE/ACM DAC*.

Andersen, E. D. & Anderson, K. D. (1998). A parallel interior-point algorithm for linear programming on a shared memory machine, *CORE Discussion Paper 9808*.

Bhardwaj, S. & Vrudhula, S. B. K. (2005). Leakage Minimization of Nano-scale Circuits in the Presence of Systematic and Random Variations, *IEEE/ACM DAC*.

Cao, Y. & Clark, L. T. (2005). Mapping statisitical process variations toward circuit performance variability: An analytical modeling approach, *IEEE/ACM DAC*.

Chang, H. & Sapatnekar, S. S. (2003). Statistical timing analysis considering spatial correlations using a single PERT-like traversal, *IEEE/ACM ICCAD*, pp. 621 – 625.

Davoodi, A. & Srivastava, A. (2006). ąśVariability-Driven Gate Sizin for Binning Yield Optimization, *IEEE/ACM DAC*.

Ferzli, I. A. & Najm, F. N. (2003). Statistical verification of power grids considering process-induced leakage current variations, *IEEE/ACM ICCAD*.

Fu, J., Luo, Z., Hong, X., Cai, Y., Tan, S.-D. & Pan, Z. (2004). A fast decoupling capacitor budgeting algorithm for robust on-chip power delivery, *Proc. Asia South Pacific Design Automation Conf. (ASPDAC)*, pp. 505–510.

Ghanta, P., Vrudhula, S., Panda, R. & Wang, J. (2005). Stochastic power grid analysis considering process variations, *Proc. European Design and Test Conf. (DATE)*, Vol. 2, pp. 964–969.

He, L., Kahng, A., Tam, K. H. & Xiong, J. (2007). Simultaneous Buffer Insertion and Wire Sizing Considering Systematic CMP Variation and Random Leff Variation, *IEEE Trans. on CAD* .

http://www.mosek.com (n.d.).

Hyvarinen, A., Karhunen, J. & Oja, E. (2001). *Independent Component Analysis*, John Wiley & Sons.

Hyvarinen, A. & Oja, E. (1997). A Fast Fixed-Point Algorithm for Independent Component Analysis, *Neural Computation* .

Karypis, G., Gupta, A. & Kumar, V. (1994). A Parallel Formulation of Interior Point Algorithms, *ACM/IEEE Conference on High Performance Networking and Computing*.

Kouroussis, D., Ferzli, I. A. & Najm, F. N. (2005). Incremental partitioning-based vectorless power grid verification, *IEEE/ACM ICCAD*.

Li, H., Qi, Z., Tan, S. X.-D., Wu, L., Cai, Y. & Hong, X. (2005). Partitioning-based approach to fast on-chip decap budgeting and minimization, *IEEE/ACM DAC*, pp. 170–175.

Mani, M., Devgan, A. & Orshansky, M. (2005). An Efficient Algorithm for Statistical Minimization of Total Power under Timing Yield Constraints, *IEEE/ACM DAC*.

Mani, M., Singh, A. & Orshansky, M. (2006). Joint Design-Time and Post-Silicon Minimization of Parametric Yield Loss using Adjustable Robust Optimization, *IEEE/ACM ICCAD*.

Orshansky, M., Milor, L., Chen, P., Keutzer, K. & Hu, C. (2002). Impact of Spatial Intrachip Gate Length Variability on the Performance of High-speed Digital Circuits, *IEEE Trans. on CAD* .

Pant, S., Blaauw, D., Zolotov, V., Sundareswaran, S. & Panda, R. (2004). A stochastic approach to power grid analysis, *IEEE/ACM DAC*, pp. 171–176.

Pant, S., D.Blaauw, Zolotov, V., S.Sundareswaran & Panda, R. (2004). A stochastic approach to power grid analysis, *IEEE/ACM DAC*.

Qian, H., Nassif, S. R. & Sapatnekar, S. S. (2005). Power Grid Analysis Using Random Walks, *IEEE Trans. on CAD* .

Shi, Y., Xiong, J., Liu, C. C. & He, L. (2007). Efficient Decoupling Capacitance Budgeting Considering Operation and Process Variations, *IEEE/ACM ICCAD*.

Sinha, D., Shenoy, N. V. & Zhou, H. (2005). Statistical Gate Sizing for Timing Yield Optimization, *IEEE/ACM ICCAD*.

Su, H., Sapatnekar, S. S. & Nassif, S. R. (2003). Optimal decoupling capacitor sizing and placement for standard-cell layout designs, *IEEE Trans. on CAD* **22**: 428–436.

Visweswariah, C., Haring, R. A. & Conn, A. R. (2000). Noise Consierations in Circuit Optimization, *IEEE Trans. on CAD* .

Visweswariah, C., Ravindran, K., Kalafala, K., Walker, S. & Narayan, S. (2004). First-order incremental block-based statistical timing analysis, *IEEE/ACM DAC*.

Zhao, M., Panda, R., Sundareswaran, S., Yan, S. & Fu, Y. (2006). A fast on-chip decoupling capacitance budgeting algorithm using macromodeling and linear programming, *IEEE/ACM DAC*.

Zheng, H., Krauter, B. & Pileggi, L. (2003). On-Package Decoupling Optimization with Package Macromodels, *Proc. IEEE Custom Integrated Circuits Conference (CICC)*.

Part 3

See the Optimal for the Uncertain: A Collection of Methods

9

Joint State and Parameter Estimation in Particle Filtering and Stochastic Optimization

Xiaojun Yang and Keyi Xing
Chang' an University
P. R. China

1. Introduction

Dynamic state-space models are useful for describing data in many different areas, such as engineering, finance mathematics, environmental data, and physical science. An important task when analyzing data by state-space models is estimation of the underlying state process based on measurements from the observation process. Bayesian filtering represents a solution of considerable importance for this type of problem definition as demonstrated by many existing algorithms based on the Kalman filter and particle filtering (PF) (Arulampalam 2002, Doucet et al. 2001, Yang et al. 2006). The PF has been extensively studied in the situation where the unknown attributes are time-varying dynamic states. Although PF have been successful in many applications, a main problem with it is how to handle the presence of the unknown static parameters, especially in models with realistically large numbers of fixed parameters.
The estimation of both the dynamic state and static parameters is commonly known in literatures as the dual estimation. Numerous papers have been written on the construction of estimation algorithms based on Markov chain Monte Carlo (MCMC) (Spall 2003). Although such methods may be effective for offline estimation, they are not suitable for online estimation because the MCMC algorithm needs to be restart at each time point. In engineering, a common trick to problem is to include the parameters as part of the state space vector. Berzuini et al. (Berzuini et al. 1997) put this approach into Bayesian estimation. However, the non-dynamics in the parameters cause the degeneracy of the algorithm. Jane and West (Jane & Mike 2001) introduced diversity in the particles by Kernel method, which is similar to replace the original static parameter with an alternative dynamic model. Polson et al (Polson & Stroud 2008) proposed a sequential parameter learning and filtering based on approximating the target posterior by a mixture of fixed lag smoothing distributions. Lee and Chia (Lee & Chia 2002) combined the particle filtering and MCMC to achieve an estimation algorithm in which the measurements are processed sequentially by particle filtering. When the degeneration occurs, the particles are rejuvenated by MCMC. Storvik (Storvic 2002) considered models with sufficient statistics for the parameters and applied particle filters to an augmented vector of states and sufficient statistics. Djuric et al (Djuric & Miguez 2002) proposed an alternative approach for a certain class of state-space model, which suppose that the marginal distribution of parameter can be analytically tractable. However, both algorithms suffer from an accumulation of error over times, albeit more slowly, leading to instability eventually. On the other hand, Andrieu et al (Andrieu et al.

2003, 2004, 2005, Yang et al. 2008) considered maximum likelihood parameter point estimation based on gradient. But in reality the graduate computation is intractable for complex nonlinear system function.

In this chapter, we propose a new algorithm that preserves the static nature of the unknown parameters. The maximum likelihood parameter estimation is performed based on particle filtering and an effective stochastic approximation gradient algorithm is used to optimize cost function. The estimation of static parameters and dynamic state variables is performed simultaneously.

2. Problem formulation

The state-space models have the form

$$\begin{aligned} x_t &\sim p(x_t | x_{t-1}, \theta) \\ y_t &\sim p(y_t | x_t, \theta) \end{aligned} \tag{1}$$

where x_t is unobserved state vector at time t, y_t is an observation at time t, $\theta \in R^m$ is m dimensional unknown static parameters vector, and $p(\cdot|\cdot)$ is generic conditional distribution. Optimal filtering consists of estimating recursively in time the sequence of posterior densities function (PDF) $p(x_t | y_{1:t})$ which summarizes all the information about the system states x_t as given by the collection of observations $y_{1:t} = (y_1, \cdots, y_t)$. For non-linear and non-Gaussian dynamic models, the particle filtering can achieve approximated estimation of PDF based on Monte Carlo simulation. Although particle filtering has been successful in many simulation experiments and in analysis of real data, a main problem with it is how to handle the presence of unknown static parameters. In this paper, we present a method referred to as point estimation, i.e. we do not aim to estimating the PDF of θ. We focus rather on the estimation of θ directly by maximum-likelihood (ML) principle. The dynamic state is estimated by particle filtering and static parameter is estimated by recursive ML method online.

Given a set of measurements $y_{0:t}$, the estimation of ML requires maximization of likelihood with respect to parameter θ. Firstly, the cost function is presented, and the likelihood of measurements $y_{0:t}$ is given by

$$\begin{aligned} p(y_{0:t}, \theta) &= p(y_t | y_{0:t-1}, \theta) p(y_{0:t-1}, \theta) \\ &= p(y_0, \theta) \prod_{k=1}^{t} p(y_k | y_{0:k-1}, \theta) \end{aligned} \tag{2}$$

where

$$\begin{aligned} p(y_k | y_{0:k-1}, \theta) &= \int p(y_k | x_k, \theta) p(x_k | y_{0:k-1}, \theta) dx_k \\ &= \int p(y_k | x_{k-1}, \theta) p(x_{k-1} | y_{0:k-1}, \theta) dx_{k-1} \end{aligned}$$

$$p(y_0, \theta) = \int p(y_0 | x_0, \theta) p(x_0) dx_0$$

In practice, one uses the log-likelihood which is numerically better behaved and satisfies

$$\begin{aligned} l(y_{0:t},\theta) &= \log p(y_{0:t},\theta) \\ &= \log p(y_0,\theta) + \sum_{k=1}^{t} \log p(y_k | y_{0:k-1},\theta) \end{aligned} \tag{3}$$

To simplify the computation, the cost function is chosen as predicted likelihood, i.e.

$$f(\theta) = p(y_t | y_{0:t-1},\theta) = \int p(y_t | x_t,\theta) p(x_t | y_{0:t-1},\theta) dx_t \tag{4}$$

However, except in a few simple cases, it is impossible to compute the optimal filter and the likelihood in closed-form, the numerical approximation schemes are required.

The problem of maximizing the cost function can be translated into finding the zeros of the gradient $\nabla f(\theta)$. A recursion procedure to estimate θ such that $\nabla f(\theta) = 0$ proceeds as follows

$$\theta_t = \theta_{t-1} + \gamma_t \hat{\nabla} f(\theta_{t-1}) \tag{5}$$

where $\hat{\nabla} f(\theta_{t-1})$ is the estimation of gradient estimated at the point θ_{t-1} and $\{\gamma_t > 0\}$ denotes a sequence of decreasing step-size. One selects a step-size sequence satisfying $\gamma_t \to 0$, $\sum_{t=1}^{\infty} \gamma_t = \infty$. Under appropriate conditions, the iteration in (5) will converge to the true value of θ in some stochastic sense. The essential part of (5) is how to obtain the gradient estimate, however, it is impossible to compute the closed-form gradient and we must resort to the numerical approximation.

The particle filtering (Gordon 1993, Doucet et al. 2001, Yang et al. 2006) is based on importance sampling where x_t is simulated sequentially from some importance distribution $q(x_t | y_{1:t})$, and the whole trajectory $x_{1:t}$ is given importance weight

$$\omega_t = {p(x_t | y_{1:t})} \Big/ {q(x_t | y_{1:t})}$$

N such sequences are simulated parallel, giving a weighted particle set $(x_t^{(i)}, \omega_t^{(i)}), i = 1, \cdots, N$ at each time point t. The problem with the particle filtering is the degeneracy phenomenon, where the variance of the importance weights can only increase over time, making the estimate unstable (Kong et al. 1994). A common trick to avoid this is to re sample from particle set with probabilities proportional to the importance weight (Gordon et al. 1993). The convergence result is surveyed in (Crisan & Doucet 2002), where the error in the approximate distribution is stable with increasing the number of particles to infinity. Given a set of weighted particle $(x_{t-1}^{(i)}, \omega_{t-1}^{(i)})$ which approximate $p(x_{t-1} | y_{0:t-1},\theta)$ and given the estimate of parameter θ_{t-1} at time $t-1$, the cost function can be approximated as follows

$$\hat{f}(\theta_{t-1}) = \hat{p}(y_t | y_{0:t},\theta_{t-1}) = \sum_{i=1}^{N} \omega_{t-1}^{(i)} p(y_t | \tilde{x}_t^{(i)},\theta_{t-1}) \tag{6}$$

where the particles $\tilde{x}_t^{(i)} \sim p(x_t | x_{t-1}^{(i)},\theta_{t-1})$ are obtained using a one-step ahead state evolution prediction.

Stochastic optimization techniques apply in the cases where a closed-form solution to the optimization problem of interest is not available and where the input information into optimization method may be contaminated with noise. One of the techniques that have attracted considerable recent attention for difficult multivariate problems is the simultaneous perturbation stochastic approximation (SPSA) method introduced by Spall (Spall 1987, 1998). SPSA is based on a highly efficient and easily implemented "simultaneous perturbation" approximation to the gradient. The SPSA technique requires all elements of θ to be varied randomly simultaneously to obtain two estimates of the cost function. Only two cost function measurements are required regardless of the dimension of the parameters be optimized. The SPSA has proven to be an effective and easy implemented algorithm and success among other finite difference methods with reduced number of estimates required for convergence (Chan et al. 2003, Doucet & Tadic 2002, Andrieu et al. 2003).

A step-by-step guide to implementation of SPSA for stochastic optimization is presented in (Spall 1998). It is assumed that $f(\theta)$ is a differentiable function of θ and that the minimum point of θ corresponding to a zero point of the gradient. In SPSA, the gradient estimate

$$\hat{\nabla} f(\theta_{t-1}) = (\hat{\nabla} f_1(\theta_{t-1}), \cdots, \hat{\nabla} f_m(\theta_{t-1}))$$

is given by

$$\hat{\nabla} f_j(\theta_{t-1}) = \frac{\hat{f}(\theta_{t-1} + c_t \Delta_t) - \hat{f}(\theta_{t-1} - c_t \Delta_t)}{2 c_t \Delta_{t,j}}$$

where c_t denotes a sequence of positive scalars such that $c_t \to 0$ and $\Delta_t = (\Delta_{t,1}, \Delta_{t,2}, \cdots, \Delta_{t,m})$ is a m-dimensional random perturbation vector. The choice of gain sequences is critical to the performance of SPSA. Careful selection of algorithm parameters a, c, A, α, r and gain sequences is required to ensure convergence. The γ_t and c_t generally take the form of $\gamma_t = a/(A+t+1)^{\alpha}$ and $c_t = c/(t+1)^{r}$. The practically effective values for α and r are 0.602 and 0.101 respectively. As a rule-of-thumb, it is effective to set c at a level approximately equal to the standard deviation of the measurement noise in $f(\theta)$. The values of a, A can be chosen together to ensure effective practical performance of the algorithm. Each components of Δ_t is usually generated from Bernoulli ± 1 distribution with probability of $\frac{1}{2}$ for each ± 1 independently.

In cases where the gradient has more than one zero point, then the algorithm may only converge to a local minimum, Spall further gives some modifications to the basic SPSA algorithm to allow it to search for the global solution among multiple local solutions[15].

3. Sampling algorithms for combined estimation of parameter and state

We present here how to incorporate maximum-likelihood algorithm within the particle filtering framework. To enhance the global convergence and Robust of the parameter estimate, for each state particle, i.e. a possible state trajectory, we produce a particle of parameter and resample correspondingly. The ultimate parameter estimate is produced by weighted sum of parameter particles. This process can alleviate the divergence of estimate of parameter. The algorithm proceeds as follows.

Step 1. Initialization:

For $i = 1,\cdots,N$, sample $x_0^{(i)} \sim p(x_0)$ and initial particles of parameters estimate $\theta_0^{(i)}$.

Assign initial important weights as $\omega_0^{(i)} = 1/N$.

The initial estimate of parameter is $\theta_0 = \sum_{i=1}^{N} \omega_0^{(i)} \theta_0^{(i)}$

Step 2. State sampling:

Given a set of weighted state and parameter particles $(x_{t-1}^{(i)}, \theta_{t-1}^{(i)}, \omega_{t-1}^{(i)})$, $i = 1,\cdots,N$ at time $t-1$, sample $\tilde{x}_t^{(i)} \sim p(x_t | x_{t-1}^{(i)}, \theta_{t-1}^{(i)})$ for $i = 1,\cdots,N$.

Step 3. Cost function evaluation:

For each parameter particle $\theta_{t-1}^{(i)}$, generate a m-dimensional simultaneous perturbation vector $\Delta_t^{(i)}$. Compute the perturbed parameter particle $(\theta_{t-1}^{(i)} + c_t \Delta_t^{(i)})$ and $(\theta_{t-1}^{(i)} - c_t \Delta_t^{(i)})$.

For $i = 1,\cdots,N$,

Sample $\tilde{x}^{(i)+} \sim p(x_t | x_{t-1}^{(i)}, \theta_{t-1}^{(i)} + c_t \Delta_t^{(i)})$ and compute the likelihood $p(y_t | \tilde{x}^{(i)+}, \theta_{t-1}^{(i)} + c_t \Delta_t^{(i)})$.

Sample $\tilde{x}^{(i)-} \sim p(x_t | x_{t-1}^{(i)}, \theta_{t-1}^{(i)} - c_t \Delta_t^{(i)})$

Compute the likelihood $p(y_t | \tilde{x}^{(i)-}, \theta_{t-1}^{(i)} - c_t \Delta_t^{(i)})$

Evaluate cost function

$$\hat{f}(\theta_{t-1}^{(i)} + c_t \Delta_t^{(i)}) = p(y_t | \tilde{x}^{(i)+}, \theta_{t-1}^{(i)} + c_t \Delta_t^{(i)})$$

$$\hat{f}(\theta_{t-1}^{(i)} - c_t \Delta_t^{(i)}) = p(y_t | \tilde{x}^{(i)-}, \theta_{t-1}^{(i)} - c_t \Delta_t^{(i)})$$

Step 4. Gradient approximation:

For each parameter particle, the corresponding gradient

$$\hat{\nabla} f(\theta_{t-1}^{(i)}) = (\hat{\nabla} f_1(\theta_{t-1}^{(i)}),\cdots,\hat{\nabla} f_m(\theta_{t-1}^{(i)}))$$

where the components of gradient

$$\hat{\nabla} f_j(\theta_{t-1}^{(i)}) = \frac{\hat{f}(\theta_{t-1}^{(i)} + c_t \Delta_t^{(i)}) - \hat{f}(\theta_{t-1}^{(i)} - c_t \Delta_t^{(i)})}{2 c_t \Delta_{t,j}^{(i)}},$$

and $\Delta_{t,j}^{(i)}$ denote the *j*-th component of $\Delta_t^{(i)}$.

Step 5. Parameter update:

For each parameter particle $\theta_t^{(i)} = \theta_{t-1}^{(i)} + \gamma_t \hat{\nabla} f(\theta_{t-1}^{(i)})$

Step 6. Re-sampling:

For each particle $(\tilde{x}_t^{(i)}, \theta_t^{(i)})$, compute the normalized importance weights as $\tilde{\omega}_t^{(i)} \propto \omega_{t-1}^{(i)} p(y_t | \tilde{x}_t^{(i)}, \theta_t^{(i)})$ at time t.

Multiply/discard particles $(\tilde{x}_t^{(i)}, \theta_t^{(i)})$ with respect to high/low importance weights $\tilde{\omega}_t^{(i)}$.

Re-assign even importance weights $\omega_t^{(i)} = 1/N$.

Step 7. Output:

The obtained weighted particles
$(x_t^{(i)}, \theta_t^{(i)}, \omega_t^{(i)}), i = 1, \cdots, N$ approximate to $p(x_t | y_{0:t}, \theta)$.
The posterior density function of state is approximated as

$$p(x_t | y_{0:t}, \theta) = \sum_{i=1}^{N} \omega_t^{(i)} \delta(x_t - x_t^{(i)})$$

The estimate of state is $x_t = \sum_{i=1}^{N} \omega_t^{(i)} x_t^{(i)}$.

The estimate of parameter is $\theta_t = \sum_{i=1}^{N} \omega_t^{(i)} \theta_t^{(i)}$

$t = t + 1$. Return to step 2.

4. Simulation results

Here, we consider the following set of equations as an illustrative example which has been analyzed before in many publications (Gordon et al. 1993, Doucet et al. 2001, Chan et al. 2003).

$$x_t = \frac{x_{t-1}}{2} + \frac{\theta_1 x_{t-1}}{1 + x_{t-1}^2} + \theta_2 \cos(0.1t) + v_t$$

$$y_t = \frac{x_t^2}{20} + w_t$$

where $x_0 \sim N(0,5)$, v_t and w_t are zero mean Gaussian random variables with variances Q_t and R_t,respectively. We use $Q_t = 10$ and $R_t = 1$. θ_1 is unknown parameter with true value $\theta_1 = 25$ and $\theta_2 = 10$. This example is severely nonlinear, both in the system and the measurement equation. Note that the form of the likelihood $p(y_t | x_t)$ adds an interesting twist to the problem.

We present two algorithms to deal with the unknown parameters. The first algorithm, titled "Augmented State", includes the parameters as part of the state vector (x_t, θ_t) which proposed in paper (Jane & Mike 2001). θ is replaced by θ_t at time t, then add an independent, zero-mean normal increment increment to the parameter at each time. That is,

$$\theta_t = \theta_{t-1} + \zeta_t$$
$$\zeta_t \sim N(0, W_t)$$

For some specified variance matrix W_t. We use $W_t = 10$ in simulations. The second algorithm is our algorithm, titled "Adaptive estimate", which includes an on-line adaptive estimation of the parameters as proposed in this paper.

We perform 50 independent Monte Carlo runs with $N = 1000$ particles in each run. The initial values of parameters are selected randomly in interval $[0,1]$.

For reference, the true states for the exemplar run are shown in Fig.1 and the measurements in Fig.2. The sequences of parameter θ_1 and θ_2 estimate are illustrated in Fig.3 and Fig.4 respectively where the solid line with the label "adaptive estimation" indicates the estimate by our algorithm, the dashed line with the label "augmented state" indicates the estimate by the first algorithm. Fig.5 shows the RMSE of dynamic state x_t by particle filtering where dashed line represents RMSE with true value of parameters, the solid line represent RMSE with augmented state estimates of parameters by the first algorithm. Fig.6 shows the RMSE of particle filtering where dashed line represents RMSE with true value of parameters, the solid line represent RMSE with adaptive estimates of parameters by our algorithm. From the simulation results, it can be seen that the parameters converge to true values quickly by the proposed algorithm and RMSE of dynamic state with adaptive estimates of parameters diminish with time and approach to RMSE with the true values of parameters.

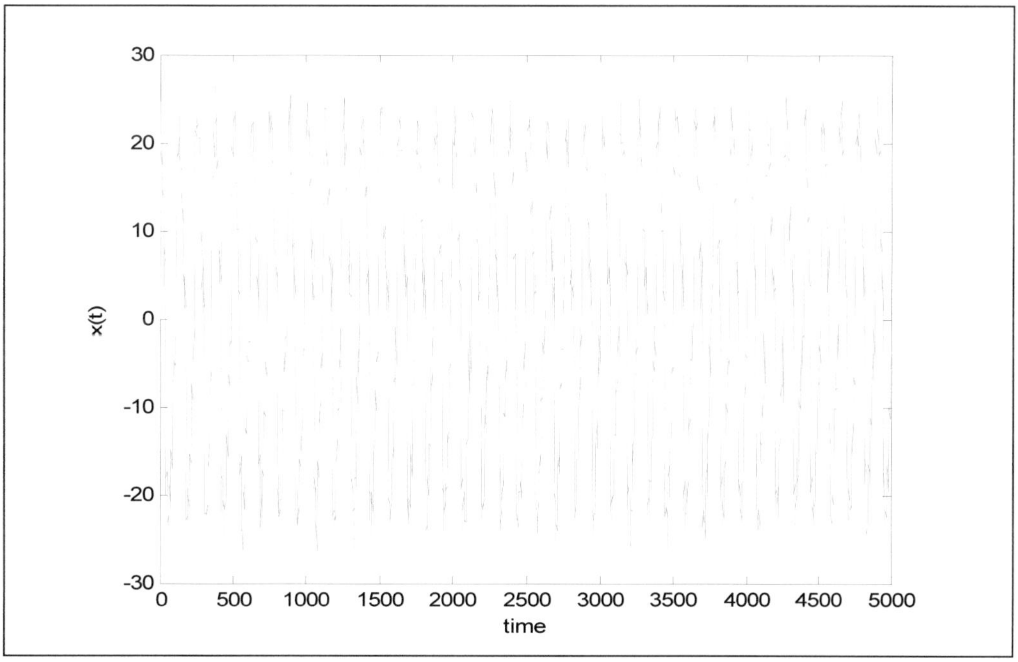

Fig. 1. Figure of the true values of state $x(t)$ as ma function of t for the exemplar run

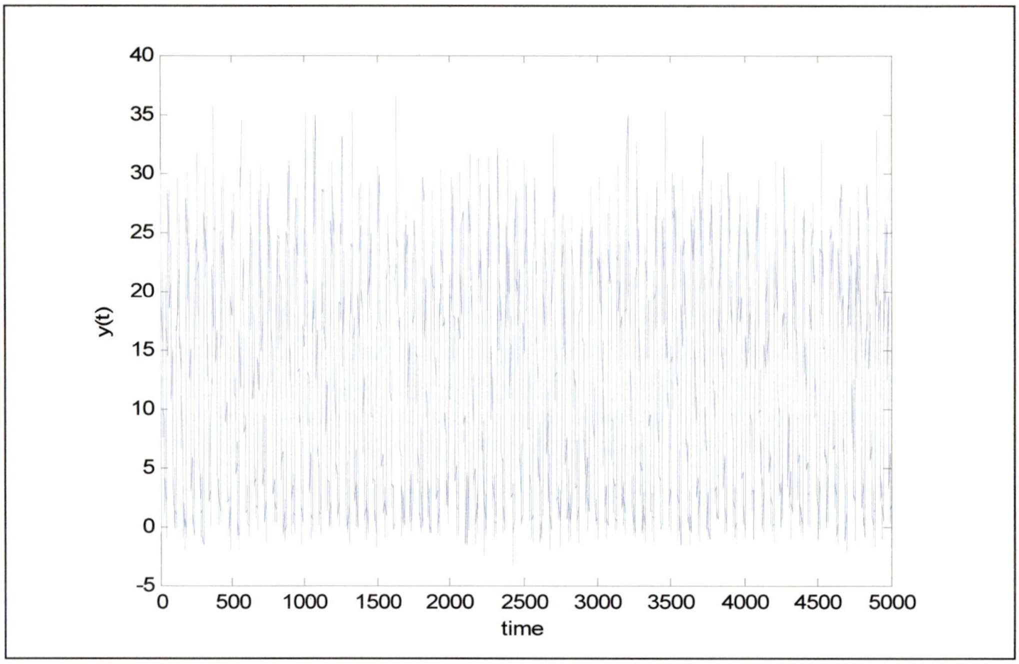

Fig. 2. Figure of the measurements $y(t)$ of the states $x(t)$ shown in Fig.1 for the same exemplar run

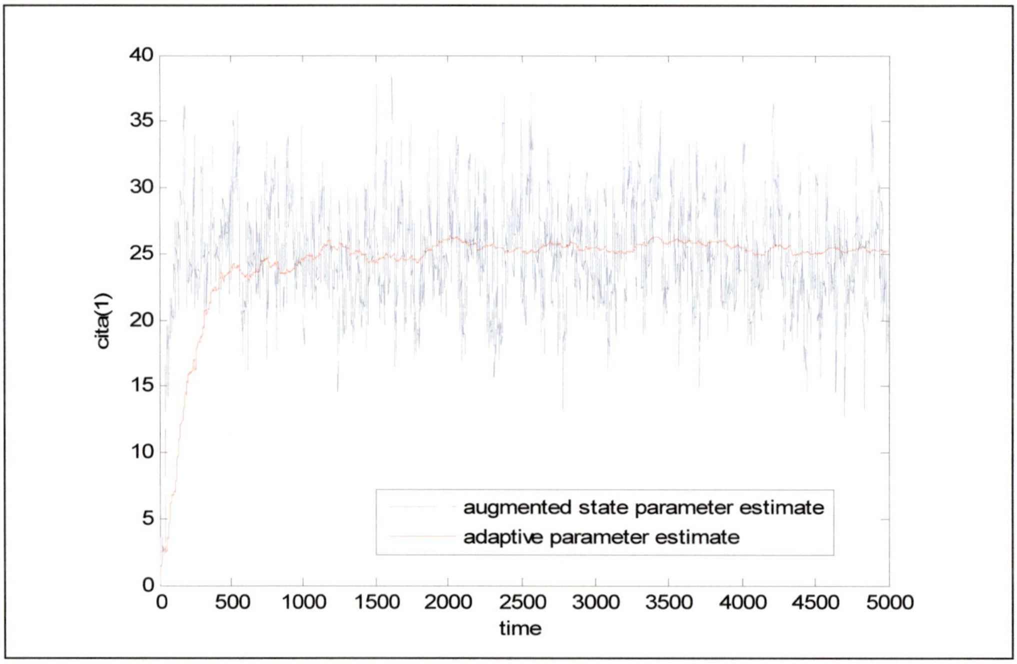

Fig. 3. Sequence of parameter θ_1 estimate over time

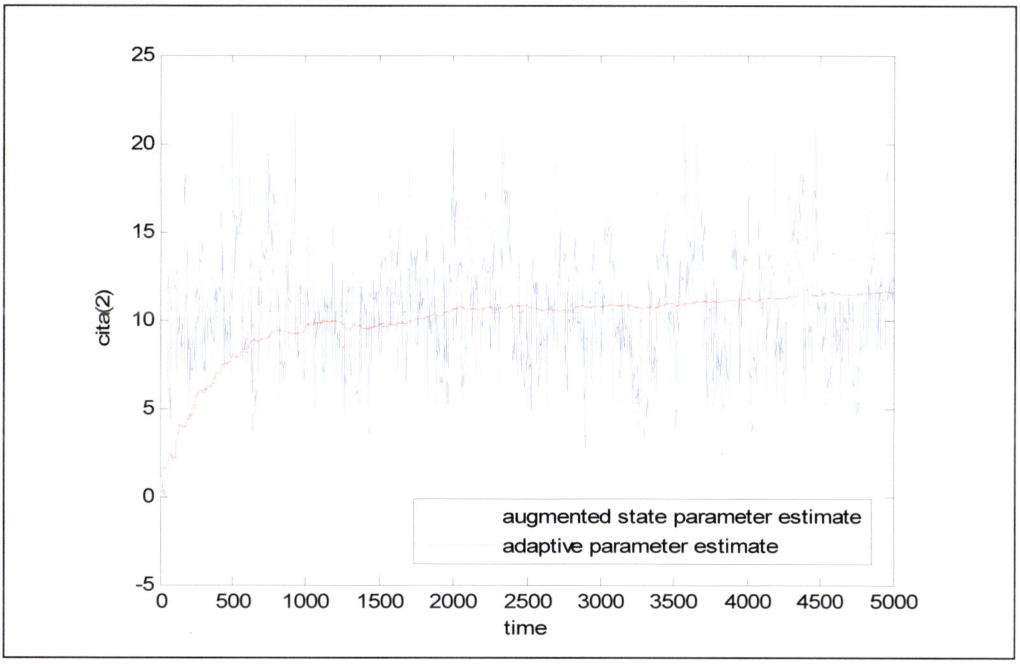

Fig. 4. Sequence of parameter θ_2 estimate over time

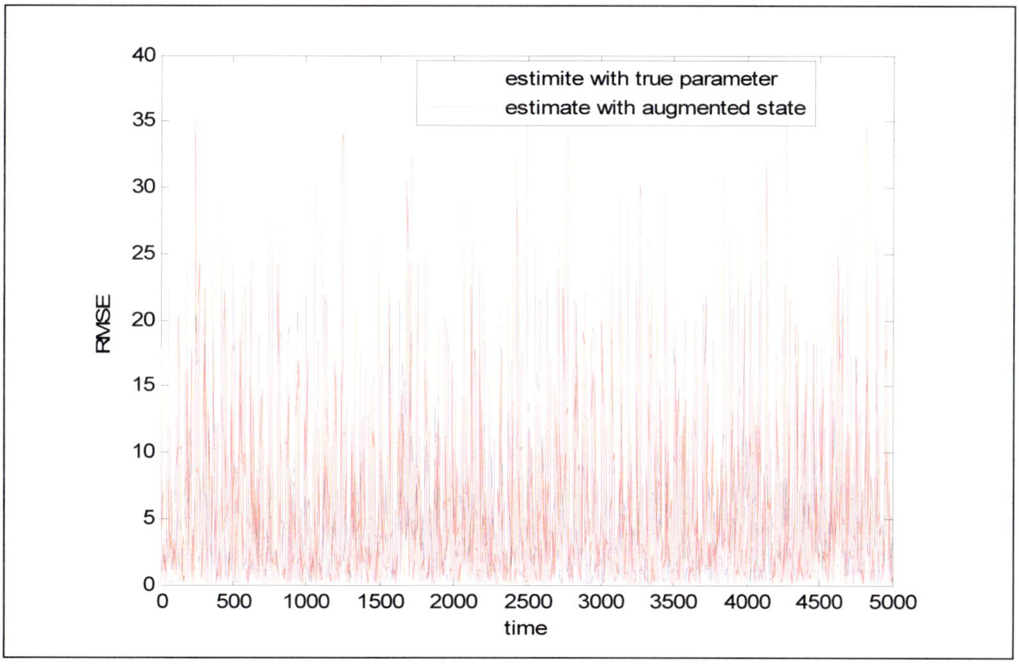

Fig. 5. RMSE of state x_t by particle filtering with true parameter and augmented state parameter estimation

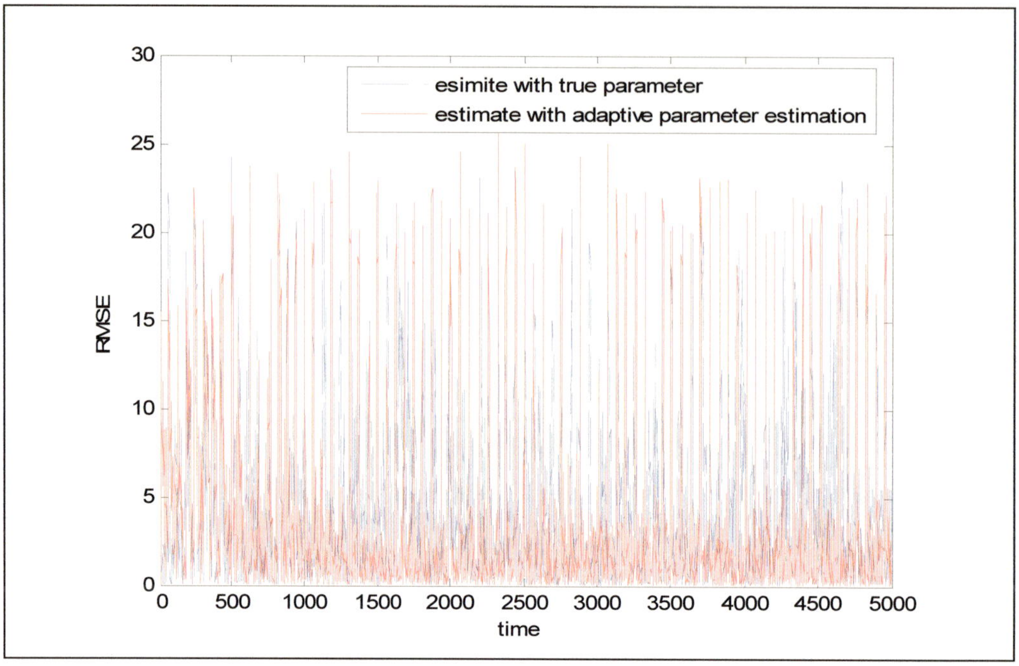

Fig. 6. RMSE of state x_t by particle filtering with true parameter and adaptive parameter estimation

We also compare the performance measure of our results with the "augmented state estimate" algorithm. The performance measure is root mean square error as follows:

$$RMS = \sqrt{\frac{1}{MT}\sum_{m=1}^{M}\sum_{t=1}^{T}(\hat{x}(m,t) - x(t))^2}$$

where $\hat{x}(m,t)$ is the estimate of $x(t)$ in the mth Monte Carlo simulation, $M = 50, T = 5000$. The performance of the first algorithm, our algorithm and the particle filtering with true parameter for various number of particles are presented in Table 1.

Algorithm / N	*800*	*1000*	*2000*
Augmented State	*0.2017*	*0.1945*	*0.1873*
Adaptive estimation	*0.1005*	*0.0996*	*0.0908*
True parameter	*0.0912*	*0.0852*	*0.0803*

Table 1. RMS performance measure for the two algorithms

5. Conclusions

In this chapter, we proposed an adaptive estimation algorithm for non-linear dynamic systems with unknown parameters based on combination of particle filtering and SPSA technique. We have demonstrated how to combine the maximum-likelihood parameter estimation with particle filtering. The estimates of parameters are obtained by state samples and maximum-likelihood estimation within particle filtering. The SPSA is used to approximate the gradient of cost function. The proposed algorithm achieves joint estimation of dynamic state and static parameters.

6. References

Andrieu, C.; Doucet, A.; & Tadic V. B. (2003). Online sampling for parameter estimation in general state space models. *Proceedings of IFAC Symposium on System Identification (SYSID 2003)*, pp.221–225, Netherlands

Andrieu, C.; Doucet, A.; Singh, S. S.; & Tadic, V. B. (2004). Particle methods for change detection, system identification, and control. *Proceeding of the IEEE*, Vol. 92, No. 3 , (March, 2004) 32-68

Andrieu, C.; doucet, A.; Tadic, V. (2005). On-Line Parameter Estimation in General State-Space Models. *Proceedings of the 44th IEEE Conference on Decision and Control*, Seville

Arulampalam, M. S. ; Maskell, S.; Gordon, N.; & Clap, T. (2002). A tutorial on particle filters for on-line nonlinear/non-Gaussian Bayesian tracking. *IEEE Transactions on Signal Processing*, Vol. 50, No. 2, (February, 2002) 174–188

Berzuini, C.; Best, N. G.; & Gilks, W. R. (1997). Dynamic conditional independence models and Markov chain Monte Carlo methods. *Journal of the American Statistical Association*, Vol. 92, No.1, 1403-1411

Chan, B. L.; Doucet, A.; & Tadic, V. B. (2003). Optimization of particle filters using simultaneous perturbation stochastic approximation. *Proceedings of IEEE International Conference on Acoustics, Speech, and Signal Processing*, pp.681-684, Hong Kong

Crisan, D.; & Doucet, A. (2002). A survey of convergence results on particle filtering methods for practitioners. *IEEE Transaction on Signal Processing*, Vol. 50, No. 3, (March, 2002) 736-746

Doucet, A.; Freitas, J. & Gordon, N. (2001). *Sequential Monte Carlo Methods in Practice*, Springer-Verlag, ISBN : 0387951466, New York

Doucet, A.; & Tadic, V. B. (2002). On-line optimization of sequential Monte Carlo methods using stochastic approximation. *Proceeding of American Control Conference*. pp.2565–2570, Anchorage

Djuric, P. M.; & Miguez, J. (2002). Sequential particle filtering in the presence of additive Gaussian noise with unkown parameters. *Proceedings of the IEEE*, Vol. 45, No. 2, (March, 2002) 23-47

Gamerman, D. (1998). Markov chain Monte Carlo for dynamic generalized models. *Biometrika*, Vol. 85, No. 1, (January, 1998) 215-227

Gordon, N. J.; Salmond, D. J.; & Smith, A. F. M. (1993). Novel approach to nonlinear/non-Gaussian Bayesian state estimation. *IEE Proceedings-F*, Vol. 140, No. 2, (February, 1993) 107-113

Jane, L.; & Mike, W. (2001). Combined parameter and state estimation in simulation-based filtering. in *Sequential Monte Carlo Methods in Practice*, Doucet, A.; Freitas, J. F. G.; & Gordon, N. J. (Eds.), Springer-Verlag, ISBN: 0387951466, New York

Kong, A.; Liu, J. S.; & Wong, W. H. (1994). Sequential imputations and Bayesian missing data problems. *Journal of the American Statistical Association*, Vol.89, No.5, (May, 1994) 278-288

Lee, D. S.; & Chia, N. K. K. (2002). A particle algorithm for sequential Bayesian parameter estimation and model selection. *IEEE Transactions on Signal Processing*, Vol. 50, No. 2, (February, 2002) 326-336

Polson, N. G.; & Stroud, J. R. (2008). Practical filtering with sequential parameter learning. *Journal of the Royal Statistical Society: Series B*, Vol.70, No. 2 413–428

Spall, J. C. (1987). A stochastic approximation technique for generating maximum likelihood parameter estimates. *Proceedings of the American Control conference*, pp.1161-1167, Chicago

Spall, J. C. (1998). Implementation of the simultaneous perturbation algorithm for stochastic optimization. *IEEE Transactions on Aerospace and Electronic Systems*, Vol. 34, No. 3, 817-823

Spall, J. C. (2003). Estimation via Markov chain Monte Carlo. *IEEE Control System Magazine*, Vol. 23 , No.2, (February, 2003) 34-45

Storvic, G. (2002). Particle filters in state space models with the presence of unknown static parameters. *IEEE Transactions on Signal Processing*, Vol. 90, No. 2, (February, 2002) 281-289

Yang, X.; Pan, Q.; & Wang, R. (2006). Development and prospect of particle filtering. *Control Theory & Applications*, Vol. 23, No. 2, 261- 67

Yang, X.; Xing, k.; & Pan Q. (2008). Joint Parameter and State Estimation in Particle Filtering and Stochastic Optimization. Journal of Control Theory & Application, Vol.6, No.2, 215-220

10

Integral Optimization of the Container Loading Problem

Rafael García-Cáceres[1], Carlos Vega-Mejía[2] and Juan Caballero-Villalobos[2]
[1]*Escuela Colombiana de Ingeniería,*
[2]*Pontificia Universidad Javeriana*
Colombia

1. Introduction

The rapid globalization of the world economy has led to the development of ample and quickly growing (aerial, maritime, terrestrial) networks for merchandise distribution in containers [Wang et al., 2008]. The transport costs afforded by the specialized companies operating in this sector are directly related to appropriate loading and efficient use of space [Xue and Lai, 1997a]. The efficient loading of a set of containers can be done technically by solving the Container Loading Problem (CLP).

CLPs are NP-Hard problems that basically consist in placing a series of rectangular boxes inside a rectangular container of known dimensions, seeking to optimize volume utilization [Pisinger, 2002], and taking into consideration the basic constraints enounced by Wäscher et al. (2007): (i) all the boxes must be totally accommodated inside the container, and (ii) boxes should not overlap. Notwithstanding, the solving of actual container loading problems can be limited or rendered inappropriate if only these two constraints are considered [Bischoff and Ratcliff, 1995; Bortfeldt and Gehring, 2001; Eley 2002].

In this sense, Bischoff and Ratcliff (1995) enounced a series of practical restrictions that are applicable to real situations: orientation and handling constraints, load stability, grouping, separation and load bearing strength of items within a container, multi-drop situations, complete shipment of certain item groups, shipment priorities, complexity of the loading arrangement, container weight limit and weight distribution within the container. According to the literature on the topic, these considerations have not been included in many of the existing approaches to the CLP problem. Some of these criteria are difficult to quantify [ibidem] due to their qualitative nature. The traditional optimization approaches, which cardinalize qualitative aspects, tend to cause loss of important criterion information. For this reason, more natural treatments such as those resulting from ordinal approaches are advisable [García et al., 2009].

The CLP has a natural correspondence with the integral optimization concept, which includes qualitative and quantitative criteria within an optimization problem [ibidem]. The CLP solving approach treated here not only considers the fundamental quantitative criteria stated by Wäscher et al. (2007), but two other important ones contributed by Bischoff and Ratcliff (1995) as well: i) not exceeding the container's weight transportation limit, and ii) once the container has been loaded, its center of gravity (COG) should be close to the geometrical center of its base (weight distribution within a container). In turn, the

qualitative criterion is the fragility of the elements packed inside the boxes. Finally, the stochastic consideration has to do with the load bearing strength of items, which results from the fragility or structural features of their contents or other reasons.
The current chapter uses the Integral Analysis Method (IAM) [García et al., 2009] to optimize the CLP. IAM adapts well to stochastic optimization problems, thus allowing the development of more complex and natural models, which are therefore closer to actual problem contexts. In section 2, the current chapter includes an analysis of the background of the problem, including the list of restrictions contributed by Bischoff and Ratcliff (1995). Section 3 develops IAM: item 3.1 introduces the quantitative assessment, which includes the mathematical model and heuristic solution to the problem, as well as the analysis of the computational results; item 3.2 addresses the qualitative analysis, and item 3.3, the integrated analysis. Finally, section 4 presents conclusions and recommendations.

2. Background

The CLP has been studied since the beginning of the sixties [Pisinger, 2002]. Our literature review, which is detailed in table 1, allowed identifying heuristic and metaheuristic methodologies as the most common approaches to solving the problem. Albeit less frequent, other approaches have made use of Mixed Integer Programming (MIP), Nonlinear Programming (NLP) and Approximation Algorithm (AA) models.
The solving technique and set of constraints considered in each of these studies can be found in tables 1 and 2, respectively. The methodologies used to treat the constraints identified by Bischoff and Ratcliff (1995) are presented in table 3. Regarding the constraints taken into consideration in the referred studies, those defined by Wäscher et al. (2007) are the most common ones: not exceeding the volume of the container and not allowing box overlapping. Few studies have addressed the constraints contributed by Bischoff and Ratcliff (1995).
The works of Eley (2002), Bortfeldt and Gehring (2001), Davies and Bischoff (1999), Xue and Lai (1997b) and Chen et al. (1995) include the most considerations, although none of them reaches the complexity treated here. These studies solve the CLP by trying to minimize the wasted space in the container. It is worthwhile mentioning that all the criteria modeled in the reviewed CLP versions were treated quantitatively, even those that could be more naturally treated in a qualitative way. Examples of these criteria are separation of items within a container, shipment priorities or loading arrangement.

3. Integral optimization of the problem

The quantitative analysis proposes a mathematical programming model and a heuristic method to solve the CLP. In the qualitative and integration analysis we applied the developments contributed by IAM.

3.1 Quantitative analysis

The works of Chen et al. (1995) and of Xue and Lai (1997b) developed MIP models which include the set of restrictions contemplated in the current work. The model detailed in section 3.1.2 is proposed for homogeneous load (all the boxes have the same dimensions when they are not bearing anything on top) and includes the stochastic consideration defined in section 3.1.1

Author	Container filling strategy					Exact methods		AA models		Heuristics and metaheuristics						
	Wall Building	Block Building	Column Building	Multi-Faced Building	Caving Degree	NLP	MIP	Next Fit	First Fit	Local Search	Greedy	Evolutionary algorithm	Genetic algorithms	Tabu Search	Tree Search	Proper of the author
Huang and He (2009b)					√						√					
Huang and He (2009a)					√											√
Chien et al. (2009)	√															√
Soak et al. (2008)										√		√				
Wang et al. (2008)		√														√
Birgin et al. (2005)						√										
Chien and Deng (2004)	√															√
Lewis et al. (2004)													√			
Bortfeldt et al. (2003)		√												√		
Lim et al. (2003)				√												√
Miyazawa and Wakabayashi (2003)								√	√							
Eley (2002)		√									√				√	
Pisinger (2002)	√														√	
Bortfeldt and Gehring (2001)	√										√		√			
Teng et al. (2001)																√
Davies and Bischoff (1999)	√	√	√													√
Xue and Lai (1997b)							√									
Xue and Lai (1997a)	√															√
Bischoff and Ratcliff (1995)			√													√
Chen et al. (1995)							√									

Table 1. CLP solving methods

Author	Constraints								
	1	2	3	4	5	6	7	8	9
Huang and He (2009b)	√	√							
Huang and He (2009a)	√	√							
Chien et al. (2009)	√	√			√				
Soak et al. (2008)	√	√							
Wang et al. (2008)	√	√							
Birgin et al. (2005)	√	√							
Chien and Deng (2004)	√	√							
Lewis et al. (2004)	√	√							
Bortfeldt et al. (2003)	√	√			√				
Lim et al. (2003)	√	√							
Miyazawa and Wakabayashi (2003)	√	√							
Eley (2002)	√	√	√						
Pisinger (2002)	√	√							
Bortfeldt and Gehring (2001)	√	√	√	√	√			√	√
Teng et al. (2001)	√	√	√		√				
Davies and Bischoff (1999)	√	√	√						
Xue and Lai (1997b)	√	√						√	
Xue and Lai (1997a)	√	√					√		
Bischoff and Ratcliff (1995)	√	√			√	√			
Chen et al. (1995)	√	√	√	√					

1. Container volume
2. Boxes cannot overlap
3. Weight distribution within a container
4. Orientation constraints
5. Load stability
6. Multi-drop situations
7. Shipment frequencies
8. Container weight limit
9. Stacking of boxes

Table 2. Constraints addressed in CLP studies

3.1.1 Defining the stochastic consideration

Boxes can be vertically compressed depending on the load they bear on top. Such deformation may depend on box content itself and on its structural features. In order to include this consideration in our MIP model we have made the following assumptions:

- Boxes might (or might not) be deformed.
- Only affecting height, deformation is homogeneous on the upper side, which bears the load.
- Boxes might be made of different materials and have diverse contents.
- The maximum load a box can support is a known feature.
- Boxes have a deformation limit

It is assumed that the deformation experimented by a box is directly proportional to the weight it bears on top. That is to say, the higher the weight, the more deformed the box will be. In this way the box reaches its maximum deformation when it is bearing the maximum permitted load. Additionally, we have included a stochastic factor that models the deformation that is not explained by the mentioned relation. The deterministic behavior of the deformation process is described in Figure 2.

Practical constraint	Quantitative nature	Qualitative nature	Authors that have included it	Applied methodology
Orientation constraints: One simple example of this constraint is the warning "This way up" that appears in certain boxes.	✓		Bortfeldt et al. (2003)	A Tabu Search metaheuristic is applied as a solution, making use of a Block Building approach which groups the boxes according to their orientation constraints.
			Bortfeldt and Gehring (2001)	Possible box rotations are handled through modifications of the wall filling method of the proposed greedy heuristic.
			Chen et al. (1995)	The model is modified according to the need for orientation constraints.
Load bearing strength of items: Depending on its structural features and on the fragility of its contents, a box may or may not tolerate the placing of weight on top.	✓	✓	Bortfeldt and Gehring (2001)	The proposed greedy heuristic's wall filling method is quantitatively modified to prevent the creation of empty spaces above boxes with weight bearing restrictions. Excessive waste of space resulting from this constraint is prevented through the incorporation of additional rules.
Handling constraints: According to the size and weight of the boxes, and to the necessary tools to store them in the container, the bigger elements may need to be placed on the floor of the container, or the heavier ones may not be allowed above a certain height.	✓		NA	NA
Load stability: If, for example, the merchandise is prone to get damaged inside the container, it might be necessary to restrict its movement beyond significant limits during transportation.	✓		Bortfeldt et al. (2003)	The blocks are built so that their base is entirely supported by another block or by the base of the container.
			Eley (2002)	Each block is built with identical elements in order to prevent the formation of empty spaces among them.
			Teng et al. (2001)	Mathematical equations are applied to minimize the system's inertial momentum.
			Bortfeldt and Gehring (2001)	The proposed wall filling method of the greedy heuristic is modified to avoid placing a box on top of another that is not supporting its bottom in its entirety.

Practical constraint	Quantitative nature	Qualitative nature	Authors that have included it	Applied methodology
			Bischoff and Ratcliff (1995)	A Column Building based heuristic solution is presented. Stability is increased through columns built with boxes of the same type, so that none of them lacks base support.
Grouping of items: Load checking and operation may be rendered easier if similar items are placed as close to one another as possible.	✓		NA	NA
Multi-drop situations: If the container is scheduled to stop several times on the way, it might result practical to group together those items having the same destiny.	✓		Bischoff and Ratcliff (1995)	A heuristic that checks all available spaces in the container before placing a box is introduced. Additional stability rules make sure all the boxes have their bases entirely supported by other boxes beneath.
Separation of items within a container: If, for example, the container is carrying both chemical and food products, the loading arrangement must prevent them from having any contact.		✓	NA	NA
Complete shipment of certain item groups: A particular shipment may include several boxes. If the decision is made to store one of them, the others might also need to be stored together.	✓		NA	NA
Shipment priorities: The shipping of certain elements might be more important than that of some other ones.	✓	✓	NA	NA
Complexity of the loading arrangement: Depending on the resulting load arrangement, special technology to unload the container (clamp or		✓	NA	NA

Practical constraint	Quantitative nature	Qualitative nature	Authors that have included it	Applied methodology
forklift trucks) might result necessary instead of manual labor. However, if the task has technical limitations, the loading arrangement must adapt to them.				
Container weight limit: The container may have a maximum capacity which cannot be exceeded.	✓		Bortfeldt and Gehring (2001)	While executing the greedy heuristic, the accumulated weight that has been loaded into the container is continuously checked. When an additional box leads to exceeding the container's weight limit, it is not stored.
			Xue and Lai (1997b)	This constraint is included in the mathematical programming section.
Weight distribution within a container: From the standpoint of the operation of a loaded container, its center of gravity should not be far from the geometrical center of its base; otherwise certain maneuvers may be impossible.	✓		Eley (2002)	The length of the container is divided in equal sections that are filled up according to each of the proposed heuristics. The sections are then exchanged in order to attain an optimum weight distribution.
			Teng et al. (2001)	During the second phase of the heuristic, the elements are tentatively swapped in order to drive the center of gravity of the system close to that of the container.
			Bortfeldt and Gehring (2001)	The load balance is handled through the greedy heuristic as follows: along the length of the container through exchanging the walls that have been built; and along the width of the container through reflecting the load arrangement of each wall.
			Davies and Bischoff (1999)	A heuristic that combines the Column, Wall and Block Building approaches is introduced. Load balance is sought by exchanging and rotating the different blocks resulting in the load arrangement.
			Chen et al. (1995)	The model is modified as to include two restrictions aimed at preventing the load balance along the container from exceeding a certain limit.

Table 3. Practical constraints defined by Bischoff and Ratcliff (1995)

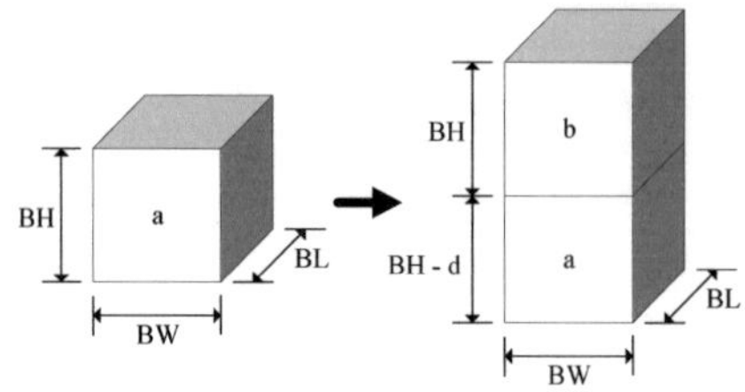

Fig. 1. Box height reduction due to top load.

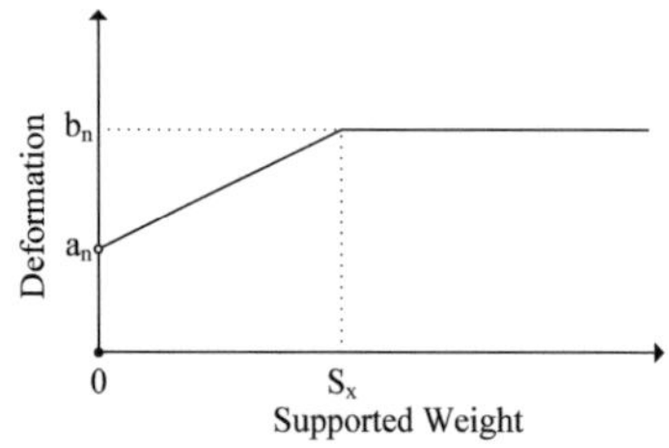

Fig. 2. Supported weight - Deformation

Deformation is modeled as follows:

$$d_{xn} = \begin{cases} 0 & \Leftrightarrow c_x = 0 \vee n = n_{max} \\ a_n + \dfrac{c_x}{S_x}(b_n - a_n) + \varepsilon_{xn} & \text{otherwise} \end{cases} \tag{1}$$

Where

n: level where box x is located; $n \in \{1,2,\dots,n_{max} = \lfloor CH/BH \rfloor\}$

d_{xn}: deformation undergone by box x at level n, $d_{xn} \geq 0$.

c_x: weight supported by box x, equaling $\sum_{i=n+1}^{n_{max}} P_{yi}$, where P_{yi} is the weight exerted by box y at level i, with $y \neq x$.

S_x: maximum weight bearable by box x, with $S_x > 0$.

a_n: minimum deterministic deformation experimented at level n.

b_n: maximum deterministic deformation experimented at level n.

ε_{xn}: stochastic parameter explaining the deformation that is not attributable to the functional relation of box x at level n. This parameter associates a different probability density function to each n, $\varepsilon_{xn} \in \mathbb{R}$ and $\theta_n^{min} \leq \varepsilon_{xn} \leq \theta_n^{max}$.

This way of modeling the deformation facilitates the simulation of instances in which one box can be more deformed than another, even when they are bearing the same weight and number of boxes. This might be the case of, for example, the different structural features of the boxes or of their contents. In sum, as a result of unknown reasons that cannot be attributed to the described function.

3.1.2 MIP model

Given that the boxes have the same dimensions, the container can be divided in multiple cells of box dimensions (Figure 3). As the model does not allow rotating the boxes, all their sides remain parallel to their corresponding container homologues. In this context, a hypothetical container can be conceived so that the boxes fit its width and length perfectly well because in practice the empty space (dotted zone in Figure 3) can be completed with filling material.

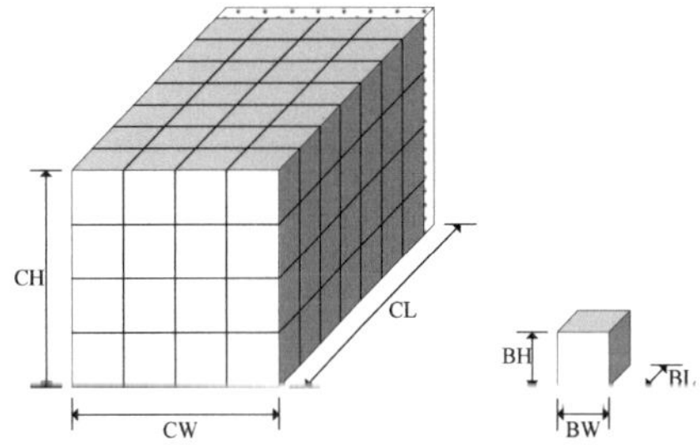

Fig. 3. Inner division of the container

The model includes the following parameters:

- I: number of boxes to be stored.
- (CL, CW, CH): dimensions of the container (length, width, height).
- (BL, BW, BH): dimensions of the boxes (length, width, height). It is assumed that the COG of each box coincides with its geometric center.
- (J, K, L): number of boxes that can be accommodated in the container along its length, width and height, respectively; where $J = \{1, \dots, j_{max} = \lfloor CL/BL \rfloor\}$, $K = \{1, \dots, k_{max} = \lfloor CW/BW \rfloor\}$ and $L = \{1, \dots, l_{max} = \lfloor CH/BH \rfloor\}$.
- P_i: weight of box i.
- S_i: maximum weight bearable by box i, being $S_i > 0$.
- P_C: maximum load capacity of the container as measured in weight.
- G: the distance between the COG of the loaded container and its base is restricted to a predetermined value (G). This distance is only measured along the length of the container (Figure 4).

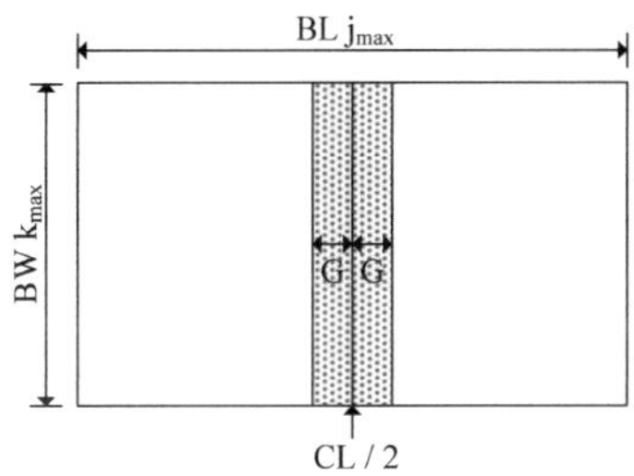

Fig. 4. Top view of the container

- A_n: minimum deterministic deformation experimented at level n of the container.
- B_n: maximum deterministic deformation experimented at level n of the container.
- f_n: probability density function that determines the stochastic deformation experimented by a box at level n of the container.
- θ_n^{min}: minimum possible value of the stochastic deformation parameter for boxes located at level n of the container.
- θ_n^{max}: maximum possible value of the stochastic deformation parameter for boxes located at level n of the container.

The model uses the following variables:

- $x_{ijkl} = \begin{cases} 1 & \text{If box } i \text{ is in cell}(j,k,l) \\ 0 & \text{Otherwise} \end{cases}$
- c_{ijkl}: total load supported by box i in cell (j,k,l).
- ε_{il}: stochastic deformation experimented by box i at level l.

- d_{ijkl}: total deformation experimented by box i in cell (j,k,l).

The model has the following constraints:

(R1) Volume capacity: the number of boxes stored in the container must not exceed the number of cells available in it:

$$\sum_{i=1}^{I}\sum_{j=1}^{j_{max}}\sum_{k=1}^{k_{max}}\sum_{l=1}^{l_{max}} x_{ijkl} \leq j_{max}k_{max}l_{max} \tag{2}$$

(R2) No box shall occupy more than one cell:

$$\sum_{j=1}^{j_{max}}\sum_{k=1}^{k_{max}}\sum_{l=1}^{l_{max}} x_{ijkl} \leq 1 \quad \forall i \in \{1,\dots,I\} \tag{3}$$

(R3) Each cell shall only be assigned to one box:

$$\sum_{i=1}^{I} x_{ijkl} \leq 1 \quad \forall j \in J; \forall k \in K; \forall l \in L \tag{4}$$

(R4) All the boxes that are not in contact with the base of the container must be supported by other boxes beneath them:

$$x_{ijkl} \leq \frac{1}{l-1}\sum_{n=1}^{l-1}\sum_{m=1,m\neq i}^{I} x_{mjkn} \quad \forall i \in \{1,\dots,I\}; \forall j \in J; \forall k \in K; l \in \{2,\dots,l_{max}\} \tag{5}$$

(R5) The total stored weight of the boxes cannot exceed the load limit of the container:

$$\sum_{i=1}^{I} P_i \sum_{j=1}^{j_{max}}\sum_{k=1}^{k_{max}}\sum_{l=1}^{l_{max}} x_{ijkl} \leq P_C \tag{6}$$

(R6) Weight distribution within the container: once the container has been loaded, its COG is calculated along its length because its stability is more compromised along its largest dimension. The distance between this point and $\frac{CL}{2}$ must not be larger than G (Figure 4). To calculate the COG of the container, it is divided in j_{max} walls of dimensions BL, BWk_{max}, BHl_{max}, each of them with weight m_j which is assumed to be exerted at the middle point of its base; that is, at $BL/2$ (Figure 5).

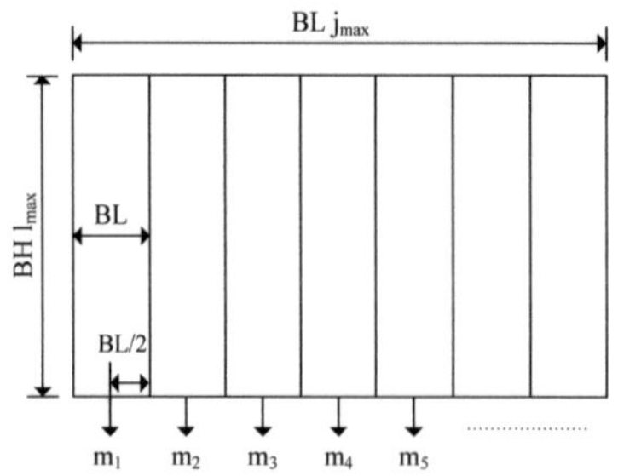

Fig. 5. Side view of the container

As a reference, we take the lower left corner as the origin of axis X. The force diagram on the base of the container is the following:

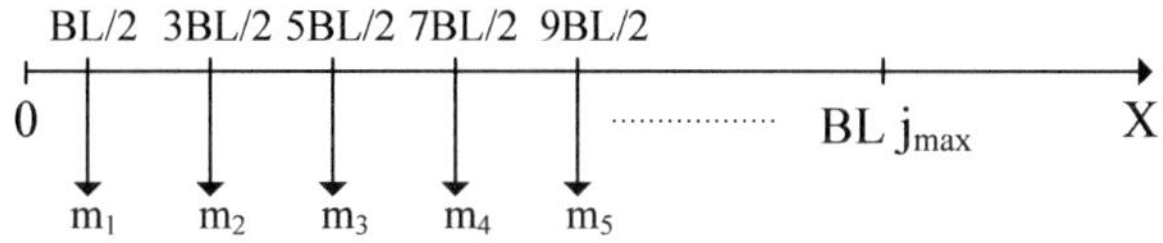

Fig. 6. Force diagram on the base of the container

Applying the equation to calculate the COG we obtain:

$$COG_X = \frac{\sum_{j=1}^{j_{max}} m_j o_j}{\sum_{j=1}^{j_{max}} m_j} \tag{7}$$

Where o_j is the distance from the center of the base of wall j to the origin, and m_j is the weight of wall j.

The distance between COG_X and $\frac{CL}{2}$ cannot be larger than G. This constraint is expressed as:

$$-G \leq \frac{\sum_{j=1}^{j_{max}} m_j o_j}{\sum_{j=1}^{j_{max}} m_j} - \frac{CL}{2} \leq G \tag{8}$$

The weight of wall j is given by the sum of the box weights stored in it:

$$m_j = \sum_{i=1}^{I} \sum_{k=1}^{k_{max}} \sum_{l=1}^{l_{max}} x_{ijkl} P_i \tag{9}$$

The distance from the center of wall j to the origin is given by:

$$o_j = BL \frac{2j-1}{2} \tag{10}$$

Replacing m_j and o_j in the constraint we obtain:

$$-G \leq \frac{\sum_{i=1}^{I} \sum_{j=1}^{j_{max}} \sum_{k=1}^{k_{max}} \sum_{l=1}^{l_{max}} \frac{BL(2j-1)}{2} x_{ijkl} P_i}{\sum_{i=1}^{I} \sum_{j=1}^{j_{max}} \sum_{k=1}^{k_{max}} \sum_{l=1}^{l_{max}} x_{ijkl} P_i} - \frac{CL}{2} \leq G \tag{11}$$

Which can be redistributed as:

$$-2G \leq BL \frac{\sum_{i=1}^{I} \sum_{j=1}^{j_{max}} \sum_{k=1}^{k_{max}} \sum_{l=1}^{l_{max}} (2j-1) x_{ijkl} P_i}{\sum_{i=1}^{I} \sum_{j=1}^{j_{max}} \sum_{k=1}^{k_{max}} \sum_{l=1}^{l_{max}} x_{ijkl} P_i} - CL \leq 2G \tag{12}$$

(R7) The weight supported by box i in cell (j,k,l) is given by the overall sum of the box weights it is bearing, that is, in those (j,k,f) cells satisfying the condition $l < f \leq l_{max}$. Said weight must not exceed the box's load bearing limit:

$$c_{ijkl} = \sum_{m=1, m \neq i}^{I} \sum_{n=l+1}^{l_{max}} x_{mjkn} P_m \quad \forall i \in \{1, \dots, I\}; \forall j \in J; \forall k \in K; \forall l \in L \tag{13}$$

$$c_{ijkl} \leq S_i \quad \forall i \in \{1, \dots, I\}; \forall j \in J; \forall k \in K; \forall l \in L \tag{14}$$

$$c_{ijkl} = 0 \quad \forall i \in \{1, \dots, I\}; \forall j \in J; \forall k \in K; l = l_{max} \tag{15}$$

As it can be seen in the constraint above, the weight supported by the boxes at the top level is zero.

(R8) Deformation of box i is calculated from the deterministic deformation range $[A_l, B_l]$ for level l, the ratio of the supported weight (c_{ijkl}/S_i) and the probability function ($f_l(\theta_l^{min}, \theta_l^{max})$) corresponding to level l where the box is located. The deformation of the boxes found at the uppermost level of the container is made equal to zero:

$$\varepsilon_{il} = f_l(\theta_l^{min}, \theta_l^{max}) \quad \forall i \in \{1, \dots, I\}; \forall l \in L \tag{16}$$

$$d_{ijkl} = A_l + \frac{(B_l - A_l)}{S_i} c_{ijkl} + \varepsilon_{il} \quad \forall i \in I; \forall j \in J; \forall k \in K; \forall l \in \{1, \dots, l_{max} - 1\} \tag{17}$$

$$d_{ijkl} = 0 \quad \forall i \in I; \forall j \in J; \forall k \in K; l = l_{max} \tag{18}$$

Finally, the objective function minimizes the empty space inside the container:

$$\min z = -BL \cdot BW \cdot \sum_{i=1}^{I} \sum_{j=1}^{j_{max}} \sum_{k=1}^{k_{max}} \sum_{l=1}^{l_{max}} (BH - d_{ijkl}) x_{ijkl} \tag{19}$$

3.1.3 Heuristic method

Although the literature review does not report the application of the GRASP (Greedy Randomized Adaptive Search Procedure) metaheuristic to solve three dimensional packing problems, it has shown very good results in combinatorial problems raised in production programming [Vega-Mejía and Caballero-Villalobos, 2010; Binato et al., 2002] and supply chain [Carreto and Baker, 2002; Delmaire et al., 1999] studies, among other research areas. In sum, the evidence of good performance of this metaheuristic for solving combinatorial problems led to its application in the current problem.

3.1.3.1 GRASP Metaheuristic

The procedure consists in an iterative process comprising two phases, namely construction and local search. In the constructive phase a feasible solution whose neighborhood is examined until reaching a local minimum is generated. At the end, the most feasible solution found is retained as the final solution of the problem [Glover et al., 2003].

In conducting the constructive phase it is necessary to define a utility function for the specific problem. Said function allows evaluating each of the elements that might be part of the initial feasible solution. When all the elements have been evaluated, a Restricted Candidate List (RCL) is elaborated with those exhibiting the best utility function. That is to say:

$$RCL = \{x | L \leq f_c(x) \leq L + \alpha(U - L)\} \quad (20)$$

Where:

- $f_c(x)$ is the utility function of element x
- α is a random number between 0 and 1.
- In case there is a problem of minimization, L is the lowest value found in the utility function, whereas U is the greatest one.

The pseudo-code proposed by Resende and González (2003) is the following:

```
PROCEDURE Constructive Phase - V
PARAMETERS
        α: numeric value between 0 and 1
        E: problem data
        c(·): utility function
VARIABLES
        x: initial solution
        C: copy of problem data
BEGIN PROCEDURE
        x ← ∅
        C ← E
        Evaluate utility function c(e),∀e ∈ C
        WHILE C ≠ ∅
                c_* ← min{c(e)|e ∈ C}
                c^* ← max{c(e)|e ∈ C}
                RCL ← {e ∈ C | c(e) ≤ c_* + α(c^* − c_*)}
                Choose from the RCL a random element s that maintains solution feasibility
                x ← x ∪ {s}
                Remove element s from C
                Evaluate utility function c(e),∀e ∈ C
        END WHILE
        RETURN x
END PROCEDURE
```

Fig. 7. GRASP - Constructive phase

This phase chooses an RCL candidate at random to add it to the initial solution, and then it empties the RCL. The process of filling and emptying the RCL is repeated until a feasible solution is obtained. Thus, the clearest advantage of the process is that the initial solution is attained step by step without affecting the feasibility of the result [Glover and Kochenberger, 2003].

The second phase of GRASP uses a local search method that improves the value of the solution found for the objective function during the constructive phase, through simple swapping of the elements of the initial solution. Said procedure is analogue to conducting searches in the close vicinity of the initial solution within the problem's solving space [Ibidem]. The local search pseudo-code is the following [Resende and González, 2003]:

```
PROCEDURE Local Search Phase
PARAMETERS
        x^0: current solution
        N(·): neighborhood of x^0
        f(·): objective function
VARIABLES
        x: improved solution
        y: solution in the vicinity of x
BEGIN PROCEDURE
        x ← x^0
        WHILE x is not a locally optimal in N(x)
                Find y ∈ N(x) such that f(y) < f(x) and y is a feasible solution
                x ← y
        END WHILE
        RETURN x
END PROCEDURE
```

Fig. 8. GRASP - Local Search

Finally, the pseudo-code for GRASP is:

```
PROCEDURE GRASP
PARAMETERS
        I: number of iterations
        α: numeric value between 0 and 1
        f(·): objective function
        c(·): utility function
VARIABLES
        E: problem data
        x: solution
        s: best solution
        u: objective function value
BEGIN PROCEDURE
        E ← Read problem data
        u = ∞
        i = 1
        WHILE i ≤ I
                x ← Constructive Phase - V (α,E,c(·))
                x ← Local Search Phase (x,N(x),f(·))
                IF f(x) < u THEN
                        u = f(x)
                        s ← x
                END IF
                i = i + 1
        END WHILE
        RETURN s
END PROCEDURE
```

Fig. 9. GRASP

3.1.3.2 Implementation of GRASP

During the constructive phase, our version of GRASP solves a relaxation of the problem at the COG constraint (12) by considering the feasibility of the latter in the local search phase, guaranteeing in this way the feasibility of the solution.

In the constructive phase of GRASP the utility function is used to find the best candidates to be placed at a given position in the container, which is filled up from bottom to top. For each available position, the utility function is defined as:

$$f_c(i,j,k,l) = \begin{cases} b_1 + \varepsilon_{i1} & \text{si } l = 1 \\ b_l + \varepsilon_{il} + \sum_{n=1}^{l-1} \sum_{m=1, m \neq i}^{I} d_{mn} & \text{si } l > 1 \end{cases} \tag{21}$$

Where:

- i: represents the box under evaluation for cell (j,k,l) of the container.
- b_l: is the maximum possible deterministic deformation experimented by a box at level l.
- ε_{il}: is the stochastic deformation that can be experimented by box i at level l.
- d_{mn}: is the deformation experimented by box m at cell (j,k,n) of the container.

When $l = 1$, that is, when the positions at the base of the container are under examination, the RCL is elaborated with those boxes that would undergo the least deformation under the maximum possible weight they can support. Considering equation (1), the utility function (21) applies the following evaluation strategy: the heaviest boxes are preferably located at the bottom level, so that the weight loaded on top of a box i (c_i), located in cell $(j,k,1)$ is equal to the maximum weight bearable by (S_i). In this way, equation (1) is reduced to $b_1 + \varepsilon_{i1}$. For the rest of the levels of the container ($l > 1$), the RCL is elaborated with those boxes that, for one thing, may be least deformed when bearing on top the maximum load they can be assigned $(b_l + \varepsilon_{il})$ at level l, and for another thing, may induce the least deformation on the boxes supporting them $(\sum_{n=1}^{l-1} \sum_{m=1,m\neq i}^{l} d_{mn})$. In this way the algorithm makes sure that each new assignation is both good and feasible for the relaxation of the problem at the load distribution constraint.

The local search phase of GRASP was conceived to minimize stored box deformation and improve weight distribution. The latter is achieved by approximating the COG of the loaded container to its geometric center at the base level, as calculated along its length as its largest dimension. The local search comprises four stages. In the first one box pairs are swapped as to reduce total deformation and therefore minimize unoccupied volume. Said swapping is carried out according to a 2-Optimal algorithm [Croes, 1958] whose pseudo-code is the following:

```
PROCEDURE Box Swapping
PARAMETERS
        x^0: current solution
        f(·): objective function
VARIABLES
        x*: improved solution
        s*: objective function value of the improved solution
BEGIN PROCEDURE
        x* ← x^0
        s* = f(x^0)
        i = 1
        WHILE i is less than the number of elements in x^0
                j = i + 1
                WHILE j is less or equal to the number of elements in x^0
                        x ← x*
                        Swap box i with box j in x
                        IF f(x) < s* AND x is a feasible solution THEN
                                x* ← x
                                s* = f(x)
                        END IF
                        j = j + 1
                END WHILE
                i = i + 1
        END WHILE
        RETURN x*,s*
END PROCEDURE
```

Fig. 10. 2-Optimal box swapping

If, at this stage, total deformation can be reduced, we will have reached a better distribution of the boxes in the container, which would eventually constitute a better utilization of total available space. The second stage is intended to check whether there is room for additional boxes. If at least one more box can be added, stage 1 is repeated. Periodically, the procedure checks compliance with the problem relaxation constraints. It finishes when all available positions in the container have been checked. The pseudo-code of the second stage is:

```
PROCEDURE Add Boxes
PARAMETERS
        E: problem data
        x^0: current solution
        f(·): objective function
VARIABLES
        result: boolean variable that determines if any boxes were added to the solution
        s^0: objective function value of the current solution
BEGIN PROCEDURE
        result = false
        WHILE there are empty positions inside the container
                FOR EACH e IN E AND NOT IN x^0
                        IF adding e to x^0 does not exceed the container's weight limit
                        AND e can be supported by the boxes below THEN
```

```
                                    x^0 ← x^0 ∪ {e}
                                    s^0 = f(x^0)
                                    Remove e from E
                                    result = true
                           END IF
                 END FOR EACH
        END WHILE
        RETURN x^0, s^0, result
END PROCEDURE
```

Fig. 11. Adding boxes to the solution

The third and fourth stages of the local search improve weight distribution within the container. In this respect, given that the container is divided in equal cells, the latter can be grouped in j_{max} walls of dimensions BL, BWk_{max}, BHl_{max}, as illustrated in Figure 12.

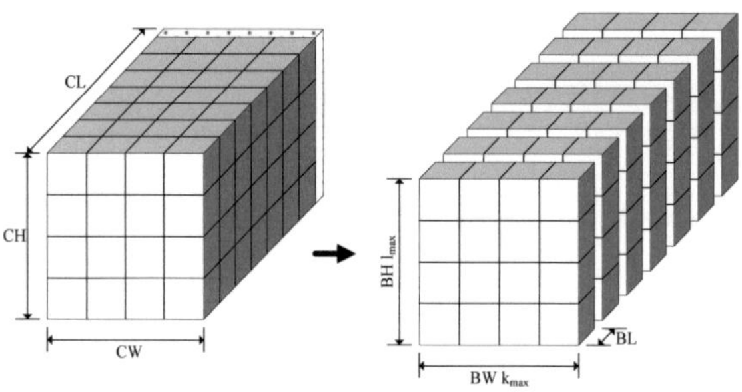

Fig. 12. Inner division of the container at stage 3 of the local search

In the third stage, these walls are swapped by the 2-Optimal algorithm, selecting for those modifications that allow driving the COG of the container to its medium length point. The pseudo-code goes as follows:

```
PROCEDURE Wall Swapping
PARAMETERS
        x^0: current solution
        CL: container length
        j_max: number of possible walls alongside the container length
        cog(·): function that calculates the COG of the loaded container
VARIABLES
        x*: improved solution
        g*: COG of the improved solution
BEGIN PROCEDURE
        x* ← x^0
        g* = cog(x^0)
        i = 1
        WHILE i is less than the number of possible walls (j_max)
                 j = i + 1
                 WHILE j is less or equal to the number of possible walls (j_max)
                          x ← x*
                          Swap boxes in wall i with those in wall j
                          g = cog(x)
                          IF g is closer to CL/2 than g* THEN
                                   x* ← x
                                   g* = g
                          END IF
                          j = j + 1
                 END WHILE
                 i = i + 1
        END WHILE
        RETURN x*, g*
END PROCEDURE
```

Fig. 13. Wall swapping

The fourth stage initiates once the 2-Optimal wall swapping has been finished. In this stage, the container is divided in k_{max} walls of dimensions BLj_{max}, BW, BHl_{max}, as illustrated in Figure 14.

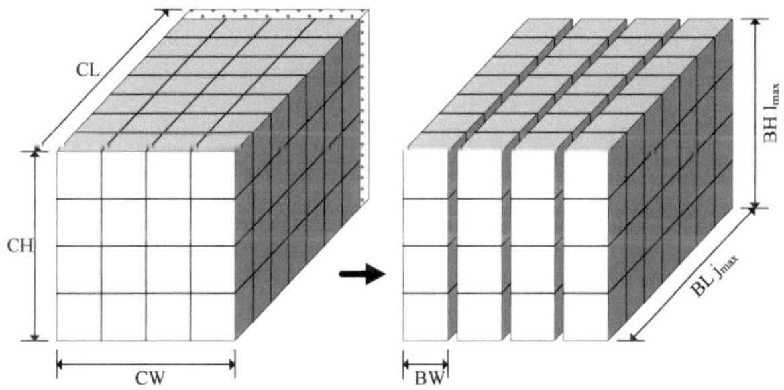

Fig. 14. Inner division of the container at stage four of the local search.

As the COG of the container is sought only along its length, the swapping of these walls is discarded because it would have no effect on the task. The incidence of these walls on the COG is analyzed by putting them back to front (reflection) as illustrated in Figure 15.

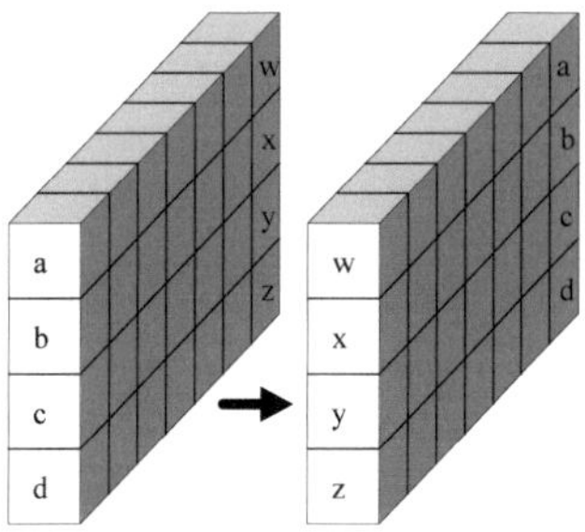

Fig. 15. Wall reflection.

The pseudo-code that is applied for this task is presented below:

```
PROCEDURE Reflect Wall
PARAMETERS
        x^0: current solution
        j_max: maximum number of available cells in the container along its length
        k: wall to reflect
VARIABLES
        W_k: set of boxes within wall k
        w^j: cell j along the container length in which box w has been placed
BEGIN PROCEDURE
        Assign to W_k all boxes that had been placed in wall k of x^0
        FOR EACH w IN W_k
                w^j = j_max − w^j + 1
        END FOR EACH
        RETURN x^0
END PROCEDURE
```

Fig. 16. Wall reflection

If at least one of these wall reflection movements drives the COG closer to the midpoint of the container's length, the third stage of the local search must be executed again. Otherwise, the local search is finished.

The pseudo-code for the local search phase is:

```
PROCEDURE Local Search Phase
PARAMETERS
        E: problem data
        x^0: current solution
        f(·): objective function
        CL: container length
        j_max: number of possible walls alongside the container's length
        k_max: number of possible walls alongside the container's width
        cog(·): function that calculates the COG of the loaded container
VARIABLES
        x*: improved solution
        g*: COG of the improved solution
BEGIN PROCEDURE
        x* ← Box Swapping (x^0, f(·))
        WHILE Add Boxes (E, x*, f(·)) = true
                x* ← Box Swapping (x*, f(·))
        END WHILE
        (x*, g*) ← Wall Swapping (x*, j_max, cog(·))
        FOR k = 1 TO k_max
                x ← x*
                x ← Reflect Wall (x, j_max, k)
                g = cog(x)
                IF g is closer to CL/2 than g* THEN
                        x* ← x
                        (x*, g*) ← Wall Swapping (x*, j_max, cog(·))
                        Set k = 0 to restart fourth stage
                END IF
        INCREMENT k
        RETURN x*
END PROCEDURE
```

Fig. 17. Local Search

Finally, the pseudo-code of the proposed GRASP metaheuristic is:

```
PROCEDURE GRASP
PARAMETERS
        I: number of iterations
        α: numeric value between 0 and 1
        f(·): objective function
        c(·): utility function
        cog(·): function that calculates the COG of the loaded container
        j_max: number of possible walls alongside the container's length
        k_max: number of possible walls alongside the container's width
VARIABLES
        E: problem data
        x: solution
        s: best solution
        u: objective function value of the best solution
BEGIN PROCEDURE
        E ← Read problem data
        u = ∞
        i = 1
        WHILE i ≤ I
                x ← Constructive Phase - V (α, E, c(·))
                x ← Local Search Phase (E, x, f(·), j_max, k_max, cog(·))
                IF f(x) < u THEN
                        u = f(x)
                        s ← x
                END IF
                i = i + 1
        END WHILE
        RETURN s
END PROCEDURE
```

Fig. 18. CLP solving GRASP

3.1.4 Computational results

The problem instances used to test the proposed heuristic procedure were generated as follows:

- The length, width and height of the container were set at 587cm, 233cm, and 220cm, respectively; corresponding to those used in previous works [Eley, 2002; Davies and Bischoff, 1999; Bischoff and Ratcliff, 1995].
- The dimensions of the boxes (length, width and height, in centimeters) were arbitrarily set at (293, 77, 55) and (72, 72, 72). The number of boxes I of each problem is:

$$I = \left\lfloor \frac{CL}{BL} \right\rfloor \cdot \left\lfloor \frac{CW}{BW} \right\rfloor \cdot \left\lfloor \frac{CH}{BH} \right\rfloor \tag{22}$$

- The weights of the I boxes as measured in kg were generated by means of a uniform distribution with parameters $a = 5$ and $b = 10$.
- Each of the I boxes' bearable weight (in kg) was estimated by multiplying its weight by a random number between 1 and 3.
- The weight limit (in kg) that can be loaded into the container was established arbitrarily as 90% of the total weight of the I boxes.
- One problem instance was generated for each box size configuration in order to perform the qualitative and integration analysis only on two problems: a 24 box one and a 72 box one.
- α values of 0.05; 0.10; 0.15 and 0.20 were used in elaborating the RCL. The realized implementation was executed 1,000 times for every instance and value of α. Each execution comprised 500 GRASP iterations.

Considering equation (1):

- For all tested instances, the parameter for maximum deterministic deformation b_n (expressed in cm) is calculated arbitrarily as shown below:

$$b_n = \frac{l_{max} - n}{\left\lceil \frac{l_{max}}{2} \right\rceil} \tag{23}$$

- For all tested instances, the parameter for minimum deterministic deformation a_n (expressed in cm) is calculated arbitrarily as shown below:

$$a_n = b_n - \frac{l_{max}}{10} \tag{24}$$

- Stochastic deformation ε_{xn} (expressed in cm) is a random number in the interval $(-a_n, a_n)$

The proposed GRASP was implemented on C# using MS Visual Studio 2005. All tests were run on a 2 GHz Dual Core processor with 3.49 GB RAM loaded with Windows XP.

The tables below summarize the results obtained in testing the instances resulting from the different values of α. The registered parameters are: percentage of container space utilized; total load weight with respect to the weight limit of the container; distance from the COG of the cargo to the center of the base of the container alongside its length; and average length of time spent in executing the solution.

Number of boxes	α	Average duration of a 500 iteration execution (sec)	Utilization of the container's space (%)			Utilization of the weight capacity of the container (%)			Distance from the COG of the loaded container to the center of the base of the container (cm)		
			Min	Max	Avg	Min	Max	Avg	Min	Max	Avg
24	0.05	16.53	89.82	90.15	89.96	98.66	99.95	99.57	0.01	16.30	2.85
	0.10	13.48	89.82	90.14	89.98	98.66	99.95	99.50	0.00	18.52	2.89
	0.15	12.12	89.86	90.17	89.98	98.66	99.95	99.56	0.01	12.79	2.92
	0.20	12.33	89.84	90.15	89.98	98.66	99.95	99.51	0.02	16.69	2.41
72	0.05	53.18	81.32	81.54	81.44	99.18	100.00	99.83	0.00	1.40	0.13
	0.10	48.51	81.36	81.53	81.43	99.23	100.00	99.87	0.00	1.66	0.15
	0.15	47.72	81.34	81.54	81.43	99.24	100.00	99.86	0.00	4.85	0.13
	0.20	48.45	81.34	81.54	81.43	99.44	100.00	99.89	0.00	1.45	0.18

Table 4. Summary of results

The qualitative analysis only made use of those results whose α value allowed an optimal utilization of the space inside the container. Such value was determined through a One-Way ANOVA applied to the results of every instance.

The 24 box problem was assessed through Levene's test conducted in Minitab, which showed no statistical evidence of homogeneity between the variances of the different values of α at a 95% confidence level. This led to applying Tamhane's test to analyze differences between means. The results, as obtained in SPSS are:

(I) alpha	(J) alpha	Mean Difference (I-J)	Std Error	Sig	95% Confidence Interval	
					Lower Bound	Upper Bound
0.05	0.10	5.1794E+03	719.2948	0.0000	3,285.0517	7,073.8021
	0.15	5.6447E+03	760.5627	0.0000	3,641.6754	7,647.7988
	0.20	3.9670E+03	748.0209	0.0000	1,997.0231	5,937.0744
0.10	0.05	-5.1794E+03	719.2948	0.0000	-7,073.8021	-3,285.0517
	0.15	4.6531E+02	742.2614	0.9890	-1,489.5696	2,420.1900
	0.20	-1.2124E+03	729.4050	0.4570	-3,133.3868	708.6305
0.15	0.05	-5.6447E+03	760.5627	0.0000	-7,647.7988	-3,641.6754
	0.10	-4.6531E+02	742.2614	0.9890	-2,420.1900	1,489.5696
	0.20	-1.6777E+03	770.1314	0.1640	-3,705.9459	350.5692
0.20	0.05	-3.9670E+03	748.0209	0.0000	-5,937.0744	-1,997.0231
	0.10	1.2124E+03	729.4050	0.4570	-708.6305	3,133.3868
	0.15	1.6777E+03	770.1314	0.1640	-350.5692	3,705.9459

Table 5. Objective function mean differences for the 24 box problem

At a 95% confidence interval, it can be concluded that, for the 24 box problem, the best objective function value is obtained with $\alpha = 0.15$. Applying the same procedure to the 72 box problem, Tamhane's test gave the following results:

(I) alpha	(J) alpha	Mean Difference (I-J)	Std, Error	Sig,	95% Confidence Interval	
					Lower Bound	Upper Bound
0.05	0.10	-2.8474E+03	439.2716	0.0000	-4,004.2949	-1,690.5171
	0.15	-3.5134E+03	436.5531	0.0000	-4,663.1334	-2,363.6766
	0.20	-2.9394E+03	427.8336	0.0000	-4,066.1716	-1,812.6444
0.10	0.05	2.8474E+03	439.2716	0.0000	1,690.5171	4,004.2949
	0.15	-6.6600E+02	445.3927	0.5810	-1,839.0072	507.0092

(I) alpha	(J) alpha	Mean Difference (I-J)	Std, Error	Sig,	95% Confidence Interval	
					Lower Bound	Upper Bound
	0.20	-9.2002E+01	436.8497	1.0000	-1,242.5138	1,058.5098
0.15	0.05	3.5134E+03	436.5531	0.0000	2,363.6766	4,663.1334
	0.10	6.6600E+02	445.3927	0.5810	-507.0092	1,839.0072
	0.20	5.7400E+02	434.1161	0.7100	-569.3141	1,717.3081
0.20	0.05	2.9394E+03	427.8336	0.0000	1,812.6444	4,066.1716
	0.10	9.2002E+01	436.8497	1.0000	-1,058.5098	1,242.5138
	0.15	-5.7400E+02	434.1161	0.7100	-1,717.3081	569.3141

Table 6. Objective function mean differences for the 72 box problem

With a 95% confidence interval, it can be concluded that, for the 72 box problem, the best objective function value is obtained with $\alpha = 0.05$.

Pareto analysis was applied to the solutions obtained for each of the two problems. Sixty six and sixty eight percent of the solutions of the 24 and 72 box problems were respectively analyzed, representing 20 alternatives of each problem. Their adjusted probabilities, as well as the expected values of the objective function and their standard deviations, all of them specified for IAM, are shown in Table 7. The load arrangement of each of the selected alternatives is shown in Appendix 1.

i	24 boxes				72 boxes			
	Frequency	$P(i), \alpha$	$E(z^i)$	σ^{Z^i}	Frequency	$P(i), \beta$	$E(z^i)$	σ^{Z^i}
1	50	0.0765	-27,130,328.4503	0	45	0.0667	-24,497,492.7011	0
2	49	0.0749	-27,069,022.1712	0	39	0.0578	-24,520,440.0663	0
3	47	0.0719	-27,079,711.8588	0	39	0.0578	-24,512,652.0699	0
4	37	0.0566	-27,071,467.0888	0	38	0.0563	-24,516,202.0138	0
5	36	0.0550	-27,066,716.6023	0	38	0.0563	-24,502,754.7084	0
6	35	0.0535	-27,068,471.0632	0	38	0.0563	-24,496,098.7389	0
7	35	0.0535	-27,088,277.5107	0	37	0.0548	-24,504,513.1559	0
8	34	0.0520	-27,072,118.7352	0	36	0.0533	-24,506,201.4630	0
9	31	0.0474	-27,052,647.8558	0	35	0.0519	-24,515,697.0110	0
10	30	0.0459	-27,066,675.3657	0	35	0.0519	-24,503,437.4409	0
11	30	0.0459	-27,093,102.3737	0	33	0.0489	-24,499,385.3670	0
12	29	0.0443	-27,075,607.8937	0	33	0.0489	-24,493,609.8728	0
13	29	0.0443	-27,070,443.4751	0	32	0.0474	-24,504,895.3574	0
14	28	0.0428	-27,075,537.4827	0	31	0.0459	-24,491,334.7171	0
15	27	0.0413	-27,065,936.3019	0	30	0.0444	-24,496,901.1626	0
16	27	0.0413	-27,059,497.8935	0	29	0.0430	-24,515,483.4574	0
17	26	0.0398	-27,070,016.2422	0	29	0.0430	-24,507,811.1248	0
18	25	0.0382	-27,091,519.0548	0	27	0.0400	-24,526,575.7616	0
19	25	0.0382	-27,071,515.1479	0	26	0.0385	-24,511,051.1289	0
20	24	0.0367	-27,052,190.1312	0	25	0.0370	-24,495,802.2597	0

α and β correspond to the joint integral index values of the alternatives associated to the cardinal result variable shown in table 11.

Table 7. Frequency, probability, expected value and deviation of the selected alternatives

3.2 Qualitative analysis

The qualitative stage is based on stochastic multicriteria acceptability analysis with ordinal SMAA-O data (Lahdelma et al., 2003). SMAA-O has been developed to support public decision making processes. According to IAM, the use of SMAA-O is restricted to ordinal variables and to the alternatives resulting from the cardinal analysis. This phase is particularly complex because of the difficulties that usually arise when defining the matrix of typical relative values that will be used as input. IAM's ordinal stage allows identifying the set of favorable weights that support each of the alternatives in a particular ranking. The most important resulting variable (indicator) featuring this analysis is the ordinal acceptability index (b_r^t), which defines its probability of acceptation of each alternative and indicates the ordinal ranking (r). Nevertheless, this indicator might prove insufficient to support the decision making process. For this reason, the technique provides two additional indicators: range values and central weight vectors, which establish the bounds of each alternative's favorable weight set and its associated centroid, respectively. In using this method, for every cardinal variable ($p(t)$), it is necessary to qualify each alternative's set of ordinal variables. Likert tables can be used to convert particular qualitative aspects into ordinal variables (Albaum, 1997). In this case, each of the original binary variables of an optimization problem has several ordinal associated variables, that are defined by the decision-makers, and that altogether allow building up the ordinal value associated to each alternative. For it to be efficient, the procedure applies the class concept (represented through index (a) in Table 10), which refers to a set of alternatives with identical utilities for all their associated ordinal variables. In the present work we have only considered one qualitative criterion, and consequently, one single analysis ranking ($r = 1$). The particular features of IAM's ordinal stage, which are explained below, are detailed in García et al. (2009).

The qualitative variable was defined as the fragility of the elements packed inside the boxes, which were then classified according to a scale ranging from 1 to 3, in which 3 indicated fragile contents, and 1, resistant ones; while 2 was assigned to boxes containing medium resistance materials.

The load arrangement of each of the alternatives corresponding to the 24 and 72 box problems was qualified according to table 8, which penalizes the boxes according to the fragility of their content and the level of the container at which they have been placed.

Box location penalization for the 24 box problem				**Box location penalization for the 72 box problem**			
Levels of the container	**Box content resistance**			**Levels of the container**	**Box content resistance**		
	1	**2**	**3**		**1**	**2**	**3**
1	1	3	3	**1**	1	2	3
2	2	1	3	**2**	2	1	2
3	3	1	2	**3**	3	3	1
4	3	2	1				

Table 8. Box location penalization

For each alternative we summed up all the penalization scores assigned to the stored boxes according to their content resistance value and location. The results were classified in four categories according to (Likert) table 9, which shows the ordinal values assigned to the different alternatives.

Table 10 shows the input of IAM's qualitative stage and its associated index of acceptability. For the two problems treated in the current work, the results show that all the weights support the alternatives corresponding to class 1 ($a = 1$) for acceptability ranking 1.

Likert table for the 24 box problem		Likert table for the 72 box problem	
Criterion	Ordinal value	Criterion	Ordinal value
If total < 37	1	If total < 109	1
If 37 ≤ total < 49	2	If 109 ≤ total < 145	2
If 49 ≤ total < 61	3	If 145 ≤ total < 181	3
If 61 ≤ total	4	If 181 ≤ total	4

Table 9. Likert tables for the 24 and 72 box problems

Ordinal parameters and indicators of the 24 box problem				Ordinal parameters and indicators of the 72 box problem			
a	*F(a)*	*Fragility, j: 1*	b_1^a	*a*	*F(a)*	*Fragility, j: 1*	b_1^a
1	t: {4, 5, 9, 10, 11, 12, 13, 14, 16, 18, 19}	1	1	1	t:{12, 17}	2	1
2	t: {1, 2, 3, 6, 7, 8, 9, 15, 17, 20}	2	0	2	t:{1, 2, 3, 4, 5, 6, 7, 8, 9, 10, 11, 13, 14, 15, 16, 18, 19, 20}	3	0

Table 10. Ordinal parameters and indicators

3.3 Integration analysis

The cardinal and ordinal analyses help determine a set of results that support the decision-making process significantly. At the same time, these results are the input of the integration procedure, which provides the indicators that are going to facilitate the analysis of the problem in a broader context. The integration analysis stage analyses what kind of valuations would make each alternative the preferred one in a particular ordinal ranking. The integration ranking (o) of each alternative is conditioned by the ordinal analysis ranking because each optimal cardinal solution may have a different ordinal ranking status. In the present case we have focused on ordinal ranking 1 (r = 1). The input of the deterministic SMAA (Lahdelma and Salminen, 2001) applied to complete the integration analysis stage of IAM is a utility matrix composed of m alternatives and two result variables (cardinal and ordinal). Thus, the process is simplified, allowing the obtention of a series of 2-dimensional central weight vectors with two ranges of mutually complementing favorable convex weights each, and of the integral acceptability indexes of each alternative. The particular features of IAM's integration analysis stage, which are explained below, are detailed in García et al. (2009).

For the integration analysis, the joint integral index is defined as $p_r(e^t)$. This value provides a comprehensive assessment of each alternative's ordinal ranking. Assuming that both cardinal and ordinal variables (listed in tables 7 and 10, respectively) are independent, the index is calculated as:

$$p_r(e^t) = p(t)b_1^t \tag{25}$$

Similar to the ordinal phase, the integration phase has a comparable set of indicators supporting the decision making process: the integral acceptability index and the weight of the result variable (qualitative and quantitative). As in the ordinal phase, in the integration phase, we have only used the acceptability index as a support indicator. The results of the integration phase are shown below.

Integration indicators of the 24 box problem			Integration indicators of the 72 box problem		
t	$p_1(e^t)$	d_1^t	t	$p_1(e^t)$	d_1^t
1	0.0765	0.0109	1	0.0667	0.0088
4	0.0566	0.9891	12	0.0489	0.9912
5, 9, 10, 11, 12, 13, 14, 16, 18, 19.	α	0	17	β	0
2, 3, 6, 7, 8, 9, 15, 17, 20.	0	0	2, 3, 4, 5, 6, 7, 8, 9, 10, 11, 13, 14, 15, 16, 18, 19, 20.	0	0

α and β correspond to the joint integral index values of the alternatives associated to the cardinal result variable.

Table 11. Results of the integration phase

The results indicate that, from the standpoint of the considerations addressed in the present analysis, alternatives 4 and 12 constitute the most favorable load arrangements for the 24 and 72 box problems, respectively.

4. Conclusions

The present work addresses CLP optimization in an integrated and actual context, including several restrictions which had not been worked out altogether in previous works. In addition, it introduces the modeling of SKU deformation and fragility content for the first time. New research perspectives have to do with the inclusion of additional considerations such as the complexity of the loading arrangement that ultimately facilitates unloading, and the management of client priority issues.

5. References

Albaum, G., 1997. The Likert scale revisited: An alternative version. Journal of the Market Research Society 39 (2), 331–348.

Binato S.; Hery W.J.; Loewenstern D. & Resende M.G.C. (2002). A GRASP for job shop scheduling. C.C. Ribeiro and P. Hansen (eds.), *Essays and Surveys in Metaheuristics*. Kluwer Academic Publishers, pp. 59-79.

Birgin E.G.; Martínez J.M. & Ronconi D.P. (2005). Optimizing the packing of cylinders into a rectangular container: A nonlinear approach. *European Journal of Operational Research*, 160, 19-33.

Bischoff E.E. & Ratcliff M.S.W. (1995). Issues in the development of approaches to container loading. *Omega, The International Journal of Management Science*, 23, 377-390.

Bortfeldt A. & Gehring H. (2001). A hybrid genetic algorithm for the container loading problem. *European Journal of Operational Research*, 131, 143-161.

Bortfeldt A.; Gehring H. & Mack D. (2003). A parallel Tabu search algorithm for solving the container loading problem. *Parallel Computing*, 29, 641-662.

Carreto C. & Baker B. (2002) A GRASP interactive approach to the vehicle routing problem with backhauls. C.C. Ribeiro and P. Hansen (eds.), *Essays and Surveys in Metaheuristics*. Kluwer Academic Publishers, pp. 185-199.

Chen C.S.; Lee S.M. & Shen Q.S. (1995). An analytical model for the container loading problem. *European Journal of Operational Research*, 80, 68-76.

Chien C-F & Deng J-F (2004). A container packing support system for determining and visualizing container packing patterns. *Decision Support Systems*, 37, 23-34.

Chien C-F; Lee C-Y; Huang Y-C & Wu W-T (2009). An efficient computational procedure for determining the container loading pattern. *Computers & Industrial Engineering*, 56, 965-978.

Croes, A. (1958) A method for solving traveling-salesman problems. *Operations Research*, 5, 791-812.

Davies A.P. & Bischoff E.E. (1999). Weight distribution considerations in container loading. *European Journal of Operational Research*, 114, 509-527.

Delmaire H., Díaz J.A.; Fernández E. & Ortega M. (1999) Reactive GRASP and Tabu Search based heuristics for the single source capacitated plant location problem. *INFOR*, 37, 194-225.

Eley M. (2002). Solving container loading problems by block arrangement. *European Journal of Operational Research*, 141, 393-409.

García R.G.; Aráoz J.A. & Palacios F. (2009). Integral Analysis Method - IAM. *European Journal of Operational Research*, 192, 891-903.

Glover F. & Kochenberger G.A. (2003). *Handbook of Metaheuristics*. Kluwer Academic Publishers. Dordrecht.

Huang W. & He K. (2009a). A caving degree approach for the single container loading problem. *European Journal of Operational Research*, 196, 93-101.

Huang W. & He K. (2009b). A new heuristic algorithm for cuboids packing with no orientation constraints. *Computers & Operations Research*, 36, 425-432.

Lahdelma, R., Salminen, P., 2001. SMAA-2: Stochastic multicriteria acceptability analysis for group decision making. *Operations Research*, 49 (3), 444–454.

Lahdelma, R., Miettinen, K., Salminen, P., 2003. Ordinal criteria in Stochastic multicriteria acceptability analysis (SMAA). *European Journal of Operational Research*, 147, 117–127.

Lewis J.E.; Ragade R.K.; Kumar A. & Biles W.E. (2004). A distributed chromosome genetic algorithm for bin-packing. *Robotics and Computer-Integrated Manufacturing*, 21, 486-495.

Lim A.; Rodrigues B. & Wang Y. (2003). A multi-faced buildup algorithm for three-dimensional packing problems. *Omega, The International Journal of Management Science*, 31, 471-481.

Miyazawa F.K. & Wakabayashi Y. (2003). Parametric on-line algorithms for packing rectangles and boxes. *European Journal of Operational Research*, 150, 281-292.

Pisinger D. (2002). Heuristics for the container loading problem. *European Journal of Operational Research*, 141, 382–392.

Resende M.G.C. & González J.L. (2003). GRASP: Procedimientos de búsqueda miopes aleatorizados y adaptativos. *Inteligencia Artificial. Revista Iberoamericana de Inteligencia Artificial*, 7, 19.

Soak S-M; Lee S-W; Yeo G-T & Jeon M-G (2008). An effective evolutionary algorithm for the multiple container packing problem. *Progress in Natural Science*, 18, 337-344.

Teng H-F; Sun S-L; Liu D-Q & Li Y-Z (2001). Layout optimization for the objects located within a rotating vessel - a three-dimensional problem with behavioral constraints. *Computers & Operations Research*, 28, 521-535.

Vega-Mejía C.A. & Caballero-Villalobos J.P. (2010). Uso combinado de GRASP y Path-Relinking en la programación de producción para minimizar la tardanza total ponderada en una máquina. *Ingeniería y Universidad*, 14, 1, 79-96.

Wang Z.; Li K.W. & Levy J.K. (2008). A heuristic for the container loading problem: A tertiary-tree-based dynamic space decomposition approach. *European Journal of Operational Research*, 191, 86–99.

Wäscher G.; Haubner H. & Schumann H. (2007). An improved typology of cutting and packing problems. *European Journal of Operational Research*, 183, 1109-1130.

Xue J. & Lai K.K. (1997a). Effective methods for a container packing operation. *Mathematical Computing Modelling*, 25, 75-84.

Xue J. & Lai K.K. (1997b). A study on cargo forwarding decisions. *Computers Industrial Engineering*, 33, 63-66.

Appendix

Bo x	Weig ht	Supported weight	Fragili ty	Bo x	Weig ht	Supported weight	Fragili ty	Bo x	Weig ht	Supported weight	Fragili ty
1	6.24	15.77	3	9	6.63	7.84	1	17	5.94	10.57	2
2	6.18	11.37	2	10	9.98	22.04	2	18	8.14	22.29	3
3	5.44	8.7	1	11	7.05	15.65	2	19	8.67	24.47	3
4	6.49	13.73	2	12	5.19	6.05	1	20	5.68	11.83	2
5	8.98	21.1	3	13	6.05	13.36	2	21	9.69	25.69	3
6	5.18	14.72	3	14	8.48	10.74	1	22	6.63	16.52	3
7	9.07	11.9	1	15	6.7	7.4	1	23	9.81	23.04	3
8	6.04	10.5	2	16	9.48	19.46	2	24	8.89	25.51	3

Table 12. Twenty four box problem

Bo x	Weight	Supported weight	Fragilit y	Bo x	Weig ht	Supported weight	Fragilit y	Bo x	Weig ht	Supported weight	Fragilit y
1	9.45	26.35	3	25	6.81	8.74	1	49	6.97	17.12	3
2	8.77	18.68	2	26	8.32	22.18	3	50	8.33	15.06	2
3	8.34	9.21	1	27	10	28.72	3	51	5.93	10.85	2
4	5.15	15	3	28	6.18	8.02	1	52	5.45	13.7	3
5	7.85	11.42	1	29	8.34	22.98	3	53	7.14	17.8	3
6	9.1	25.15	3	30	6.63	11.93	2	54	7.74	11.19	1
7	8.03	20.94	3	31	7.84	23.09	3	55	6.06	7.73	1
8	5.76	13.36	2	32	8.9	12.9	1	56	6.81	16.73	3
9	6.09	17.38	3	33	8.11	8.4	1	57	7.12	17.03	3
10	6.47	10.9	2	34	7.11	19.14	3	58	6.96	12.48	2
11	6.36	15.77	3	35	6.12	13.51	2	59	6.39	15.9	3
12	6.13	16.88	3	36	8.57	24.31	3	60	7.72	20.83	3
13	6.2	9.52	1	37	6.42	16.4	3	61	6.08	17.02	3
14	7.42	8.26	1	38	8.63	10.3	1	62	6.6	17.06	3
15	5.89	9.96	2	39	8.94	25.73	3	63	8.62	19.75	2
16	8.03	20.89	3	40	7.27	16.43	2	64	9.72	10.55	1
17	7.3	18.41	3	41	5.04	6.77	1	65	9.13	10.62	1
18	7.9	16.57	2	42	8.48	9.08	1	66	8.51	9.55	1
19	9.73	15.56	1	43	8.4	21.39	3	67	6.37	7	1
20	8.21	16.72	2	44	9.01	18.43	2	68	7.22	15.79	2
21	8.08	10.91	1	45	7.63	14.2	2	69	5.41	15.55	3
22	9.76	15.37	1	46	9.4	10.67	1	70	8.04	23.06	3
23	7.11	15.77	2	47	9.87	14.65	1	71	6.12	13.22	2
24	6.3	10.25	1	48	9.75	22.31	2	72	6.56	11.65	2

Table 13. Seventy two box problem

Position representation (X,Y,Z)	Position representation (X,Y,Z)	Position representation (X,Y,Z)	Position representation (X,Y,Z)
1,1,1 = 1	1,1,2 = 7	1,1,3 = 13	1,1,4 = 19
1,2,1 = 2	1,2,2 = 8	1,2,3 = 14	1,2,4 = 20
1,3,1 = 3	1,3,2 = 9	1,3,3 = 15	1,3,4 = 21
2,1,1 = 4	2,1,2 = 10	2,1,3 = 16	2,1,4 = 22
2,2,1 = 5	2,2,2 = 11	2,2,3 = 17	2,2,4 = 23
2,3,1 = 6	2,3,2 = 12	2,3,3 = 18	2,3,4 = 24

Table 14. List of positions inside the container for 24 boxes

Position representation (X,Y,Z)	Position representation (X,Y,Z)	Position representation (X,Y,Z)	Position representation (X,Y,Z)
1,1,1 = 1	3,3,1 = 19	5,2,2 = 37	7,1,3 = 55
2,1,1 = 2	4,3,1 = 20	6,2,2 = 38	8,1,3 = 56
3,1,1 = 3	5,3,1 = 21	7,2,2 = 39	1,2,3 = 57
4,1,1 = 4	6,3,1 = 22	8,2,2 = 40	2,2,3 = 58
5,1,1 = 5	7,3,1 = 23	1,3,2 = 41	3,2,3 = 59
6,1,1 = 6	8,3,1 = 24	2,3,2 = 42	4,2,3 = 60
7,1,1 = 7	1,1,2 = 25	3,3,2 = 43	5,2,3 = 61
8,1,1 = 8	2,1,2 = 26	4,3,2 = 44	6,2,3 = 62
1,2,1 = 9	3,1,2 = 27	5,3,2 = 45	7,2,3 = 63
2,2,1 = 10	4,1,2 = 28	6,3,2 = 46	8,2,3 = 64
3,2,1 = 11	5,1,2 = 29	7,3,2 = 47	1,3,3 = 65
4,2,1 = 12	6,1,2 = 30	8,3,2 = 48	2,3,3 = 66
5,2,1 = 13	7,1,2 = 31	1,1,3 = 49	3,3,3 = 67
6,2,1 = 14	8,1,2 = 32	2,1,3 = 50	4,3,3 = 68
7,2,1 = 15	1,2,2 = 33	3,1,3 = 51	5,3,3 = 69
8,2,1 = 16	2,2,2 = 34	4,1,3 = 52	6,3,3 = 70
1,3,1 = 17	3,2,2 = 35	5,1,3 = 53	7,3,3 = 71
2,3,1 = 18	4,2,2 = 36	6,1,3 = 54	8,3,3 = 72

Table 15. List of positions inside the container for 72 boxes

i	Load arrangement (position - box)	Ordinal criterion total
1	1-24; 2-11; 3-5; 4-18; 5-13; 6-21; 7-10; 8-2; 9-6, 10-19; 11-9; 12 23; 13-17; 14-7; 15-20; 16-1; 17-12; 18-22; 19-15; 20-0; 21-4; 22-8; 23-0; 24-3	39
2	1-18; 2-21; 3-24; 4-16; 5-4; 6-23; 7-2; 8-19; 9-14; 10-1; 11-11; 12-13; 13-20; 14-8; 15-15; 16-9; 17-22; 18-3; 19-6; 20-5; 21-0; 22-12; 23-0; 24-17	40
3	1-21; 2-23; 3-24; 4-11; 5-19; 6-10; 7-18; 8-2; 9-4; 10-9; 11-5; 12-13; 13-7; 14-15; 15-20; 16-6; 17-8; 18-17; 19-12; 20-0; 21-1; 22-0; 23-22; 24-3	38
4	1-10; 2-11; 3-19; 4-24; 5-21; 6-5; 7-22; 8-6; 9-18; 10-16; 11-13; 12-12; 13-17; 14-15; 15-9; 16-2; 17-8; 18-20; 19-7; 20-0; 21-3; 22-1; 23-4; 24-0	36
5	1-18; 2-19; 3-10; 4-6; 5-23; 6-21; 7-11; 8-24; 9-20; 10-17; 11-13; 12-16; 13-15; 14-3; 15-22; 16-14; 17-4; 18-8; 19-1; 20-9; 21-0; 22-0; 23-12; 24-2	33
6	1-10; 2-23; 3-18; 4-7; 5-24; 6-16; 7-1; 8-20; 9-11; 10-12; 11-13; 12-4; 13-19; 14-5; 15-9; 16-8; 17-15; 18-22; 19-17; 20-0; 21-2; 22-0; 23-6; 24-3	43
7	1-19; 2-13; 3-23; 4-5; 5-21; 6-22; 7-24; 8-8; 9-11; 10-7; 11-18; 12-1; 13-14; 14-2; 15-3; 16-17;	37

i	Load arrangement (position - box)	Ordinal criterion total
	17-15; 18-12; 19-20; 20-0; 21-4; 22-6; 23-9; 24-0	
8	1-18; 2-24; 3-21; 4-4; 5-19; 6-23; 7-5; 8-7; 9-15; 10-22; 11-10; 12-1; 13-13; 14-12; 15-3; 16-17; 17-2; 18-6; 19-20; 20-8; 21-0; 22-0; 23-11; 24-9	38
9	1-21; 2-19; 3-22; 4-5; 5-11; 6-24; 7-16; 8-4; 9-17; 10-13; 11-6; 12-10; 13-7; 14-20; 15-12; 16-2; 17-15; 18-8; 19-1; 20-9; 21-0; 22-3; 23-0; 24-14	30
10	1-19; 2-21; 3-1; 4-24; 5-16; 6-18; 7-5; 8-22; 9-9; 10-7; 11-4; 12-11; 13-2; 14-15; 15-8; 16-12; 17-17; 18-10; 19-13; 20-3; 21-0; 22-6; 23-20; 24-0	36
11	1-21; 2-6; 3-19; 4-18; 5-10; 6-24; 7-4; 8-3; 9-23; 10-2; 11-5; 12-22; 13-8; 14-14; 15-17; 16-9; 17-20; 18-11; 19-13; 20-0; 21-1; 22-0; 23-12; 24-15	34
12	1-18; 2-24; 3-23; 4-5; 5-19; 6-4; 7-6; 8-8; 9-21; 10-7; 11-11; 12-3; 13-2; 14-16; 15-17; 16-15; 17-1; 18-20; 19-9; 20-0; 21-13; 22-12; 23-22; 24-0	36
13	1-21; 2-18; 3-10; 4-5; 5-23; 6-22; 7-11; 8-20; 9-1; 10-4; 11-19; 12-24; 13-6; 14-3; 15-8; 16-13; 17-15; 18-12; 19-9; 20-0; 21-14; 22-2; 23-17; 24-0	34
14	1-23; 2-5; 3-10; 4-21; 5-19; 6-18; 7-6; 8-14; 9-24; 10-4; 11-22; 12-1; 13-15; 14-20; 15-3; 16-9; 17-2; 18-8; 19-13; 20-0; 21-11; 22-12; 23-17; 24-0	36
15	1-16; 2-11; 3-10; 4-5; 5-23; 6-24; 7-6; 8-13; 9-19; 10-1; 11-22; 12-14; 13-9; 14-3; 15-2; 16-20; 17-7; 18-12; 19-17; 20-0; 21-15; 22-8; 23-4; 24-0	41
16	1-18; 2-10; 3-22; 4-24; 5-1; 6-19; 7-11; 8-13; 9-21; 10-23; 11-9; 12-6; 13-14; 14-20; 15-17; 16-8; 17-4; 18-15; 19-3; 20-12; 21-0; 22-5; 23-0; 24-2	34
17	1-20; 2-24; 3-21; 4-10; 5-23; 6-19; 7-22; 8-5; 9-13; 10-6; 11-11; 12-14; 13-12; 14-8; 15-2; 16-18; 17-9; 18-4; 19-0; 20-15; 21-17; 22-3; 23-1; 24-0	38
18	1-24; 2-21; 3-1; 4-5; 5-22; 6-23; 7-13; 8-10; 9-18; 10-11; 11-16; 12-4; 13-9; 14-14; 15-20; 16-12; 17-6; 18-17; 19-3; 20-2; 21-0; 22-8; 23-0; 24-15	30
19	1-23; 2-7; 3-19; 4-18; 5-16; 6-5; 7-24; 8-17; 9-4; 10-8; 11-22; 12-10; 13-20; 14-12; 15-2; 16-11; 17-15; 18-3; 19-1; 20-0; 21-9; 22-0; 23-13; 24-6	36
20	1-23; 2-18; 3-16; 4-24; 5-10; 6-21; 7-22; 8-13; 9-14; 10-4; 11-19; 12-1; 13-6; 14-17; 15-11; 16-9; 17-3; 18-20; 19-8; 20-2; 21-0; 22-12; 23-15; 24-0	37

Table 16. Twenty four box problem alternatives selected for IAM

i	Load arrangement (position - box)	Ordinal criterion total
1	1-58; 2-35; 3-7; 4-8; 5-1; 6-17; 7-10; 8-53; 9-26; 10-44; 11-38; 12-31; 13-40; 14-11; 15-34; 16-36; 17-16; 18-61; 19-27; 20-68; 21-29; 22-30; 23-56; 24-12; 25-71; 26-5; 27-24; 28-28; 29-37; 30-57; 31-20; 32-33; 33-55; 34-51; 35-42; 36-14; 37-72; 38-52; 39-49; 40-45; 41-19; 42-9; 43-48; 44-66; 45-50; 46-59; 47-62; 48-41; 49-0; 50-4; 51-39; 52-13; 53-22; 54-60; 55-0; 56-18; 57-0; 58-69; 59-0; 60-21; 61-2; 62-32; 63-67; 64-6; 65-3; 66-63; 67-25; 68-15; 69-23; 70-0; 71-70; 72-0	159
2	1-10; 2-4; 3-11; 4-57; 5-22; 6-53; 7-69; 8-49; 9-2; 10-39; 11-71; 12-18; 13-27; 14-17; 15-37; 16-67; 17-72; 18-44; 19-1; 20-29; 21-61; 22-26; 23-60; 24-48; 25-28; 26-30; 27-7; 28-5; 29-25; 30-16; 31-13; 32-20; 33-52; 34-43; 35-12; 36-51; 37-50; 38-3; 39-59; 40-24; 41-45; 42-9; 43-58; 44-15; 45-8; 46-47; 47-14; 48-40; 49-0; 50-35; 51-54; 52-66; 53-0; 54-0; 55-32; 56-42; 57-70; 58-36; 59-55; 60-21; 61-62; 62-23; 63-34; 64-0; 65-0; 66-33; 67-31; 68-41; 69-38; 70-68; 71-56; 72-0	147
3	1-50; 2-48; 3-68; 4-31; 5-40; 6-2; 7-61; 8-58; 9-52; 10-18; 11-59; 12-43; 13-9; 14-45; 15-1; 16-12; 17-21; 18-72; 19-7; 20-24; 21-6; 22-66; 23-51; 24-4; 25-49; 26-8; 27-11; 28-63; 29-20; 30-25; 31-39; 32-34; 33-69; 34-10; 35-26; 36-44; 37-13; 38-37; 39-36; 40-55; 41-30; 42-35; 43-33; 44-42;	147

i	Load arrangement (position - box)	Ordinal criterion total
	45-29; 46-70; 47-3; 48-57; 49-15; 50-41; 51-38; 52-16; 53-17; 54-14; 55-28; 56-0; 57-71; 58-32; 59-53; 60-46; 61-65; 62-67; 63-62; 64-56; 65-0; 66-0; 67-54; 68-0; 69-23; 70-0; 71-0; 72-5	
4	1-62; 2-26; 3-36; 4-16; 5-11; 6-40; 7-20; 8-17; 9-31; 10-21; 11-4; 12-29; 13-39; 14-37; 15-27; 16-69; 17-48; 18-59; 19-71; 20-56; 21-6; 22-63; 23-30; 24-9; 25-53; 26-33; 27-15; 28-57; 29-55; 30-28; 31-8; 32-10; 33-13; 34-12; 35-67; 36-34; 37-47; 38-50; 39-49; 40-51; 41-38; 42-5; 43-52; 44-1; 45-42; 46-35; 47-60; 48-58; 49-23; 50-70; 51-14; 52-72; 53-45; 54-41; 55-46; 56-43; 57-54; 58-0; 59-61; 60-24; 61-3; 62-7; 63-25; 64-18; 65-68; 66-0; 67-0; 68-0; 69-2; 70-44; 71-0; 72-0	157
5	1-1; 2-2; 3-60; 4-56; 5-9; 6-50; 7-37; 8-39; 9-4; 10-72; 11-45; 12-28; 13-53; 14-30; 15-43; 16-36; 17-58; 18-16; 19-48; 20-11; 21-64; 22-17; 23-29; 24-5; 25-52; 26-18; 27-44; 28-12; 29-63; 30-23; 31-40; 32-70; 33-55; 34-62; 35-69; 36-67; 37-61; 38-42; 39-25; 40-13; 41-35; 42-54; 43-7; 44-47; 45-32; 46-20; 47-24; 48-3; 49-38; 50-10; 51-51; 52-21; 53-26; 54-49; 55-57; 56-71; 57-34; 58-41; 59-14; 60-0; 61-68; 62-0; 63-8; 64-6; 65-0; 66-66; 67-59; 68-15; 69-0; 70-33; 71-0; 72-0	146
6	1-31; 2-27; 3-41; 4-57; 5-18; 6-17; 7-66; 8-6; 9-36; 10-16; 11-2; 12-65; 13-12; 14-50; 15-45; 16-39; 17-4; 18-44; 19-5; 20-30; 21-34; 22-49; 23-26; 24-20; 25-46; 26-37; 27-67; 28-10; 29-68; 30-48; 31-29; 32-52; 33-21; 34-28; 35-22; 36-61; 37-58; 38-70; 39-15; 40-51; 41-60; 42-55; 43-3; 44-56; 45-35; 46-53; 47-11; 48-62; 49-13; 50-40; 51-0; 52-54; 53-7; 54-38; 55-0; 56-71; 57-63; 58-25; 59-8; 60-0; 61-14; 62-0; 63-23; 64-19; 65-72; 66-24; 67-0; 68-0; 69-9; 70-59; 71-43; 72-69	155
7	1-44; 2-4; 3-2; 4-32; 5-20; 6-57; 7-53; 8-29; 9-26; 10-59; 11-48; 12-17; 13-60; 14-37; 15-22; 16-36; 17-61; 18-72; 19-69; 20-21; 21-68; 22-14; 23-39; 24-6; 25-43; 26-56; 27-38; 28-23; 29-63; 30-45; 31-58; 32-28; 33-49; 34-71; 35-66; 36-46; 37-7; 38-5; 39-67; 40-33; 41-18; 42-9; 43-47; 44-35; 45-50; 46-70; 47-30; 48-52; 49-65; 50-51; 51-15; 52-0; 53-13; 54-34; 55-12; 56-55; 57-42; 58-3; 59-41; 60-40; 61-8; 62-0; 63-24; 64-10; 65-31; 66-0; 67-0; 68-0; 69-25; 70-0; 71-11; 72-62	147
8	1-64; 2-39; 3-35; 4-29; 5-45; 6-48; 7-18; 8-72; 9-70; 10-62; 11-27; 12-43; 13-16; 14-56; 15-58; 16-6; 17-11; 18-61; 19-53; 20-31; 21-51; 22-34; 23-68; 24-47; 25-42; 26-37; 27-30; 28-36; 29-12; 30-49; 31-54; 32-55; 33-24; 34-67; 35-52; 36-20; 37-17; 38-9; 39-25; 40-8; 41-50; 42-26; 43-10; 44-57; 45-44; 46-60; 47-15; 48-59; 49-0; 50-65; 51-13; 52-2; 53-69; 54-3; 55-21; 56-0; 57-7; 58-0; 59-71; 60-33; 61-66; 62-14; 63-0; 64-4; 65-0; 66-40; 67-63; 68-41; 69-0; 70-46; 71-23; 72-28	160
9	1-60; 2-56; 3-18; 4-25; 5-34; 6-71; 7-57; 8-17; 9-70; 10-20; 11-9; 12-31; 13-65; 14-68; 15-6; 16-1; 17-40; 18-39; 19-30; 20-36; 21-52; 22-11; 23-2; 24-61; 25-49; 26-15; 27-35; 28-54; 29-32; 30-14; 31-53; 32-10; 33-45; 34-42; 35-37; 36-47; 37-50; 38-16; 39-26; 40-7; 41-24; 42-69; 43-29; 44-27; 45-67; 46-41; 47-21; 48-19; 49-33; 50-12; 51-38; 52-0; 53-5; 54-0; 55-72; 56-44; 57-51; 58-13; 59-66; 60-4; 61-0; 62-23; 63-43; 64-28; 65-59; 66-8; 67-0; 68-58; 69-0; 70-62; 71-55; 72-0	148
10	1-16; 2-59; 3-56; 4-50; 5-39; 6-60; 7-7; 8-21; 9-51; 10-57; 11-17; 12-19; 13-29; 14-48; 15-27; 16-53; 17-34; 18-35; 19-70; 20-43; 21-71; 22-20; 23-64; 24-26; 25-66; 26-4; 27-11; 28-10; 29-31; 30-41; 31-28; 32-23; 33-72; 34-62; 35-32; 36-40; 37-36; 38-6; 39-13; 40-38; 41-69; 42-61; 43-33; 44-5; 45-30; 46-52; 47-42; 48-24; 49-18, 50-22; 51-8; 52-58; 53-9; 54-55; 55-12; 56-0; 57-0; 58-67; 59-37; 60-15; 61-0; 62-3; 63-0; 64-2; 65-54; 66-49; 67-14; 68-25; 69-0; 70-68; 71-0; 72-63	153
11	1-57; 2-26; 3-29; 4-1; 5-22; 6-71; 7-48; 8-31; 9-56; 10-45; 11-53; 12-14; 13-17; 14-15; 15-27; 16-36; 17-18; 18-4; 19-20; 20-62; 21-3; 22-16; 23-12; 24-23; 25-50; 26-47; 27-65; 28-33; 29-61; 30-11; 31-35; 32-21; 33-6; 34-72; 35-7; 36-68; 37-30; 38-19; 39-10; 40-40; 41-55; 42-58; 43-5; 44-70; 45-52; 46-41; 47-59; 48-24; 49-28; 50-49; 51-39; 52-9; 53-43; 54-69; 55-38; 56-54; 57-13; 58-8; 59-63; 60-0; 61-34; 62-0; 63-67; 64-51; 65-0; 66-60; 67-0; 68-66; 69-0; 70-0; 71-25; 72-37	155
12	1-59; 2-6; 3-26; 4-56; 5-32; 6-42; 7-57; 8-29; 9-68; 10-17; 11-53; 12-70; 13-67; 14-1; 15-39; 16-36; 17-8; 18-60; 19-2; 20-11; 21-51; 22-3; 23-34; 24-54; 25-31; 26-18; 27-35; 28-48; 29-52; 30-4; 31-15; 32-40; 33-61; 34-5; 35-64; 36-7; 37-24; 38-46; 39-38; 40-13; 41-62; 42-71; 43-49; 44-65; 45-63; 46-33; 47-12; 48-66; 49-37; 50-72; 51-69; 52-41; 53-55; 54-0; 55-23; 56-21; 57-50; 58-58; 59-10; 60-9; 61-0; 62-45; 63-47; 64-25; 65-0; 66-14; 67-20; 68-28; 69-0; 70-0; 71-30; 72-0	138
13	1-50; 2-6; 3-59; 4-44; 5-17; 6-43; 7-45; 8-68; 9-48; 10-57; 11-3; 12-69; 13-1; 14-7; 15-27; 16-8; 17-31; 18-53; 19-54; 20-11; 21-23; 22-40; 23-2; 24-70; 25-61; 26-46; 27-28; 28-26; 29-58; 30-62;	154

i	Load arrangement (position - box)	Ordinal criterion total
	31-15; 32-56; 33-36; 34-35; 35-72; 36-52; 37-67; 38-32; 39-20; 40-55; 41-66; 42-30; 43-41; 44-34; 45-13; 46-29; 47-4; 48-37; 49-39; 50-51; 51-0; 52-12; 53-33; 54-9; 55-16; 56-18; 57-25; 58-24; 59-0; 60-14; 61-49; 62-22; 63-42; 64-0; 65-0; 66-5; 67-71; 68-0; 69-63; 70-10; 71-21; 72-0	
14	1-2; 2-66; 3-61; 4-5; 5-44; 6-12; 7-69; 8-62; 9-43; 10-63; 11-72; 12-18; 13-37; 14-60; 15-1; 16-49; 17-53; 18-45; 19-16; 20-19; 21-50; 22-59; 23-20; 24-56; 25-38; 26-15; 27-57; 28-24; 29-22; 30-10; 31-71; 32-41; 33-58; 34-31; 35-55; 36-54; 37-68; 38-29; 39-34; 40-64; 41-40; 42-51; 43-46; 44-67; 45-8; 46-28; 47-26; 48-21; 49-3; 50-0; 51-33; 52-0; 53-7; 54-23; 55-35; 56-11; 57-32; 58-42; 59-0; 60-4; 61-0; 62-14; 63-52; 64-9; 65-30; 66-0; 67-70; 68-13; 69-25; 70-0; 71-17; 72-36	152
15	1-12; 2-6; 3-1; 4-68; 5-32; 6-29; 7-27; 8-31; 9-17; 10-44; 11-70; 12-2; 13-62; 14-18; 15-63; 16-26; 17-42; 18-51; 19-36; 20-49; 21-57; 22-47; 23-67; 24-54; 25-28; 26-59; 27-71; 28-4; 29-61; 30-43; 31-52; 32-10; 33-3; 34-14; 35-50; 36-66; 37-25; 38-13; 39-34; 40-30; 41-24; 42-37; 43-56; 44-21; 45-69; 46-5; 47-15; 48-45; 49-9; 50-55; 51-35; 52-23; 53-8; 54-11; 55-53; 56-38; 57-60; 58-33; 59-39; 60-20; 61-58; 62-41; 63-40; 64-7; 65-0; 66-0; 67-16; 68-0; 69-65; 70-0; 71-0; 72-0	157
16	1-43; 2-63; 3-47; 4-69; 5-59; 6-23; 7-6; 8-11; 9-71; 10-60; 11-18; 12-48; 13-5; 14-55; 15-56; 16-33; 17-25; 18-45; 19-16; 20-24; 21-57; 22-1; 23-7; 24-58; 25-21; 26-39; 27-72; 28-37; 29-31; 30-61; 31-70; 32-36; 33-52; 34-34; 35-49; 36-44; 37-41; 38-28; 39-10; 40-13; 41-35; 42-4; 43-20; 44-3; 45-68; 46-29; 47-40; 48-32; 49-17; 50-15; 51-8; 52-53; 53-62; 54-51; 55-30; 56-67; 57-0; 58-38; 59-14; 60-9; 61-12; 62-0; 63-66; 64-0; 65-0; 66-2; 67-65; 68-0; 69-42; 70-54; 71-27; 72-0	149
17	1-50; 2-26; 3-32; 4-51; 5-34; 6-17; 7-58; 8-63; 9-16; 10-43; 11-12; 12-59; 13-1; 14-72; 15-44; 16-60; 17-68; 18-22; 19-19; 20-52; 21-57; 22-36; 23-70; 24-20; 25-10; 26-5; 27-66; 28-23; 29-62; 30-42; 31-41; 32-55; 33-18; 34-71; 35-54; 36-21; 37-8; 38-13; 39-47; 40-61; 41-29; 42-37; 43-14; 44-67; 45-69; 46-27; 47-11; 48-24; 49-9; 50-45; 51-0; 52-0; 53-38; 54-35; 55-4; 56-28; 57-49; 58-0; 59-30; 60-15; 61-3; 62-0; 63-33; 64-6; 65-40; 66-53; 67-0; 68-56; 69-25; 70-31; 71-7; 72-0	142
18	1-69; 2-70; 3-27; 4-20; 5-19; 6-62; 7-39; 8-40; 9-12; 10-63; 11-53; 12-31; 13-56; 14-16; 15-17; 16-43; 17-13; 18-44; 19-71; 20-18; 21-58; 22-49; 23-66; 24-29; 25-26; 26-15; 27-38; 28-7; 29-11; 30-35; 31-72; 32-24; 33-52; 34-42; 35-60; 36-61; 37-36; 38-22; 39-57; 40-1; 41-33; 42-6; 43-54; 44-14; 45-9; 46-51; 47-8; 48-25; 49-41; 50-46; 51-68; 52-5; 53-59; 54-10; 55-32; 56-30; 57-28; 58-37; 59-3; 60-55; 61-45; 62-65; 63-34; 64-4; 65-0; 66-23; 67-0; 68-0; 69-0; 70-67; 71-0; 72-0	154
19	1-68; 2-57; 3-38; 4-20; 5-21; 6-34; 7-4; 8-6; 9-59; 10-44; 11-9; 12-47; 13-16; 14-69; 15-48; 16-70; 17-53; 18-1; 19-39; 20-31; 21-56; 22-35; 23-29; 24-45; 25-8; 26-62; 27-49; 28-43; 29-26; 30-67; 31-51; 32-30; 33-28; 34-11; 35-54; 36-55; 37-46; 38-33; 39-27; 40-7; 41-60; 42-72; 43-36; 44-10; 45-3; 46-12; 47-63; 48-17; 49-52; 50-25; 51-0; 52-23; 53-0; 54-41; 55-14; 56-18; 57-71; 58-15; 59-42; 60-0; 61-61; 62-0; 63-65; 64-37; 65-5; 66-24; 67-40; 68-32; 69-0; 70-13; 71-58; 72-0	153
20	1-44; 2-34; 3-32; 4-6; 5-50; 6-60; 7-24; 8-5; 9-29; 10-17; 11-20; 12-1; 13-16; 14-14; 15-63; 16-37; 17-52; 18-43; 19-48; 20-7; 21-68; 22-69; 23-2; 24-62; 25-57; 26-61; 27-15; 28-64; 29-56; 30-35; 31-21; 32-41; 33-4; 34-65; 35-38; 36-11; 37-66; 38-59; 39-30; 40-53; 41-31; 42-36; 43-67; 44-40; 45-39; 46-54; 47-9; 48-72; 49-55; 50-58; 51-25; 52-8; 53-49; 54-13; 55-0; 56-28; 57-0; 58-33; 59-12; 60-46; 61-3; 62-0; 63-0; 64-23; 65-0; 66-0; 67-71; 68-70; 69-51; 70-45; 71-10; 72-19	147

Table 17. Seventy two box problem selected alternatives for IAM

11

Understanding Protein-Ligand Interactions Using Simulated Annealing in Dimensionally Reduced Fingerprint Representation

Ravi K. Nandigam and Sangtae Kim
Purdue University School of Chemical Engineering
USA

1. Introduction

Structure-based drug design is a rational approach for drug discovery based on understanding of the three dimensional structural interactions between a target protein and the drug-like ligands. The underlying premise is that good drug-like molecules must possess structural and chemical features complementary to that of the target receptor, which is usually a protein involved in the disease process. The process first involves identification of the protein target that is of interest. The structure of the target protein is then determined using experimental procedures like NMR, X-ray crystallography or computational approaches like homology modeling. After determining the structure of the target, the structural knowledge is used to systematically search the chemical space for compounds (or ligands) that would bind to the protein in the desired binding mode using docking techniques. These compounds are scored and ranked using scoring functions that take into account factors that could influence the nature of the binding such as steric and electrochemical interactions, exposed surface area, molecular weight, etc. The challenge in the search for the desired ligands is the ability to accurately model and analyze the protein-ligand binding by understanding the structural and chemical characteristics of the protein's binding site from theory, computation and experiment.

The amount of protein-ligand structural data available in public domain and corporate databanks increased exponentially during the last two decades due to significant advances in high throughput experimental techniques and computation power. In addition, there are many more structures that remain undisclosed due to proprietary interests. It is expected to have many more X-ray crystal structures to be available in the near future due to advances in high-throughput techniques and other experimental sophistications. In addition, there are also structures that are computationally generated through docking, or similar techniques. A typical virtual chemical library screen could generate a library of structures containing thousands to millions of small molecules docked onto a target protein in silico (Lyne, 2002). As discussed before the key to success in the rational drug design process is the proper understanding of the receptor site and the mode(s) in which ligands bind to the receptor by leveraging the available structural data. Traditionally, this is done by making logical deductions after visually inspecting the protein ligand complex on a computer or sometimes aided by software tools like LIGPLOT (Wallace et al., 1995) that generate two dimensional schematic representations of the interactions. However the traditional approach is impractical when the number of structures to be analyzed is very large. In such scenarios, there is requirement for an automated way of detecting the various interaction patterns between the protein and the ligand, representing them in an efficient manner such that different protein ligand complexes can be compared and if possible correlated with their actual binding constants. The interaction patterns so identified from the structural data can eventually help to develop virtual screening and other design tools to aid the search for new drugs i.e. ligands with desired characteristics.

1.1 Structural Interaction Fingerprint (SIFt)

Fingerprint based approaches have been developed recently in the cheminformatics domain to mine, analyze, organize and visualize the vast structural binding data. They involve representing the three dimensional protein-ligand structural binding information into a one-dimensional vector by encoding the nature of interactions between binding site residues and the ligand as in Structural Interaction Fingerprint or SIFt (Deng et al., 2004; Chuaqui et al., 2005; Singh et al., 2006). Since the binding information is encoded in a 1D fingerprint, advanced filtering, clustering, and machine learning methods may be applied to identify patterns underlying the binding data, thereby enhancing the ability to make useful implications that are not apparent by looking at individual structures. There are also other fingerprint approaches published in literature such as atom-pairs based interaction fingerprint (Pérez-Nueno VI et al., 2009), pharmacophore based fingerprint (Sato et al., 2010), etc. This chapter demonstrates the use of advanced mathematical and statistical learning techniques to enhance the understanding of binding interactions from fingerprints. Though the methods explained here are in the context of SIFt, they can be applied to other fingerprint approaches.

A SIFt is generated from a protein-ligand complex by first identifying the key residues of the receptor protein, which are the residues that could potentially be involved in binding with a ligand. The key residues are identifying by performing a rigorous search among all known protein-ligand complexes of the target protein for residues that are involved in binding in at least one complex. The next step involves representing of each key residue by a bit pattern corresponding to the kind of interaction that is being made at that residue by the ligand. The first bit is a master bit that checks if an interaction is present at all or not. The second and third bits check if the interaction is with the main chain or side chain portions of the residue. The next four bits characterize the chemical nature of the interaction. The fourth and fifth bits are turned 'on' or 'off' corresponding to whether the residue is involved in a polar or non-polar interaction respectively, while one of the sixth and seventh bits is turned 'on' if there is a hydrogen bond interaction depending on whether the residue has a functional group that is an acceptor or a donor. The bit strings from all the residues are concatenated to form a fingerprint (called SIFt) which is a unique representation for that protein-ligand complex, as shown in Figure 1.

The overall pattern of interactions in a set of structures can be represented by an interaction profile where each element or entry in the profile speaks about the nature of interactions of the entire set. A profile based on the conservation or frequency of a bit over the set of fingerprints was used in (Chuaqui et al., 2005). They demonstrated by comparing the profiles of protein complexes belonging to different kinase targets viz. p38 and CDK2, one

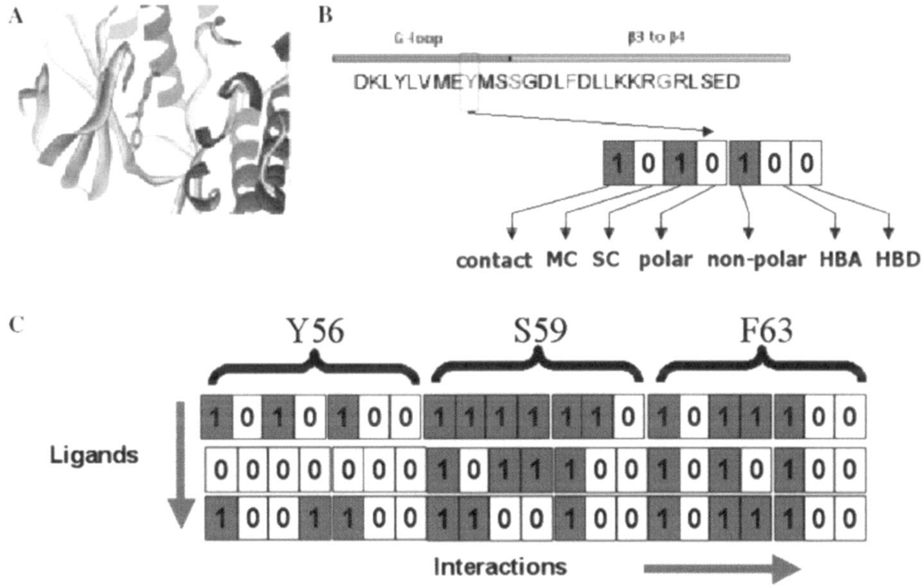

Fig. 1. An illustrative showing the SIFt methodology. (A) identify the key binding residues of the receptor protein in the complex. (B) represent each key residue by a bit string according to the kind of interaction at that residue. (C) concatenate 7-bit strings of all key residues to form a unique fingerprint, called SIFt. (Figure reprinted in part with permission from Singh J et al., 2005).

can identify the characteristic role played by the individual interactions in the overall binding. Interaction fingerprints and profile-based methods have been applied to virtual screening, library design, and the analysis of large numbers of X-ray structures to identify interaction patterns that may influence inhibitor potency and selectivity. The evolution of interaction fingerprint and profile approaches and their application to docking, scoring, and the analysis of ligand-receptor interactions has been comprehensively reviewed recently by Brewerton (Brewerton, 2008).

1.2 Weighted interactions profile

The original plain fingerprint is a simplified representation of protein-ligand interactions with all interactions being treated identical. But in reality the various possible interactions at different residues might have different contributions towards the overall binding. As an example, it is well-known that in kinases the interactions at the hinge region are critical for binding compared to interactions at other regions. Likewise, a hydrogen bond interaction could have a different impact compared to a polar or nonpolar interaction. By not capturing the information pertaining to the interactions differently from each other, their relative importance information is in effect lost. Hence the fingerprint representation is inefficient due to underrepresentation of significant interaction information and overrepresentation of insignificant interaction information. A new weighted interactions based approach called weighted Structural Interaction Fingerprint (wSIFt) was introduced in (Nandigam et al., 2009) to address this inefficiency of fingerprint representation. In the wSIFt method a robust representation signifying the relative importance of ligand receptor interactions is captured in the form of a weights vector called weighted profile, where each weight corresponds to the importance of that interaction in overall binding. The weighted profile incorporates empirically determined weights fit from inhibitor potency data. The profile weights are determined such that the fingerprint similarity between docked poses and the weighted profile is in effect a residue-specific QSAR based on the relative importance of ligand-receptor interactions for determining potency.

The chapter describes the wSIFt methodology developed by Nandigam et al. to determine a weighted profile capturing the significance of interactions. The weights are determined using a statistical learning technique from structural data and experimental potency data such that the similarity between the weighted profile and a SIFt (called wSIFt score) is positively correlated with its experimentally determined inhibition potency. The mathematical formulation to determine the weights is an optimization problem with the objective to be maximized being the correlation between the wSIFt score and the inhibitor potency. Since the objective function is complex and non-linear, and the number of variables (i.e. weights) to determine is very large, a stochastic optimization technique (Simulated Annealing) is applied. The dimensionality of SIFt interaction bits is large and the representation contains linearly interdependent interaction bits and hence a dimensionality reduction technique called Nonnegative Matrix Factorization (NMF) is combined with the stochastic optimization stage. The subsequent sections of the chapter describe the methods including the strategy of the overall algorithm, dimensionality reduction and Simulated Annealing, followed by results and analysis of the weights.

2. Methods

2.1 Overall approach

The weighted profile is assumed to contain non-negative weights with values ranging between 0 and 1 at positions that have a 1 in at least one of the SIFts, and a value of 0 at positions that do not have a 1 in at least one of the SIFts (as shown in Figure. 2).

SIFt 1	1	0	0	1	1	0	0	1	0	1
SIFt 2	1	1	0	0	1	0	1	0	0	1
SIFt 3	1	1	0	0	1	0	1	0	0	1
SIFt 4	1	1	0	0	1	0	1	1	0	1
SIFt 5	0	0	0	1	1	0	0	1	0	1
W-Profile	w_1	w_2	0	w_4	w_5	0	w_7	w_8	0	w_{10}

Fig. 2. Illustration of weighted profile for a set of interaction fingerprints.

The objective is to determine the weights such that the computed weights will represent the significance of each interaction in contributing toward overall protein-ligand binding. This can be achieved by statistically learning the weights from a training set such that the similarity between the weighted profile and SIFt is positively correlated with the inhibition potency. The reasoning behind the proposed approach is that the interactions appearing more frequently in high potent compounds are supposedly more important, and so in order to boost the w-SIFt score of the high potent compounds the weights for those interactions will be calculated to be higher. Likewise, interactions that appear more frequently in less potent compounds are supposedly less important, and so in order to decrease the w-SIFt score of the less potent compounds these interactions' weights will be lower. Thus the overall weights in the weighted profile so determined will represent the importance associated with each SIFt interaction bit in the protein-ligand binding potency. The Tanimoto score is used here as the metric to measure the similarity between the weighted profile and SIFt, and for a given SIFt we call this metric the w-SIFt score. Thus a protein-ligand complex with a higher w-SIFt score implies that it comprises of interactions predominantly at higher weight bit positions and so the ligand would be a strong inhibitor of the protein, and likewise a complex with lower w-SIFt score implies that it comprises of interactions mainly at lower weight bit positions and so the ligand would be a weak inhibitor. The proposed strategy to determine the weighted profile can be graphically visualized as in Figure 3. Suppose the SIFts can be represented as points in a high dimensional hyperspace, the desired weighted profile should be more similar to the high potent compounds and less similar to the low potent compounds. In other words the weighted profile should be as closer as possible to the high potent compounds and as farther as possible to the low potent compounds in the SIFt coordinate space.

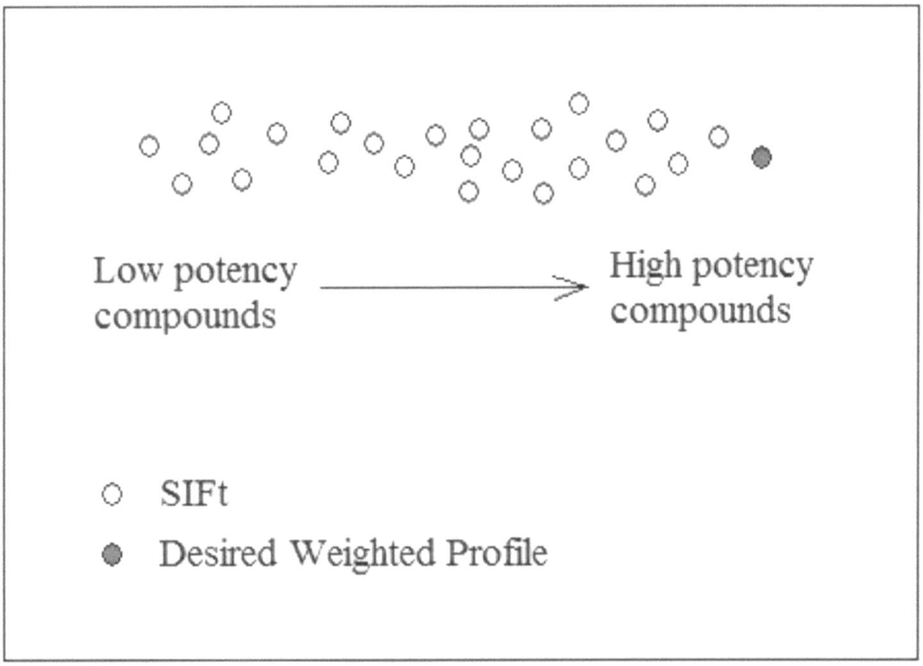

Fig. 3. Illustration of proposed weighted profile relative to the high potent and low potent SIFts in a hypothetical high dimensional hyperspace.

2.2 Mathematical objective function

Assume $\mathbf{s}$ represents a SIFt in a vector form and $\mathbf{w}$ represents the weighted profile. The w-SIFt score, let us call T_w, is defined as the Tanimoto similarity between the SIFt and the profile. i.e.

$$T_w = \frac{\mathbf{s} \cdot \mathbf{w}}{\mathbf{s} \cdot \mathbf{s} + \mathbf{w} \cdot \mathbf{w} - \mathbf{s} \cdot \mathbf{w}}.$$

The weights of the profile will be determined so as to obtain a w-SIFt score that correlates well with the experimentally determined potencies. We constrain the weights to be positive since in principle they represent the significance of the corresponding interactions. The objective of determining the weights can be mathematically stated as follows.

To determine $\mathbf{w}$ *so that* $T_w \propto -Log(IC50)$, *with* $w_i \geq 0$.

i.e. find $\mathbf{w}$ that corresponds to a straight line fit between T_w and $-Log(IC50)$ with highest correlation. The Pearson's correlation coefficient is chosen here to measure the extent of correlation. So, the objective function is formulated as,

$$\underset{w_i \text{ s.t. } w_i \geq 0}{Maximize} \quad CorrCoef(T_w, -Log(IC50)) \tag{1}$$

where $CorrCoef(x,y) = \dfrac{\mathrm{cov}(x,y)}{\sqrt{\mathrm{var}(x) \cdot \mathrm{var}(y)}}$

Since the objective function is complex and non-linear, and the number of variables (i.e. weights) to alter is very large, we apply a stochastic optimization technique *viz.* Simulated Annealing (Kirkpatrick, Gelatt et al. 1983). The energy function for Simulated Annealing is defined here as the negative of the objective function defined in Equation 1.

$$E_w = -CorrCoef\left(Tw, -Log(IC50)\right) \tag{2}$$

2.3 Linear dimensionality reduction

The dimensionality of the SIFt bits is the number of binding region residues times the number of interaction bits per residue. Typically this number is high, for e.g. in the case of P38α the number of bits in SIFt is 560 as discussed in the Dataset Generation subsection. Even after eliminating the zero valued bit positions the number of bit positions whose weights need to be determined is large. However not all the interactions at the non-zero bit positions are independent of each other, as there could be co-occurrences (i.e. two bits simultaneously 'on' or 'off') and cross-occurrences (i.e. bits that are complementary to each other). There could also be additional statistically significant dependencies between bit pairs, i.e. two bit positions positively or negatively highly correlated within the data. So a dimensionality reduction technique is used here to reduce if not eliminate these interdependencies and eventually compress the number of SIFt bits to a considerably smaller number without losing significant information. Thus, by doing so the number of weight parameters to be determined in the weighted profile is also significantly reduced. As the interdependencies in the SIFt are linear, we choose a linear dimensionality reduction technique for the data compression. The values of the SIFts in the reduced space need not be binary, but have to be positive. We now only have as many weights to be determined as the dimension of the reduced space. After determining the weights in the lower dimensional space, the weights in the higher dimensional space (i.e. the original weights of the SIFts) can be obtained by an inverse transformation.

A linear dimensionality reduction technique involves transformation or rotation of the vector coordinate space such that the original data vector of higher dimensionality can be represented by another vector of lower dimensionality. Assume the original SIFt vector is represented as $\mathbf{s}^h$ of dimensionality n, let $\mathbf{s}^l$ be its representation in a lower vector space of dimensionality r, and $\mathbf{L}$ be the dimensionality reduction transformation. Then,

$$\mathbf{s}^h \approx \mathbf{L} \cdot \mathbf{s}^l$$

Suppose the full SIFt dataset is represented as an $n \times m$ matrix, $\mathbf{S}^h$ where m is the number of SIFts. During linear dimensionality reduction the matrix $\mathbf{S}^h$ is in effect factorized into two sub-matrices $\mathbf{L}$ and $\mathbf{S}^l$ of size $n \times r$ and $r \times m$ respectively *i.e.*

$$\underbrace{\mathbf{S}^h}_{n\times m} \approx \underbrace{\mathbf{L}}_{n\times r} \cdot \underbrace{\mathbf{S}^l}_{r\times m} \qquad \text{where } (n+m)r < nm$$

The matrix $\mathbf{S}^l$ represents the m SIFts in the lower dimensional space.
Dimensionality reduction techniques such as Nonnegative Matrix Factorization (NMF), Principal Component Analysis (PCA), and Vector Quantization (VQ) differ in the nature of the factor matrices. NMF involves a factorization such that the end sub-matrices are nonnegative. PCA involves a factorization such that the $\mathbf{L}$ matrix corresponds to a transformation into the Eigen vector coordinate system, whereas in VQ the factorization is such that the vectors of the transformed matrix are all unary. NMF is used here for dimensionality reduction of the SIFt space as the nonnegative constraint imposed in this method helps to preserve the underlying physical interpretation of the weights.
Lee and Seung (Lee and Seung 1999) demonstrated that NMF involves parts based learning of objects, and is very effective and meaningful for dimensionality reduction in applications like image processing and text mining. NMF has been applied in several recent works in the context of computational biology and bioinformatics. Gao and Church (Gao and Church 2005) applied NMF as an unsupervised classification method for cancer identification based on gene expression data, and found the method to be effective over other clustering techniques. Brunet et al. (Brunet et al., 2004) have also used NMF on cancer related microarray data. The basis vectors in their work, called meta genes, represented distinct molecular patterns thus enabling them to extract meaningful biological information. In Ref. (Kim and Tidor 2003) NMF was used on a large dataset of genome-wide expression measurements of yeast and was able to detect local features in the expression space that mapped to functional cellular subsystems. Recently, Devarajan (Devarajan 2008) provided a review of recent NMF applications in the context of biological informatics
When NMF is applied to SIFts, the basis vectors represent underlying patterns of interactions between protein and the ligands as explained in Results section. The algorithm for solving NMF based on the following update rules as described by Lee and Seung (Lee and Seung 2001) is used here for the dimensionality reduction.

$$L_{ia} \leftarrow L_{ia} \frac{\left(S^h S^{lT}\right)_{ia}}{\left(L S^h S^{lT}\right)_{ia}} \tag{3}$$

$$L_{ia} \leftarrow \frac{L_{ia}}{\sum_j L_{ja}} \tag{4}$$

$$S^l_{a\mu} \leftarrow L_{a\mu} \frac{\left(L^T S^h\right)_{a\mu}}{\left(L^T L S^l\right)_{a\mu}} \tag{5}$$

The update in Equation (4) is for ensuring uniqueness of the NMF submatrices. The convergence criterion for the algorithm is the Euclidean distance $\left\| S^h - LS^l \right\|$.

2.4 Determining weights using Simulated Annealing

After the NMF dimensionality reduction is completed the SIFts training data is initially transformed into the reduced space. Initial guess values are assigned to the weights in the lower r-dimensional space which are back transformed into the higher n-dimensional space using the equation $\mathbf{w}^h = \mathbf{L} \cdot \mathbf{w}^l$. The w-SIFt score is then calculated which is used to evaluate the objective function in Equation 2. A new weights vector $\mathbf{w}^l + \Delta\,\mathbf{w}$ is determined and the objective function is reevaluated. The new weights vector is accepted if the new objective value is better, otherwise it is accepted with a probability $p = \exp(-(E_{w,new} - E_w)/T)$ where T is a global parameter called the temperature which is gradually reduced to a very small value ~ 0 during the course of the algorithm.

Since the weights in the higher dimension are supposed to be nonnegative, the weights in the lower dimension are constrained to be nonnegative. The nonnegativity constraint of the NMF algorithm helps to retain the nonnegative values of the SIFt data in the lower dimension and conversely nonnegative weights in the lower dimensions ensures nonnegative weights in the higher dimension. Maintaining the constraint of nonnegative weights in the higher dimension would have been a challenge, if other dimensionality reduction techniques such as Principal Component Analysis were used because of the possible encoding of the data to negative values in the lower dimension. Fig. 4. summarizes the overall workflow involving NMF dimensionality reduction stage and the determination of weights stage using simulated annealing.

2.5 Dataset generation

A dataset of P38α inhibitors whose potency (IC50) values and two-dimensional chemical structure have been reported in literature is considered to begin with. However, in order to generate SIFts for these inhibitors we should identify the *accurate* three-dimensional structure of the ligands binding into the protein which is a huge challenge. A rigorous search to determine the most likely binding pose of the ligand by binding energy minimization is not practical because of the combinatorial complexity of the conformational and positional search space of the ligand and the protein. The six degrees of translational and rotational freedom of the ligand, along with the internal conformational degrees of freedom of both the ligand and the protein, makes the search space extremely large. Consider as an example a simple system comprising a ligand with four rotatable bonds and six rigid body alignment parameters, the search space can be estimated as follows (Taylor et al., 2002): The alignment parameters are used to place the ligand relative to the protein in a

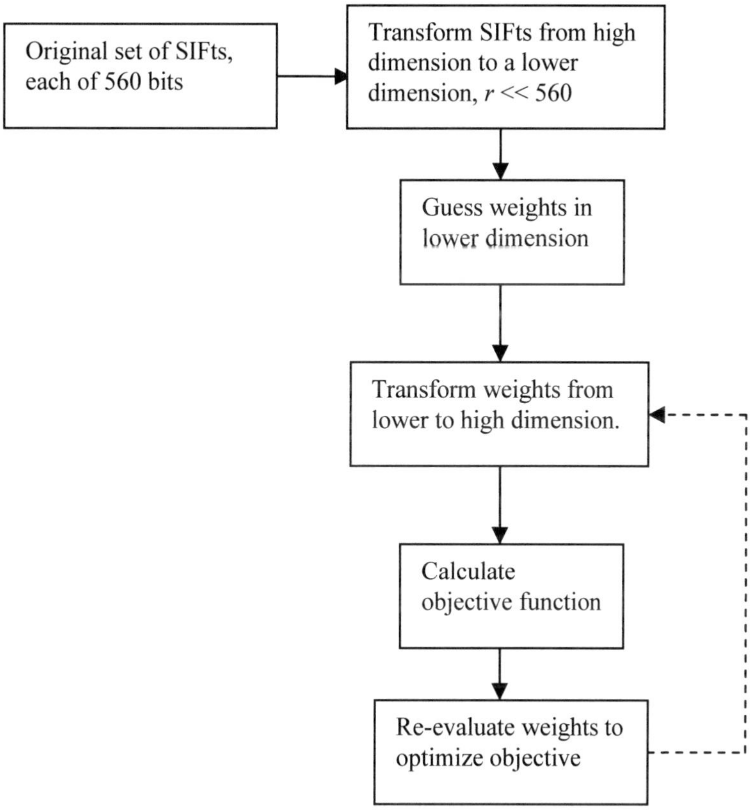

Fig. 4. The workflow involving dimensionality reduction and weights calculation.

cubic active site of size 10^3 Å^3. If the angles are considered in 10 degree increments and translational parameters on a 0.5 Å grid there are approximately 4×10^8 rigid body degrees of freedom to sample, corresponding to 6×10^{14} configurations (including the four rotatable torsions) to be searched. The search would take approximately 2,000,000 years of computational time at a rate of 10 configurations per second. So, the search process of docking algorithms implement some way of exploring only a partial region of the search domain thereby making the search implementation feasible. Molecular docking programs use heuristic search approaches based on molecular dynamics, monte carlo methods, genetic algorithms, fragment based methods, point complementarity methods, distance geometry methods, etc. However since these programs are heuristic the docked structure results are not reliable and so need to be cross-checked by other means such as comparing with experimentally determined binding poses of structurally similar ligands.

For the inhibitors above, all stable three-dimensional conformations are first generated using Omega program (Openeye Scientifc Software, NM) and these conformations are searched against known ligands of P38α using ROCS. The known ligands here are the ligands whose binding conformation with P38α has been confirmed experimentally and is available in the PDB. Only those inhibitors with a conformation closely matching with the known ligands are considered further for docking, whereas the remaining inhibitors are discarded because the resulting poses from docking cannot be verified for accuracy. Glide docking program (Schrodinger, NY) is used here to obtain the likely docking poses for the selected inhibitors.

After comparing the docking results with the binding pose of the corresponding known ligand using SIFts, only those ligands are finally retained whose binding pose matches closely with that of the known ligand and hence can be considered to be accurate. More information regarding the generation of the accurate binding poses from the two-dimensional inhibitor structures can be found in Nandigam et al. The final SIFt dataset considered here consisted of 89 protein-ligand structures of P38α. The active site of P38α consists of 56 residues with each residue being represented by 10 bits, making SIFt a 560 bit vector.

2.6 Cross-validating weights

The methodology described in the previous section involves a dimensionality reduction step that requires knowing *a priori* the dimensionality of the reduced space. Since we do not know the exact value of the reduced dimensionality in the case of SIFts, we build weighted profile models based on some guess values of the reduced space dimensionality using a training set and validate the models on a validation set. The guess value that generates a weights vector model that has the least validation error is chosen as the accurate dimensionality of the reduced space. This is because a model with the least validation error would theoretically also generate the least predictive error (Hastie et al., 2003).

Since the available SIFt dataset is small to split into separate training and validation sets, a five-fold cross validation method is used to generate training and test sets. The dataset of 89 SIFts is divided into a training set (both for training and cross validation) of 80 SIFts, and a test set (for final testing) of 9 SIFts. The 80 SIFts are further divided into 5 training-validation set pairs. In the cross validation procedure, a model is built for each of the five training sets and is validated against its corresponding validation set. The validation error of an individual model is the sum of squared differences between the model prediction values and the experimental $-Log(IC50)$ values for the validation set. The overall cross-validation error for a given dimensionality guess is taken as the average of validation errors of the five individual models constructed from the five training-validation set pairs.

The following steps outline the 5-fold cross-validation procedure.

1. Divide the overall dataset into five training and validation sets.
2. Consider a set of r values.
3. For each r, run the dimensionality reduction algorithm and then calculate five sets of weights corresponding to the five training sets.
4. Validate wSIFt scores of the five validation sets calculated based on the above weights by comparing against the experimental potency values.

3. Results

The cross validation errors calculated for various guess values of dimensionality for the reduced space are shown in Figure 3. The results show that a value of 20 for the reduced dimensionality corresponds to the least overall cross validation error, implying that the given P38α SIFt data can be efficiently translated as a combination of 20 linearly independent vectors. Figure 4 shows a heat map representation of the transformation **L** which is a graphical illustration of the 20 basis vectors in terms of the original 560 bits. Each of these basis vectors represents an 'interaction pattern' which is a combination of individual interactions that were found to co-occur in the original SIFt data. Each entry in

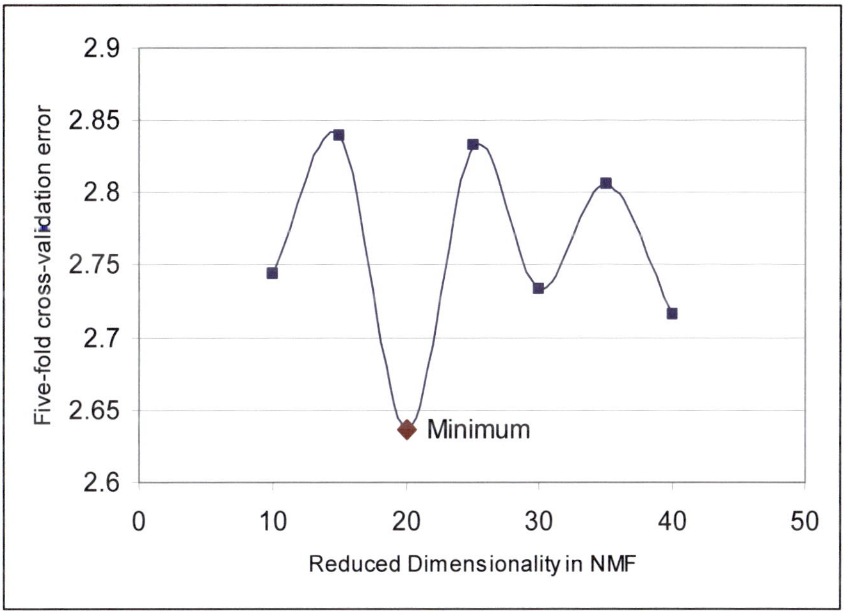

Fig. 3. The cross validation error of models built using different values of the lower dimensionality in NMF.

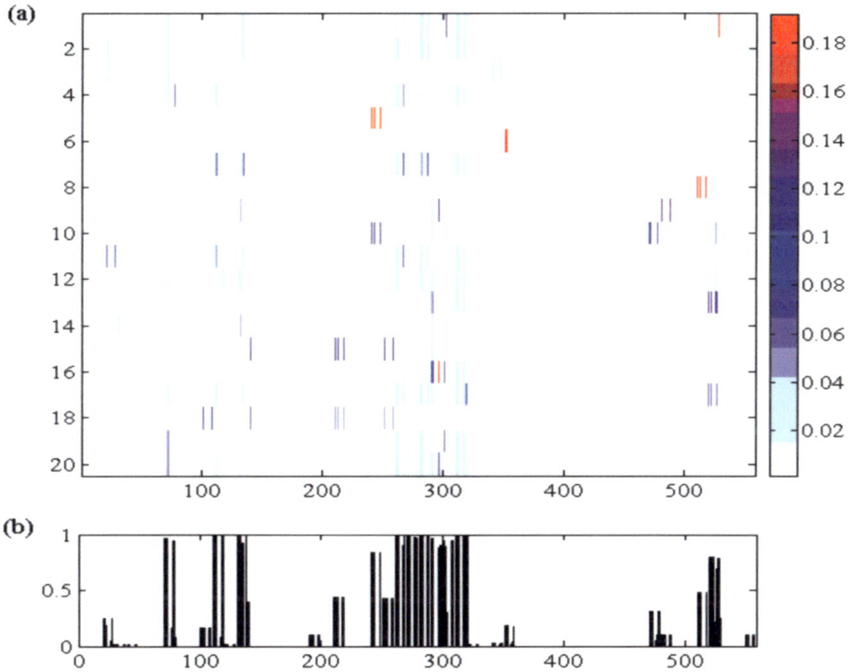

Fig. 4. (a) Heatmap of the transformation matrix ($\mathbf{L}$) from 560 bit-space to a lower dimensional space (of size 20). The panel on the right shows the numerical value range for the colors in the heatmap. (b) The average of all the SIFts in the entire dataset.

the basis vector corresponds to the importance of that particular bit in that pattern of interactions. Thus the basis vectors represent a meaningful combination of interactions due to the nonnegative restriction on the elements of $\mathbf{L}$ matrix. Also, since the transformation matrix, $\mathbf{L}$, is nonnegative we simply need to restrict our weights in the lower dimensional space to be positive in order to satisfy the criterion that the weights in the original 560 bit space should be nonnegative.

The weight values of the weighted profile are provided as supplementary information in (Nandigam et al, 2009). The weights at the fingerprint positions corresponding to the contact bit of all the residues is shown in Figure 5. By looking at the weight values at the residue positions and the average SIFt values in Figure 5, it can be deduced that the weights are 'learnt' based on the supposed contribution of the interactions towards potency rather than mere frequency of interaction occurrence. In Figure 6(a), the w-SIFt scores of the training compounds, computed using the final weights model, are plotted against $-Log(IC50)$ values. The SIFt training data is categorized into three classes (colored blue, yellow and red in the figure) for better illustration and subsequent box plot analysis. The points in blue, yellow and red correspond to highly potent, moderately potent, and least potent compounds respectively. Figure 6(b) is the corresponding box plot representation showing the mean, quantiles, and outliers of the weighted profile scores (w-SIFt scores) for the three classes.

In Figure 6(c) w-SIFt scores of the 9 SIFts from final test set and the 80 SIFts from the training set are compared with the potencies. The w-SIFt scoring metric seems to perform well on the final test set too. The analysis done in Figure 6(a-b) is repeated for molecular weight and the docking score, in order to compare the performance of w-SIFt against other ligand parameters. Figure 7(a) shows the scatter plot of the molecular weight against the $-Log(IC50)$ values, whereas Figure 7(b) is its corresponding box plot. Figure 7(c) is the scatter plot of -docking score against the $-Log(IC50)$ values with its respective box plot shown in Figure 7(d). The figures show that the molecular weight ($R = 0.2929$) and docking score ($R = 0.3415$) bear some correlation with the potencies though the deviation from the straight-line fit seems to be higher as evidenced in the respective box plots. The w-SIFt score definitely seems to a better metric for assessing the experimental potency of the ligand from the interaction fingerprint.

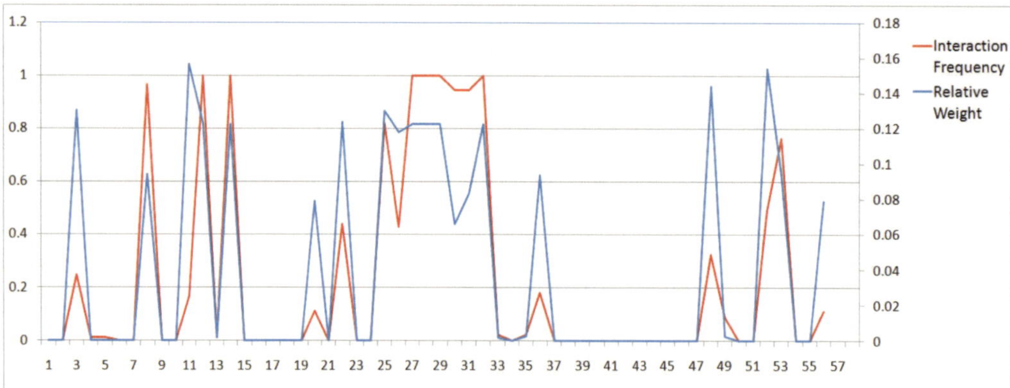

Fig. 5. The weighted profile showing the contact-bit weight at each of the residues as determined from the algorithm.

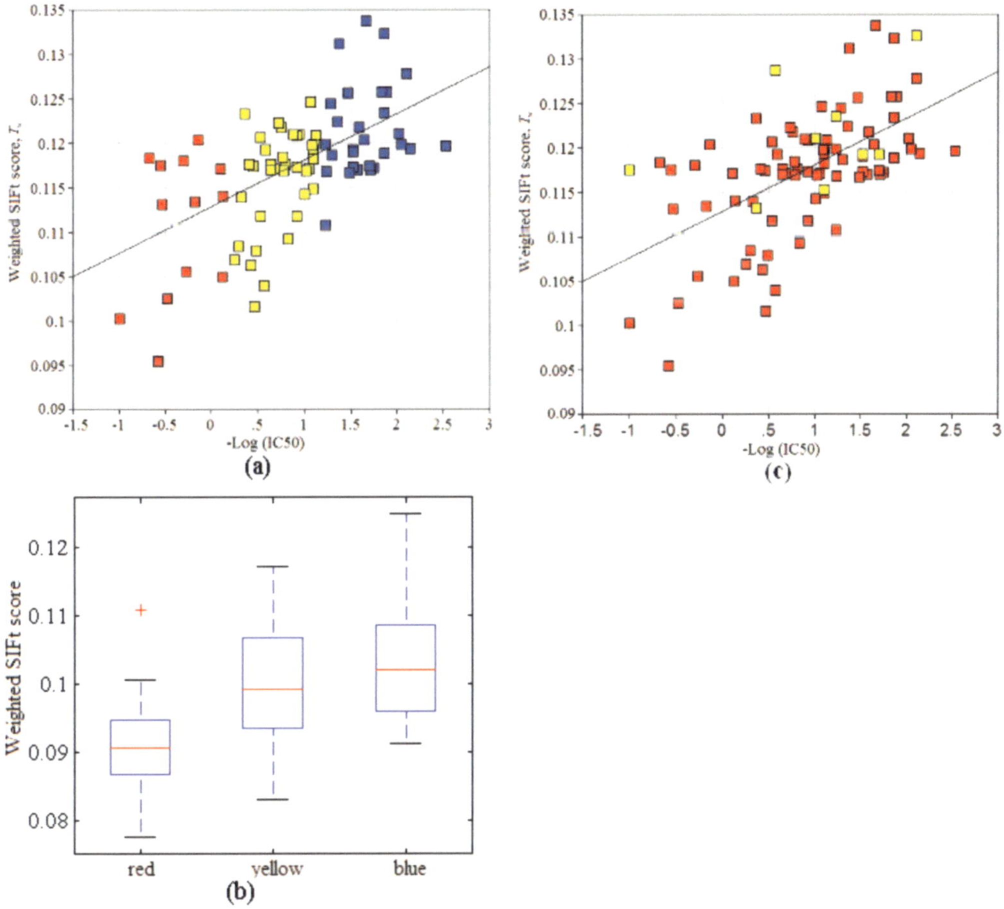

Fig. 6.(a) Scatter plot of the weighted SIFt scores against $-Log(IC50)$ for training data. The points in blue, yellow, and red correspond to the most potent, moderately potent, and least potent compounds. The correlation coefficient, $R = 0.6040$. (b) Box plots of the distribution of the Weighted SIFt scores with respect to potency classes. (c) Scatter plot of the weighted profile scores against $-Log(IC50)$ for training (in red) and testing (in yellow) compounds.

4. Discussion

Typical physics based or empirical scoring functions are difficult to interpret: it is often not possible to extract information on what residues are driving potency and which interactions are more dispensable. The visual interpretation of the profile weights as illustrated in the previous section is perhaps the most powerful feature of the weighted interaction profiles described in this chapter.

The binding pocket of P38α with a ligand bound to it (PDB 1BL7) is shown in Figure 8(a), with the key binding residues highlighted with purple, cyan or white. It is observed that the weights illustrated in Figure 5 in fact reflect the relative importance of specific interactions in determining the potency of the P38α inhibitors considered in this study. In Figure 8(a),

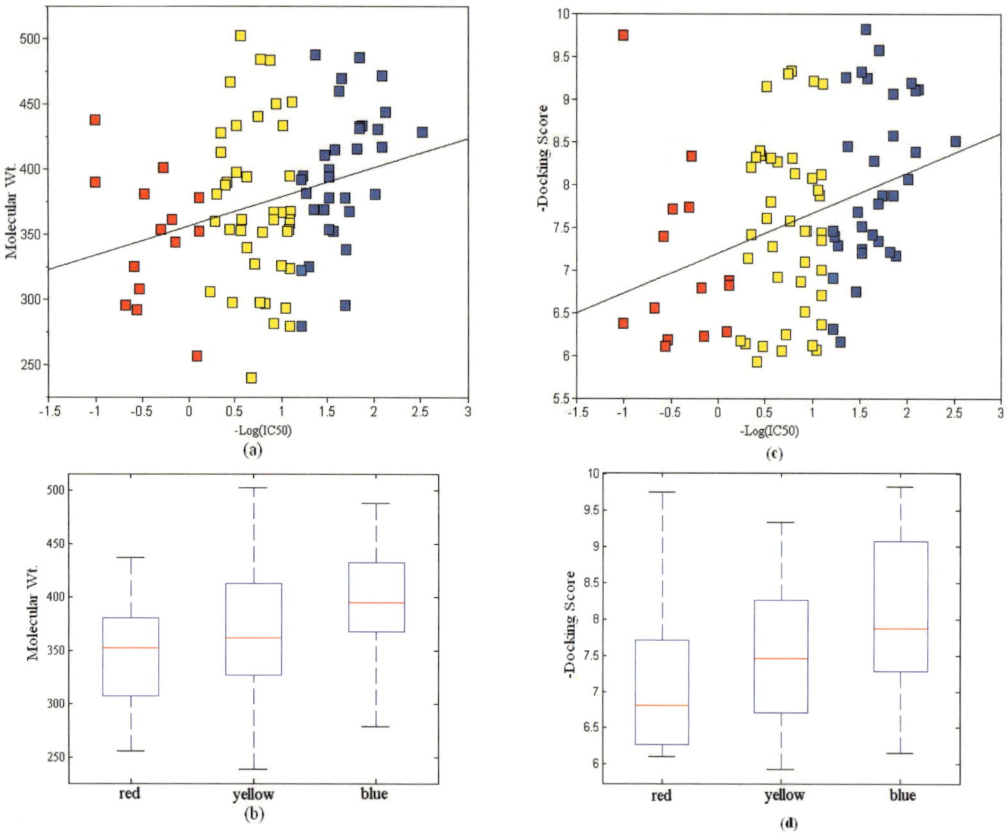

Fig. 7.(a) Scatter plot of the molecular weight against $-Log(IC50)$. The points in blue, yellow, and red correspond to the most potent, moderately potent, and least potent compounds. The correlation coefficient, $R = 0.2929$. (b) Box plots of the distribution of molecular weight with respect to potency classes. (c) Scatter plot of the -docking score against $-Log(IC50)$. The points in blue, yellow, and red correspond to the most potent, moderately potent, and least potent compounds. The correlation coefficient, $R = 0.3415$. (d) Box plots of the distribution of the -docking scores with respect to potency classes.

the most highly weighted residues are in purple; those with intermediate weight in cyan, and those least important for potency are colored white. The majority of ATP competitive kinase inhibitors interact with the hinge region of the kinase via at least one hydrogen bond (Chuaqui, Deng et al. 2005) mimicking the interactions made by the adenine moiety of ATP. In fact, these interactions are often used as constraints for filtering poses from docking experiments (Lyne, Kenny et al. 2004; Chuaqui, Deng et al. 2005). Not surprisingly, interactions with Met109, the key hydrogen-bonding residue in the hinge for P38α, are weighted heavily. In addition, Ala51 that makes hydrophobic contact with the typically heteroaromatic hinge binding substituents is identified as important for potency. Another nearly canonical interaction observed in the majority of kinase inhibitor co-crystal structures is with the conserved residue Lys53.

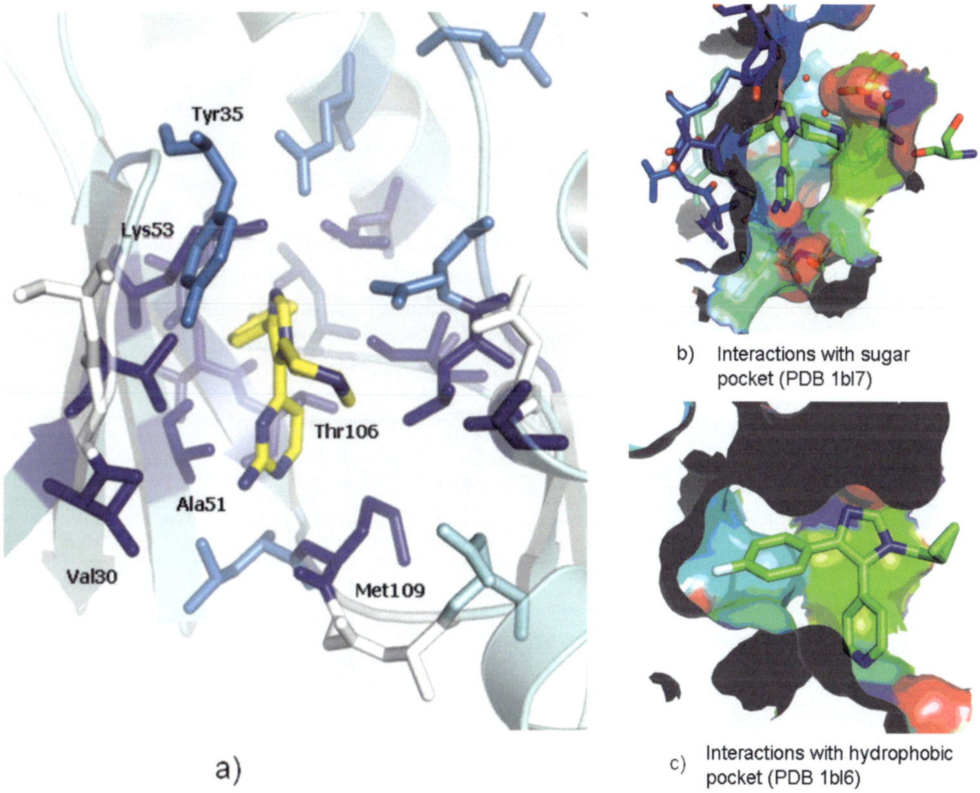

Fig. 8. (a) P38α with the key residues colored according to their weights. The residues in purple are the most highly weighted followed by residues in cyan, and the residues in white are the least weighted residues. Also shown in the figure are the labels for the residues referred to in the Discussion section. The sugar pocket (b) and hydrophobic pocket (c) are identified from the w-SIFt analysis as important regions for potency.

In addition to these highly conserved interactions, the hydrophobic pocket and sugar pocket regions of the ATP binding site received high weights. As is shown for example in Figure 8(b), inhibitors with substituents interacting with sugar pocket residues demonstrated increased potency over unsubstituted examples. Targeting the sugar pocket is a common strategy in kinase inhibitor design although it is not necessary to achieve potent activity in many kinases. The current analysis, however, indicates that this is an important region for p38α inhibition. In contrast, interaction with the P-loop of the kinase is not as important. The hydrophobic (or selectivity) pocket shown in Figure 8(c) was the final region that was identified in our analysis as being critical for potency. The small Thr106 gatekeeper residue in P38α permits access to the hydrophobic pocket unlike in kinases with bulky gatekeeper residues, e.g., CDK2 (Phe) or Akt (Met). Many P38α inhibitors exploit this region with substituted phenyl groups that contact a cluster of hydrophobic residues lining the pocket. The weights determined from our analysis highlight the importance of these interactions for achieving potency against P38α. Finally, interactions with the hinge toward the solvent channel of P38α were in comparison much less important for potency. As substitution toward solvent is typically aimed at improving inhibitor solubility, physical properties, and selectivity (Fitzgerald, Patel et al. 2003), it is not surprising that the weights determined from potency alone are not high. However, inhibitors with solvent channel substituents that made hydrophobic contacts with Val30 did receive relatively high weights in our analysis.

In addition to being interpretable, we have demonstrated that with an optimized set of target-specific weights, weighted profiles are able to rank order compounds based on potency. The weighted SIFt scoring function could be used as a virtual screening tool for mining potent compounds from chemical databases. The first step of the virtual screening protocol would involve docking the inhibitors against the target protein and determining accurate poses based on a SIFt based filter as demonstrated by Deng et al. (Deng, Chuaqui et al. 2004). The weighted profile and the SIFts of the docked poses are now used to compute the w-SIFt score, which is used as a ranking criterion.

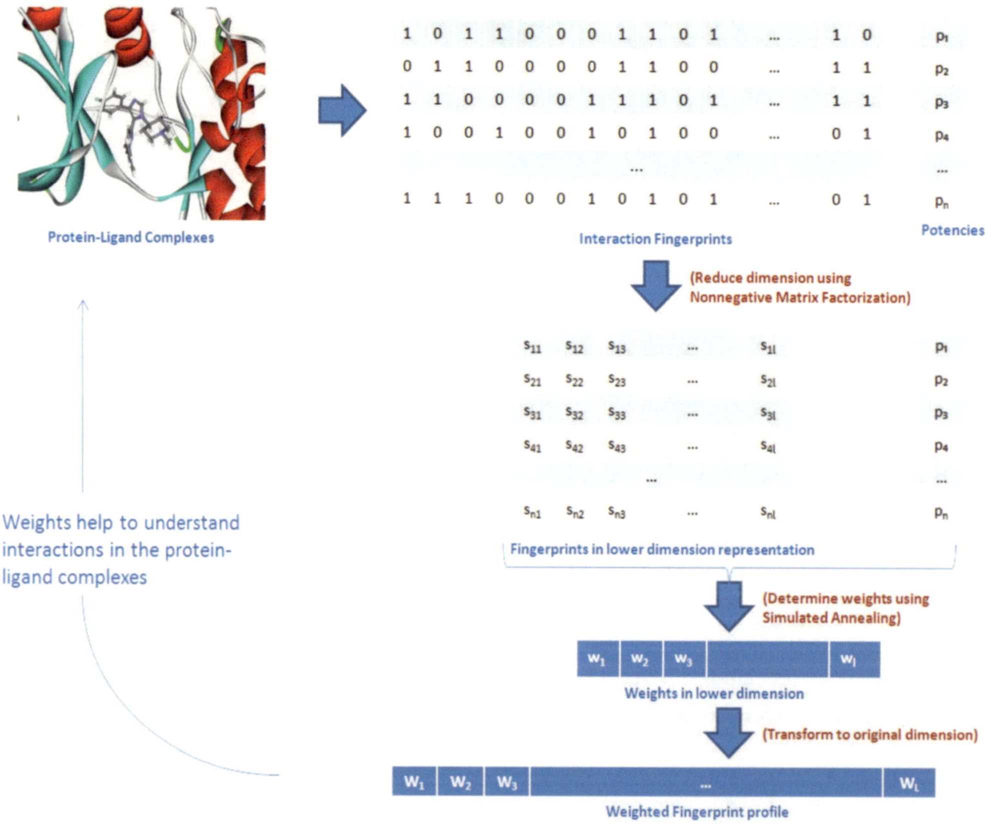

Fig. 9. Illustrative figure summarizing the full workflow involving determining SIFts from protein-ligand complexes, dimensionality reduction, weights determination, and interpretation of weights for better understanding of protein-ligand interactions.

Figure 9 shows a summary of the overall algorithm starting with the generation of SIFts from protein-ligand structures followed by the dimensionality reduction, and calculation of weights using simulated annealing, The weights so determined in turn help the understanding of the protein-ligand interactions which eventually will be useful for designing more efficient virtual screening algorithms to search for better binding ligands.

The concept of weighting the bits in SIFt can be extended to determine other criteria such as selectivity of a compound towards two targets. Rather than training the weights for learning experimental potency values, the weights now have to be trained for learning the relative potencies expressed as $\Delta(-Log(IC50))$ for example. The w-SIFt scoring function however suffers from the shortcoming that it is entirely based on assigning potency to protein-ligand binding interactions and does not include terms to delineate entropic contributions. There is however scope to combine the concept of weighting the interactions with other important ligand based terms like polar surface area, molecular weight, etc that also play a critical role in protein-ligand binding.

5. References

Glide. New York, Schrodinger Inc.

Omega. Santa Fe, NM, OpenEye Scientific Software.

Brewerton, S. C. (2008). "The use of protein-ligand interaction fingerprints in docking." Current Opinion in Drug Discovery & Development 11(11): 356-364.

Brunet, J. P., P. Tamayo, et al. (2004). "Metagenes and molecular pattern discovery using matrix factorization." Proc Natl Acad Sci 101: 4164-4169.

Chuaqui, C., Z. Deng, et al. (2005). "Interaction profiles of protein kinase-inhibitor complexes and their application to virtual screening." Journal of Medicinal Chemistry 48(1): 121-133.

Deng, Z., C. Chuaqui, et al. (2004). "Structural Interaction Fingerprint (SIFt): A novel method for analyzing three-dimensional protein-ligand binding interactions." Journal of Medicinal Chemistry 47(2): 337-344.

Devarajan, K. (2008). "Nonnegative Matrix Factorization: An Analytical and Interpretive Tool in Computational Biology." PLoS Comput Biol 4(7).

Fitzgerald, C. E., S. B. Patel, et al. (2003). "Structural basis for p38 alpha MAP kinase quinazolinone and pyridol-pyrimidine inhibitor specificity." Nature Structural Biology 10(9): 764-769.

Gao, Y. and G. Church (2005). "Improving molecular cancer class discovery through sparse non-negative matrix factorization." Bioinformatics 21: 3970-3975.

Hastie, T., R. Tibshirani, et al. (2003). The elements of statistical learning, Springer.

Kim, P. M. and B. Tidor (2003). "Subsystem identification through dimensionality reduction of large-scale gene expression data." Genome Res. 13: 1706-1718.

Kirkpatrick, S., C. D. Gelatt, et al. (1983). "Optimization by Simulated Annealing." Science 220(4598): 671-680.

Lee, D. D. and H. S. Seung (1999). "Learning the parts of objects by non-negative matrix factorization." Nature 401(6755): 788-791.

Lee, D. D. and H. S. Seung (2001). "Algorithms for Non-negative Matrix Factorization." Advanced in Neural Information Processing Systems 13: Proceedings of the 2000 Conference. MIT Press: 556-562.

Lyne, P. D. (2002). "Structure-based virtual screening: an overview." Drug Discovery Today 7(20): 1047-1055.

Lyne, P. D., P. W. Kenny, et al. (2004). "Identification of compounds with nanomolar binding affinity for checkpoint kinase-1 using knowledge-based virtual screening." Journal of Medicinal Chemistry 47(8): 1962-1968.

Nandigam, R. K., S. Kim, et al. (2009). "Position Specific Interaction Dependent Scoring Technique for Virtual Screening Based on Weighted Protein-Ligand Interaction Fingerprint Profiles." J. Chem. Inf. Model. 49(5): 1185-1192.

Pérez-Nueno VI, Rabal O, et al. (2009). "APIF: a new interaction fingerprint based on atom pairs and its application to virtual screening." J. Chem. Inf. Model. 49(5): 1245-1260.

Sato, T., T. Honma, et al. (2010). "Combining Machine Learning and Pharmacophore-Based Interaction Fingerprint for in Silico Screening." J. Chem. Inf. Model. 50(1): 170-185.

Singh, J., Z. Deng, et al. (2006). "Structural interaction fingerprints: A new approach to organizing, mining, analyzing, and designing protein-small molecule complexes." Chemical Biology & Drug Design 67(1): 5-12.

Taylor, R. D., P. J. Jewsbury, et al. (2002). "A review of protein-small molecule docking methods." Journal of Computer-Aided Molecular Design 16(3): 151-166.

Wallace, A. C., R. A. Laskowski, et al. (1995). "LIGPLOT - A program to generate schematic diagrams of protein-ligand interactions." Protein Engineering 8(2): 127-134.

12

Comparison among Different Sale-Bidding Strategies to Hedge against Risk in a Multi-Market Environment

Daniele Menniti, Nadia Scordino, Nicola Sorrentino and Antonio Violi
University of Calabria, Dep. of Electronic, Computer and System Science
via Pietro Bucci, 87036 Arcavacata di Rende (CS),
Italy

1. Introduction

With deregulation in the electricity market industry, competition was introduced among Generation Companies (GenCos), which no longer enjoyed guaranteed rates of return, like in old regulated environment, since price of electricity was no more fixed but varying according to market conditions. The price of electricity GenCos receive in the new competitive market depends on many factors of uncertainty: other GenCos bidding strategies, congestion in transmission, power demand, volatility of spot price of electricity (Liu & Wu, 2006). Scheduling decisions of GenCos are then a determinant factor of their own profitability, which nonetheless depends on either how much a GenCo is able to evaluate market risks or how it can manage such risks. Risk management is the process of achieving a desired return/profit through a particular strategy, which should take into account all the aforementioned factors of uncertainty. However, the complexity of the problem is so high that only strategies taking into account a subset of the above uncertainty factors were proposed in the literature. In order to reduce spot price volatility, diversification and portfolio optimization in physical trading markets were proposed (see e.g. (Liu & Wu, 2006)). Other GenCos bidding strategies and congestion management were conversely embedded in several algorithms based on game theory and evolutionary programming (see e.g. (Bydc, 2003) through (Jia et al., 2007)). Nonetheless the problem of demand forecasting was faced from different points of view (Darbellay, 2001), (Kirschen, 2003) but only in very few cases it was introduced in a risk management formulation (Zhou Ming, 2003) through (Conejo et al., 2008). In particular (Menniti et al. 2007) formulates a stochastic optimization problem with recourse as a tool to decide how much energy to bid in a multi-session market, with the aim to maximize the overall profit and minimize the risk of achieving revenues lower than a given threshold, with risk measured by the Conditional Value at Risk. (Conejo et al., 2008) utilizes a stochastic optimization problem with recourse very similar to the one in (Menniti et al., 2007), which nonetheless addresses the problem of a power producer facing the possibility of signing forward contracts as a form of protection against pool price volatility but at the cost of lower expected profits and considering only one market session over three of the present proposal.

This paper proposes a comparison among different sale-bidding strategies embedding risk due to daily-price volatility and to uncertainty typical of a process of bids acceptance, as well as delivery risk due to transmission congestion, taking into account zonal spot prices. The GenCo was modeled as a price taker, its price bids coincide with marginal costs and thus only energy bids were represented as decision variables. Each sale-bidding strategy then consists of the hourly energy quantities to bid for the 24 hours of the next day in a multi-session market, with the aim of maximizing overall profits and minimizing risk exposure. The convenience of a strategy was evaluated in terms of *efficient frontier* (Liu & Wu, 2006), that is the set of non-dominated solutions, in terms of maximum expected profit and minimum risk of profit variation, for varying values of risk aversion, whereas risk of profit variation was modelled using a discrete formulation of the Conditional Value at Risk (Rockafellar & Uryasev, 2000). The efficient frontiers relating to different sale-bidding strategies were produced by means of an enhanced formulation of the proposal in (Menniti et al. 2007) of a mixed-integer multi-stage stochastic programming problem with recourse. The problem is stochastic since it takes into account volatility of spot prices, modeled with a set of discrete variables, whereas a set of relating outcomes of these discrete variables is called scenario (Birge & Louveaux, 1997).

Besides the stochastic nature of the proposed optimization problem, it is worth to underline the need for a multi-stage formulation. Bidding strategies in energy and reserve markets are consecutive: the decision on the quantity of energy to bid in reserve market is a consequence of the clearing of previous markets, from which different levels (multi-stage) of decisions. The possibility to dynamically decide the quantity of energy to bid (*multi-stage decision strategy*), depending on the acceptances in preceding markets, allows to reduce risk in comparison to other strategies, such as *fixed-mix* and *greedy* (Dempster et al., 2002), (Fleten et al. (2002). In fact, according to a *fixed-mix* strategy, bids are percentages of the available capacity and *a priori* decided. Nonetheless a *greedy* strategy is a particular fixed-mix chance in which the whole production capability is devoted to the forecasted most convenient market session. Simulations were carried out in order to set up the efficient frontiers for multi-stage, fixed-mix and greedy strategies, applying the enhanced multi-stage stochastic programming problem to the Italian Power Exchange (IPEx) framework, and using field data of historical trends in the Italian market.

2. Italian market structure overview

In this section a description is provided of the basic Italian market structure which, like most of electricity markets, presents two alternatives to trade energy: Power Exchange and (physical) forward market.

2.1 Power exchange

Power Exchange is managed by a market operator, GME (www.mercatoelettrico.org), which determines the generation units to be deployed and how much energy each selected unit should produce to meet power demand. From a GenCo's point of view, selling energy in the Power Exchange (PEx) means to submit a bid (price and quantity) and get either of the two alternative results: (1) PEx accepts the bid and pays the Market Clearing Price (MCP) for the actual energy output of the GenCo; (2) PEx rejects the bid, and the GenCo sells nothing in the spot market. MCP depends on bids of all market participants, as well as on demand of energy, and is therefore uncertain. Unlike other European energy markets, e.g. Powernext in

France or EEX in Germany, GME Power Exchange is not a merely financial market with the sole purpose of determining prices and quantities, but an actually physical market, where physical injection and consumption schedules of energy are defined as a result of a clearing process.

To clear the market, a zonal model is used to manage network congestions, thus zonal prices will value producer bids.

Moreover, the Italian Power Exchange is made up of three sessions the *Day-Ahead Market*, the *Intraday Market* and the *Ancillary Services Market*, which are described in detail below for completeness sake.

The *Day-Ahead Market* (DAM) takes place in the morning of the "day-ahead" of the day of delivery. At the end of the offer/bid submission sitting, GME activates the market solution process. For each hour of the following day, the market algorithm accepts offers/bids so as to maximize the value of transactions, while satisfying transmission limits on capacity between zones. DAM clearing energy quantities and prices define the injection and consumption schedules for each hour of the following day.

The *Intraday Market* (IM) is not configured as a trading market, since participants submit demand offers or supply bids only to revise schedules resulting from the Day-Ahead Market. This market takes place immediately after the Day-Ahead Market, usually in the afternoon. The process of acceptance of offers/bids in the Intraday Market is similar to that described for the Day-Ahead Market. However, in the Intraday Market, also accepted offers/bids referring to consumption points are remunerated at zonal clearing prices and not at unique market clearing prices of the IM, like in the DAM.

The need for an Intraday Market after the Day-Ahead Market arises because of the use of simple offers/bids: since the 24 hourly schedules of injection or consumption are determined independently of each other, they are not guaranteed to be jointly consistent with constraints of production units. As an example, suppose a unit with a start-up time of 2 hours submits 24 supply bids for 100 MWh at given prices for the 24 hours of the next day, and all bids are accepted but one, at 7 a.m. The daily generation schedule resulting from the market would be then unfeasible for such a unit, whereas it cannot be shut-down at 7:00 and started-up at 8:00. The availability of an Intraday Market will thus allow that unit to submit appropriate demand/supply bids in order to revise previous unfeasible schedules.

The *Ancillary Services Market* (ASM) is the session within which market participants submit offers/bids to increase or decrease energy injection or consumption. The Italian TSO, TERNA (ex GRTN), uses these offers/bids *a) as-planned,* to correct any schedule violating transmission limits and to create reserve margins for the following day; *b)* in *real-time,* to re-establish an equilibrium between demand and production of energy, in the case of deviations from schedules. Unlike what happens in energy markets, offers/bids in the Ancillary Services Market are remunerated at the offered price rather than at the corresponding hourly zonal price.

The more the number of units in a GenCo ownership and of instances of market sessions, the higher the complexity level of the decision problem to be solved and the more risky the bidding operation. A valid means to control and reduce risk is diversification. Diversification is to engage in a wide variety of markets so that the exposure to the risk of any particular market is limited (Liu & Wu, 2006). Applying this concept to energy trading in an electricity market, diversification means to trade energy through different physical trading approaches, in which actual physical energy is traded, such as spot and contract markets.

2.2 Contract market

In a contract market, GenCos trade energy by way of signing physical forward contracts with their counterparties (e.g., energy consumers). Specific details, such as trading quantity (MW), trading duration (h), trading price (€/MWh), and delivery point are bilaterally negotiated between GenCo and consumer. Bilateral contracts are signed before the actual trading period, which means that trading quantity and price are set in advance, however they are embedded within the DAM session. In fact, when supply bids and consumption offers are checked for compliance with transmission constraints in the DAM, also bilateral contracts are embedded, with maximum priority of price, i.e. respectively zero-price supply bids and price-independent demand offers. If at least one transmission limit is violated, i.e. there is scarcity of transmission capacity, market is split into two or more zones. In this case, each zone z has a different clearing price P_z and this implies that: i) there is a value of transmission right between zones x and y, equal to P_y-P_x, i.e. the bilateral contract is required to pay/receive such a fee to/from TERNA for flows which contribute to congestion/congestion-relief on the grid. Transmission rights are assigned to bilateral contracts until exhaustion of transmission capacity and thus to the most competitive offers/bids submitted in the market. The bilateral contract will pay a fee for the transmission right, P_y-P_x, for the quantity of electricity quoted in the contract. Congestion and the resulting zonal prices are thus uncertain and unpredictable, and this makes risky inter-zonal bilateral contracts, whereas only intra-zonal contracts are risk-free in such a market.

3. Decision approach for the formulation of sale-bidding strategies

The tool used in this paper, already proposed by the authors elsewhere (Menniti et al. 2007), and here enhanced by the introduction of new decision variables and relating constraints, is to be used on a daily basis, the day ahead the DAM, IM and ASM sessions take place, by a GenCo which decides to recur to bidding diversification in order to maximize overall profits and minimize risk exposure. The GenCo is also supposed to honor a *physical forward contract*, in the remainder *bilateral contract*, according to a daily load profile at a given price. As an improvement of the stochastic programming problem presented in (Menniti et al. 2007), the GenCo can decide to which production units refer the bilateral contract, given that a number of units in its ownership are located in different zones and that the price cleared in a zone may differ from that of another zone because of delivery risk due to transmission congestions. As a result of the optimality of the adopted strategy, the bilateral contract will be then honored by units placed in the zones where zonal prices result the lowest, producing energy where it is more convenient and thus minimizing delivery risk. The interested reader is referred to Appendix C for a more detailed treatment of the constraints of the problem (equations (16)-(33)), whereas the objective function which drives the optimal choice of energy to bid in a multi-session market is formulated in the following section.

3.1 Objective function of the problem

As said above, the aim of the paper is proposing a way to define a sale-bidding strategy for a GenCo who wants to maximize overall expected profits over the operating day and conversely minimize risk exposure. For this reason, the authors considered in (Menniti et al. 2007) a risk-reward structure for the objective function, which is a choice of modeling widely used in many applicative contexts characterized by a high level of uncertainty,

(Conejo et al., 2008), (De Giorgi, 2005). This choice consists in a weighted sum of two terms: the expected overall profit and the Conditional Value at Risk on possible losses occurring in the entire planning horizon of one day:

$$\max \text{E[Profit]- } \kappa \text{CVaR} \tag{1}$$

where κ is a user-defined trade-off value, called in the remainder the *risk aversion parameter*, which models how much the GenCo is averse to risk, whereas high values of κ model a conservative approach, i.e. low propensity to risk. For each scenario, i.e. for each likely realization of the discrete variables modeled by an intuitive scenario tree, the overall profit for the entire planning horizon of one day is defined as the difference between revenues and costs. Revenues and costs depend on prices and on the energy actually cleared, thus not known in advance and modeled as expected values. Let η_{it}^{s}, π_{it}^{l}, and θ_{it}^{v} denote probabilities of occurrence of outcomes *s*, *l* and *v*, respectively related to the DAM, IM and ASM sessions, for each period *t* and for the zone which generation unit *i* belongs to. The expected value of overall profits can then be defined as:

$$\text{E[Profit]} = \sum_{i=1}^{I}\sum_{t=1}^{T}\sum_{v=1}^{V}\theta_{it}^{v}(R_{it}^{v} - C_{it}^{v}) + \sum_{t=1}^{T} R_{t}^{Bil} \tag{2}$$

with θ_{t}^{Bil} being the revenue due to bilateral contract at time *t*, a constant quantity not dependent on the decision variables.
Moreover, let λ_{it}^{s}, μ_{it}^{l}, and ζ_{it}^{v} denote outcomes of random clearing prices in the DAM, IM and ASM at the *t*-th hour for the zone which generation unit *i* belongs to. Overall revenues for generation unit *i* at time *t* according to outcome *v* are then:

$$R_{it}^{v} = R_{itDAM}^{p(p(v))} + R_{itAM}^{p(v)} + R_{itASM}^{v} \quad \forall v, \forall i, \forall t \tag{3}$$

Where:

$$R_{itDAM}^{s} = \lambda_{it}^{s}\gamma_{it}^{s}x_{it} \quad \forall s, \forall i, \forall t \tag{4}$$

$$R_{itAM}^{l} = \mu_{it}^{l}\delta_{it}^{+l}y_{it}^{+p(l)} \quad \forall l, \forall i, \forall t \tag{5}$$

$$R_{itASM}^{v} = \zeta_{it}^{v}\rho_{it}^{v}z_{it}^{p(v)} \quad \forall v, \forall i, \forall t \tag{6}$$

Overall cost related to generator *i* at time *t* according to outcome *v* is instead:

$$C_{it}^{v} = C_{\text{itProd}}^{v} + C_{\text{itSU}} + C_{\text{itSD}} + C_{itAM}^{p(v)} \quad \forall v, \forall i, \forall t \tag{7}$$

where:

$$C_{\text{itProd}}^{v} = (\alpha_i U_{it} + \beta_i Q_{it}^{v}) \quad \forall v, \forall i, \forall t \tag{8}$$

is the production cost of unit *i* at time *t*, whereas α_i and β_i are coefficients of the production-cost function of unit *i*, constant for each hour *t*. It should be noted that power output Q_{it}^{v} becomes zero whereas unit *i* is not committed, i.e. binary variable U_{it} is equal to zero, as stated by constraints (16) and (25) provided in the Appendix C. Production-cost function was approximated with such a linear function since we are dealing with marginal costs.

$$C_{itSU} = SU_i \Delta_{it}^{+} \quad \forall i, \forall t \tag{9}$$

$$C_{itSD} = SD_i \Delta_{it}^{-} \quad \forall i, \forall t \tag{10}$$

with C_{itSU} and C_{itSD} the start-up and shut-down costs incurred if unit i is going to be started-up/shut-down at the t-th hour, whereas SU_i and SD_i are linear cost coefficients. Finally, Δ_{it}^{+} and Δ_{it}^{-} are binary variables, respectively equal to 1 if unit i is going to be started-up/shut-down at the t-th hour, 0 otherwise;

$$C_{itAM}^{l} = \mu_{it}^{l} \delta_{it}^{l-} y_{it}^{p(l)-} \quad \forall l, \forall i, \forall t \tag{11}$$

When the GenCo buys energy on the IM, the purchase cost (11) has an expression similar to IM revenues (5): the bid of energy accepted in the IM, $\delta_{it}^{l-} y_{it}^{p(l)-}$, will be remunerated at the zonal clearing price, μ_{it}^{l} (depending on the zone unit i belongs to). As to the term CVaR in (1), a discrete formulation is given in Appendix B.

The solution of the stochastic optimization programming problem (1), (16)-(33) for different values of the risk aversion parameter κ, provides the efficient frontier for any adopted bidding strategy, which represents how the expected profit augments as CVaR increases (see Fig. 10 of the case study).

4. Numerical results

This section presents the results obtained simulating different bid strategies adopted by a small GenCo operating in the Italian PEx, which was supposed to own 3 thermo-electrical units, with operational features provided in Tab. 1, whose last row indicates where units are located. Note that the minimum power output of all units, $Q_i^{\min}$, is 0 MW. The zonal clearing prices of the Italian Power Exchange (IPEx) in January 2005 were considered for simulation (www.mercatoelettrico.org). Moreover, the GenCo serves a bilateral contract

	Unit 1	Unit 2	Unit 3
SU [€]	805	805	805
SD [€]	43	43	43
UT_i [h]	4	4	4
DT_i [h]	4	4	4
α_i [€]	892	892	892
β_i [€/MWh]	14	14	14
$Q_i^{\max}$ [MW]	500	400	280
$Q_i^{\min}$ [MW]	0	0	0
Location Zone	North	Middle North	Sardinia

Table 1. Units data

which is supposed to absorb 40% of the daily power production of the GenCo, according to the daily consumption profile shown in Fig. 1.

The remainder of the section is organized as follows: first, field data of historical trends in the Italian PEx during January 2005 were reported and analyzed. Using the heuristic procedure for scenario generation explained in Appendix A, 300 scenarios for prices and percentages of acceptance were generated. A comparison among three different strategies, multi-stage, fixed-mix and greedy, was then proposed and commented, in terms of efficient frontiers, resulting from the use of the proposed optimization tool.

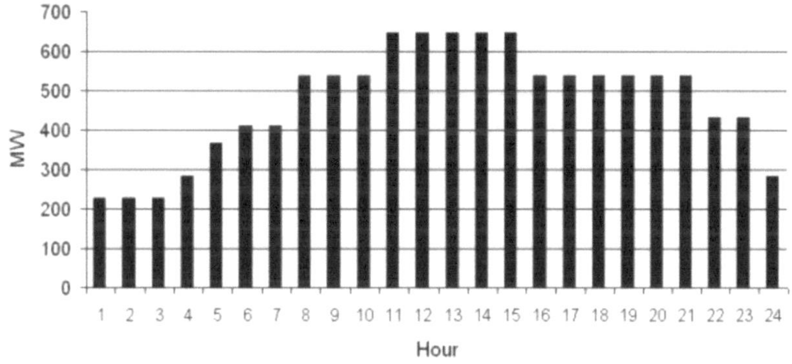

Fig. 1. Reference load profile (Q_{bil})

4.1 Italian market data

Mean hourly prices averaged over all zones in the Day-Ahead Market during January 2005 were plotted in Fig. 2, which highlights a high inter hour volatility, with values of prices ranging from a minimum of €/MWh 31.32 (4 a.m.) to a maximum of €/MWh 114.21 (7 p.m.).

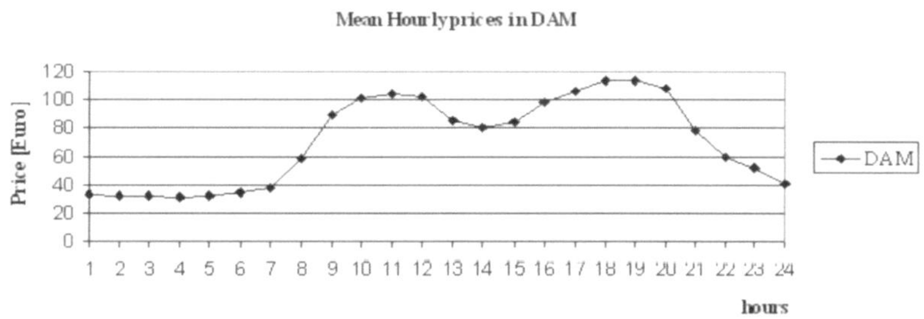

Fig. 2. Mean hourly prices [€/MWh] in the Italian Day-Ahead Market over January 2005

Fig. 3 compares mean monthly prices, always averaged over all zones, in the Day-Ahead Market and Intraday Market over 2005, from which it can be noticed how prices were quite similar in the DAM and IM, whereas during January DAM mean price resulted 2.27% higher than IM mean price, and this feature was taken into account within the scenario tree generation, as described in Appendix A. Conversely, Fig. 4 depicts mean hourly prices of DAM and ASM over January 2005. Mean hourly prices of ASM were derived as the average over zones of "the last" zonal hourly bids accepted in the ASM (that is bids with the highest prices).

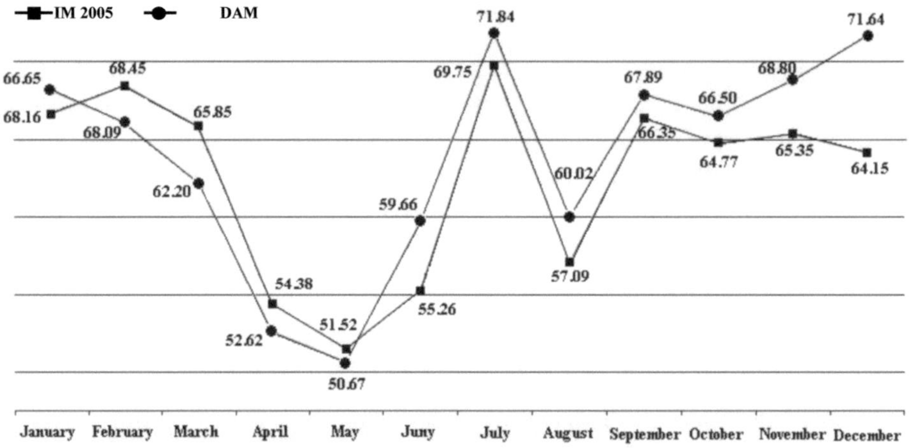

Fig. 3. Mean monthly prices [€/MWh] in the Italian Day-Ahead Market and Intraday Market over 2005

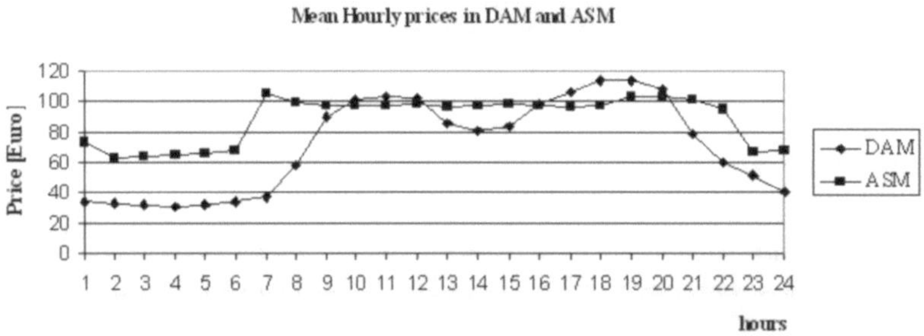

Fig. 4. Mean hourly prices [€/MWh] in the Italian Day-Ahead Market and Ancillary Service Market over January 2005

4.2 Comparison among multi-stage, fixed-mix, and greedy strategies

The enhanced stochastic optimization problem was implemented on a Pentium 4, 1.8 GHz with 1056 GB of RAM using AIMMS (www.aimms.com) as modeling environment and ILOG CPLEX 10 (www.ilog.com) as optimization solver. The size of the mixed-integer linear programming problem (1), (16-33) expressed as the number of continuous variables, binary variables and constraints is provided in Tab. 2. More in detail, I, T, S, L and V are respectively the number of units, the number of time intervals, and the number of likely outcomes of the Day-Ahead Market, of the Intraday Market and of the Ancillary Services Market. The CPU time required to solve the stochastic problem was of 1175.38 sec per strategy, therefore suitable for practical implementations.

Starting from all the previous assumptions, the purpose of the following simulation was twofold: *i)* showing effects of risk aversion on a sale-bidding strategy by a GenCo operating in different market sessions; *ii)* comparing the effectiveness of the proposed multi-stage decisional approach with other realistic classic strategies, such as fixed-mix and greedy. These two classic strategies are similar since both decide a priori the offers of energy in each market session as predetermined percentages of the available capacity of production. However, according to a greedy strategy, values assumed for these percentages were chosen so as to concentrate profits in a "greedy" way in one of the three markets of IPEx, and

Continuos decision variables	I T(2+2S+L+V)=29 664
Binary variables	I T(3+2S)=1656
Constraints	I T(7+5S+L+2V)+I+T=54 531

Table 2. Problem size

assumed in the paper equal to 100% for offers in the DAM, and 0% in the IM and ASM. Differently, for a fixed-mix strategy, offers were "distributed "in the DAM, IM and ASM according to different predetermined percentage, assumed equal to 80%, 5% and 15% respectively, these percentage reflecting the real trend of the Italian Market over 2005.

Moreover, a fixed-mix and a greedy strategy also differ for the way in which offers are managed in the IM and ASM. In fact, with a fixed-mix strategy, when an offer is refused by a generic market session, the residual capacity of production may be offered in other subsequent market sessions, always according to the programmed percentages, which for a greedy strategy are instead 0%.

According to the above assumptions, offers in the DAM, IM, and ASM obviously vary as a function of the particular strategy chosen, as Fig. 5 shows for a generic value of the risk aversion parameter (κ=0.5). For κ=0.5 most of offers are committed in the DAM if a greedy strategy is adopted, whilst correspondingly offers decrease if we move from a greedy towards a multi-stage strategy, in favor of offers in the more remunerative Ancillary Service Market (Stage 3).

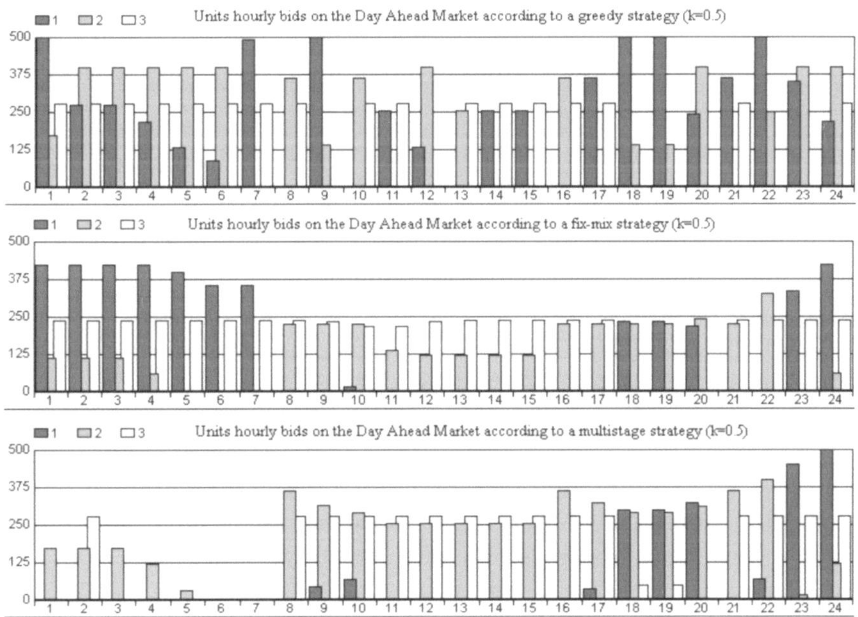

Fig. 5. Energy bids in the DAM in MWh as a function of greedy, fixed-mix, and multi-stage strategies, for κ=0.5

Moreover, observing the generic strategy, the decision of which units to commit is a function of the geographic position of units themselves, whereas unit 2 belongs to Middle-North and presents offers higher than unit 3, which belongs to Sardinia, where prices were higher than in Middle-North.
Obviously, how offers are distributed over sessions and over 24 hours also depends on the aversion to risk modeled by the κ parameter. Simulations for varying values of the risk aversion parameter (ranging from 0 (full acceptance of risk) to 1 (maximum aversion to risk) with a step of 0.1) were performed. Calling *efficient frontier* the set of solutions for different values of risk aversion (Liu & Wu, 2006), a comparison among the efficient frontiers obtained adopting multi-stage, fixed-mix and greedy strategies was reported in Tab. 3, and Fig. 6. Each point of Fig. 6 represents the most profitable sale-bidding strategy as a function of a given risk level or, equivalently, the less risky sale-bidding strategy as a function of a given value of profitability. Moreover, focusing attention on a generic strategy, it is evident that a non-conservative approach, which corresponds to low values of κ, allows higher potential gains, although a higher risk value as well.
With the purpose of highlighting the validity of a multi-stage decisional approach versus other "non-recursive" approaches, Fig. 6 proves that the efficient frontier of a multi-stage strategy dominates the others, in terms of both profitability and risk. With non-recursive approach we denote the impossibility to "recur" to successive decisions to "correct" likely losses due to undesired realizations of variables of previous stages. This result can be attributed to the possibility actually offered by a multi-stage stochastic strategy, i.e. to take into account different likely scenarios and to dynamically correct previous decisions according to the observed outcomes of the market clearing process.

	Multistage		Fixed-Mix		Greedy	
κ	*E[Profit]*	*CVaR*	*E[Profit]*	*CVaR*	*E[Profit]*	*CVaR*
0	621978	51754.8	282471.3	64916.5	208544.6	44870.86
0.10	621745.1	39608.43	282471.3	39623.87	208420.9	28721.51
0.20	621332.1	37463.89	282471.3	39623.87	208416.8	28685.03
0.30	621085.8	36311.77	282471.3	39623.87	208416	28681.49
0.40	621085.8	36311.77	282471.3	39623.87	208416	28681.49
0.50	620916	35910.5	282464.9	39608.43	208416	28681.41
0.60	620916	35910.5	282464.9	39608.43	208416	28681.41
0.70	620179.7	34835.55	282464.9	39608.43	208416	28681.41
0.80	617893.5	31747.6	282464.9	39608.43	208407	28668.94
0.90	613996.5	27249.12	282464.9	39608.43	208372.8	28626.79
1	613996.5	27249.12	282464.9	39608.43	207258.6	27495.31

Table 3. Expected profit and CVaR as a function of varying values of the risk aversion parameter according to multistage, fixed-mix and greedy strategies

Simulations for intermediate values of κ, not reported here for brevity sake, obviously produced different intermediate schedules, thus a clear conclusion can be drawn: the GenCo should make a decision on its desired level of risk before solving its scheduling problem and then bidding in the electric energy market.

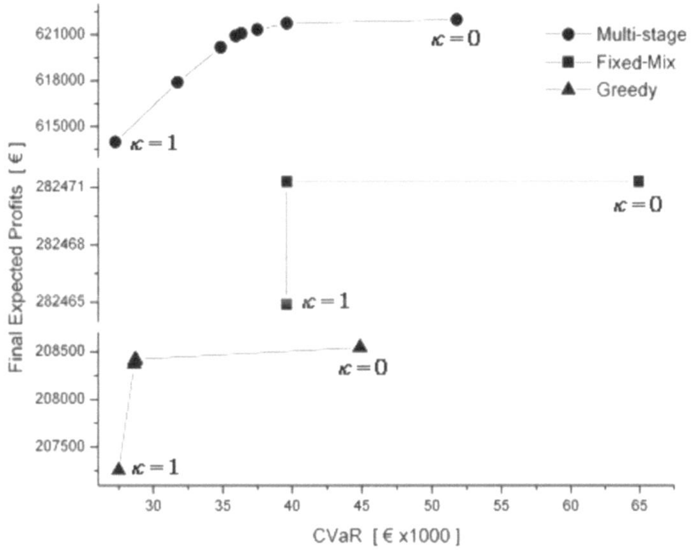

Fig. 6. Efficient frontiers for multistage, fixed-mix and greedy strategies

5. Conclusions

A multi-stage strategy represents the best trade-off in terms of maximum expected profit and minimum risk of profit volatility in comparison with other strategies, such as fixed-mix or greedy, which do not allow to "recur" to successive decisions to "correct" likely losses due to undesired previous outcomes. The appropriate behaviour of the proposed multi-stage strategy is demonstrated through a case study based on field record of the Italian PEx, in which it was shown that the efficient frontier of the multi-stage strategy dominates the efficient frontiers of the other two strategies analyzed.

6. Appendix A: Heuristic procedure for scenario generation

A GenCo which recurs to bidding diversification in the DAM, IM and ASM must decide within different succeeding time horizons "how much energy must be bid" and "at which price". The first decision, "how much energy must be bid" in each market session, was modeled by means of continuous decision variables, whereas price bids in the DAM and IM were not considered as decision variables, having assumed that the GenCo is a price-taker and has no capability of altering the electricity price. In particular, the evolution of the random clearing prices of DAM and IM was modeled by an intuitive scenario tree (see Fig. 7), and a zonal model was adopted thus taking into account also delivery risk due to transmission congestion (Liu & Wu, 2006). Differently from DAM and IM, according to the "pay as bid" mechanism, bids accepted in the ASM are remunerated at the price bid, which clearly represents a decision variable. For the sake of simplicity, as a first step of this research activity, ASM price bids were assumed in the paper as input data, within nodes of the third stage, but they were not considered stochastic variables such as DAM and IM clearing prices, thus they do not vary with the scenario, but only with hours and zones. This means that a unit belonging to zone A is supposed to bid at a different price in comparison with a unit located in zone B at the same *t*-th hour.

Besides uncertainty of the clearing zonal prices of DAM and IM, the above mentioned scenario also captures the uncertainty relating the acceptance of energy bids, respectively, γ_{it}^{s}, (δ_{it}^{l+}, δ_{it}^{l-}), and ρ_{it}^{v}, over the three different time horizons associated to DAM, IM and ASM sessions.

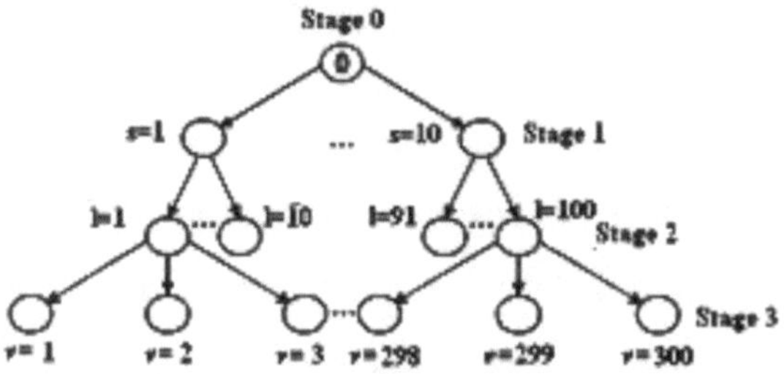

Fig. 7. Scenario tree formulation.

Root-node stands for stage 0, and embeds no uncertainty. Stages 1-3 model the three market sessions of Power Exchange and are thus associated with the sequential decision process. Each generic node *k* has a unique immediate predecessor p(*k*) in the preceding stage and a finite number of successors in the next stage, but the root-node. Nodes without any successor are called the *leaves* of the tree. They are in a one-to-one correspondence with each scenario, whereas a scenario is a path from root-node to a leaf and represents a joint outcome over all market sessions. At each hour *t*=1..T and for each zone, each node captures the evolution of random decision variables by which uncertainty is represented, i.e. percentages of bids accepted in the corresponding marker session, clearing prices and relating probabilities of occurrence.

The heuristic procedure given below receives historical time series data as input and generates the scenario tree used for simulation as output.

Step 1 For each *t*-th hour and zone *z*.

1.1 Observe $P_{z_t}^{DAM\min}$ and $P_{z_t}^{DAM\max}$.

1.2 Devide the corresponding range into 10 sub-ranges of equal amplitude, as depicted in Fig. 8.

1.3 Observe, for each *s*-th sub-range, $P_{z_t}^{s\min}, P_{z_t}^{s\max}$, and calculate $P_{zt}^{s\ mean}$.

1.4 Compute the probability of occurrence of $P_{zt}^{s\ mean}$.

Step 2 Assign γ_{it}^{s}=0 for *s*=1-4, γ_{it}^{s}=0.5 for *s*=5-6, γ_{it}^{s}=1 for *s*=7-10.

Step 3 For each *s*-th node of DAM, *t*-th hour and zone *z*,

3.1 scale $P_{zt}^{s\ mean}$ by ten scaling factors opportunely chosen.

3.2 Compute the occurrence probability of the *l*-th hourly zonal IM clearing price as 1/10 of the occurrence probability of the price of the predecessor node p(*l*), for the same hour and the same zone.

3.3 Assign $\delta_{it}^{l+}, \delta_{it}^{l-}$ =0 for *l*=the first 4 sons of p(*l*), $\delta_{it}^{l+}, \delta_{it}^{l-}$ =0.5 for *l*=sons 5-6 of p(*l*), $\delta_{it}^{l+}, \delta_{it}^{l-}$ =1 for the remaining sons of p(*l*).

Step 4 For each *t*-th hour and zone *z*

4.1 Observe the last price bid accepted in the ASM and store it in each ν-th node of the scenario tree.

4.2 Compute the occurrence probability of the ν-th hourly ASM price as 4/10, 2/10 and 4/10 of the occurrence probability of the price of the predecessor node p(ν), for the same hour and the same zone.

4.3 Assign to each triplet of nodes in ASM with the same predecessor p(ν) ρ_{it}^{v} =0 for ν=the first son of p(ν), ρ_{it}^{v} =0.5 for l=second son of p(ν), ρ_{it}^{v} =1 for p(ν) last son.

With reference to Stage 1 (DAM session) and focusing attention on each hour *t* and zone *z*, excluding Sundays and Saturday evening, we observed which minimum and maximum zonal prices, $P_{zt}^{DAM\min}$ and $P_{zt}^{DAM\max}$, occurred over the days of January 2005 in the Italian DAM (Step 1.1). We divided the corresponding range into 10 sub-ranges of equal amplitude, each with a lower and upper bound, respectively $P_{z_t}^{s\min}, P_{z_t}^{s\max}$ (Step 1.2). For each *s*-th sub-range, the relating mean price, $P_{zt}^{s\ mean}$, was calculated (Step 1.3), having thus generated *s*=10 likely hourly zonal clearing prices, as depicted in Fig. 8, each corresponding to a node of Stage 1.

The probability of occurrence of $P_{zt}^{s\ mean}$ was calculated as the number of prices at the *t*-th hour belonged to interval *s* over all the observed days, divided by the number of observed days (Step 1.4). Step 1 was iterated for each hour *t*, with *t*=1..24, and for each of the 7 zones of the Italian PEx. Step 2 gives value to percentages of bid acceptance for DAM, γ_{it}^{s}, at each *t*-th hour, and for each zone unit *i* belongs to. In particular, γ_{it}^{s} =0 for *s*=1-4, γ_{it}^{s} =0.5 for *s*=5-6, γ_{it}^{s} =1 for *s*=7-10.

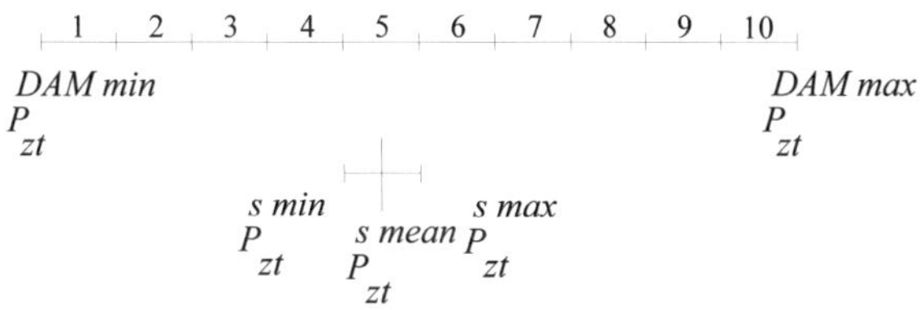

Fig. 8. Formulation of scenario tree for prices.

Generation of 10 outcomes of zonal clearing prices for the DAM.

Each node belonging to Stage 1 has also 10 sons, belonging to Stage 2, and, for these last, prices were derived as follows. From the monthly trading report of January 2005 (www.mercatoelettrico.org), it was observed that clearing prices of the DAM averaged greater than the corresponding IM clearing prices (2.27%). This behavior was replicated in the generation of the L=100 IM clearing prices by scaling the $P_{zt}^{s\ mean}$ clearing prices of each s-th father node (DAM) by ten different factors (assumed less than 1 for seven over ten son nodes and greater than 1 for the remaining nodes, (Step 3.1)). For each *l*-th hourly zonal IM clearing price the occurrence probability was computed as 1/10 of the occurrence probability of the price of the predecessor node p(*l*), for the same hour and the same zone (Step 3.2). Percentage of bid acceptance for IM, δ_{it}^{l+} and δ_{it}^{l-}, were assumed equal to 0 for 4 nodes, 0.5 for 2 nodes, *1* for the rest of the nodes, all sons of the same predecessor, p(*l*) (Step 3.3).

Finally, Stage 3 models the ASM session. Each *l*-th predecessor node belonging to the IM (Stage 2) has 3 sons in the ASM and this because the only differentiation among ASM nodes

was simulated by the different percentage of acceptance of a bid, ρ_{it}^{v}. In fact, ρ_{it}^{v} was assumed equal to 0, 0.5 or 1, respectively meaning bid is refused, unit is marginal, or bid price is less than the highest forecasted accepted price bid. Hourly prices vary with hours and zones, whereas they do not vary with nodes and, for a given hour *t*, and a given zone *z*, they were assumed equal to the value of the average, over all the days of January 2005, of the last (i.e. the highest) accepted price bid in the ASM (Step 4.1). For each triplet of nodes in the ASM, probabilities of occurrence were assumed equal to 0.4, 0.2, and 0.4 respectively of the probabilities of the price in the predecessor node p(v) of the IM, for the same hour and the same zone (Step 4.2). Moreover, each triplet of nodes in ASM with the same predecessor p(v) will have percentage of bid acceptance ρ_{it}^{v}=0 for v=the first son of p(v), ρ_{it}^{v}=0.5 for *l*=second son of p(v), ρ_{it}^{v}=1 for p(v) last son.
The overall scenario tree has then V=300 leaves, each corresponding to a scenario, that is a likely evolution of uncertain outcomes of the multi-session market.

7. Appendix B: CVaR as risk measure in energy trading

With an evaluation on a 24-hour time-frame, CVaR was here chosen to detect the risk of loss or, at least, the risk of achieving revenues lower than a given threshold for a GenCo which trades energy in both Power Exchange and Contract market. A discrete version (12) for CVaR was formulated elsewhere (Menniti et al., 2007), considering a confidence level ε equal to 0.95. As demonstrated elsewhere (Ahmed, 2006), CVaR is a risk measure which preserves convexity, and its linear relaxation still maintains this convexity feature.

$$CVaR_{\varepsilon} = VaR_{\varepsilon} + \frac{1}{1-\varepsilon} E\left\{\max\left[Loss^{v} - VaR_{\varepsilon}, 0\right]\right\} \tag{12}$$

where $Loss^{v}$ is a loss function, here assumed as the opposite of the profit function, $Profit^{v}$. Since uncertainty of market prices was represented by means of a finite set V of likely scenarios, (12) can be linearized using a set of auxiliary variables and constraints as follows:

$$CVaR_{\varepsilon} = VaR_{\varepsilon} + \frac{1}{1-\varepsilon} \sum_{v=1}^{V} \theta^{v} \sigma^{v} \tag{13}$$

with θ^{v} the probability that scenario v can occur, and:

$$\sigma^{v} \geq Loss^{v} - VaR_{\varepsilon} \qquad \forall v = 1..V \tag{14}$$

$$\sigma^{v} \geq 0 \qquad \forall v = 1..V \tag{15}$$

8. Appendix C: mixed-integer multi-stage stochastic problem for the formulation of sale-bidding strategies- constraints of the problem

Classical multi-period problems with unit commitment include provisions for modeling restrictions on the operation of thermal generation units. These restrictions include most notably minimum/maximum power output limits, ramping limitations, and minimum up- and down-time constraints (Shahidehpour et al., 2002), (Conejo et al., 2002). Because we do not implement the presence of hydro generation units and do note devote our attention at

the process of scheduling of tertiary reserves and its later deployment through generation re-dispatch, we do not thus model ramping limitations.
Constraints of the stochastic programming problem modeling the decision problem faced by the GenCo are formulated below as.

$$x_{it} + x_{it}^{bil} \le Q_i^{\max} U_{it} \quad \forall i, \forall t \tag{16}$$

$$\sum_{i=1}^{I} x_{it}^{bil} = Q_t^{bil} \quad \forall t \tag{17}$$

$$y_{it}^{s+} \le Q_i^{\max} U_{it} - \gamma_{it}^{s} x_{it} - x_{it}^{bil} \quad \forall i, \forall t, \forall s \tag{18}$$

$$y_{it}^{s-} \le \gamma_{it}^{s} x_{it} \quad \forall i, \forall t, \forall s \tag{19}$$

$$y_{it}^{s+} \le M \varphi_{it}^{s+} \quad \forall i, \forall t, \forall s \tag{20}$$

$$y_{it}^{s-} \le M \varphi_{it}^{s-} \quad \forall i, \forall t, \forall s \tag{21}$$

$$\varphi_{it}^{s+} + \varphi_{it}^{s-} \le 1 \quad \forall i, \forall t, \forall s \tag{22}$$

$$z_{it}^{l} \le Q_i^{\max} U_{it} - \gamma_{it}^{p(l)} x_{it} - x_{it}^{bil} - \delta_{it}^{l+} y_{it}^{p(l)+} + \delta_{it}^{l-} y_{it}^{p(l)-} \quad \forall i, \forall t, \forall l \tag{23}$$

$$Q_{it}^{v} = x_{it}^{bil} + \gamma_{it}^{p(p(v))} x_{it} + \delta_{it}^{p(v)+} y_{it}^{p(p(v))+} - \delta_{it}^{p(v)-} y_{it}^{p(p(v))-} + \rho_{it}^{v} z_{it}^{p(v)} \quad \forall i, \forall t, \forall v \tag{24}$$

$$Q_i^{\min} U_{it} \le Q_{it}^{v} \quad \forall i, \forall t, \forall v \tag{25}$$

$$\sum_{\mathrm{t=1}}^{\mathrm{G_i}} (1\text{-}U_{it}) = 0 \quad \forall i \tag{26}$$

$$\sum_{l=t}^{\mathrm{t+UT_i-1}} U_{il} \ge UT_i \, \Delta_{it}^{+} \quad \forall i, \forall t = G_i + 1..\mathrm{T\text{-}UT_i} + 1 \tag{27}$$

$$\sum_{l=t}^{\mathrm{t+UT_i-1}} U_{il} \ge UT_i \, \Delta_{it}^{+} \quad \forall i, \forall t = G_i + 1..\mathrm{T\text{-}UT_i} + 1 \tag{28}$$

where $G_i = \min[\mathrm{T}, (\mathrm{UT_i\text{-}R_i^0}) U_{i0}]$.

$$\sum_{\mathrm{t=1}}^{\mathrm{F_i}} U_{it} = 0 \quad \forall i \tag{29}$$

$$\sum_{l=t}^{\mathrm{t+DT_i-1}} U_{il} \ge DT_i \, \Delta_{it}^{-} \quad \forall i, \forall t = F_i + 1..\mathrm{T\text{-}DT_i} + 1 \tag{30}$$

$$\sum_{l=t}^{T}(1-U_{il}-\Delta_{it}^{-})\geq 0 \quad \forall i,\forall t=\text{T-DT}_{\text{i}}+2..\text{T} \tag{31}$$

where $F_i = \min\ [\text{T}, (\text{DT}_\text{i}\text{-S}_\text{i}^0)(1-U_{i0})]$.

$$\Delta_{it}^{+}-\Delta_{it}^{-}=U_{it+1}-U_{it} \quad \forall i,\forall t \tag{32}$$

$$\Delta_{it}^{+}+\Delta_{it}^{-}\leq 1 \quad \forall i,\forall t \tag{33}$$

7.1 First Stage constraints: bidding in the Day-Ahead Market

Constraints (16) require that the sum of a bid of unit i in the DAM, x_{it}, and of the production to satisfy the bilateral contract, x_{it}^{bil}, must not be exceeded the unit maximum power output, $Q_i^{\max}$ at the t-th hour.

Constraints (17) guarantee the satisfaction of the bilateral contract by means of zero-price bids in the DAM (x_{it}^{bil}).

7.2 Second Stage constraints: bidding in the Intraday Market

Constraints (18) say that unit i can sell in the IM at most its maximum capacity, $Q_i^{\max}$, decreased of the accepted bid in the previous DAM, $\gamma_{it}^{s}x_{it}+x_{it}^{bil}$.

Constraints (19) limit the purchase bid of unit i to the only quantity already accepted in the DAM, $\gamma_{it}^{s}x_{it}$. Moreover, in order to avoid buying and selling bids in the IM at the same hour by the same unit, we introduced additional binary variables, φ_{it}^{s+} and φ_{it}^{s-}, and sets of constraints (20)-(22).

7.3 Third Stage constraints: bidding in the Ancillary Services Market

Also in the ASM session, the GenCo may commit still unused units or increase the output of one or more units already committed for other sessions, under constraints (23) which impose to respect unit maximum output.

7.4 Other constraints

Constraints (24) express the energy produced by each unit i, Q_{it}^{v}, at each period t and for each likely outcome ν, as the sum of all the energy effectively sold over the three market sessions and by bilateral contract.

Production Q_{it}^{v} is also constrained (25) by the minimum power output of unit i, whereas unit i is committed ($U_{it}=1$) for period t under scenario ν.

Constraints (26)-(28) represent linear expressions of minimum up-time constraints (Conejo et al., 2002). In particular, set of equations (26) is related to the initial status of the units. Set of equations (27) ensure the satisfaction of minimum up-time constraints during all likely sets of consecutive periods of size UT_i. Finally, set of equations (28) is essential for the last $UT_{i\text{-}1}$ periods, i.e. if a unit is started-up in one of these periods, it must still remain on-line during next periods.

Similarly to (26)-(28), constraints (29)-(31) formulate the minimum down-time constraints (Conejo et al., 2002). Equations (29)-(31) are identical to (26)-(28) just changing U_{it}, Δ_{it}^{-}, DT_i, and S_i^0 with (1-U_{it}), Δ_{it}^{+}, UT_i, and R_i^0, respectively.

Finally, constraints (32) and (33) are necessary to model the start-up and shut-down status of units and to avoid the simultaneous commitment and decommitment of a unit (Conejo et al., 2002).

9. References

Liu M. & Wu F. F. (2006) Managing Price Risk in a Multimarket Environment, *IEEE Trans. Power Syst.*, Vol. 21, No. 4, (2006) (1512-1519), 0885-8950.

Byde A. (2003) Applying evolutionary game theory to auction mechanism design, *Proceedings of Internatonal Conference on E-Commerce,* pp. 347- 354, 0-7695-1969-5, Newport Beach, California, June 2003, IEEE Computer society, Newport Beach

Reeves D. M., Wellman M. P., MacKie-Mason J. K. & Osepayshvili A. (2003) Exploring bidding strategies for market-based scheduling, *Proceedings of the Fourth ACM Conference on Electronic Commerce,* pp. 115-124, 0-7695-1969-5, San Diego, June 2003, San Diego

Wen F. & David A. K. (2001) Optimal bidding strategies and modeling of imperfect information among competitive generators, *IEEE Trans. Power Syst,* Vol. 16, No.1, (2001), (15-21), 0885-8950

Jia D., Cheng H., Zhang W., Hu Z., Yan J. & Chen M. (2007). A new game theory-based solution methodology for generation maintenance strategy, *European Transactions on Electrical Power,* (2007) (www.interscience.wiley.com) DOI: 10.1002/etep.208

Darbellay G. A. & Slama M. (2001), Forecasting the short-term demand for electricity: Do neural networks stand a better chance? *International Journal of Forecasting,* Vol.16, No.1, (2001) (71-83), 0169-2070

Kirschen D.S. (2003) Demand-side view of electricity markets, *IEEE Trans. Power Syst,* Vol. 18, No.2, (2003), (520- 527), 0885-8950

Zhou Ming, Li Gengyiu', Min Liu, Wen F.S. & Ni Y.X.(2003) Research on electricity procurement strategy for the electric utilities in power markets, *Proceedings of the Sixth International Conference on Advances in Power System Control, Operation and Management,* pp. 327- 332, 0-86341-328-5, APSCOM 2003, Hong Kong, November 2003

Shahidehpour M., Yamin H. & Li Z. (2002), *Market operations in electric power systems,* Wiley Interscience, 9780471224129, New York

Lo K.L. & Wu Y.K. (2003) Risk assessment due to local demand forecast uncertainty in the competitive supply industry, *IEE Proc.-Gener. Transm. Distrib.,* pp. 573-581http://ieeexplore.ieee.org/xpl/tocresult.jsp?isnumber=27637&isYear=2003, 978-0-88986-689-8

Birge JR. & Louveaux FV. (1997), *Introduction to stochastic programming,* 0387982175, New York Springer

Menniti D., Scordino N., Sorrentino N. & Violi A. (2007) Managing Price Risk while bidding in a multimarket environment, *Proceedings of the IEEE Power Engineering Society General Meeting,,* pp. 1-10, 978-1-905593-36-1, Florida, June 2007, IEEE, Tampa

Conejo A.J., Garcia-Bertrand R., Carrion M., Caballero A., & de Andres A. (2008)Optimal Involvement in Futures Markets of a Power Producer, *IEEE Trans. Power Syst.,* Vol. 23, No.2, (703-711), 0885-8950

Rockafellar R. & Uryasev S. (2000) Optimization of conditional value-at risk , *The Journal of Risk,* Vol. 2, No.3 (21 –41)

Dempster, M. A. H., Schenk-Hoppé, K. R. and Evstigneev, Igor V. (2002), Exponential Growth of Fixed-Mix Strategies in Stationary Asset Markets, U. of Cambridge, Working Paper No. WP 01/2002. http://ssrn.com/abstract=307095

Fleten S. E., Høyland K. & Wallace S. W. (2002) The performance of stochastic dynamic and fixed mix portfolio models, *European Journal of Operational Research,* Vol. http://www.sciencedirect.com/science?_ob=PublicationURL&_tockey=%23TOC%235963%232002%23998599998%23296610%23FLA%23&_cdi=5963&_pubType=J&view=c&_auth=y&_acct=C000061349&_version=1&_urlVersion=0&_userid=7166485&md5=2db43444afc040a21334ff4fc8cbce6c140, No.1 (2002) (37-49), 0377-2217

www.mercatoelettrico.org

De Giorgi E. (2005), Reward-risk portfolio selection and stochastic dominance, Journal of Banking & Finance, *Vol. 29, No.4 (2005) (895-926), 0378-4266*

AIMMS User's Guide, Paragon Software, www.aimms.com

CPLEX Optimizer, ILOG Software, www.ilog.com

Ahmed S. (2006),Convexity and decomposition of mean-risk stochastic programs, Mathematical Programming, *Vol. 106 (433-446), 1436-4646*

Conejo A. J., Nogales F. J. & Arroyo J. M. (2002), Price-Taker Bidding Strategy Under Price Uncertainty, IEEE Trans. Power Syst., *Vol. 17, No.4 (1081 – 1088), 0885-8950*

13

Chance Constrained Programming and Its Applications to Energy Management

Wim van Ackooij[1], Riadh Zorgati[2], René Henrion[3] and Andris Möller[4]
[1,2]*EDF R&D, Department OSIRIS, 1 avenue du Général de Gaulle ;*
F-92141 Clamart Cedex
[3,4]*Weierstrass Institute Berlin, Mohrenstraße 39, 10117 Berlin*
[1,2]*France*
[3,4]*Germany*

1. Introduction

Chance Constrained Programming belongs to the major approaches for dealing with random parameters in optimization problems. Typical areas of application are engineering and finance, where uncertainties like product demand, meteorological or demographic conditions, currency exchange rates etc. enter the inequalities describing the proper working of a system under consideration. The main difficulty of such models is due to (optimal) decisions that have to be taken prior to the observation of random parameters. In this situation, one can hardly find any decision which would definitely exclude later constraint violation caused by unexpected random effects. Sometimes, such constraint violation can be balanced afterwards by some compensating decisions taken in a second stage. For instance, making recourse to pumped storage plants or buying energy on the liberalized market is an option for power generating companies that are faced with unforeseen peaks of electrical load. As long as the costs of compensating decisions are known, these may be considered as a penalization for constraint violation. This idea leads to the important class of *twostage* or *multistage stochastic programs* Birge & Louveaux (1997); Kall & Wallace (1994); Ruszczyński & Shapiro (2003).
In many applications, however, compensations simply do not exist (e.g., for safety relevant restrictions like levels of a water reservoir) or cannot be modeled by costs in any reasonable way. In such circumstances, one would rather insist on decisions guaranteeing feasibility 'as much as possible'. This loose term refers once more to the fact that constraint violation can almost never be avoided because of unexpected extreme events. On the other hand, when knowing or approximating the distribution of the random parameter, it makes sense to call decisions feasible (in a stochastic meaning) whenever they are feasible with high probability, i.e., only a low percentage of realizations of the random parameter leads to constraint violation under this fixed decision. A generic way to express such a *probabilistic* or *chance constraint* as an inequality is

$$\mathbb{P}(h(x,\xi) \geq 0) \geq p. \tag{1}$$

Here, x and ξ are decision and random vectors, respectively, "$h(x,\xi) \geq 0$" refers to a finite system of inequalities and $\mathbb{P}$ is a probability measure. The value $p \in [0,1]$ is called the probability level, and it is chosen by the decision maker in order to model the safety

requirements. In the following we tacitly assume that (1) represents a constraint inside an optimization problem where some objective function $f(x)$ has to be minimized. Since the role of f is as in conventional optimization problems, we shall focus our attention to the special type of constraint as given by (1).
Sometimes, the probability level is strictly fixed from the very beginning (e.g., $p = 0.95, 0.99$ etc.). In other situations, the decision maker may only have a vague idea of a properly chosen level. Of course, he is aware that higher values of p lead to fewer feasible decisions x in (1), hence to optimal solutions at higher costs. Fortunately, it turns out that usually p can be increased over quite a wide range without affecting too much the optimal value of some problem, until it closely approaches 1 and then a strong increase of costs becomes evident. In this way, models with chance constraints can also give a hint to a good compromise between costs and safety.
Formally, the chance constraint (1) may be written as a usual inequality constraint:

$$\alpha(x) \geq p, \quad \text{where} \quad \alpha(x) := \mathbb{P}(h(x,\xi) \geq 0). \tag{2}$$

In contrast to conventional optimization problems, however, the challenge posed by chance constraints consists in the fact that the function α is not given explicitly. Therefore neither theoretical properties (continuity, differentiability, concavity) nor suitable algorithmic approaches are evident. Not surprisingly, there does not exist a general solution method for chance constrained programs. The choice strongly depends on how random and decision variables interact in the constraint model. Sometimes a linear programming solver will do the job. In other models, one has to have access to values and gradients of multidimensional distribution functions (e.g., the reservoir management model of Section 6). Of particular interest is the application of algorithms from convex optimization. Convexity of chance constraints, however, does not only depend on convexity properties of the constraint function h in (1) but also of the distribution of the random parameter ξ. The question of whether this distribution is continuous or discrete is another crucial aspect for algorithmic treatment. The biggest challenges from the algorithmic and theoretical points of view arise in chance constraints where random and decision variables cannot be decoupled.
All issues discussed up to now illustrate the close tie between algorithmic and structural properties. Some of these shall be briefly presented in the following sections. The chapter is organized as follows: Section 2 is dedicated to a discussion of structural properties of chance constraints. Section 3 will illustrate the importance of stochastic programming in general and chance constrained programming in particular for energy management problems. Moreover, we will present the generic look and feel of such problems. This will be further developed in Section 4. In Section 5 recent results on CCP for Energy management structured problems will be discussed. These results are illustrated on a typical example in Section 6, that also shows that CCP can be tractable/interesting for some problems in EM and with some research effort could become a very important tool for EM under uncertainty. Finally Section 7 sketches some perspectives.
Among the numerous applications of chance constrained programming one may find areas like water resource management, circuit manufacturing, chemical engineering, telecommunications, finance and Energy management. For basic monographs on this topic, we refer to Prékopa (2003) and relevant chapters in Ruszczyński & Shapiro (2003), Shapiro et al. (2009).

2. Models and structural properties

The properties of a concrete chance constrained optimization problem mainly hinge on the following items:

- Distribution of the random vector (e.g., continuous or discrete distribution, independent or correlated components)
- Type of constraint system (e.g., linear, separated random vector, coupled random and decision vectors)
- Type of chance constraints (individual or joint)

Different combinations of elements from these basic categories may lead to mathematical objects with drastically different theoretical properties and algorithmical requirements.

2.1 Models

The most important models in practical applications of chance constraints are linear in the random vector. This means that the constraint mapping h in (1) takes one of the forms

$$h(x,\xi) = g(x) - A\xi \quad \text{or} \quad h(x,\xi) = A(\xi)g(x) - b, \tag{3}$$

where A and $A(\xi)$ are determinstic or stochastic matrices, respectively, g is a mapping just depending on the decision vector x and b is a vector of appropriate size. The basic difference between both models is that in the first case the random vector appears separated from the decision vector, whereas both are coupled in the second model. Both models have numerous applications in engineering and, in particular, in energy management.
The chance constraint (1) can be written more explicitly as

$$\mathbb{P}(h_j(x,\xi) \geq 0 \quad (j = 1,\ldots,m)) \geq p. \tag{4}$$

Since here, the probability is taken over the whole stochastic inequality system, one also calls this a *joint* chance constraint. Alternatively, one could turn each component of the stochastic inequality system into several chance constraints individually, and thereby allowing individual probability levels for each chance constraint:

$$\mathbb{P}(h_j(x,\xi) \geq 0) \geq p_j \quad (j = 1,\ldots,m) \tag{5}$$

Such *individual* chance constraints, though formally yielding a larger system of m inequalities as compared to just one inequality in the joint case, may lead to much easier mathematical models in some special cases (see Section 2.2). Care has to be taken, however, with a correct interpretation of results for these two models. If one is interested in decisions guaranteeing satisfaction of the whole stochastic inequality system at the given probability level, then a formal solution via the individual model, though appealing for its simplicity, may result in completely unreliable optimal decisions (see, e.g., van Ackooij et al. (2010c)). On the other hand, individual chance constraints may be used to derive upper and lower bounds for the optimal value in an optimization problem with joint chance constraints. More precisely, if x is feasible for (4), then x is feasible for (5) too provided that $p \geq p_j$ for all j. Conversely, if x is feasible for (5), then x is feasible for (4) too provided that $\sum_{j=1}^{m} p_j \geq p + m - 1$.
Finally, it has to be mentioned that the chance constraint (1) is of static type. This means that, if decision and random vector represent discrete time processes, then the decision policy would

be designed in a way that it does not react on previously observed realizations of the random vector. Dynamic models for chance constraints lead to new challenges and complications which are outside the scope of this presentation. For a recently proposed approach in this direction, we refer to Henrion et al. (2010).

2.2 Random right-hand side

An important special case of the linear separated model (first case of (3)) arises if the linear transformation A reduces to the identity such that the chance constraint gets the form of random right-hand side. Then, the probability function of (2) can be written as a composition

$$\alpha(x) = \mathbb{P}(g(x) \geq \xi) = F_\xi(g(x)), \tag{6}$$

where F_ξ is the cumulative multivariate distribution function of the random vector ξ. This special structure has the advantage that the effort of verifying analytical properties or of implementing numerical algorithms for the solution of chance constrained problems can be focussed on distribution functions which are well-studied objects in stochastics. The composition formula $\alpha = F_\xi \circ g$ allows one to transfer properties like continuity, (local or global) Lipschitz continuity or differentiability from F_ξ and g to α. Since the mapping g is typically given in analytical form and thus its properties are well understood from the beginning, it remains to check or to rely on known analogous properties of F_ξ. For instance, F_ξ is always continuous if the random vector ξ has a density. Differentiability and convexity are a more involved issues but can be checked for important classes of distributions (see Sections 2.3 and 2.4).

Under random right-hand side the model of individual chance constraints (5) becomes

$$\alpha_j(x) = \mathbb{P}(g_j(x) \geq \xi_j) = F_{\xi_j}(g_j(x)) \geq p_j \quad (j = 1, \ldots, m),$$

where now F_{ξ_j} refers to the one-dimensional distribution function of the component ξ_j. As one-dimensional distribution functions can be inverted via the concept of quantile, the individual chance constraints can be rewritten as

$$\alpha_j(x) \geq p_j \Longleftrightarrow g_j(x) \geq q^{(j)}_{p_j} \quad (j = 1, \ldots, m),$$

where $q^{(j)}_{p_j} := \inf\{\tau | F_{\xi_j}(\tau) \geq p_j\}$ is the p_j- quantile of F_{ξ_j}. In other words: individual chance constraints with random right hand side inherit their structure from the underlying stochastic constraint. If the latter was linear then the induced individual chance constraints will be linear too.

Another important special case under random right-hand side arises if the random vector ξ has independent components, then the calculation of α breaks down to one dimensional distribution values again:

$$\alpha(x) = F_{\xi_1}(g_1(x)) \cdots F_{\xi_m}(g_m(x)).$$

Although the constraint $\alpha(x) \geq p$ cannot be further simplified to an explicit constraint involving just the g_j (as was possible for individual chance constraints), one may still benefit from the fact that one dimensional distribution functions are usually easy to calculate. On the other hand, the independence assumption is often not reasonable in practice.

2.3 Multivariate normal distribution

Perhaps the most important special case in practical applications arises from joint chance constraints with random right-hand side having a regular multivariate normal distribution. We shall use the standard notation $\xi \sim \mathcal{N}(\mu, \Sigma)$ to indicate that ξ has a multivariate normal distribution with mean vector μ and covariance matrix Σ. Such normal distribution is called regular if Σ is positive definite. According to (6) the constraint with random right-hand side takes the form $F_\xi(g(x)) \geq p$ then. As g is explicitly given by a formula, in general, the evaluation of such constraints by optimization algorithms requires the calculation of $F_\xi, \nabla F_\xi \ldots$, i.e., of values and (higher order) derivatives of a nondegenerate multivariate normal distribution function. Fortunately, gradients of such distribution functions can be reduced analytically to some lower dimensional multivariate normal distribution functions (see Prékopa (1995), p. 204). The precise formula can be found in Lemma 0.5 below. Thus, proceeding by induction for higher order derivatives (see also Section 5.2.4), the whole optimization issue hinges upon the evaluation of nondegenerate normal distribution functions in this situation. Much progress has been made in computing such distributions functions be it by using specially designed techniques of numerical integration (Genz & Bretz (2009)) or be it by developping efficient lower and upper bounds for their values combined with adapted simulation techniques (Bukszár & Szántai (2002); Szántai & Habib (1998)). Using those methods at hand, it is possible to deal with joint chance constraints under normally distributed random right-hand side with moderate precision in moderate dimension of ξ of say up to a few hundred.

It is important to observe that, given a tool for calculating multivariate normal distribution functions, it is not only possible to deal with the special case of random right-hand side but also with the more general linear models introduced in (3). If, for instance, ξ has a multivariate normal distribution with mean vector μ and covariance matrix Ξ, then the linearly transformed random vector $\eta := A\xi$ will have a multivariate normal distribution too with mean vector $A\mu$ and covariance matrix $A\Xi A^T$. Consequently, the first model in (3) can be written without loss of generality in the special form with random right-hand side η and one is back to the situation discussed before. A similar argument applies to the second model in (3). However, one must be aware of the fact that a linear transformation of the random vector may change the normal distribution from a nondegenerate one (i.e., with positive definite covariance matrix) to a singular one. This is necessarily the case, for instance, if the number of rows in A exceeds the dimension of the random vector as is typical for instance in network problems. Then, algorithms for calculating singular normal distribution functions Genz & Kwong (2000), for calculating normal probabilities of convex sets (in particular: polyhedra) Deák (1986) or for reducing singular normal distribution functions to regular ones via an efficient inclusion-exclusion formula Henrion & Römisch (2010) can be applied. At the same time, it is also possible to obtain gradients with respect to the decision variable x in the models (3) via reduction to the calculus of values of multivariate normal distribution functions pretty much the same way (though possibly more involved) as in the case of random right-hand side. As an instance of such models which are different from random right-hand side, we discuss two-sided chance constraints with multivariate normal distribution in Section 5.2. We note that beyond normal distributions and models of type (3) gradients of probability functions α in (2) may be very difficult to obtain. For a general, abstract gradient formula, we refer to Uryasev (1995).

2.4 Convexity

Convexity is a basic issue for theory (structure, stability) and algorithms (convergence towards global solutions) in any optimization problem. In chance constrained programming, the first question one could deal with is convexity of the feasible set defined say by a very simple probabilistic constraint of the type

$$\{x|\mathbb{P}(\xi \leq x) \geq p\} = \{x|F_{\xi}(x) \geq p\}. \tag{7}$$

It is well known that such a set is convex if F_{ξ} is a quasiconcave function. Although distribution functions can never be concave or convex (due to being bounded by zero and one) it turns out that many of them are quasiconcave. The left plot of Figure 1 shows the graph of the bivariate normal distribution function with independent components. It is neither concave nor convex, but all of its upper level sets are convex (the boundary of the upper level set corresponding to the level $p = 0.5$ is depicted by a curve on the graph). For algorithmic

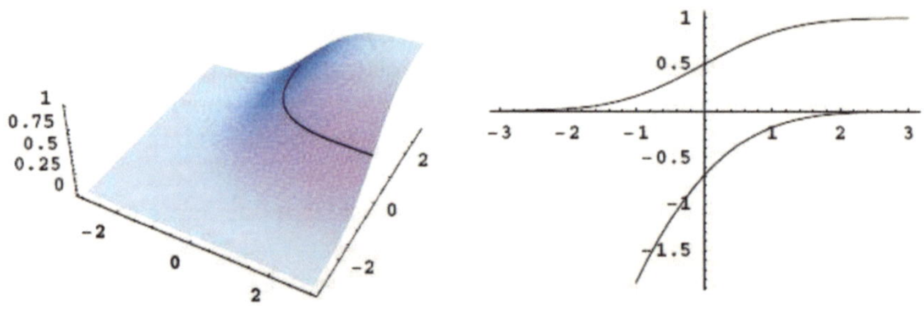

Fig. 1. Bivariate normal distribution function (left) and standard normal distribution and its logarithm (right).

purposes it is often desirable to know that the function defining an inequality constraint of type '$\geq$' is not just quasiconcave but actually concave. As mentioned above, this cannot hold for inequalities of type (7). However, a suitable transformation might do the job. Indeed, it turns out that most of the prominent multivariate distribution functions (e.g., multivariate normal, uniform distribution on convex compact sets, Dirichlet, Pareto, etc.) share the property of being log-concave, i.e., $\log F_{\xi}$ is concave (an illustration for the one-dimensional normal distribution and its log is given in the right plot of Figure 1). The key for verifying such a nontrivial property for the distribution function is to check the same property of log-concavity for the density of F_{ξ}, if it exists. The latter task is easy in general. For instance, a nondegenerate normal density is proportional to the exponential of a concave function, hence multivariate normal distributions are logarithmically concave. The mentioned result is a consequence of a celebrated theorem due to Prékopa (1995). Now, when F_{ξ} is log-concave, (7) may be equivalently rewritten as a concave inequality constraint $\{x| \log F_{\xi}(x) \geq \log p\}$ or equivalently as a convex inequality constraint $\{x| - \log F_{\xi}(x) \leq -\log p\}$. The same conclusions on convexity can be drawn for more general chance constraints of linear separated type

$$\{x|\mathbb{P}(Bx \geq A\xi) \geq p\},$$

i.e., the set of feasible decisions can be described by the convex inequality constraint

$$\{x| - \log F_{A\xi}(Bx) \leq - \log p\}$$

for the same family of distributions of ξ having log-concave densities.
Things become more involved in the feasible set

$$\{x|\mathbb{P}(A(\xi)g(x) - b) \geq p\} \tag{8}$$

of the coupled model (right case of (3)). A classical result by van de Panne & Popp (1963) and by Kataoka (1963) states that if the random matrix $A(\xi)$ reduces to just one line $A_1(\xi)$, the mapping g is the identity (i.e., $g(x) = x$), ξ has a regular multivariate normal distribution and $p \geq 0.5$, then the set (8) is convex. A first difference with the log-concavity properties stated above is that convexity of the feasible set does no longer hold true for arbitrary probability levels but only for sufficiently large ones. This, however, is not a severe restriction because in practice one is interested in large probability levels anyway (e.g., $p \geq 0.95$). This classical result has been generalized later on to other than normal distributions of ξ (e.g., elliptically symmetric or symmetric log-concave, Lagoa et al. (2005)) and to nonlinear mappings $g(x)$ (see Henrion (2007)).
Evidently, the previous results can be immediately applied to the feasible set of individual chance constraints:

$$\{x|\mathbb{P}(A_j(\xi)g(x) - b_j) \geq p_j \quad (j = 1, \ldots, m)\}.$$

Indeed, since the intersection of convex sets is convex again, it follows from the previously mentioned result for one single row $A_1(\xi)$ that this feasible set induced by a whole random matrix is convex provided that $p_j \geq 0.5$ for $j = 1, \ldots, m$. Not surprisingly, things are not that evident for the joint chance constraint (8) if $A(\xi)$ has more than just one line. Convexity results can then be found under the assumption of ξ having a normal distribution with specially structured covariance matrix (see Henrion & Strugarek (2008); Prékopa (1995)). Convexity in the general case is an open question.

2.5 Compactness

Compactness of the feasible domain is a very interesting property to check, since non-empty and compact feasible sets guarantee the existence of solutions and allow us to derive stability of results. It is interesting to observe that compactness of the coupled chance constraint (8) can be derived in case of a normal distribution without enforcing it by additional exterior deterministic constraints on the decision vector (e.g., box constraints). To be more precise, let the rows A_i of A in (8) be normally distributed according to $A_i \sim \mathcal{N}(\mu_i, \Sigma_i)$ with positive definite covariance matrices Σ_i for $i = 1, ..., m$. Assuming that g is a homeomorphism (e.g., $g(x) = x$), then, (8) is compact provided that $p > \min_i \Phi_1(\sqrt{\mu_i^T \Sigma_i^{-1} \mu_i})$. Here, Φ_1 refers to the one-dimensional standard normal distribution function and, hence, the critical probability level beyond which compactness is guaranteed can be calculated explicitly from the distribution parameters of ξ. As a consequence, the Weierstrass Theorem ensures the existence of a solution to the optimization problem

$$\min\{f(x) \mid x \text{ satisfies } (8)\},$$

whenever the objective function f is continuous.

2.6 Discrete distributions

The setting of joint chance constraints with random right-hand side and nondegenerate multivariate normal distribution enjoys many desirable features such as differentiability or convexity (via log-concavity). Of course, other settings may have practical importance too. For instance, the distribution of the random right-hand side could be other than normal. The cases of multivariate Gamma or Dirichlet distributions are discussed in Prékopa (1995), Section 6.6. Here, log-concavity remains an important tool.
Things become different, however, when passing to discrete distributions. These are of interest for at least two reasons: first, the problem to be solved could have been directly modeled by discrete random variables (see, e.g., Beraldi & Ruszczyński (2002)). Second, there may be a need to approximate continuous distributions (e.g., multivariate normal) by discrete ones, for instance when treating probabilistic constraints in two stage models with scenario formulations Ruszczyński (2002). A key issue in discrete chance constrained programming is finding the so called p-efficient points (introduced in Prékopa (1990)) of the distribution function F_ξ of ξ. These are points z such that $F_\xi(z) \geq p$ and the relations $F_\xi(y) \geq p,\, y \leq z$ (partial order of vectors) imply that $y = z$. One easily observes that all the information about the p-level set of F_ξ is contained in these points because

$$\{y | F_\xi(y) \geq p\} = \bigcup_{z \in E} (z + \mathbb{R}^s_+),$$

where E is the set of p-efficient points and $\mathbb{R}^s_+$ is the positive orthant in the space of the random vector. In the case of ξ having integer-valued components and $p \in (0,1)$, P is a finite set (see Theorem 1 in Dentcheva et al. (2000)). Algorithms for enumerating or generating p-efficient points are described, for instance, in Beraldi & Ruszczyński (2002); Dentcheva et al. (2000); Prékopa (2003); Prékopa et al. (1998). It is interesting to note that the log-concavity concept, even if not directly applicable, can be adapted with useful consequences to discrete distributions as well (see Dentcheva et al. (2000)).
Another powerful approach to solve chance constrained programs with discrete distributions via integer programming methods has been recently reported in Luedtke & Ahmed (2008).

3. Randomness and energy management optimization problems

In the electrical power industry, it is important to guarantee at each time step, the equilibrium between the offer and demand and hence avoid shortage supply. This is a major concern, whatever the time horizon. The traditional Unit Commitment Problem (UCP) consists of defining the minimal-cost power generation schedule for a given set of power plants satisfying at each time step the equilibrium between the production and the demand while respecting physical constraints. This problem, in a deterministic setting, is a challenging large-size, non-convex, non-linear optimization problem, due to many thermal and hydro power-plants constraints, which introduce discontinuous operation domains and give non-convex dynamic constraints. It has been solved satisfactory in an industrial way (Batut & Renaud (1992); Cohen & Zhu (1983); Lemaréchal & Sagastizábal (1994); Merlin & Sandrin (1983)).
Many uncertainties strongly impact the electrical power industry and should be taken into account in this problem. Uncertainty consists of the load charge curve and the hydraulic-inflows of each reservoir, both of which are climate sensitive (temperature and

cloud cover). Moreover, we have to consider the availability of the power plants, which are subject to random failure, the prices on both electricity and gas markets and wind generation. Extending, in the context of electricity markets, the traditional UCP leads to a modern Energy Management Problem (EMP). This modern version consists of optimizing the production planning, while keeping supply shortage risk under bounds, using both financial (interruption options, futures and markets) and physical (thermal and hydraulic production units) assets (Zorgati et al. (2009)). For economical reasons, one key point, which requires significant effort deals with the definition of an efficient Water Reservoir Management Problem. Such a problem can be considered as a sub problem of any EMP. Since the original deterministic UCP is already challenging, needless to say, adding uncertainty has not made things easier. Hence, in a logic of price decomposition (or optimization assets against market prices) we will typically consider subproblems of the huge EMP. It is important to note that the structures that occur in these subproblems are quite general and occur in many other Energy management problems. We refer to Section 4 for more on these structures.
When generally considering Optimization Problems encountered in Energy management, we can state that they are characterized by challenging key features such as:

- the stochastic nature of the problem, due to the uncertainty affecting the electrical system
- the stochastic nature of several physical constraints
- the nature of the decision variables of the problem (real, integer, binary/logical)
- the huge number of variables and constraints
- the non-linear (and non-convex) nature of many constraints
- bilateral constraints
- we are looking for closed loop strategies, i.e., decisions that adapt whenever the outcome of randomness is observed.

Considering the related Energy Management optimization Problems (EMOP) and a large class of other problems[1] such as long run marginal costs of energetic commodities or gas management, we clearly obtain the following generic structure of many EMOP:

$$\begin{aligned} \min \quad & f[c(x,\xi)] \\ s.t. \quad & b_l(\xi_\delta) \leq A(\xi_\alpha)x + \theta(\xi) \leq b_u(\xi_\delta) \\ & Px \leq h \\ & x \in X, \end{aligned} \tag{9}$$

where

- f is a risk measure on the cost function c,
- x are the controls of the problem,
- $A(\xi_\alpha)$ the matrix of the problem affected by random processes ξ_α and describing either
  - the offer. In this case α is the type of assets we consider, e.g., thermal, hydro, Futures, contracts, wind, etc...
  - a network. In this case α can be associated to coal mines, roads, gas compression stations, pipes and reservoirs, etc...

[1] with time horizons ranging from long to short term

- the (bilateral) stochastic inequality $b_l(\xi_\delta) \leq A(\xi_\alpha)x + \theta(\xi) \leq b_u(\xi_\delta)$ has to be given a meaning. For instance by using a probability constraints, i.e., $\mathbb{P}[b_l(\xi_\delta \leq A(\xi_\alpha)x + \theta(\xi) \leq b_u(\xi_\delta)] \geq p$ or by using Robust Optimization.
- the (possible void) deterministic constraints $Px \leq h$ models any polyhedral set of constraints on x
- $b_l(\xi_\delta)$ the demand affected by the random process ξ_δ. In that case b_u would be infinity. In the case of hydro management, b_l and b_u would be the lower and upper bounds on the reservoir capacity respectively.
- $\xi = [\xi_\alpha; \xi_\delta]$ is the concatenation of ξ_α and ξ_δ. Alternatively we can write $\xi = \Xi(\xi_\alpha, \xi_\delta)$ as some global random process, reflecting complex correlations and dependencies. We have expressed this feature through the use of the function Ξ.

All other specific constraints such as those appearing in water reservoir management or the nature of the controls are symbolically described by the set X. Such a set can contain all dynamic constraints on power plants for example (see Langrene et al. (2010) for the difficulties induced by such constraints).
We can distinguish three main classes of problems depending on the nature of randomness of the above stochastic inequalities:

- Only the right member b is random. We can think of coal, gas, hydro production or water reservoir management problems. In such problems, the matrix describes the topology of a system or a network and is considered fixed.
- Only the matrix A is random. This case occurs, in gas problems when considering investments on the network.
- Both A and b are random. This is the case in unit commitment and hedging problems.

4. Structure of energy management optimization problems

The general problem (9) can be declined in various subproblems. Each of these subproblems contains key features such as bilateral chance-constraints, random matrices with singularities and binary variables. The point of moving to subproblems is that these do not contain all problematic features of problem (9) at once. We can hence consider specific and adapted algorithms and methods. These models of the different subproblems often come with a robust counterpart or even an approximate chance constrained model. The results of the latter models can be compared with results obtained, using a chance-constraint formulation.
This section will detail the general structure derived from Energy management optimization problems. These structures are however far more general and can be found in many other problems. As such, the derived algorithms can be applied to problems from other contexts as well. The typical considered problems have the form

$$\begin{array}{ll} \min_x & c^\mathsf{T} x \\ s.t. & \mathbb{P}[b_l^k(\xi) \leq A^k(\xi)x + \theta^k(\xi) \leq b_u^k(\xi)] \geq p_k \; \forall k = 1,...,K \\ & Qx \leq q \\ & x \in \mathbb{R}^{n_r} \times \{0,1\}^{n_b}, \end{array} \tag{10}$$

where the problem (10) can have unilateral (either b_l or b_u is $\pm\infty$) or bilateral constraints for any of the K (joint) chance constraints. Moreover, $n_r + n_b = n$, where n is the problem

dimension and either n_r or n_b can be zero. The matrix can be deterministic, as well as θ, b_l or b_u but never all together.
Assuming the law θ centered, and absence of uncertainty, problem (10) is basically an extension of the linear (mixed-integer) program:

$$\begin{aligned} \min_x \quad & c^\mathsf{T} x \\ s.t. \quad & b_l \leq Ax \leq b_u \\ & Qx \leq q \\ & x \in \mathbb{R}^{n_r} \times \{0,1\}^{n_b}, \end{aligned} \tag{11}$$

Since model (10) is quite general, we will give some specific versions of this model and point out the structure of the submodels.

4.1 Shortage supply hedging

In a simplified version of the stochastic unit-commitment problem we can only focus on shortage supply hedging under randomness on power plant generation and customer load. In such a setting, prices and randomness on hydro reservoirs would be considered absent (in order to simplify). This leads to a version of model (10), wherein the random matrix $A(\xi)$ has the following form :

$$A(\xi) = \begin{pmatrix} A^\theta(\xi_\theta) & A^\eta(\xi_\eta) & A^\mu(\xi_\mu) & A^\sigma(\xi_\sigma) & A^\varepsilon(\xi_\varepsilon), \end{pmatrix}$$

where $\theta, \eta, \mu, \sigma, \varepsilon$ stand for type of assets, respectively thermal, hydro, markets, contracts and renewable. The decisions x in this problem relate to production decisions on various assets. The lines of the matrix would typically correspond to different time steps in our problem and the entries of the matrix would correspond to random availability coefficients. The thermal coefficient matrix would typically have the following sparse random structure:

$$A^\alpha(\xi_\alpha) = \begin{pmatrix} a_{11}^\alpha & \dots & a_{1N^\alpha}^\alpha & \dots & 0 & \dots & 0 & \dots & 0 & \dots & 0 \\ & & & \ddots & & & & \ddots & & & \\ 0 & \dots & 0 & \dots & a_{i1}^\alpha & \dots & a_{iN^\alpha}^\alpha & \dots & 0 & \dots & 0 \\ & & & \ddots & & & & \ddots & & & \\ 0 & \dots & 0 & \dots & 0 & \dots & 0 & \dots & a_{m1}^\alpha & \dots & a_{mN^\alpha}^\alpha \end{pmatrix}.$$

A natural first idea is to use a unilateral probabilistic constraint for this model, i.e., we will assume that $b_l(\xi_\delta)$ is the random load. This would correspond to the idea that we are looking to produce a sufficient quantity (and avoid shortage supply) in most cases as randomness will affect our system after decision making. We can also argue that we would like to produce not too far from the load in a sufficient amount of cases. In that case $\theta(\xi)$ would be the negative customer load and b_l and b_u two bandwidth parameters (e.g., $\pm 500MW$). One can also imagine a series of such probabilistic constraints with increasing probability level and increasing margins. We refer to Zorgati et al. (2009) and Zorgati & van Ackooij (2010) for more on this model.
Variations of this model would consist of considering individual chance constraints rather than joint ones. The danger of such a model would be that we might avoid shortage supply with a sufficient level for each time step, but never on the global time horizon. Another

variation consists in considering that we decide on what asset to use and assume that it produces at its random maximal level. This greatly simplifies that problem as it ejects (or neglects) dynamic constraints on thermal plants. It also simplifies the hydro sub-problem as now, one only needs to know plausible hydro production trajectories, which can be pre-computed. This reduces problem (10) to a stochastic knapsack problem. Robust versions of which can be found in Klopfenstein (2007); Klopfenstein & Nace (2007; 2008).

4.2 Singularities in the random matrix?

In Section 4.1 we have seen that an important problem to consider, due to the random failure process that affects thermal units, is the following:

$$\begin{array}{ll} \min_x & c^{\mathsf{T}} x \\ s.c. & \mathbb{P}[A(\xi)x \geq b] \geq p \\ & x \geq 0 \end{array} \tag{12}$$

This problem generalizes the first one since it suffices to add the random b vector to the random matrix and introduce a single variable $x_{n+1} = -1$. Therefore the global setting wherein both the right member and the matrix are random can be reduced to problem (12). However as seen in Section 4.1 the random matrix might have many (non-random) zeros and hence a priori has a distribution with many singularities. It can however be reformulated as a random-vector problem and do away with the singularities. This reformulation is very useful when we want to compute the probabilities for each x. To this end, let us define the following operator T, $T(x) = \mathrm{diag}((x^{\mathsf{T}}, ..., x^{\mathsf{T}})^{\mathsf{T}})$. We can remark that T is actually a linear operator. We also define the following matrix operation $A \mapsto A^{\odot}$, which we shall call the vector transform, by $A^{\odot} = (A_{11}, ..., A_{1n}, A_{21}, ..., A_{nn})^{\mathsf{T}}$. Then the system in equation (12) can also be rewritten as follows

$$\mathbb{P}[T(x)A^{\odot} \geq b] \geq p. \tag{13}$$

What is very interesting about this transform is that if the original A matrix contained some non-random zero components due to a formulation issue, as is the case for the thermal production matrix A^{θ} then applying this transform we can actually place the zero components in the $T(x)$ decision matrix and obtain a random vector $A^{\odot}$ that does not contain any singularities. Moreover if we assume that $A^{\odot}$ is actually a normally distributed random vector with covariance matrix Σ, then computing the probability (13) comes down to computing a multivariate normal cumulative distribution function having covariance matrix $T(x)\Sigma T(x)^T$. One can therefore see that the number of columns of matrix A doesn't really matter here as the probability that has to be computed is normal of dimension the number of rows of A.

4.3 Hydro reservoir management

The hydro subproblem of problem (10) is of particular interest as it has a structure that is common to many other network flow problems with randomness. Indeed, in such problems, we typically have righthand side randomness. In particular matrix A describes the topology of the systems, i.e., the flow constraints. Randomness occurs as in each node of the network random quantities are withdrawn (customer load in a coal-mine investment model with random load) or added (random water inflows in a hydro reservoir model). The cost vector can describe investment and transportation costs (coal-mine model, Lepaul (2009)) or water turbining costs (where we assume that volume dependent water values are available). Further deterministic constraints describe non-random parts of the model, such as reservoirs that are not impacted by random inflows, or nodes in the network not subject to random load (mines, roads). We refer to van Ackooij et al. (2010b;c) for more information on the hydro reservoir model. This subproblems also offers an alternative formulation as robust optimization (see Appariagliato et al. (2006)).

5. Chance constrained programming results for EM

When considering chance constrained optimization problems, such as the EMP (9) two important paths can be taken. We can either try to solve the problem exactly or we can try to find a good approximation of the problem. In the first setting it is important to dispose of a way to evaluate the probability constraint for any x quickly and dispose of a way to compute gradients (see van Ackooij et al. (2010c)), second derivatives (van Ackooij et al. (2010b)) and exploit information in the covariance matrices of the uncertainty factors (see van Ackooij et al. (2010a)) combined with Prékopa's LP method (Prékopa (1995)). In the second approach, the difficulty resides in finding a good approximation of the chance-constraint. This can be typically done by bounding the contraint. The advantage often resides in the fact that the approximation holds for all laws. Hence, we can obtain convex approximations of a CCP. In EM, for some problems with random matrices the decision vector contains binary variables. Such stochastic knapsack problems can be solved approximately by combining inner and outer bounds on the probability measure (see Zorgati & van Ackooij (2008; 2010)). Another approach is Robust Knapsack problems, such as those considered in Klopfenstein (2007); Klopfenstein & Nace (2007; 2008). These approaches can also be handsomely compared on the same problem. Such approximation schemes can also be used in a continuous setting, i.e., one wherein the decision vector x is real (see Zorgati et al. (2010)). The advantage of using such approximation techniques is that they transform the potentially non-convex chance constraint problem (if we take exotic laws) into a conic quadratic problem. The price of which is an approximation.
In this section we will discuss both paths.

5.1 Approximate chance constrained programming: Bounds

5.1.1 Minimal information about uncertainties

Two major questions have to be investigated in the aim of taking uncertainties into account in the optimization process. First, some knowledge about random processes has to be available. Secondly, provided that such knowledge is available, how can we integrate the associated information into the optimization process? These questions are key questions in stochastic optimization and are in practice very difficult.
Since laws are not precisely known or very complex, we aim to approximately solve the problem. We choose here a very simplistic solution based on minimal available information about uncertainties. We assume that, for any random parameter r, we know the average $r_{mean} = \mathbb{E}(r)$, the maximal value, r_{max} and its minimal value r_{min}, all derived from historically observed values.
No further hypothesis are made about the underlying random process. We will just suppose that all uncertain coefficients of the matrix A and vector b are bounded independent random variables. Boundedness is not a restrictive assumption as all borelian random variables are tight and can therefore be assumed to be almost bounded.

5.1.2 Conic approximations of individual chance constraint

Approximate solution of the probabilistic model can be obtained using the following result, the proof of which follows from an application of Hoeffding's Theorem (Hoeffding (1963)) and can be found in Zorgati et al. (2010) for each individual chance constraint, i.e., each line of the individual chance constrained stochastic matrix inequality system:

Lemma 0.1. *Let $a_j, b, j = 1, ..., n$ be almost surely bounded independent random variables and let A denote the random vector a. We will note these bounds by a_j^{min}, b^{min} and a_j^{max}, b^{max}. Furthermore we define the (semi positive definite) diagonal matrix Δ as $\Delta = \mathrm{diag}((a_1^{max} - a_1^{min}, ..., a_n^{max} - a_n^{min})^{\mathsf{T}})$. Any individual chance constraint*

$$\mathbb{P}[\langle A(\xi), x\rangle \geq b(\xi^{\delta})] \geq \alpha \tag{14}$$

can be bounded by the 2 following convex conic quadratic inequalities:

$$\begin{aligned} \langle \mathbb{E}[A(\xi)], x\rangle\rangle - \sqrt{(1/2)|\ln(1-\alpha)|}\, \|\Delta x + \delta_b\| &\geq \mathbb{E}(b) \\ \langle \mathbb{E}[A(\xi)], x\rangle\rangle &\geq \mathbb{E}(b), \end{aligned}$$

where bounded means that the feasible set of equation (14) contains the feasible set of the 2 convex conic inequalities.

As a consequence, the individualized and unilateralized version of the constraints in the general problem (10) related to time step i:

$$\begin{aligned} \mathbb{P}(\langle A_i, x\rangle \leq b_l + \theta_i(\xi)) &\geq \beta_i \\ \mathbb{P}(\langle A_i, x\rangle \geq b_u + \theta_i(\xi)) &\geq \beta_i \end{aligned}$$

can be approximated by

$$\begin{aligned} \langle A_i, x\rangle &\leq b_l + \mathbb{E}(\theta_i) + \sqrt{(1/2)\,|\ln 1 - \beta_i| R_i} \\ \langle A_i, x\rangle &\leq b_l + \mathbb{E}(\theta_i) \\ \langle A_i, x\rangle &\geq b_u + \mathbb{E}(\theta_i) + \sqrt{(1/2)\,|\ln 1 - \beta_i| R_i} \\ \langle A_i, x\rangle &\geq b_u + \mathbb{E}(\theta_i), \end{aligned}$$

where $R_i = [max(\theta_i) - min(\theta_i)]^2$
If the initial problem has m constraints and mn variables, the convex approximation using the result leads to a problem with $m(2n+5)$ constraints and mn variables.
This result implies that any individual chance-constrained optimization problem of the form (10) can be approximated by the convex conic quadratic problem :

$$\begin{aligned} \min_x \quad & c^t x \\ \text{s.t.} \quad & \|\tilde{A}_l x + \tilde{b}_l\|_2 \leq \tilde{f}_{l^t} x + \tilde{d}_l, l = 1, ..., L, \end{aligned}$$

since, by Lemma 0.1, any linear constraint corresponds to a particular case of conic quadratic constraint with null matrix A_i and null vector b_i and any positivity constraint can also be written in a conic quadratic form (with $f_i = 0$ (Alizadeh & Goldfarb (2001); Lobo et al. (1998))).

Then, by applying Schur's complement theorem, it is easy to give the Semi-Definite version of this conic quadratic approximation :

Corollary 0.2. *Any individual chance constraint:*

$$\mathbb{P}[\langle A_i(\xi), x\rangle \geq b_i(\xi_\delta)] \geq \alpha_i,\ \forall i \in I$$

can be bounded by the following semi-definite condition:

$$\begin{bmatrix} (\tilde{f}_l^t x + \tilde{d}_l)I & \tilde{A}_l x + \tilde{b}_l \\ (\tilde{A}_l x + \tilde{b}_l)^t & \tilde{f}_l^t x + \tilde{d}_l \end{bmatrix} \succeq 0,\ l \in (1, L),$$

where notations are as in Lemma 0.1

5.1.3 Approximations in the combinatorial case : Stochastic Knapsack problems

As indicated earlier, when problem (10) only contains binary decisions, we are facing a stochastic multi-knapsack problem. By considering individual chance constraints, using finite subadditivity of the probability measure and the inclusion-exclusion principle, we show that thanks to Hoeffding's inequality, any chance constraint can be approximated by an "outer" bound for m odd and by a "inner" bound for m even. This leads to a robust mixed inner-outer algorithm that allows us to approximately solve our binary chance-constrained program and, in general, any stochastic Multi-Knapsack Problem, i.e., canonical problems of the form

$$\begin{array}{ll} \min_{x\in\{0,1\}^n} & c^{\mathsf{T}} x \\ s.t. & \mathbb{P}[A(\xi)x \geq b] \geq 1 - p \end{array} \tag{15}$$

We refer to Zorgati & van Ackooij (2010) for the proofs of the theorems in this paragraph.

5.1.3.1 Method 1 : Mixed Inner Outer approximation (AMIO)

The following approximation is based on Hoeffding's inequality.

Lemma 0.3. *Let u be the all-one vector. Assuming $\langle \mathbb{E}(A_i), u\rangle \leq b_i$ and fixing $\tau_i \geq 0$ such that $b_i = \tau_i + \langle \mathbb{E}(A_i), u\rangle$, we obtain*

$$\mathbb{P}[\langle A_i, x\rangle \geq b_i] \leq \exp(-\frac{2\tau_i^2}{\sum_{j=1}^n (\bar{a}_{ij} - \underline{a}_{ij})^2}).$$

Whenever $\langle \mathbb{E}(A_i), u\rangle > b_i$, we obtain

$$\mathbb{P}[\langle A_i, x\rangle \geq b_i] \geq 1 - \exp(-\frac{2\tau^2}{\sum_{j=1}^n (\bar{a}_{ij} - \underline{a}_{ij})^2}),$$

where $\tau = \min_x \langle \mathbb{E}(A_i), x\rangle - b_i$.

Lemma 0.4. *Define* $\tau_i(x) = b_i - \langle \mathbb{E}(A_i), x \rangle$. *Let x be a feasible solution of the following problem*

$$\begin{aligned} \min_{(x,z)\in\{0,1\}^{n+m}} \quad & c^{\mathsf{T}} x \\ \text{s.t.} \quad & -\hat{C}_i z_i + (1-z_i)\ln(1-p) \le \frac{-2(b_i - \langle \mathbb{E}(A_i), x\rangle)^2}{\sum_{j=1}^n (\bar{a}_{ij} - \underline{a}_{ij})^2} \\ & \frac{-2(b_i - \langle \mathbb{E}(A_i), x\rangle)^2}{\sum_{j=1}^n (\bar{a}_{ij} - \underline{a}_{ij})^2} \le \ln(p) + C(1-z_i) \\ & -M_i z_i \le \tau_i(x) \le M_i(1-z_i) \end{aligned} \qquad (16)$$

where C is such that $\exp(C) \ge \frac{1}{p}$, $\hat{C}_i = 2\frac{M_i^2}{\sum_{j=1}^n (\bar{a}_{ij} - \underline{a}_{ij})^2}$ *and* M_i *some big constant such that* $\tau_i(x) \in [-M_i, M_i]\ \forall x$, *then x is feasible for the canonical problem on constraint i if* $\tau_i(x) \le 0$. *If x is a feasible solution for constraint i of the canonical problem (15) and* $\tau_i(x) \ge 0$ *then x is feasible for constraint i for (16).*

We will call the problem (16) the mixed-inner-outer approximation (MIO) of the canonical problem. It is a linear problem if we remark that z_i is binary, and the fact that the first constraint is active whenever $z_i = 0$ and the second when $z_i = 1$. Indeed the following problem is equivalent to MIO :

$$\begin{aligned} \min_{(x,z)\in\{0,1\}^{n+m}} \quad & c^{\mathsf{T}} x \\ \text{s.t.} \quad & -\tau_i(x) \ge \sqrt{-\frac{1}{2}\sum_{j=1}^n (\bar{a}_{ij} - \underline{a}_{ij})^2 \ln(p) z_i} \\ & \tau_i(x) \ge -M_i z_i \\ & -\tau_i(x) \ge -\sqrt{\frac{1}{2}\sum_{j=1}^n (\bar{a}_{ij} - \underline{a}_{ij})^2 \hat{C}_i z_i} + \sqrt{-\frac{1}{2}\sum_{j=1}^n (\bar{a}_{ij} - \underline{a}_{ij})^2 \ln(1-p)(1-z_i)} \\ & -\tau_i(x) \ge -M_i(1-z_i) \end{aligned} \qquad (17)$$

The interpretation is noteworthy since the ratios inside the constraints are the expected difference between load and the production normalized by the total power available at time step k. Indeed on some constraints we will have enforced the original constraint, therefore obtaining a feasible, but potentially costly solution. However on some other constraints we will have relaxed the original constraint, therefore obtaining a potentially non-feasible but cheap solution. On some examples, this allows us to approximate rather accurately the optimal cost.

We will speak of the augmented MIO problem whenever the objective function is replaced by $\min_{x,z} c^T x - a^T z$, for some positive vector a. The point in adding the additional a vector is giving additional value to the event $\tau_i(x) \le 0$, which is the average version of what we wish to achieve with our chance constraint! The more negative $\tau_i(x)$, the likelier the chance constraint is satisfied.

5.1.3.2 Method 2 : Robust Knapsack Formulation (RKP(Γ))

Following Klopfenstein & Nace (2008), we can build a Robust Knapsack version of our problem (10) $RKP(\Gamma)$. We thus obtain

$$\begin{aligned} \min \quad & c^T x \\ s.t. \quad & \sum_{j \in S} \underline{a}_{ij} x_j + \sum_{j \notin S} \overline{a}_{ij} x_j \geq b_i \forall i \forall S \subset \{1, ..., n\}, |S| = \Gamma. \end{aligned}$$

Here Γ is a hardness parameter. Taking for instance $\Gamma = n$ gives the full-robust solution, i.e., whatever the realization of uncertainty the chance-constraint is satisfied. If the above problem is infeasible for $\Gamma = 0$ there is no solution to problem (15) either. The problem $RKP(\Gamma)$ can be solved using a dynamic programming algorithm as indicated in Klopfenstein & Nace (2008). The main difficulty in these approximations is that for many Γ the $RKP(\Gamma)$ problem may be infeasible.

5.2 Gradients for two-sided chance constraints under multivariate normal distribution

In the hydro sub-problem that we consider (Section 4.3), probabilistic constraints are induced by two-sided stochastic inequalities. Indeed we have seen that it is of the following form:

$$\min\{c^\mathsf{T} x \mid \mathbb{P}(Ax + a \leq L\xi \leq Bx + b) \geq p\}, \tag{18}$$

where A, B, L and a, b, c are matrices and vectors, respectively, of appropriate orders. Assuming inflows normally distributed, these inequalities bound a normally distributed random vector by some decision-dependent functions. More precisely the probabilistic constraint may take the form

$$\mathbb{P}(\alpha(x) \leq \xi \leq \beta(x)) \geq p.$$

We refer to van Ackooij et al. (2010c) for more on these methods.

Here, ξ is a random vector having a regular multivariate normal distribution, $\mathbb{P}$ denotes the probability measure, $p \in (0, 1)$ is a probability level and x refers to a decision vector. In geometric terms, it is required that the probability of some x-dependent rectangle be not smaller than p. In order to determine an optimal decision x^* in the context of an optimization problem, one has to have access to values and derivatives of this probability function. As far as values are concerned, one may employ numerical algorithms designed for the calculus of normal distribution functions Szántai (2000), of normal probabilities of general convex sets Déak (1980) or directly of rectangles Genz (1992). However, none of these algorithms provides gradients of the probability function with respect to changes of the lower and upper limit of the rectangle. In case of one-sided constraints (i.e., $\alpha = -\infty$, so that one is dealing with distribution functions), there is no problem to reduce the computation of the gradient to that of a value of a distribution function (see Lemma 0.5 below). Formally, one could also do so with gradients of two-sided constraints by exploiting a representation of rectangle probabilities in terms of distribution functions (see (19)) and then taking derivatives of the latter ones term by term. We note that such representation allowing for reduction of derivatives to those of distribution functions is available even for general polyhedra Henrion & Römisch (2010). This approach, however, becomes impractical already in small dimension. For example in the case of an n-dimensional rectangle, the number of terms in the representation equals 2^n.

5.2.1 Constraints induced by rectangular sets and multivariate normal distributions

We present a simple formula for the derivative of the normal probability of rectangles with respect to their lower and upper limits. In particular, this formula allows to reduce the problem to the same calculus of probabilities of rectangles (in one dimension less). Consequently, the same algorithm in Genz (1992) can be used for computing values and derivatives of the probability function introduced above.

Let ξ be some n-dimensional random vector having a nondegenerate multivariate normal distribution with mean vector μ and covariance matrix Σ. We will write $\xi \sim \mathcal{N}(\mu, \Sigma)$ for short. Denote by

$$\Phi_{\xi}(z) := \mathbb{P}(\xi \leq z) \quad \forall z \in \mathbb{R}^n$$

its cumulative distribution function (with $\mathbb{P}$ referring to the underlying probability measure). We further introduce the rectangle probability function

$$F_{\xi}(a,b) := \mathbb{P}(a \leq \xi \leq b) \quad \forall a,b \in \mathbb{R}^n : a \leq b.$$

The following relation is well known to hold whenever $a \leq b$:

$$F_{\xi}(a,b) = \sum_{i_1,\ldots,i_n \in \{0,1\}} (-1)^{\left[n+\sum_{j=1}^{n} i_j\right]} \Phi_{\xi}(y_{i_1},\ldots,y_{i_n}), \tag{19}$$

where

$$y_{i_j} := \begin{cases} a_j & \text{if } i_j = 0 \\ b_j & \text{if } i_j = 1 \end{cases}.$$

For instance, if $n = 2$, the probability of the rectangle $[a,b]$ calculates via the distribution function as

$$F_{\xi}(a,b) = \Phi_{\xi}(a_1,a_2) - \Phi_{\xi}(a_1,b_2) - \Phi_{\xi}(b_1,a_2) + \Phi_{\xi}(b_1,b_2).$$

The following lemma can be found (in its equivalent form for standard normal distributions) in Prékopa (1995). It shows how the derivative of a multivariate normal distribution can be reduced to values of a different multivariate normal distribution (in one dimension less):

Lemma 0.5. *Assume that $\xi \sim \mathcal{N}(\mu, \Sigma)$ with some positive definite covariance matrix $\Sigma = \left(\sigma_{ij}\right)$. Then, Φ_{ξ} is contiuously differentiable and*

$$\frac{\partial \Phi_{\xi}}{\partial z_i}(z) = f_{\xi_i}(z_i) \cdot \Phi_{\tilde{\xi}(z_i)}(z_1,\ldots,z_{i-1},z_{i+1}\ldots,z_s) \quad (i = 1,\ldots,n).$$

Here, f_{ξ_i} denotes the one-dimensional probability density of the component ξ_i, $\tilde{\xi}(z_i)$ is an $n-1$-dimensional random vector distributed according to $\tilde{\xi}(z_i) \sim \mathcal{N}(\hat{\mu}, \hat{\Sigma})$, $\hat{\mu}$ results from the vector $\mu + \sigma_{ii}^{-1}(z_i - \mu_i)\sigma_i$ by deleting component i and $\hat{\Sigma}$ results from the matrix $\Sigma - \sigma_{ii}^{-1}\sigma_i\sigma_i^T$ by deleting row i and column i, where σ_i refers to column i of Σ.

In the next theorem, we generalize Lemma 0.5 to the case of probability functions F_{ξ} defined by rectangles. In particular, the presented formula allows to again reduce the derivative of F_{ξ} to the calculus of values of a similar function induced by a different normally distributed random vector. The proof of the theorem can be found in van Ackooij et al. (2010c)

Theorem 0.6. *Assume that $\xi \sim \mathcal{N}(\mu, \Sigma)$ with some positive definite covariance matrix Σ. Then, for $i = 1, \ldots, n$,*

$$\frac{\partial}{\partial b_i} F_\xi(a, b) = f_{\xi_i}(b_i)\, F_{\tilde{\xi}(b_i)}(\tilde{a}, \tilde{b}) \tag{20}$$

$$\frac{\partial}{\partial a_i} F_\xi(a, b) = -f_{\xi_i}(a_i)\, F_{\tilde{\xi}(a_i)}(\tilde{a}, \tilde{b}). \tag{21}$$

Here, f_{ξ_i} is as in Lemma 0.5, $\tilde{\xi}(b_i), \tilde{\xi}(a_i)$, are $n-1$-dimensional random vectors distributed according to $\tilde{\xi}(b_i), \tilde{\xi}(a_i) \sim \mathcal{N}(\hat{\mu}, \hat{\Sigma})$ such that $\hat{\mu}$ results from the vector $\mu + \sigma_{ii}^{-1}(b_i - \mu_i)\sigma_i$ (in case of b_i) or from the vector $\mu + \sigma_{ii}^{-1}(a_i - \mu_i)\sigma_i$ (in case of a_i) by deleting component i and $\hat{\Sigma}$ is defined as in Lemma 0.5. Moreover $\tilde{a}$ and $\tilde{b}$ result from a and b by deleting the respective component i.

In order to demonstrate the impact of the derived formula, we consider the optimization problem (18). Given that ξ (and so $L\xi$ too) has a multivariate normal distribution, we know from Prékopa (1995) that the function

$$x \mapsto \log \mathbb{P}(Ax \leq L\xi \leq Bx) \tag{22}$$

is concave. This allows to rewrite the optimization problem as a convex one:

$$\min\{c^T x \mid -\log \mathbb{P}(Ax + a \leq L\xi \leq Bx + b) \leq -\log p\}$$

Now one can apply, for instance, a supporting hyperplane type method as described in Prékopa (1995) in order to solve this problem. This requires, apart from functional values, also to calculate gradients of the function (22) which amounts to determine partial derivatives of the function $F_\xi(Ax, Bx)$ introduced above. The latter task can efficiently be realized with the aid of the formula given in Corollary 0.8. It resides in the fact that we rely on the same algorithm as used for determining values of F_ξ.

5.2.2 Convexity of rectangular constraint problems?

When looking at the definition of the function h in (4), we can see that we are dealing here with the special case

$$h(x, \xi) := Ax + B\xi - c, \tag{23}$$

of separated linear constraints. In (23), A and B may represent matrices which describe how releases x and inflows ξ accumulate over time and how reservoirs are interconnected. The vector c provides certain lower and upper levels in the reservoirs which have to be respected (possibly time-dependent).

Defining the linearly transformed random variable $\eta := -B\xi$, we may rewrite the probabilistic constraint associated with (23) as

$$\mathbb{P}(Ax + B\xi \geq c) \geq p \Longleftrightarrow \mathbb{P}(Ax - c \geq \eta) \geq p \Longleftrightarrow F_\eta(Ax - c) \geq p, \tag{24}$$

where F_η refers to the (multivariate) distribution function of η. This means, the probabilistic constraint is equivalent to a single inequality in the decision vector x which can be evaluated (e.g., in the framework of a nonlinear optimization code) if one is able to cope with multivariate distribution functions.

Clearly, problem (18) can be cast into the equivalent problem

$$\min\left\{\langle d,x\rangle\,|F_\eta\left(u\right)\geq p,\ u=Ax-c\right\}. \tag{25}$$

The key observation for a numerical treatment of (25) in the framework of convex optimization is that many prominent multivariate distribution functions (e.g., regular and singular normal, Dirichlet, Gamma, Wishart uniform etc.) share the property of *log-concavity*:

$$\log F_\eta\left(\lambda_1 u_1+\lambda_2 u_2\right)\geq\lambda_1\log F_\eta\left(u_1\right)+\lambda_2\log F_\eta\left(u_2\right)\quad\forall u_1,u_2\ \forall\lambda_1,\lambda_2\geq 0:\lambda_1+\lambda_2=1.$$

The verification of log-concavity for distribution functions is based on the celebrated Theorem by Prékopa (see Prékopa (1973)) stating that a distribution function is log-concave if and only if the density function has this property (see Henrion & Strugarek (2008)), for these distributions one may pass to the equivalent (by monotonicity of log) optimization problem

$$\min\left\{\langle d,x\rangle\,|\log F_\eta\left(u\right)\geq\log p,\ u=Ax-c\right\}. \tag{26}$$

5.2.3 A cutting planes algorithms for joint chance constrained programming

Being that $\log F_\eta$ is a concave function, (26) becomes a convex optimization problem[2]. This can be solved, for instance, by means of the cutting plane method. As it is well-known, the following ingredients are required for the application of the cutting plane method:

- a Slater point $(\hat{x},\hat{u})$ satisfying $F_\eta\left(\hat{u}\right)>p,\ \hat{u}=A\hat{x}-c$
- a procedure to calculate the distribution function F_η in order to determine in each iteration k a point $\tilde{u}_k$ on the line segment $[u_k,\hat{u}]$ satisfying $F_\eta\left(\tilde{u}_k\right)=p$. Here, u_k is part of the current iterate (x_k,u_k).
- a procedure to calculate the gradient ∇F_η in order to add in each iteration k a cut $\left\langle\nabla F_\eta\left(\tilde{u}_k\right),u-\tilde{u}_k\right\rangle\geq 0$.
- a linear programming solver for solving (26) but with the nonlinear constraint $\log F_\eta\left(u\right)$ replaced by the accumulated cuts (linear constraints) from the previous item.

The last requirement being standard, we adress the first three items in the following subsections. From now on we restrict our considerations to the - most important case - of normally distributed random vectors. For the calculation of other distributions like t-distribution, Gamma-distribution, Dirichlet-distribution or Exponential distribution, we refer to Genz (2002), Szántai (1996), Gouda & Szántai (2004) and Olieman & van Putten (2006).

5.2.3.1 Calculation of multi-variate normal distribution functions

As mentioned before, we assume from now on that η obeys a multi-variate normal distribution. We write $\eta\sim\mathcal{N}\left(\mu,\Sigma\right)$ to say that the expectation of η equals μ and the covariance matrix equals Σ. Codes for calculating the associated distribution function F_η typically assume that η be standardized, such that $\mu=0$ and $\Sigma_{ii}=1$ (i.e., Σ is actually a correlation matrix). This standardization is easily carried out by introducing the transformed random vector

$$\tilde{\eta}:=T\left(\eta-\mu\right),$$

[2] alternatively we may impose (u,x) to be in some general convex set and problem (26) remains a convex optimization problem

where T is a diagonal matrix with entries $\Sigma_{ii}^{-1/2}$. Then, $\tilde{\eta} \sim \mathcal{N}(0, R)$, where R is the correlation matrix associated with Σ. Then, the relation between the values of the original and the standardized distribution functions is given by

$$F_\eta(u) = \mathbb{P}(\eta \leq u) = \mathbb{P}(\tilde{\eta} \leq T(u - \mu)) = F_{\tilde{\eta}}(T(u - \mu)).$$

Therefore, it is sufficient to have access to algorithms calculating standardized distribution functions. For algorithms doing this job we refer as examples to Szántai (2000) or Genz (1992); Genz & Kwong (2000). The difference between the two approaches is that the first one relies on a combination of simulation and efficient probability bounds from modern graph theory, whereas the second one employs a clever scheme of numerical integration. There is one peculiarity to be respected in our model: the random vector η was already obtained from the original random vector ξ via a linear transformation: $\eta = -B\xi$ (see (24)). Of course, assuming that already ξ had a multi-variate distribution, say $\xi \sim \mathcal{N}(\mu', \Sigma')$ we know that so has η and we even know how the parameters of η's distribution are related to those of ξ:

$$\mu = -B\mu' \quad and \quad \Sigma = B\Sigma' B^T. \tag{27}$$

Many algorithms for calculating multi-variate normal distributions (such as Szántai (2000)) assume that this distribution is regular, i.e., the covariance matrix is positive definite. There is not much loss of generality to assume that original random vectors in practical applications, such as our ξ, follow indeed a regular normal distribution. However, in our optimization problem (26), we deal with the transformed random vector η rather than with ξ and it is clear that the transformation of covariance matrices in (27) destroys the regularity of the covariance matrix whenever B does not have full rank. But such is typically the case in network problems and it will turn out to be also the case in our application to water reservoirs due to considering lower and upper reservoir levels simultaneously. Then, one may benefit from the algorithm presented in Genz (1992) (see also Genz & Kwong (2000)). We mention that algorithms for calculating regular normal distributions can also be applied to problems with singular normal distributions (by using some efficient inclusion-exclusion formula presented in Bukszár et al. (2004)) and then turn out to be very fast but they require the determination of all vertices of a polyhedron which limits its use to small dimensions.

5.2.3.2 Calculation of gradients to multi-variate normal distribution functions

By combining the results of Theorem 0.6 with those from Corollary 0.8, computing the gradients of the chance constraint in problem (18) comes down to evaluation normal densities in dimension one and multi-variate normal density functions. The same remarks as those made in Section 5.2.3.1 apply however.

5.2.3.3 Determination of a Slater point

Given the probability level p one actually does not know in advance whether or not the optimization problem (25) has a feasible solution at all. Indeed, choosing a too large safety level p may lead to an empty feasible set. Much less one has direct access to a Slater point which strictly satisfies the probabilistic constraint. In order to get more information here, one may solve the following auxiliary problem which is also called 'max p'-problem:

$$\max \left\{ p | F_\eta(u) \geq p, \ u = Ax - c \right\}. \tag{28}$$

This looks pretty much the same as (25) but the difference is that the objective now is to maximize the safety level (rather than minimize some cost function) and that optimization takes place with respect to variables (x,u,p) (whereas in (25) p was fixed). Nevertheless, one may transform (28) again into a convex optimization problem. First, apply the same logarithmic transformation as above:

$$\max\left\{p \mid \log F_\eta(u) \geq \log p,\ u = Ax - c\right\}. \tag{29}$$

Here, the mapping $\log F_\eta(u) - \log p$ defining the inequality constraint is not concave in both variables (u,p) simultaneously. However, (29) is easily seen to be equivalent with

$$\max\left\{p' \mid \log F_\eta(u) \geq p',\ u = Ax - c\right\}. \tag{30}$$

Indeed, (x^*,u^*,p^*) is a solution of (29) if and only if $\left(x^*,u^*,e^{p^*}\right)$ is a solution of (30). On the other hand, (30) is a convex problem because the mapping $\log F_\eta(u) - p'$ defining the inequality constraint now is concave in both variables (u,p') simultaneously. Of course, now one is formally faced again with the four items required for a cutting plane method mentioned above. However, the last three items are covered by the same arguments as before (calculus of F_η, ∇F_η and linear optimization solver). Concerning the first item, the Slater point, this problem is solved very easily for (29) or (30), respectively, because the safety level is no longer fixed but becomes a variable. So it suffices to put in (30)

$$\left(\hat{x},\hat{u},\hat{p}'\right) := \left(0,-c,\log F_\eta(-c) - \varepsilon\right)$$

for some sufficiently small $\varepsilon > 0$ to see that

$$\log F_\eta(\hat{u}) > \hat{p}' \quad and \quad \hat{u} = A\hat{x} - c.$$

Once, (30) (and thus (29)) is solved, the optimal solution (x^*,u^*,p^*) of (29) can be used to derive a Slater point for the original optimization problem (25). Indeed, if it turns out that the maximum possible probability level p^* is smaller than the level p chosen by the decision maker in (25), then this latter program will not have any feasible solution at all and the decision maker will have to adjust (reduce) his safety level. Otherwise, if $p^* > p$, then (x^*,u^*) may obviously be used as a Slater point for the original problem (25). A part from the meaning of the 'max p'-problem for the determination of a Slater point in the original problem, its solution provides useful additional insight: indeed, the associated part x^* of its solution indicates the most robust decision possible. In the application to water reservoirs it will represent the most robust release control in order to keep the level constraints of the reservoir with maximum possible probability. Of course, this robust control will come at a significantly higher price (in terms of the cost function $c^\mathsf{T}x$ in (25)).

5.2.4 Second order derivatives

If one is interested in applying second order solution methods to increase the efficiency of the solution process, one has to work out second derivatives of the probability function φ (where notations are as in corollary 0.8) on the basis of the gradients obtained in theorem 1 of van Ackooij et al. (2010c). The results (van Ackooij et al. (2010b)), which follow from a straight-forward second application of theorem 1 in van Ackooij et al. (2010c) are collected in the following lemma.

Lemma 0.7. *Let ξ be a Gaussian random vector with mean μ and variance-covariance matrix Σ. We define the mapping $F_\xi(a,b) = \mathbb{P}[a \leq \xi \leq b]$ for any rectangle, i.e., $a \leq b$. Let D^i_n denote the n dimensional identity matrix from which the ith row has been deleted. Define $\mu^{c(i,z)} = D^i_n(\mu + \Sigma^{-1}_{i,i}(z-\mu_i)\Sigma_i)$ and $\Sigma^{c(i)} = D^i_n(\Sigma - \Sigma^{-1}_{i,i}\Sigma_i\Sigma_i^\mathsf{T})(D^i_n)^\mathsf{T}$, where Σ_i is the ith column of Σ. We define $\xi^{c(i,z)}$ as the Gaussian random variable with mean $\mu^{c(i,z)}$ and covariance matrix $\Sigma^{c(i)}$. The following holds:*

$$
\begin{aligned}
\frac{\partial^2}{\partial a_j \partial a_i} F_\xi(a,b) &= f_{\mu^{c(i,a_i)},\Sigma^{c(i)}_{j,j}}(a_j) f_{\mu_i,\Sigma_{i,i}}(a_i) F_{(\xi^{c(i,a_i)})^{c(j,a_j)}}(D^j_{n-1}D^i_n a, D^j_{n-1}D^i_n b)\ \forall j \neq i \\
\frac{\partial^2}{\partial b_j \partial a_i} F_\xi(a,b) &= -f_{\mu^{c(i,a_i)},\Sigma^{c(i)}_{j,j}}(b_j) f_{\mu_i,\Sigma_{i,i}}(a_i) F_{(\xi^{c(i,a_i)})^{c(j,b_j)}}(D^j_{n-1}D^i_n a, D^j_{n-1}D^i_n b)\ \forall i,j \\
\frac{\partial^2}{\partial b_j \partial b_i} F_\xi(a,b) &= f_{\mu^{c(i,b_i)},\Sigma^{c(i)}_{j,j}}(b_j) f_{\mu_i,\Sigma_{i,i}}(b_i) F_{(\xi^{c(i,b_i)})^{c(j,b_j)}}(D^j_{n-1}D^i_n a, D^j_{n-1}D^i_n b)\ \forall j \neq i,
\end{aligned}
$$

where $f_{\mu,\sigma}(x)$ is the standard gaussian density. Moreover, whenever $j = i$ and z is a or b we have:

$$
\begin{aligned}
\frac{\partial^2}{\partial z_i^2} F_\xi(a,b) &= -\frac{z_i - \mu_i}{\Sigma^2_{i,i}} f_{\mu_i,\Sigma_{i,i}}(z_i) F_{\xi^{c(i,z_i)}}(D^i_n a, D^i_n b) \\
&+ f_{\mu_i,\Sigma_{i,i}}(z_i)(D^i_n \Sigma^{-1}_{i,i}\Sigma_i)^\mathsf{T}(\nabla_{D^i_n a} F_{\xi^{c(i,z_i)}}(D^i_n a, D^i_n b) + \nabla_{D^i_n b} F_{\xi^{c(i,z_i)}}(D^i_n a, D^i_n b))
\end{aligned}
$$

The following corollary follows trivially from lemma 0.7 and theorem 1 of van Ackooij et al. (2010c).

Corollary 0.8. *Let ξ be a Gaussian Random variable of dimension n. Let x, A,B,a,b be vectors and matrices of appropriate dimension. Define furthermore, $\alpha = Ax + a$ and $\beta = Bx + b$. Now consider the mapping $\varphi : x \mapsto \mathbb{P}[a + Ax \leq \xi \leq Bx + b]$. We have:*

$$
\begin{aligned}
\nabla \varphi &= \nabla_\alpha F_\xi(\alpha,\beta)^\mathsf{T} A + \nabla_\beta F_\xi(\alpha,\beta)^\mathsf{T} B \\
\triangle \varphi &= A^\mathsf{T} \triangle_{\alpha\alpha} F_\xi(\alpha,\beta) A + A^\mathsf{T} \triangle_{\alpha\beta} F_\xi(\alpha,\beta) B + B^\mathsf{T} \triangle_{\beta\alpha} F_\xi(\alpha,\beta) A + B^\mathsf{T} \triangle_{\beta\beta} F_\xi(\alpha,\beta) B.
\end{aligned}
$$

6. Illustration : Feasibility of CCP for EMOP

In this section we will consider the hydro reservoir management example from van Ackooij et al. (2010b). We will consider a discretized time horizon. To this end let τ denote the set of (homogeneous) time steps. Let Δt be this time step size expressed in hours.

6.1 Topology

A hydro valley can be seen as a set of connected reservoirs. We can therefore represent this with a directed graph. Let $\mathcal{N}$ be the set of nodes and let A (of size $|\mathcal{N}| \times |\mathcal{N}|$) be the connection matrix, i.e., $A_{n,m} = 1$ whenever water released from reservoir n will flow into reservoir m. We will assume that D is the flow duration matrix, i.e., D_m is the amount of time (measured in time steps) it takes for water to flow from reservoir m to its child. Let $\mathcal{T} := \left\{g^i, i = 1,...,N_\mathcal{T}\right\}$ denote the set of turbines and $\mathcal{P} := \left\{p^i, i = 1,...,N_\mathcal{P}\right\}$ denote the set of pumping stations. We furthermore introduce the mapping $\sigma_\mathcal{T} : \{1,...,N_\mathcal{T}\} \to \mathcal{N}$ ($\sigma_\mathcal{P} : \{1,...,N_\mathcal{P}\} \to \mathcal{N}$) attributing to each turbine (pumping station) the reservoir number to which it belongs. We will also introduce the sets $\mathcal{A}(n) = \{m \in \mathcal{N} : A_{m,n} = 1\}$ and $\mathcal{F}(n) = \{m \in \mathcal{N} : A_{n,m} = 1\}$. The set $\mathcal{A}(n)$ is empty for top reservoirs and the set $\mathcal{F}(n)$ for bottom reservoirs.

6.2 Controls

We will assume that each turbine (and pumping station) can be controlled for each time step. To this end we introduce the variables $x^i(t)$ for each $t \in \tau$ and $i = 1, ..., N_{\mathcal{T}}$. In a similar way we introduce the variables $y^i(t)$ for the pumping stations. The units are in m^3/h. Furthermore we assume that each of these variables are bounded from below by zero and from above by $\overline{x}^i$ ($\overline{y}^i$ respectively).

6.3 Water values

Let $\pi_n(V)$ be a given discretization of the water levels of reservoir n, i.e., $\pi_n(V) = \left\{V_0^n = V_{min}^n, ..., V_{K_n}^n = V_{max}^n\right\}$. We assume that a water value $W_i^n(t)$ (in €$/m^3$) is attributed to each interval $[V_{i-1}^n, V_i^n)$, $i = 1, ..., K_n$. We introduce two real variables $z_{x,i}^n(t)$ and $\gamma_{x,i}^n(t)$ for each time step $t \in \tau$, each $i = 1, ..., K_n$ and for each reservoir. We similarly introduce $z_{y,i}^n(t)$ and $\gamma_{y,i}^n(t)$ for turbining. In fact $z_i^n(t)$ represents the part of the water turbined ($z_{x,i}^n(t)$) / pumped ($z_{y,i}^n(t)$)that falls in the interval $[V_{i-1}^n, V_i^n)$. We impose the following constraints for each $n \in \mathcal{N}$ and $t \in \tau$:

$$
\begin{aligned}
\sum_{i=1}^{K_n} z_{x,i}^n(t) = \Delta t \sum_{j \in \sigma_{\mathcal{T}}^{-1}[n]} x^j(t)\,,\ \sum_{i=1}^{K_n} z_{y,i}^n(t) &= \Delta t \sum_{j \in \sigma_{\mathcal{P}}^{-1}[n]} y^j(t) \\
(z_{x,i}^n(t) - \mathbb{E}\left(V^n(t)\right) - V_{i-1}^n + \gamma_{x,i}^n(t)) z_{x,i}^n(t) &\leq 0 \ \forall i = 1, ..., K_n \\
(z_{y,i}^n(t) - V_i^n + \mathbb{E}\left(V^n(t)\right) + \gamma_{y,i}^n(t)) z_{y,i}^n(t) &\leq 0 \ \forall i = 1, ..., K_n \\
0 \leq z_{u,i}^n(t) &\leq (V_i^n - V_{i-1}^n) \ \forall i = 1, ..., K_n \ u \in \{x, y\} \quad (31) \\
\gamma_{u,i}^n(t) &\geq 0 \ \forall \ \forall i = 1, ..., K_n \ u \in \{x, y\}
\end{aligned}
$$

In fact $z_{x,i}^n(t)$ represents the part of the water turbined that falls in the interval $[V_{i-1}^n, V_i^n)$. A natural constraint is $z_{x,i}^n(t) \leq \max(V^n(t) - V_{i-1}^n, 0)$. However, in our example, $V^n(t)$ is random. Fortunately, when combining this with an objective function that we wish to optimize in expectation, the constraint becomes $z_{x,i}^n(t) \leq \max(\mathbb{E}\left(V^n(t)\right) - V_{i-1}^n, 0)$, hence erasing randomness from the objective function. The quadratic constraints arise as it is easily seen that the following problems are equivalent $\min_x \{f(x) : g(x) \leq [h(x)]^+\}$ and $\min_{x,\lambda \geq 0} \{f(x) : (g(x) - h(x) + \lambda) g(x) \leq 0\}$. In our numerical example (Section 6.7) we use a constant watervalue, removing the quadratic constraints.

6.4 Random inflows

We will assume that inflows (in m^3/h) in reservoirs are the result of some stochastic process. Let $A^n(t)$ denote this stochastic process for reservoir n. Not all reservoirs will have stochastic inflows, some of them will have deterministic inflows (typically zero). This can be explained by the fact that top reservoirs have random inflows due to the melting of snow in the high mountains, whereas rain can be neglected for lower reservoirs. Let $\mathcal{N}^r \subseteq \mathcal{N}$ denote the set of reservoirs receiving random inflows. We will assume that the stochastic inflow process is the sum of a deterministic trend s_t^n and a causal process (Shumway & Stoffer (2000)) generated by Gaussian innovations. To this end let $\zeta^n(t)$ be a gaussian white noise process, where

$(\zeta^{k_1}(t), ..., \zeta^{k_l})$ is a Gaussian random vector of zero average and variance-covariance matrix $\Sigma(t)$ ($\{k_1, ..., k_l\} = \mathcal{N}^r$). We will assume independence between time steps of the ζ vector. Since $A^n(t)$ is a causal process, we can write it as follows

$$A^n(t) = s_t^n + \sum_{j=0}^{\infty} \psi_j^n \zeta^n(t-j) = s_t^n + \sum_{j=t}^{\infty} \psi_j^n \zeta^n(t-j) + \sum_{j=0}^{t-1} \psi_j^n \zeta^n(t-j),$$

for some coefficient vector ψ^n. We will assume that randomness before $t = 0$ is known and as such we can assume WLOG that the random inflow process can be written as

$$A^n(t) = s_t^n + \sum_{j=0}^{t-1} \psi_j^n \zeta^n(t-j).$$

6.5 Flow constraints and volume bounds

Each reservoir is subject to flow constraints induced by pumping and turbining. The following equilibrium constraint applies

$$\begin{aligned} V_n(t) &= V_n(t-1) + \sum_{m \in \mathcal{A}(n)} \sum_{i \in \sigma_{\mathcal{T}}^{-1}[m]} x^i(t - D_m)\Delta t - \sum_{i \in \sigma_{\mathcal{T}}^{-1}[n]} x^i(t)\Delta t \\ &+ \sum_{m \in \mathcal{F}(n)} \sum_{i \in \sigma_{\mathcal{P}}^{-1}[m]} y^i(t)\Delta t - \sum_{i \in \sigma_{\mathcal{P}}^{-1}[n]} y^i(t)\Delta t + s_t^n \Delta t + \sum_{j=0}^{t-1} \psi_j^n \zeta^n(t-j)\Delta t. \end{aligned} \tag{32}$$

The above equation is entirely deterministic except for the reservoirs $n \in \mathcal{N}^r$. In order to deal with this randomness and reservoir bounds we will therefore add the following constraints

$$\mathbb{P}[V_{min}^n(t) \leq V^n(t) \leq V_{max}^n(t)\ \forall t \in \tau, n \in \mathcal{N}^r] \geq p \tag{33}$$

$$V_{min}^n(t) \leq V^n(t) \leq V_{max}^n(t)\ \forall t \in \tau, n \in \mathcal{N} \setminus \mathcal{N}^r, \tag{34}$$

this is a joint chance constraint.

6.6 Objective function

Often, in reality, each reservoir only has a single turbine. The power output of turbining x m^3/s is given by a function $\rho(x)$. This function is strictly increasing and concave, i.e., $\rho'(x) \geq 0$ and $\rho''(x) \leq 0$. In our model we have split this range into several subsections (hence several turbines), each with efficiency $\rho_i = \rho'(s_i^*)/3600$ (MWh/m^3) for some s_i^* in each section. We can thus remark that for any two turbines i_1 and i_2 belonging to the same reservoir we either have $\rho_{i_1} \geq \rho_{i_2}$ or vice versa. This approximation comes down to approximating $\rho(x)$ by a piece-wise linear function.
We assume given a time dependent price signal $\lambda(t)$ (in €/MWh). The following objective function has to be minimized:

$$\sum_{t \in \tau} \sum_{n \in \mathcal{N}} \sum_{i=1}^{K_n} (W_i^n(t)(z_{x,i}^n(t) - z_{y,i}^n(t)) - \sum_{t \in \tau} \lambda(t)\Delta t(\sum_{i=1}^{N_{\mathcal{T}}} \rho_i(t)x^i(t) - \sum_{i=1}^{N_{\mathcal{P}}} \frac{1}{\theta_i(t)} y^i(t)),$$

where the first part corresponds to the cost of using water expressed by the water-values, and $\theta^i(t)$ is the efficiency of pumping.

6.7 Numerical example

Plugging some numerical values in the problem defined in this section 6. We can consider for example 24 time steps of 2 hours each, the valley 2 (Left) and $AR(3)$ uncertainty on inflows. More importantly that the actual numerical values (which can be found in van Ackooij et al. (2010b)), is a comparison of the individual chance constrained model (5) and the joint constrained model (4).

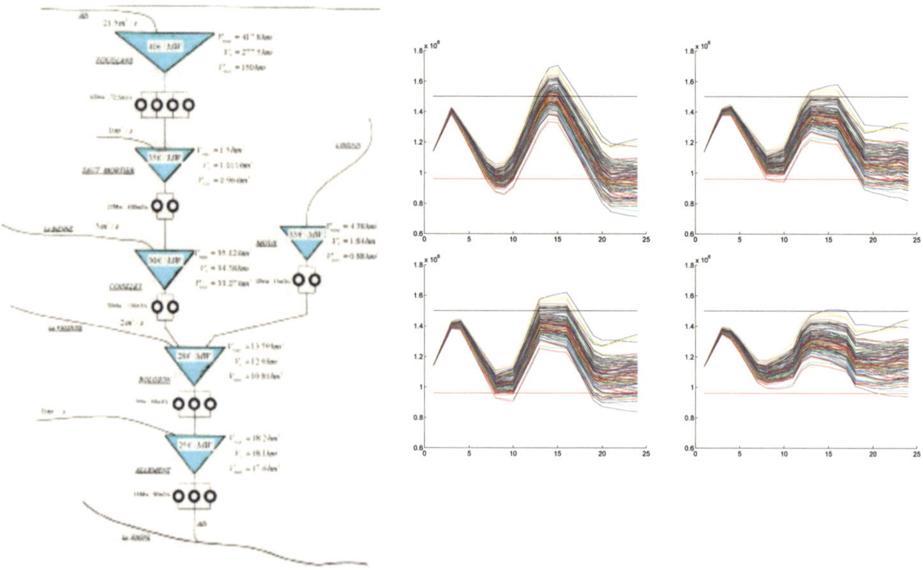

Fig. 2. (Left) The hydro Valley. (Right) : Water trajectories for reservoir "Saut Mortier". From top left to bottom right, solutions of problems (11), (4), (5) and (28).

Table 1 shows optimal costs and number of violations. Figure 2 shows simulations of water trajectories. Clearly we observe the advantage of using joint chance constrained programming. The additional cost with respect to the deterministic solution is only small, but robustness can be fine tuned. A full robust solution (max-p problem) turns out quite costly. Finally individual chance constrained programming can not be used to mimic joint chance constraints as we have no control over the number of violations over a period of time.

Item / Problem	(11)	(4)	(5)	(28)
nbViolation	100	20	35	2
Cost (€)	$-1.0478e^5$	$-1.0340e^5$	$-1.0422e^5$	$-9.9176e^4$

Table 1. Comparison of costs and number of violations

One can come up with a robust counterpart of problem (10), by defining an elipsoidal uncertainty set $\mathcal{E}$ for η. It can be easily seen that constraints (18) (derived from (33)) can be transformed in $Ax + a \leq \inf \mathcal{E}$ and $Bx + b \geq \sup \mathcal{E}$, where the latter has to be understood in the partial order of $\mathbb{R}^n$. Unfortunately, even when the uncertainty set $\mathcal{E}$ is very well calibrated, i.e., $\mathbb{P}(\mathcal{E}) = p$, the solution is often over-robust. Even worse, for larger values of p this often leads to an empty feasible set of the robust problem, even though solutions of (4) exist.
We can observe that the speed of Genz' code is not independent of the "nature" of a and b (see Lemma 0.7). The "shape" of the covariance matrix of ξ is pointed downwards. It seems that

whenever a and b mimic this shape, i.e., $a_1 \leq ... \leq a_n$, that evaluating $F_\xi(a, b)$ is about 20 times faster than having a uniform a and b.
Since this valley is a realistic example from Energy management exact joint-CCP can be tractable for problems. Moreover clearly the interest has been shown over an individual chance constraint formulation.

7. Perspectives / transgressing frontiers

Perspectives contain three main axis: The first axis is concerned with improved bounds for approximate chance constrained programming. Currently we have used Hoeffding's bound, but far better bounds exists. One could think of the bounds derived in Ben-Tal et al. (2009). By combining different bounding techniques and different levels of available information we can derive a whole class of approximate algorithms, much in the style of the MIO algorithm exposed here. A second important question to answer is that of classification of the solution. Is the approximate solution far from the optimal one?
A second axis is concerned with working on exact joint chance constraint programming for the separated linear setting. In particular efficient derivative formulae have to be derived for the case of a random matrix. Further clear extensions concern such questions for the case of other laws. Often laws in a problem are of a different nature and such special cases have to be considered. From an algorithmic perspective, instead of using a cutting planes idea, one could use a bundle method to hopefully improve computation times and stability. A second point that needs investigations is an improved use of Genz' code by using preconditioning and exploiting the observed shaping/computation time effect. Finally we could combine the use of Genz' code with Prekopa's LP estimation method for probability measures to increase the size of the model or improve the speed.
A third axis consists of considering the mixed integer formulation of (10). If the relaxed problem has good properties (convexity, etc..). We could, in theory apply a branch and bound technique combined with cuts, lift&projects, etc... But one could equally consider this a special case of discrete randomness.

8. References

Alizadeh, F. & Goldfarb, D. (2001). Second-order cone programming, *Technical Report RRR 51-2001, Available at http://rutcor.rutgers.edu/pub/rrr/reports2001/51.ps* .

Appariagliato, R., Vial, J. & Zorgati, R. (2006). Weekly management of a hydraulic valley by robust optimization., *19th international symposium on Mathematical programming, Rio de Janeiro* .

Batut, J. & Renaud, A. (1992). Daily scheduling with transmission constraints: A new class of algorithms, *IEEE Transactions on Power Systems* 7(3): 982–989.

Ben-Tal, A., Ghaoui, L. E. & Nemirovski, A. (2009). *Robust Optimization*, Princeton University Press.

Beraldi, P. & Ruszczyński, A. (2002). A branch and bound method for stochastic integer problems under probabilistic constraints., *Optimization Methods and Software* 17: 359–382.

Birge, J. & Louveaux, F. (1997). *Introduction to Stochastic Programming*, Springer, New York.

Bukszár, J., R. Henrion, M. H. & Szántai, T. (2004). Polyhedral inclusion-exclusion, *Preprint No. 913, Weierstrass Institute Berlin* .

Bukszár, J. & Szántai, T. (2002). Probability bounds given by hypercherry trees, *Optimization Methods and Software* 17: 409–422.

Cohen, G. & Zhu, D. (1983). Decomposition-coordination methods in large-scale optimization problems. the non-differentiable case and the use of augmented Lagrangians, *Large Scale Systems, Theory and Applications* 1.

Déak, I. (1980). Three digit accurate multiple normal probabilities, *Numerische Mathematik* 35: 369–380.

Deák, I. (1986). Computing probabilities of rectangles in case of multidimensional distribution., *Journal of Statistical Computation and Simulation* 26: 101–114.

Dentcheva, D., Prékopa, A. & Ruszczyński, A. (2000). Concavity and efficient points for discrete distributions in stochastic programming, *Mathematical Programming* 89: 55–79.

Genz, A. (1992). Numerical computation of multivariate normal probabilities, *J. Comp. Graph Stat.* 1: 141–149.

Genz, A. (2002). Methods for the computation of multivariate t-probabilities, *J. Comp. Graph. Stat.* 11: 950–971.

Genz, A. & Bretz, F. (2009). *Computation of multivariate normal and t probabilities.*, number 195 in *Lecture Notes in Statistics*, Springer, Dordrecht.

Genz, A. & Kwong, K.-S. (2000). Numerical evaluation of singular multivariate normal distributions, *J. Stat. Comp. Simul.* 68: 1–21.

Gouda, A. & Szántai, T. (2004). New sampling techniques for calculation of dirichlet probabilities, *Central European Journal of Operations Research* 12: 389–403.

Henrion, R. (2007). Structural properties of linear probabilistic constraints, *Optimization* 56(4): 425–440.

Henrion, R., Andrieu, L. & Römisch, W. (2010). A model for dynamic chance constraints in hydro power management, *European Journal of Operations Research* 207: 579–589.

Henrion, R. & Römisch, W. (2010). Lipschitz and differentiability properties of quasi-concave and singular normal distribution functions, *Annals of Operations Research* 177: 115–125.

Henrion, R. & Strugarek, C. (2008). Convexity of chance constraints with independent random variables, *Computational Optimization and Applications* 41: 263–276.

Hoeffding, W. (1963). Probability inequalities for sums of bounded random variables, *Journal of the American Statistical society* 58(301): 13–30.

Kall, P. & Wallace, S. (1994). *Stochastic Programming*, Wiley, New York.

Kataoka, S. (1963). A stochastic programming model, *Econometrica* 31: 181–196.

Klopfenstein, O. (2007). Tractable algorithms for chance-constrained combinatorial problems, *www.optimization-online.org* .

Klopfenstein, O. & Nace, D. (2007). Polyhedral aspects of a robust knapsack problem, *www.optimization-online.org* .

Klopfenstein, O. & Nace, D. (2008). A robust approach to the chance-constrained knapsack problem, *Operations Research Letters* 36: 628–632.

Lagoa, C., Li, X. & Sznaier, M. (2005). Probabilistically constrained linear programs and risk-adjusted controller design, *SIAM Journal on Control and Optimization* 15: 938–951.

Langrene, N., van Ackooij, W. & Bréant, F. (2010). Dynamic constraints for aggregated units: Formulation and application, *To Appear : IEEE transactions on Power Systems* p. 8.

Lemaréchal, C. & Sagastizábal, C. (1994). An approach to variable metric bundle methods, *Lecture Notes in Control and Information Science* 197: 144–162.

Lepaul, S. (2009). Stochastic approach for an endogenous capacity expansion long-term world coal market model, 32nd *IAEE International Conference, Energy, Economy, Environment: The Global View (June 21-24)* .

Lobo, M., Vandenberghe, L., Boyd, S. & Lebret, H. (1998). Applications of second-order cone programming, *Linear Algebra and its Applications* 284: 193–228.

Luedtke, J. & Ahmed, S. (2008). A sample approximation approach for optimization with probabilistic constraints, *SIAM Journal on Optimization* 19: 674–699.

Merlin, A. & Sandrin, P. (1983). A new method for unit commitment at electricité de france, *IEEE Transactions Power App. Syst.* PAS-102: 1218–1225.

Olieman, N. & van Putten, B. (2006). Estimation method of multivariate exponential probabilities based on a simplex coordinates transform, *Stochastic Programming E-Print Series (SPEPS)* 6.

Prékopa, A. (1973). On logarithmic concave measures and functions, *Acta Scientiarium Mathematicarum (Szeged)* 34: 335–343.

Prékopa, A. (1990). Sharp bound on probabilities using linear programming., *Operations Research* 38: 227–239.

Prékopa, A. (1995). *Stochastic Programming*, Kluwer, Dordrecht.

Prékopa, A. (2003). *Probabilistic programming. In Ruszczyński & Shapiro (2003) (Chapter 5).*

Prékopa, A., Vizvári, B. & Badics, T. (1998). Programming under probabilistic constraint with discrete random variable., *In (F. Giannessi et al. eds.): New Trends in Mathematical Programming* pp. 235–255.

Ruszczyński, A. (2002). Probabilistic programming with discrete distributions and precedence constrained knapsack polyhedra., *Mathematical Programming* 93: 195–215.

Ruszczyński, A. & Shapiro, A. (2003). *Stochastic Programming*, Vol. 10 of *Handbooks in Operations Research and Management Science*, Elsevier, Amsterdam.

Shapiro, A., Dentcheva, D. & Ruszczyński, A. (2009). *Lectures on Stochastic Programming. Modeling and Theory*, Vol. 9 of *MPS-SIAM series on optimization*, SIAM and MPS, Philadelphia.

Shumway, R. & Stoffer, D. (2000). *Time Series Analysis and Its Applications*, 1st edn, Springer.

Szántai, T. (1996). Evaluation of a special multivariate gamma distribution, *Mathematical Programming Study* 27: 1–16.

Szántai, T. (2000). Improved bounds and simulation procedures on the value of the multivariate normal probability distribution function, *Annals of Operations Research* 100: 85–101.

Szántai, T. & Habib, A. (1998). On the k-out-of-r-from-n probabilities., *In (F. Giannessi et al. eds.) New Trends in Mathematical Programming* 36: 289–303.

Uryasev, S. (1995). Derivatives of probability functions and some applications, *Annals of Operations Research* 56: 287–311.

van Ackooij, W., Henrion, R., Möller, A. & Zorgati, R. (2010a). Early evaluation of chance-constrained programming for energy management optimization problems, *Technical Report : H-R36-2010-00447-EN* p. 103.

van Ackooij, W., Henrion, R., Möller, A. & Zorgati, R. (2010b). Joint chance constrained programming for hydro reservoir management, *Submitted : EngOpt2010, 2nd International Conference on Engineering optimization* .

van Ackooij, W., Henrion, R., Möller, A. & Zorgati, R. (2010c). On probabilistic constraints induced by rectangular sets and multivariate normal distributions, *Mathematical Methods of Operations Research* 71(3): 535–549.

van de Panne, C. & Popp, W. (1963). Minimum-cost cattle feed under probabilistic protein constraints, *Managment Science* 9: 405–430.

Zorgati, R. & van Ackooij, W. (2008). Optimizing financial and physical assets with chance-constrained programming in the electrical industry, *EngOpt2008, International Conference on Engineering optimization* .

Zorgati, R. & van Ackooij, W. (2010). Optimizing financial and physical assets with chance-constrained programming in the electrical industry, *to Appear in : Optimization and Engineering* Accepted.

Zorgati, R., van Ackooij, W. & Apparigliato, R. (2009). Supply shortage hedging : estimating the electrical power margin for optimizing financial and physical assets with chance-constrained programming, *IEEE Transactions on Power Systems* 24(2): 533–540.

Zorgati, R., van Ackooij, W. & Gorge, A. (2010). Uncertainties on power systems. probabilistic approach and conic approximation, *PMAPS2010, 11th international Conference on Probabilistic Methods applied to Power systems (Prize Paper Award)* p. 8.

14

Highway Transportation Project Evaluation and Selection Incorporating Risk and Uncertainty

Zongzhi Li, Sunil Madanu and Sang Hyuk Lee
Illinois Institute of Technology
United States

1. Introduction

Over the past two decades, transportation agencies worldwide have developed various highway asset management systems such as pavement, bridge, maintenance, safety, and congestion management systems as analytical tools to help them make cost-effective investment decisions. In general, each management system generally performs the following tasks: i) establishing highway system goals and performance measures, ii) monitoring the performance of physical highway assets and system operations, iii) predicting performance trends over time, iv) recommending candidate projects to address system needs, v) carrying out project evaluation, vi) conducting project selection, and vii) providing feedback to refine the analysis in subsequent decision cycles (FHWA, 1987, 1991).

1.1 Current approaches for highway project evaluation

As one of the key tasks involved in the highway investment decision-making process, project evaluation is concerned with realistically estimating project-level life-cycle costs and benefits of different types of highway projects. Different highway facilities such as pavements and bridges have different useful service lives. In order to compare the merit of different projects on an equal basis, the life-cycle cost analysis approach needs to be adopted to evaluate the total economic worth of the initial construction cost and discounted future maintenance and rehabilitation costs in the facility life-cycle. As related to pavement project evaluation, the Federal Highway Administration (FHWA) made a concerted effort for the use of life-cycle cost analysis in highway pavement design (FHWA, 1998). Hicks and Epps (1999) explored alternative pavement life-cycle design strategies with a logical comparison between conventional mixtures and the mixture containing asphalt rubber pavement materials. Wilde et al. (1999) introduced a life-cycle cost analysis framework for rigid pavement design. Abaza (2002) developed an optimal life-cycle cost analysis model for flexible pavements. Falls and Tighe (2003) enhanced life-cycle cost analysis through the development of cost models using the Alberta roadway maintenance and rehabilitation analysis application. Labi and Sinha (2005) and Peshkin et al. (2005) studied systematic preventive maintenance and the optimum timing strategies to achieve minimum pavement life-cycle costs. Chan et al. (2008) evaluated life-cycle cost analysis practices in Michigan. For bridge project evaluation, Purvis et al. (1994) performed life-cycle cost analysis of bridge deck protection and rehabilitation. Mohammadi et al. (1995) introduced the concept of incorporating life-cycle costs into highway bridge planning and design. Hawk (2003) developed a bridge life-cycle cost analysis software tool for bridge project evaluation. In recent years, researchers began to utilize the risk-based life-cycle cost analysis approach to establish mathematical expectations of highway project benefits. For instance, Tighe (2001) performed a probabilistic life-cycle cost analysis of pavement projects by incorporating mean, variance, and probability distribution for typical construction variables, such as pavement structural thickness and costs. Reigle et al. (2005) incorporated risk considerations into the pavement life-cycle cost analysis model. Setunge et al. (2005) developed a methodology for risk-based life-cycle cost analysis of alternative rehabilitation treatments for highway bridges using Monte Carlo simulation.

1.2 Current approaches for highway project selection

One of the key steps using the asset management systems for highway investment decision-making is to conduct project selection. Specifically, this process aims at selecting a subset of mixed types of highway projects from all candidate projects proposed to address the needs of a highway network to achieve maximized total benefits under budget and other constraints. Techniques for network-level project selection are classified as ranking, prioritization, and optimization. Optimization models are popular because of the inherent mathematical rigor. Over the last two decades, various optimization models have been developed to support highway project selection. Widely used optimization techniques include integer programming (Isa Al-Subhi et al., 1989; Weissmann et al., 1990; Zimmerman, 1995; Neumann, 1997), mixed integer nonlinear programming (Ouyang and S.M. Madanat, 2004), goal/compromise programming (Geoffroy and Shufon, 1992; Ravirala and Grivas, 1995), and multi-objective optimization (Teng and Tzeng, 1996; Li and Sinha, 2004).

1.3 Limitations of current approaches

When applying risk-based analysis approaches for project evaluation, in many instances it might not be possible to establish a meaningful probability distribution to possible outcomes of a specific input factor such as construction, rehabilitation, and maintenance costs and traffic growth due to lacking of pertinent information. That is, the input factors are under uncertainty with no definable probability distributions. Consequently, the mathematical expectation of the input factor cannot be established. Further, risk and uncertainty inherited with input factors for project level life-cycle benefit/cost analysis may vary from project to project. Some projects may only involve risk cases for some input factors, whereas other projects may only experience uncertainty cases for some input factors. In more general situations, a project may face mixed cases of certainty, risk, and uncertainty concerning all input factors for the computation. This necessitates developing a new uncertainty-based methodology for highway project level life-cycle benefit/cost analysis that could rigorously handle such general situations.

Network-level project selection is also affected by several important factors. One of such factors is the available budget for the multi-year project selection period. In the current practice, state transportation agencies generally maintain a number of management programs to handle issues related to pavement preservation, bridge preservation, safety improvements, roadside improvements, system expansion/ new construction, Intelligent Transportation Systems (ITS), maintenance, etc. A certain level of budget is designated to each management program per year and the program-specific budget is not to be transferred across different programs for use. For instance, budget for the pavement preservation program supposedly is not used for the bridge preservation program, and vice versa. In a multi-year project selection period, the multi-year budgets for each management program may be treated in two ways: either being treated as yearly-constrained budgets or as a cumulative budget for all years combined.

In addition to considering alternative budget constraint scenarios for each management program, the program-specific budget in each year is inherent with uncertainty. Investment decisions are usually made based on an estimated budget years ahead of the project selection period. As time passes by updated budget information would be available, project selection decisions must be updated accordingly to maintain realistic results. This is because if the actually available budgets are higher than the initially estimated budgets, additional projects might be selected. Otherwise, some of the projects selected using the initial budgets must be removed to avoid any budget violation. In either case, the question becomes what rational approach needs to be followed to ensure that the increase in total project benefits can be maximized with additional budgets, while the reduction in total project benefits could be minimized with budget cuts. Therefore, the issue of budget uncertainty needs to be explicitly addressed.

For mitigating traffic disruption at the construction stage, multiple projects within one highway segment or across multiple highway segments might be tied together for actual implementation. In some occasions, the project grouping could be extended to a freeway/ major urban arterial corridor. In the project selection process, selecting any one of such projects necessitates the selection of all constituent projects in the same project group. Otherwise, all projects in the same project group would be declined. The projects grouped by highway segment or by corridor could be associated with different types of physical highway assets or system operations that would request funding from different management programs in a single year or across multiple years. In addition, some large-scale projects might have a chance to be postponed for a few years due to reasons such as right-of-way acquisition, design changes, and significant environmental impacts. As such, project selection could be carried out using segment-based, corridor-based or deferment-based project implementation approaches.

The next section introduces a new method for highway project evaluation that considers certainty, risk, and uncertainty associated with input factors for the computation. A stochastic optimization model is then introduced to explicitly consider alternative budget constraint scenarios, budget uncertainty, and project implementation approaches for network-level highway project selection. Further, a computational study is conducted to assess impacts of risk and uncertainty considerations in estimating project life-cycle benefits and on network-level project selection. Discussions and recommendations of usefulness of the proposed method and model are provided in the last section.

2. Proposed method for project evaluation

The section starts with the discussion of common agency cost and user cost categories for pavement and bridge facilities, respectively. It then introduces a project level life-cycle cost analysis approach for computing agency costs and user costs, as well as estimating overall project level life-cycle benefits for pavements and bridges. Next, risk and uncertainty issues associated with input factors for the computation are addressed. The last part of this section provides a generalized framework for uncertainty-based highway project level life-cycle benefit/cost analysis where the input factors are under certainty, risk, and uncertainty.

2.1 Pavement and bridge life-cycle agency and user costs

In this study, the pavement or bridge life-cycle is defined as the time interval between two consecutive construction events. Maintenance and rehabilitation treatments are performed within the pavement or bridge life-cycle. The pavement and bridge life-cycle agency cost and user cost components are briefly discussed in the following:

Pavement life-cycle agency costs

Cost analysis is a cardinal element of any highway project life-cycle benefit/cost analysis. All costs incurred over pavement life-cycle including those of construction, rehabilitation, and maintenance treatments need to be included into the analysis.

Bridge life-cycle agency costs

Bridge agency costs are primarily involved with costs of bridge design and construction/ replacement, deck and superstructure rehabilitation and replacement, and maintenance treatments.

Pavement/bridge life-cycle user costs

User costs are incurred by highway users in the pavement or bridge life-cycle. User cost components mainly include costs of vehicle operation, travel time, vehicle crashes, and vehicle air emissions (FHWA, 2000; AASHTO, 2003). Each user cost component consists of two cost categories: user cost under normal operation conditions and excessive user cost due to work zones (FHWA, 1998).

2.2 Pavement/bridge life-cycle activity profiles and user cost profiles

Pavement/Bridge Life-Cycle Activity Profiles

The pavement or bridge life-cycle activity profile refers to the frequency, timing, and magnitude of construction, rehabilitation, and maintenance treatments within its life-cycle. A typical life-cycle activity profile represents the most cost-effective way of implementing strategically coordinated treatments to achieve the intended service life. In practice, pavement life-cycle activity profiles are determined using preset time intervals for treatments and condition triggers for treatments, respectively. Many state transportation agencies currently use preset time intervals because of lacking consensus in condition trigger values and consistency in pavement condition data. With respect to bridge life-cycle activity profiles, the preset time interval approach is also commonly used. Table 1 lists the typical frequency and timing of major treatments in pavement and bridge service lives used by the FHWA, American Association of State Highway and Transportation Officials (AASHTO), and state transportation agencies (FHWA, 1987, 1991; Gion et al, 1993; INDOT, 2002; AASHTO, 2003).

The life-cycle agency costs for each type of pavements or bridges can be quantified on the basis of the proposed life-cycle activity profile as Table 1. For a specific pavement or bridge project, the construction, rehabilitation, and maintenance costs in the pavement or bridge life-cycle can be estimated using historical data on the unit rates of construction, rehabilitation, and maintenance treatments multiplied by the project size. A geometric growth rate represented by a constant percent of annual growth can be used to establish annual routine maintenance costs for future years based on the first year routine maintenance cost within an interval between two major treatments.

Facility	Material Type		Service Life (Year)	Treatment Frequency	Timing
Pavement	Flexible		40	Thin overlay + Thick HMA overlay	15th year 30th or 33rd year
	Rigid		40	PCC joint sealing + PCC joint sealing + PCC repair techniques + Thick HMA overlay + HMA crack sealing	7th year 15th year 23rd year 30th year 37th year
				PCC overlay + PCC joint sealing	30th year 35th year
Bridge	Concrete	Channel Beam	35	Deck rehabilitation	20th year
		T-Beam/ Girder	70	Deck rehabilitation + Superstructure replacement	20th, 55th year 35th year
		Slab	60	Deck rehabilitation	30th, 45th year
	Prestressed Concrete	Box-Beam	65	Deck rehabilitation + Deck replacement	20th, 50th year 35th year
		Box Girder	50	Deck rehabilitation	20th, 35th year
	Steel	Box-Beam/ Girder	70	Deck rehabilitation + Deck replacement	20th, 55th year 35th year
		Truss	80	Deck rehabilitation + Deck replacement	25th, 65th year 40th year

Table 1. Typical Frequency and Timing of Major Treatments in Pavement and Bridge Life-Cycles

Pavement/Bridge Life-Cycle Annual User Cost Profiles

For each user cost component, the first year user costs under normal operation conditions within an interval between two major treatments can be calculated. A geometric growth rate can be used for estimating annual user costs in future years within the same interval based on the first year user costs. The excessive user costs caused by project work zones such as delay costs need to be considered for the year involving major treatments.

2.3 Estimation of project level life-cycle benefits

The typical life-cycle activity profile for pavements or bridges represents the most cost-effective investment strategy to manage pavement or bridge facilities. If any needed treatment fails to be timely implemented as per the typical life-cycle activity profile, an early termination of the service life is expected. As such, the typical life-cycle activity profile can be used as the base case activity profile and the case with early service-life termination can be considered as an alternative case activity profile. For each type of pavements or bridges, the reduction in life-cycle agency costs of the base case activity profile compared with the alternative case activity profile can be computed as project level life-cycle agency benefits of timing implementing the needed project. Similarly, the decrease in life-cycle user costs according to the base case activity profile against the alternative case activity profile can be estimated as the project level life-cycle user benefits.

Figure 1 illustrates an example of base case and alternative case activity profiles for the steel-box beam bridge and the method for estimating project level life-cycle agency benefits and user benefits by keeping the typical life-cycle activity profile for the bridge. For the base case life-cycle activity profile, agency costs in the T-year bridge service life consist of initial bridge construction cost C_{CON} in year 0, first deck rehabilitation cost $C_{DECK\ REH1}$ in year t_1, deck replacement cost $C_{DECK\ REP}$ in year t_2, second deck rehabilitation cost $C_{DECK\ REH2}$ in year t_3, and annual routine maintenance costs. The annual routine maintenance costs between two major treatments in the bridge life-cycle will gradually increase over time due to the combined effect of higher traffic demand, aging materials, climate conditions, and other non-load related factors. Different geometric gradient growth rates are used for intervals between year 0 and t_1, t_1 and t_2, t_2 and t_3, and t_3 and T, respectively.

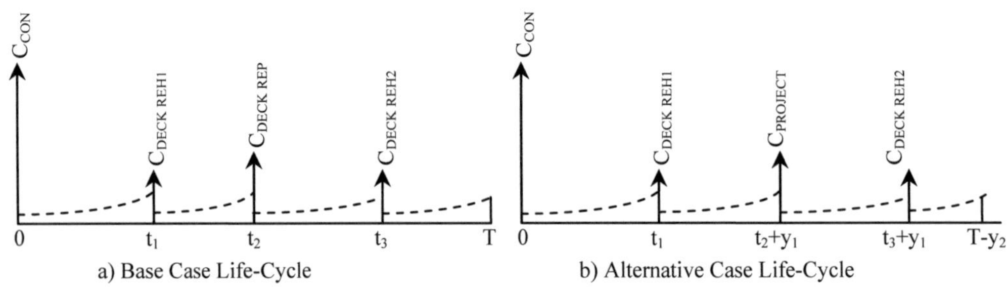

Fig. 1. Illustration of Base Case and Alternative Case Life-Cycles for the Steel- Box Beam Bridge

For the alternative life-cycle activity profile, it is assumed that the deck replacement project (with the cost of $C_{PROJECT}$) is actually implemented y_1 years after year t_2 as the base case profile, namely, $C_{DECK\ REP}$ in year t_2 is replaced by $C_{PROJECT}$ in year t_2+y_1. This will defer the second deck rehabilitation by y_1 years. Due to postponing deck replacement and the second deck rehabilitation, the bridge service life may experience an early termination of y_2 years. As for the annual routine maintenance costs, different geometric gradient growth rates are used for intervals between year 0 and t_1, t_1 and t_2+y_1, t_2+y_1 and t_3+y_1, and t_3+y_1 and $T-y_2$, correspondingly. In particular, the annual routine maintenance cost profiles for the base case and alternative case profiles are identical from year 0 to year t_2. The project level life-cycle agency benefits are estimated as the reduction in bridge life-cycle agency costs quantified according to the base case activity profile compared with the alternative case activity profile. The primary user cost items include vehicle operating costs, travel time, vehicle crashes, and vehicle air emissions. For each user cost item, the base case and alternative case annual user cost profiles in bridge life-cycle follow a pattern similar to the profile of annual routine maintenance costs in bridge life-cycle. In either the base case profile or alternative case profile, the "first year" user cost amounts immediately after the major treatments including bridge construction, first deck rehabilitation, deck replacement, and second deck rehabilitation are directly computed on the basis of the unit user cost in constant dollars per vehicle mile of travel (VMT) and the annual VMT. The unit user cost per VMT is estimated according to average travel speed and roadway condition. Geometric growth rate is then applied to the "first year" user cost amount for each interval between two major treatments to establish the annual user cost amounts for subsequent years within the interval. Additional work zone related costs are estimated using the procedures in FHWA (1988, 2000) and AASHTO (2003), and added to the annual user cost amounts for the years in which major treatments are implemented. This ultimately establishes the base case and alternative case annual user cost profiles for vehicle operating costs, travel time, vehicle crashes, and vehicle air emissions, respectively.

For each user cost item, the annual user cost profiles for the base case and alternative case are identical from year 0 to t_2 and are different for the remaining years in the bridge life-cycle. The travel demand in terms of annual VMT for a specific year after year t_2 could be different between the base case and alternative case due to the fact that the traffic volume, i.e., annual average daily traffic (AADT) and/or travel distance associated with the bridge might change for the two cases. The consumer surplus concept is employed to separately compute the user benefits by comparing the base case and alternative case annual user cost profiles for intervals from year t_2 to t_2+y_1, t_2+y_1 to t_3, t_3 to t_3+y_2, t_3+y_2, $T-y_2$, and $T-y_2$ to T. The total project level life-cycle user benefits are the aggregation of individual user benefit items associated with reductions in vehicle operating costs, travel time, vehicle crashes, and vehicle air emissions in the bridge life-cycle. With equal weights assigned for agency benefits and user benefits, the total project level life-cycle benefits by keeping the typical life-cycle activity profile for the bridge are established by combining the two sets of benefits.

2.4 Estimation of project level life-cycle benefits in perpetuity

The project level life-cycle benefits in perpetuity can be quantified on the basis of the base case and alternative life-cycle activity profiles. As the base case life-cycle activity profile represents the most cost-effective investment strategy, investment decisions are always made with the intention to keep abreast of the base case life-cycle activity profile. For the base case life-cycle activity profile in perpetuity, the base case typical facility life-cycle is assumed to be repeated an infinite number of times. For the alternative case life-cycle activity profile in perpetuity, early termination of service life may occur in the first life-cycle, in the first and second life-cycles or in the first several life cycles. After experiencing early service life terminations, the base case typical facility life-cycle is expected to be resumed back for the subsequent life cycles in perpetuity horizon. This is because that the base case life-cycle profile represents the most cost-effective investment strategy that the decision-maker always aims to achieve. Without loss of generality, the alternative case life-cycle profile in perpetuity in this study adopts early terminations for the first two life-cycles and the base case life-cycle profile is used for subsequent life cycles in perpetuity horizon. The reduction in project level life-cycle agency costs between the base case and the alternative case life-cycle activity profiles in perpetuity is computed to establish project level life-cycle agency benefits in perpetuity.

Similarly, the reduction in project level life-cycle user costs between the base case and the alternative case life-cycle annual user cost profiles in perpetuity for vehicle operating costs, travel time, vehicle crashes, and vehicle air emissions can be separately computed and summed up to establish project level life-cycle user benefits in perpetuity. With equal weights considered for agency benefits and user benefits, they can be directly added to establish overall project level life-cycle benefits in perpetuity.

2.5 Risk considerations in estimating project level life-cycle benefits

Primary Input Factors under Risk Considerations

Project construction, rehabilitation, and maintenance costs may not remain as predicted. Traffic demand may not follow the projected path. Discount rate may fluctuate over time during the pavement or bridge life-cycle. Such variations will in turn result in changes in the overall project level life-cycle benefits. In this study, the unit rates of project construction, rehabilitation, and maintenance treatments, traffic growth rates, and discount rates are primary input factors considered for probabilistic risk assessments.

Selection of Probability Distributions for the Input Factors under Risk Considerations

The minimum and maximum values of above input factors under risk considerations are bounded by non-negative values. For each of the risk factors, the distribution of its possible outcomes could be either symmetric or skewed. Such distribution characteristics can be readily modeled by the Beta distribution that is continuous over a finite range and also allows for virtually any degree of skewness and kurtosis. The Beta distribution has four parameters- lower bound (L), upper bound (H), and two shape parameters α and β, with density function given by

$$f(x|\alpha,\beta,L,H)=\frac{\Gamma(\alpha+\beta)\cdot(x-L)^{\alpha-1}\cdot(H-x)^{\beta-1}}{\Gamma(\alpha)\cdot\Gamma(\beta)\cdot(H-L)^{\alpha+\beta-1}} \quad (L\le x\le H) \tag{1}$$

where the Γ-functions serve to normalize the distribution so that the area under the density function from L to H is exactly one.
The mean and variance of the Beta distribution are given as

$$\mu=\frac{\alpha}{\alpha+\beta} \text{ and } \sigma^2=\frac{\alpha\beta}{(\alpha+\beta)^2(\alpha+\beta+1)}. \tag{2}$$

Using Simulation for Probabilistic Risk Assessments

Simulation is essentially a rigorous extension of sensitivity analysis that uses randomly sampled values from the input probability distribution to calculate discrete outputs. Two types of sampling techniques are commonly used to perform simulations. The first type is the Monte Carlo sampling technique that uses random numbers to select values from the probability distribution. The second type is the Latin Hypercube sampling technique where the probability scale of the cumulative distribution curve is divided into an equal number of probability ranges. The number of ranges used is equal to the number of iterations performed in the simulation. The Latin Hypercube sampling technique is likely to achieve convergence in fewer iterations as compared to those of the Monte Carlo sampling technique (FHWA, 1998).

2.6 Uncertainty considerations in estimating project level life-cycle benefits

As a practical matter, the input factors under risk considerations may not be readily characterized using reliable probability distributions. Consequently, a meaningful mathematical expectation for each factor cannot be established and this invalidates risk-based analysis. Shackle's model introduced herein is well suited to handle each input factor under uncertainty where no probability distribution can be readily established for a number of possible outcomes (Shackle, 1949).

In general, Shackle's model overcomes the limitation of inability to establish the mathematical expectation of possible outcomes of each input factor for project level life-cycle benefit/cost analysis according to the following procedure. First, it uses degree of surprise as a measure of uncertainty associated with the possible outcomes in place of probability distribution. Then, it introduces a priority index by jointly evaluating each known outcome and the associated degree of surprise pair. Next, it identifies two outcomes of the input factor maintaining the maximum priority indices, one on the gain side and the other on the loss side from the expected outcome $X_{(E)}$. The expected outcome could be the average value or the mode of all known possible outcomes, but it is not the mathematical expectation as outcome probabilities are unknown. The two outcomes need to be standardized to remove the associated degrees of surprise. The absolute deviations of two outcomes relative to the expected outcome are terms as standardized focus gain x_{SFG} and standardized focus loss x_{SFL} from the expected outcome $X_{(E)}$. This model yields a triple < x_{SFL}, $X_{(E)}$, x_{SFG}> for each input factor under uncertainty. More details of Shackle's model are in Ford and Ghose (1998), Young (2001), Li and Sinha (2004, 2006), and Li and Madanu (2009).

To simplify the application of Shackle's model for uncertainty-based analysis, the grand average of simulation outputs from multiple iterations of replicated simulation runs can be used as the expected outcome $X_{(E)}$ for an input factor under uncertainty:

$$X_{(E)} = \frac{\sum_{m=1}^{M}\sum_{n=1}^{N} X_i}{M \times N} \tag{3}$$

where

X_i = A simulation output representing a possible outcome

N = Number of iterations in each simulation run, and

M = Number of replicated simulation runs.

If higher valued outcomes are preferred for an input factor, the absolute deviation of the average value of simulation outputs that are lower than the expected outcome can used as standardized focus loss value x_{SFL} and the absolute deviation of the average value of simulation outputs that are equal or higher than the expected outcome can used as standardized focus gain value x_{SFG} for the input factor under uncertainty.

$$x_{SFL} = \left| \frac{\sum_{m=1}^{M}\sum_{n=1}^{N_r} X_i}{M \times N_r} - X_{(E)} \right| \tag{4}$$

$$x_{SFG} = \left| \frac{\sum_{m=1}^{M}\left(\sum_{n=1}^{N} X_i - \sum_{n=1}^{N_r} X_i\right)}{M \times (N - N_r)} - X_{(E)} \right| \tag{5}$$

where

N_r = Number of simulation outputs in the rth simulation run such that $X_i < X_{(E)}$ if a higher outcome value is preferred for the input factor.

In some cases, lower outcome values are preferred for an input factor such as the discount rate. The N_r for computing the standardized focus loss value x_{SFL} and the standardized focus gain value x_{SFG} thus refers to number of simulation outputs in the rth simulation run such that $X_i > X_{(E)}$.

As an extension of Shackle's model dealing with the input factor under uncertainty, a decision rule is introduced to help compute a single value X for the input factor based on the triple $< x_{SFL}, X_{(E)}, x_{SFG}>$ that can be used for estimating project benefits. Assuming that the decision-maker only tolerates loss from the expected outcome for the input factor under uncertainty by ΔX and if higher outcome values are preferred, the decision rule is set as

$$X = \begin{cases} X_{(E)}, & \text{if } x_{SFL} \leqslant \Delta X \\ \dfrac{X_{(E)} - x_{SFL}}{[1 - \Delta X / X_{(E)}]}, & \text{otherwise} \end{cases} \tag{6}$$

When lower outcome values are preferred for an input factor, the decision rule is revised to

$$X = \begin{cases} X_{(E)}, & \text{if } x_{SFL} \leqslant \Delta X \\ \dfrac{X_{(E)} + x_{SFL}}{[1 + \Delta X / X_{(E)}]}, & \text{otherwise} \end{cases} \tag{7}$$

If the standardized focus loss x_{SFL} from the expected outcome $X_{(E)}$ does not exceed ΔX, the expected outcome value will be utilized for the input factor for the computation. This will produce an identical input factor value for both uncertainty-based and risk-based analyses. If the standardized focus loss x_{SFL} from the expected outcome $X_{(E)}$ exceeds ΔX, a penalty is applied to derive a unique value for the input factor. Different tolerance levels ΔX's may be used for different input factors under uncertainty.

2.7 A generalized framework for project evaluation under certainty, risk, and uncertainty

Figure 2 shows a generalized framework for project evaluation under *certainty* (the input factor is purely deterministic with single value), *risk* (the input factor has a number of possible outcomes with a known probability distribution), and *uncertainty* (the input factor has a number of possible outcomes with unknown probabilities). If an input factor is under certainty, the single value of the factor can be used for the computation. If an input factor is under risk, the mathematical expectation of the factor can be utilized for the computation. If an input factor is under uncertainty, the single value of the factor determined according to the decision rule extended from Shackle's model can be adopted for the computation.

By using values of input factors determined under certainty, risk or uncertainty, the proposed framework helps establish project level life-cycle agency benefits and user benefits concerning decrease in agency costs, reduction in vehicle operating costs, shortening of travel time, decrease in vehicle crashes, and cutback of vehicle air emissions in perpetuity horizon, respectively. The combination of certainty, risk, and uncertainty cases for input factors may vary by project benefit item for the same project and may also vary for different types of highway projects.

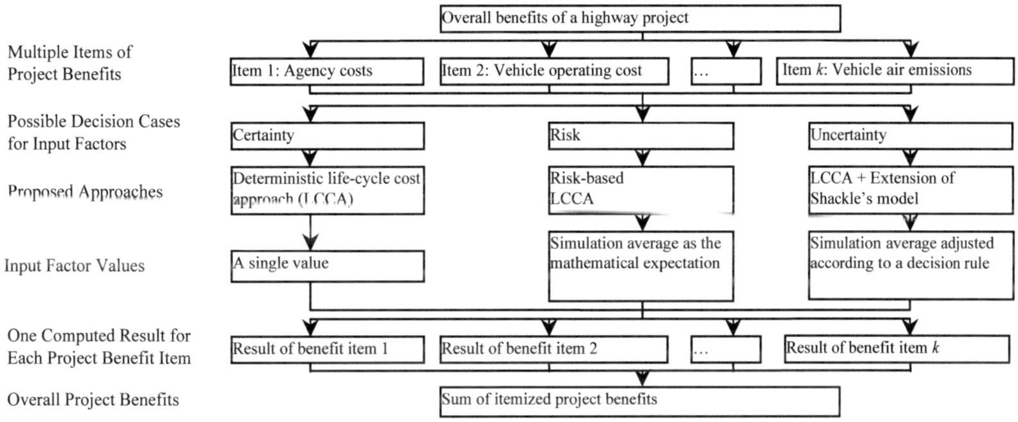

Fig. 2. A Generalized Framework for Project Evaluation under Certainty, Risk, and Uncertainty

3. Proposed model for project selection

This section begins with a basic deterministic optimization formulation for network-level project selection subject to the constraints of available budgets and integrality of decision variables under yearly-constrained and cumulative budget scenarios, respectively. It then introduces a stochastic model augmented from the basic model by incorporating budget uncertainty using recourse functions. The stochastic model is further enhanced to incorporate options of using segment-based, corridor-based, and deferment-based project implementation approaches for project selection.

3.1 A basic optimization model

In general, optimization models for project selection can be formulated as the 0/1 integer multi-choice multidimensional Knapsack problem (MCMDKP). Multi-choice corresponds to multiple categories of budgets designated for different management programs to address the needs of physical highway assets and system operations. While multi-dimension refers to a multi-year analysis period (Martello and Toth, 1990). The objective is to select a subset from all economically feasible candidate projects to achieve maximized total benefits under various constraints. The 0/1 value of a decision variable implies rejection or selection of a proposed project.

Denote:

x_i = Decision variable for project i, $i = 1, 2,\ldots, N$

a_i = Benefits of project i, $i = 1, 2, \ldots, N$

c_{ikt} = Costs of project i using budget from management program k in year t

X = Decision vector for all decision variables, $X= [x_1, x_2,\ldots, x_N]^T$

A = Vector of benefits of N projects, $A = [a_1, a_2,\ldots, a_N]^T$

C_{kt} = Vector of costs of N projects using budget from management program k in year t, $C_{kt} = [c_{1kt}, c_{2kt},\ldots, c_{Nkt}]^T$

i = $1, 2,\ldots, N$

$k \quad = 1, 2,\ldots, K$
$t \quad = 1, 2,\ldots, M.$

Note: The superscript "T" of the vector refers to the transpose of the vector.

A basic deterministic optimization model as a MCMDKP formulation under the yearly-constrained budget scenario is given below:

$$\text{Maximize} A^{T}.X \tag{8}$$

$$\text{Subject to} C_{kt}^{T}.X \leq B_{kt} \tag{9}$$

X is a decision vector with 0/1 integer decision variables.

As Equation (8), the objective function of the model essentially helps select a subset from all candidate projects to achieve maximized total benefits. Equation (9) lists budget constraints by management program and by analysis year. The 0/1 integrality constraints for the decision variables in the decision vector are used for rejection or selection of individual projects. For the cumulative budget scenario, budget constraints by analysis year are reduced to a single period constraint. Only the budget constraints by management program are retained. The notations B_{kt} is replaced by $\sum_{t=1}^{M} B_{kt}$, accordingly.

3.2 A stochastic model incorporating budget uncertainty

This section first discusses the proposed method for addressing the budget uncertainty issue and then introduces a stochastic model extended from the basic optimization model to handle budget uncertainty using recourse functions.

Treatments of Budget Uncertainty

As Figure 3, consider a multi-year project selection period of t_{Ω} years. The transportation agency makes first round of investment decisions many years ahead of the project implementation period using estimated budgets for all years. With time elapsing, updated budget information on the first few years of the multi-year project selection period would become available that motivates the agency to refine the investment decisions. In each refined decision-making process, the annual budget for each management program for the first few years that can be accurately determined is treated as a deterministic value, while the budgets for the remaining years without accurate information are still processed as stochastic budgets.

Assuming that the multi-year budgets are refined Ω times and each time an increasing number of years with accurate budget information from the first analysis year onward is obtained. Hence, Ω-decision stages are involved. Without loss of generality, we assume a discrete probability distribution of budget possibilities for each year where no accurate budget estimates are available. For the first stage decisions, the multi-program, multi-year budget matrix is comprised of the expected budgets for all years that can be best estimated at the time of decision-making. For the second stage decisions, accurate information on budgets for years 0 to t_1 is known and the budgets are treated as deterministic, and there are ($p_2=s_2.s_3.\ldots.s_{(L-1)}.s_L.s_{(L+1)}.\ldots.s_{\Omega}$) possible budget combinations for the remaining years from t_1+1 to t_{Ω}. For the generic stage L decisions, budgets up to year $t_{(L-1)}$ are deterministic and there are ($p_L=s_L.s_{L+1}\ldots.s_{\Omega}$) possible combinations for years $t_{(L-1)}$+1 to t_{Ω}. The final stage has deterministic budgets up to year $t_{(\Omega-1)}$ and $p_{\Omega}=s_{\Omega}$ budget possibilities from year $t_{(\Omega-1)}$+1 to t_{Ω}.

Year	1 to t_1	t_1+1 to t_2	...	$t_{(L-2)}$+1 to $t_{(L-1)}$	$t_{(L-1)}$+1 to t_L	t_L+1 to $t_{(L+1)}$	...	$t_{(\Omega-1)}$+1 to t_Ω
Budget	1 possibility	s_2 possibilities	...	$s_{(L-1)}$ possibilities	s_L possibilities	$s_{(L+1)}$ possibilities	...	s_Ω possibilities

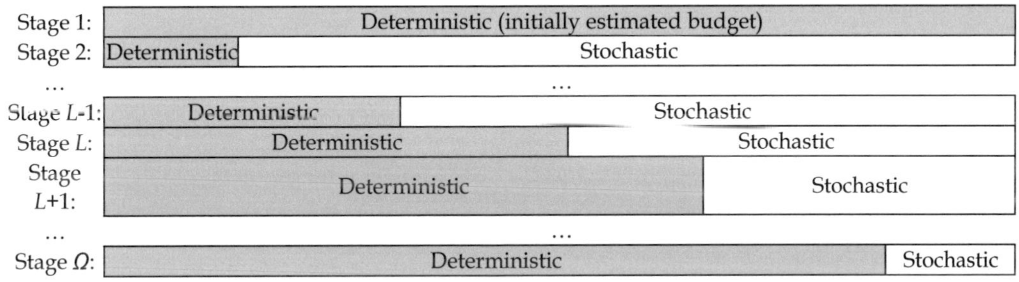

Fig. 3. Budget Attributes in an Ω-Stage Recourse Project Selection Process

A Stochastic Optimization Model Using Budget Recourse Functions

The stochastic model with Ω-stage budget recourses is formulated as a deterministic equivalent program that combines first stage decisions using the initially estimated budgets with expected values of recourse functions for the remaining (Ω -1) stages (Birge and Louveaux, 1997, Li *et al.*, 2010).

Denote:

x_i = Decision variable for project i, $i = 1, 2,\ldots, N$

a_i = Benefits of project i, $i = 1, 2, \ldots, N$

c_{ikt} = Costs of project i using budgets from management program k in year t

ξ_L = Randomness associated with budgets in stage L and decision space

$X_L(p)$ = Decision vector using budget $B_{kt}^L(p)$ in stage L, $X_L(p) = [x_1, x_2,\ldots, x_N]^T$

A = Vector of benefits of N projects, $A = [a_1, a_2,\ldots, a_N]^T$

C_{kt} = Vector of costs of N projects using budget from management program k in year t, $C_{kt} = [c_{1kt}, c_{2kt},\ldots, c_{Nkt}]^T$

$Q(X_L(p), \xi_L)$ = Recourse function in stage L

$E_{\xi_2}[Q(X_L(p), \xi_L)]$ = Mathematical expectation of the recourse function in stage L

$B_{kt}^L(p)$ = The pth possibility of budget for management program k in year t in stage L

$p(B_{kt}^L(p))$ = Probability of having budget scenario $B_{kt}^L(p)$ occur in stage L

$E(B_{kt}^L)$ = Expected budget in stage L, where $E(B_{kt}^L) = \sum_{p=1}^{p_L} \left[P\left(B_{kt}^L(p)\right) \cdot B_{kt}^L(p) \right]$

p = $1, 2,\ldots, p_L$, where $p_L = s_L \cdot s_{L+1} \cdots s_\Omega$

L = $1, 2,\ldots, \Omega$

i = $1, 2,\ldots, N$

k = $1, 2,\ldots, K$

t = $1, 2,\ldots, M$.

The stochastic model with Ω-stage budget recourses under yearly-constrained budgets is as

Maximize
$$A^T.X_1 + \sum_{\omega=2}^{\Omega} E_{\xi_\omega}\left[Q_\omega\left(X_\omega(p), \xi_\omega\right)\right] \quad (10)$$

Stage 1

Subject to
$$C_{kt}^T.X_1 \leq E(B^1_{kt}) \quad (11)$$

X_1 is a decision vector with 0/1 integer elements.

Stage 2

$$E_{\xi_2}[Q_2(X_2(p), \xi_2)] = \max \{ A^T . X_2(p) \mid B_{kt}^2(p) = E(B_{kt}^2) \} \quad (12)$$

$$\text{Subject to } C_{kt}^T . X_2(p) \le B^2_{kt}(p) \quad (13)$$

$$X_1 + X_2(p) \le 1 \quad (14)$$

X_1 and $X_2(p)$ are decision vectors with 0/1 integer elements.

...

Stage L

$$E_{\xi_L}[Q_L(X_L(p), \xi_L)] = \max \{ A^T . X_L(p) \mid B_{kt}^L(p) = E(B_{kt}^L) \} \quad (15)$$

Subject to

$$C_{kt}^T . X_L(p) \le B_{kt}{}^L(p) \quad (16)$$

$$X_1 + X_2(p) + \ldots + X_L(p) \le 1 \quad (17)$$

$X_1, X_2(p), \ldots, X_L(p)$ are decision vectors with 0/1 integer elements.

...

Stage Ω

$$E_{\xi_\Omega}[Q_\Omega(X_\Omega(p), \xi_\Omega)] = \max \{ A^T . X_\Omega(p) \mid B_{kt}^\Omega(p) = E(B_{kt}^\Omega) \} \quad (18)$$

Subject to

$$C_{kt}^T . X_\Omega(p) \le B_{kt}{}^\Omega(p) \quad (19)$$

$$X_1 + X_2(p) + \ldots + X_L(p) + \ldots + X_\Omega(p) \le 1 \quad (20)$$

$X_1, X_2(p), \ldots, X_L(p), \ldots, X_\Omega(p)$ are decision vectors with 0/1 integer elements.

In the objective function as Equation (10), the first term is for total project benefits in the first stage decisions using initially estimated budgets and the second term is for the expected value of total project benefits for the remaining (*Ω* -1)-stage recourse decisions. Equations (11), (13), (16), and (19) are employed to hold budget constraints by management program and by project implementation year for the investment decisions at each stage. Equations (12), (15), and (18) compute the expected values of optimal project benefits that use one possible budget closest to the budget updated following the preceding decision stage. Equations (14), (17), and (20) ensure that one highway project is selected at most once in the multi-stage decision process.

For the cumulative budget constraint scenario, budget constraints by management program are still maintained. The notations $B_{kt}{}^L(p)$, $p(B_{kt}{}^L(p))$, and $E(B_{kt}{}^L)$ are replaced by $\sum_{t=1}^{M} B_{kt}^L(p)$, $p(\sum_{t=1}^{M} B_{kt}^L(p))$, and $E(\sum_{t=1}^{M} B_{kt}^L)$, where $E(\sum_{t=1}^{M} B_{kt}^L) = \sum_{p=1}^{P_L}[p(\sum_{t=1}^{M} B_{kt}^L(p)).\sum_{t=1}^{M} B_{kt}^L(p)]$ ($L = 1, 2, \ldots, \Omega$), respectively.

The Enhanced Stochastic Model using Alternative Project Implementation Approaches

This section first discusses alternative project implementation approaches, including jointly implementing candidate projects by highway segment, by freeway/ major urban arterial corridor or deferring the implementation of some large-scale projects. The basic stochastic model presented in the previous section is enhanced to accommodate alternative project implementation approaches for project selection.

Segment-Based Project Implementation Approach. As discussed in the problem statement section, multiple projects within one highway segment or across multiple highway segments might be tied together for actual implementation to reduce traffic disruption at the construction stage. The first step for applying this approach is to identify the list of highway segments in the highway network to be considered for segment-based project implementation. Next, all projects within one highway segment or across multiple highway segments are tied together to form one "project group" and they are either all rejected or selected for implementation. For example, if three projects $(i+1)$, $(i+2)$, and $(i+3)$ belong to one "project group" S_g, the respective 0/1 decision variables $x_{(i+1)}$, $x_{(i+2)}$, and $x_{(i+3)}$ are replaced by one 0/1 decision variable x_{S_g}. For those isolated projects that do not belong to any of the identified "project groups", they are still treated as stand-alone projects that are designated with unique 0/1 decision variables.

Suppose that g "project groups" are identified from N candidate projects as

$1, 2, \ldots, i$ (i isolated projects),

$i+1, i+2, \ldots, i+n_1$ (n_1 projects in "project group" S_1),

$i+n_1+1, i+n_1+2, \ldots, i+n_1+n_2$ (n_2 projects in "project group" S_2),

$i+n_1+n_2+1, i+n_1+n_2+2, \ldots, i+n_1+n_2+n_3$ (n_3 projects in "project group" S_3),

...

$i+n_1+n_2+\ldots+n_{g-2}+1$, $i+n_1+n_2+\ldots+n_{g-2}+2, \ldots$, $i+n_1+n_2+\ldots+n_{g-2}+n_{g-1}$ (n_{g-1} projects in "project group" S_{g-1}), $i+n_1+n_2+\ldots+n_{g-2}+n_{g-1}+1$, $i+n_1+n_2+\ldots+n_{g-2}+n_{g-1}+2$, ..., N ($N-i-n_{g-1}$ projects in "project group" S_g).

The decision vector in stage L decisions $X_L(p) = [x_1, x_2, \ldots, x_i, \ldots, x_N]^T$ in the stochastic model is thus replaced by $X_L(p) = [x_1, x_2, \ldots, x_i, x_{S_1}, x_{S_2}, x_{S_3}, \ldots, x_{S_{g-1}}, x_{S_g}]^T$ ($L = 1, 2, \ldots, \Omega$). This implies that the basic stochastic model could still be used, but size of the decision vector $X_L(p)$ is reduced from having N decision variables to $(i+g)$ decision variables. Each decision variable still takes a 0/1 integer value representing the rejection or selection of an isolated project or multiple projects in a segment-based "project group". The benefits of all constituent projects of each segment-based "project group" are directly added together to establish the overall benefits of the "project group".

Corridor-Based Project Implementation Approach. As an extension of segment-based project implementation approach, the tie-ins of multiple projects within one or more highway segments could be further expanded to a freeway or an urban arterial corridor. First, the list of corridors in the network to be considered for corridor-based project selection is identified. Then, all candidate projects in the same corridor that are grouped by segment are further grouped into one corridor-based "grand project group". In the project selection process, all constituent projects in the same "grand project group" are either all rejected or selected for implementation. For those isolated projects that do not belong to any of the identified segment-based "project groups" or corridor-based "grand project groups", they are still treated as stand-alone projects with unique decision variables assigned.

Suppose that N candidate projects are classified as 1, 2, ... i isolated projects and S_1, S_2, S_3, S_4,..., S_{g-2}, S_{g-1}, S_g segment-based "project groups". The corresponding decision vector in stage L decisions is $X_L(p)= [x_1, x_2,..., x_i, x_{S_1}, x_{S_2}, x_{S_3}, x_{S_4},..., x_{S_{g-2}}, x_{S_{g-1}}, x_{S_g}]^T$ (L = 1, 2,..., Ω).

Further assume that all projects in "project groups" S_2 and S_3 are in one freeway corridor and all projects in "project groups" S_{g-1} and S_g are in one urban arterial corridor. This creates two corridor-based "grand project groups" for possible implementation: "grand project group" C_1 that combines "project groups" S_2 and S_3; and "grand project group" C_2 that joins "project groups" S_{g-1} and S_g. Hence, the decision vector in stage L decisions $X_L(p)= [x_1, x_2,..., x_i, x_{S_1}, x_{S_2}, x_{S_3}, x_{S_4},..., x_{S_{g-2}}, x_{S_{g-1}}, x_{S_g}]^T$ in the stochastic model that uses segment-based project implementation approach for project selection is further reduced to $X_L(p)= [x_1, x_2,..., x_i, x_{S_1}, x_{C_1}, x_{S_4},..., x_{S_{g-2}}, x_{C_2}]^T$ (L = 1, 2,..., Ω).

This implies that the enhanced stochastic model incorporating segment-based project implementation approach can still be used for the stochastic model utilizing corridor-based project implementation approach. However, the size of the decision vector $X_L(p)$ is reduced from having $(i+g)$ decision variables to $(i+g\text{-}2)$ decision variables. Each decision variable still takes a 0/1 integer value representing the rejection/ selection of an isolated project, multiple projects in a segment-based "project group" or multiple projects in a corridor-based "grand project group". The benefits of all constituent projects of each corridor-based "grand project group" are directly added together to obtain the overall benefits of the "grand project group".

Deferment-Based Project Implementation Approach. As discussed in the problem statement section, some large-scale projects may have a high risk of being deferred for a few years due to various reasons. In this study, the proposed deferment-based project implementation approach considers a fixed number of years of delays in implementing large-scale projects with project costs exceeding a threshold value.

In the application of the deferment-based project implementation approach, the basic stochastic model essentially remains unchanged and the decision vector in stage L decisions $X_L(p)= [x_1, x_2,..., x_N]^T$ in the stochastic model is kept the same. For projects involving deferred implementation, the project benefits and costs are adjusted according to the number of years of deferment. In the project selection process, the deferred projects would compete for funding with other unaffected projects in the newly designated implementation years using the adjusted project benefits and costs.

3.3 Model solution algorithm

This section first presents a theorem of Lagrange multipliers and briefly discusses the essential part of the proposed heuristic algorithm extended from the heuristic of Volgenant and Zoon (1990), which uses two Lagrange multipliers, on how (suboptimal) values for multiple Lagrange multipliers can be determined. It then discusses the improvement of the upper bound for the optimum of the proposed model.

Theorem of the Lagrange multipliers

The stage L optimization can be reformulated as

$$\text{Objective} \qquad \text{maximize } z(X_L) = A^T.X_L \tag{21}$$

Subject to $$C_{kt}^{T}.X_L \le B_{kt}^{L} \tag{22}$$

where X_L is stage L decision vector with zero/one integer elements for rejecting or selecting individual projects.

Given non-negative, real Lagrange multipliers λ_{kt}, the Lagrange relaxation of (21), $z_{LR}(\lambda_{kt})$, can be written as

Objective $$z_{LR}(\lambda_{kt}) = \text{maximize } A^T.X_L + \sum_{k=1}^{K}\sum_{t=1}^{M}\left[\lambda_{kt}\left(B_{kt}^{L} - C_{kt}^{T}.X_L\right)\right]$$

$$= \text{maximize } \left(A^T - \sum_{k=1}^{K}\sum_{t=1}^{M}\left(\lambda_{kt}.C_{kt}^{T}\right)\right)X_L + \sum_{k=1}^{K}\sum_{t=1}^{M}\left(\lambda_{kt}.B_{kt}^{L}\right) \tag{23}$$

Subject to X_L with zero/one integer elements.

Because $\sum_{k=1}^{K}\sum_{t=1}^{M}\left(\lambda_{kt}\cdot B_{kt}^{L}\right)$ in (23) is a constant, optimization can just be concentrated on the first term, namely, maximizing

$$\left(A^T - \sum_{k=1}^{K}\sum_{t=1}^{M}\left(\lambda_{kt}.C_{kt}^{T}\right)\right)X_L . \tag{24}$$

The solution to (24) is X_L^*, where

$$X_L^* = \begin{cases} 1, \text{ if } \left(A^T - \sum_{k=1}^{K}\sum_{t=1}^{M}\left(\lambda_{kt}\cdot C_{kt}^{L}\right)\right) > 0 \\ 0, \text{ otherwise} \end{cases} \tag{25}$$

Then, X_L^* maximizes $z(Y_L) = A^T.X_L$, subject to X_L with zero/one integer elements.

In order to obtain optimal solution by maximizing $z(X_L) = A^T.X_L$, only subject to X_L with zero/one integer elements, the following condition needs to be satisfied

$$\sum_{k=1}^{K}\sum_{t=1}^{M}\left[\lambda_{kt}.\left(B_{kt}^{L} - C_{kt}^{T}.X_L\right)\right] = 0 \tag{26}$$

In this regard, stage L optimization operations need to focus on determining Lagrange multipliers λ_{kt} such that i) X_L^* obtained in (25) is feasible to the original model, i.e., $C_{kt}^{T}.X_L \le B_{kt}^{L}$ is valid, and ii) condition (26) is satisfied to maintain optimality to the original model as Equations (21) and (22).

The Heuristic Algorithm

At the recourse decision stage L, the heuristic initializes the Lagrange multiplier values to zero and all variables to the value one so that Equation (25) is satisfied. In general this solution is not feasible, because constraints of the proposed model as Equation (22) are violated. In each of the iterations, the constraint that has the largest ratio of the remaining total benefits and costs is first determined. Then the corresponding multiplier value is increased as much as necessary to violate Equation (25) for just one variable, the variable will be reset to zero. This step is repeated until the solution has become feasible. An improvement step 'polishes' the solution obtained.

Denote X^*_L is the optimal decision vector at stage L, $s(X'_{(L-1)})$is the set of projects selected at stage L-1, $s(X'_L)$ is the set of projects selected at stage L, $S(X'_L)$ is the set of projects selected at stage L-1 so that each of these projects has at least uses budegt from year 1 to $t_{(L-1)}$, where budget at stage L remains the same as that at stage L-1 for period from year 1 to $t_{(L-1)}$, which means that project $i \in s(X'_{(L-1)})$ and $c_{ikt} > 0$ for any k and at least one t (t =1, 2 … $t_{(L-1)}$) and $S(X'_L) \subseteq s(X'_{(L-1)})$, and $S(X''_L)$ is the set of projects not selected at stage L-1, or selected projects that do not use budget between year 1 and year $t_{(L-1)}$ (complement of $S(X'_L)$). In full, the heuristic has the following steps:

Step 0 (initialize and normalize)

- For stage 1, set $X^*_0 = \{0, 0, \ldots, 0\}$ (No project selected at stage 0). Hence, $s(X'_0) = S(X'_1) = \phi$.
- For stage L, use budget $B_{kt}{}^L = B_{kt}{}^L(p)$ for computation such that $\Delta B^L(p)$= min $\{ \sum_{k=1}^{K}\sum_{t=1}^{M}[B^L_{kt}(p) - E(B^L_{kt})]^2 \}$ and perform the following calculations for project $i \in S(X'_L)$: i) sort the projects by benefits (A_i) in descending order, set λ_{kt} = 0 for all k, t and x_i = 1; ii) normalize cost and budget matrices by setting $c'_{ikt} = \frac{c_{ikt}}{B^L_{kt}}$ for all k, t and $B_{kt}{}^L$ = 1 for all k, t; and iii) compare sum of normalized costs with normalized budgets $C_{kt} = \sum_{i=1}^{N} c'_{ikt}$. If $C_{kt} \le 1$ for all k, t, go to Step 4. Otherwise, go to Step 1.

Step 1 (determine the most violated constraint k, t)

Set C'_{kt} = maximum $\{C_{kt}\}$ for all k, t

Step 2 (compute the increase of Lagrange multiplier value λ_{kt})

$$\theta_i = \begin{cases} \dfrac{A_i - \sum_{k=1}^{K}\sum_{t=1}^{M}(\lambda_{kt}.c'_{ikt})}{\sum_{k=1}^{K}\sum_{t=1}^{M}(c'_{ikt}.\frac{C_{kt}}{C'_{kt}})}, c'_{ikt} > 0 & \text{for all project } i \in S(X'_L) \\ \infty, \text{otherwise} \end{cases}$$

Select project $i \in S(X'_L)$ that has the minimum θ_i and let $\theta'_i = \min\{\theta_1, \theta_2, \ldots, \theta_i, \ldots\}$

Step 3 (increase λ_{kt} by $\theta'_i.(C_{kt}/C'_{kt})$ and reset x_i the value zero)

Let $\lambda_{kt} = \lambda_{kt} + \left(\theta'_i.\frac{C_{kt}}{C'_{kt}}\right)$ and $C_{kt} = C_{kt} - c'_{ikt}$ for all k, t;

Reset x_i = 0 for project $i \in S(X'_L)$ and shift project i from $S(X'_L)$ to $S(X''_L)$

If $C_{kt} \le 1$ for all k, t, go to Step 4. Otherwise, go to Step 1.

Step 4 (improve the solution)

For the feasible solution obtained in Step 3, check whether the projects with zero-variable values can have the value one without violating the constraints $C_{kt} \le 1$. When this is the case, choose the project with highest benefits and add it to the selected project list. Repeat this step until no project with zero-variable value can be found and stop. Update the set of projects selected at stage L, $s(X'_L)$= $\{i \mid$ for all x_i = 1$\}$, and this establishes an improved solution.

Step 5 (further improved solution with budget carryover)

In each year of the multiyear project implementation period, a small amount of budget might be left after project selection. Such amount could be carried over to the immediate following year one year at a time to repeat Steps 1 to 4 to further improve the solution. Update the set of projects selected at stage L, $s(X'_L)=\{i \mid \text{for all } x_i = 1\}$, and this finds an improved solution with budget carryover.

If $L = \Omega$, stop. X^*_L is final. Otherwise, repeat Steps 1-5.

The budget categories K and project implementation years M are much smaller than number of projects N. Practically, 3 budget possibilities for each year may be considered to represent low, medium, and high budget levels. This gives possible budget combinations for stages 1, 2, 3,..., and Ω to be $p_1=1$, $p_2=3^{M-1}$, $p_3=3^{M-2}$, ...with stage 2 having the highest possible combinations. At each stage, the computational complexity for executing Steps 1-4 is $O(MN^2)$ and the extended Step 5 for budget carryover require M iterations. The Ω-stage recourses need at most M iterations. Thus, the computing time of the heuristic is $O(M^3N^2)$.

3.4 Improvements of the upper bound

Let X_L^s be the solution obtained in Step 3 of the above algorithm, we could substitute this solution to Equation (23). Then, an upper bound for the objective function z^U is given by

$$z^U = A^T.X_L^s + \sum_{k=1}^{K}\sum_{t=1}^{M}\left[\lambda_{kt}.\left(B_{kt} - C_{kt}^T.X_L^s\right)\right] \tag{27}$$

The upper bound depends on the non-violated budget constraints with positive Lagrange multipliers. At the beginning of each iteration, suppose that more than one non-violated constraints have positive Lagrange multipliers. Denote I^s be the index of the constraint with the largest value of $\lambda_{kt}.\left(B_{kt} - C_{kt}^T.X_L^s\right)$. The question is then whether the value of Lagrange multiplier $\lambda_{kt(Is)}$ can be chosen smaller so that the influence of constraint I^s in the computation of the upper bound for the objective function is reduced. Obviously, there is no influence if the multiplier value is set to zero. However, if a smaller value of $\lambda_{kt(Is)}$ is used, some other Lagrange multiplier value must be increased in order to satisfy the condition in Equation (18). In the proposed algorithm, we have heuristically chosen the multiplier $\lambda_{kt(i')}$ that is associated with the selected project maintaining the least extent of loss in "benefit-to-cost" ratio if removed, where the index i' is determined by $\theta'_i = \min\{\theta_1, \theta_2, \ldots, \theta_i, \ldots\}$ in Step 2. In the execution of the proposed algorithm, only the decision variable x_i with the value one is set to zero, i.e., a project selected previously is removed in the current iteration. For the two non-violated constraints with positive multipliers $\lambda_{kt(Is)}$ and $\lambda_{kt(i')}$, the tradeoffs of decreasing $\lambda_{kt(Is)}$ and increasing $\lambda_{kt(i')}$ satisfy the following conditions:

$$b_i - \sum_{k=1}^{K}\sum_{t=1}^{M}(\lambda_{kt}.c_{ikt}) + \alpha_1.c_{ikt(I^s)}.\left(\frac{C_{kt}}{C'_{kt}}\right) - \alpha_2.c_{ikt(i')}.\left(\frac{C_{kt}}{C'_{kt}}\right) \leq 0, \text{ for all } x_i = 0 \tag{28}$$

$$b_i - \sum_{k=1}^{K}\sum_{t=1}^{M}(\lambda_{kt}.c_{ikt}) + \alpha_1.c_{ikt(I^s)}.\left(\frac{C_{kt}}{C'_{kt}}\right) - \alpha_2.c_{ikt(i')}.\left(\frac{C_{kt}}{C'_{kt}}\right) \geq 0, \text{ for all } x_i = 1 \tag{29}$$

where α_1 and α_2 are respective changes in the values of $\lambda_{kt(Is)}$ and $\lambda_{kt(i')}$.

For a specific project i with $x_i= 1$, the decision variable x_i will be changed from one to zero only when Equation (29) holds with equality. For the purpose of determining (α_1, α_2) pair, two conditions must be satisfied: i) α_1 is maximal; and ii) Equation (29) holds with equality. Having obtained the values of α_1 and α_2, a project i with $x_i = 1$ that satisfies the equality condition is removed by setting its decision variable x_i to zero. The values of α_1 and α_2 can be determined by the following procedure:

The inequalities in (28) and (29) define the lower and upper boundaries of the feasible region for (α_1, α_2) pair. The lower bound function $f_L(\alpha_1)$ and upper bound function $f_U(\alpha_1)$ for α_1, can be defined as

$$f_L(\alpha_1) = \max\left\{\left[b_i - \sum_{k=1}^{K}\sum_{t=1}^{M}(\lambda_{kt}.c_{ikt}) + \alpha_1.c_{ikt(I^s)}.(\frac{C_{kt}}{C'_{kt}})\right] / \sum_{k=1}^{K}\sum_{t=1}^{M}\left[c_{ikt}.(\frac{C_{kt}}{C'_{kt}})\right]\right\}, \text{ for all } x_i = 0 \quad (30)$$

$$f_U(\alpha_1) = \min\left\{\left[b_i - \sum_{k=1}^{K}\sum_{t=1}^{M}(\lambda_{kt}.c_{ikt}) + \alpha_1.c_{ikt(I^s)}.(\frac{C_{kt}}{C'_{kt}})\right] / \sum_{k=1}^{K}\sum_{t=1}^{M}\left[c_{ikt}.(\frac{C_{kt}}{C'_{kt}})\right]\right\}, \text{ for all } x_i = 1 \quad (31)$$

This is identical to determine the α_1 value such that the function $g(\alpha_1) = f_U(\alpha_1) - f_L(\alpha_1)$ reaches zero value. The function is continuous and piecewise linear that requires a computational complexity of O(N), where N is total number of projects. A numerical method that combines the secant and bisection methods for the computation of zero of the function $g(\alpha_1)$ can be found in Bus and Dekker (1975).

4. Impacts of the proposed method and model on project evaluation and selection

4.1 Comparison of estimated project benefits for project-level impact assessments

Project-level impact assessments compare project level life-cycle benefits separately estimated using the deterministic, risk-based, and the uncertainty-based project level life-cycle cost analysis approaches. For the application of deterministic project level life-cycle benefit/cost analysis, project benefits are calculated by assuming that all input factors are under certainty and each input factor has a single value. These values are directly used for the computation.

For the application of risk-based project level life-cycle benefit/cost analysis, project benefits are calculated by assuming that input factors regarding unit rates of construction, rehabilitation, and maintenance treatments, traffic growth rates, and discount rates are all under risk. The remaining input factors such as pavement or bridge service life and timing of treatments are still treated as being under certainty with single values. Monte Carlo simulations are executed to establish the grand average values of simulation outputs as mathematical expectations of input factors under risk. The single values of input factors under certainty and the grand average values of input factors under risk are used for the computation.

For the application of the uncertainty-based methodology, project benefits are calculated by assuming that the input factors regarding unit rates of construction, rehabilitation, and maintenance treatments, traffic growth rates, and discount rates are all under uncertainty or under mixed cases of risk and uncertainty. The remaining input factors are still considered under certainty with single values. For the input factor under risk, the grand average value as the mathematical expectation is established using Monte Carlo simulation outputs. For the input factor under uncertainty, the grand average value of simulation outputs is adjusted according to the preset decision rule. The single values of input factors under certainty, the grand average values of input factors under risk, and the adjusted grand average values of input factors under uncertainty are used for the computation.

4.2 Comparison of project selection for network-level impact assessments

In order to assess the network-level impacts of adopting different approaches for project benefit estimation, the three sets of project benefits computed using the deterministic, risk-based, and uncertainty-based approaches are separately applied to a stochastic optimization model for network-level project selection. The network-level impacts are assessed by cross comparison of the overall benefits of selected projects and consistency matching rates of project selection using the three different sets of project benefits with the actual project selection and programming practice. This section briefly discusses the stochastic optimization formulation for finding the optimal subset of highway projects from all candidate projects to achieve maximized total project level life-cycle benefits where there is stochasticity in the available budget.

Consider a state transportation agency that carries out highway network-level project selection over a future project implementation period of t_Ω years. The agency makes first round of investment decisions many years prior to project implementation using an estimated budget for all years. With time elapsing, updated budget information on the first few years of the multi-year project selection and programming period becomes available that motivates the agency to refine the investment decisions. In each refined decision-making process, the annual budget for the first few years that can be accurately determined is treated as a deterministic value, while the budget for the remaining years without accurate information is still handled as a stochastic budget.

5. A computational study

A computational study is conducted to examine the impacts of using deterministic, risk-based, and uncertainty-based project level life-cycle cost analysis approaches on computing the benefits of individual highway projects. The computed project benefits are used to assess the network-level impacts of adopting different project level life-cycle cost analysis approaches on project selection results.

5.1 Data sources

Data collection and processing for highway project evaluation

For assessing the project-level impacts of using deterministic, risk-based, and uncertainty based project level life-cycle cost analysis approaches for project benefit estimation, historical data on the Indiana state highways for period 1990-2006 were collected to establish the base case life-cycle activity profiles and annual user cost profiles for different types of pavements and bridges. The data items collected mainly included project type and size; unit rates of construction, rehabilitation, and maintenance treatments; unite rates of vehicle operating costs, travel time, crashes, and air emissions; traffic volume and growth rates; discount rates, etc. Table 2 presents Beta distribution parameters established for those factors on the basis of historical data.

Furthermore, eleven-year data on 7,380 candidate projects (grouped into 5,068 contracts) proposed for Indiana state highway programming during 1996-2006 were collected for applying the deterministic, risk-based, and uncertainty based project level life-cycle cost analysis approaches for project benefit estimation. For each pavement or bridge project, base case and alternative case life-cycle activity profiles and annual user cost profiles were established. As described in the proposed methodology, the agency benefits and user

Input Factors		Mean	Standard Deviation	Beta Distribution Parameters			
				L	H	α	β
Flexible Pavement Cost (1990, $/lane-mile)	Construction	1,353,537	694,614	588,385	3,165,840	2.49	4.50
	Rehabilitation	155,287	509,879	29,147	1,119,863	2.56	4.50
	Resurfacing	52,938	19,689	26,364	101,602	2.56	4.50
	Routine maintenance	138	499	4	2,186	2.27	4.50
Rigid Pavement Cost (1990, $/lane-mile)	Construction	1,334,841	763,709	674,299	2,947,173	2.25	4.50
	Rehabilitation	383,704	242,260	57,952	2,052,896	2.41	4.50
	Routine maintenance	323	204	4	1,981	3.10	4.50
All Pavement Cost (1990, $/lane-mile)	Preventive maintenance	4,120	6,544	186	21,999	2.56	4.50
Concrete Bridge Cost (1990, $/ft^2)	Deck	62	42	0.1	387	2.39	4.50
	Superstructure	110	82	0.2	372	2.39	4.50
	Substructure	115	92	0.1	372	2.39	4.50
Steel Bridge Cost (1990, $/ft^2)	Deck	86	59	0.4	734	2.17	4.50
	Superstructure	171	75	0.4	734	2.17	4.50
	Substructure	206	99	0.4	734	2.17	4.50
Annual Routine Maintenance Growth		3%	1%	1%	5%	4.50	4.50
Annual Traffic Growth		2%	1%	1%	3%	4.50	4.50
Discount Rate		4%	1%	3%	5%	4.50	4.50

Table 2. Input Values of Factors for Risk and Uncertainty-Based Project Benefit Analysis

benefits associated with reduction in vehicle operating costs, shortening of travel time, decrease in vehicle crashes, and cutback of vehicle air emissions for each project were separately estimated by comparing the respective base case and alternative case life-cycle profiles. For the application of the deterministic life-cycle cost analysis approach, the single values of all input factors were utilized for estimating the project level life-cycle benefits.

For the application of the risk-based life-cycle cost analysis approach, Beta distribution parameter values for the input factors regarding unit rates of construction, rehabilitation, and maintenance treatments; traffic growth rates; and discount rates were applied in 10 simulation runs, each with 1,000 iterations using the @RISK software, Version 4.5 (Palisade, 2007). The Latin Hypercube stratified sampling technique was used in the simulations to reach faster convergence. The grand average of simulation runs for each risk factor was adopted for computing the mathematical expectations of agency benefits and user benefits.

When conducting risk-based analysis, it was found that project benefits related to decrease in agency costs, reduction in vehicle operating costs, and cutback of vehicle air emissions were not very sensitive to the variations of simulation outputs of the input factors under risk. However, travel time and vehicle crash reductions varied considerably with the simulation outputs of the factors. For this reason, the project user benefits concerning travel time and vehicle crash reductions were further estimated using the uncertainty-based analysis approach. Specifically, the grand average values of simulation runs for unit rates of construction, rehabilitation, and maintenance treatments, traffic growth rates, and discount rates were adjusted according to the preset decision rules as the proposed methodology for uncertainty-based analysis. The adjusted values were used to compute the benefits of travel time and vehicle crash reductions under uncertainty.

Data Collection and Processing for Network-Level Highway Project Selection

The three sets of project level life-cycle benefits estimated for the 7,380 candidate projects were used to assess the network-level impacts of using deterministic, risk-based, and uncertainty-based project level life-cycle cost analysis approaches for estimating project benefits on project selection results.

Additional data on available budgets by highway asset management program and by project implementation year for period 1996-2006 were collected. The annual average budget was approximately 700 million dollars with 4 percent increment per year. The initially estimated budget for the project implementation period was found to have being updated three times by the Indiana Department of Transportation (DOT). This provided 4-stage budget recourses in the application of the stochastic optimization model for project section. The budget adjustments were mainly made on pavement preservation, bridge preservation, system expansion, and maintenance programs, with changes varying from -32 percent to +60 percent.

Optimization Model Solution

For the purpose of this computational study, the solution algorithm developed based on the LaGrangian relaxation technique was implemented using a customized computer code.

5.2 Summary of estimated project level life-cycle benefits

Table 3 lists project level life-cycle benefits of some pavement and bridge projects. On average, the present worth amounts of project level life-cycle benefits estimated using

Contract No.	Let Year	Lanes	Length (Miles)	AADT	Work Type	Project Cost	Project Benefits Estimated under		
							Certainty	Risk	Uncertainty
12021	2000	4	0.11	69,200	Bridge widening	2,291,000	6,959,434	11,703,264	11,703,264
12040	2000	4	0.50	32,630	Pavement resurfacing	4,620,000	4,776,319	6,927,669	6,365,844
12077	2000	2	2.06	3,170	Pavement resurfacing	3,000,000	9,436,804	15,545,501	15,545,501
12158	1999	2	3.70	16,770	Added travel lanes	750,000	3,036,253	5,405,621	4,806,134
20694	1996	2	1.34	3,420	Flexible pave. replace	51,000	43,704	131,989	131,989
21743	1996	4	0.40	25,310	Pavement rehabilitation	696,000	1,271,574	1,878,375	1,878,375
21749	1998	2	13.63	4,190	Pavement resurfacing	11,573,000	38,024,319	63,943,225	63,943,225
21825	1996	4	2.53	11,150	Pavement rehabilitation	151,000	504,574	1,033,274	1,505,738
21931	1996	4	0.78	2,664	Rigid pavement replace	196,000	705,235	736,046	736,046
21944	1996	2	9.46	1,100	Pavement rehabilitation	131,000	239,334	353,545	353,545
22026	1996	2	0.15	8,291	Bridge widening	108,000	267,380	299,746	254,516
22032	1996	4	6.30	12,274	Pavement resurfacing	754,000	1,743,188	2,753,259	2,559,337
22044	1996	2	1.10	13,994	Pavement resurfacing	2,757,000	6,169,067	6,773,242	5,702,627
22119	1998	4	0.10	27,700	Pavement rehabilitation	264,000	445,933	658,734	658,734
22264	1996	2	1.13	7,843	Pavement resurfacing	1,226,000	3,566,566	7,164,611	6,450,209
...	...	...	...	...	...	...	...	...	...

Table 3. Project Level Life-Cycle Benefits of Some Pavement and Bridge Projects Computed Using Deterministic, Risk-Based, and Uncertainty-Based Analysis Approaches (1990 Constant Dollars)

deterministic, risk-based, and uncertainty-based analysis approaches for the 7,380 projects are 4.18, 7.14, and 6.64 million dollars per project (in 1990 constant dollars), respectively. The average benefit-to-cost ratios are 3.24, 5.54, and 5.16, correspondingly. The significant difference between the project benefits estimated using the deterministic analysis approach and risk-based analysis approach is mainly attributable to large standard deviations of input factors considered for probabilistic risk assessments. The comparable results of project benefits computed using the risk-based analysis approach and uncertainty-based analysis approach are intuitive. This is because the grand average of simulation outputs for each input factor under uncertainty is adjusted only if the deviation between the grand average as the expected outcome and standardized focus loss value exceeds the preset threshold level. The input factor values for risk-based and uncertainty-based analyses will be identical if no adjustment is made.

5.3 Comparisons of project selection results

Comparison of Total Benefits of Selected Projects

Figure 4 illustrates the total benefits of projects selected using the optimization model based on three sets of estimated project benefits (deterministic, risk-based, and uncertainty-based),

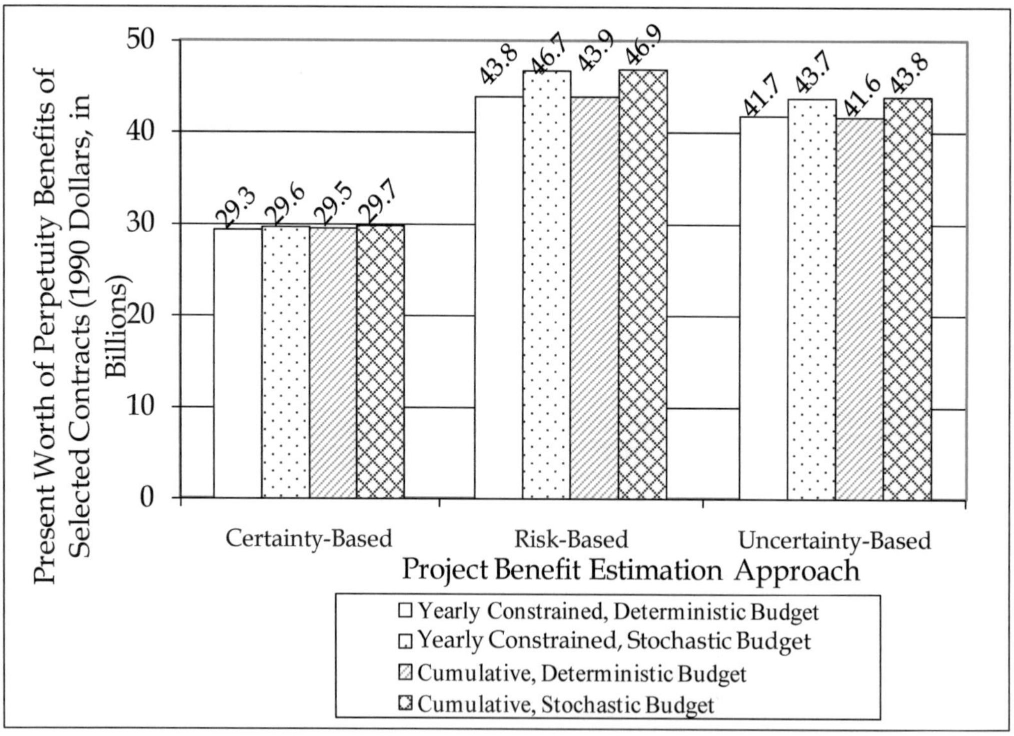

Fig. 4. Comparison of Total Benefits of Selected Projects Using Deterministic and Stochastic Budgets under Yearly Constrained and Cumulative Budget Scenarios (1996-2006)

two types of budgets (deterministic and stochastic), and two budget constraint scenarios (yearly constrained and cumulative). Regardless of budget types and budget constraint scenarios, the total benefits of selected projects are the lowest for project benefits estimated using the deterministic analysis approach and are the highest for project benefits computed using the risk-based analysis approach.

Despite approaches used for computing project benefits and types of budgets used in the optimization model, the project selection using the cumulative budget scenario generally yielded higher total benefits. The results are not unexpected. The cumulative budget scenario does not have year-by-year budget restrictions as those added to the yearly constrained budget scenario. This entails more flexibility to the optimization model in conducting project selection, leading to increases in the total project benefits.

Comparison of Number of Selected Contracts

Table 4 presents the comparison of contracts selected using the three sets of project benefits, two types of budgets, and two budget constraint scenarios. The matching rates were established in reference to the contracts being authorized by the Indiana DOT. One match is counted if a contract is both selected in the optimization model application and also authorized by the Indiana DOT.

Year	No. of Contracts	Indiana DOT Authorized	Yearly Constrained Budget						Cumulative Budget						All Methods Matched with Indiana DOT	
			Deterministic			Stochastic			Deterministic			Stochastic				
			M_D	M_R	M_U	M_D	M_R	M_U	M_D	M_R	M_U	M_D	M_R	M_U	No.	%
1996	464	443	433	390	388	437	390	394	439	411	414	439	412	415	319	72%
1997	412	358	387	338	344	386	336	343	390	370	372	390	369	374	250	70%
1998	429	275	408	351	363	409	353	361	413	375	377	414	377	377	187	68%
1999	411	323	376	322	333	381	322	332	388	352	352	388	351	352	203	63%
2000	610	578	576	506	516	579	504	514	582	544	544	586	546	546	416	72%
2001	418	412	395	348	358	396	343	356	393	363	363	393	360	366	289	70%
2002	422	421	399	343	343	398	339	343	402	373	373	406	373	377	291	69%
2003	469	461	437	373	381	440	371	375	444	413	414	446	413	418	315	68%
2004	649	648	608	519	531	615	521	528	612	578	580	613	578	581	463	71%
2005	408	406	380	337	339	384	337	340	387	355	359	389	357	364	282	69%
2006	376	375	355	302	307	353	303	303	357	333	336	359	334	338	259	69%
Total	5,068	4,700	4,754	3,871	4,203	4,778	3,896	4,189	4,807	4,625	4,484	4,823	4,660	4,508		
Total Match with Indiana DOT			4,400	3,828	3,889	4,421	3,817	3,877	4,451	4,129	4,145	4,466	4,131	4,168	3,274	
% Match with Indiana DOT			94%	81%	83%	94%	81%	82%	95%	88%	88%	95%	88%	89%		70%

Note: M_D, M_R, and M_U - Project benefits estimated using deterministic based, risk-based, and uncertainty-based analysis approaches, respectively.

Table 4. Summary of Consistency in Contract Selection Results under Different Extents of Risk and Uncertainty Considerations

For the deterministic budget, the average matching rates for the three sets of estimated project benefits and two budget constraint scenarios are 81-95 percent. Irrespective of using project benefits estimated by the deterministic, risk-based or uncertainty-based life-cycle cost analysis approach, the use of cumulative budget constraint scenario in the optimization model for project selection resulted in the selection of a higher number of contracts and with a higher matching rate. The net increases in the matching rates for the cumulative budget scenario as opposed to the yearly constrained budget scenario are 1 percent for deterministic project benefits, 7 percent for risk-based project benefits, and 5 percent for uncertainty-based project benefits, respectively. The relative increases in the matching rates resulted from the use of the cumulative budget scenario versus the yearly constrained budget scenario are 1%/94% = 1.1 percent for deterministic based project benefits, 7%/81% = 9 percent for risk-based project benefits, and 5%/83% = 6 percent for uncertainty-based project benefits, correspondingly.

For the stochastic budget, the average matching rates for the three sets of estimated project benefits and two budget constraint scenarios also range from 81-95 percent. The use of cumulative budget constraint scenario in the optimization model for project selection resulted in the selection of a higher number of contracts and with a higher matching rate. The increases in the matching rates for the cumulative budget scenario as opposed to the yearly constrained budget scenario are 1 percent for deterministic based project benefits, 7 percent for risk-based project benefits, and 7 percent for uncertainty-based project benefits, respectively. The relative increases in the matching rates are 1%/94% = 1.1 percent, 7%/81% = 9 percent, and 7%/82% = 8.5 percent, correspondingly.

Irrespective of budget types and budget constraint scenarios, the use of project benefits estimated by the deterministic life-cycle cost analysis approach for project selection produced a higher percentage of matching rate as compared to matching rates established for project benefits estimated by risk-based and uncertainty-based analysis approaches. The matching rates for project benefits estimated using the uncertainty-based analysis approach are slightly higher than those of the project benefits computed by the risk-based analysis approach. In particular, increases in the matching rates are 2 percent for yearly constrained deterministic budget, 2 percent for yearly constrained stochastic budget, 0 percent for cumulative deterministic budget, and 1 percent for cumulative stochastic budget, respectively. The relative increases in the matching rates are 2%/81% = 2.5 percent, 2%/81% = 2.5 percent, 0%/82% = 0 percent, and 1%/88% = 1.1 percent, accordingly.

Without regard to using different approaches for project benefit estimation and employing different types of budgets and budget constraint scenarios in the optimization model for project selection, the average matching rate between projects selected using the optimization model and actually authorized by the Indiana DOT for the eleven-year analysis period is 70 percent. After removing this portion of matching rate invariant to approaches used for project benefit analysis and types of budgets and budget constraint scenarios used in the optimization model for project selection, the relative increases in the matching rates of project selection resulted from the use of uncertainty-based analysis approach versus the risk-based analysis approach for project benefit estimation are 2%/(81%-70%) = 18 percent for yearly constrained deterministic budget, 2%/(81%-70%) = 18 percent for yearly constrained stochastic budget, 0%/(82%-70%) = 0 percent for cumulative deterministic budget, and 1%/(88%-70%) = 9 percent for cumulative stochastic budget, accordingly.

6. Summary, conclusion, and recommendations

A new method is introduced for highway project evaluation that handles certainty, risk, and uncertainty inherited with input factors for the computation. Also, a stochastic model is proposed for project selection that rigorously addresses issues of alternative budget constraint scenario, budget uncertainty, and project implementation approach considerations. A computational study is conducted to assess the impacts of risk and uncertainty considerations in estimating project level life-cycle benefits and on the results of network-level project selection.

The computational study results have revealed that using project level life-cycle benefits estimated by the proposed uncertainty-base analysis approach yielded a higher percentage of matching rate with the actual programming practice as compared to the matching rate of using the project benefits computed by the risk-based analysis approach. The relative increase in matching rate with uncertainty considerations is up to 2.5 percent. After removing the portion of matching rate invariant to approaches used for project benefit estimation and types of budgets and budget constraint scenarios considered in the optimization model for project selection, the relative increase in the matching rate is as high as 18 percent. The difference is quite significant. The proposed methodology offers a means for transportation agencies to explicitly address uncertainty issues in project level life-cycle benefit/cost analysis that would enhance the existing risk-based life-cycle cost analysis approach.

Application of the proposed method and model requires collecting a large amount of data. This may limit the method and model application primarily to large-scale transportation agencies that maintain sufficient historical data on highway system preservation, expansion, operations, and expenditures. In addition, the customized Beta distribution parameters need to be updated over time to reflect changes in the values of input factors for the analysis. Moreover, the equally assigned weights for project level life-cycle agency benefits and user benefits may be adjusted to assess the impact of such changes on the estimated project benefits and on the results of network-level project selection.

7. References

AASHTO. (2003). *User Benefit Analysis for Highways*. American Association of State Highway and Transportation Officials, Washington, D.C.

Abaza, K.A. (2002). Optimum Flexible Pavement Life-Cycle Analysis Model. *ASCE Journal of Transportation Engineering* 128(6), 542-549.

Birge, J.R. &Louveaux, F. (1997). *Introduction to Stochastic Programming*. Springer-Verlag, New York, NY.

Bus, J.C.P. & Dekker, T.J. (1975). Two Efficient Algorithms with Guaranteed Convergence for Finding a Zero of a Function. *ACM Transactions on Mathematical Software* 1, 330-345.

Chan, A.; Keoleian, G. & Gabler, E. (2008). Evaluation of Life-Cycle Cost Analysis Practices Used by the Michigan Department of Transportation. *ASCE Journal of Transportation Engineering* 134(6), 236-245.

Falls, L.C. & Tighe, S. (2003). Improving LCCA through the Development of Cost Models Using the Alberta Roadway Rehabilitation and Maintenance Analysis. Transportation Research Board 82nd Annual Meeting, Washington, Washington, D.C.

FHWA. (1987). *Bridge Management Systems*. Demonstration Project No. 71. Federal Highway Administration, U.S. Department of Transportation, Washington, D.C.

FHWA. (1991). *Pavement Management Systems*. Federal Highway Administration, U.S. Department of transportation, Washington, D.C.

FHWA. (1998). *Life-Cycle Cost Analysis in Pavement Design-In Search of Better Investment Decisions*. Federal Highway Administration, U.S. Department of transportation, Washington, D.C.

FHWA. (2000). Highway Economic Requirements System. Federal Highway Administration, U.S. Department of transportation, Washington, D.C.

Ford, J.L. & Ghose, S. (1998). Lottery Designs to Discriminate between Shackle's Theory, Expected Utility Theory and Non-Expected Utility Theories. *Annals of Operations Research*. Kluwer Academic Publishers, Norwell, MA.

Geoffroy, D.N. & Shufon, J.J. (1992). Network Level Pavement Management in New York State: A Goal-Oriented Approach. *Transportation Research Record* 1344, 57-65.

Gion, L.C.; Gough, J.; Sinha, K.C. & Woods, R.E. (1993). *User's Manual for the Implementation of the Indiana Bridge Management System*. Purdue University, West Lafayette, IN.

Hawk, H. (2003). Bridge Life Cycle Cost Analysis. *NCHRP Report 483*. National Academies Press, Washington, D.C.

Hicks, R.G. & Epps, J.A. (1999). Life Cycle Cost Analysis of Asphalt-Rubber Paving Materials. Final Report Volumes 1 and II to Rubber Pavements Association, Tempe, AZ.

INDOT. (2002). *Indiana Department of Transportation Design Manual*. Indiana Department of Transportation, Indianapolis, IN.

Isa Al-Subhi, K.M.; Johnston, D.W. & Farid, F. (1989). Optimizing System-Level Bridge Maintenance, Rehabilitation, and Replacement Decisions. North Carolina State University, Raleigh, NC.

Labi, S. & Sinha, K.C. (2005). Life-Cycle Evaluation of Flexible Pavement Preventive Maintenance. *ASCE Journal of Transportation Engineering* 131(10), 744-751.

Li, Z. & Sinha, K.C. (2004). A Methodology for Multicriteria Decision Making in Highway Asset Management. *Transportation Research Record* 1885, 79-87.

Li, Z. & Sinha, K.C. (2006). Application of Shackle's Model for Highway Project Evaluation under Uncertainty. Proceedings of the 9th International Conference on Applications of Advanced Technology in Transportation, 67-73.

Li, Z. &Madanu, S. (2009). Highway Project-Level Life-Cycle Benefit/Cost Analysis under Certainty, Risk, and Uncertainty: A Methodology with Case Study. *ASCE Journal of Transportation Engineering* 135(8), 516-526.

Li, Z.; Madanu, S.; Wang, Y.; Abbas, M. & Zhou, B. (2010). A Heuristic Approach for Selecting Highway Investment Alternatives. *Wiley Journal of Computer-Aided Civil and Infrastructure Engineering* 25(6), 427-439.

Martello, S. & Toth, P. (1990). *Knapsack Problems: Algorithms and Computer Implementations.* John Wiley & Sons, Chichester, UK.

Mohammadi, J.; Guralnick, S.A. & Yan, L. (1995). Incorporating Life-Cycle Costs in Highway-Bridge Planning and Design. *ASCE Journal of Transportation Engineering* 121(5), 417-424.

Neumann, L.A. (1997). Methods for Capital Programming and Project Selection. *NCHRP Synthesis* 243. National Academy Press, Washington, D.C.

Ouyang, Y. & Madanat, S.M. (2004). Optimal Scheduling of Rehabilitation Activities for Multiple Pavement Facilities: Exact and Approximation Solutions. *Transportation Research Part A* 38(5), 347-365.

Palisade (2007). @Risk Software, Version 4.5. Palisade Corporation, Ithaca, NY.

Peshkin, D.G.; Hoerner, T.E. & Zimmerman, K.A. (2005). Optimal Timing of Pavement Preventive Maintenance Treatment Applications. *NCHRP Report* 523. National Academies Press, Washington, D.C.

Purvis, R.L.; Babaei, K.; Clear, K.C. & Markow, M.J. (1994). Life-Cycle Cost Analysis for Protection and Rehabilitation of Concrete Bridges Relative to Reinforcement Corrosion. *SHRP-S-377.* National Academies Press, Washington, D.C.

Ravirala, V. &Grivas, D.A. (1995). Goal-Programming Methodology for Integrating Pavement and Bridge Programs. *ASCE Journal of Transportation Engineering* 121(4), 345-351.

Reigle, J.A. & Zaniewski, J.P. (2005). Risk-Based Life-Cycle Cost Analysis for Project-Level Pavement Management. *Transportation Research Record* 1816, 34-42.

Setunge, S.; Kumar, A.; Nezamian, A.; De Sliva, S. & Lokuge, W. (RMIT); Carse, A.; Spathonis, J. & Chandler, L. (QDMR); Gilbert, D. (QDPW); Johnson, B. (Ove Arup); Jeary, A. (UWS); & Pham, L. (CSIRO). (2005). Whole of Life Cycle Cost Analysis in Bridge Rehabilitation. *Report 2002-005-C-03.* RMIT University, Melbourne, Australia.

Shackle, G.L.S. (1949). *Expectation in Economics,* 2nd Edition. Cambridge University Press, Cambridge, United Kingdom.

Teng, J.Y. & Tzeng, G.H. (1996). A Multiobjective Programming Approach for Selecting Non-Independent Transportation Investment Alternatives. *Transportation Research Part B* 30(4), 291-307.

Tighe, S. (2001). Guidelines for Probabilistic Pavement Life Cycle Cost Analysis. *Transportation Research Record* 1769, 28-38.

Volgenant, A. & Zoon, J.A. (1990). An Improved Heuristic for Multidimensional 0-1 Knapsack Problems. *Journal of the Operational Research Society* 41(10), 963-970.

Weissmann, J.; Harrison, R.; Burns, N.H. & Hudson, W.R. (1990). Selecting Rehabilitation and Replacement Bridge Projects, Extending the Life of Bridges. *ASTM STP* 1100, 3-17.

Wilde, J.W.; Waalkes, S. & Harrison, R. (1999). Life Cycle Cost Analysis of Portland Cement Concrete Pavements. *FHWA/TX-00/0-1739-1.* The University of Texas at Austin, TX.

Young, R.A. (2001). Uncertainty and the Environment: Implications for Decision Making and Environmental Policy. Edward Elgar, Cheltenham, United Kingdom.

Zimmerman, K.A. (1995). Pavement Management Methodologies to Select Projects and Recommend Preservation Treatments. NCHRP Synthesis 222. National Academy Press, Washington, D.C.

Part 4

The Survival of the Algorithmically Fittest

15

Global Optimization of Conventional and Holey Double-Clad Fibres by Stochastic Search

Ioannis Dritsas, Tong Sun and Ken Grattan
City University London
UK

1. Introduction

High power fibre lasers (HPFLs) find applications in the material processing, automotive, medical, telecoms and defence industries. Over 1kW of output power [1] has been demonstrated as the race to scale up the power while maintaining excellent beam quality and achieving impressive power conversion efficiency is ongoing. During the mature stages of the HPFLs technology, the automated simulation-based optimization of HPFLs is expected to contribute significantly to the formulation of optimal designs and to improve intuition for the conception of new fibre lasers. This chapter researches the common ground between computational photonics and direct search optimization methods with the prospect to propose optimized fibre designs for HPFLs.

Published work on the subject of pump light enhancement in the active core of cladding pumped fibres could be categorized as follows:

a. Pump absorption ion system optimization [2-5]
b. Pumping techniques focusing on how to couple more power into the inner cladding [6-10]
c. Fibre designs that focus on maximizing the overlap between the coupled pump light and absorbent core volume [11-15]
d. Holistic solutions that attempt to address (b) and (c) simultaneously [16-18]

Schemes in (c) are usually compatible with categories (b) and (d) meaning that the special fibres proposed by (c) can be pumped by schemes in (b) or they can be modified for use in the schemes of category (d) to further increase the pump absorption.

In category (b), Koplow *et al* [9] list a set of pumping schemes evaluation criteria and propose an embedded mirror side pumping scheme after discussing the contemporary pumping methods. Their technique initially appeared attractive and for that it was tested numerically within the computation environment of the simulation method proposed in [19]. It was found, however, that it does not benefit from the fibre cross section optimization because it reduces the percentage of higher order modes resulting in absorption degradation. Another side pumping technique which, in contrast with the previous, did not require machining of the pumped fibre was proposed by Polynkin *et al* [8]. A DCF was pumped via evanescent field coupling. This scheme appears to be fully compatible with the incorporation of optimized fibre topologies in place of the conventional circular inner cladding with centred core. Lassila [6] proposed a scalable side pumping scheme that could benefit from tailored axially symmetrical (presumably as far as the inner cladding is concerned) cross sections.

A pump absorption enhancing scheme that could fit in category (c) was proposed by Baek *et al* [14]. The authors incorporated a long period fibre grating (LPFG) in a cladding pumped configuration and measured a 35% increase in pump absorption as a direct result of the LPFG. A similar approach based on the reflection of the residual pump light was reported by Jeong *et al* [15]. The free end of the single-end pumped DCF was shaped into a right-angled cone that reflected more than 55% of the unabsorbed pump light that offered an 18% increase in absorbed pump power. This is one more scheme which could benefit from optimised fibre topologies. Recently, the use of a large area helical core was proposed [11] for the enhancement of pump absorption and simultaneous rejection of high order lasing modes naturally suggesting that optimized helical solid-state holes (that may be fabricated by rotation just like the helical core) could exhibit a similar tapering effect [19] as that reported here. This could avoid the need to increase the core area when increasing the inner clad area [12] to accept more pump power.

In the category of holistic solutions, Kouznetsov and Moloney proposed [16] and modelled analytically [17] the tapered slab delivery of multimode pump light to a small diameter inner cladding. This scheme combines the specially designed pump waveguide and corresponding inner cladding that could also fit in the shallow-angle single pumping category listed in [9]. It benefits highly from the coupling of multimode light into a narrow inner cladding while potential drawbacks are the leakage of high order pump modes and the fabrication difficulties. An alternative approach is demonstrated experimentally by Peterka *et al* [18]. The proposed DCF is single-end pumped and has a double-D cross section with the core at the centre of its half section. The input side is processed so that signal and pump delivery fibres can be spliced on the two specially fabricated facets. Overall, a promising way forward appears to be the development of generic and modular solutions within categories (a), (b) and (c) and then the synergistic combination of the three. This would act as a practical two stage approach that could amplify the pump absorption enhancement and consecutively the laser output power.

The results reported in this chapter fit in the aforementioned second category of pump absorption enhancing schemes. The interpretation of the original NM algorithm [20] as well as the deterministic cross section shape perturbation technique [21] are presented in this chapter in the form of structured pseudocode-functions. The proposed notation serves as the background for the development and validation of improved methods. Furthermore, additional fibre topology encoding schemes at higher dimensions are introduced and a modern interpretation of NM is given prior to the proposal of stochastically enhanced NM forms described in pseudocode syntax. The proposed algorithms are compared with commercial implementations of the genetic algorithm (GA) [22], generalised pattern search (GPS) [23-27] and mesh adaptive direct search (MADS) [28-29] methods that are also tested here for their performance and suitability. All the aforementioned algorithms share a set of common characteristics: they can operate exclusively on the function values (zeroth-order or derivative free or direct search methods) and they were tuned to their most parsimonious instances to the extent that their global convergence properties were not compromised. Here, the term global convergence is used to mean first order convergence to a point far enough from an arbitrary starting point. It does not mean convergence to a point $x_*: f(x_*) \le f(x),\ \forall x \in \Re^n$ adhering to the terminology in the extensive review for direct search methods by Kolda *et al.* A third common characteristic is that they all call a 3-dimentional (3-D) fibre simulation method, described and validated in [19], in order to evaluate the objective function.

The contributions made in this chapter are summarized below:

- First reported stochastic simulation-based optimization of DCF topologies (to the best of the authors knowledge)
- Pseudocode descriptions of proposed algorithms for ease of verification and/or use by other researchers
- Benchmarking of several optimization algorithms with an emphasis on their statistical nature
- An optimization problem description scheme that allows the incorporation of inhomogeneous independent variables
- The proposal of perturbed stochastic search patterns as generalizations of the simplex formation pattern with possible applicability in pattern search algorithms
- The concept of implicitly constrained optimization via perturbed pattern search
- The proposal of the enhanced stochastically perturbed Nelder-Mead (ESPNM) method for implicitly constrained global optimization with simple bounds
- The unified description of NM, NM's stochastic forms, GPS and MADS methods based on the pattern search concept
- Mostly globally (as opposed to mostly locally in [21]) optimized DCF designs with an emphasis on manufacturability and modular design

The next section describes a set of optimization schemes on relatively low dimensions and compares NM, NM's stochastic variants (simple sampling Monte Carlo techniques), GA, GPS and MADS methods. Section 3 focuses on optimization schemes and algorithms in higher dimensions, introduces the perturbed patterns for simple and importance sampling Monte Carlo optimization and compares the locally introduced algorithms. The simulation parameters as well as the settings of each algorithm are given in section 4 where the optimization results for DCFs with polymer as well as air outer cladding are also discussed. Finally, section 5 concludes this chapter.

2. Bound-constrained zeroth-order optimization algorithms

The optimization problem considered in this chapter is

$$\min_{\mathbf{P}\in\mathbf{\Omega}} \mathrm{f}(\mathbf{P}),\ \mathrm{f}:\Re^n \to \Re \cup \{\infty\} \tag{1}$$

$$\text{where, } \mathrm{f}(\mathbf{P}) = -P_{abs,tot}(\mathbf{P}), \tag{2}$$

$\mathbf{P}$ is a point in $\Re^n$, n is the number of variables and $\mathbf{\Omega}$ is the bounded function domain. Equation (2) gives the objective function which maps a DCF topology to the corresponding negative total absorbed pump power value [19]. The current notation partly adheres to that of [23] by assuming that

$$\mathbf{\Omega} = \{\mathbf{P} \in \Re^n : l \le \mathbf{P} \le u\} \text{ where } l,u \in \{\Re \cup \{\pm\infty\}\}^n . \tag{3}$$

The optimization domain $\mathbf{\Omega}$ constitutes a declaration of the computational bounds and physically meaningful function domain. It acts as a barrier when applying the optimization algorithm not to f but to f_{Ω} where

$$f_{\Omega} = \begin{cases} f(\mathbf{P}) & \text{if}\, \mathbf{P} \in \mathbf{\Omega} \\ \infty & \text{otherwise} \end{cases}. \tag{4}$$

The current work attempts to solve a simulation-based optimization problem where the objective function can be evaluated to only a few significant figures. This observation along with the noise that may be present in the computed function values or the expense of these computations render the calculation of derivatives impossible or impractical. Hence there is a need to treat the optimization problem with direct search methods.

The GA, GPS and MADS methods are implemented here via the commercially available 'genetic algorithm and direct search toolbox' within the MATLAB technical computing environment. The amount of subjective evaluation of the aforementioned algorithms was kept to a minimum by carefully tuning their parameters so that both global convergence and low computational cost are served in a well balanced way. Moreover, directly comparable sets of optimizations were performed by each method in order to gain statistical insight into the benefits of each algorithm and build intuition into their performance for a more objective judgment.

The NM simplicial search method has been comprehensively studied theoretically [30-32], extensively applied mostly in chemistry but also in optics [33-34], criticized for its inadequacies [35], remedied [36], enhanced [37,38] and even stochastically incorporated [39]. However, all theoretical improvements have led to a reduction in its computational efficiency. The main strength of the original algorithm is that when it succeeds it offers the best efficiency indicating that the most successful modifications of the simplex descent concept, with applications in computationally intensive problems, are expected to be those that maintain the number of function evaluations required to a minimum. Due to NM's susceptibility to different interpretations and the need to clearly and concisely describe the NM-based methods proposed here, its current interpretation is crystallized in algorithm NM and associated subalgorithms NM_SimplexGener, FuncEval, SmxAssessm and NM_Step. The later follows the modern practice examined by Lagarias [30] and is described in section 3 as a subset of subalgorithm ESPNM_Step introduced there. Algorithm NM shows distinctively its two main operations being the generation of the initial simplex ($\mathbf{S}_0$) along orthogonal directions around the start point (at line 3) and the line search procedure recursively executed (at line 10) by calling NM_Step during an iteration (while loop: lines 8-12). The descent path is governed by the descent coefficient set {reflection, expansion, contraction, shrinkage} assigned in line 6. Line 2 of algorithm NM implies that the generation of the initial simplex (a polytope in $\Re^n$ with $n+1$ vertices - the minimum statistical information required to capture first order information) is essentially a pattern search operation along all n-directions denoted by the column vectors of the $n \times n$ pattern matrix (Ξ_{NM}) which in this case is practically the identity matrix ($\Xi_{\mathrm{NM}} \equiv \mathbf{I}_{n \times n}$). The initial simplex is generated by the subalgorithm NM_SimplexGener with respect to the start point and vector $\mathbf{M}$ where the mesh sizes of the all independent variables are stored. In this way, the simultaneous optimization of inhomogeneous variables (of different physical meaning, units, mesh size) is practically implemented. An example is the case where the diameter and refractive index of an embedded hole are simultaneously optimized. Essentially, this is the integration of a parametric optimization procedure into a more robust non-parametric optimization scheme.

An important implication of subalgorithm NM_SimplexGener is that it should form a nondegenerate initial ($j = 0$) simplex. That is,

$$\operatorname{vol}\left(\mathbf{S}_j\right) = \frac{\left|\det\left(\mathbf{P}_1^{(j)} - \mathbf{P}_{n+1}^{(j)}, \mathbf{P}_2^{(j)} - \mathbf{P}_{n+1}^{(j)}, \cdots, \mathbf{P}_n^{(j)} - \mathbf{P}_{n+1}^{(j)}\right)\right|}{n!} > 0 \tag{5}$$

The satisfaction of inequality (5) is important in order to conserve the numerical integrity of the 'flexible polytope' when descending in $\Re^n$ and avoid convergence to a non-minimizer after collapsing one or more of its vertices on the hyperplane of others [35].

A simple sampling Monte Carlo approach is exercised here by means of the stochastic Nelder-Mead method (SNM) with the prospect to increase NM's efficiency and probability to find a global minimizer in low dimensions. The SNM method is partly implemented by substituting line 2 in algorithm NM with

Algorithm NM. Interpretation of the modern Nelder-Mead (NM) method:

$$\left[\mathbf{P}_l, \mathrm{f}_l, \sigma_j\right] = \mathrm{NM}\left(\mathbf{P}_1, \mathbf{M}, \sigma_{halt}, \mathbf{\Omega}\right)$$

Input: (start point $\mathbf{P}_1 = \left[p_{1,1}\, p_{2,1} \cdots p_{n,1}\right]^{\mathrm{T}}$ *in* $\Re^n$*, mesh size vector* $\mathbf{M} = \left[m_1\, m_2 \cdots m_n\right]^{\mathrm{T}}$*, stopping value for the halting criterion and optimization domain* $\mathbf{\Omega} = \left[\mathbf{B}_1\, \mathbf{B}_2 \cdots \mathbf{B}_n\right]^{\mathrm{T}}$ *where* $\mathbf{B}_i = \left[p_{i,\min}\, p_{i,\max}\right]^{\mathrm{T}} |_{i=1,2,\ldots,n}$ *(bounds)). Output: [optimal point, corresponding function value, standard deviation of* $\left\{\mathrm{f}_i |_{i=1,2,\ldots,n+1;\, i\neq h}\right\}$ *after the last iteration].*

1 $j := 0$ — *// iteration index*

2 $\Xi_{\mathrm{NM}} := \left[\xi_1\, \xi_2 \cdots \xi_n\right] \equiv \mathbf{I}_{n\times n}$ — *// initial simplex formation pattern*

3 ***call*** $\left[\mathbf{S}_0\right] = \mathrm{NM\_SimplexGener}\left(\mathbf{P}_1, \Xi_{\mathrm{NM}}, \mathbf{M}, n\right)$ — *//* nondegenerate *initial simplex*

4 ***for*** each $\left\{\mathbf{P}_i |_{i=1,2,\ldots,n+1}\right\}$ ***call*** s$\left[f_i\right] = \mathrm{FuncEval}\left(\mathbf{P}_i, \mathbf{\Omega}\right)$ ***endfor*** — *// objective function evaluations*

5 $\mathbf{F}_j := \left[f_1\, f_2 \cdots f_{n+1}\right]_{1\times(n+1)}$ — *// initial objective matrix*

6 $\{r, e, c, s\} := \{1, 2, 1/2, 1/2\}$ — *// descent coefficients standard values*

7 ***call*** $\left[\mathrm{f}_h, \mathrm{f}_l, \mathbf{P}_h, \mathbf{P}_l, \bar{\mathrm{f}}, \bar{\mathbf{P}}\right] = \mathrm{SmxAssessm}\left(\mathbf{S}_j, \mathbf{F}_j\right)$ — *// current simplex (* $\mathbf{S}_j$ *) assessment*

8 ***while*** $\left(\sigma_j \geq \sigma_{halt}\right)$ *// where,* $\sigma_j = \left(\left\langle\left(\mathrm{f}_i - \bar{\mathrm{f}}\right)^2 |_{i=1,2,\ldots,n+1;\, i\neq h}\right\rangle\right)^{1/2}$ *(descent halting criterion)*

9 $\quad j := j + 1$ — *// increment*

10 $\quad$ ***call*** $\left[\mathbf{S}_j, \mathbf{F}_j, step\right] = \mathrm{NM\_Step}\left(\mathbf{P}_h, \mathbf{P}_l, \bar{\mathbf{P}}, \mathbf{\Omega}, f_h, f_l, r, e, c, s, \mathbf{S}_j, \mathbf{F}_j\right)$ — *// NM step*

11 $\quad$ ***call*** $\left[\mathrm{f}_h, \mathrm{f}_l, \mathbf{P}_h, \mathbf{P}_l, \bar{\mathrm{f}}, \bar{\mathbf{P}}\right] = \mathrm{SmxAssessm}\left(\mathbf{S}, \mathbf{F}\right)$ — *// simplex assessment*

12 ***endwhile*** — *// end of iteration loop*

13 ***return*** $\mathbf{P}_l, f_l, \sigma_j$ — *// output.*

Subalgorithm NM_SimplexGener. NM initial simplex generation:

$$[\mathbf{S}_0] = \text{NM\_SimplexGener}(\mathbf{P}_1, \Xi_{\text{NM}}, \mathbf{M}, n)$$

Input: (start point $\mathbf{P}_1$*, NM pattern, mesh size vector and length of* $\mathbf{P}_1$*). Output: [initial simplex matrix].*

for each simplex vertex in the set $\{\mathbf{P}_i\,|_{i=2,3,\ldots,n+1}\}$
    $\mathbf{P}_i := \mathbf{P}_1 + (\mathbf{M} \circ \xi_{i-1})$
    //where, $\circ : [a_{ij}]_{m\times n} \circ [b_{ij}]_{m\times n} = [a_{ij}b_{ij}]_{m\times n}$
endfor
    $\mathbf{S}_0 := [\mathbf{P}_1\,\mathbf{P}_2 \cdots \mathbf{P}_{n+1}]_{n\times(n+1)}\,|_{\text{vol}(\mathbf{S}_0)>0}$
return $\mathbf{S}_0$ *// output.*

Subalgorithm FuncEval. Objective function evaluation:

$$[f_i] = \text{FuncEval}(\mathbf{P}_i, \mathbf{\Omega})$$

Input: (point in $\Re^n$*, bounds). Output: [function value].*

if $\mathbf{P}_i \in \mathbf{\Omega}$ ***then***
    $f_i := \text{f}(\mathbf{P}_i)$ // compute (simulate)
else
    $f_i := +\infty$ // assign a large positive value
endif
return f_i //output.

Subalgorithm SmxAssessm. Simplex assessment:

$$[\text{f}_h, \text{f}_l, \mathbf{P}_h, \mathbf{P}_l, \bar{\text{f}}, \bar{\mathbf{P}}] = \text{SmxAssessm}(\mathbf{S}, \mathbf{F})$$

Input: (simplex, objective matrices). Output: [worse, best function values, corresponding points, mean function value and centroid for $i \neq h$*].*

$\text{f}_h := \max\{\text{f}_i\,|_{i=1,2,\ldots,n+1}\}$; ***assign*** $\mathbf{P}_h\,|_{\text{f}_h \equiv \text{f}(\mathbf{P}_h)}$
$\text{f}_l := \min\{\text{f}_i\,|_{i=1,2,\ldots,n+1}\}$; ***assign*** $\mathbf{P}_l\,|_{\text{f}_l \equiv \text{f}(\mathbf{P}_l)}$
$\bar{\text{f}} := \langle \text{f}_i\,|_{i=1,2,\ldots,n+1;\, i\neq h} \rangle$; $\bar{\mathbf{P}} := \langle \mathbf{P}_i\,|_{i=1,2,\ldots,n+1;\, i\neq h} \rangle$
return $\text{f}_h, \mathbf{P}_h, \text{f}_l, \mathbf{P}_l, \bar{\text{f}}, \bar{\mathbf{P}}$ *// output.*

$$\Xi_{\mathrm{SNM}} = \left(\xi_1, \xi_2, \ldots, \xi_n\right)_{n\times n} = \begin{bmatrix} m_1 & 0 & \cdots & 0 \\ 0 & m_2 & \cdots & 0 \\ \vdots & \vdots & & \vdots \\ 0 & 0 & \cdots & m_n \end{bmatrix} \tag{6}$$

where $\left\{m_i \mid_{i=1,2,\ldots,n}\right\} \in \left[-1,1\right]$ is a set of uniformly distributed pseudorandom numbers. A short description of the pseudorandom number generator used is given in section 4. SNM can use subalgorithm NM_SimplexGener to generate the initial simplex after substituting Ξ_{NM} with Ξ_{SNM} in the set of input arguments. During the generation of $\mathbf{S}_0$ around $\mathbf{P}_1$, on the basis of Ξ_{SNM}, a set of randomly signed orthogonal directions are searched while the initial mesh sizes fluctuate randomly as well (between zero and their nominal values stored in $\mathbf{M}$). The second and last part of the SNM implementation is to discard line 6 of algorithm NM and to add the following line

$$\boldsymbol{assign}\ \left\{r,e,c,s\right\}_j \in \left\{\left[0.5,1\right],\left[2,4\right],\left[0.25,0.5\right],\left[0.3,0.7\right]\right\} \tag{7}$$

just before line 10. The later means that the descent coefficients are recursively set to uniformly distributed random values within the designated ranges. With regard to the modern understanding of the Nelder-Mead algorithm, the descent coefficients must satisfy the conditions $r \in \left(0,+\infty\right)$, $e \in \left\{\left(1,+\infty\right) \cap \left(r,+\infty\right)\right\}$, $c \in [0,1]$ and $s \in [0,1]$. According to Lagarias [30], the condition $r \in \left(0,+\infty\right)$ is not stated explicitly in the original paper by Nelder and Mead but is implicit in the presentation of the original algorithm [20].

A significant role during an optimization is played by the corresponding optimization problem encoding key which orderly stores the independent variables of a fibre topology in a column vector (point $\mathbf{P}$ in $\Re^n$) that is read by the fibre simulator. The construction of the computation grid and/or the setting of the simulation parameters involved in the evaluation of the objective function are then based on the information encoded in the coordinates of $\mathbf{P}$. For fixed perimetric lines of laminas participating in a DCF cross section, the following encoding keys are used in this chapter:

$$\mathbf{P} = \left(y, z, y_{h,1}, z_{h,1}, y_{h,2}, z_{h,2}, \cdots y_{h,N}, z_{h,N}\right)^{\mathrm{T}} \tag{8}$$

in $\Re^{2(N+1)}$ for an inner cladding topology embedding N-holes and a single active core. The first pair $\left(y,z\right)$ of elements represents the coordinates of the core centroid on the cross section plane while each pair in the set $\left\{\left(y_{h,i}, z_{h,i}\right)\mid_{i=1,2,\ldots,N}\right\}$, appearing in $\mathbf{P}$, represents the centroid coordinates of the i-th hole. Equation (8) encodes a fibre topology according to the 'Offset' optimization scheme under which the centroid coordinates of each involved lamina is optimized independently. Following the same notation, the point

$$\mathbf{P} = \left(y, z, y_{h,1}, z_{h,1}, \cdots, y_{h,N}, z_{h,N}, d_1, \cdots, d_N\right)^{\mathrm{T}} \tag{9}$$

in $\Re^{3N+2}$ encodes the same topology under the 'Offset-Diameter' scheme that, in addition to (8), allows the simultaneous optimization of circular hole diameters or square hole side lengths. Furthermore, the point

$$\mathbf{P} = \left(y, z, y_{h,1}, z_{h,1}, \cdots, y_{h,N}, z_{h,N}, A_1, \cdots, A_N, B_1, \cdots, B_N\right)^{\mathrm{T}} \tag{10}$$

in $\Re^{2(2N+1)}$ allows, in addition to (8), the independent optimization of the horizontal and vertical characteristic dimension of each hole (major-minor axis of an ellipse for initially circular holes and length-height of a parallelepiped for initially square holes). Encoding keys (9) and (10) demonstrate the need for individually defined mesh sizes tailored to the domains within which the search for optimal values is desired. This view is reinforced by

$$\mathbf{P} = \left(y, z, y_{h1}, z_{h1}, \cdots, y_{hN}, z_{hN}, A_1, \cdots, A_N, B_1, \cdots, B_N, R_1, \cdots, R_N\right)^{\mathrm{T}} \tag{11}$$

that includes variables representing refractive index values. The independent variables in (11) are inhomogeneous not only in terms of corresponding mesh size and domain but also in physical meaning and units. In this case, point $\mathbf{P}$ in $\Re^{5N+2}$ represents the 'Offset-Major-Minor-Index' optimization scheme that expands (9) by including the refractive indices $\left\{R_i \,|_{i=1,2,\ldots,N}\right\}$ of dielectric holes embedded in the inner cladding.

Four groups of thirty optimizations are executed next in each of the $\Re^{10}$ and $\Re^{18}$ spaces in order to compare the performance of SNM variants with algorithm NM and in relation to the dimensionality of the optimization space. To avoid fragmentation, it is thought adequate for the current discussion to report that all optimizations were initiated from the same start point. The later represents a double-clad design with a polymer outer cladding and four rods embedded in the inner cladding (solid-state circular dielectric holes) assumed to be made of CBYA alloy glass with a refractive index of 1.430 [40,19].

Figure 1 demonstrates the $\Re^{10}$ sets of optimizations executed following different strategies. The type of search strategy is denoted by the {Initial simplex, Descent coefficients} pair where the letter D denotes deterministic as opposed to S denoting stochastic implementation. The initial circular inner cladding topology with centred core included four symmetrically embedded circular holes at the corners of a centred square and absorbed $P_{abs,tot}$ =8.60W. Due to the high number of optimizations required, lower resolution than in

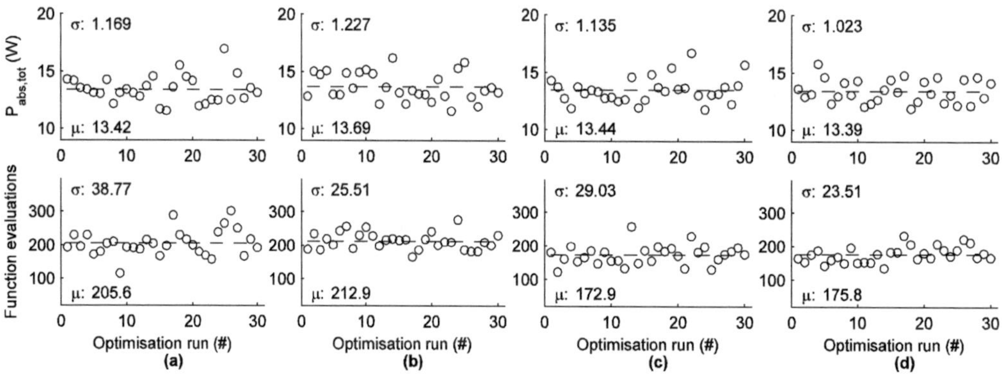

Fig. 1. Four groups of 30 optimizations in $\Re^{10}$ from the same starting point and under different optimization strategies: (a) SNM{D,D} ≡ NM (here for variable mesh size). (b) SNM{S,D}. (c) SNM{D,S}. (d) SNM{S,S}.

section 4 was used here after verifying that approximately the same trends were followed. The fibre was 1cm long and 126 rays carried the pump energy while the rest of the parameters were kept constant. The graphs along the first row of figure 1 plot the values of the total absorbed pump power (optimized as a function of the core and hole offsets) while those along the second row present the corresponding number of objective function evaluations recorded prior to convergence. The mean value (μ - dashed line) and standard deviation (σ) of the plotted values is also reported in each graph. Figure 1(a) (1st column) reveals the influence of the mesh size random variance on the NM results. The SNM{S, D} strategy results are shown in figure 1(b) where the initial simplex vertices are formed stochastically while the simplex descent is based on deterministic coefficient values. Figure 1(c) corresponds to the case of constant initial simplex (that of the first optimization in figure 1(a)) but this time the value of each optimization coefficient is recursively and randomly determined prior to each iteration during the simplex descent (SNM{D, S} strategy). Finally, figure 1(d) presents the results for the case where both the initial simplex and descent coefficients are randomly determined (SNM{S, S}). All optimizations in figure 1 were initiated from the same start point. The results variations observed in figures 1(b)-(d) are attributed solely to the stochastic nature of SNM while those in figure 1(a) originate from the mesh size variations. The best performing optimization strategy in $\Re^{10}$ can be chosen on different criteria serving different applications. The strategy that delivers acceptably optimized objective function values with minimum uncertainty is preferred here. It offers the smallest spread of objective function values for the second lowest mean number of function evaluations.

Figure 2 presents the corresponding study in $\Re^{18}$ where the area and the ellipticity of the four holes are optimized in addition to the core and hole offsets previously optimized in $\Re^{10}$. The four examined strategies are presented here in the same order as in figure 1. Strategy (b) is preferred in this case because it offered the highest mean absorption at the highest certainty. This comes at the cost of the maximum mean number of function evaluations exhibiting this time the strongest spread around their mean value. In both $\Re^{10}$ and $\Re^{18}$ spaces it appears that SNM{D, S} offers the lowest number of function evaluations and, more importantly, a slower growth in function evaluations with increasing dimensions [29]. This is a highly desired feature for the optimization of expensive objective functions.

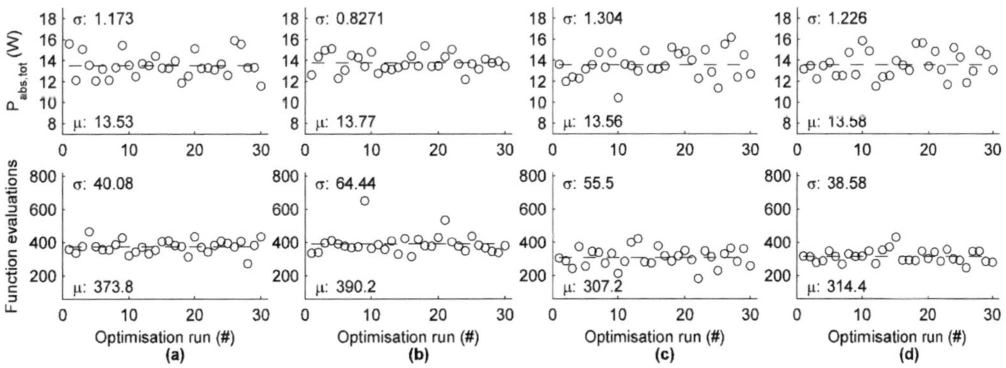

Fig. 2. Four groups of 30 optimizations in $\Re^{18}$ from the same starting point and under different optimization strategies: (a) SNM{D,D} ≡ NM. (b) SNM{S,D}. (c) SNM{D,S}. (d) SNM{S,S}.

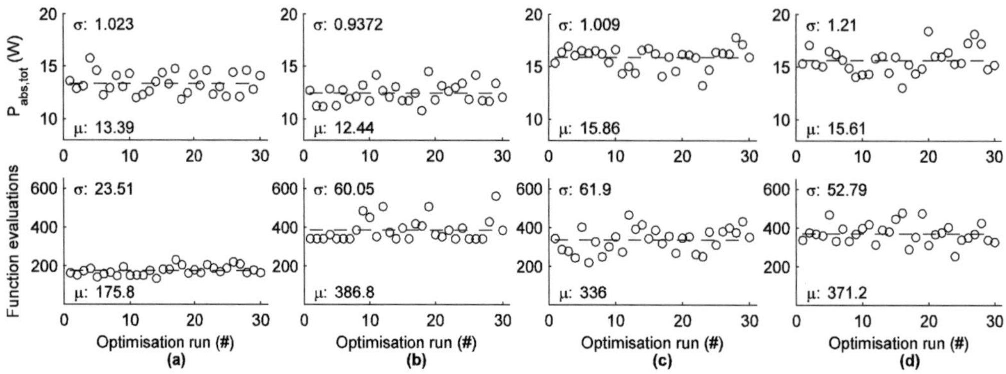

Fig. 3. Four groups of 30 optimizations in $\Re^{10}$ from the same starting point and driven by different algorithms: SNM{S,S}, GA{Np1}, GPS{Np1,2N}, MADS{Np1,2N}.

The fittest SNM strategies are compared next with three global optimization methods operating in $\Re^{10}$ and $\Re^{18}$ in figures 3 and 4 correspondingly. Figure 3(a) plots again the results for algorithm SNM{S, S} while figures 3(b)-(d) report the corresponding results from GA, GPS and MADS methods. The detailed set-up of each method is reported in section 4. The expression GA{Np1} denotes that each GA optimization started with (n+1) initial population members generated by random sampling of $\mathbf{\Omega}$. By GPS{Np1, 2N} it is meant that the search pattern includes $n+1$ directions and that the poll pattern matrix stores $2n$ directions. GPS and MADS algorithms implement two distinct steps namely the search and poll. The search step can be absent or be a pattern search or any other heuristic or Monte Carlo method [41] or preferably a method that uses inexpensive surrogates to approximate the objective function [42]. The search step adopted in this work implements a pattern search along the directions denoted by the column vectors in the pattern matrix

$$\Xi_{\text{GPS,Search}} \equiv \Xi_{\text{GPS,Np1}} = \begin{bmatrix} 1 & 0 & \cdots & 0 & -1 \\ 0 & 1 & \cdots & 0 & -1 \\ \vdots & \vdots & & \vdots & \vdots \\ 0 & 0 & \cdots & 1 & -1 \end{bmatrix}_{n\times(n+1)} . \quad (12)$$

The poll step is a compulsory pattern search that is closely linked to the convergence theory of pattern search algorithms [29]. The adopted poll patterns are represented by the column vectors in

$$\Xi_{\text{GPS,Poll}} \equiv \Xi_{\text{GPS,2N}} = \begin{bmatrix} 1 & 0 & \cdots & 0 & -1 & 0 & \cdots & 0 \\ 0 & 1 & \cdots & 0 & 0 & -1 & \cdots & 0 \\ \vdots & \vdots & & \vdots & \vdots & \vdots & & \vdots \\ 0 & 0 & \cdots & 1 & 0 & 0 & \cdots & -1 \end{bmatrix}_{n\times 2n} . \quad (13)$$

The GPS algorithm invokes the poll step only when the search step fails to produce a point in $\Re^n$ that improves the optimal function value recorded so far. After a poll step, the mesh size is adapted (contracts after an unsuccessful poll and expands after a successful poll) and

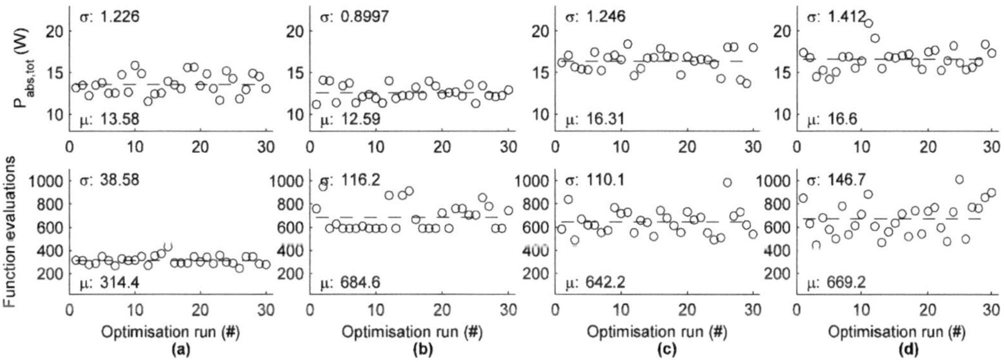

Fig. 4. Four groups of 30 optimizations in $\Re^{18}$ from the same starting point and driven by different algorithms: SNM{S,S}, GA{Np1}, GPS{Np1,2N}, MADS{Np1,2N}.

a new iteration begins. MADS is a stochastic form of GPS. The $\Xi_{\text{MADS,Search}} \equiv \Xi_{\text{MADS,Np1}}$ pattern matrix stores $n+1$ randomly generated column vectors while $\Xi_{\text{MADS,Poll}} \equiv \Xi_{\text{MADS,2N}}$ is generated using a random permutation of an $(n \times n)$ linearly independent lower triangular matrix. Both of the above patterns are regenerated prior to each iteration according to MALAB's documentation.

Before discussing the results in figure 3, it is informative to note that the variations in the GPS optimization results are due to the use of a different mesh size for each optimization whilst all other results exhibit variations originating from the stochastic nature of the corresponding algorithm. SNM, GA, GPS and MADS achieved an average objective improvement of 56%, 45%, 84% and 81% correspondingly. In $\Re^{18}$ (figure 4) the corresponding percentages are 58%, 46%, 90% and 93%. It is obvious at this stage that GPS and MADS managed to find optimizers located in deeper valleys indicating global convergence with higher probability than GA and SNM. On the computational expense front in $\Re^{10}$ the GA, GPS and MADS were correspondingly 121%, 91% and 111% more expensive than SNM while in $\Re^{18}$ they were 118%, 104% and 113% more expensive than SNM. The GA is consistently the most expensive method. The reported results agree with other benchmark results [43,44] and although GA promises global convergence when evolving a large initial population [45], it is not preferred here due to it being unsuitable for the optimization of expensive functions. The above analysis indicates that in the examined dimensions the most efficient strategy would be to use SNM as a first stage optimization tool, a numerical telescope that can relatively inexpensively designate the vicinity that offers the highest probability to contain a global optimizer. A second stage search with the significantly more expensive GPS of MADS methods is then justified in the SNM designated subdomains. Nevertheless, and in agreement with section 4 results, the SNM method offers the best case efficiency when it succeeds in finding a global optimizer.

3. Implicitly constrained zeroth-order optimization algorithms with simple bounds

The stochastic forms of NM proposed in this section solve optimization problems in higher dimensions that are difficult to treat or incompatible with GA, GPs and MADS. In addition they achieve global convergence at low computational cost. The 'Offset-Perimeter' encoding key ([21] gives a schematic representation) is used to map a variable perimetric line shape for each lamina comprising a fibre cross section. Under this scheme, the shape of a given cross section can be fully optimized but at a considerably higher computational cost. The dimensionality of the objective function domain increases by at least an order of magnitude depending on the sampling density of each lamina perimeter included in a cross section. A fibre topology that includes N-holes in the inner cladding is represented in $\Re^{2(n_c+n_{h1}+\ldots+n_{hN}+1)}$ by a single point of the form

$$\mathbf{P}=\left(y,z,y_{c,1},\cdots,y_{c,n_c},z_{c,1},\cdots,z_{c,n_c},y_{h1,1},\cdots,y_{h1,n_{h1}},z_{h1,1},\cdots,z_{h1,n_{h1}},\cdots,\right.$$
$$\left.y_{hN,1},\cdots,y_{hN,n_{h1}},z_{hN,1},\cdots,z_{hN,n_{hN}}\right)^{\mathrm{T}} \tag{14}$$

where n_c is the number of points that sample the inner cladding perimeter and $n_{hi}\,|_{i=1,2,\ldots,N}$ is the i-th hole perimetric point set population. The aforementioned encoding key includes the core centre coordinates but does not optimize the hole offsets. However, this is a feature that could be included into the coordinates set of $\mathbf{P}$.

Even for a low resolution polygonic approximation of a smooth perimeter, all the previously compared algorithms generate trial points that abruptly perturb a smooth start point and lack physical integrity and/or manufacturability. Examples of such perturbations are given in figures 5(a)-(c) showing typical trial points that the corresponding algorithms NM, GPS, MADS may generate during an optimization. Most representative trial points are those of the GA algorithm shown in figures 5(d), 5(e) for two different bounding configurations. It becomes obvious that GA scrambles randomly the start point coordinates failing to produce children or members of the initial population with physical integrity. Figure 5(e) suggests that a scheme capable of generating smooth perturbations is needed. An effort was

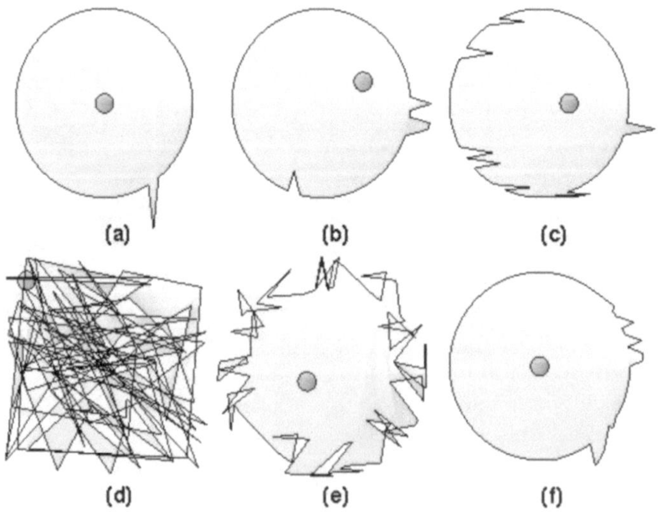

Fig. 5. Trial points (or initial population members). (a) NM. (b) GPS. (c) MADS. (d) GA with own population, bounded within [-4,4]mm (e) GA with own population, bounded within the ± 50μm zone from start point. (f) GA with PNM initial population.

made to construct suitable constrains that would force the mapped coordinates to change in groups forming smooth, local and able to propagate perturbations along the perimeter of a lamina but it appears that this is a non-functioning approach.

Although algorithm NM is not meant for constrained optimization it was found that it can be modified to perform implicitly constrained optimization. The outline of the related process is that after generating a suitable pattern, the vertices of the initial simplex could obey pattern imprinted constraints which propagate all the way to the convergence point at the end of a descent. The simplest implementation of the above concept is implemented via the perturbed Nelder-Mead (PNM) algorithm and by virtue of subalgorithms PNM_PattGener and PNM_SimplexGener. The former of the subalgorithms generates a pattern of the form

$$\Xi_{\mathrm{PNM}} = \begin{bmatrix} \nu_2 & \nu_1 & 0 & \dots & 0 \\ \nu_3 & \nu_2 & \nu_1 & \dots & 0 \\ 0 & \nu_3 & \nu_2 & \dots & 0 \\ 0 & 0 & \nu_3 & \dots & 0 \\ \vdots & \vdots & \vdots & & \vdots \\ 0 & 0 & 0 & \dots & \nu_1 \\ 0 & 0 & 0 & \dots & \nu_2 \end{bmatrix}_{n \times n} \tag{15}$$

when the perturbed element group population is $k = 3$. Equation (15) demonstrates essentially the propagation of a constant disturbance involving k-elements along the length of the additive identity ($n \times 1$ zero vector). In line 1 of PNM_PattGener, the set $\{\nu_q\} \in \left(0, 1/\sigma_{\mathrm{N}}\sqrt{2\pi}\right)|_{q=1,2,\dots,k}$ with statistical median $\nu_\mu = \nu_{(k+1)/2}$, follows the normal distribution $\mathrm{N}\left(\mu, \sigma_{\mathrm{N}}^2\right)$ where σ_N is the predefined standard deviation of the distribution with a probability density function shown in the line 1 comment. It is notable that $\Xi_{\mathrm{PNM}} \equiv \Xi_{\mathrm{NM}} = \mathbf{I}$ when $k = 1$ and $\sigma_N = 1/\sqrt{2\pi}$, indicating that Ξ_{PNM} is a generalization of

Algorithm PNM. The Perturbed Nelder-Mead (PNM) method:

$$\left[\mathbf{P}_l, \mathrm{f}_l, \sigma_j\right] = \mathrm{PNM}\left(\mathbf{P}_1, M, \sigma_{halt}, \mathbf{\Omega}, \sigma_N, k\right)$$

Input: (as in algorithm NM but with scalar mesh size and in addition, standard deviation of the normal distribution and perturbed element set population (odd positive integer: $k = 2\tau + 1; \tau \in Z^*$)). Output: [as in algorithm NM].

1 // same as in algorithm NM

2 ***call*** $\left[\Xi_{\mathrm{PNM}}\right] = \mathrm{PNM\_PattGener}\left(n, \sigma_N, k\right)$ // PNM pattern generation

3 ***call*** $\left[\mathbf{S}_0\right] = \mathrm{PNM\_SmxGener}\left(\mathbf{P}_1, \Xi_{\mathrm{PNM}}, M, n\right)$ // *initial simplex generation*

1-13 // same as in algorithm NM

Subalgorithm PNM_PattGener. Perturbed Nelder-Mead (PNM) pattern generation:

$$[\Xi_{\text{PNM}}] = \text{PNM\_PattGener}(n, \sigma_N, k)$$

Input: (number of variables, standard deviation of the normal distribution, perturbed element set population (odd positive integer: $k = 2\tau + 1; \tau \in Z^*$)). Output: [PNM pattern matrix].

$\mathbf{N} := [\nu_1 \nu_2 \cdots \nu_k]^{\text{T}} |_{k=2\tau+1; \tau \in Z^*}$ //where $\{\nu_q |_{q=1,2,\ldots,k}\} = \left(1/\sigma_{\text{N}}\sqrt{2\pi}\right)\exp\left[-(q-\mu)^2\left(2\sigma_{\text{N}}^2\right)^{-1}\right]$

$\varepsilon := (k-1)/2$ // *number of variables in either bell shape branch excluding the median* (μ)

for each PNM pattern-matrix column in the set $\{\xi_i |_{i=1,2,3,\ldots,n}\}$

$\quad \xi_i := (\xi_1, \xi_2, \ldots, \xi_n)^{\text{T}} \equiv (0,0,\ldots,0)^{\text{T}}$ // *additive identity* ($n \times 1$ *zero vector*)

$\quad \left[\left(\xi_{i-\varepsilon}, \xi_{i-(\varepsilon-1)}, \cdots, \xi_{i-1}, \xi_i, \xi_{i+1}, \cdots, \xi_{i+(\varepsilon-1)}, \xi_{i+\varepsilon}\right)^{\text{T}}\right]_{k \times 1} := \mathbf{N}$ // *bell shaped perturbation*

endfor

$\Xi_{\text{PNM}} := (\xi_1, \xi_2, \cdots, \xi_n)_{n \times n}$ // *PNM pattern matrix*

return Ξ_{PNM} //*output.*

Subalgorithm PNM_SmxGener. PNM initial simplex generation:

$$[\mathbf{S}_0] = \text{PNM\_SmxGener}(\mathbf{P}_1, \Xi_{\text{PNM}}, M, n)$$

Input: (start point $\mathbf{P}_1$, PNM pattern, mesh size and length of $\mathbf{P}_1$). Output: [initial simplex matrix].

for each simplex vertex in the set $\{\mathbf{P}_i |_{i=2,3,\ldots,n+1}\}$

$\quad \mathbf{P}_i := \mathbf{P}_1 + M(1/\xi_{\max,i-1})\xi_{i-1}$

$\quad\quad$ // *where,* $\xi_{\max,i-1} = \max\{\xi_{w,i-1} |_{w=1,2,\ldots,n}\}$

endfor

$\mathbf{S}_0 := [\mathbf{P}_1 \mathbf{P}_2 \cdots \mathbf{P}_{n+1}]_{n \times (n+1)} |_{\text{vol}(\mathbf{S}_0)>0}$

return $\mathbf{S}_0$ // *output.*

Ξ_{NM}. Subalgorithm PNM_SmxGener returns the initial simplex vertices as a result of the superposition between the start point ($\mathbf{P}_1$) and the search directions stored in Ξ_{PNM}. The practical outcome is the propagation of a bell-shaped perturbation along the elements in $\mathbf{P}_1$ and is illustrated in figure 6 which assumes that $k = 3$ and shows clearly the n-steps of the perturbation propagation process which generates the initial simplex vertices $\mathbf{P}_2$ to $\mathbf{P}_{n+1}$. Also clearly demonstrated is that a set of vertices created at the start and the end of the process bare a perturbation that is abrupt at one end. This is a drawback of the described technique that has a small overall effect though due to the comparatively small number of vertices baring such a non-smooth perturbation. Soon after the start of the simplex decent, the abruptly perturbed vertices are naturally substituted by newly discovered and better performing smoothly perturbed vertices. The only damage made is the comparatively small reduction in the probability to capture optimal vertices right from the start of the process. The height of the bell shape is controlled, in subalgorithm PNM_SmxGener, via the mesh size M while its full-width half-maximum is set via σ_N. The factor $1/\xi_{\max}$, used in line 2, normalizes the bell-shaped perturbation, stored in the pattern, to the maximum value of 1 in order to scale the perturbation height to the predefined mesh size M. A set of decoded initial simplex vertices is given in figure 7(a) where the start point was a cross section with circular inner cladding embedding an offset circular hole and an offset core. For completeness, figure 5(f) shows a child produced by GA after having been initiated with the same initial population that comprised the initial simplex vertices in PNM. Here the child's features have been improved compared to figures 5(d), 5(e) but still the GA algorithm appears unable to generate a smooth optimizer.

Following the proposal of SNM method in section 2, algorithm PNM naturally suggests its stochastic version SPNM which can be implemented by the simultaneous random assignment of (M, σ_N) and/or the simplex descent coefficients. The random assignment of (σ_N, M) is implemented just before the generation of Ξ_{SPNM} which now stores, as opposed to Ξ_{PNM}, a set of directions that still smoothly but this time randomly perturb the

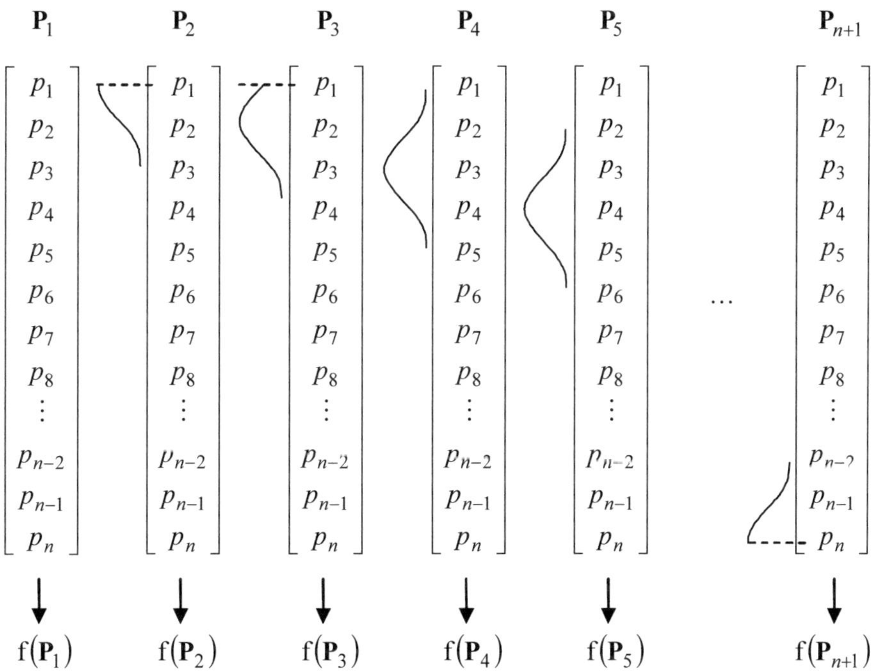

Fig. 6. Illustration of the bell shape propagation in the nonrandomized initial simplex generation scheme for perturbed vertex elements number $k = 3$. Under this scheme, the shape of the perturbation propagates along the whole vertex in n-steps while preserving its shape.

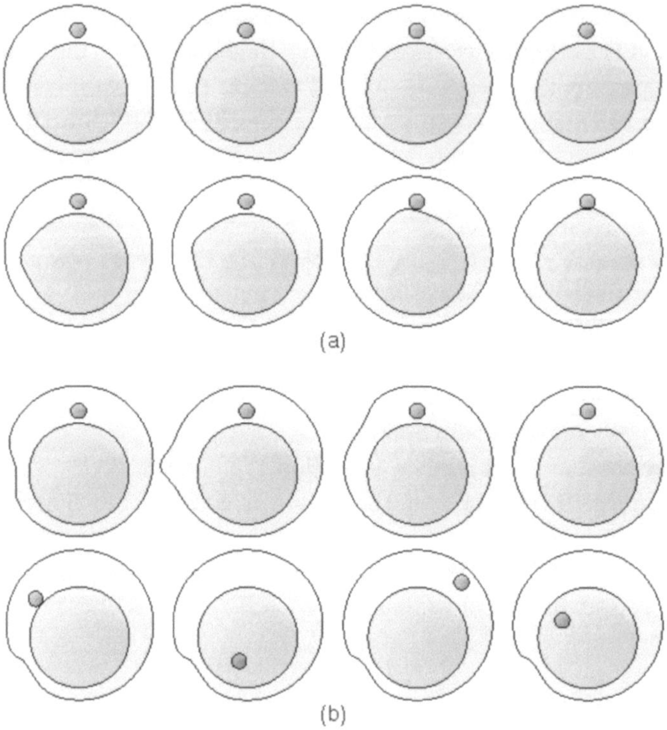

Fig. 7. Propagation instances of a perturbation envelope. (a) PNM method. (b) ESPNM method stochastic envelope (1st row) and random core offsets inside a selected vertex (importance sampling- 2nd row).

additive identity. Both PNM and SPNM algorithms still call the same iteration subalgorithm (NM_Step) as NM and SNM do. The assignment of the random M, σ_N parameter values is implemented as in algorithm ESPNM (enhanced stochastically permuted NM) proposed next. Algorithm ESPNM enhances SPNM method by dynamically and preferentially forming the initial and also intermediate (during a descent) simplices as well as conditionally and adaptively regenerating the intermediate simplices. The implementation of ESPNM method is described in algorithm ESPNM and associated subalgorithms ESPNM_PattGener, ESPNM_SmxObjGener and ESPNM_Step. Subalgorithm ESPNM_PattGrner generates a simplex formation pattern of the type

$$\Xi_{\mathrm{ESPNM}} = \begin{bmatrix} v_{1,1} & 0 & \cdots & 0 & 1 & \cdots & 1 \\ \vdots & v_{1,2} & \cdots & 0 & 1 & \cdots & 1 \\ v_{k,1} & \vdots & & 0 & 0 & \cdots & 0 \\ 0 & v_{k,2} & \cdots & 0 & 0 & \cdots & 0 \\ \vdots & \vdots & & \vdots & \vdots & & \vdots \\ 0 & 0 & \cdots & v_{1,n-(k-1)} & 0 & \cdots & 0 \\ \vdots & \vdots & & \vdots & 0 & \cdots & 0 \\ 0 & 0 & \cdots & v_{k,n-(k-1)} & 0 & \cdots & 0 \end{bmatrix}_{n\times n} . \tag{16}$$

Algorithm ESPNM. Enhanced stochastically perturbed Nelder-Mead (ESPNM) method:

$$\left[\mathbf{P}_l, \mathrm{f}_l, \sigma_j\right] = \mathrm{ESPNM}\left(\mathbf{P}_1, M, \sigma_{halt}, \mathbf{\Omega}, \sigma_{\mathrm{N}}, k, \upsilon_m\right)$$

Input: (as in algorithm PNM, max consecutive shrinkages(>=2)). Output: [as in algorithm NM].

$j := 0$ // *iteration index*

$\left[\Xi_{\mathrm{ESPNM}}\right] = \mathrm{ESPNM\_PattGener}\left(n, \sigma_N, k\right)$ // stochastically permuted pattern

call $\left[\mathbf{S}_j, \mathbf{F}_j\right] = \mathrm{ESPNM\_SmxObjGener}\left(\mathbf{P}_1, \Xi_{\mathrm{ESPNM}}, \mathbf{\Omega}, M, n, k\right)$ // stochastic simplex

$\upsilon_c := 0$ // *consecutive shrinkages number initialization*

call $\left[\mathrm{f}_h, \mathrm{f}_l, \mathbf{P}_h, \mathbf{P}_l, \bar{\mathrm{f}}, \bar{\mathbf{P}}\right] = \mathrm{SmxAssessm}\left(\mathbf{S}_j, \mathbf{F}_j\right)$ // *current simplex (* $\mathbf{S}_j$ *) assessment*

while $\left(\sigma_j \geq \sigma_{halt}\right)$ // *where,* $\sigma_j = \left(\left\langle\left(\mathrm{f}_i - \bar{\mathrm{f}}\right)^2 \big|_{i=1,2,\ldots,n+1; i\neq h}\right\rangle\right)^{1/2}$ *(descent halting criterion)*

  $j := j + 1$ // increment

  assign $\{r, e, c, s\}_j \in \{[0.5,1], [2,4], [0.25,0.5], [0.3,0.7]\}$ // *random, uniformly distributed*

  call

$\left[\mathbf{S}_j, \mathbf{F}_j, step, \upsilon_c\right] = \mathrm{ESPNM\_Step}\left(\mathbf{P}_h, \mathbf{P}_l, \bar{\mathbf{P}}, \mathbf{\Omega}, f_h, f_l, r, e, c, s, \mathbf{S}_j, \mathbf{F}_j, \mathbf{P}_1, \Xi_{\mathrm{ESPNM}}, M, n, k, \upsilon_c, \upsilon_m\right)$

call $\left[\mathrm{f}_h, \mathrm{f}_l, \mathbf{P}_h, \mathbf{P}_l, \bar{\mathrm{f}}, \bar{\mathbf{P}}\right] = \mathrm{SmxAssessm}\left(\mathbf{S}, \mathbf{F}\right)$ // simplex assessment

endwhile // *end of iteration loop*

return $\mathbf{P}_l, f_l, \sigma_j$ // *output.*

The concept behind Ξ_{ESPNM} is that it stores a leftmost set of direction vectors that propagate the perturbation envelope starting from the first element in $\mathbf{P}_1$ (1st column of Ξ_{ESPNM}) and stopping when the opposite end of the envelope reaches the last element ($\left[n-(k-1)\right]$-th column). In this way there remain $k-1$ unfilled columns in Ξ_{ESPNM} ($\left[n-(k-2)\right]$-th to n-th column) that are assigned as shown. The later, in conjunction with subalgorithm ESPNM_SmxObjGener, will allow the selection of the best vertex so far ($\mathbf{P}_{opt}$) and its subsequent perturbation with emphasis to its most influential elements (importance sampling). In this case, the aforementioned influential elements are the first two chosen on the basis that they control the offset of the active core where the pump photons absorption takes place. Subalgorithm ESPNM_SmxObjGener describes the stochastic assignment of each perturbation propagation instance along $\mathbf{P}_1$ (line 4). In addition to the simplex matrix it also returns the objective matrix since the simplex is generated dynamically based on the feedback from the function evaluations. Then it evaluates the objective function at the perturbed vertices and selects the fittest ($\mathbf{P}_{opt}$) amongst them (line 8). Its final operation is to randomly scramble the core offset along positive directions within the optimal cross section, represented by the decoded $\mathbf{P}_{opt}$, in search for objective improving coordinates (lines 9-13). The initial polytope generated in this way is again a numerically non-degenerate structure.

Subalgorithm ESPNM_PattGener. ESPNM pattern generation:

$$\left[\Xi_{\text{ESPNM}}\right] = \text{ESPNM\_PattGener}\left(n, \sigma_N, k\right)$$

Input: (number of variables, maximum standard deviation of the normal distribution and number of perturbed variables (odd positive integer)). Output: [EPSNM pattern matrix].

$\varepsilon := (k-1)/2$ // number of variables in either branch of the normal distribution

assign $\left\{\sigma_{\text{N},i}\,|_{i=1,2,\ldots,n-2\varepsilon}\right\} \in \left[\sigma_{\text{N}}/2, \sigma_{\text{N}}\right]$ // uniformly distributed random values

for each ESPNM pattern matrix column vector in the set $\left\{\xi_{i-\varepsilon}\,|_{i=\varepsilon+1,\ldots,n-\varepsilon}\right\}$

  $\mathbf{N}_{i-\varepsilon} := \left(\nu_1, \nu_2, \cdots, \nu_k\right)^{\text{T}}\,|_{k=2\tau+1;\tau\in Z^*}$ // $\left\{\nu_q\,|_{q=1,2,\ldots,k}\right\} = \text{N}\left(\mu, \sigma^2_{\text{N},i-\varepsilon}\right) \in \left(0, 1/\sigma_{\text{N},i-\varepsilon}\sqrt{2\pi}\right)$

  $\xi_{i-\varepsilon} := \left(\xi_1, \xi_2, \cdots, \xi_n\right)^{\text{T}} \equiv \left(0, 0, \ldots, 0\right)^{\text{T}}$ // additive identity ($n \times 1$ zero vector)

  $\left[\left(\xi_{i-\varepsilon}, \xi_{i-(\varepsilon-1)}, \cdots, \xi_{i-1}, \xi_i, \xi_{i+1}, \cdots, \xi_{i+(\varepsilon-1)}, \xi_{i+\varepsilon}\right)^{\text{T}}\right]_{k\times 1} := \mathbf{N}_{i-\varepsilon}$ // bell shaped perturbation

endfor

for each ESPNM pattern matrix columns in the set $\left\{\xi_i\,|_{i=n-(k-2), n-(k-3), \ldots, n}\right\}$ // $k-1$ vectors

  $\xi_i := \left(\xi_1, \xi_2, \cdots, \xi_n\right)^{\text{T}} = \left[\left(1, 1, 0, 0, \ldots, 0\right)\right]^{\text{T}}$ // preferential perturbation pattern vectors

endfor

$\Xi_{\text{ESPNM}} := \left(\xi_1, \xi_2, \cdots, \xi_n\right)_{n\times n}$ // *ESPNM pattern matrix*

return Ξ_{ESPNM} // output.

Using this technique in high dimensions means that the initial simplex is formed by a search process with an extra element of intelligence which is the selective collection of information within a subset of dimensions offering higher probability to deliver substantially optimized objective function values and\or second order information. In other words, a subset of simplex vertices record a certain space of higher interest, while keeping the coordinates in the rest of the dimensions frozen, adding an element of exploratory search right from the start of the process. The aforementioned assignment process of the initial simplex is graphically illustrated in figure 8 for a small number of perturbed elements $k=5$ selected to assist the demonstration of the selective randomization concept. It is also assumed there that $\mathbf{P}_3$ performed optimally amongst the vertices from $\mathbf{P}_1$ to $\mathbf{P}_{n+1-(k-1)}$ and as shown it is vertex $\mathbf{P}_3$ that is further processed and used as the basis to assign the remaining $k-1$ vertices of the initial simplex ($\mathbf{S}_0$).The top two elements of each of the vertices $\mathbf{P}_{n+1-(k-2)}$ to $\mathbf{P}_{n+1}$ in figure 8 show the way the represented core centre coordinates are randomly altered to capture further and better focused objective function information in the sub-dimensions of higher probability to capture optimal objective function values. A schematic visualization of the above process is given in figure 7(b) where the cross sections shown

Subalgorithm ESPNM_SmxObjGener. ESPNM simplex, objective matrices generation:

$$[\mathbf{S},\mathbf{F}] = \text{ESPNM\_SmxObjGener}(\mathbf{P}_1, \Xi_{\text{ESPNM}}, \mathbf{\Omega}, M, n, k)$$

Input: (start point $\mathbf{P}_1$*, ESPNM pattern ,optimization domain, mesh size, length of* $\mathbf{P}_1$ *and number of perturbed variables). Output: [simplex and objective matrices].*

assign $\left\{a_i \mid_{i=1,2,\ldots,n-(k-1)}\right\} \in [-M, M]$ *// uniformly distributed random bell-amplitude values*

assign $\left\{m_i \mid_{i=1,2,\ldots,2(k-1)}\right\} \in [-M, M]$ *// uniformly distributed random mesh size values*

for each simplex vertex in the set $\left\{\mathbf{P}_i \mid_{i=2,3,\ldots,(n+1)-(k-1)}\right\}$ *// perturbation propagation loop*

    $\mathbf{P}_i := \mathbf{P}_1 + a_i\left(1/\xi_{\max,i-1}\right)\boldsymbol{\xi}_{i-1}$ *//where,* $\xi_{\max,i-1} = \max\left\{\xi_{w,i-1} \mid_{w=1,2,\ldots,n}\right\}$

    call $[f_i] = \text{FuncEval}(\mathbf{P}_i, \mathbf{\Omega})$ *// function evaluation at the simplex vertices*

endfor

call $[f_1] = \text{FuncEval}(\mathbf{P}_1, \mathbf{\Omega})$ *// function evaluation at the start point*

$f_{opt} := \min\left\{f_i \mid i = 1,2,\ldots,(n+1)-(k-1)\right\}$; ***assign*** $\mathbf{P}_{opt} \mid_{f_{opt}=f(\mathbf{P}_{opt})}$ *// optimal vertex selection*

for each simplex vertex in the set $\left\{\mathbf{P}_i \mid_{i=(n+1)-(k-2),(n+1)-(k-3),\ldots,n+1}\right\}$

    $\xi_{1,i-1} := \xi_{1,i-1} m_{2(i-n+k-2)-1}$; $\xi_{2,i-1} := \xi_{2,i-1} m_{2(i-n+k-2)}$

    $\mathbf{P}_i := \mathbf{P}_{opt} + \boldsymbol{\xi}_{i-1}$ *// stochastic perturbation of core centre coordinates in selected* $\mathbf{P}_{opt}$

    call $[f_i] = \text{FuncEval}(\mathbf{P}_i, \mathbf{\Omega})$ *// function evaluation at the perturbed* $\mathbf{P}_{opt}$

endfor

$\mathbf{S} := \left[\mathbf{P}_1 \mathbf{P}_2 \cdots \mathbf{P}_{n+1}\right]_{n\times(n+1)} \mid_{\text{vol}(\mathbf{S})>0}$; $\mathbf{F} := \left[f_1 f_2 \cdots f_{n+1}\right]_{1\times(n+1)}$ *// simplex; objective matrices*

return $\mathbf{S},\mathbf{F}$ *// output.*

along the first row are instances of the stochastic bell shape propagation while the second row shows the importance sampling process [46] which is practically a uniformly random search for improved core offsets in the vicinity of $\mathbf{P}_{opt}$. The aforementioned process is invoked once by algorithm ESPNM during the initial simplex ($\mathbf{S}_0$) generation at line 3 and then recursively during the line search process (simplex descent) at line 21 of subalgorithm ESPNM_Step. The later is executed conditionally in the vicinity of the currently best vertex ($\mathbf{P}_l$) when subsequent shrinkages are recorded indicating descent on a problematic landscape (noisy, discontinuous, nonconvex with many narrow and deep basins). It is also executed adaptively by halving the mesh size prior each new simplex generation around the preserved $\mathbf{P}_l$ in order to accelerate convergence (ESPNM_Step line 20). This process resembles the mesh size contraction in GPS and MADS and places ESPNM in the class of methods that optimize a function by iterative processes executed on a tower of meshes [29]. An important aspect of the initial simplex generation at line 3 of algorithm ESPNM is to choose appropriate values for M and σ_N parameters such that the initial simplex spans an

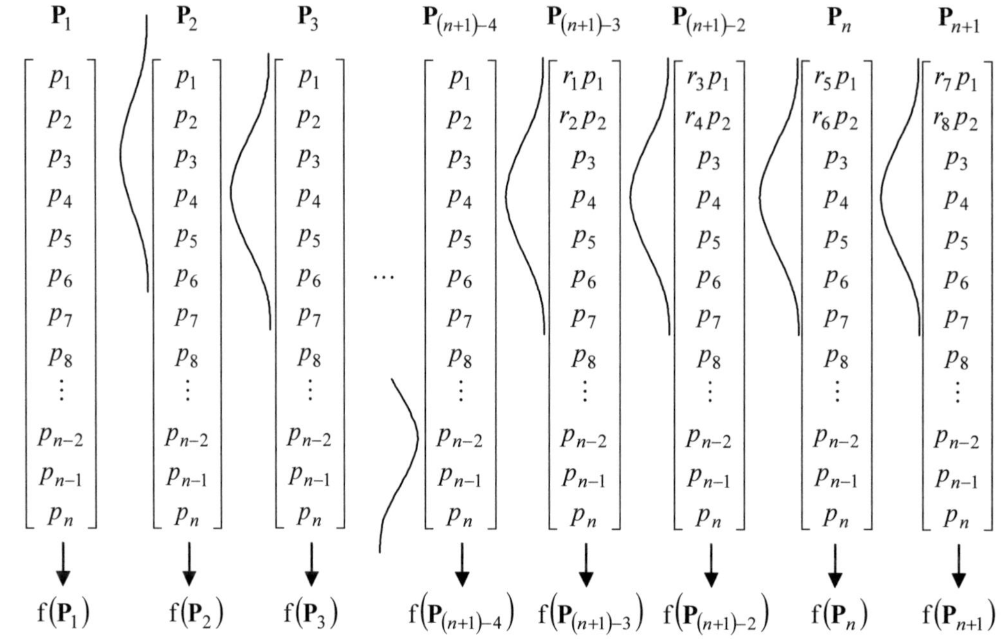

Fig. 8. Illustration of the selectively randomized initial simplex generation scheme for perturbed vertex elements number $k = 5$. The last four ($k-1$) simplex vertices are versions of the vertex ($\mathbf{P}_3$) that was the optimal point found. containing the core centre coordinates altered by the set of normally distributed pseudorandom coefficients $\{r_1, r_2, \dots, r_8\}$.

area that includes many valleys (nonconvex objective function) as opposed to forming a small initial simplex with all its vertices located inside a single valley. The latter will almost certainly result in local convergence.

Subalgorithm ESPNM_Step implements a line search operation that guides the simplex when descending in $\Re^n$. The aforementioned subalgorithm NM_Step is a subset of ESPNM_Step formed by removing the if-then-else-endif module (lines 19-25) after keeping lines 23 and 24. It includes a stronger expansion condition (line 4) and strict inequalities (lines 11 and 12). Also, the seven input arguments are removed as well as the last output argument. In previous work [21], the weaker expansion condition was used in NM_step($f_e < f_l$ as in the original algorithm [20]).

Subalgorithm ESPNM_Step. Interpretation of the ESPNM step operation:

$$\left[\mathbf{S}_j, \mathbf{F}_j, step, \upsilon_c\right] = \text{ESPNM\_Step}\left(\mathbf{P}_h, \mathbf{P}_l, \overline{\mathbf{P}}, \boldsymbol{\Omega}, f_h, f_l, r, e, c, s, \mathbf{S}_j, \mathbf{F}_j, \mathbf{P}_1, \Xi_{\text{ESPNM}}, M, n, k, \upsilon_c, \upsilon_m\right)$$

Input: (worse, best points, centre of polytope excluding $\mathbf{P}_h$*, bounds, highest, lowest function values, reflection, expansion, contraction, shrinkage coefficients, current simplex, objective matrices, start point* $\mathbf{P}_1$*, ESPNM pattern, mesh size, length of* $\mathbf{P}_1$*, number of perturbed variables, consecutive and max consecutive shrinkages). Output: [current simplex, objective matrices, operation step, consecutive shrinkages].*

1 $\mathbf{P}_r := (1+r)\overline{\mathbf{P}} - r\mathbf{P}_h$; ***call*** $[f_r] = \text{FuncEval}(\mathbf{P}_r, \mathbf{\Omega})$ // *calculate; evaluate reflection point*
2 ***if*** $(f_r < f_l)$ ***then***
3     $\mathbf{P}_e := e\mathbf{P}_r + (1-e)\overline{\mathbf{P}}$; ***call*** $[f_e] = \text{FuncEval}(\mathbf{P}_e, \mathbf{\Omega})$ //*calculate; evaluate expansion point*
4   ***if*** $[(f_e < f_l)\text{AND}(f_e < f_r)]$ ***then*** // *stronger expansion condition (modern NM)*
5         $\mathbf{P}_h := \mathbf{P}_e$ in $\mathbf{S}_j$; $f_h := f_e$ in $\mathbf{F}_j$; *step* := 'expansion' // *expansion operation*
6   ***else***
7   s $\mathbf{P}_h := \mathbf{P}_r$ in $\mathbf{S}_j$; $f_h := f_r$ in $\mathbf{F}_j$; *step* := 'reflection' // *reflection*
8   ***endif***
9 ***else***
10     $f_m := \max\{f_i \,|_{i=1,2,\ldots,n+1;\, i\neq h}\}$
11   ***if*** $(f_r \geq f_m)$ ***then***
12   ***if*** $(f_r < f_h)$ ***then***
13             $\mathbf{P}_h := \mathbf{P}_r$ // improved $\mathbf{P}_h$ to be used in line 16
14             $\mathbf{P}_h := \mathbf{P}_r$ in $\mathbf{S}_j$; $f_h := f_r$ in $\mathbf{F}_j$; *step* := 'reflection' // *reflection*
15   ***endif***
16         $\mathbf{P}_c := c\mathbf{P}_h + (1-c)\overline{\mathbf{P}}$; ***call*** $[f_c] = \text{FuncEval}(\mathbf{P}_c, \mathbf{\Omega})$ // *contraction point*
17   ***if*** $(f_c > f_h)$ ***then***
18             $\{\mathbf{P}_i := c(\mathbf{P}_i + \mathbf{P}_l)\,|_{i=1,2,\ldots,n+1;\, i\neq l}\}$; *step* := 'shrinkage' ; $\upsilon_c := \upsilon_c + 1$ // *shrinkage*
19   ***if*** $(\upsilon_{cons} = \upsilon_{\max})$ ***then***
20                 $\mathbf{P}_1 := \mathbf{P}_l$; $M := M/2$; $\upsilon_c := 0$ // *preservation; adaptation; reset*
21   ***call*** $[\mathbf{S}_j, \mathbf{F}_j] = \text{ESPNM\_SmxObjGener}(\mathbf{P}_1, \Xi_{\text{ESPNM}}, \mathbf{\Omega}, M, n, k)$ // *new smx*
22   ***else***
23   ***for*** each $\{\mathbf{P}_i \,|_{i=1,2,\ldots,n+1;\, i\neq l}\}$ ***call*** $[f_i] = \text{FuncEval}(\mathbf{P}_i, \mathbf{\Omega})$ ***endfor***
24                 $\mathbf{F}_j := [f_1\, f_2 \cdots f_{n+1}]_{1\times(n+1)}$ // evaluation of shrunk simplex
25   ***endif***
26   ***else***
27             $\mathbf{P}_h := \mathbf{P}_c$ in $\mathbf{S}_j$; $f_h := f_c$ in $\mathbf{F}_j$; *step* := 'contraction' // *contraction*
28   ***endif***
29   ***else***
30             $\mathbf{P}_h := \mathbf{P}_r$ in $\mathbf{S}_j$; $f_h := f_r$ in $\mathbf{F}_j$; *step* := 'reflection' // *reflection*
31   ***endif***
32 ***endif***
33 ***return*** $\mathbf{S}_j$, $\mathbf{F}_j$, *step* , υ_c // output.

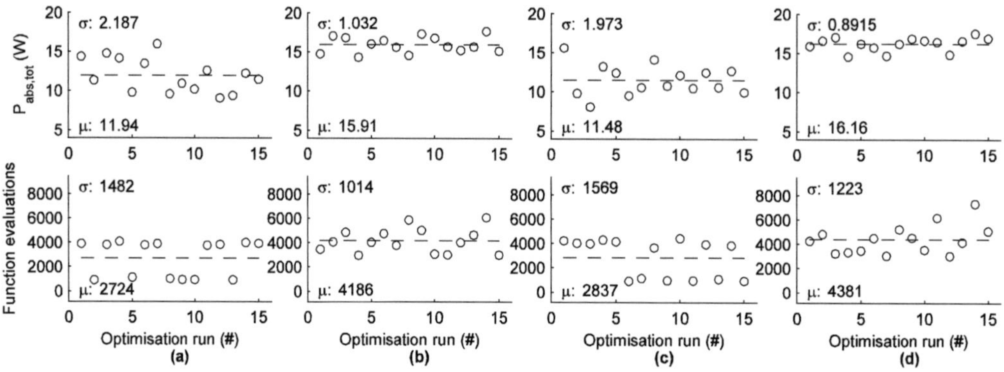

Fig. 9. Four groups of 15 optimizations in $\Re^{182}$ from the same starting point and driven by different algorithms: (a) SPNM{D,D} ≡ PNM. (b) ESPNM{S,D}. (c) SPNM{D,S}. (d) ESPNM{S,S}.

Figure 9 presents a comparison of the algorithms proposed in this section. The {*, *} notation denotes {simplex generation, descent coefficients} pairs that can be either deterministically (D) or stochastically (S) assigned. The corresponding start point was a circular non-holey inner cladding with a centred core which absorbed 5.6W of pump power. The reported results indicate that the best performing algorithm is ESPNM{S, S} because it delivered, on average, the optimal function values exhibiting at the same time the lowest spread around their mean value. It demonstrated a 152% improvement of the mean $P_{abs,tot}$ compared to the 113% offered by PNM for a 61% increase in computation cost over PNM.

4. Optimization results

The inner cladding of a conventional DCF has a numerical aperture (NA) of 0.48 while the core NA is 0.175. The core doping density is 20,000ppm-by-volume, the launched pump power is 100W and the fibre length is 10cm for all the optimization results presented in this section. The pump light has a random modal content, its energy is propagated via 288 rays in 10 time steps and the absorption computation grid of the active core is comprised of 100 volume elements. The pump light wavelength is λ_p =975nm at which the Yb^{+3} (Er^{+3}-Yb^{+3} ion system) absorption cross section is $2.1\times10^{-24}\mathrm{m}^2$. The simulated fibres are single-end pumped by a 600μm diameter pure silica core (standard fibre bundled pump delivery fibre) and NA of 0.48 when pumping a fibre with polymer outer clad or it is assumed to be surrounded by an air outer cladding when pumping a double-clad fibre which also has an air outer cladding. This work focuses on a set of fibre topologies that are thoroughly optimized and computationally compared on a common basis that avoids confusion and develops intuition into their absorption trends. Although space restrictions did not allow comprehensive parametric optimization, a sample of parametric optimization results in $\Re^{10}$ is presented in figure 10 which shows a set of fairly similar optimizers exhibiting almost identical absorption characteristics. Algorithm NM converged to the reported shapes for different pairs of fibre length and pump power values correspondingly. The optimization process started from the same initial cross section and run under the same settings. Figure 10 demonstrates the generality of the optimization results reported in tables 1-4 which are approximately valid within the ranges [0.1, 1]W and [0.1, 1]m of pump power and fibre length correspondingly.

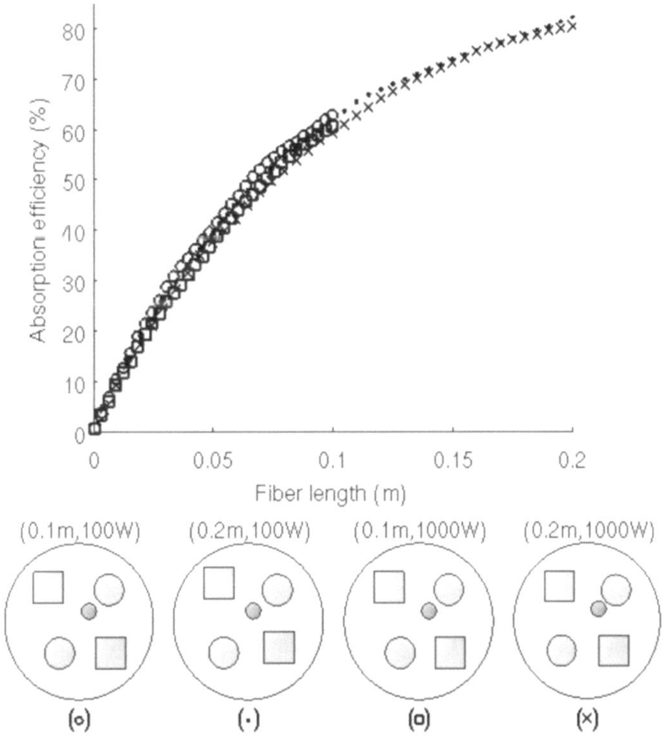

Fig. 10. Absorption performance of four convergence points resulting from optimization runs under different fibre length and pump power values.

The computing platform used for the optimizations reported in this chapter, is the same as the platform described in reference [19]. The CPU time consumed for the objective function evaluation at each start point is shown in the tables of this chapter for a more informative presentation. The strongest influence on the recorded CPU times originates from the total number of scattering operations which fluctuates slightly during an optimization. The computational efficiency of the 3-D fibre simulation method used was compared in [19] with other methods reported in the literature.

All Mote Carlo algorithms proposed in this chapter made use of the built-in MATLAB random number generator to produce the required sequences of uniformly distributed pseudorandom numbers. The built in function is based on the random number generator by Marsaglia and Zaman [47] which was specifically designed to produce floating point values and uses a lagged Fibonacci generator with a cache of 32 floating point numbers between 0 and 1 combined with a separate, independent random integer generator based on bitwise logical operations. As a result, MATLAB's built-in generator has a period of 2^{1492} (number of values produced before the sequence begins to repeat itself) and can theoretically generate all numbers between 2^{-53} and $1-2^{-53}$, all with equal probability to occur.

Figure 11 demonstrates the effort to optimize the offset of the core inside a circular (1st row figures) and a square (2nd row figures) inner cladding. The CPU time required for a single function evaluation for the circular fibre was approximately 28s on the MATLAB platform. Figures 11(a) and 11(e) show the corresponding pump power absorption surfaces generated by sampling the total absorbed pump power ($P_{abs,tot}$) calculated at 49 nodes (by moving

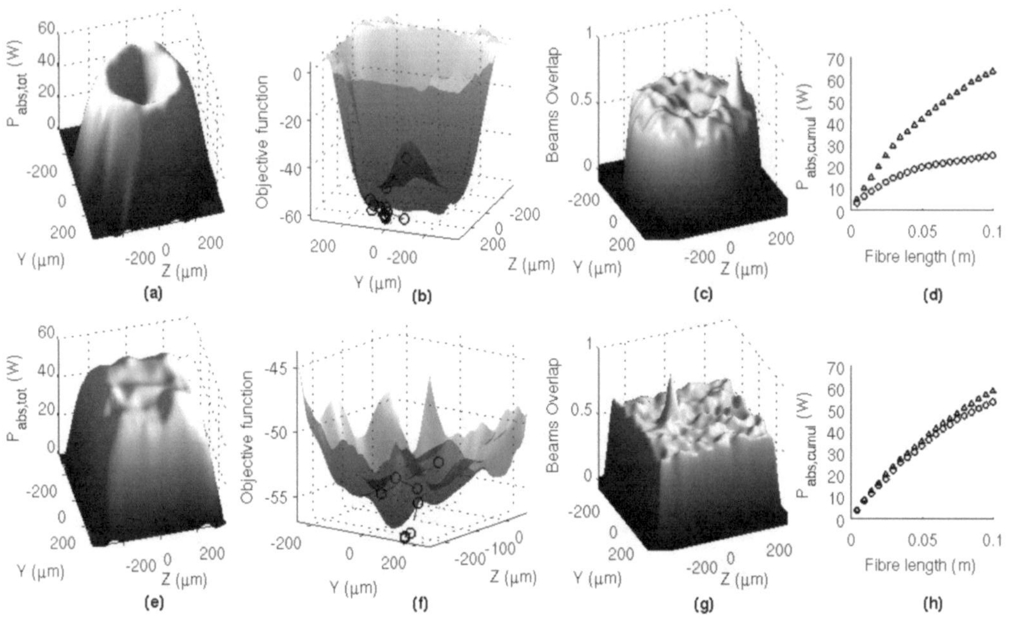

Fig. 11. Core offset optimization (in $\Re^2$) inside a circular (1st row) and a square inner-clad (2nd row). (a),(e) Transverse distribution of total absorbed power. (b),(f) Interpolated objective function surface and simplex descent path on the actual surface. (c),(g) Beam overlap images. (d),(h) Cumulative absorption of the initial guess (circles) and the convergence point (triangles).

the core on each one) of a Cartesian grid covering a square area 4900μm² and interpolating the values on a 784 nodes grid covering the same area. This information is plotted here in order to observe the behaviour of the referred to as the modern interpretation of the Nelder-Mead algorithm adopted in this work. For the circular inner cladding, the $P_{abs,tot}$ values exhibit the well known symmetrical distribution around the centre of the cross section with the peak appearing near the inner-to-outer cladding interface. Figure 11(b) shows the surface that plots the corresponding values ($-P_{abs,tot}$) of the objective function and the path followed by the lowest vertex of the simplex (which is a triangle here in $\Re^2$). The descent started from the region of the initial guess which was the centre of the cross section $\left(y_{c,init}, z_{c,init}\right)$=(0, 0)μm and the algorithm converged at the point $\left(y_{c,opt}, z_{c,opt}\right)$=(-38, -203)μm denoting that the optimum offset of the core from the centre is approximately at a distance of 69% of its radius for the considered operation point.

The corresponding path for the square DCF is shown in figure 11(f) on a fragment of the objective function surface. Here the simplex started again from the cross section centre and converged this time to the point $\left(y_{c,opt}, z_{c,opt}\right)$=(-24, 126)μm where the core is situated at a distance from the centre that is approximately 21% of the inner cladding side length. In both figures it is apparent that the direct search method achieved better landscape resolutions and at lower computation cost than those achieved through the initial evaluation of $P_{abs,tot}$ at the grid nodes. Furthermore, figure 11(b) suggests graphically that first-order convergence from an arbitrary starting point (global convergence) is achieved at a point

$\mathbf{P}_{optim} \in \Re^2$ very close to an optimizer x_* that is a stationary point of the objective function satisfying the second-order sufficiency condition ($\exists x_* : \nabla^2 f(x_*) > 0$ for a differentiable function). The spatial distribution of $P_{abs,tot}$ across the cross section plane of the circular DCF is also clearly followed by the lowest order standing wave that developed in the beam overlap image in figure 11(c). The corresponding surface for the square DCF shows the improved scrambling of the modes achieved by this cross section. The peak standing high above the rest on each surface denotes the location of the core within the inner cladding. Figure 11(d) shows the dramatic improvement of absorption in the offset core of the circular DCF which is the direct result of the simplex descent to a deep valley while figure 11(h) demonstrates that there is comparatively little room for improvement when offsetting the core within a square DCF.

Table 1 presents the results from the simultaneous optimization of the cross section and refractive index performed mostly by the stochastic variants of NM at relatively low dimensions. The listed schemes (column 5) optimized the offset, size, shape and refractive index of an encompassed lamina while the shape of the inner cladding remained constant. These results represent a telescopic view into the considered optimization domains facilitated by the parsimonious nature of NM and SNM methods. All dielectric holes shown are assumed to be made of CBYA alloy-glass [40] apart from the row 3 optimizer representing an attempt to search for improved refractive index values. The increased CPU times recorded for the most complicated and absorbent topologies is due to the correspondingly larger number of scatterings occurring inside them. The optimal cross section in table 1 is the row 8 optimizer, found by stochastic search in $\Re^{18}$ where the offset as well as ellipticity and size of four large area holes were allowed to vary independently. The single hole designs demonstrated high potential to achieving optimal absorption while when square shapes for the inner cladding or embedded holes were used, the absorption dropped considerably. The same was the case when air holes or hexagonal CBYA holes of variable offset and size were optimized (not shown). As far as the preliminary results in table 1 are considered, the cross sections worth to invest on in terms of computational expense for further optimization by the MADS method appear to be the:

- Four elliptical holes scheme (row 8)
- Circular hole topologies because they are easier to manufacture and showed improved absorption potential (row 6) after initiating a second optimization from a previous optimizer (row 5)
- Single large-hole cross section due to its simplicity and good performance.

The most promising topologies from table 1 are taken to the next level for optimization by MADS which promises to deliver global optimizers with higher probability but a significant increase in computational cost is expected. Prior to discussing the results in table 2 it is useful to describe the algorithmic settings of GA, MADS and GPS methods because they had an impact on all corresponding results. The optimizations executed by GA in section 2 started with $n+1$ members in the initial population (to match the number of vertices maintained by a simplex), the elite population size was set to the nearest integer of $(n+1)/10$, the cross over factor was 0.8, the migration factor was 0.2 and the migration interval was set to 20. With the need to make the GPS and MADS as computationally efficient as possible with a minimum negative impact on their global convergence properties, they were set up as follows. Neither complete search nor complete poll

Start point	Opti-mizer	Start point $P_{abs,tot}$ (W)	Opti-mizer $P_{abs,tot}$ (W)	Encoding scheme	Algorithm	Optimi-zation space	Func Evals (#)	Start point t_{CPU} (s)
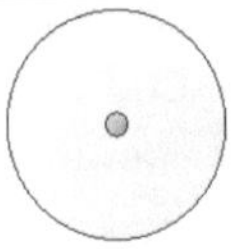	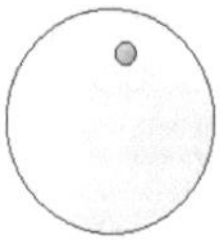	25.3	63.8	Offset	NM	$\Re^2$	78	27.6
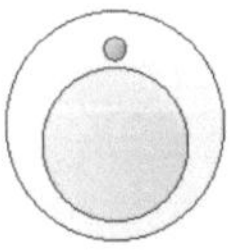	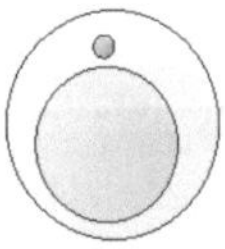	63.6	69.1	Offset-Diameter	SNM {S, S}	$\Re^5$	335	65.8
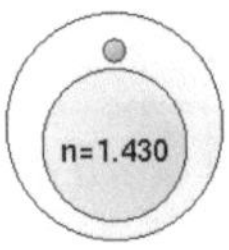		63.6	69.5	Offset-Diameter - index	NM	$\Re^6$	328	65.8
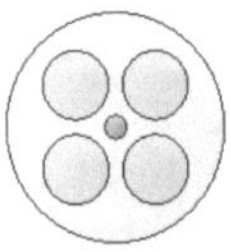	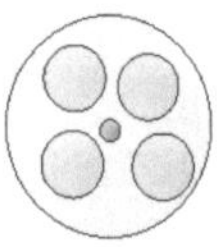	57.9	64.6	Offset	SNM {S, S}	$\Re^{10}$	227	109.0
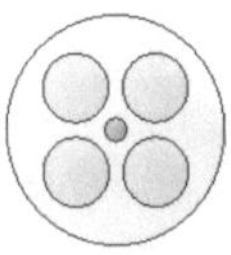	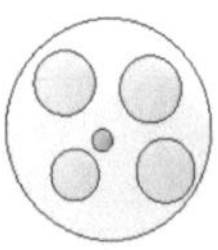	57.9	67.0	Offset-Diameter	SNM {S, D}	$\Re^{14}$	304	109.0
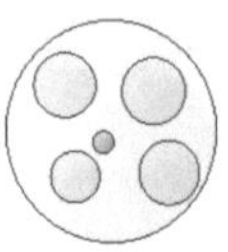	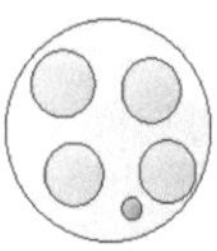	67.0	69.8	Offset-Diameter	SNM {S, D}	$\Re^{14}$	425	101.7
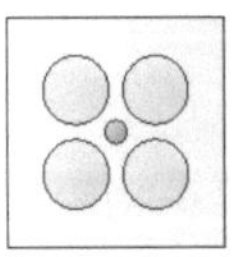	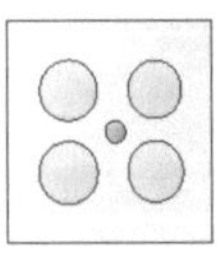	54.4	58.6	Offset-Diameter	SNM {S, D}	$\Re^{14}$	306	84.7
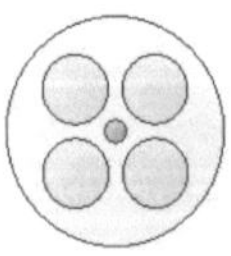	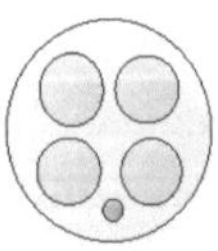	57.9	70.7	Offset-Major-Minor	SNM {S, D}	$\Re^{18}$	558	109.0
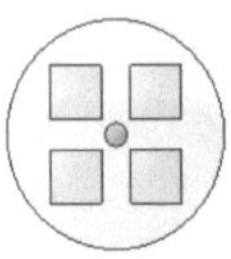	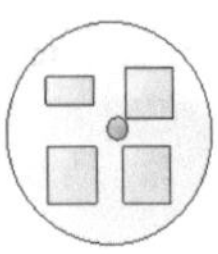	56.2	65.0	Offset-Major-Minor	SNM {S, D}	$\Re^{18}$	412	91.3
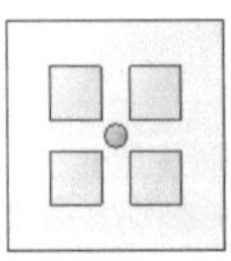	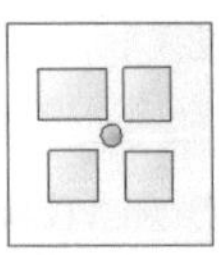	54.7	59.3	Offset-Major-Minor	SNM {S, D}	$\Re^{18}$	355	76.4

Table 1. Optimization results for polymer outer-clad and holey inner-clad with NM variants.

Start point	Opti-mizer	Start point $P_{abs,tot}$ (W)	Opti-mizer $P_{abs,tot}$ (W)	Encoding scheme	Algorithm	Optimi-zation space	Func Evals (#)	Start point t_{CPU} (s)
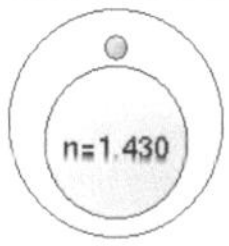		63.6	71.1	Offset-Major-Minor -Index	MADS {Np1, 2N}	$\Re^7$	112	65.8
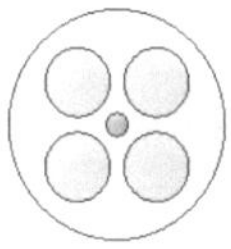	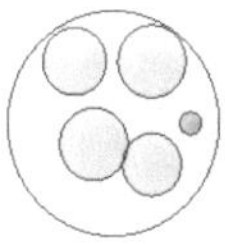	57.9	71.0	Offset-Diameter	MADS {Np1, 2N}	$\Re^{14}$	441	109.0
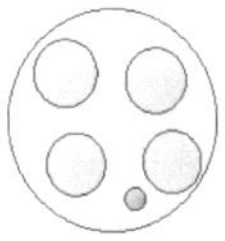	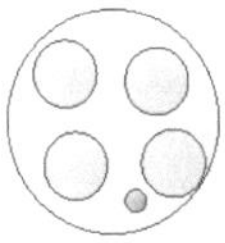	69.8	69.8	Offset-Diameter	MADS {Np1, 2N}	$\Re^{14}$	235	97.3
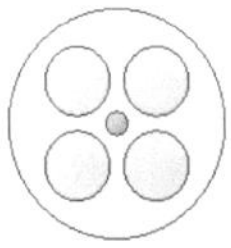	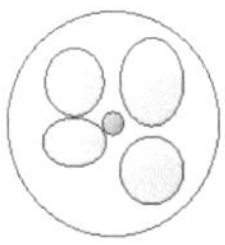	57.9	65.3	Offset-Major-Minor	MADS {Np1, 2N}	$\Re^{18}$	452	109.5

Table 2. MADS optimization results for polymer outer-clad and holey inner-clad.

operations were allowed resulting in an opportunistic style of direct search iteration that stops as soon as a better point has been found. Also, the first direction of search after a successful poll or search step is set to be the one that was successful in the previous iteration (exploratory search tactic). A so called tabu list that records the already visited points was maintained so that the expense of unnecessary function re-evaluations would be avoided. This added a tabu search metaheuristic element to MADS and GPS that was found to offer up to approximately 40% reduction in function evaluations. Tabu search is not recommended for stochastic functions but in this case the stochastic noise was suppressed. One other setting that can reduce the computation expense is to accelerate the rate at which the mesh size is adapted after a non-successful iteration. This setting was not enabled in this work because it was found to significantly reduce the probability to discover a global optimizer (at a benefit of 20% reduction in function evaluations). The last setting, shared by all optimization methods used here is the minimization halting criterion. In order to achieve an equally economical minimization that avoids unnecessary function evaluations at the vicinity of an already well approximated optimizer, all halting criterions were set to stop the minimization when saturation in the improvement of the lowest recorded objective function value as a function of the number of iterations was observed. Regarding MATLAB's 'Genetic Algorithm and Direct Search Toolbox' used to implement the GA, GPS, and MADS optimizations, it was found via observation that the above halting condition was satisfied for 'Function Tolerance' (a parameter compared against the cumulative change in the best function value over a number of iterations) values of 10^{-6}, 10^{-7} and 10^{-4} correspondingly. In algorithm NM and all its forms proposed in sections 2 and 3, the saturation of the fittest function value was observed for

$$\sigma_{halt} \cong (1/10)\sigma_0 \tag{17}$$

where σ_0 is the standard deviation of the initial objective matrix elements excluding the highest value. The success of (17) depends on the standard deviation of the function values, stored in the initial objective matrix ($\mathbf{F}_0$), not being too large so that the simplex will reach the neighbourhood of an optimizer before the condition $\sigma_j \geq \sigma_{halt}$ is satisfied at the end of the *j*-th iteration. When the aforementioned criterion fails to halt the simplex after acceptably approximating an optimizer, then the descent halts after a relatively small number of iterations and a large improvement in the objective (row 1 in table 3, row 5 in table 4). Then the process is restarted using the discovered point as a new start point (row 2 in table 3, row 6 in table 4). In this way, the inherent tendency of NM (and proposed NM-based methods) to perform unnecessary iterations after having adequately approximated an optimizer was avoided.

Start point	Opti-mizer	Start point $P_{abs,tot}$ (W)	Opti-mizer $P_{abs,tot}$ (W)	Encoding scheme	Algorithm	Optimi-zation space	Func Evals (#)	Start point t_{CPU} (s)
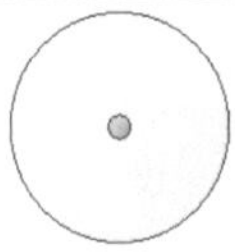	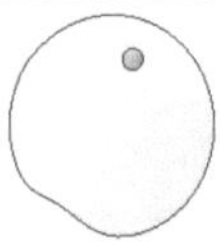	25.3	64.8	Offset-Perimeter	ESPNM {S, S}	$\Re^{182}$	727	27.6
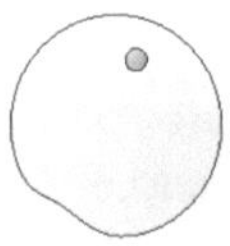	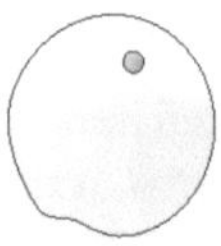	64.8	68.7	Offset-Perimeter	ESPNM {S, S}	$\Re^{182}$	9196	27.2
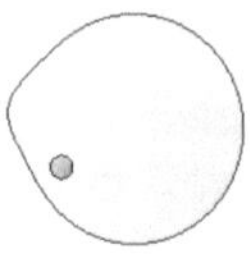		61.5	67.2	Offset-Perimeter	ESPNM {S, S}	$\Re^{182}$	11662	26.1
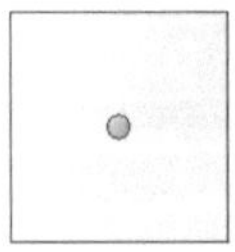	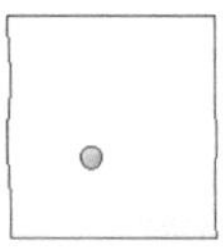	53.5	61.3	Offset-Perimeter	ESPNM {S, S}	$\Re^{186}$	10146	28.8
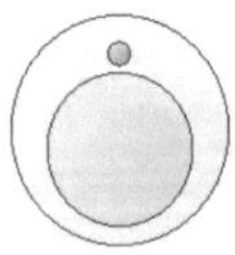	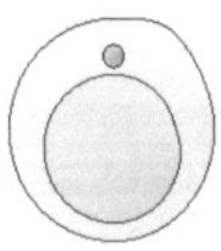	63.6	69.7	Offset-Perimeter	ESPNM {S, S}	$\Re^{362}$	1238	65.8

Table 3. Optimization results for polymer outer cladding with algorithm ESPNM.

After the direct comparison of several algorithms in section 2, the MADS method was chosen as the most successful at lower dimensions in terms of probability to find global optimizers. The most distinctive topologies listed in table 1 are re-optimized in table 2 under MADS. The 1st row of table 2 shows the results from an attempt to optimize the same start point as in row 3 of table1 but this time with an added dimension. The discovered optimizer outperformed all optimizers from table 1 showing that an offset core topology with a single large hole of optimal ellipticity delivers the strongest pump absorption. Although the refractive index was independently varied during the optimization, the MADS algorithm converged to an optimizer with the exactly the same hole refractive index, a manifestation of the discrete nature of pattern search. One other aspect of the MADS algorithm is that it demonstrates an inherent tendency to preferentially search along those directions that exhibit the stronger influence on the objective function values. The results in row 4 disappointed because although the start point was the same as in row 8 of table 1, the MADS algorithm converged to an optimizer in $\Re^{18}$ that was strongly outperformed by the SNM found optimizer (for a higher cost though this time). This observation suggests that a surprisingly low number of function evaluations is a sign of local convergence. However, the discovered optimizer indicates that if a centred core topology is sought after then the design parameters of the holes can be optimized for improved absorption strength. Row 2 in table 2 shows a successful optimization in $\Re^{14}$ that improved over the later suggesting that the optimization of the hole-ellipticity may not be justified if it is significantly more difficult to manufacture. An interesting result is reported in row 3 of table 2 where MADS converged to the start point after about 1/3 of the expected number of function evaluations. This behaviour of MADS was observed several times and showed that its success depends strongly on starting the process from a point far away from an optimizer, a property which is not shared by SNM as suggested by the results in row 6 of table 1.

Remaining in the class of topologies with polymer outer cladding, table 3 presents the optimization of inner cladding and hole perimeters along with the core offset at high dimensions. The two-stage optimization (rows 1,2) of a circular inner cladding with centred core resulted in a cross section with a minor spiral deformation to the inner cladding perimeter and an offset core. Row 3 adopted a start point resembling the spiral fibre proposed by Kouznetsov and Moloney [48] and converged to an inner cladding shape that is a perturbed spiral shape with the core located closer to the centre. The optimizer in row 3 suggests that a spiral cross section can be further improved. Row 4 demonstrates that a square fibre has limited prospects for competitive improvement while row 5 shows a case of local convergence in $\Re^{362}$ where a global optimization is potentially very expensive due to the high dimensions.

Finally, table 4 presents a set of optimization attempts for double-clad topologies with air outer cladding. The CPU times recorded here are much higher than in the polymer outer cladding case because the air-clad designs support higher order modes (rays of higher transmission angles under the absorption model in [19]) resulting in significantly increased number of scattering operations on the dielectric interfaces. An interesting finding was that an optimized polymer hole (row 2) can be very efficient in decoupling the pump light from its volume. In this way the pump modes are forced to propagate inside the significantly reduced inner cladding volume with a dramatic effect on the increase of the pump photons overlap with the active core volume. This design can be used with moderate pump power levels though due to the low damage threshold of a polymer. However, it has been demonstrated that high glass-transition temperature thermoplastic polymers can be thermally co-drawn into micro-sized structures without cracking or delamination [49]. A direct comparison between MADS and ESPNM is provided by the results in rows 3 and 4 where a dodecagon shaped inner cladding with offset core is optimized. The two algorithms converged to optimizers of the same absorption performance but ESPNM did so at a significantly lower cost. The dodecagon shape was chosen due to the small number of perimetric sampling points involved which did not allow MADS to generate trial points without physical meaning (or lacking manufacturability), contrary to the cases in figure 5. Furthermore, an air outer cladding may be easier to fabricate around a polygonic inner cladding by means of a comb of suitably shaped air holes.

Start point	Opti-mizer	Start point $P_{abs,tot}$ (W)	Opti-mizer $P_{abs,tot}$ (W)	Encoding scheme	Algorithm	Optimi-zation space	Func Evals (#)	Start point t_{CPU} (s)
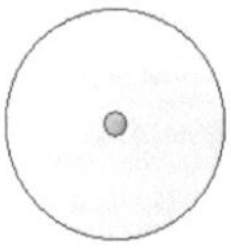	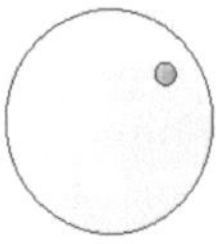	28.1	66.7	Offset	NM	$\Re^2$	68	58.9
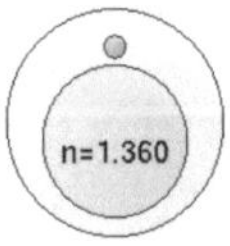		71.3	76.3	Offset-Major-Minor -Index	MADS {Np1, 2N}	$\Re^7$	126	155.7
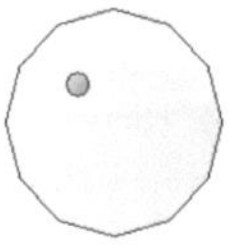	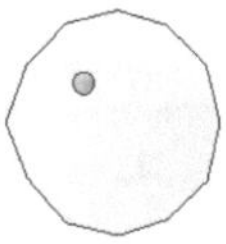	71.3	73.4	Offset-Perimeter	ESPNM {S, S}	$\Re^{26}$	629	55.3
	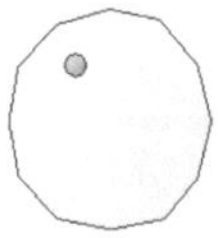	71.3	73.4	Offset-Perimeter	MADS {Np1, 2N}	$\Re^{26}$	898	55.3
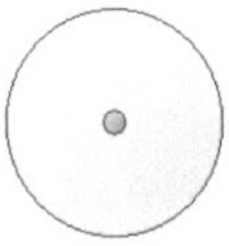	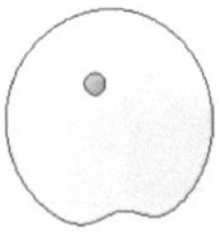	28.1	71.2	Offset-Perimeter	ESPNM {S, S}	$\Re^{182}$	669	58.9
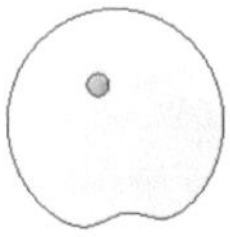	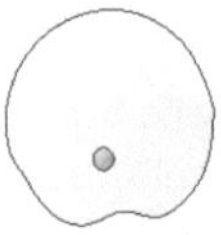	71.2	73.9	Offset-Perimeter	ESPNM {S, S}	$\Re^{182}$	11199	60.0

Table 4. Optimization results for air outer cladding.

The predictions reported here may be compared to the 35% pump absorption enhancement reported by Baek *et al* [14] and to the 18% improvement measured by Jeong *et al* [15] for a circular fibre with centred core. Based on the current results, in the case of polymer coated DCFs, it is predicted that the optimizer in row 1 of table 2 can offer an approximate enhancement of 180% compared to a conventional circular DCF with centred core. Against a conventional circular DCF with optimally offset core (table 1, row 1 optimizer), an enhancement of 11% is predicted. For the air outer cladding case, assuming high power operation (no polymer holes), a 160% improvement (table 4, row 6 optimizer) is predicted against a centred circular DCF and 10% enhancement compared to the circular optimizer with optimally offset core.

5. Summary

Several stochastic algorithms based on the deterministic Nelder-Mead method were proposed and benchmarked against pattern search methods and a genetic algorithm. In low dimensions, the proposed Monte Carlo NM variants offered improved computational efficiency via a simple sampling approach. Implicitly constrained search combined with importance sampling offered efficient global convergence in high dimensions. Smoothly perturbed patterns were proposed that may find theoretical support for constrained optimization. The fittest algorithms were applied to the cross section geometry and corresponding refractive index profile optimization. The identified advantages of the aforementioned pump absorption enhancement concept were:

- In the case of the holey DCFs the size of the inner cladding can be scaled to accept more pump power without the need to increase the core size. The solid state holes can be correspondingly scaled to retain their pump light tapering effect into the core volume.
- The proposed holey cross sections are compatible with the helical core concept and most side pumping schemes. Multi-core ribbon lasers [12] may also benefit from optimized solid-state holes
- No fibre machining is needed while also compatibility with standard fibre manufacturing is maintained

The main limitation may be the low fabrication tolerance implied by the complexity of most proposed topologies. On the front of correctly predicting their relative absorption performance, limitations are imposed by error levels induced by stochastic and numerical noise during optimization as well as simulation inaccuracies induced during function evaluations.

6. References

[1] Jeong Y, Sahu J, Payne D and Nilsson J 2004 Ytterbium-doped large-core fiber laser with 1.36 kW continuous-wave output power *Optics Express* 12 6088-92

[2] Yahel E, Hess O and Hardy A A 2006 Modeling and Optimization of High-Power Nd^{3+}-Yb^{3+} Codoped Fiber Lasers *IEEE J. Lightwave Technol.* 24 1601-9

[3] Yahel E and Hardy A 2003 Modeling High-Power Er^{3+}-Yb^{3+} Codoped Fibre Lasers *IEEE J. Lightwave Technol.* 21 2044–52

[4] Vienne G G, Caplen E J, Dong L, Minelly D J, Nilson J and Payne N D 1998 Fabrication and Characterization of Yb^{+3}:Er^{+3} Phosphosilicate Fibres for Lasers *IEEE J. Lightwave Technol.* 16 1990–2001

[5] Federighi M and Di Pasquale F 1995 The Effect of Pair-Induced Energy Transfer on the Performance of Silica waveguide Amplifiers with High Er^{3+}/Yb^{3+} Concentrations *IEEE Photonics Tech. Lett.* 7 303–5

[6] Lassila E, Hernberg R and Alahautala T 2006 Axially symmetric fiber side pumping *Optics Express* 14 8638-43

[7] Yan P, Gong M, Li C, Ou P, Xu A 2005 Distributed pumping multifiber series fiber laser *Optics Express* 13 2699-706

[8] Polynkin P, Temyanko V, Mansuripur M and Peyghambarian N 2004 Efficient and Scalable Side Pumping Scheme or Short High-Power Optical Fiber Lasers and Amplifiers *IEEE Photonics Tech. Lett.* 16 2024-26

[9] Koplow J P, Moore S W and Kliner D A V 2003 A New method for Side Pumping of Double-Clad Fiber Sources *J. Quantum Electr.* 39 529-40

[10] Koplow J P, Goldberg L, and Dahv A. V. Kliner D A V 1998 Compact 1-W Yb-Doped Double-Cladding Fiber Amplifier Using V-Groove Side-Pumping *IEEE Photonics Tech. Lett.* 10 793-5

[11] Wang P, Cooper L J, Sahu J K and Clarkson 2006 Efficient single-mode operation of a cladding-pumped ytterbium-doped helical-core fiber laser *Optics Letters* 31 226-8

[12] Wang P, Clarkson W A, Shen D Y, Copper L J and Sahu J K 2006 Novel concepts for high-power fibre lasers *Solid state lasers and amplifiers II: Proc. SPIE* (Strasbourg, France, 5-6 April 2006) Vol. 6190, 61900I (Apr. 17, 2006) ed A. Sennaroglu *et al* pp 1-12

[13] Jiang Z and Marciante J R 2006 Mode-area scaling of helical-core, dual-clad fiber lasers and amplifiers using an improved bend-loss model *J. Opt. Soc. Am. B* 23 2051-8

[14] Baek S, Roh S, Jeong Y and Lee B 2006 Experimental Demonstration of Enhancing Pump Absorption Rate in Cladding-Pumped Ytterbium-Doped Fiber Lasers Using Pump-Coupling Long-Period Fiber Gratings *IEEE Photonics Tech. Lett.* 18 700-2

[15] Jeong Y, Baek S, Nilsson J and Lee B 2006 Simple and compact, all-fibre retro-reflector for cladding-pumped fibre lasers *Electronics Letters* 42 15-6

[16] Kouznetsov D and Moloney J V 2003 Highly Efficient, High-Gain, Short-Length, and Power-Scalable Incoherent Diode Slab-Pumped Fiber Amplifier/Laser *J. Quantum Electr.* 39 1452-61

[17] Kouznetsov D and Moloney J V 2004 Slab Delivery of Incoherent Pump Light to Double-Clad Fiber Amplifiers: An Analytic Approach *J. Quantum Electr.* 40 378-83

[18] Peterka P, Kašík I, Matejec V, Kubeek V and Dvo1áek P 2006 Experimental demonstration of novel end-pumping method for double-clad fiber devices *Optics Letters* 31 3240-2

[19] Dritsas I, Sun T and Grattan K T V 2006 Numerical simulation based optimization of the absorption efficiency in double-clad fibres *IoP J. Opt. A: Pure Appl. Opt.* 8 49-61

[20] Nelder J A and Mead R 1965 A simplex method for function minimization *Computer Journal* 7 308-13

[21] Dritsas I, Sun T and Grattan K T V 2006 Double-clad fibre numerical optimization with a simplex method *Solid state lasers and amplifiers II: Proc. SPIE* (Strasbourg, France, 5-6 April 2006) Vol. 6190, 61900L (Apr. 17, 2006) ed A. Sennaroglu *et al* pp 1-12

[22] Conn A R, Gould N I M and Toint P L 1991 A Globally Convergent Augmented Lagrangian Algorithm for Optimization with General Constraints and Simple Bounds *SIAM J. Numer. Analysis* 28 545-72

[23] Audet C and Dennis J E, jr. 2003 Analysis of generalized pattern searches *SIAM J. Optim.*, 13 889-903

[24] Lewis R M and Torczon V 2002 A globally convergent augmented lagrangian pattern search algorithm for optimization with general constraints and simple bounds *SIAM J. Optim.*, 12 1075-89

[25] Lewis R M and Torczon V 2000 Pattern Search Methods for Linearly Constrained Minimization *SIAM J. Optim.*, 10 917-41

[26] Lewis R M and Torczon V 1999 Pattern Search Algorithms for Bound Constrained Minimization *SIAM J. Optim.*, 9 1082-99

[27] Torczon V 1997 On the Convergence of Pattern Search Algorithms *SIAM J. Optim.*, 7 1-25

[28] Audet C and Dennis J E, jr. 2006 Mesh adaptive direct search algorithms for constrained optimization *SIAM J. Optim.*, 17 188–217

[29] Abramson M A, Audet C and Dennis J E, jr. 2006 Nonlinear Programming by Mesh Adaptive Direct searches *SIAG/OPT Views-and-news* vol 17 no 1 pp 2-11
[30] Lagarias J C, Reeds J A, Wright M H and Wright P E 1998 Convergence Properties of the Nelder-Mead Simplex Method in Low Dimensions *SIAM J. Optim.*, 9 112-47
[31] Kolda T G, Lewis R M and Torczon V 2004 Optimization by Direct Search: New Perspectives on Some Classical and Modern Methods *SIAM Review* 45 385-482
[32] Torczon V 1991 On the convergence of the multidirectional search algorithm *SIAM J. Optim.*, 1 123-45
[33] Teng C-H, Chen Y-S and Hsu W-H 2006 Camera self-calibration method suitable for variant camera constraints *Applied Optics* 45 688-96
[34] Lhommé F, Caucheteur C, Chah K, Blondel M and Mégret P 2005 Synthesis of fiber Bragg grating parameters from experimental reflectivity: a simplex approach and its application to the determination of temperature-dependent properties *Applied Optics* 44 493-7
[35] McKinnon K I M 1998 Convergence of the Nelder-Mead simplex method to a nonstationary point *SIAM J. Optim.* 9 148–58
[36] Kelley C T 1999 Detection and remediation of stagnation in the Nelder-Mead algorithm using a sufficient decrease condition *SIAM J. Optim.*, 10 43–55
[37] Tseng P 1999 Fortified-descent simplicial search method: A general approach *SIAM J. Optim.*, 10 269–88
[38] Zhang R and Shi F G 2004 A Novel Algorithm for Fiber-Optic Alignment Automation *IEEE Trans. Advance. Packaging* 27 173–8
[39] Lin J Wu Y Huang T S 2004 Articulate Hand Motion Capturing Based on a Monte Carlo Nelder-Mead Simplex Tracker *Proceedings of the 17th International Conference on Pattern Recognition* (ICPR'04-23-26 Aug.) 4 pp 975-978
[40] Zhang L, Gan F and Wang P 1994 Evaluation of refractive-index and material dispersion in fluoride glasses *Applied Optics* 33 50–6
[41] Amar J G 2006 The Monte Carlo Method in Science and Engineering *IEEE Computing in Science & Engineering* vol 8 no 2 pp 9-19
[42] Bandler J W, Koziel S and Madsen K 2006 Space Mapping for Engineering Optimization *SIAG/OPT Views-and-news* vol 17 no 1 pp 19-26
[43] Renders J-M and Flasse S P 1996 Hybrid methods using genetic algorithms for global optimization *IEEE Trans. Systems, Man and Cybernetics, Part B* 26 243–58
[44] Wessel S, Trebst S and Troyer M 2005 A renormalization approach to simulations of quantum effects in nanoscale magnetic systems *SIAM J. Multiscale model simul.* 4 237-49
[45] Wen M and Yao J 2006 Birefringent filter design by use of a modified genetic algorithm *Applied Optics* 45 3940-50
[46] Luijten E 2006 Fluid Simulation with the Geometric Cluster Monte Carlo Algorithm *IEEE Computing in Science & Engineering* vol 8 no 2 pp 20-9
[47] Marsaglia G and Zaman A 1991 A new class of random number generators *Ann. Appl. Probab.* 3 462–80
[48] Kouznetsov D and Moloney J 2002 Efficiency of pump absorption in double-clad fibre amplifiers. II. Broken circular symmetry *J. Opt. Soc. Am. B* 19 1259–63

[49] Temelkuran B, Hart S D, Benoit G, Joannopoulos J D and Fink Y 2002 Wavelength-scalable hollow optical fibres with large photonic bandgaps for CO2 laser transmission *Nature* 420 650-3

16

Global and Dynamic Optimization using the Artificial Chemical Process Paradigm and Fast Monte Carlo Methods for the Solution of Population Balance Models

Roberto Irizarry
DuPont Electronic Technologies. 14 T.W. Alexander Drive P.O. Box 13999. Research Triangle Park, NC 27709-3999. USA

1. Introduction

Global and dynamic optimization of engineering problems usually involves complex physico-chemical models as constraints. These models are in general highly non-linear, resulting in multimodal optimization problems. The model may have discontinuous behavior and/or include a very large set of variables. As the complexity of the systems increases, equation-free modeling is becoming more common (Kevrekidis, Gear and Hummer, 2004). For example, in particle dynamics, population balance models are sometimes more effectively solved by the Monte Carlo method.

Stochastic global optimization methods are very important algorithms for the solution of these types of problems. They have been successfully applied to solve challenging problems that cannot be solved using gradient based methods. Stochastic optimization methods have also been used in many algorithms, in which solution of optimization problems is part of the algorithm. Global stochastic optimization strategies have been utilized in learning phase of pattern recognition algorithms using fuzzy logic (Irizarry, 2005b) and neuro-fuzzy systems (Lin, 2008). These methods have been used for the optimization of complex engineering designs involving computational fluid mechanics such as aerodynamics applications (Duvigneau and Visonneau, 2004). Other applications include the determination of molecular structures, including protein structure prediction and protein-small molecule interactions among others (Sahinis, 2009). Batch scheduling problems are another type of problem were stochastic optimization can be very efficient (Liu et al., 2010).

In particular, the solution of dynamic optimization problems is also of great industrial importance for process development and process optimization, since most processes are dynamic. In this type of problem an optimal profile function is sought (vs. an optimal value for a set of variables). For example, in a fed-batch fermenter, the feed-rate schedule is optimized to maximize production of antibiotics, vitamins, enzymes, and other products (Banga et al., 2003). Another example is the determination of optimal temperature profiles in crystallization processes to control crystal size distribution (Ma, Tafti and Braatz, 2002). Dynamic optimization is also of central importance to the application of process control using model predictive control (Banga, Irizarry-Rivera and Seider, 1998; Pistikopoulos, 2009). Model predictive control provides a sequence of control actions over a future time horizon by solving a dynamic optimization problem that covers past and future behavior of the system.

The genetic algorithm (GA) (Holland, 1975; Goldberg, 1989) and simulated annealing (SA) (Kirkpatrick, Gelatt and Vecchi, 1983; Ingber, 1993) are classical stochastic optimization methods used in many applications and new algorithm developments. GA is based on emulating Darwinian evolution in populations. Evolutionary strategies also focus on real decision variables problems using Darwinian evolution concepts (Schwefel, 1995). In these population-based methods, a large set of configurations forms a population, with new generations created by selection, crossover and mutation operators acting on the current population. This evolution process will increase the fitness of the population to a near optimal value. These algorithms strongly depend on the parameters and types of selection, crossover and mutation mechanisms selected. These operators are continuously being improved and redefined for specific applications and problems (as one of many examples see Tang, Sun and Yang, 2010). Other algorithms like the ant colony (Dorigo and Stutzle, 2004)) and particle swarm optimization (Kennedy and Eberhart, 2001) are inspired by cooperative phenomena of animal behavior or agents.

Simulated annealing was designed for combinatorial optimization problems using concepts from statistical physics. In this case, a very low-energy configuration may be achieved by starting at a high temperature and then gradually lowering the temperature using a cooling schedule. The performance of these algorithms depends strongly on the selection of the cooling schedule, which in general needs to be tuned for specific problems. Furthermore, SA does not consider how to select a step change for the next trial solution, which is critical to the success of the algorithm. This needs to be defined by the user for the problem at hand.

This chapter discussed an alternative for global optimization methodology based on a different paradigm known as the artificial chemical process (Irizarry, 2004). The paradigm has been used to design robust dynamic optimization algorithms (Irizarry, 2005a; Irizarry, 2006) and fuzzy logic algorithms (Irizarry, 2005b). Fast MC algorithms of population balance models are also reviewed (Irizarry, 2007a; Irizarry, 2007b). These coarse graining algorithms accelerate simulation speed by an order of magnitude without loss of accuracy, making optimization of these systems feasible in real time. Unlike other lumping or coarse graining strategies, in this strategy the particle integrity is not lost in the coarsening process. This increase in speed allows the efficient solution of parameter identification problems (Irizarry, 2010) and dynamic optimization problems. The LARES algorithm is described in Section 2. A general purpose algorithm to solve dynamic optimization problems is described in Section 3. Section 4 considers fast MC simulation algorithms for the simulation of population balance models. Fast MC strategies are discussed in Section 5. Section 6 discusses how to combines the algorithms into a hybrid strategy to solve problems involving multiple time scales and inherently stochastic variables.

2. Global optimization using the artificial chemical process paradigm

In this section an optimization algorithm called LARES is reviewed. This algorithm is based on an artificial chemical optimization paradigm introduced in 2004 (Irizarry, 2004). To apply the algorithm, the first step is to encode all decision variables, θ, into a set of integer variables with a very small range of possible values (i.e., 2–10). The integer variables are called **molecules**, and their respective values are called **states**. As a motivating example consider a case were θ is a vector of real variables. The real decision variables can be encoded using a binary representation (similar to GA). Unlike GA, in this encoding each bit of the string is associated with a molecule variable with two possible values (0 and 1), which represents the value of a specific bit in the binary encoding (see Figure 1). In general, any type of decision variables (including real, integer, logical, and combinatorial) can be encoded into a set of molecules, making the algorithm very flexible.

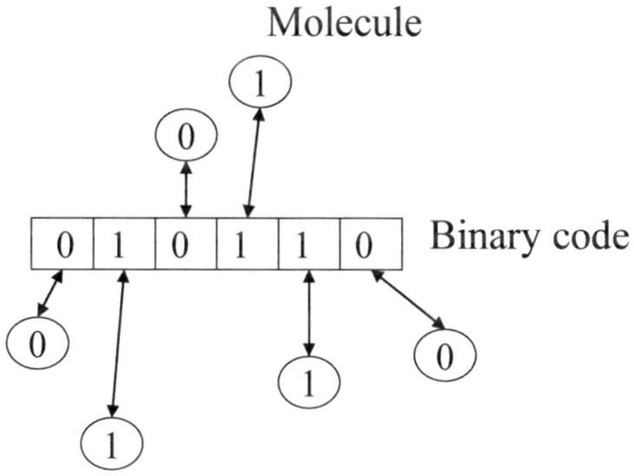

Fig. 1. The concept of molecules for binary encoding of a real variable

Given the decision vector represented as a set of molecules, the LARES algorithm operates on these molecules to create new trial states. At each iteration of the algorithm, a subset of molecules will change state (value) to generate a new trial vector. The artificial chemical plant concept is based on the fact that chemical reactors convert a low-quality material into a high-value product by a series of reactions, feedback loops, and separation steps. The following algorithm is based on an abstraction of those steps.

2.1 The LARES artificial chemical plant paradigm

The LARES algorithm is an iterative improvement methodology, which considers one solution at a time. Given the decision variables encoded into molecules, the algorithm generates a movement of some molecules between four compartments or sets (called L, AR, E, and S). The four compartments are shown in Figure 2 (panel 1). The algorithm starts with all molecules assigned to a set L with an initial state. At each iteration, a set of rules determines the event to be triggered next. Each event is a stochastic subprocess whereby a subset of molecules is moved from one compartment to another. When molecules reach one specific compartment (AR), their state is changed (similar to a reactor in a real chemical plant). The set of rules for the next event selection are based on the previous values of the objective function and the objective function of the best value found so far.

Before describing the algorithm in detail, the different types of possible triggered events are described. Let x_j^g be the state of the molecule j for the best value found so far (or initial trial), and $x^g = (x_1^g, \ldots, x_V^g)$ the vector of molecular states for the best value found. Let F be the objective function to be minimized. Figure 2 panel 2 shows an example of the state of six molecules for the best value found so far. One possible event consists of a set of molecules being transferred from the Load tank (L set) to the Activation Reactor (AR set), in which the molecules change state to a new random state, $x_j^a \neq x_j^g \; \forall j \in AR$. The state of molecules will not change while they are inside AR. An example of this type of event is shown in Figure 2 panel 2, where molecules 1 and 4 were moved from L to AR and their states changed from 0 to 1 and 1 to 0, respectively (compare panel 1 and panel 2). This event generates a new trial vector as shown in Figure 2 panel 3, the performance of which is evaluated. In another type of event in a different iteration, some reacted molecules can be sent to the Extraction unit (E set) where they are deactivated back into their previous state upon entering the reactor ($x_j^t = x_j^g \ \forall j \in E$). These extracted molecules could be sent to the Separation unit (S set) or recycled back into the Activation Reactor, where the molecules are reactivated to a new state $x_j^a \neq x_j^g \ \forall j \in E$. At each iteration, a trial vector consists of the activated molecules in AR and the deactivated molecules in the other three sets: $x_j^t = x_j^a \neq x_j^g \ \forall j \in AR$, $x_j^t = x_j^g \ \forall j \notin AR$. If, after any event in the current iteration, a "good batch" is accomplished (i.e., a better objective function is found, $F(\theta_t) \leq F(\theta_b)$, the activation reactor can be emptied into the separator unit, S. In this case all molecules conserve the new state ($x_j^g = x_j^a \ \forall j \in AR$), and a new "batch" is then started. The algorithm is described in detail in the next section.

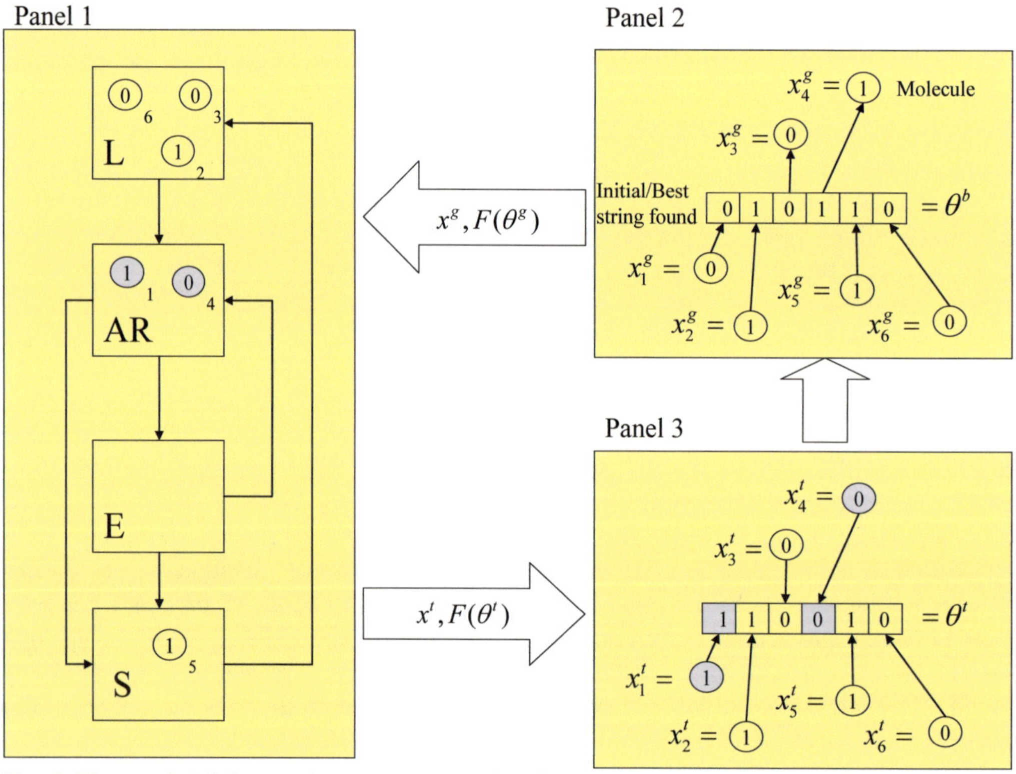

Fig. 2. The artificial chemical process in panel 1 changes the state of the molecules in panel 2 to a new trial state in panel 3 by transferring some molecules from L to AR and changing the states of the molecules in AR.

2.2 LARES algorithm

Initialization: The algorithm starts by initializing x^g randomly and placing all molecule variables in L.

Outer loop: Perturbation to form AR.

1. Select the number of molecules, N, to be extracted from L and added to the AR set ($N = rF_1$, where and r is a random number uniformly distributed in (0,1)).
2. Select N random molecules from L and add them to the AR set. For each selected molecule j, select a new state $x_j^a \neq x_j^g$ randomly.
3. Form a new trial vector using

$$x_j^t = \begin{cases} x_j^g & if\ x_j \notin AR \\ x_j^a & if\ x_j \in AR \end{cases} \tag{1}$$

4. If performance is improved, accept the trial state as the new best solution (ground state). $x^g \leftarrow x^t$. Send all AR molecules to the S set. Go to Step 1.
5. Set parameters: $RP = F(x^t)$, $|AR|_0 = |AR|$.
6. Inner loop: Iterative improvement of AR
   6.1 Select the number of molecules, M, to be extracted from AR to form E ($M = rF_2$, where F_2 is an algorithm parameter, and r is a random number.)
   6.2 Select M random molecules from AR and transfer them to the E set. Return the state of all molecules j in E to the state of the best solution found, $x_j^t = x_j^g$, and build the trial vector as in Step 3 using Eq. (1).
   6.3 If the performance is improved, $x^g \leftarrow x^t$, and go to step 1.
   6.4 *Improvement criterion for AR:*
      6.4.1 If $F(x^t) \leq RP$, add all molecules in E to S and update $RP = F(x^t)$.
      6.4.2 If $F(x^t) > RP$, generate a new activated state for all elements in E ($x_j = x_j^a \neq x_j^g, \forall j \in E$) and transfer all molecules in E to AR ($E = \varnothing$)
   6.5 Exit the inner loop if AR is too small or if the ratio of the number of iterations relative to the initial size of AR exceeds a given parameter, RRT. Otherwise go to Step 6.1.
7. If the size of L is less than a parameter LT, transfer all S molecules to L.

In Step 1, $F_1 = V \times c_0$; in Step 6.1 $F_2 = |AR|_0 \times c_i$. In both cases, if the number of molecules selected is larger than the set, all molecules in the set are selected. The parameters used for this algorithm are: RRT = 1.0, c_o = 0.3, c_i = 0.25, LT = V/2.

The algorithm was shown to be fast and robust when tested with problems of different degrees of multi-modality, discontinuity and flatness. The molecular representation allows the solution of a large class of problems. This structure is general in purpose but also has the flexibility to add problem-specific features. For example, the "locality" of these operators allows the inclusion of bias in the sub-set formation (Steps 3 and 11) or the transformation rule (Step 5).

2.3 Algorithm performance

This algorithm has been tested and extensively utilized to solve many optimization problems. Its performance in some of the test problems is reviewed in this section. The multi-modal random problem generator of Spears (Spears, 1998) was utilized to test LARES over various degrees of modality for binary representation. The problem generator generates a set of *P* random *V*-bit strings representing the location of the *P* peaks in space. To evaluate the performance of an arbitrary string, the nearest peak is located (in Hamming space). Then the fitness of the bit string *c* is calculated as the number of bits the string has in common with that nearest peak, divided by *V*. The optimum fitness for an individual is 1.0.

$$f(c) = \frac{1}{V}\max_{i=1}^{P}\{V - Hamming(c, Peak_i)\} \tag{2}$$

The objective function used in LARES was $F(c) = 1 - f(c)$, while $-F(c)$ was used for the fitness function in GA simulations.
Table 1 shows the results for four study cases. For each set of parameters *V* and *P*, 20 random problems were generated in each case. Each algorithm was run on each problem generated. LARES found the global maximum in all cases ($f(c^*) = 0$), while GA failed to find the global maximum for cases 3 and 4, and μGA failed to find the global maximum in three out of four cases. For the first case, LARES converged to a global optimum in 78 function evaluations on average, while GA converged in 900 function evaluations and μGA converged in less than 350 function evaluations. For the second case, LARES found the global maximum in 647 evaluations on average, while GA converged in approximately 3,700 evaluations and μGA failed to find the global maximum in 20,000 function evaluations (see Figure 3). For the third and fourth study cases, LARES was the only algorithm that converged to the global maximum in nearly 30,000 function evaluations. This behavior was explored systematically by De Jong et al. (1997). In their analysis, the authors found that for $V = 20$, the simple GA will converge in less than 5,000 function evaluations. For $V = 100$, many trials failed to find the global optimum after 20,000 evaluations.
The algorithm has also being tested with Boolean satisfiability problems (SAT), which refers to the task of finding a truth assignment that makes a Boolean expression true. The Boolean satisfiability problem generator of Mitchel et al. (1992) was used to test the performance of LARES in solving random problems with different levels of epistasis. The model assumes a conjunctive normal form of the Boolean expression with C clauses. All clauses are also assumed to consist of the same number of literals, L. The vector of variables *V* is represented as a binary string.
A random problem is generated to create C random clauses. Each clause is generated by randomly selecting L variables, and then each variable is negated with probability 0.5. Once a random L-SAT problem is defined, the fitness function, *f*, is given by the fraction of clauses that are satisfied by the assignment. Note that the main goal of this section is to study LARES with different levels of epistasis. For practical solution of this type of problem, methods such as GSAT (Selman and Kautz, 1993) and WSAT (Gottlieb et al., 2002) have been specially developed.

V	P	Number of Iterations	GA	μGA	LARES
20	20	20,000	0	0	0
100	20	20,000	0	0.03	0
1000	20	30,000	0.16	0.29	0
1000	200	30,000	0.16	0.29	0

Table 1. Comparison of LARES performance with GA for the multi-modal random problem generator.

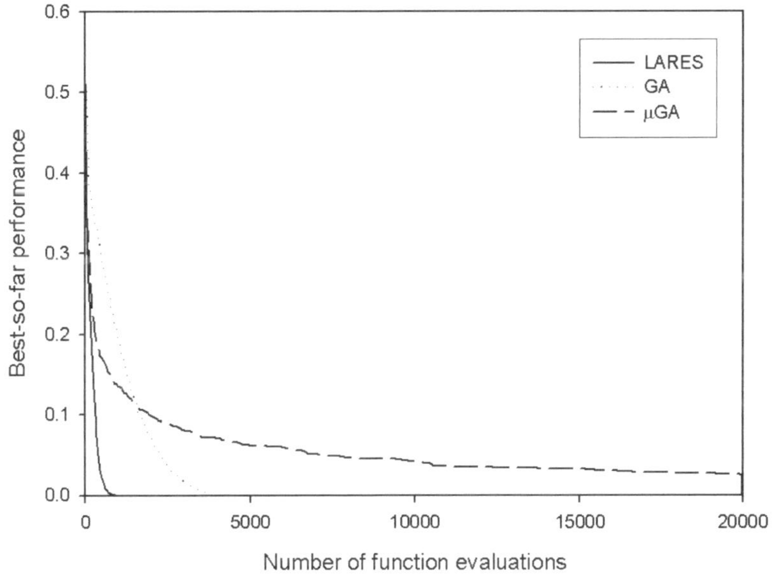

Fig. 3. Average best-so-far curves for LARES, GA and μGA using a multi-modal problem generator with V = 100 and P = 20.

Table 2 shows the solution of a series of L-SAT random problems using LARES and GA. Each test consists of an average of over 20 randomly generated problems. In all simulations, the length of clauses, L, had a fixed value of 3. The number of variables, *V*, was also fixed at a value of 100. The number of clauses was used as a parameter in the simulation, ranging from 200 to 2400. LARES was faster than GA in all cases, but in the last two cases GA found a slightly better solution while μGA found a slightly worse solution to the L-SAT problem (see Figure 9). These results indicate that LARES also behaves very well with problems involving different levels of epistasis.

The LARES algorithm was also applied to a very challenging test bed used by many authors to test real function optimization algorithms. Binary encoding was used to represent real variables. The algorithm was compared with GA using the same test bed, starting with the same initial guesses, and performing the same number of iterations. Comparisons are also made with other methods specifically designed for real-function optimization reported in the literature. Although literature in this field is extensive, few studies involve methods that are efficient for real function optimization. Reported algorithms include Differential Evolution (DE) (Storn and Price, 1997), the Breeder Genetic Algorithm (BGA) (12 Mühlenbein and Schlierkamp-Voosen, 1993), Evolutionary Algorithm with Soft Genetic operators (EASY) (Voigt, 1995), the Line-up Competition Algorithm (LCA) (Yan and Ma, 2001), Continuous Ant Colony Optimization (CACO) (Mathur et al., 2000), Adaptive Simulated Annealing (ASA) (Ingber and Rosen, 1992), Very Fast Simulated Annealing (VFSA) (Ingber, 1993), Guided Evolutionary Simulated Annealing (GESA) (Yip and Pao, 1995) and Covariance Matrix Adaptation Evolution Strategy (CMA-ES) (Hansen, Muller and Koumoutsakos, 2003). In summary, LARES had better performance than GA in most instances, and in many cases the speed of LARES is comparable to that of methods specially designed to operate with real-value optimization problems.

Number of classes, C	Number of iterations	GA	μGA	LARES
200	30,000	0	0	0.0003
1200	30,000	0.0433	0.050	0.0469
2400	30,000	0.0651	0.071	0.0675

Table 2. Comparison of LARES and GA performance with the LSAT random problem generator

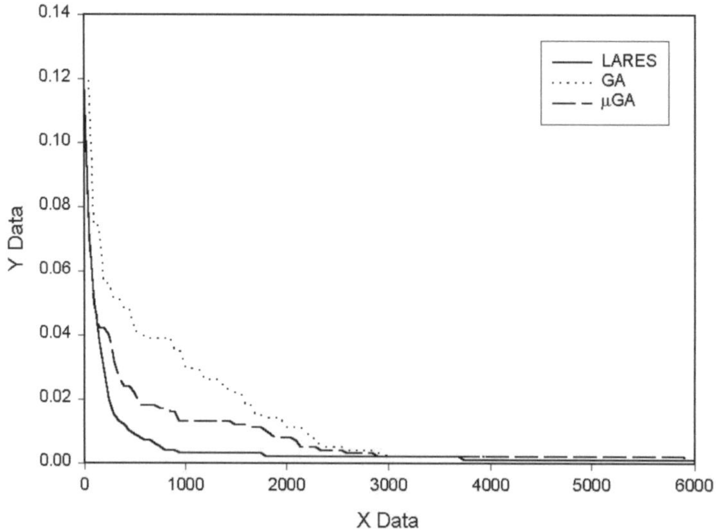

Fig. 4. Average best-so-far curves for LARES, GA, and μGA using a L-SAT problem with C = 200, L = 3, and V = 100.

3. Solution of dynamic optimization problems using LARES

As discussed in the introduction, dynamic optimization is a very important type of optimization problem in operation research and engineering, since many systems of interest are dynamic. In particular, most processes in the chemical industry are batch processes in which optimal reactant addition (and/or temperature) profiles determine product quality. Dynamic optimization is also used in model predictive control systems. These types of problems are more effectively solved using stochastic optimization methods that can escape from local minima and are not affected by singularities. In Banga, Irizarry-Rivera, and Seider (1998), an efficient and robust algorithm was developed to solve dynamic optimization problems using a flexible parametrization of the control law, consisting of a piecewise variable-length linear function. This method resulted in a big improvement over the more traditional piecewise constant approximations (Roubos et al., 1999; Luus, 2000). A generalized algorithm that uses LARES with a very flexible control law representation has also been considered (Irizarry, 2005a). This algorithm is reviewed in this section.
Unlike standard optimization to determine the optimal value of a set of real variables, in dynamic optimization, we seek an optimal function $u(t)$ or a set of functions $u_i(t)$, i= 1,M. The dynamic optimization problem for a single control law can be formulated as:

Find u(t) over $t \in [t_o, t_f]$ such that

$$\min_{u(t)} F(x(t_f)) \tag{3a}$$

subject to:

$$\frac{dx}{dt} = \Psi(x(t), u(t), t) \tag{3b}$$

$$x(t_o) = x_o \tag{3c}$$

$$h(x(t), u(t)) = 0 \tag{3d}$$

$$c(x(t), u(t)) \leq 0 \tag{3e}$$

$$u^L \leq u(t) \leq u^U \tag{3f}$$

where F is the performance index, u is the control law, and x the vector of state variables. The set of constraints consists of the dynamic model (Eqn. 3b), the initial conditions of the state variables (Eqn. 3c), the equality constraints (Eqn. 3d), the inequality constraints (Eqn. 3e), and bounds on the control variables (Eqn. 3f). Different methods to solve this type of problem have been reviewed recently by Banga et al. (2003).

3.1 LARES-PR algorithm

The previously introduced algorithm (Irizarry, 2005; Irizarry, 2006) consists of interfacing the LARES algorithm with a generalized representation of the control law. This procedure decodes the LARES decision variables (molecules) into a flexible representation of the control law based on three key elements: (a) variable-length segments, (b) the use of finite element trial functions to represent the control function in each segment (Zienkiewics, 1977), and (c) switching between different representations to model each segment with different functions. Figure 5 shows an example in which the possible profile is represented by three segments of different lengths. In the first segment, the control function is modeled with a quadratic finite element. The second segment is modeled with a constant function (step function). The third segment is modeled with a linear finite element. In this representation, the segment sizes, the type of function representing each segment, and the adjustable parameters of the selected function for each segment are all decision variables of the optimization problem to be solved. This representation spans a large functional space in which smooth regions, drastic changes in functionality, singularities, and discontinuities of the control function can be found as part of the solution for the optimization problem with a reduced number of decision variables.

The unknown control profile is encoded according to the following procedure. For the segments represented with *finite elements,* the node values of the finite element are part of the decision variables. Molecules are assigned to encode each of these variables using binary encoding. The function selection for each segment is then performed as follows. The data structure starts with all segments represented by finite-element function using the highest order of elements to be considered in the analysis. Then, a logical variable is defined for each segment, which is used as a switching mechanism. The logical variable can replace the

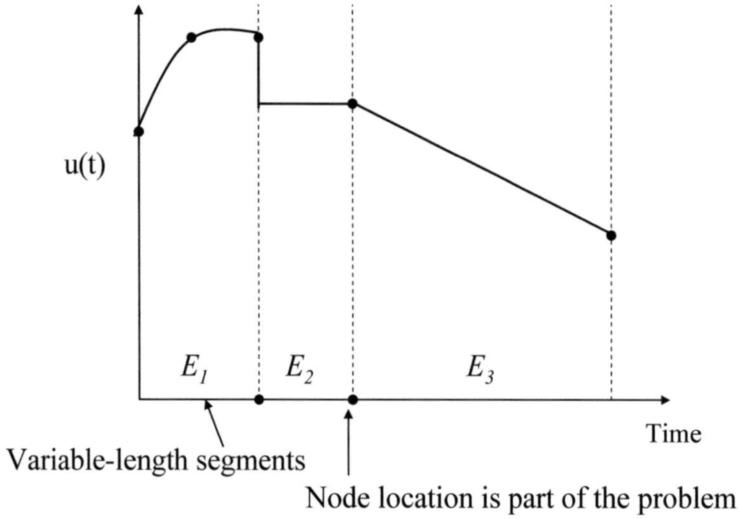

Fig. 5. Profile representation: generalized structure.

element with a lower-order element or with user-defined functions over the same segment interval. Figure 6 illustrates the hybrid formulation. This example consists of quadratic finite elements with three nodes representing each element. The logical variable with state $\delta = (1,1,2,3,0)$ replaces the first two elements with lower-order linear elements (eliminating the middle node as a variable), the third and fourth elements are replaced with user-specified functions, and element 5 is represented with a quadratic element. The combinatorial variables for each finite element, δ_i, is an integer number whose range equals the number of possible functions to be used. One molecule is selected for each combinatorial variable. The number of states for the molecule equals the number of possible functions that can represent a segment.

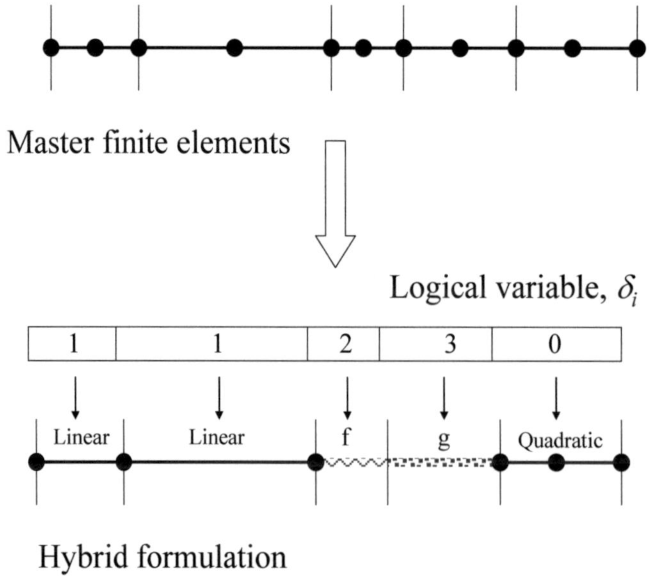

Fig. 6. Encoding a hybrid formulation.

The encoding of the segment size is the most difficult aspect of this formulation. The size of each segment is a component of the decision variables of the optimization problem, represented by a partition $\tau_1....\tau_N$. For each trial solution, a new partition is generated (τ_i^t , where the sequence is in increasing order, $\tau_i^t \le \tau_{i+1}^t$). These variables cannot be encoded directly into LARES, and if standard binary encoding of these parameters in the range $\tau_i \in [0,t_f]$ is utilized, this constraint will be violated frequently during LARES iterations. This problem is avoided by the following two-step procedure, called *Moving Partition (MP) transformation* (Irizarry, 2005a). First, computational variables are chosen for each partition variable ($s_i \in \left[0,1\right]$ to represent each τ_i). Mapping from this computational domain to the physical domain is made with the help of the disjoint segments, each one around the partition of the best solution found. Let τ_i^b be the sequence for the best solution found. Then the following boundaries are calculated:

$$\tau_i^{L,b} \equiv \tau_i^b - \beta \cdot \left(\tau_i^b - \tau_{i-1}^b\right) / 2 \tag{4}$$

$$\tau_i^{U,b} \equiv \tau_i^b + \beta \cdot \left(\tau_{i+1}^b - \tau_i^b\right) / 2 \tag{5}$$

where the parameter β is used to control the gap between the disjoint segments. With this boundary for each partition node and the trial vector, s_i^t , the actual trial partition is calculated from the following MP mapping, $T_i : [0,1] \to [\tau_i^{L,b}, \tau_i^{U,b}]$, defined as follows:

$$\tau_i^t = \tau_i^{L,b} + s_i^t \cdot \left(\tau_i^{U,b} - \tau_i^{L,b}\right) \tag{6}$$

The MP is shown schematically in Figure 7. As shown in this figure, the trial variables $s_1,...s_N$ are not in ascending order ($s_2 < s_1$), but the trial partition values, $\tau_1,...\tau_N$ are in ascending order ($\tau_1 < \tau_2$).

With this description of the control law, the LARES-PR algorithm can be described as follows:

LARES-PR algorithm. The overall algorithm is discussed in Irizarry (2005). It consists of interfacing this profile representation with LARES. After a new trial molecular state from LARES, the procedure described in this section consists of (1) decoding, (2) applying MP transformation, (3) building the control law determined by element type, size, and parameters, (4) integrating the model, and (5) feedback to LARES regarding the performance of the control

3.2 Simulation results

LARES-PR performance has been studied with a set of benchmark problems with low sensitivity of the objective function, bang-bang behaviors, singular arc, and discontinuities in the optimal profile. In all cases, the algorithm has proven to be efficient and robust. Figure 8 shows the solution of four optimization problems used by several authors as benchmark problems. The Van der Pol oscillator problem has been studied by Vassiliadis (1993), Tanartkit and Biegler (1995), Banga, Irizarry-Rivera and Seider (1998), and Vassiliadis et al. (1999). This problem was solved using the generalized control function, where each element can be represented by either linear or quadratic Lagrange polynomials. The optimal profile is shown in Figure 8a, with an improved performance index over other methods using only four elements and a smoother profile compared to previous results reported in the literature.

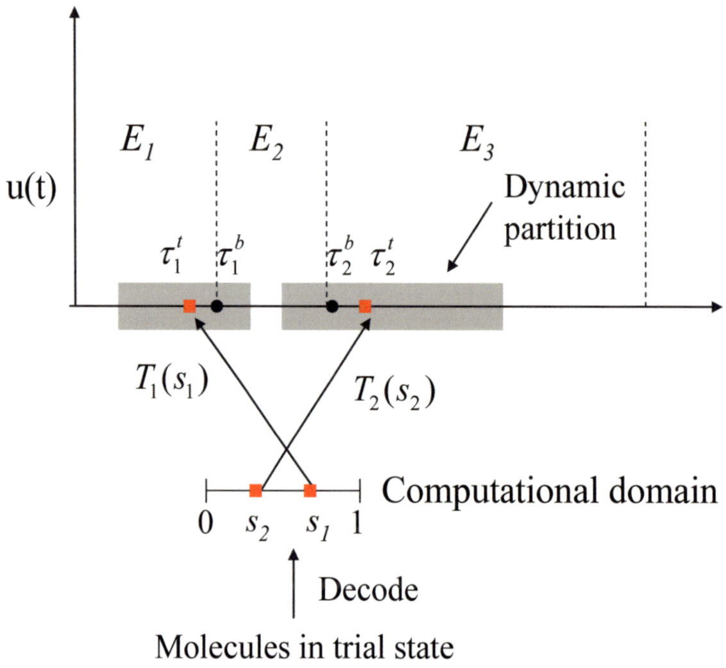

Fig. 7. Moving partition transformation. Each variable in a computational domain is mapped into a corresponding space/time subdomain.

The second case shown in Figure 8b is a plug-flow reactor with singular arc. In this problem, a plug-flow reactor packed with a mixture of catalysts is used to perform the reaction $A \Leftrightarrow B \Leftrightarrow C$. The fraction of catalyst is adjusted throughout the reactor to maximize the product C. This problem was solved using the generalized control law approximation with three possible functions for the element E_i: δ_i = {1, 2, 3} = {u(t) = constant finite element, u(t) = u_{max}, u(t) = u_{min}}. The optimal control law is shown in Figure 8b. Figure 8c shows the optimal production of secreted protein in a fed-batch reactor. This problem consists of a bioreactor operated in fed-batch mode studied by Park and Ramirez (1988), Luus (1992), Banga, Irizarry-Rivera and Seider (1988), Vassiliadis et al. (1999), and Sarkar and Modak (2003). This problem shows very low performance index sensitivity of the control profile, often leading to computational difficulties particularly when gradient-based algorithms are used. The fed-batch reactor problem was also solved using the generalized control law approximation, with three possible functions for the element E_i: δ_i = {1, 2, 3} = {u(t) = quadratic finite element, u(t) = u_{max}, u(t) = u_{min}}with 10 elements. The control law gives a global optimum for this problem.

Figure 8d shows the optimal profile for the bang-bang control problem (see Irizarry 2005a for a detailed description of the problem). To solve this problem, eight elements were used, and the function approximation of each element is either a linear interpolation function or the bang-bang constant functions δ_i={1, 2, 3}={u(t)=linear trial function, u(t)= u_{max}, u(t)= u_{min}}. LARES-PR found the correct bang-bang feature as part of the solution, that is, δ^*= {4,3,4,3,4,3,4}. This is an important element of the proposed method, which can be used with general-purpose approximation functions or with problem-specific functionalities for which the proposed algorithm will identify problem features in addition to the solution.

In most cases, the near optimum value (less than 0.5% of global optimum) was found in less than 1,000–10,000 function evaluations. The algorithm continues to refine the solution at a slower rate, resulting in very accurate solutions. In most cases, a very accurate solution can be found in 50,000–100,000 iterations. The results demonstrate that LARES-PR is robust and has fast convergence properties when compared with other stochastic optimization methods.

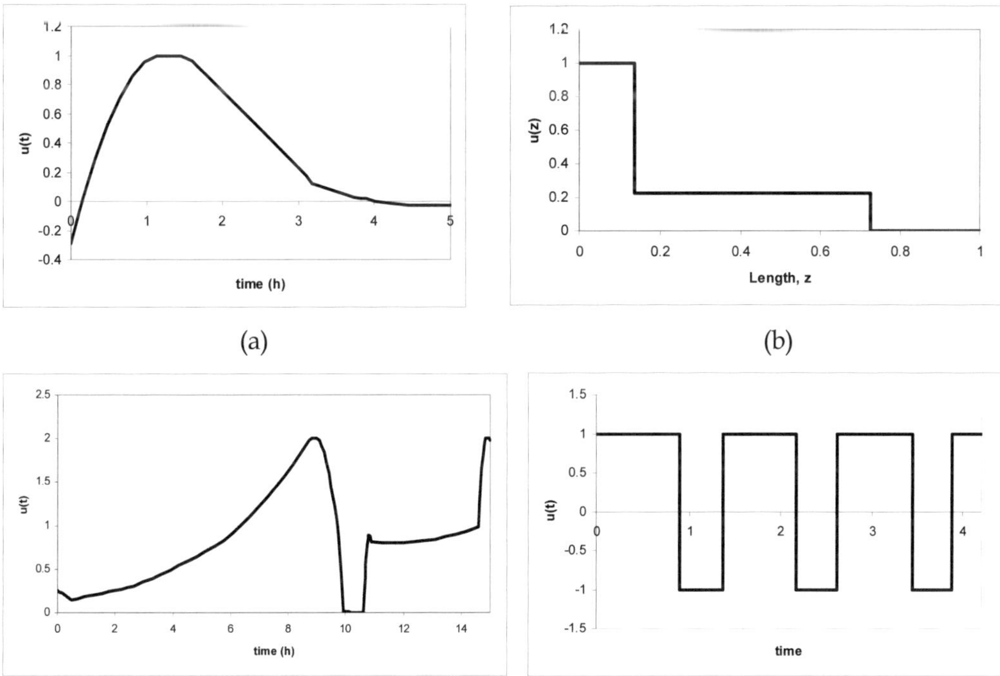

(a) (b)

(c) (d)

Fig. 8. Optimal profiles: (a) Van der Pol oscillator problem, (b) plug-flow reactor with singular arc, (c) fed-batch bioreactor, (d) bang-bang control problem.

LARES-PR has also being applied to large-scale optimal control problems with discrete-time dynamics and multiple control laws. The dynamic integrated climate-economy (DICE) model for global warming (Nordhaus, 1994) is a model of a very important problem, which posed several challenges in finding the optimal profile. This model consists of maximizing the discounted sum of per capita utilities consumption subject to the dynamics of emissions, economic impact, and economic cost of policies to control global warming. Moles, Banga and Keller (2004) made an extensive study of optimal policy with a modified version of this model using different global optimization algorithms (ICRS, LJ, DE, SRES, GLOBAL, GCSOLVE). As discussed in Moles, Banga and Keller (2004), the numerical solution of this multimodal NLP is very challenging, due to the non-convexities and discontinuous nature of the dynamics.

As the time horizon is discrete, the dynamic optimization problem can be formulated as a standard NLP problem with the value of the control laws at each discrete time as a decision variable. Using this approach, the number of decision variables increases as the time horizon, N_t, increases (number of decision variables = N_t*N_u), resulting in a large-scale nonlinear optimization problem. Alternatively, the profile representation of LARES-PR can be utilized to represent the control law with a very small set of decision variables.

Figure 9 shows the performance of LARES, DE, CRS, and LARES-PR in solving the original DICE model for a time horizon of 50 decades. As shown in Figure 9, LARES and LARES-PR are faster than DE and CRS in converging to a near global optimum. In particular, LARES-PR was much faster than all methods with a high-quality solution: The best value found for each algorithm was: W^* = 966.91767 (DE), 966.91632 (LARES-PR), 966.91353 (LARES), and 966.69733 (ICRS). When the number of finite elements was increased from five to eight, the solution was improved to almost identical to the DE results in fewer iterations, with W^* = 966.91711 (LARES-PR).

LARES-PR effectively solved this problem, which consisted of finding the optimal functionality of two simultaneous control laws. To implement multiple control laws, a representation is defined for each unknown profile (PR_1 and PR_2).

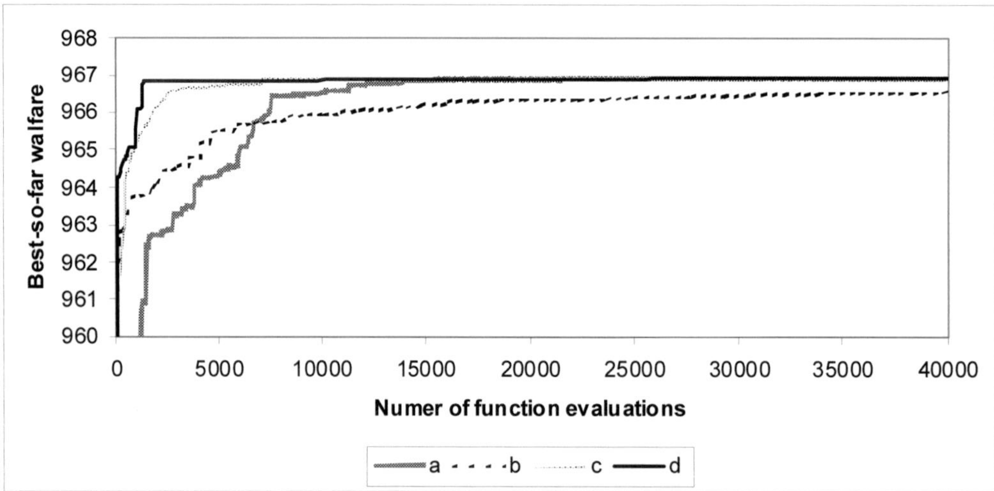

Fig. 9. Performance for the DICE climate-economy discrete time model: (a) DE, (b) CRS, (c) LARES, (d) LARES-PR.

4. Monte Carlo methods for population balance problems

A great majority of products are composed of finely divided solids or contain finely divided particles as part of their composition. One example is metallic microparticles and nanoparticles used in electronic ink compositions. Another example is the dispersion of pigments in paints. Most pharmaceutical products include a crystallization of organic powders. The particle size distribution, shape, and composition of these finely divided particles control the properties of the final product. Therefore, the understanding of these particles and how they form is of great importance (Irizarry, 2010a). The macroscopic modeling of particle formation consists of formulating population balance equations for the problem at hand. When optimization of these systems is pursued, the population balance equations appear as part of the constraints (Irizarry, 2005; Irizarry, 2006).

Population balance models are continuity equations of a particle population evolving by different mechanisms (such as aggregation, breakage, nucleation, and growth). The continuous population balance equation, PBE, is a deterministic integro-differential equation that describes the dynamics of a particle density function as a function of continuous particle properties (i.e. volume, particle radius, surface area, etc.). As the dimensionality of the PBE increases, the direct numerical solution of these equations becomes more difficult. For a multidimensional population balance equation, the Monte Carlo (MC) solution is an attractive alternative (and in many cases the only option). In these methods, the system evolution is modeled by a simple stochastic game, which is robust and easy to implement (Gillespie, 1975; Garcia et al., 1987). For systems close to the thermodynamic limit, both the MC solution and the direct numerical solution of the PBE converge to the same results. In many situations of practical interest, the MC solution may become very slow. Several optimization approaches have been developed to increase the MC simulation speed. The point ensemble Monte Carlo (PEMC) algorithm and the τ–PEMC algorithm developed in 2007 (Irizarry, 2007a; Irizarry, 2007b) are approximated MC methods that increase simulation speed by orders of magnitude when compared with existing MC methods.

Population balance models can be formulated as discrete events Markov processes (also known as a jump Markov process). The standard exact simulation method (exact MC) for jump Markov processes consists of selecting the time for the next event and the type of event sequentially until a final time is reached (one trajectory). Many trajectories are calculated to generate the probability distribution function of the Markov process variables. This simulation method uses the propensity functions of each event, E_s, defined as follows:

$R(E_s)\, dt \equiv$ the probability that the event E_s occurs in the time interval (t, t + dt).

The time for the next event, τ, is sampled from an exponential distribution:

$$P(\tau) = R_\Sigma \exp[R_\Sigma \tau]\,. \tag{7}$$

where R_Σ is the total propensity of all possible events ($R_\Sigma = \sum_i R(E_i)$). The probability of the event, E_i, occurring next (i.e. that particles will aggregate) is proportional to the event propensity, $R(E_i)$:

$$P(E_i) = R(E_i) / R_\Sigma\,. \tag{8}$$

In the inverse method, this distribution is sampled using a uniform random variable $r \in (0,1)$ and then solving the following equation:

$$\sum_{i=1}^{f} R(E_i) < r\, R_\Sigma \le \sum_{i=1}^{f+1} R(E_i) \tag{9}$$

where $E_i, i = 1,T$ is the indexed list of all possible events, and T is the total number of events. The solution of this equation, E_f, is the next event to be executed at time $t+\tau$. Alternatively, the acceptance-rejection method can be used to sample the next event [5].

This simulation procedure has been used to develop the stochastic simulation algorithm, SSA, for chemical kinetics (Gillespie, 1976; Gillespie, 1977). In this method the firing of a chemical reaction represents a discrete chemical kinetic event of the Markov process. This algorithm is also known as kinetic Monte Carlo (KMC). The exact MC has also been used for the MC solution of population balance models. In many situations of practical interest, the MC solution may become very slow, especially when the number of particles in the simulation box is increased and the total number of events becomes very large or when the computational cost of calculating all the rates, R_{Σ} is large. In these cases the calculation of Eqs. (1) and (3) becomes very computationally expensive, slowing down the generation of trajectories.
To further accelerate the MC simulation of population balance models, a new approach was introduced in 2007 (Irizarry, 2007a; Irizarry, 2007b). These algorithms are based on the construction of a jump Markov process called PERP, which approximates the actual jump Markov model. These algorithms are shown to reduce CPU time by orders of magnitude without sacrificing simulation accuracy, when compared with optimized exact MC methods. Unlike other coarse graining (or lumping) strategies in which information and identity is lost, in these algorithms, the history of each particle is retained while a coarse view of the process is taken. These two algorithms are summarized in the next section.

5. Fast Monte Carlo algorithms

The PEMC and τ-PEMC algorithms are based on the simulation of an approximated jump Markov process called PERP (Irizarry, 2007a; Irizarry, 2007b). This approximated Markov process is based on three ideas. First, the total population is "discretized" into subpopulations of particles with sizes of specified intervals. Each subpopulation is viewed as a "chemical species" with the number of particles in the subpopulation representing the number of molecules of that species in the simulation volume. Second, the inter-particle interactions (i.e. aggregation, nucleation, breakage) are viewed as a set of special types of reaction, in which the reaction products are allocated stochastically to the existing species using probability functions that are mass conserving on average. Third, the original set of subpopulations is coupled with the system of "chemical species". The PERP Markov process is described next.

5.1 PERP Markov process and PEMC algorithm

The first step in this approximated Markov process is the partition of the particles in the simulation volume into a set of sub-ensembles, Φ_i , called point ensembles. This partition is made using a set of M grid points of representative sizes $v_1,\dots v_M$. All simulation particles in an interval around the grid point v_i are allocated in point ensemble Φ_i. Let N_i be the number of particles in point ensemble Φ_i. The state vector is then defined as $(\boldsymbol{N},\boldsymbol{\Phi})$ were $\boldsymbol{N}=(N_1,N_2,\dots,N_M)^T$ and $\Phi=(\Phi_1,\Phi_2,\dots,\Phi_M)^T$. Here, each grid point is viewed as a chemical pseudo-specie, S_i, with N_i molecules in the simulation volume. For example, Figure 10 shows a size-dependent partition of 17 particles (each with a set of different properties) into five point ensembles. The five pseudo-species $(S_1,S_2,\dots,S_5)$ defined by this partition have (3, 4, 6, 3, 1) molecules in the simulation volume.

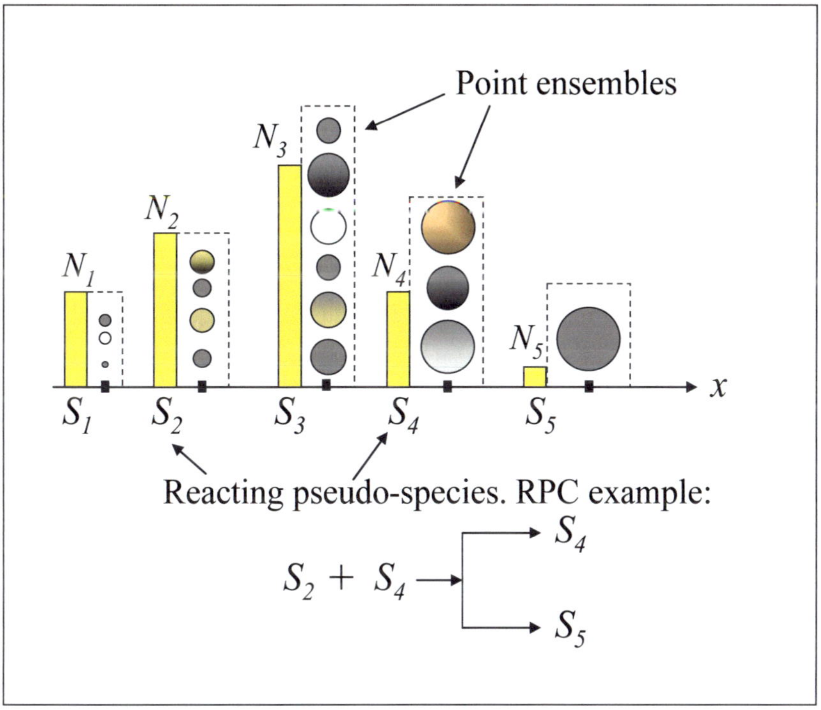

Fig. 10. Schematic of PERP jump Markov model

In this approximated process, the discrete events consist of a set of "reaction channels" where the reaction part involves the pseudo-species to mimic the actual particle event (i.e. aggregation between two particles). Unlike standard reaction channels of chemical kinetics, the product component consists of several steps, some of them also stochastic processes.

In the exact Markov process, an event, E, is defined in terms of the possible interactions between the simulation particles. For example, an aggregation between two particles i and j is an event that creates a new particle in the simulation volume ($E: x_{new} = x_i + x_j$) and eliminates the mother particles from the simulation volume. The reactant component of the RPC mimics the same event, but between the pseudo-species instead of actual particles. For example, the events representing the aggregation mechanism in the original Markov process are replaced by an "aggregation reaction" of pseudo-species ($E_s : S_i + S_j$) in the PERP Markov process. In the case of aggregation, the propensity function for these "reaction channels" is given by:

$$R(E_s) = \left(1 - \frac{1}{2}\delta_{ij}\right) N_i N_j q(v_i, v_j) / V_s \tag{10}$$

The propensity functions for other mechanisms have also been described (Irizarry, 2007a). Notice that the propensity of each event in the PERP Markov process is given only in terms of $\boldsymbol{N}$. For the aggregation case discussed here, the PERP event is summarized in the following algorithm:

Algorithm M1: Fire an aggregation RPC event: $E_f = S_i + S_j$ with $(v_i + v_j) \in [v_k, v_{k+1}]$.

1. Reduce N_i and N_j by one.
2. Select random particles, *n and m*, from point ensembles *i* and *j* ($x_n \in \Phi_i$ and $x_m \in \Phi_j$).
3. Form a new particle from the mother particles, $x_{new} = x_n + x_m$.
4. Eliminate the particles *n* and *m* from their ensembles.
5. Find the product sub-specie $S_p : p = k$ with probably P_f or $p = k + 1$ otherwise.
6. Allocate the new particle to the product point ensemble $x_{new} \in \Phi_p$, increase N_p by one.

The product pseudo-specie S_{new} in the current event is determined by letting the landing interval $\left[v_k, v_{k+1}\right]$ be defined as the interval such that $v_{new} = v_i + v_j \in \left[v_k, v_{k+1}\right]$. The product pseudo-specie is S_k ($S_{new} = S_k$) with probability P_s. In this case, the number of molecules N_k is increased by one, and x_{new} is allocated to Φ_k. Otherwise $S_{new} = S_{k+1}$, N_{k+1} is increased by one, and x_{new} is allocated to Φ_{k+1}. The product probability parameter, P_s, is calculated using the mass conservation equation for this landing interval: $v_k P_s + v_{k+1}(1 - P_s) = v_{new}$. All these events in the product component of the RPC are simply called PERP events. RPCs can be defined for any mechanism (Irizarry, 2007a)
The PEMC algorithm is the exact MC simulation of the approximated PERP Markov process. A detailed description of these steps has been published (Irizarry, 2007b). Let $E_i, i = 1,..,T$ be the list of all possible RPCs describing the population balance model at hand. The PEMC method is summarized in the following algorithm:

Algorithm M2: PEMC (one iteration).

1. Find the time to fire the next RPC using Eq. (7). Update the time $t = t + \tau$.
2. Find the RPC to be fired next solving Eq. (9).
3. Fire the selected PERP event (Algorithm M1)

These steps are repeated until the final time is reached. This algorithm is very fast because the set of RPCs is more compact than the set of all possible events between particles, making the calculations of Eq. (7) and (9) very fast.

5.2 τ-PEMC

The τ–PEMC algorithm is a τ-leap solution of the approximated PERP Markov process. The τ-leap method is an approximated stochastic simulation, were many events are fired at once over the time interval. Consider a coarser time interval, τ, such that many events occur in this interval, but small enough that the propensity functions will not change appreciably during τ. When this condition is satisfied, all reaction channels can be considered as independent events (Gillespie, 2001), and the number of firings for each reaction, E_j, is a Poisson random variable with distribution $P_{PD}\left(k_j; R(E_j), \tau\right)$, where

$$P_{PD}\left(k; a, \tau\right) = \frac{e^{-a\tau}}{k!}\left(a\tau\right)^k \tag{11}$$

The accuracy and speed of the method depends on the selection of time τ during the simulation (Gillespie and Petzold, 2003). Since the Poisson distribution is not bounded, it could generate negative values for the concentration.

Another improvement to the method is to replace the Poisson distribution with a binomial distribution (Tian and Burrage, 2004; Chatterjee, Vlachos, and Katsoulakis, 2005):

$$P_{BD}\left(k;p,k_{\max}\right)=\frac{k_{\max}}{k!\left(k_{\max}-k\right)!}p^{k}\left(1-p\right)^{k_{\max}-k} \tag{12}$$

In this case the number of firings for each reaction, k_j, is sampled from a binomial random variable with distribution $P_{PD}\left(k_j;p_j,k_{\max}^{j}\right)$, where $k_{\max}^{j}$ is the maximum number of times reaction j can be fired (after consuming the limiting component). The firing probability for E_j is $p_j = R(E_j)\tau / k_{\max}^{j}$. The binomial distribution eliminates the problem of negative concentrations and is more robust with respect to larger τ values.

The PERP process can be simulated using the τ-leap method, as previously described (Irizarry, 2007b). A pseudo-code for this algorithm is described as follows:

Algorithm M3: τ-PEMC (one iteration)

1. Select the time parameter, τ .
2. For each RPC, E_s , take a sample k_s from a binomial distribution (Eq. (12)) using the parameter $p = R(E_s)\tau / k_{\max}^{s}$.
3. Fire each PERP event, E_s , k_s times (execute algorithm M1 k_s consecutive times).

Continue steps 1-3 until the final time is reached.

5.3 Performance of the PEMC algorithm with complex kernels

The numerical accuracy of these algorithms has been studied with complex coagulation kernels of physical relevance. Numerical results are compared with the generalized approximation method (GA) developed by Piskunov and Golubev (2002) and Piskunov et al. (2002). The values for the second moment by the GA method are considered the most accurate existing numerical results in the literature. They are used here as benchmark values. The following kernels are considered:

i. The Brownian kernel,

$$q_B(u,v)=\left(u^{1/3}+v^{1/3}\right)\left(u^{-1/3}+v^{-1/3}\right) \tag{13}$$

ii. The coagulation kernel simulating the process of migration and coalescence of particles on a heated substrate,

$$q_+(u,v)=u^{2/3}+v^{2/3} \tag{14}$$

iii. The gravitational coagulation of particles in the Stokes regime,

$$q_C(u,v)=\left(u^{1/3}+v^{1/3}\right)^2\left|u^{2/3}-v^{2/3}\right| \tag{15}$$

For the gravitational kernel, some moments diverge after a critical point that depends on initial conditions. The critical point for the initial conditions used here is in the range of 0.5–0.8 (Piskunov et al., 2002).

The initial conditions used in the simulation for q_B and q_+ kernels are a mono-disperse solution with unit particle volume and unit total particle concentration. For the case of q_C, the following initial conditions are utilized: $n(v,0)=0.5\delta(v-1)+0.25\delta(v-2)$. In Table 3, the CPU time and final second moments of the simulations for different methods are compared as a function of kernel type and number of particles. For the τ-PEMC, two representative coarse-graining factors (f = 100 and f = 1,000) were examined. All calculations were performed using Visual Fortran 6.6 on an Intel Pentium M 1.6 GHz machine with 504 MB RAM. Table 3 shows that τ-PEMC can be 14–44 times faster than PEMC.

For kernel q_B, the τ-PEMC method gives accurate results in all cases with a coarse-graining factor f = 100. For the case f = 1,000, the number of particles had to be increased to 50,000 to generate accurate second moments (see Table 3). The q_+ kernel is more computationally challenging than the Brownian kernel, resulting in a wider distribution. Numerical results presented previously (Irizarry, 2007a) show that PEMC also quickly converges to the GA values. Table 3 shows the solution convergence to the exact value as a function of increasing the number of particles. For the factor f = 1000, large deviations of the second moments were observed even when a large number of particles was utilized. Good results were obtained for f = *100*.

For the q_C kernel, some moments diverge at a critical value (gelling point). For the initial conditions used here, this critical value is believed to be between 0.5 and 0.8 (Piskunov et al., 2002). Unlike most numerical methods, the PEMC gives accurate results for all times, especially at time 0.6, where all discretization methods diverge (see Irizarry, 2007a). The τ-PEMC method can converge to the exact solution for times far from the critical point (time ≤ 0.4). When the time reaches the critical point, the errors for the second moment were quite large in all cases.

		PEMC		τ-PEMC	f=10^2	τ-PEMC	f=10^3	AR		GA
Kernel	N_p	*CPU*	$m_2(t_f)$	*CPU*	$m_2(t_f)$	*CPU*	$m_2(t_f)$	*CPU*	$m_2(t_f)$	$m_2(t_f)$
q_B	10,000	3.68	412	0.22	413	0.06	364	0.18	413	416
	20,000	7.24	415	0.45	414	0.12	381	0.35	420	
	50,000	18.12	416	1.11	415	0.51	400	0.89	414	
q_+	10,000	5.75	2.15E+5	0.52	1.90E+5	0.13	7.45E+4	331.1	2.10E+5	2.29E+5
	20,000	11.52	2.20E+5	1.01	2.03E+5	0.24	1.14E+5	662.7	2.24E+5	
	50,000	28.74	2.37E+5	2.49	2.29E+5	0.57	1.74E+5	1642.2	2.39E+5	
q_C	10,000	0.36	33.00	0.02	9.02	0.006	0.0	70.2	6E+3	23.27
	20,000	0.73	28.50	0.06	12.2	0.02	4.36	115.6	5E+3	
	50,000	1.76	23.30	0.18	15.7	0.05	7.16	290.0	5E+3	

Table 3. Comparison of second moments at final time t_f and *CPU* times between *τ-PEMC* and *PEMC* for kernels q_B, q_+, and q_C. Numerical results are compared with the generalized approximation method (*GA*) and the acceptance-rejection *MC* method (*AR*).

These results show that the τ-PEMC method generates accurate results if τ is selected to be small enough and the number of particles large enough. For the cases studied here,

N_p = 20,000 and f = *100*, give very accurate results for all kernels (away from gelling points). For simulations near gelling points, the performance of the τ-PEMC deteriorates, and the PEMC should be used in this case.

Table 3 also shows results using the acceptance rejection (AR) method of Garcia et. al. (1987) for comparison. For the coagulation case, this method is very attractive because it is simple to implement and avoids calculation of all interactions between particles, making the method very computationally efficient. As noticed by other authors, the CPU time and accuracy of this method depends drastically on the problem (kernel and initial conditions). As shown in Table 1, for some cases the AR method can be very efficient (q_B) while in other cases the CPU time is very high (q_+). Additionally, the AR method diverges for the q_C kernel, also shown in Table 3.

6. Hybrid Monte Carlo algorithm for population balance models with stochastic and deterministic variables

Most MC implementations of population balance models have focused on the solution of the PBE to approximate macroscopic variables. Less attention has been focused on the solution of population balance models where some species are far from the thermodynamic limit (very dilute or finite) and other species can be considered deterministic (high concentration). In this case the MC is more accurate than direct numerical solution, which ignores the inherent fluctuations of the system. This type of problem often results in a stochastic system that contains both stochastic and deterministic variables with multiple timescales for the different mechanisms. In this case, the direct MC simulation will be accurate but very ineffective in terms of CPU time. Furthermore, most of the computational time is spent sampling the fast events. This type of situation has been considered in the case of chemical kinetics and biological systems for which efficient hybrid algorithms have been developed to solve multi-scale problems (Salis and Kaznessis, 2005; Kaznessis, 2006; Haseltine and Rawlings, 2002; Haseltine and Rawlings, 2005). In these algorithms, the fast processes are approximated by continuous models, and the slow processes are solved by the exact MC method in a hybrid algorithm.

Disparate scales in population balance models may arise because some species are concentrated while others are very dilute. For accurate simulation of the dilute species, a large number of simulation particles are needed. In this case, the exact MC methods become very slow. A recently introduced hybrid strategy (Irizarry, 2010b) is reviewed. In this strategy, the τ-PEMC is used for the parts of the system than can be considered large, and the PEMC is used for the stochastic events.

6.1 Hybrid algorithms in chemical kinetics

The hybrid strategy for chemical kinetic problems (Salis and Kaznessis, 2005; Kaznessis, 2006; Haseltine and Rawlings, 2002) is based on partitioning between fast and slow reactions. To split the system between slow and fast events, the following criteria for fast events are utilized:

1. The fast events occur many times in a small time interval.
2. The effect of these events on the number of particles and the propensity functions is small relative to the total propensity function and the total number of particles.

The slow processes are simulated using SSA, while the fast processes are integrated using the Langevin equations. To make this hybrid simulation self-consistent, the coupling between both processes must be considered. If we look at the interval between the previous slow event at time t_o and the time for the next slow event ($t_o+\tau$), the following equation is satisfied:

$$\int_{t_0}^{t+\tau} R_{\Sigma}^{slow} dt + \ln(r) = 0 \qquad (16)$$

where r is a random number from the uniform distribution (*0, 1*). This equation replaces Eq. (7) for the time of the next slow event. In the interval $[t_o, t_o+\tau]$, the dynamics of the fast system can be integrated in a seamless way since by definition no slow events are present in this interval. Thus, Eq. (16) becomes a constraint in the hybrid strategy that needs to be monitored while integrating the fast process.

As previously discussed (Salis and Kaznessis, 2005), one way to implement this constraint is to notice that the integral term is monotonically increases, and the second term is a negative term. Therefore, the time for the next slow event can by found by monitoring the zero crossing of the residual equation:

$$RES(t) \equiv \int_{t_0}^{t_0+t} R_{\Sigma}^{slow} dt + \ln(r) \qquad (17)$$

6.2 Hybrid algorithm in multi-scale MC simulation of particulate processes

The hybrid strategy described in Section 6.1 is utilized with the slow mechanisms simulated using the PEMC algorithm. Instead of approximating the fast mechanism with a continuous model, as in the case of chemical kinetics, the τ-PEMC algorithm is utilized to model the fast mechanisms. The τ-PEMC method allows for coarse simulation in time while maintaining individual particle properties, in contrast to continuous models such as Langevin equations in which particle integrity is lost. The hybrid algorithm consists of the τ-leap integration of the PERP Markov process for fast events while monitoring the residual Eq. (17) for the firing of the next slow event of the PERP Markov process. This process is shown schematically in Figure 11. The detailed description of the algorithm is given in Irizarry (2010b).

6.3 Simulation results

Consider a system with two type of particles, A and B. B particles are much smaller than A particles. A particles can grow by an aggregation mechanism. B particles are stable from aggregation with other B particles but can condense on the surface of growing A particles. Furthermore, it is assumed that B particles are very dilute compared to A particles. These conditions make A-B condensation events a stochastic process, while A-A aggregation events can be approximated as continuous events.

Figure 12 shows five instances of the test problem for the case $W = 100$ (See Irizarry, 2010b for details). As shown in Figures 12a and 12b, the condensation of B monomers (measured with parameters x_1 defined in Irizarry, 2010b) is a stochastic process with considerable variability between trajectories, while the aggregation of A particles can be approximated as deterministic. In this case all A-particle size distribution trajectories of the second moment are almost identical. The PEMC is used as a benchmark for the accurate stochastic simulation. As there are disparate rates between condensation and aggregation, the hybrid

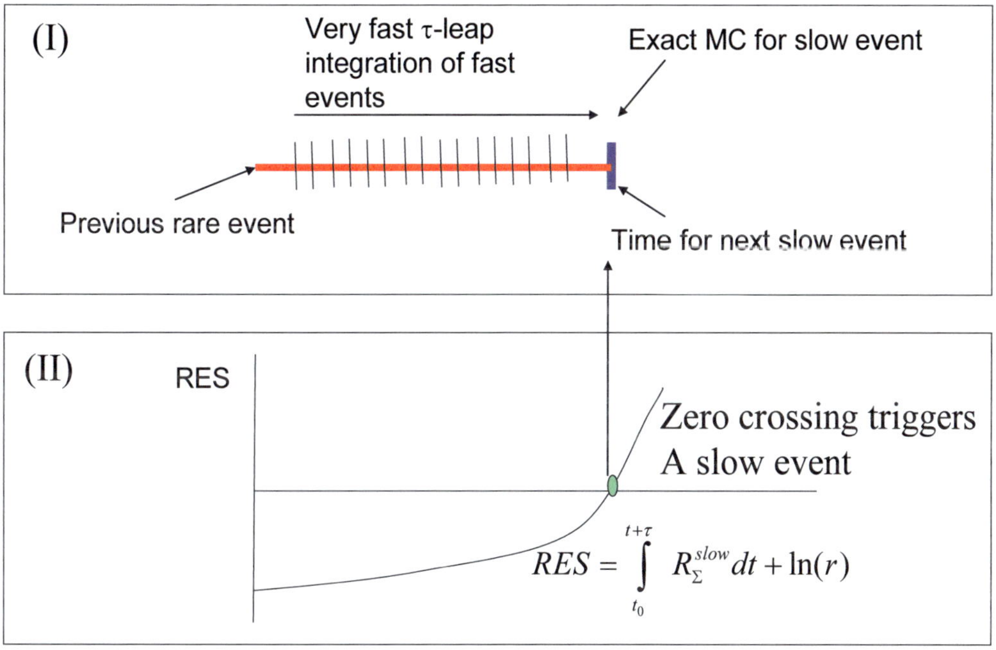

Fig. 11. Schematic of the hybrid algorithm. Integrate fast processes (panel I) while monitoring for the next slow event (panel II). At a zero crossing, a PEMC iteration is executed.

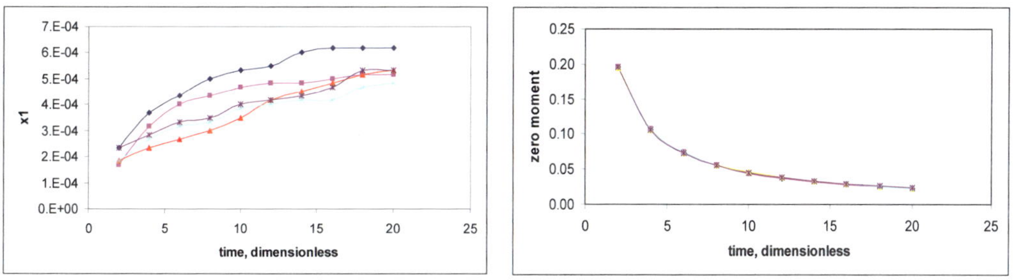

(a) (b)

Fig. 12. Five PEMC trajectories of the test problem with W = 100. (a) The fraction of B in A-B particles is stochastic A-B (parameter x_1). (b) Zero moment of the The size distribution of the main population (A) is deterministic.

algorithm can be utilized. As the rate of aggregation is reduced with time, the hybrid algorithm correctly switches to a PEMC simulation of the entire system. The hybrid algorithm can simulate stochastic variables (A-B) at speeds approaching τ-PEMC.

The statistics of the condensation of B monomers for the case *W = 100* is summarized in Table 4 for 1,000 simulations. The histogram of the parameter x_1 (which measures the concentration of B particles on A particles) for the hybrid-PEMC and PEMC solutions is shown in Figure 13. The hybrid and PEMC solutions are in excellent agreement. This result is remarkable considering that condensation events are very rare (~30 condensation events vs. ~60,000 aggregation events). The box plot for these parameters is shown in Figure 14. An analysis of variance was performed to compare the population generated by both methods.

For the case of x_1, both simulations are statistically equivalent. The hybrid algorithm is 17 times faster than the PEMC algorithm per trajectory. This increase in speed is very important, since many trajectories (~10^3) are needed to generate good statistics for the slow process. If the model is used for optimization, many design instances are needed (~10^4), each consisting of many trajectories, resulting in a very large number of simulations (~10^7). In this case any increase in the simulation speed of a trajectory will have a tremendous impact on the total simulation speed.

	PEMC	Hybrid-PEMC
Average value of x_1	5.20×10^{-4}	5.13×10^{-4}
Standard deviation of x_1	8.9×10^{-5}	9.0×10^{-5}
Average number of slow aggregation events	58,623	58,629
Average number of condensation events	31.2	30.8

Table 4. A comparison of hybrid-PEMC and PEMC for the test problem with $W = 100$ (Average of 1,000 trajectories).

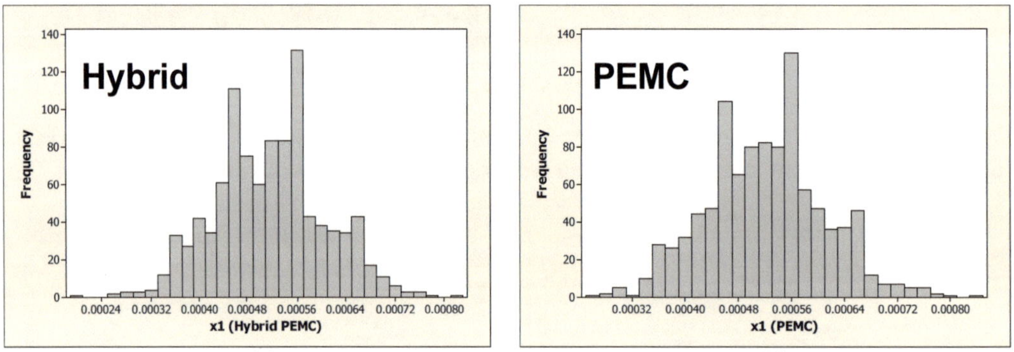

(a) (b)

Fig. 13. Histogram of the x_1 parameter for the test problem with W=100 (1,000 trajectories). (a) Hybrid-PEMC and (b) PEMC.

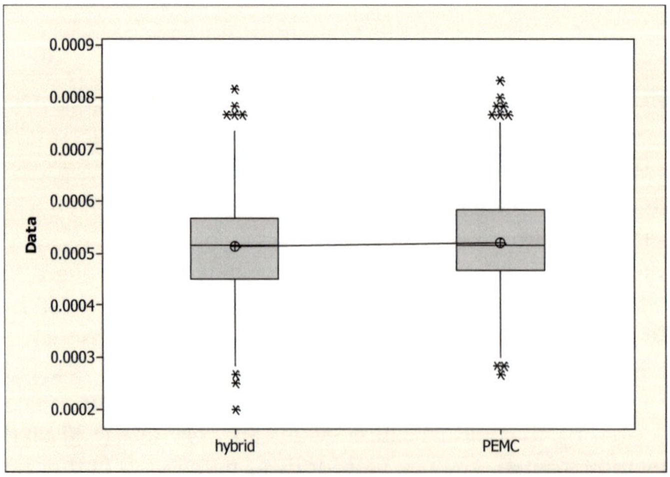

Fig. 14. A box-plot comparison of the hybrid-PEMC and PEMC solutions (W=100).

Hybrid and MC simulations produce statistically equivalent results, but the hybrid's increase in computational speed allows optimization problems involving these types of models to be solved very efficiently.

7. Conclusions and discussion

This chapter reviewed the artificial chemical process paradigm for global optimization. The LARES algorithm is very robust and efficient, converging to near-global optimal solutions when solving different classes of problems with different degrees of multi-modality, epistasis, flatness, and discontinuities. Future research will consider the use of the ACP paradigm in the development of new problem-specific algorithms. The algorithm was utilized to develop dynamic optimization strategies, LARES-PR and hybrid LARES-PR. The power of the algorithm lies in its utilization of a generalized approximation of the control function, composed of variable-length segments of finite elements of different orders or using specified functions. This generalized representation of the trial control law is possible due to the two-step encoding of the decision variables and the capability of LARES for multiple encoding. Multiple encoding allows the inclusion of different types of problem-specific finite elements (constant, linear, quadratic, etc.) and/or specialized functions to approximate the control law without any tailoring of the optimization algorithm. This approach is particularly effective for the solution of problems in which manipulated variables experience transition from smooth variations over time to discrete changes. Numerical experiments demonstrate that this algorithm is robust in finding global optimums for the different types of problems and definitions of the generalized control law introduced in this work.

To accelerate optimization of systems that use MC simulations as part of their constraints, a new general-purpose MC algorithm for the dynamics of the particulate process was proposed, PEMC. The method has been shown to reduce CPU time without sacrificing simulation accuracy. While a coarse view of the process is taken, particle history is retained. The method was extended with the τ-PEMC method, proposed to further improve CPU time with negligible simulation errors. As with the original PEMC, internal coordinates can be handled effectively. The CPU times reported here show that accurate results can be achieved with simulation times less than a second using a low-end PC. These results demonstrate the feasibility of stochastic optimization using PEMC and τ-PEMC. A new hybrid strategy was developed to solve stochastic population balance models with multiple time scales. This self-consistent hybrid method combines the PEMC and τ-PEMC algorithms to accelerate simulation time while capturing the stochastic nature of the slow process. The simulation speed and accuracy of the hybrid strategy depends on the selection of the τ parameter, the criteria for the partition between slow and fast events, and the grid quality of the point ensembles.

8. References

Banga J. R., Balsa-Canto E., Moles C. G., and Alonso A. A. (2003), Dynamic optimization of bioreactors: a review, *Proceedings of the Indian Academy of Science* Part A, 69, 257-266.

Banga J. R., Irizarry-Rivera R., and Seider W. D. (1998), Stochastic optimization for optimal and model-predictive control, *Computers & Chemical Engineering*, 22, 603-612.

Banga J.R., Irizarry R., and, Seider W.D., (1998) Stochastic optimization for optimal and model-predictive control, *Computers Chem. Engng.* 22: 603-612.

Chatterjee, A., Vlachos, D.G. and Katsoulakis M.A. (2005) Binomial distribution based τ-leap accelerated stochastic simulation. *J. Chem. Phys.*, 122 024112.

Cuthrell J.E. and L.T. Biegler (1989), Simultaneous optimization and solution methods for batch reactor control profiles, *Comput. Chem. Engng.*, 13, 49-62.

De Jong, K.A., M.A. Potter, and W.M. Spears (1997). Using Problem Generators to Explore the Effects of Epistasis. Proceedings of the Int'l Conference on Genetic Algorithms.

Dorigo, M. and Stutzle T. (2004) Ant colony optimization. Bambridge, MA; MIT Press.

Duvigneau R. and Visonneau M. (2004) Hybrid genetic algorithms and artificial neural networks for complex design optimization in CFD, *Int. J. Numer. Meth. Fluids*, 44, 1257-1278.

Garcia, A.L., van den Broek, C., Aertsens, A., and Serneels, (1987) A Monte Carlo method of coagulation. *Physica* (1987) 143A, 535-546.

Gillespie, D. T. (1975), An Exact Method for Numerically Simulating the Stochastic Coalescence Process in a Cloud. *J. Atmos. Sci.* 32 1977-.

Gillespie, D.T. (1077) Exact stochastic simulation of coupled chemical reactions. *J. Phys. Chem.* 81 2340–2361.

Gillespie, D.T. (1976) A general method for numerically simulating the stochastic time evolution of coupled chemical reactions. *Journal of Computational Physics* 22 403–434.

Gillespie, D.T. (2001) Approximate accelerated simulation of chemically reacting systems. *J. Chem. Phys.* 115, 1716-1733.

Gillespie, D.T. and Petzold (2003) Improved leap-size selection for accelerated stochastic simulation. L.R., *J. Chem. Phys.* 119 (2003) 8229-8234.

Goldberg, D.E. (1989), Genetic Algorithms in Search, Optimization and Machine Learning. Reading, MA:Addison-Wesley.

Gottlieb J., E. Marchiori and C. Rossi (2002), Evolutionary Algorithms for the Satisfiability Problem, *Evolutionary Computation* 10(1), 25-49.

H. Salis and Y. Kaznessis (2005) Accurate hybrid stochastic simulation of a system of coupled chemical or biochemical reactions *J. Chem. Phys.* 122 54103-1-13.

Hansen N., S.D. Muller and P. Koumoutsakos (2003), Reducing the Time Complexity of the Derandomized Evolution Strategy with Covariance Matrix Adaptation (CMA-ES), *Evolutionary Computation*, 11(1), 1-18.

Haseltine E.L. and Rawlings J.B., *J. Chem. Phys.* 117 (2002) 6959-6969.

Haseltine E.L. and Rawlings J.B., *J. Chem. Phys.* 123 (2005) 164115 -1–15.

Holland, J. H. (1975). Adaptation in natural and artificial systems. Ann Arbor: University of Michigan Press.

Ingber, L. (1993), Simulated Annealing: Practice versus Theory, *J. Mathl. Comput. Modelling* 18(11), 29-57.

Ingber, L. and B. Rosen (1992), Genetic Algorithms and Very Fast Simulated Reannealing: A Comparison, *J. of Mathematical and Computer Modeling* 16(11), 87-100.

Irizarry R. (2004) LARES: An Artificial Chemical Process Approach for Optimization, *Evolutionary Computation Journal*, 12 (4), 435-460.

Irizarry R. (2005a) A Generalized Framework for Solving Dynamic Optimization Problems using the Artificial Chemical Process Paradigm: Applications to Particulate

Processes and Discrete Dynamic Systems, *Chemical Engineering Science*, 60, 5663-5681.

Irizarry R. (2005b) Fuzzy classification with an artificial chemical process, *Chemical Engineering Science*, 60, 399-412.

Irizarry R. (2006) Hybrid Dynamic Optimization using Artificial Chemical Process: Extended LARES-PR, *Industrial & Engineering Chemistry Research*, 45, 8400-8412.

Irizarry R. (2007a) Fast Monte Carlo Methodology for Multivariate Particulate Systems-I: Point Ensemble Monte Carlo. *Chemical Engineering Science*, 63, 7649 - 7664.

Irizarry R. (2007b)Fast Monte Carlo Methodology for Multivariate Particulate Systems-II: τ-PEMC., *Chemical Engineering Science* 63, 7665 - 7675.

Irizarry R. (2010a) Simulated dynamic optical response strategy for model identification of metal colloid synthesis. *Ind. Eng. Chem. Res.*, 49, 5588–5602.

Irizarry R. (2010b) Multi-time scale point ensemble Monte Carlo method for the solution of stochastic population balance models. *Proc. 4th International Conference on Population Balance Modeling* September 15-17 2010, Berlin, Germany, 771-788.

Kaznessis Y. N. (2006) Multi-scale models for gene network engineering, *Chem. Eng. Sci.* 61 940 - 953.

Kennedy, J. and Eberhart, R.C. (2001) Swarm intelligence. Silicon Valley, LA.H.: Morgan Kaufmann Publishers.

Kevrekidis I. G., Gear C.W., and Hummer G. (2004), Equation-Free: The Computer-Aided Analysis of Complex Multiscale Systems, *AIChE J.*, 50, 1346-1355.

Kirkpatrick, S., C.D. Gelatt, Jr. and M.P. Vecchi (1983), Optimization by Simulated Annealing, *Science* 220(4598), 671-680.

Liu B., Wanga L., Liud Y., Qiane B., Jin Y. (2010) An effective hybrid particle swarm optimization for batch scheduling of polypropylene processes, *Computers and Chemical Engineering*, 34 (2010) 518–528.

Luus, R. (1992), On the application of iterative dynamic programming to singular optimal control problems, *IEEE Transac. Autom. Control* 37(11), 1802-1806.

Luus, R. (2000), Iterative dynamic programming. London, UK; Chapman and Hall/CRC.

Ma D. L., Tafti D. K., and Braatz R. D. (2002), Optimal control and simulation of multidimensional cystallization process, *Comput. Chem. Engng.* 26, 1103-1116.

Mathur M., S.B. Karale, S. Priye, V.K. Jayaraman and Kulkarni B.D. (2000), Ant Colony Approach for Continuous Optimization, *Ind. Eng. Chem. Res.* 39, 3814-3822.

Mitchell, D., B. Selman, and H. Levesque (1992). Hard and easy distributions of SAT problems. In Proceedings of the Tenth National Conference in Artificial Intelligence, 459-465. AAAI Press/The MIT Press.

Moles C.G., Banga J.R., Keller K. (2004), Solving nonconvex climate control problems: pitfalls and algorithm performances, *Applied Soft Computing, in press.*

Mühlenbein, H. and D. Schlierkamp-Voosen (1993), Predictive Models for the Breeder Genetic Algorithm, I. Continuous Parameter Optimization, *Evolutionary Computation* 1(1), 25-49.

Nordhaus, W.D. (1994), Managing the Global Commons: The Economics of climate change. MIT press, Cambridge, Massachusetts.

Park S. and Ramirez W. F. (1988), Optimal production of secreted protein in fed-batch reactors, *A.I.Ch.E. J.*, 34, 1550-1558.

Pistikopoulos E.N. (2009) Perspectives in multiparametric programming and explicit model predictive control, *AIChE J.*, 55, 1918.

Roubos J. A., van Straten G., and van Boxtel A. J. B. (1999), An evolutionary strategy for fed-batch bioreactor optimization; concepts and performance, *J. of Biotechnology,* 67(2/3), 173-178.

Sahinidis N.V. (2009) optimization techniques in molecular structure and function elucidation, *Computers and Chemical Engineering*, 33, 2055-2062.

Sarkar D. and Modak J. M. (2003a), Optimization of fed-batch bioreactors using genetics algorithms, *Chemical Engineering Science,* 58, 2283-2296.

Schwefel, H.P. (1995), Evolution and Optimum Seeking, John Wiley.

Selman, B. and H. Kautz (1993). An Empirical Study of Greedy Local Search for Satisfiability Testing. Proceedings of the Eleventh National Conference on Artificial Intelligence (AAAI-93), Washington, D.C.

Spears, W.M. (1998). The Role of Mutation and Recombination in Evolutionary Algorithms. Ph.D. Dissertation, George Mason University, Fairfax, Virginia.

Storn, R. and K. Price (1997), Differential Evolution- A Simple and Efficient Heuristic for Global Optimization over Continuous Spaces, *Journal of Global Optimization* 11, 341-359.

Tanartkit P. and Biegler L. T. (1995), Stable decomposition for dynamic optimization, *I &EC Res.*, 34, 1253-1266.

Tanartkit P. and L.T. Biegler (1996), A nested, simultaneous approach for dynamic optimization problems-I, *Comput. Chem. Engng.*, 20, 735-741.

Tang K., Sun T., Tang J. (2010) An improved genetic algorithm based on a novel selection strategy for nonlinear programming problems. *Computers and chemical engineering* (article in press).

Tian, T. and Burrage, K., *J. Chem. Phys.* 121, (2004) 10356-10356.

Tomshine J. and Kaznessis Y.N. (2006) Optimization of a Stochastically Simulated Gene Network Model via Simulated Annealing. *Biophysical Journal* 91 (2006) 3196–3205.

Vassiliadis V. (1993). Computational solution of dynamic optimization problems with general differential-algebraic constraints. PhD Thesis, Imperial College, University of London, UK.

Vassiliadis V. S., Canto E. B., and Banga J. R. (1999), Second-order sensitivities of general dynamic systems with application to optimal control problems, *Chemical Engineering Science*, 54, 3851-3860.

Voigt, H. M. (1995), Soft Genetic Operators in Evolutionary Computation, Evolution and Biology Computation, Lecture Notes in Computer Science 899, Springer, Berlin, pp.123-141.

Yan L. and D. Ma (2001), Global optimization of non-convex nonlinear programs using Line-up Competition Algorithm, *Computers and Chemical Engineering* 25, 1601-1610.

Yip, P. and Y.H. Pao (1995), Combinatorial Optimization with the Use of Guided Evolutionary Simulated Annealing, *IEEE Transactions on Neural Networks*, 6(2), 290-295.

Zienkiewics O. C., The finite Element Method, third ed. McGraw Hill, New York (1977).

Parameter Optimization for Simulating Runoff from Highlatitude River Basins Using Land Surface Model and Global Data Sets

Yeugeniy M. Gusev and Olga N. Nasonova
Institute of Water Problems, Russian Academy of Sciences
Russian Federation

1. Introduction

Currently, high latitude regions characterized by a long and severe cold season are receiving more and more attention from the hydrometeorological modelling community (Bowling et al., 2000; Slater et al., 2001; Bowling et al., 2003; Nijssen et al., 2003; Etchevers et al., 2004; Su et al., 2005; Tian et al., 2007; etc.) because these regions are among the most sensitive to natural and anthropogenic effects and it is necessary to predict the consequences of such effects. At the same time, northern regions are poorly covered with measurements, which are necessary to provide the atmospheric forcing data and to estimate the land surface parameters for model simulations. One of the possible ways to provide a model with input data is to apply, along with existing measurements, available global datasets, which contain meteorological data, land-use information, and soil and vegetation characteristics.

Nowadays there are a lot of global data sets, which differ in spatial and temporal resolution, as well as in accuracy and reliability (e.g., Meeson et al., 1995; Hall et al., 2003; Zhao & Dirmeyer, 2003). Differences in global datasets are connected with uneven coverage of the land surface with ground-based observation systems, difficulties in collecting measurements, the problems with instruments, differences in procedures of filling in the missing data and interpolation of point measurements into grid boxes (Zhao & Dirmeyer, 2003). Nevertheless, this source of information is quite attractive for modellers (as it saves them from a quite difficult time- and labour-consuming procedure of model input data preparation) and global datasets are widely used for atmospheric and hydrological applications (e.g., Oki et al., 1999; Nijssen et al., 2001; Su et al., 2005).

However, the accuracy of most streamflow hydrograph simulations in high latitudes is not high, in spite of a good model structure and calibration of a number of model parameters against measured river runoff from the whole basin under study or from its sub-basins or small catchments, located within the basin. This raises a question: where can one find the potentialities to improve the agreement between observed and simulated streamflow hydrographs? We believe that one of such potentialities is to introduce adjustment factors for the most influencing atmospheric forcing data, along with the land surface characteristics, into a set of calibrated parameters.

As a matter of fact, according to the logic of construction and operation of hydrological and land surface models, both the land surface parameters and forcing data represent input information, which can suffer from errors and uncertainties. If the forcing data are based on reanalysis products, they contain systematic errors (which reflect the biases and errors in the underlying general circulation models), resulting in errors in simulated heat and water balance components (Zhao & Dirmeyer, 2003; Nasonova et al., 2008). If the forcing data are derived from in situ measurements, their accuracy depends on density and representativity of meteorological stations, and interpolation techniques used to obtain gridded data. In this case, the accuracy of forcing data can be rather low due to low accuracy of precipitation (especially snowfall) measurements, insufficient gauge density, and absence of incoming radiation observations. This is a typical situation of the northern regions.

One of the ways to improve measured precipitation is an application of different correction factors (the major of which is wind correction) to measured precipitation. However, this is not a trivial way. Wind corrections can be estimated by means of different regression equations for different types of precipitation (solid, liquid, and mixed) and gauges using observed wind speed and air temperature (Goodison et al., 1998; Yang & Ohata, 2001). These equations allow one to take into account wind-induced undercatch of precipitation and provide estimates of wind correction factor of positive sign. The equations are recommended for wind speeds lower than 6.5 m s^{-1} at the gauge height, and in the absence of blizzards (Goodison et al., 1998). At the same time it is known that in Arctic and sub-Arctic climates, snowfalls typically occur under strong winds and blizzard conditions. A number of investigations of measurement techniques for solid and mixed precipitation in pan-Arctic regions have shown that in windy conditions with snow on the ground, blowing snow from the ground enters the gauges causing "false" precipitation (Bryazgin & Dement'ev, 1996; Bogdanova et al., 2002a,b). Annual "false" precipitation in some pan-Arctic regions can reach 30-40% of the measured annual totals. Evidently, that in this case, "overcatch" of snowfall takes place rather than "undercatch", and the wind correction factor should be negative. Bogdanova et al. (2002 a,b) suggests a bias-correction model for the Tretyakov gauge allowing an estimation of the amount of false snow, which depends not only on air temperature and wind speed, but also on the state of snow cover surface (fresh snow, old snow, snow compressed by wind etc.), weather conditions (blizzard, blowing snow), duration of blizzard, the degree to which the gauges are sheltered from surroundings and so on. The main difficulties associated with application of this model we see in a large amount of input data required, some of which may be inaccessible, particularly, characteristics of the blizzard condition and the state of the snow cover surface.

One more source of uncertainties in forcing data is associated with a 'point' character of measurements of meteorological variables, when their spatial distribution is needed. Generally, point measurements are distributed in space over the catchment by interpolation techniques. In the case of sparse observational network, inadequate gauge density may provide unrepresentative interpolated estimates of meteorological variables (especially precipitation). This also contributes to errors in runoff simulations.

As to incoming fluxes of shortwave and longwave radiation, they are not measured at regular networks and their values are estimated using, in particular, standard meteorological observations. Such estimates are not free from uncertainties. Uncertainties in the estimates of shortwave radiation are mainly caused by the necessity to take into account cloudiness. For this purpose empirical formulae are used. These formulae, firstly, are not universal and, secondly, need information both on the amount and the type of clouds. The data on the clouds' type are often inaccessible; the information on the amount of clouds is not very accurate because of visual character of observations. For calculating incoming longwave radiation, a lot of empirical formulae have been developed. However, as a rule, they were derived under milder climate conditions (compared to Arctic and sub-Arctic climate) and their application to the regions with a severe climate results in strong biases (Gusev et al., 2006a). At the same time the sensitivity of snowmelt-driven streamflow to incoming longwave radiation is rather high, because this radiation greatly influences the rate of snow processes.

One of the ways to solve the problem of uncertainties in the major forcing data is calibration of these data within the accuracy of their measurement or estimation. It should be noted that the idea of calibration of the main forcings is not novel. Calibration of precipitation and potential evapotranspiration (representing the forcing data for some hydrological models) was performed in Gan et al. (2006) for SAC-SMA model. Xia (2007) has shown that in the cold regions in the Northeast United States, where measured precipitation has large systematic biases, calibration of a land surface model using observed annual streamflow can be successful, if model parameters and precipitation biases are calibrated simultaneously. It is reasonable to expect that this statement will be also valid for other cold regions.

The aim of the present study is to reveal to what extent optimization (within reasonable bounds) of the most important land surface parameters and adjustment factors for atmospheric forcings can improve simulating river runoff in high latitudes by a physically based land surface model (LSM) SWAP (Soil Water - Atmosphere - Plants).

2. Methodology

2.1 Model SWAP

The land surface model SWAP represents a physically based model describing the processes of heat and water exchange within a soil–vegetation/snow cover–atmosphere system (SVAS). Different versions of SWAP were detailed in a number of publications (e.g. Gusev & Nasonova 1998, 2002, 2003, 2004a; Gusev et al. 2006b). The last version of SWAP treats the following processes: interception of liquid and solid precipitation by vegetation; evaporation, melting and freezing of intercepted precipitation, including refreezing of melt water; formation of snow cover at the forest floor and at the open site during the cold season; partitioning of non-intercepted precipitation or water yield of snow cover between surface runoff and infiltration into a soil; formation of the water balance of aeration zone including transpiration, soil evaporation, water exchange with underneath layers and dynamics of soil water storage; water table dynamics; formation of the heat balance and thermal regime of SVAS; soil freezing and thawing.

The model can be applied both for point (or grid box) simulations of vertical fluxes and state variables of SVAS in atmospheric science applications (Gusev & Nasonova, 1998, 2004; Gusev et al., 2004) and for simulating streamflow at different scales — from small catchments to continental-scale river basins located in different natural conditions (Gusev & Nasonova, 2000, 2002, 2003; Boone et al., 2004; Gusev et al., 2006a). In the case of a small river basin (up to the order of 10^3–10^4 km^2), a kinematic wave equation is used to simulate runoff at the basin outlet. In the case of a larger river basin, the basin area is divided into a number of computational grid boxes connected by a river network. Runoff is modelled for each grid box and then transformed by a river routing model to simulate streamflow at the river basin outlet (with accounting for a contributing area of each box). Such a transformation may be performed by different ways. Herein, a simple linear transfer model in river channels to simulate river discharge is used (Oki et al., 1999).

The basic equation for this model is the conservation equation of the water storage in a river channel of each computational grid box, which can be written as

$$\frac{dS_r}{dt} = Y_{in} - Y_{out} \tag{1}$$

where S_r is the water storage in a river channel located within a grid box, Y_{in} is the sum of runoff, generated within a grid box, and inflow from neighbouring grid boxes, Y_{out} is the streamflow at a grid box outlet. The directions of lateral water flow among grid boxes may be determined on the basis of Total Runoff Integrating Pathways (TRIP) (Oki & Sud, 1998). The value of Y_{in} is usually assumed to be constant within the computational time step Δt, used for description of runoff transformation in the channel network. Parameterization of Y_{out} is based on the following equation

$$Y_{out} = \frac{u_e}{d_c} S_r \tag{2}$$

where u_e and d_c are the effective velocity and the distance between grid boxes, respectively. Mean global value u_e is approximately 0.35 - 0.36 m s^{-1} (Oki et al., 1999). Via substitution of (2) into (1) and solving the obtained equation, the following recurrence relation that describes water dynamics in the river channel is derived

$$S_r(t_{i+1}) = C_{\Delta t} S_r(t_i) + (1 - C_{\Delta t}) \frac{d_c Y_{in}}{u_e} \quad , \quad C_{\Delta t} = \exp(-\frac{u_e}{d_c} \Delta t) \quad , \quad \Delta t = t_{i+1} - t_i \tag{3}$$

where $S_r(t_i)$ and $S_r(t_{i+1})$ are the water storages in the channel at time steps t_i and t_{i+1}. On the basis of (1-3) and in accordance with the channel network connecting computational boxes and schematized in the form of graph, the dynamics of the water storages in the channel of each grid box, streamflow at the box outlet and river discharge are calculated.

During the last 10 years, different versions of SWAP were validated against observations including characteristics both related to energy balance or thermal regime of SVAS (sensible and latent heat fluxes, ground heat flux, net radiation, upward longwave and shortwave radiation, surface temperature, soil freezing and thawing depths) and related to hydrological cycle or water regime of SVAS (surface and total runoff from a catchment, river discharge, soil water storage in different layers, evapotranspiration, snow evaporation, intercepted precipitation, water table depth, snow density, snow depth and snow water equivalent, water yield of snow cover). The model validations were performed for "point" experimental sites and for catchments and river basins of different areas (from 10^{-1} to 10^5 km^2) on a long-term basis and under different natural conditions (e.g., Gusev & Nasonova 1998, 2000, 2002, 2003, 2004; Gusev et al., 2006a; Boone et al., 2004). The results have demonstrated that SWAP is able to reproduce (without calibration) heat and water exchange processes occurring in SVAS under different natural conditions adequately, provided that input data of high quality are available. In the case of streamflow simulation, the accuracy of modelling can be increased due to optimization of model parameters, which influence runoff to the greatest extent, using streamflow observations. This approach is very effective if measurements required for parameter estimation are absent (Nasonova et al., 2009). This situation is typical of most northern river basins of Russia.

2.2 Study basins and their schematization

Three river basins, located in the northeast of the European part of Russia (Figure 1), were chosen for investigation: the Mezen River basin (area: 78 000 km^2), the Pechora River basin (area: 312 000 km^2) and the Northern (Severnaya) Dvina River basin (area: 348 000 km^2). All three basins represent flat forested planes. Forests (with the predominance of coniferous species) cover nearly 80% of the area of each basin.

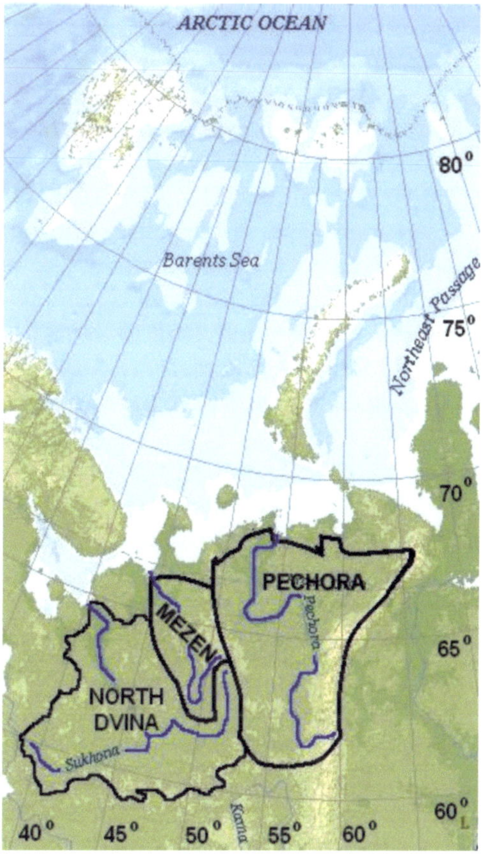

Fig. 1. Location of the three river basins

The climate in the study region is characterized by a short (3-4 months) cool summer and long (5–7 months) cold winter with a stable snow cover and soil freezing. There is a permafrost in some areas. Mean air temperature of January ranges across the basins from -13 to -17°C, mean air temperature of July is 14-17°C. Mean annual precipitation varies from 650 to 800 mm over the Mezen and the Northern Dvina basins and from 400 to 600 mm over the Pechora basin. Nearly 30-40% of precipitation falls as snow. Mean annual streamflow is 310, 360 and 400 mm/year, respectively, for the Northern Dvina, Mezen and Pechora Rivers. Streamflow of each river can be mainly characterized as snowmelt (up to 50-80%) and rain driven. Their annual hydrographs have maximum flood peaks in spring (caused by spring snowmelt), low baseflow during winter and summer periods, and relatively small flood peaks in autumn (caused by rainfall, along with low evapotranspiration).

For modelling purposes, the Mezen River basin (from the head of the river down to the Malonisogorskaya gauging station) was represented by ten 1°×1° computational grid boxes in accordance with a global river channel network TRIP (Figure 2). The Pechora River basin (down to the Oksino gauging station) was schematized by 57 (Figure 3) and the Northern Dvina River basin (down to the Ust-Pinega gauging station) by 62 one-degree grid boxes (Figure 4). Such a spatial resolution seems to be insufficient for hydrological applications. However, it may be acceptable, provided that subgrid effects are taken into account in model parameterizations (e.g., in SWAP, spatial heterogeneity of soil hydraulic conductivity at saturation is taken into account (Gusev & Nasonova, 1998)). This is confirmed by the results of participation of SWAP in the international Rhone-aggregation LSM intercomparison project (Rhone-AGG) (Boone et al., 2004). The main goals of the project were to investigate how participating LSMs simulate the water balance components of the Rhone River basin (covering 86 000 km^2 and characterized by a wide variety of natural conditions) compared to observations, and to examine the impact of changing the spatial resolution of the basin schematization on the simulations. For the SWAP model, it was found that differences in the basin-averaged annual runoff and evapotranspiration simulated with spatial resolution 8x8 km and 1°×1° were not more than 3.5 and 1.0%, respectively. This fact allows us to assume that coarse (1-degree) spatial resolution will not lead to significant errors in the simulated runoff from the chosen river basins.

2.3 Atmospheric forcing data

Atmospheric forcing data for the SWAP model represent near-surface meteorology including air temperature and humidity, precipitation, incoming shortwave and longwave radiation, air pressure and wind speed. Here, three versions of atmospheric forcing data were used: (1) global reanalysis dataset, (2) global reanalysis product hybridized with observations, and (3) measurements from meteorological stations located within the basins.

2.3.1 Global datasets

Global atmospheric forcing data were taken from 3-hourly near-surface meteorological datasets with 1-degree spatial resolution produced for the Second Global Wetness Project (GSWP-2) (Dirmeyer et al., 2002; Zhao & Dirmeyer, 2003) for the period from 1 July 1982 to 31 December 1995. The first version of global data used here (hereafter, referred to as "Version-1") is based on pure reanalysis product produced by the National Centres for Environmental Prediction/Department of Energy (NCEP/DOE) (Kanamitsu et al., 2002). As it was above mentioned, any reanalysis product contains systematic errors. One of the possible ways to solve this problem is to combine (hybridize) the 3-hourly reanalysis estimates with global gridded observations. The latter are usually available at lower spatial resolution and cannot be directly used in LSMs. Hybridization of NCEP/DOE reanalysis product with global gridded datasets from observations, presented in the International Satellite Land-Surface Climatology Project (ISLSCP) Initiative II (Hall et al., 2003), was performed for the GSWP-2 project (Zhao & Dirmeyer, 2003). Fully hybridized meteorological data, provided within the framework of GSWP-2 and recommended for baseline simulations, we used as the second version of atmospheric forcing data (hereafter, referred to as "Version-2") (see Zhao & Dirmeyer (2003) for more details).

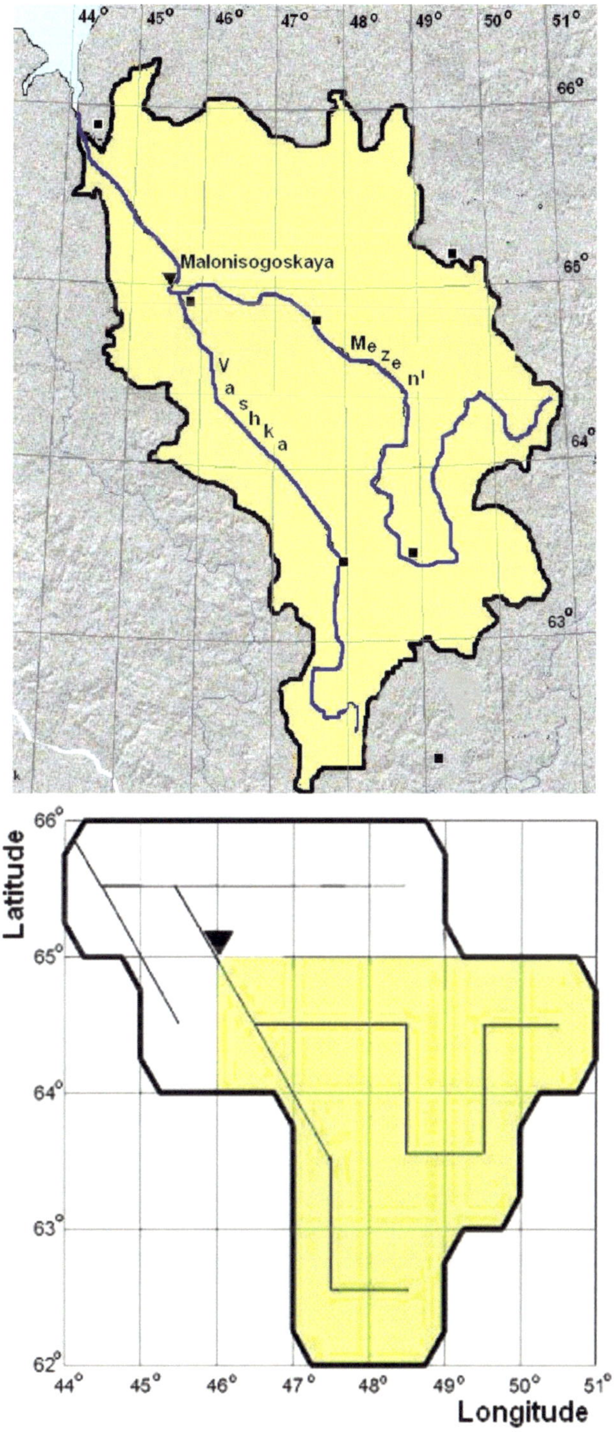

Fig. 2. The Mezen River basin and its schematization for streamflow modelling. Streamflow gauging station location (triangle) and meteorological stations (squares)

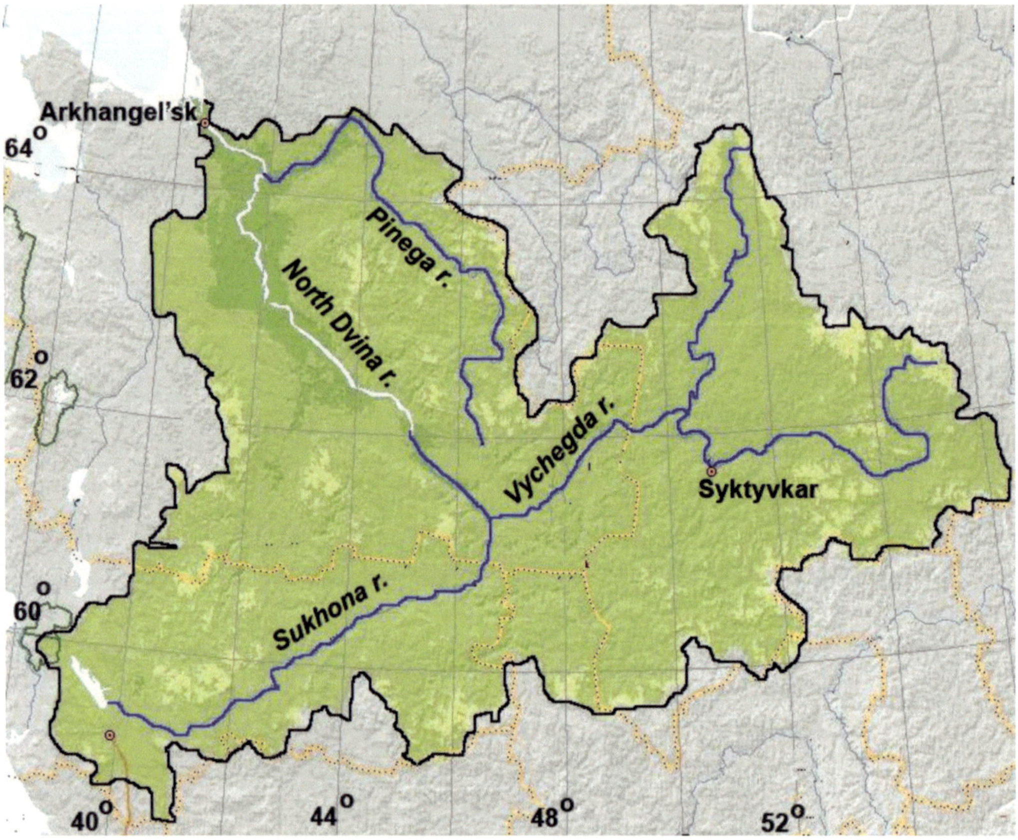

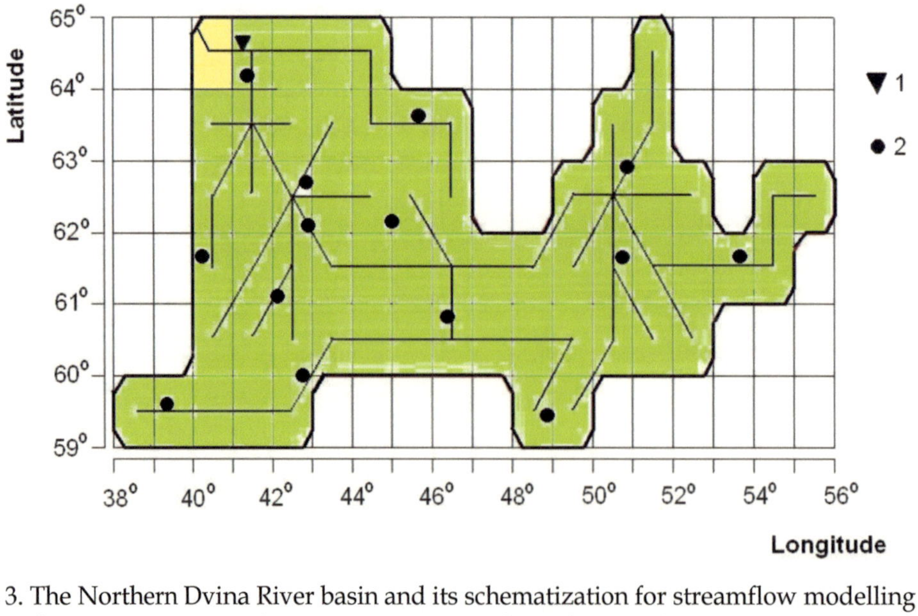

Fig. 3. The Northern Dvina River basin and its schematization for streamflow modelling (1 is streamflow gauging station locations, 2 is meteorological station locations)

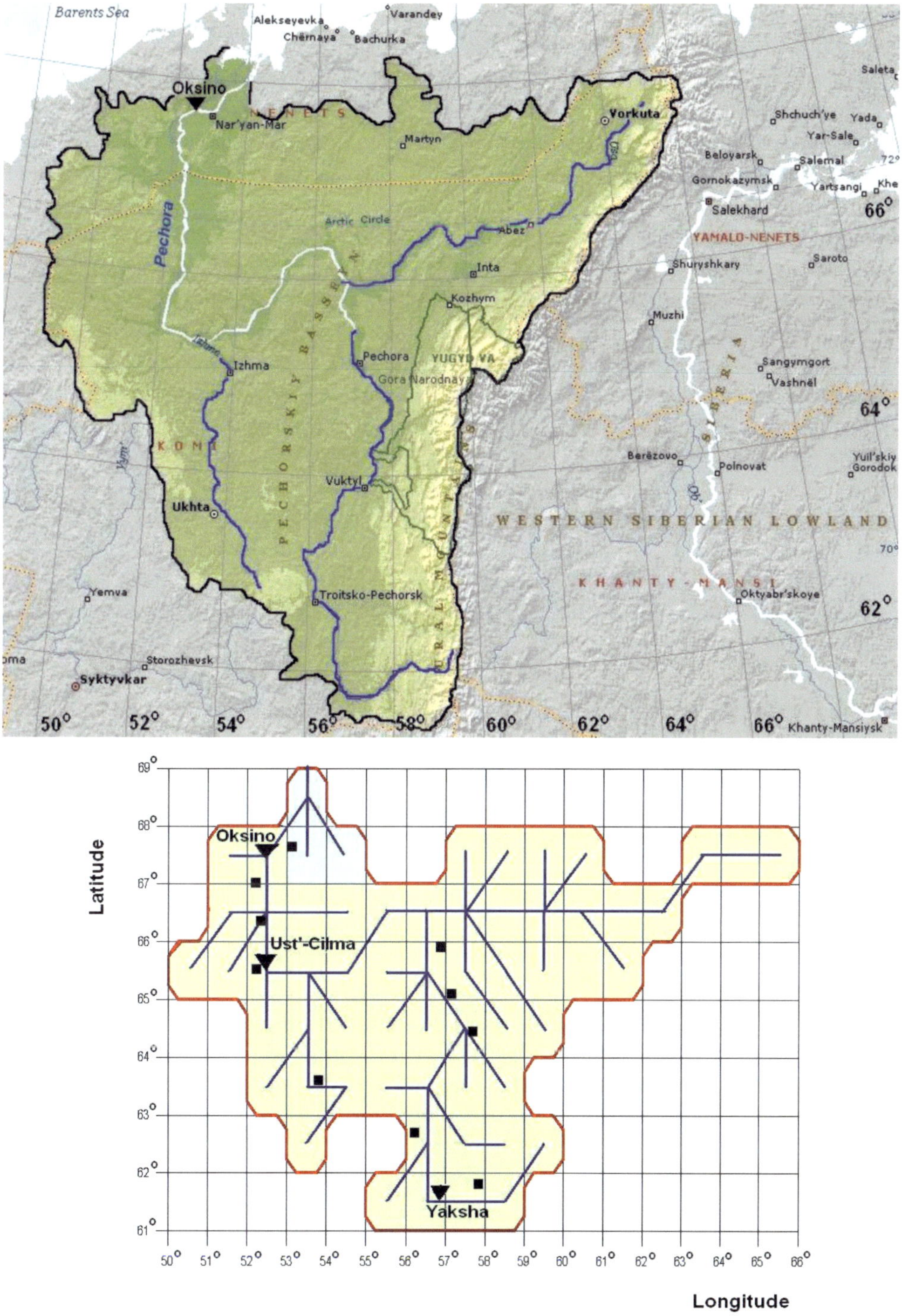

Fig. 4. The Pechora River basin and its schematization for streamflow modelling. Streamflow gauging station locations (triangles) and meteorological stations (squares)

2.3.2 Meteorological observations

Locations of meteorological stations over the basins are shown in Figures 2-4. Meteorological observations are far from perfect, especially snowfall measurements, which can suffer both from positive and negative biases due to overcatch or undercatch of snow by precipitation gauges. At the same time, in high latitudes, where snow is a significant contributor to formation of annual streamflow hydrograph, the accuracy of snowfall measurements is of great importance. Besides that, distribution and density of meteorological stations over the Mezen River and the Pechora River basins cannot be treated as satisfactory. Most of the stations are situated along the rivers and may be not representative for watershed areas. Insufficient density of meteorological observations, their possible non-representativeness, along with the necessity of their spatial interpolation to the computational grid boxes, can lead to uncertainties and biases in forcing data for model simulations. This mostly concerns precipitation due to its complicated stochastic nature resulting in the great problem of estimating area averages from point measurements. Incoming fluxes of shortwave and longwave radiation were not measured at meteorological stations, they were derived from standard meteorological observations using techniques, described in Gusev et al. (2006a).

Interpolation of meteorological observations to the centers of grid boxes was performed using the kriging procedure (Globus, 1987). The classic kriging procedure was slightly modified. Its description can be found in Gusev et al. (2008). The obtained forcing data set will be referred to as "Version-3".

2.4 Land surface parameter datasets

The soil and vegetation parameters were prepared using global one-degree datasets provided within the framework of GSWP-2 (Dirmeyer et al., 2002). Global one-degree vegetation datasets contained information on the land surface types in accordance with the International Global Biosphere Project (IGBP) classification, which includes 17 types of the land surface, and their fractions within each one-degree grid box, as well as time-varying monthly values of biophysical parameters (leaf area index, greenness fraction, roughness length, zero-plane displacement height, snow-free albedo, root depth) for 1982-1995. Global one-degree soil datasets included data on sand, clay, silt and organic matter fractions; texture classes (12 soil texture classes according to the classification of US Department of Agriculture (USDA)); depth of active soil column and soil hydrophysical parameters (porosity, field capacity, wilting point, hydraulic conductivity at saturation, saturated matric potential, B-exponent parameter, soil snow-free albedo) for each grid box. First of all, the values of the soil and vegetation parameters were analyzed and checked for consistency (they must be reasonable and in a good agreement with each other) as it was described in Gusev et al. (2006b). In so doing, some corrections were performed. In addition, several SWAP model specific parameters were derived. As a result, a set of a priori parameters was obtained.

The last group of data represents topographic characteristics including mean elevation of grid boxes, taken from the EROS (Earth Resources Observation Systems) Data Centre (EDC), and the slopes of the surface of each box in the meridianal and latitudinal directions, required for the simulation of runoff transformation within a box. The latter were derived from mean elevations of neighbouring grid boxes.

2.5 Optimization procedure

The goal of a model parameter optimization procedure is to find the values of parameters that minimize an objective function *Ext*, which is a measure of the discrepancy between the model outputs and observations. The objective function is usually expressed as

$$Ext = \frac{1}{\Delta t}\sum_{t=1}^{\Delta t} w_t \left|Cal_t \quad Obs_t\right|^{l} \tag{4}$$

where Cal_t and Obs_t are, respectively, the simulated and measured values of output variable (here, daily river runoff *R*), which is used for parameter optimization, at time *t*; Δt is the length of optimization period; *l* is a parameter, equalled to 1 or 2; w_t is the time-varying weight. The values of the two last characteristics depend on the goals of the users. In particular, if correct runoff reproduction is important for each moment of a year, parameters l=2 and w_t=1 are used (these values will be used here). When correct simulation of spring flood hydrograph is of the most importance, the values of w_t must be higher for the spring compared to the rest seasons.

Overview of different methods of finding the minimum of the objective function *Ext* is given in a number of publications (e.g., Törn & Zilinskas, 1989; Pintér, 1996). As it was shown there, when the objective function does not have an analytical expression (as in the present study), application of minimization techniques like a gradient search (Jacobs, 1977) is impossible. In this case, methods of direct search are usually used if *Ext* is a single-extremum function; otherwise, methods of global optimization are applied (Rosenbrock, 1960; Powell, 1964; Nelder & Mead, 1965; Solomatine et al., 1999; Duan, 2003). Many of them are based on the statistical methods of finding the extremum of *Ext* (vector of optimized parameters) (Rastrigin, 1968; Gupta et al., 1998; Solomatine et al., 1999). It should be noted, that the method of blind random search in the parameter space with the pseudo-uniform distribution of points is n-times (where n is the total number of parameters) as effective as the method of search on the deterministic grid (Rastrigin, 1968).

Here, optimization of parameter values was performed using an automatic procedure for two different global optimization algorithms. The first one, based on ideas from Bastidas et.al. (1999) and Solomatine et.al. (1999) and detailed in Gusev et al. (2008), applies a statistical method for direct search of the optimum (or Random Search Technique - RST) of an objective function. The second one is the Shuffled Complex Evolution algorithm (SCE-UA) developed by Duan et al. (1992). The SCE-UA has been found to be robust, effective, and an efficient optimization algorithm (Duan et al., 2003) and it is widely used in hydrological modelling. Two objective functions were calculated during optimization: *Ext*=1-*Eff*, where *Eff* is the Nash–Sutcliffe coefficient of efficiency (Nash & Sutcliffe, 1970), and the relative value of systematic error *Bias* (mean difference between the modelled and observed values of the output variable normalized by the mean observed value):

$$Eff = 1 - \frac{\sum_{\Omega}(x_{sim} - x_{obs})^2}{\sum_{\Omega}(x_{obs} - \overline{x}_{obs})^2} \tag{5}$$

$$Bias = \frac{\sum_{\Omega}(x_{sim} - x_{obs})}{\sum_{\Omega} x_{obs}} \cdot 100\ \% \tag{6}$$

where x_{sim} and x_{obs} are simulated and observed values of a variable x and Ω is a discrete sample set of variable x.

Application of *Bias* along with *Eff* was motivated by the fact that maximum values of *Eff* do not guarantee low *Bias*. This becomes clear if *Eff* is expressed in the terms of root-mean-square error RMSE

$$Eff = 1 - \left(\frac{\text{RMSE}}{\text{STD}_{obs}}\right)^2 \tag{7}$$

where STD is the observed standard deviation. Since RMSE includes the systematic and random errors, the same value of RMSE (and, evidently, *Eff*) may correspond to different values of the systematic error (bias). Consequently, among the sets of "optimal" parameters corresponding to the lowest RMSE (or the highest *Eff*) one should select the parameter set that provides the lowest bias.

2.5.1 RST

Random search technique (RST) has several stages (Gusev et al. 2008). At the first stage, sufficiently wide feasible parameter space is specified by fixing the lower and upper parameter bounds defined from the maximum plausible ranges for the parameters based on physical reasoning. A prescribed number of model runs (realizations) are performed using different values of calibrated parameters, which are determined within their fixed bounds using a generator of uniformly distributed random numbers. For each realization, streamflow simulation and estimation of *Ext* and *Bias* are carried out. Then, the "best" realizations, i.e. with the lowest values of *Ext* and near-zero values of *Bias*, are selected and corresponding values of calibrated parameters are used to reduce ("manually") the feasible parameter space. At the next stage, a new search of the optimum of the objective functions is performed for the reduced parameter space that allows one to reduce the number of realizations. This is especially important for a large set of optimized parameters, because if the feasible parameter space is fixed during optimization, the number of realizations needed to find the optimum with the specified accuracy grows exponentially with an increase in the number of parameters (Solomatine et al., 1999). If it is necessary, further reduction of parameter space may be done and searching the optimum may be continued until there will be no progress in minimization of *Ext*. When the optimization procedure is stopped, N points (N=4-5) with the lowest values of *Ext* and near-zero values of *Bias* are selected. The values of optimized parameters corresponding to these points are averaged (with the weights that may differ from 1.0). The obtained mean values of parameters are considered to be optimal and their standard deviations, divided by $\sqrt{N}$, allows one to assess the accuracy of estimating the optimal values of model parameters. Figure 5 illustrates the described optimization algorithm for the case of two parameters X and Y.

Figure 5b gives an example of relation between *Ext* and *Bias* obtained from a large number of model runs within the boundaries of Region-1 at the first stage of realization of algorithm.

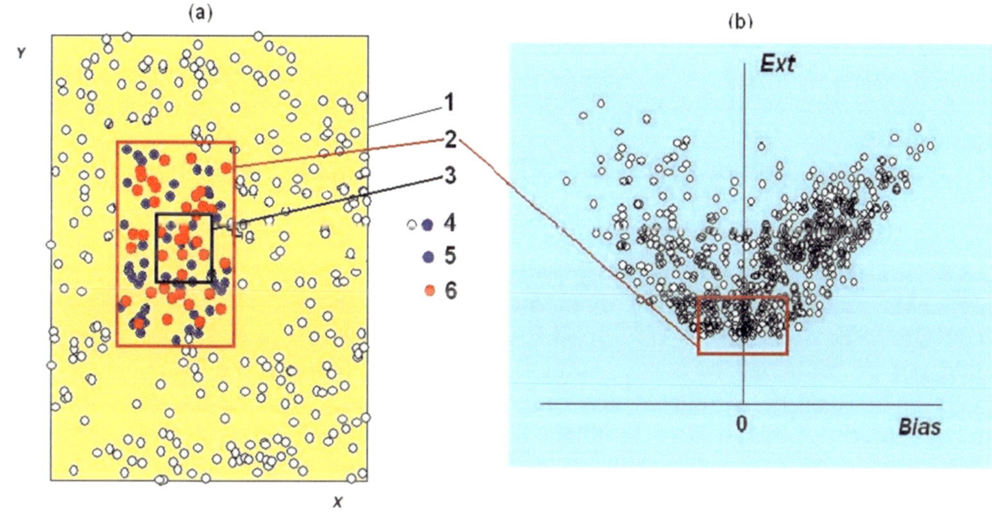

Fig. 5. An example of a direct search of the minimum of the objective function *Ext* (b) for 2-dimentional case (a). Here, 1 is the boundary of Region-1 with initial population of quasi-random points (4) with coordinates (*X*, *Y*); 2 is the boundary of Region-2 with the best points (5) from the initial population; 6 – points from the repeated optimization within the boundaries of Region-2; 3 is the boundary of Region-3 with the best points (close to optimal) generated during the repeated optimization.

Selecting the group with the "best" realizations, i.e. with the lowest values of *Ext* and near-zero values of *Bias* (marked in Figure 5b by the red rectangle), and the corresponding range of the parameter values (the red rectangle in Figure 5a), we reduce the feasible parameter space (from Region-1 to Region-2) and continue to search optimal values of the parameters within the new boundaries. If it is necessary, further reduction of parameter space (from Region-2 to Region-3 in Figure 5a) may be done and searching the optimum may be continued until there will be no progress in minimization of *Ext*.

2.5.2 SCE-UA

The SCE-UA algorithm has been described in detail in Duan et al. (1992). At the first step, the SCE-UA selects an initial population of optimized parameters by random sampling throughout the feasible parameter space for *n* parameters, based on given parameter ranges. For each point, the objective function values are calculated. Then, the population is partitioned into several communities (complexes), each consisting of 2*n*+1 points, based on the corresponding objective function values. Each community is made to evolve independently for a prescribed number of times based on the downhill simplex method (Nelder and Mead, 1965). The communities are periodically consolidated into a single group and the population is shuffled to share information and partitioned into new communities. As the search progresses, the entire population tends to converge toward the neighbourhood of global optimum, provided the initial population size is sufficiently large. The evolution and shuffling steps are repeated until a prescribed convergence criterion is satisfied.

SCE-UA is a single-objective optimization algorithm. To apply SCE-UA for our two objective functions *Ext* and *Bias*, we decided to minimize *Ext* under condition that the

absolute value of *Bias* did not exceed 5%. If the fulfilment of this condition resulted in relatively low *Eff* ($Eff<0.9 \cdot Eff_0$, where Eff_0 is the efficiency without this condition, i.e. the efficiency corresponding to global optimum), we removed this condition and the point with $Eff=Eff_0$ was treated as an optimum. Evidently, that in this case absolute value of *Bias* is larger than 5%.
The distributive diskette for the SCE-UA code was taken from the site http://www.sahra.arizona.edu/software/.

2.5.3 Selection of parameters to be optimized

Since LSMs usually contain a lot of model parameters, the procedure for selection of parameters to be optimized is very important. The total number of optimized parameters should not be too small to ensure sufficient degrees of freedom for obtaining a good agreement between the simulated and observed daily streamflow. At the same time the number should not be too large to obtain the steady values of the calibrated parameters under a reasonable number of realizations. Evidently, those parameters, whose changes influence daily streamflow to the greatest extent, should be calibrated.
Our significant experience has shown that in high latitudes the following SWAP model parameters can be calibrated: (1) soil hydrophysical parameters: hydraulic conductivity at saturation K_0, parameters describing the dependence of soil water potential φ on soil moisture W (B-exponent parameter and saturated matric potential φ_0 in the parameterization of function $\varphi(W)$ by Clapp and Hornberger (1978)), plant wilting point W_{wp}, field capacity W_{fc}, soil porosity W_{sat}, soil column thickness h_0 (here, the depth from the soil surface to the upper impermeable layer); (2) vegetation parameters: the root layer depth h_r, the leaf area index LAI, the snow-free vegetation albedo α_{sum}, the vegetation albedo in the winter period (with snow on tree crowns) α_{win}; (3) albedo of snow on the ground α_{sn}; (4) parameters controlling the transformation of runoff both within a grid box (the Manning roughness coefficient n) and in a river channel network (effective velocity of water movement in a channel u_e).
Only seven land surface parameters from the above listed were chosen for calibration: K_0, h_0, h_r, α_{sum}, α_{sn}, n, and u_e (the other parameters were taken from the GSWP-2 global datasets) because of the following reasons. The hydraulic conductivity at saturation K_0 is one of the most important parameters of SWAP because it controls partitioning of water reaching the soil surface between infiltration and surface runoff. Besides that, in SWAP, subgrid effects are taken into account through K_0. Thus, when modelling infiltration and surface runoff, subgrid spatial variability of K_0 is considered by using not only mean value of K_0 for each grid box, but also root-mean-square deviation (Gusev and Nasonova, 1998). SWAP is also sensitive to the soil column thickness h_0, which, affecting the total soil water storage, controls to a great extent (along with some other factors) the partitioning of water entering a soil between an increment of soil water storage and drainage from the soil column. The root layer thickness h_r affects the maximum water storage available for transpiration, which occurs from this layer. The parameter α_{sum} determines the amount of non-reflected incoming solar radiation, which influences heat and water exchange at the land-atmosphere interface. The value of alb_{sn} influences energy balance at the snow surface and, consequently, the rate of snow formation processes, in particular, snow evaporation, snow accumulation and snowmelt; this is especially important for formation of flood peaks of streamflow hydrograph in spring. The shape of the streamflow hydrograph is also influenced by the parameters n and u_e.

Since the sensitivity of runoff, simulated by SWAP, to the parameters *B* and φ_0 is not significant, they were excluded from the list of calibrated parameters. As to W_{wp}, W_{fc}, W_{sat}, and LAI, analysis of their values, taken from the global datasets, has shown that they are quite reasonable for the three river basins and their calibration within narrow physically meaningful bounds will hardly improve the quality of runoff simulation. Besides that, first attempts of model calibration have shown correlation between the impact of these parameters and the parameters h_0 and h_r on the value of $Ext(\vec{par})$ (where $\vec{par}$ is the vector of calibrated parameters) (in particular, decrease in W_{fc} together with increase in h_r does not practically change *Ext*) that makes the search of the optimum of *Ext* using the indicated parameters extremely complicated.

The meteorological forcing data, as it was mentioned in Introduction, suffer from uncertainties and errors, therefore some authors began to calibrate the most influencing meteorological characteristics along with parameters of hydrological and land surface models (Gan et al., 2006; Xia, 2007). Since precipitation and incoming radiation influence runoff formation to the greatest extent, we decided to use the following adjustment factors for these forcings: k_{lp}, k_{sp}, k_{sw} and k_{lw} for rainfall, snowfall, shortwave and longwave radiation, respectively.

To reduce the list of calibrated parameters the following steps were undertaken. When adjustment factors for forcing data are involved in the process of parameter optimization, one of the four parameters α_{sum}, α_{sn}, α_{win} and k_{sw} must be excluded from the list because in the model these parameters are presented as a product of the corresponding albedo and the intensity of shortwave radiation. The parameter α_{win} with rather realistic values for the river basins was excluded. The parameters α_{sn}, n, u_e and the adjustment factors k_{sw}, k_{lw}, k_{lp} and k_{sp} were assumed to be the same for all the basin grid boxes, while the values of K_0, h_0, h_r and α_{sum} varied from a box to a box that resulted in a great number of parameters, which require calibration. To reduce the number of calibrated parameters and to increase their stability, instead of K_0, h_r and α_{sum} for each grid box, we decided to calibrate their adjustment factors k_{K0}, k_{hr} and $k_{\alpha sum}$, which were taken to be constant for the entire basin. In addition, we set $h_0=k_{h0}\cdot h_r$ for each box, where k_{h0} is also an adjustment factor taken to be constant for each basin. As a result, the total number of calibrated parameters was reduced to 11: seven for the land surface: k_{K0}, k_{hr}, $k_{\alpha sum}$, k_{h0}, α_{sn}, n, u_e and four for the forcing data: k_{sw}, k_{lw}, k_{lp} and k_{sp}.

2.6 Model calibration and validation

Daily streamflow hydrographs, measured at the Malonisogorskaya gauging station (Figure 2b), the Ust-Pinega station (Figure 3b) and the Oksino station (Figure 4b) during the period of 1986-1995 and taken from the GRDC (Global Runoff Data Centre) database, were used for parameter optimization and validation. The period from 1986 to 1990 was used for parameter optimization, which was performed for each river basin and for each version of the forcing data. To reveal the impact of optimization of adjustment factors for forcing data we performed calibration with and without application of the adjustment factors. In the former case, 11 parameters were calibrated, while in the latter case 8 (11 minus 4 adjustment factors and plus α_{win}) parameters.

Validation of the model with different sets of parameter values was performed for the period of 1991-1995. The results of daily streamflow simulations were compared with observations and with each other. The agreement between simulated and observed streamflow for each river basin was estimated at daily time scale using several goodness-of-fit statistics: the Nash-Sutcliffe coefficient of efficiency *Eff*, systematic error *Bias* and the coefficient of correlation *r*. Hydrographs were also compared visually to reveal how the model reproduces the shape of hydrograph, including timing of peaks, recession slopes and low flows.

The agreement between simulations and observations is usually considered to be satisfactory if $Eff > 0.5$ (if $Eff = 1$ the simulation is ideal). If $Eff < 0$, temporal variability of variable x is reproduced badly (in this case, a simple averaging of observations is better than model simulation). Generally speaking, the threshold values of *Eff* characterizing the quality of simulations are subjective and depend on the problem to be solved. The scale of accuracy commonly used for evaluation of the quality of streamflow forecasts is as follows (Appolov et al., 1974): the accuracy is regarded as "good" when $Eff \geq 0.75$, as "satisfactory" when $0.36 \leq Eff < 0.75$, and as "unsatisfactory" when $Eff < 0.36$. As to the *Bias*, it should be taken into account, that a systematic error in daily, monthly, and annual values of the measured river runoff is on the average not less than 5% (this value can be much greater for flood periods). Therefore, we can assume that when $|Bias| \leq 5\%$, the quality of modelling can be considered as "good".

3. Results

3.1 Comparison of RST and SCE-UA optimization algorithms

Optimization of 11 model parameters using RST and SCE-UA optimization algorithms allowed us to compare their effectiveness. Four sets of optimal values of calibrated parameters were obtained for each river by application of RST and SCE-UA algorithms for Version 1 and Version 2 of forcing data. Then streamflow simulations were performed using the optimized parameter values. Table 1 summarizes the results of comparison of simulated and measured daily streamflow for the calibration and validation periods and for the entire calculational period.

Analysis of the results shows that application of the two different optimization algorithms for the same set of calibrated parameters gives closely consistent values of daily *Eff* and *Bias*. On average, RST-set of optimal parameters results in daily *Eff* equalled to 0.82, 0.81 and 0.81 for the calibration, the validation and the entire 1986-1995 period, respectively, while absolute *Bias* for the same periods is 1.8%, 5.8% and 2.6% respectively. Application of SCE-UA provides *Eff* equalled to 0.83, 0.82 and 0.83, while absolute *Bias* is 3.6%, 2.6% and 1.8%, respectively, for the calibration, the validation and the entire periods. Visual comparison of hydrographs reveals negligible differences. The differences can be explained by a limited number of realizations in both cases. These results mean that RST calibration technique is as effective as SCE-UA. The advantage of the former is that a user can interfere in the process of calibration and to speed up it by analyzing the preliminary results and reducing the feasible parameter space. For example, calibration of parameters for the Northern Dvina River by SCE-UA technique took us about two weeks against 2-3 days by RST (increase of the number of realizations in the latter case could improve the results, which are somewhat worse than in the former case, especially with respect to the validation period). If the time is not limited, it is more convenient to use the SCE-UA procedure, which does not need user interference and, consequently, depends on a user's experience to a less extent and is a less labour-consuming procedure.

River	Optimization algorithm	Version 1			Version 2		
		Bias,%	*Eff*	*r*	*Bias*, %	*Eff*	*r*
Calibration period (1986-1990)							
Mezen	RST	-4	0.72	0.85	-1	0.80	0.89
	SCE-UA	-6	0.75	0.87	2	0.83	0.91
Pechora	RST	-	-	-	0	0.89	0.94
	SCE- UA	0	0.87	0.94	4	0.85	0.92
Northern Dvina	RST	4	0.84	0.93	0	0.87	0.93
	SCE-UA	6	0.85	0.93	0	0.89	0.94
Validation period (1991-1995)							
Mezen	RST	-7	0.82	0.91	1	0.84	0.91
	SCE-UA	2	0.73	0.86	6	0.82	0.91
Pechora	RST	-	-	-	-6	0.75	0.88
	SCE- UA	-6	0.85	0.92	-1	0.76	0.87
Northern Dvina	RST	-11	0.80	0.90	4	0.85	0.92
	SCE-UA	-3	0.90	0.95	1	0.90	0.95
Entire period (1986-1995)							
Mezen	RST	-5	0.75	0.87	0	0.82	0.90
	SCE-UA	-1	0.74	0.86	4	0.82	0.91
Pechora	RST	-	-	-	-3	0.81	0.91
	SCE- UA	-3	0.86	0.93	2	0.80	0.90
Northern Dvina	RST	-3	0.81	0.91	2	0.86	0.93
	SCE-UA	1	0.88	0.94	1	0.90	0.95

Table 1. Statistical estimation of two optimization algorithms

3.2 Streamflow simulations with different sets of forcing data and optimal parameters

Table 2 summarizes the results of statistical estimation of agreement between measured and modelled daily streamflow for three rivers in different model runs with three versions of forcing data and with different sets of parameter values: a priori estimated parameters (Run-1) and optimized parameters without (Run-2) and with (Run-3) involving adjustment factors for forcing data. Optimization was performed by SCE-UA procedure.

Comparison of Run-1 and Run-2 results shows that calibration of eight model parameters has resulted in substantial improvement of the quality of streamflow simulations for each version of forcing data as compared to a priori estimated parameters. This is clearly seen from Figure 6, which shows the results averaged over three rivers. Thus, in Run-1, *Eff* was mainly negative, while in Run-2 mean *Eff* reached 64%, 72% and 84%, respectively, for Version 1, Version 2 and Version 3 of forcing data for the calibration period. The corresponding values of *r* were 0.87, 0.89 and 0.92, while the mean absolute *Bias* was 28%, 26% and 5%. Therefore, the best progress was archived for Version 3 of forcing data (when real observations form meteorological stations were used). As to the global forcing datasets, hybridized product was better than reanalysis one in terms of efficiency, while differences in the mean values of *r* and *Bias* were rather small. If we consider the validation period, the statistics for Version 3 was again the best. At the same time the quality of model performance using Version 1 of forcing data was even higher than with Version 2. For the entire period, the results for Version 1 and Version 2 were nearly the same. All this mean

Model run	River	Version 1			Version 2			Version 3		
		Bias,%	*Eff*	*r*	*Bias*, %	*Eff*	*r*	*Bias*, %	*Eff*	*r*
Calibration period (1986-1990)										
Run-1	Mezen	32	0.45	0.84	30	-0.34	0.83	-47	0.00	0.35
	Pechora	-28	-0.26	0.19	3	-0.66	0.45	-60	-0.16	0.25
	Northern Dvina	68	-0.68	0.76	56	-0.93	0.83	-46	0.29	0.69
	Mean	**43**	**-0.16**	**0.60**	**30**	**-0.64**	**0.70**	**51**	**0.04**	**0.43**
Run-2	Mezen	26	0.58	0.78	33	0.70	0.87	-3	0.82	0.91
	Pechora	0	0.83	0.91	1	0.78	0.89	-11	0.83	0.92
	Northern Dvina	57	0.52	0.91	45	0.67	0.91	0	0.88	0.94
	Mean	**28**	**0.64**	**0.87**	**26**	**0.72**	**0.89**	**5**	**0.84**	**0.92**
Run-3	Mezen	-6	0.75	0.87	2	0.83	0.91	0	0.90	0.95
	Pechora	0	0.87	0.94	4	0.85	0.92	3	0.92	0.96
	Northern Dvina	6	0.85	0.93	0	0.89	0.94	-4	0.89	0.94
	Mean	**4**	**0.82**	**0.91**	**2**	**0.86**	**0.92**	**2**	**0.90**	**0.95**
Validation period (1991-1995)										
Run-1	Mezen	38	0.37	0.79	42	-0.34	0.86	-43	0.14	0.46
	Pechora	-23	-0.03	0.36	2	-0.56	0.51	-57	0.05	0.50
	Northern Dvina	48	-0.38	0.64	55	-0.62	0.80	-40	0.40	0.75
	Mean	**36**	**-0.01**	**0.60**	**33**	**-0.51**	**0.72**	**47**	**0.20**	**0.57**
Run-2	Mezen	31	0.71	0.87	42	0.69	0.87	-7	0.86	0.93
	Pechora	-5	0.79	0.89	2	0.71	0.86	-11	0.69	0.84
	Northern Dvina	38	0.71	0.90	53	0.68	0.91	0	0.90	0.95
	Mean	**25**	**0.74**	**0.89**	**32**	**0.69**	**0.88**	**6**	**0.82**	**0.91**
Run-3	Mezen	2	0.73	0.86	6	0.82	0.91	-4	0.90	0.95
	Pechora	-6	0.85	0.92	-1	0.76	0.87	3	0.76	0.89
	Northern Dvina	-3	0.90	0.95	1	0.90	0.95	-5	0.89	0.95
	Mean	**4**	**0.83**	**0.91**	**3**	**0.83**	**0.91**	**4**	**0.85**	**0.93**
Entire period (1986-1995)										
Run-1	Mezen	35	0.41	0.81	36	-0.34	0.85	-45	0.08	0.40
	Pechora	-25	-0.13	0.29	3	-0.60	0.49	-59	-0.04	0.40
	Northern Dvina	58	-0.50	0.69	56	-0.74	0.81	-45	0.36	0.72
	Mean	**39**	**-0.07**	**0.60**	**32**	**-0.56**	**0.72**	**50**	**0.13**	**0.51**
Run-2	Mezen	29	0.66	0.83	38	0.69	0.87	-5	0.84	0.92
	Pechora	-3	0.81	0.90	2	0.75	0.87	-11	0.76	0.87
	Northern Dvina	47	0.64	0.90	49	0.67	0.91	0	0.89	0.95
	Mean	**26**	**0.70**	**0.88**	**30**	**0.70**	**0.88**	**5**	**0.83**	**0.91**
Run-3	Mezen	-1	0.74	0.86	4	0.82	0.91	-2	0.90	0.95
	Pechora	-3	0.86	0.93	2	0.80	0.90	3	0.83	0.92
	Northern Dvina	2	0.88	0.94	1	0.90	0.95	-4	0.89	0.95
	Mean	**2**	**0.83**	**0.91**	**2**	**0.84**	**0.92**	**3**	**0.87**	**0.94**

Table 2. Statistical evaluation of different model runs. Mean *Bias* was obtained for absolute values

that, first, forcing data based on real meteorology are of better quality than forcing data taken from the global datasets; second, high correlation between measured and simulated streamflow in all three cases, along with lower values of *Eff* and *Bias* in Version 1 and Version 2 compared to Version 3, confirms that global forcing data contain systematic errors (in spite of hybridization of pure reanalysis product with observations, which was undertaken to decrease the errors); third, these errors are not compensated by optimization of the land surface parameters, therefore to reduce their impact on streamflow simulations the adjustment factors for the key forcing data are required.

Further improvement of the above results was archived by means of involving adjustment factors for forcing data in the process of parameter optimization. This is confirmed by comparison of the results from Run-2 and Run-3 (see Figure 6 and Table 2). For Version 1

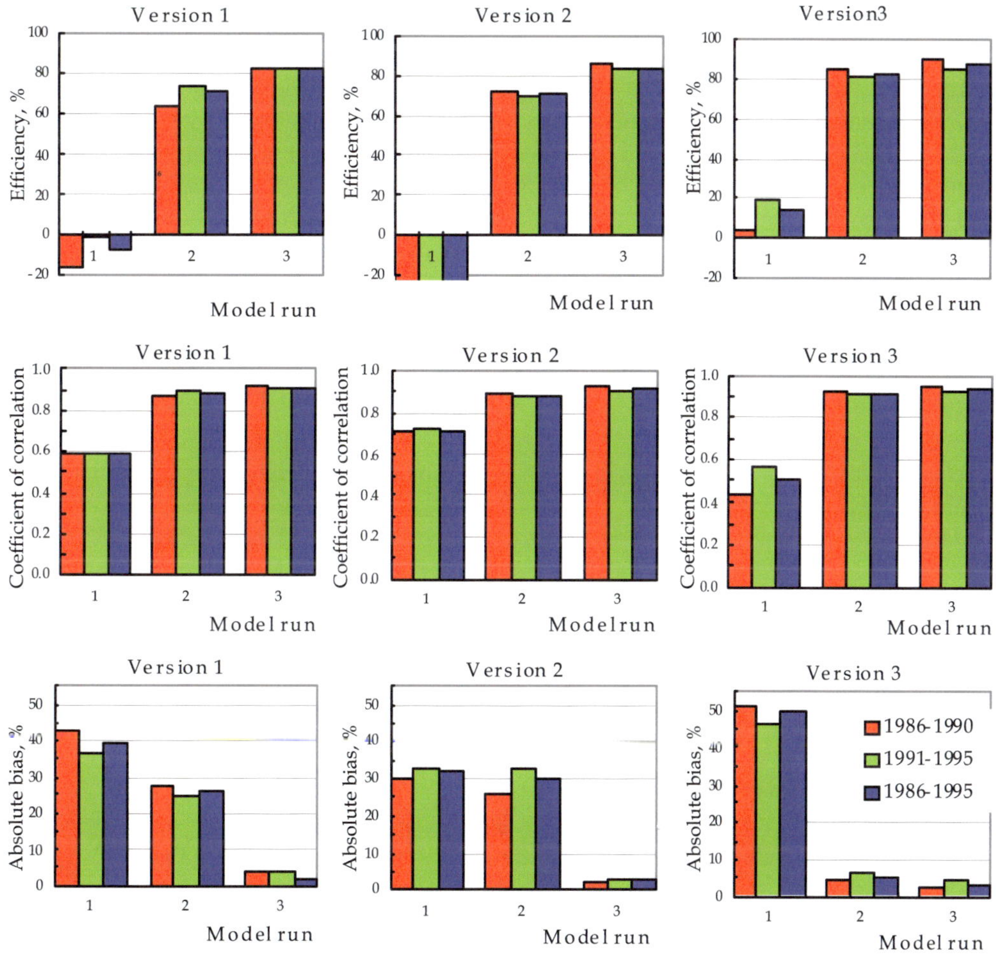

Fig. 6. Averaged over the three considered rivers daily efficiency, coefficient of correlation and absolute value of *Bias* from a priori simulations (model run 1) and calibrated results without (model run 2) and with (model run 3) application of adjustment factors for forcing data for the calibration period (red), the validation period (green) and the entire period (blue). The results are given for three versions of forcing data. All statistics are averaged over the three rivers.

and Version 2, the progress in model performance was significant, especially with respect to *Eff* and *Bias*. For the entire calculational period, mean *Eff* increased by 13-14% and mean absolute Bias decreased by 24-28% as a result of calibration of adjustment factors for forcing data. For Version 3, the improvement in mean *Eff* was only 4% and in mean absolute bias 2%. Therefore the quality of forcing data based on observations from meteorological stations, on average, was rather good. At the same time for the Mezen River and Pechora River, increase in *Eff* and decrease in absolute *Bias* sometimes reached 7-9%, while for the Northern Dvina the differences were much smaller, i.e. in the latter case the quality of forcing data was higher.

The obtained results have shown that optimization of model parameters and adjustment factors for forcing data makes it possible to use global datasets for streamflow simulations and to obtain results of a good quality. The lower the quality of input data the more effectiveness of such optimization. This is clearly illustrated by Figure 7 where hydrographs simulated for the Northern Dvina River in different model runs are compared with the measured hydrograph for the period of 1986-1995. The grey hydrographs were simulated without any optimization. Their agreement with measurements is very poor. Differences between grey hydrographs in the upper and middle panels are due to differences in the global atmospheric forcing data (the values of model parameters are the same here). In these cases both forcing data and model parameters (which were also taken from global datasets) contribute to the low accuracy of streamflow simulation. In the bottom panel, poor simulation (without calibration) is due to inadequate values of a priori estimated model parameters (taken from global datasets), while real meteorology, as it was shown above, is rather good. Optimization of parameter values allowed us greatly improve the modelled hydrographs (compare grey lines with blue lines in all panels). Further improvement was made by means of simultaneous optimization of model parameters and adjustment factors for forcing data (compare blue lines with green lines). Coincidence of green and blue hydrographs in the bottom panel confirms the above made conclusion that there is no necessity to use the adjustment factors for forcing data if the quality of forcing data is rather high.

At last, Figure 8 shows that it is possible to obtain a good accuracy of streamflow simulations using any of three versions of forcing data if optimization of model parameters and (if it is necessary) adjustment factors has been performed in a proper way. As can be seen from Figure 8, three hydrographs modelled by SWAP using different versions of forcing data are in a good agreement with each other and with measured hydrograph.

4. Conclusions

The main conclusions from this investigation can be summarized as follows.

- Direct application of the global data on meteorological characteristics and land surface parameters, developed within the framework of the ISLSCIP-II and GSWP-2 projects, for simulating streamflow for three northern rivers, located in the European part of Russia, by the LSM SWAP leads to poor results (low Nash-Sutcliffe efficiencies and large biases). Optimization helps to compensate to some extent uncertainties and shortcomings in input data and model parameters. Uncertainties and errors in forcing data can be partly compensated by application of adjustment factors for those meteorological characteristics, which influence runoff generation to a greater extent. Calibration of such factors together with model parameters allows one to reduce the influence of systematic errors in forcing data on optimization of model parameters and

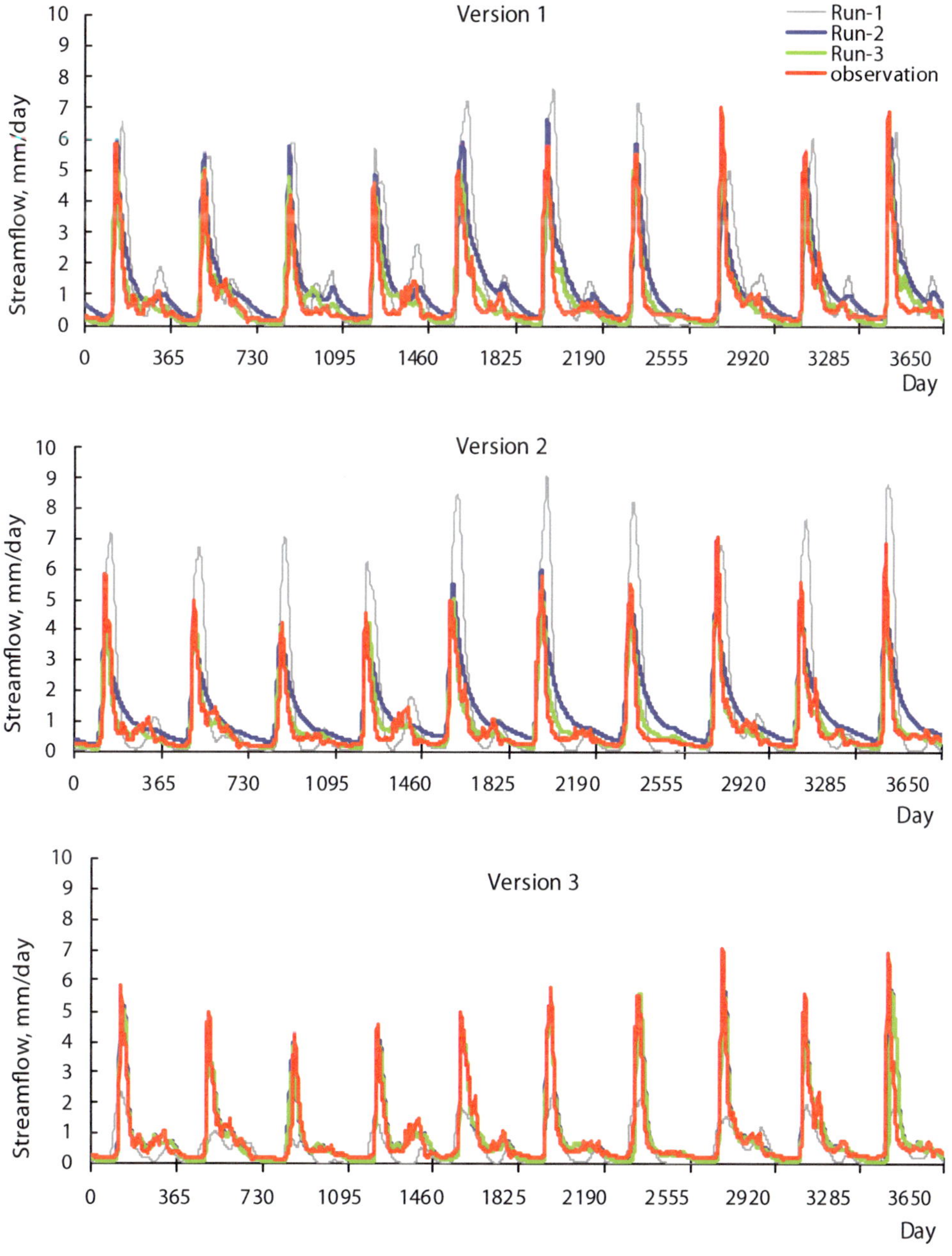

Fig. 7. Measured and simulated streamflow of the Northern Dvina River. Simulations were performed for three versions of forcing data using a priori (Run-1) estimated parameters and optimized parameters without (Run-2) and with (Run-3) application of adjustment factors for forcing data. The days are numbered from the 1 January 1986.

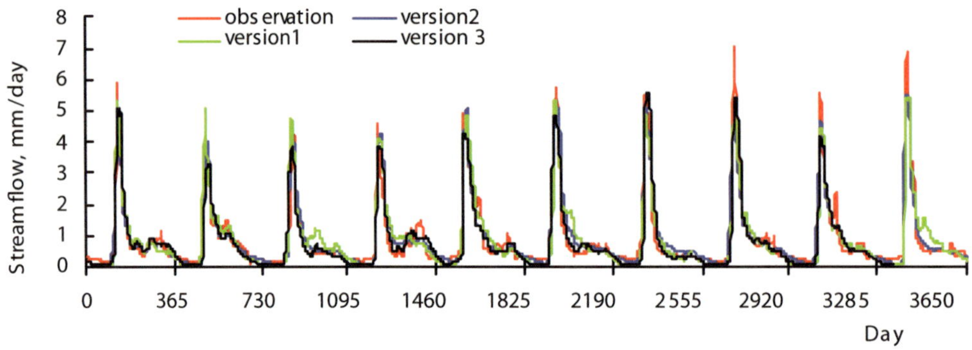

Fig. 8. Measured and simulated (Run-3) streamflow of the Northern Dvina River. The days are numbered from the 1 January 1986.

on model performance. All calibrated parameters should be kept within a reasonable range so as not to violate physical constraints while providing a close match between simulated and measured daily streamflow.

- Forcing data based on real meteorology from the meteorological stations located within a basin require adjustment factors only in the case of low quality of data (if the density of measurements is poor, or location of the stations cannot provide the study basin with representative information, or measurements contain errors etc.).
- Application of two different global optimization algorithms (RST and SCE-UA) has shown that both algorithms lead to practically the same results. The advantage of the former is that a user can interfere in the process of calibration and to speed up it by analyzing the preliminary results and reducing the feasible parameter space. SCE-UA does not need user interference and, consequently, depends on a user's experience to a less extent and is a less labour-consuming procedure. At the same time SCE-UA is a more time-consuming procedure, but if the time is not limited, it is more convenient to use SCE-UA optimization technique.
- Application of the LSM SWAP with global parameter datasets and with different versions of atmospheric forcing data (based on (1) global reanalysis product, (2) global reanalysis product hybridized with gridded observations and (3) real meteorology from meteorological stations) allows one to reproduce hydrographs of the northern rivers of the European part of Russia after optimization of a set of model parameters and adjustment factors for forcing data with a good accuracy, which is confirmed by statistical estimation of agreement between simulated and measured hydrographs and their visual comparison.

Future research should be concentrated on the solution of the following problems. First, development of methodology for predicting changes in river runoff due to climate change and anthropogenic effects. Second, development of methods for modelling river runoff in ungauged basins, i.e. when streamflow measurements are absent and it is not possible to perform optimization of model parameters and to validate the results. These problems are difficult; however, the possible ways for their solutions may be as follows. The former problem can be solved on the base of application of LSMs, along with climate forecast generators and land use scenarios of a high spatial and temporal resolution. The second problem can be solved on the base of LSMs and construction of relations between calibrated model parameters and natural characteristics of river basins.

5. Acknowledgements

This work was supported by the Russian Foundation for Basic Research (Grant 11-05-00015) and Federal Agency of Science and Innovations of Russian Federation (Project No. 02.740.11.0336). We also acknowledge the Global Runoff Data Centre (D - 56068 Koblenz, Germany) for providing us with daily streamflow measurements.

6. References

Appolov, B.A.; Kalinin, G.P. & Komarov, V.D. (1974). *Hydrological Forecasts Course*, Gidrometeoizdat, Leningrad, USSR (in Russian)

Bastidas, L.A.; Gupta, H.V.; Sorooshian, S. et al. (1999). Sensitivity Analysis of a Land Surface Scheme using Multi-Criteria Methods. *J. Geophys. Res.*, Vol. 104, No. D16, 19481-19490, ISSN: 0148-0227

Bogdanova, E.G.; Golubev, V.S.; Ilyin, B.M. & Dragomilova I.V. (2002b). A new model for bias correction of precipitation measurements, and its application to polar regions of Russia. *Russian Meteorol. Hydrol.* No. 10, 68–94, ISSN: 1068-3739

Bogdanova, E.G.; Ilyin, B.M. & Dragomilova, I.V. (2002a). Application of a comprehensive bias correction model to precipitation measured at Russian North Pole drifting stations. *J. Hydrometeorol*, Vol. 3, 700–713, ISSN: 1525-755X

Boone, A.; Habets, F.; Noilhan, J.; Clark, D.; Dirmeyer, P.; Fox, S.; Gusev, Y.; Haddeland, I.; Koster, R.; Lohmann, D.; Mahanama, S.; Mitchell, K.; Nasonova, O.; Niu, G.-Y.; Pitman, A.; Polcher, J.; Shmakin, A.B.; Tanaka, K.; van den Hurk, B.; Verant, S.; Verseghy, D.; Viterbo, P. & Yang, Z.-L. (2004). The Rhone-aggregation land surface scheme intercomparison project: An overview. *J. Climate*, Vol. 17, 187-208, ISSN: 0894-8755

Bowling, L.C.; Lettenmaier, D.P. & Matheussen B.V. (2000). Hydroclimatology of the Arctic drainage basin. In: The Freshwater Budget of the Arctic Ocean, E.L. Lewis et al. (Eds.), 57- 90, Springer, ISBN: 978-0-7923-6440-5, New York

Bowling, L.C.; Lettenmaier, D.P.; Nijssen, B.; Graham, L.P.; Clark, D.B.; El Maayar, M.; Essery, R.; Goers, S.; Habets, F.; van den Hurk, B.; Jin, J.; Kahan, D.; Lohmann, D.; Mahanama, S.; Mocko, D.; Nasonova, O.; Samuelsson, P.; Shmakin, A.B.; Takata, K.; Verseghy, D.; Viterbo, P.; Xia, Y.; Ma, X.; Xue, Y. & Yang, Z.-L. (2003). Simulation of high latitude hydrological processes in the Torne- Kalix basin: PILPS Phase 2(e): 1. Experiment description and summary intercomparisons. *Global Plan. Change*, Vol. 38, 1 -30, ISSN: 0921-8181

Bryazgin, N.N. & Dement'ev, A.A. (1996). *Dangerous meteorological events in Russian Arctic*, Gidrometeoizdat, ISBN: 5286012167, 9785286012169, St. Petersburg, (in Russian).

Clapp, R.B. & Hornberger, G.M. (1978). Empirical equations for some soil hydraulic properties. *Water Resour. Res.* Vol. 14, No. 4, 601-604, ISSN: 0043-1397

Dirmeyer, P.; Gao, X. & Oki, T. (2002). *The Second Global Soil Wetness Project. Science and Implementation Plan*, IGPO Publication Series, Silver Spring: International GEWEX Project Office, 37, 75 pp.

Duan, Q. (2003). Global optimization for watershed model calibration, In: *Calibration of Watershed Models*, Duan Q. et al. (Eds.), 89–104, AGU Water Sci. & App. 6, ISBN: 087590355X, Washington, DC

Duan, Q.; Sorooshian S. & Gupta V.K. (1992). Effective and efficient global optimization for conceptual rainfall runoff models. *Water Resour. Res.*, Vol. 28, No. 4, 1015–1031, ISSN: 0043-1397

Etchevers, P.; Martin, E.; Brown, R.; Fierz, C.; Lejeune, Y.; Bazile, E.; Boone, A.; Dai, Y.-J.; Essery, R.; Fernandez, A.; Gusev, Ye.; Jordan, R.; Koren, V.; Kowalczyk, E.; Nasonova, O.N.; Pyles, R.D.; Schlosser, A.; Shmakin A.B.; Smirnova, T. G.; Strasser, U.; Verseghy, D.; Yamazaki, T. & Yang, Z.-L. (2004). Validation of the energy budget of an alpine snowpack simulated by several snow models (SnowMIP project). *Annals of Glaciology*, Vol. 38, 150-158, ISSN: 0260-3055

Gan, T.Y.; Gusev, Ye.; Burges, S.J. & Nasonova, O. (2006). Performance comparison of a complex, physics-based land surface model and a conceptual, lumped-parameter hydrological model at the basin-scale. *IAHS Publ.* No. 307, 196-207, ISSN: 0144-7815

Globus, A.M. (1987). *Soil-hydrophysical information for agroecological models*, Leningrad, Gigrometeoizdat, (in Russian)

Goodison, B.E.; Louie, P.Y.T. & Yang, D. (1998). *WMO solid precipitation intercomparison. Final Report*, World Meteorol. Org., Instruments and Observing Methods Rep. 67, WMO/TD 872, 212 pp.

Gupta, H.V.; Sorooshian, S. & Yapo, P.O. (1998). Toward improved calibration of hydrologic models: Multiple and non-commensurable measures of information, *Water Resour. Res.*, Vol. 34, No. 4, 751-763, ISSN: 0043-1397

Gusev, Ye.M. & Nasonova, O.N. (1998). The land surface parameterization scheme SWAP: description and partial validation. *Global Plan. Change*, Vol. 19, No. 1-4, 63-86, ISSN: 0921-8181

Gusev, Ye.M. & Nasonova, O.N. (2000). An experience of modelling heat and water exchange at the land surface on a large river basin scale. *J. Hydrol.*, Vol. 233, No. 1-4, 1-18, ISSN: 0022-1694

Gusev, Ye.M. & Nasonova, O.N. (2002). The simulation of heat and water exchange at the land-atmosphere interface for the boreal grassland by the land-surface model SWAP. *Hydrol. Proc.*, Vol. 16, No. 10, 1893-1919, ISSN: 0885-6087

Gusev, Ye.M. & Nasonova, O.N. (2003). Modelling heat and water exchange in the boreal spruce forest by the land-surface model SWAP. *J. Hydrol.*, Vol. 280, No. 1-4, 162-191, ISSN: 0022-1694

Gusev, E.M. & Nasonova, O.N. (2004). Simulation of heat and water exchange at the land–atmosphere interface on a local scale for permafrost territories. *Eurasian Soil Sci.*, Vol. 37, No. 9, 1077–1092, ISSN: 0032-180X

Gusev, E.M.; Nasonova, O.N. & Dzhogan, L.Ya. (2006a). The Simulation of runoff from small catchments in the permafrost zone by the SWAP model. *Water Resour.*, Vol. 33, No. 2, 115–126, ISSN: 0321-0596

Gusev, E.M.; Nasonova, O.N.; Dzhogan, L.Ya. & Kovalev, E.E. (2008). The Application of the land surface model for calculating river runoff in high latitudes. *Water Resour.*, Vol. 35, No. 2, 171–184, ISSN: 0321-0596

Gusev, E.M.; Nasonova, O.N. & Kovalev, E.E. (2006b). Modeling the components of heat and water balance for the land surface of the globe. *WaterResour.*, Vol. 33, No. 6, 616-627, ISSN: 0321-0596

Gusev, E.M.; Nasonova, O.N. & Mohanty, B.P. (2004). Estimation of radiation, heat, and water exchange between steppe ecosystems and the atmosphere in the SWAP model. *Izvestiya RAN, Atmospheric and Oceanic Physics*, Vol. 40, No. 3, 291–305, ISSN: 0002-3515

Hall, F. G.; Meeson, B.; Los, S.; Steyaert, L.; Brown de Colstoun, E. & Landis, D. (2003). *ISLSCP Initiative II*, NASA DVD/CD-ROM

Jacobs, D.A.H. (1977). *The State of The Art in Numerical Analysis*, Academic Press, ISBN: 0123786509, London

Kanamitsu, M.; Ebisuzaki, W.; Woollen, J.; Yang, S.-K.; Hnilo, J.J.; Fiorino, M. & Potter, G.L. (2002). NCEP-DOE AMIP-II reanalysis (R-2). *Bull. Amer. Meteor. Soc.*, 83, 1631-1648, ISSN: 0003-0007

Meeson, B.W.; Corprew, F.E.; McManus, J.M.P.; Myers, D.M.; Closs, J.W.; Sun, K.J.; Sunday, D.J. & Sellers, P.J. (1995). *ISLSCP Initiative I - Global data sets for land-atmosphere models, 1987-1988*, Volumes 1-5, Published on CD-ROM by NASA (USA_NASA_GDAAC_ISLSCP_001 - USA_NASA_GDAAC_ISLSCP_005).

Nash, J.E. & Sutcliffe, J.V. (1970). River flow forecasting through conceptual models: 1 A discussion of principles. *J. Hydrol.*, Vol. 10, No. 3, 282-290, ISSN: 0022-1694

Nasonova, O.N.; Gusev, E.M. & Kovalev, E.E. (2008). Global evaluation of the components of heat and water balances of the land. *Izvestiya RAN, Seriya georgaphicheskaya*, No. 1, 8-19 (in Russian), ISSN: 0373-2444

Nasonova O.N.; Gusev Ye.M. & Kovalev Ye.E. (2009). Investigating the ability of a land surface model to simulate streamflow with the accuracy of hydrological models: A case study using MOPEX materials. *J. Hydrometeorol.*, Vol. 10, No 5, 1128-1150, ISSN: 1525-755X

Nelder, J.A. & Mead R.A. (1965). Simplex method for function minimization. *Comput. J.*, Vol. 7, No. 4, 308–313, ISSN: 0010-4620

Nijssen, B.; O'Donnell, G.M.; Lettenmaier, D.P.; Lohmann D. & Wood, E.F. (2001). Predicting the discharge of global rivers. *J. Climate*, Vol. 14, 3307-3323, ISSN: 0894-8755

Nijssen, B.; Bowling, L.C.; Lettenmaier, D.P.; Clark, D.B.; El Maayar, M.; Essery, R.; Goers, S.; Gusev, Y.M.; Habets, F.; van den Hurk, B.; Jin, J.; Kahan, D.; Lohmann, D.; Ma, X.; Mahanama, S.; Mocko, D.; Nasonova, O.; Niu, G.; Samuelsson, P.; Shmakin, A.B.; Takata, K.; Verseghy, D.; Viterbo, P.; Xia, Y.; Xue, Y. & Yang, Z. (2003). Simulation of high-latitude hydrological processes in the Torne– Kalix basin: PILPS Phase 2(e): 2. Comparison with observations. *Global Plan. Change*, Vol. 38, 31– 53, ISSN: 0921-8181

Oki, T.; Nishimura, T. & Dirmeyer, P. (1999). Assessment of annual runoff from land surface models using Total Runoff Integrating Pathways (TRIP). *J Meteorol. Soc. of Japan*, Vol. 77, No. 1B, 235-255, ISSN: 0026-1165

Oki, T. & Sud, Y.C. (1998). Design of Total Runoff Integrating Pathways (TRIP) – A global river channel network. *Earth Interactions*, Vol. 2, 1-37, ISSN: 1087-3562

Pintér J. (1996). *Global Optimization in Action*, Kluwer, ISBN: 978-0-7923-3757-7, Dordrecht

Powell, M.J.D. (1964). An efficient method of finding the minimum of a function of several variables without calculating derivatives. *Comput. J.*, Vol. 7, 155–162, ISSN: 0010-4620

Rastrigin, L.A. (1968). *Statistical methods of searching*, Nauka, Moscow (in Russian)

Rosenbrock, H.H. (1960). An automatic method for finding the greatest or least value of a function. *Comput. J.*, Vol. 3, 175–184, ISSN: 0010-4620

Slater, A.G.; Schlosser, C.A.; Desborough, C.E.; Pitman, A.J.; Henderson-Sellers, A.; Robock, A.; Vinnikov, K. Ya.; Mitchell, K.; Boone, A.; Braden, H.; Chen, F.; Cox, P.M.; deRosney, P.; Dickinson, R.E.; Dai, Y.-J.; Duan, Q.; Entin, J.; Etchevers, P.; Gedney, N.; Gusev, Ye.M.; Habets, F.; Kim, J.; Koren, V.; Kowalczyk, E.A.; Nasonova, O.N.; Noilhan, J.; Schaake, S.; Shmakin, A.B.; Smirnova, T.G.; Verseghy, D.; Wetzel, P.; Xue, Y.; Yang, Z.-L. & Zeng, Q. (2001). The representation of snow in land surface schemes: results from PILPS 2(d). *J. Hydrometeorol.*, Vol. 2, 7-25, ISSN: 1525-755X

Solomatine, D.P.; Dibike, Y.B. & Kukuric, N. (1999). Automatic calibration of groundwater models using global optimization techniques. *Hydrological Sciences J.*, Vol. 44, No. 6, 879-894, ISSN: 0262-6667

Su, F.; Adam, J.C.; Bowling, L.C. & Lettenmaier, D.P. (2005). Streamflow simulations of the terrestrial Arctic domain. *J. Geophys. Res.*, Vol. 110, No. D08112, doi:10.1029/2004JD005518, ISSN: 0148-0227

Törn, A. & Zilinskas, A. (1989). *Global Optimization*, Springer-Verlag, ISBN: 3540508716, Berlin

Tian, X.; Dai, A.; Yang, D. & Xie, Z. (2007). Effects of precipitation-bias corrections on surface hydrology over northern latitudes. *J. Geophys. Res.*, Vol. 112, No. D14101, doi:10.1029/2007JD008420, ISSN: 0148-0227

Xia, Y. (2007). Calibration of LaD model in the northeast United States using observed annual streamflow. *J. Hydrometeorol.*, Vol. 8, 1098-1110, ISSN: 1525-755X

Yang, D. & Ohata, T. (2001). A bias-corrected Siberian regional precipitation climatology. *J. Hydrometeorol.* Vol. 2, 122 – 139, ISSN: 1525-755X

Zhao, M. & Dirmeyer, P.A. (2003). *Production and Analysis of GSWP-2 near-surface meteorology data sets*. COLA Technical Report, 159, 38 pp.

18

Evaluation of Stochastic Global Optimization Methods in the Design of Complex Distillation Configurations

Julián Cabrera-Ruiz[1], Erick Yair Miranda-Galindo[1], Juan Gabriel Segovia-Hernández[1], Salvador Hernández[1] and Adrián Bonilla-Petriciolet[2]
[1]*Universidad de Guanajuato, Chemical Engineering Department, Campus Guanajuato, C.P. 36050, Guanajuato,*
[2]*Instituto Tecnológico de Aguascalientes, Chemical Engineering Department, C.P. 20256, Aguascalientes,*
México

1. Introduction

Distillation is a widely used separation process and is a very large consumer of energy. In process design, a significant amount of research work has been done to improve the energy efficiency of distillation systems in terms of either the design of optimal distillation schemes or for improving internal column efficiency. Still, the optimal design of multicomponent distillation systems remains one of the most challenging problems in process engineering (Kim & Wankat, 2004). The economic importance of distillation separations has been a driving force for the research in synthesis procedures for more than 30 years. For the separation of an N-component mixture into N pure products, as the number of components increases, the number of possible simple column configurations sharply increases. Therefore, the design and optimization of a distillation column involves the selection of the configuration and the operating conditions to minimize the total investment and operation cost (Yeomans & Grossmann, 2000). The global optimization of a complex distillation system is usually characterized as being of large problem size, since the significant number of strongly nonlinear equations results in serious difficulty in solving the model. Moreover, good initial values are needed for solving the NLP subproblems. Until now, several strategies have been proposed to address this optimization problem. For example, Andrecovich & Westerberg (1985) proposed a mixed-integer linear programming (MILP) model for synthesizing sharp separation sequences. Later, Paules & Floudas (1990) and Aggarwal & Floudas (1990) developed mixed-integer nonlinear programming (MINLP) models for heat-integrated and nonsharp distillation sequences using linear mass balances. In other study, Novak et al. (1996) proposed superstructure MINLP optimization approaches using short-cut models for heat-integrated distillation. Smith & Pantelides (1995) and Bauer & Stichlmair (1998) developed MINLP models using rigorous tray-by-tray models for zeotropic and azeotropic mixtures. Also, Dunnebier & Pantelides (1999) have used rigorous tray-by-tray MINLP models to solve complex column configuration distillation sequences. So far, most of the available mathematical programming models are based on simplified performance models of the distillation columns, including linear mass balance equations, short-cut models, and aggregated models (see for example, Papalexandri & Pistikopoulos, 1996; Caballero & Grossmann, 1999). While some of these methods can provide useful results in terms of preliminary designs or bounds for process synthesis, it is clear that it would be desirable to directly incorporate rigorous models in the design procedures in order to increase their industrial relevance and scope of application, particularly, for nonideal mixtures. Regarding the rigorous MINLP synthesis models by Bauer & Stichlmair (1998), Smith & Pantelides (1995), and Dünnebier & Pantelides (1999), all of them use modifications of the single-column MINLP model proposed by Viswanathan & Grossmann (1993) for optimizing the feed tray location and number of trays. These rigorous MINLP synthesis models exhibit significant computational difficulties such as the introduction of equations that can become singular, the solution of many redundant equations, and the requirement of a good initialization point. So, the presence of nonlinearities and nonconvexities in the MESH equations and thermodynamic equilibrium equations, as well as the convergence difficulties when deleting non-existing columns or column sections, are common problems to the tray-by-tray models based on the model by Viswanathan & Grossmann (1993). In summary, these difficulties translate into high computational times and the requirement of good initial guesses and bounds on the design variables to achieve model convergence.

In general, the optimal design of distillation systems is a highly non-linear and multivariable problem, with the presence of both continuous and discontinuous design variables. In addition, the objective function used as optimization criterion is generally non-convex with several local optimums and subject to several constraints. The use of stochastic optimizers, which deals with multi-modal and non-convex problems, can be an effective way to face the challenging characteristics involved in the design of distillation columns. Stochastic global optimization algorithms are capable of solving, robustly and efficiently, the challenging multi-modal optimization problem, and they appear to be a suitable alternative for the design and optimization of complex separation schemes (Martínez-Iranzo et al., 2009). These optimization methods have several features that make them attractive for solving optimization problems with modular simulators, where the model of each unit is only available in an implicit form (i.e., black-box model). First, due to the fact that they are based on direct search strategies, it is not necessary to have explicit information on the mathematical model or its derivatives. Secondly, the search for the optimal solution is not limited to one point but rather relies on several points simultaneously; therefore, the knowledge of initial feasible points is not required.

In this chapter, we have implemented several stochastic global optimization methods to obtain the design and optimization of three distillation sequences: multicomponent conventional distillation system (Figure 1), thermally coupled reactive scheme with side stripper (Figure 2), and a dividing wall distillation column (Figure 3). Specifically, these stochastic optimization methods are: Simulated Annealing (SA), Harmony Search (HS) and Genetic Algorithms (GA). In recent years, the range of applicability of optimization has been widened and progress has improved in different areas. Effective search methods, such as genetic algorithms, simulated annealing and harmony search, for global optimization have been developed, and problems with complex analysis model and various types of constraints and non-convex objective functions have been investigated (Costa et al., 2000).

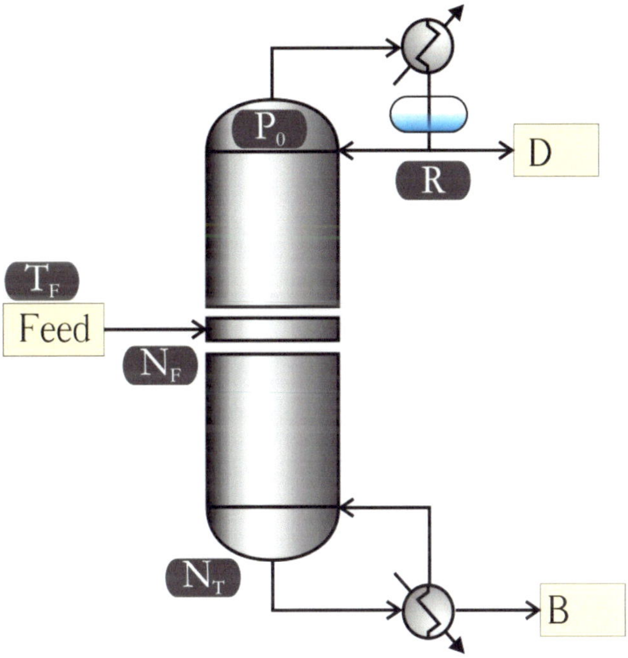

Fig. 1. Schematic representation of a multicomponent conventional distillation column. Nomenclature of this figure is given in section 8 of this chapter.

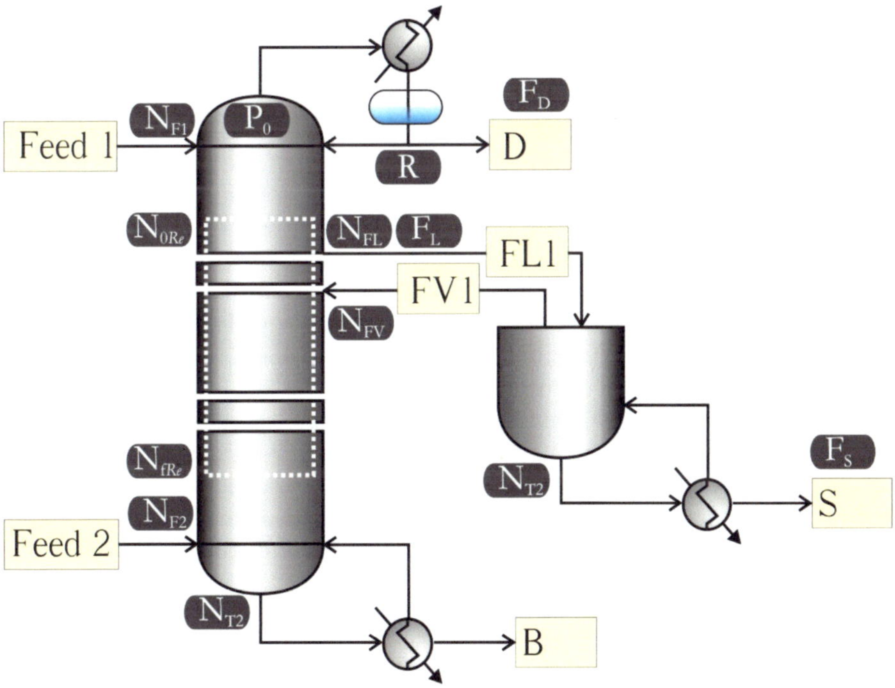

Fig. 2. Schematic representation of a thermally coupled reactive distillation sequence with side stripper (TCRDS-SS). Nomenclature of this figure is given in section 8 of this chapter.

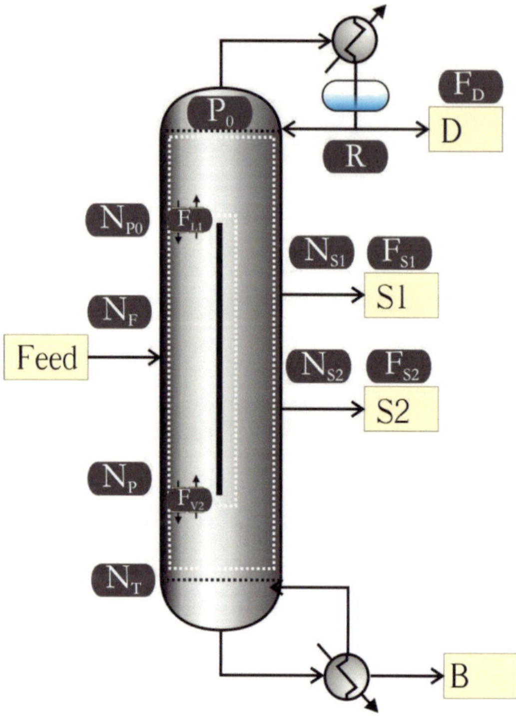

Fig. 3. Schematic representation of a dividing wall distillation column (DWC).
Nomenclature of this figure is given in section 8 of this chapter.

We select SA, HS and GA for this study because they have shown their merits in large-scale search, approaching the global optimum quickly and steadily. These optimization methods have several features that make them attractive for solving optimization problems with modular simulators, where the model of each unit is only available in an implicit form.

On the other hand, literature indicates that, when operating conditions are properly chosen, the thermally coupled reactive scheme with side stripper and dividing wall distillation column can produce important energy savings compared with conventional distillation sequences (Kiss et al., 2010). Some studies have demonstrated that this kind of sequences has energy savings of about 30% over conventional schemes (Triantafyllou & Smith, 1992; Hernández & Jiménez, 1996). Therefore, we have studied the design of these distillation schemes using stochastic global optimization methods coupled to the Aspen One Aspen Plus process simulator for the evaluation of the objective function, ensuring that all results obtained are rigorous. To the best of our knowledge, the evaluation and comparison of stochastic global optimization methods have not been reported for process design of distillation configurations. Therefore, our results permit to identify the capabilities and limitations of these optimization strategies in the process design applications.

2. Description of stochastic global optimization methods used for the design of distillation schemes

Stochastic optimization methods are optimization algorithms which incorporate probabilistic (i.e., random) elements to diversify and intensify the search space of decision variables. Further, the injected randomness may provide the necessary impetus to move away from a local solution when searching for a global optimum. Stochastic optimization methods of this kind include: simulated annealing, harmony search, swarm intelligence (e.g., ant colony optimization, particle swarm optimization), evolutionary algorithms (e.g., genetic algorithms, differential evolution), among others. In this study, we use three optimization methods: Simulated Annealing (SA), Genetic Algorithms (GA) and Harmony Search (HS). Note that SA and GA are classical stochastic optimization methods and have been used for process design (Vazquez-Castillo et al., 2009), while HS is a novel stochastic optimization method with few chemical engineering applications (Geem, 2009). In general, all methods have the attributes of a good optimization strategy such as generality, efficiency, reliability and ease of use. A brief description of these algorithms is provided in the following section.

2.1 Simulated annealing

Simulated annealing mimics the thermodynamic process of cooling of molten metals to attain the lowest free energy state (Kirkpatrick et al., 1983). Starting with an initial solution, the algorithm performs a stochastic partial search of the space defined for decision variables. In minimization problems, uphill moves are occasionally accepted with a probability controlled by the parameter called annealing temperature: T_{SA}. The probability of acceptance of uphill moves decreases as T_{SA} decreases. At high T_{SA}, the search is almost random, while at low T_{SA} the search becomes selective where good moves are favored. The core of this algorithm is the Metropolis criterion (Metropolis et al., 1983), which is used to accept or reject uphill movements with an acceptance probability given by

$$M(T_{SA}) = \min\left\{1, \exp\left(\frac{-\Delta f}{T_{SA}}\right)\right\} \quad (1)$$

where Δf is the change in objective function value from the current point to new point.
The objective function is evaluated at the trial point, and its value is compared to the objective value at the starting/current point. Eq. (1) is used to accept or reject the trial point. If this trial point is accepted, the algorithm continues the search using that point; otherwise, another trial point is generated within the neighborhood of the starting/current point. A fall in T_{SA} is imposed upon the system using a proper cooling schedule. Thus, as T_{SA} declines, downhill moves are less likely to be accepted and SA focuses on the most promising area for optimization. These iterative steps are performed until the specified stopping criterion is satisfied. Figure 4 shows a flowchart of this algorithm. Until now, SA algorithm has been successfully used in several chemical engineering application (e.g., Rangaiah, 2001; Bonilla-Petriciolet et al., 2006; Wei-Zhong & Xi-Gang, 2009). In our work, we have used the SA subroutine of MATLAB®.
The random numbers rand can be uniformly distributed in the interval [0, 1]. If rand < $M(T_{SA})$, the trial point is accepted, otherwise the starting/current point is used to start the next step. The temperature T_{SA} can be considered a control parameter. The initial temperature Ti is related with the standard deviation of the random perturbation and the final temperature T_f, with the order of magnitude of the desired accuracy, will give the location of the optimum solution.

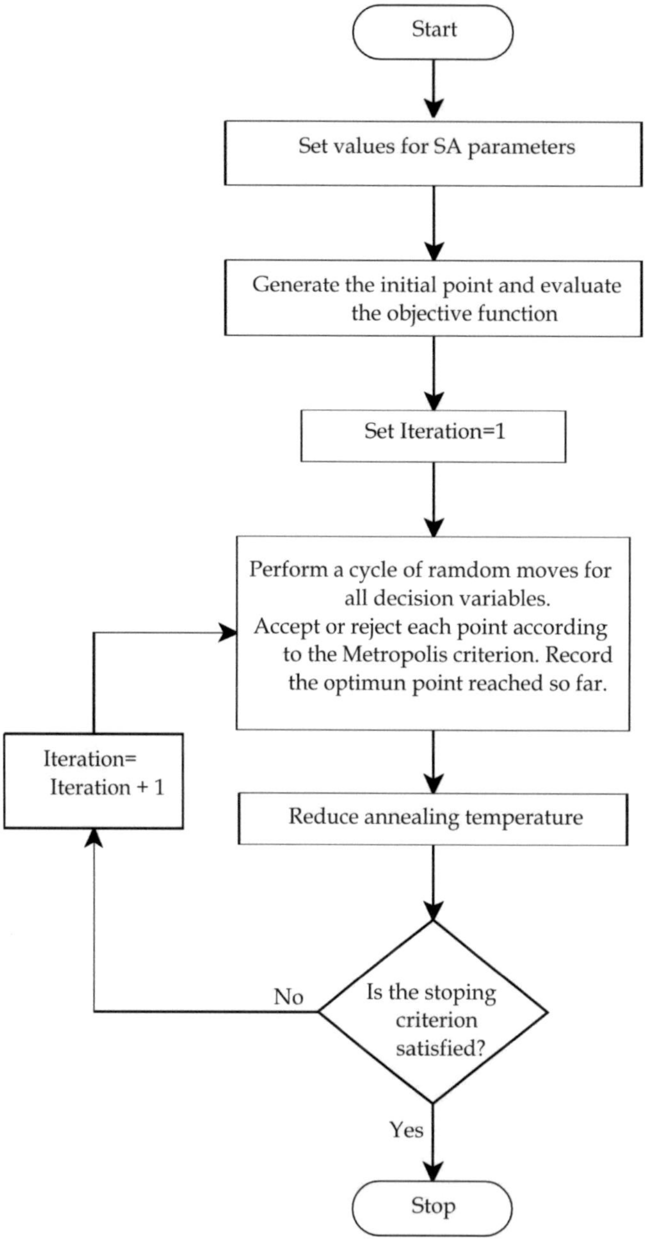

Fig. 4. Flowchart of Simulated Annealing stochastic optimization method.

2.2 Genetic Algorithm

Genetic algorithm (GA) is a stochastic technique that simulates natural evolution on the solution space of the optimization problems. It operates on a population of potential solutions (i.e., individuals) in each iteration (i.e., generation). By combining some individuals of the current population according to predefined operations, a new population that contains better individuals is produced as the next generation. The first step of GA is to create randomly an initial population of N_{pop} solutions in the feasible region. GA works on this population and combines (crossover) and modifies (mutation) some chromosomes according to specified genetic operations, to generate a new population with better characteristics. Individuals for reproduction are selected based on their objective function values and the Darwinian principle of the survival of the fittest (Holland, 1975). Genetic operators are used to create new individuals for the next population from those selected individuals of the current population, and they serve as searching mechanisms in GA. In particular, crossover forms two new individuals by first choosing two individuals from the mating pool (containing the selected individuals) and then swapping different parts of genetic information between them. This combining (crossover) operation takes place with a user-defined crossover probability (P_{cros}) so that some parents remain unchanged even if they are chosen for reproduction. Mutation is a unary operator that creates a new solution by a random change in an individual. It provides a guarantee that the probability of searching any given string will never be zero and acting as a safety net to recover good genetic material which may be lost through the action of selection and crossover. The mutation procedure proceeds with a probability P_{mut}. Selection, crossover and mutation procedures are recursively used to improve the population and to identify promising areas for optimization. This algorithm terminates when the user-specified criterion is satisfied. Usually, GA stops after evolving for the specified number of generations (Gen_{max}). The GA subroutine used in this study is from the OptimToolbox of MATLAB®. Details about the GA strategy and applications can be found in Holland (1975) and Figure 5 provides the corresponding general flowchart of GA.

2.3 Harmony Search

Harmony Search (HS) was first developed by Geem et al. (2001). This relatively new heuristic optimization algorithm has been applied to solve many optimization problems, e.g.: benchmark optimization problems, water distribution network, groundwater modeling, energy-saving dispatch, among others. HS is a music-based metaheuristic optimization algorithm and is inspired by the observation that the aim of music is to search for a perfect state of harmony (Geem, 2009). This harmony in music is analogous to find the optimal solution in an optimization process.

Like genetic algorithms and particle swarm optimization, harmony search is not a gradient-based search, so it avoids most of the pitfalls of any gradient-based search algorithms. Thus, it has fewer mathematical requirements and, subsequently, can be used to deal with complex objective functions with continuous or discontinuous and linear or nonlinear constraints. On the other hand, harmony search could be potentially more efficient than genetic algorithms because harmony search does not use binary encoding and decoding, but it has multiple solution vectors. Therefore, HS can be faster during each iteration and its implementation is also easier.

HS can be explained in more detail with the aid of the discussion of the improvisation process by a musician. When a musician is improvising, he or she has three possible choices: (1) play any piece of music (a series of pitches in harmony) exactly from his or her memory; (2) play something similar to a known piece (thus adjusting the pitch slightly); or (3) compose new or random notes. If we formalize these three options for optimization, we have three corresponding components: usage of harmony memory, pitch adjusting, and randomization.

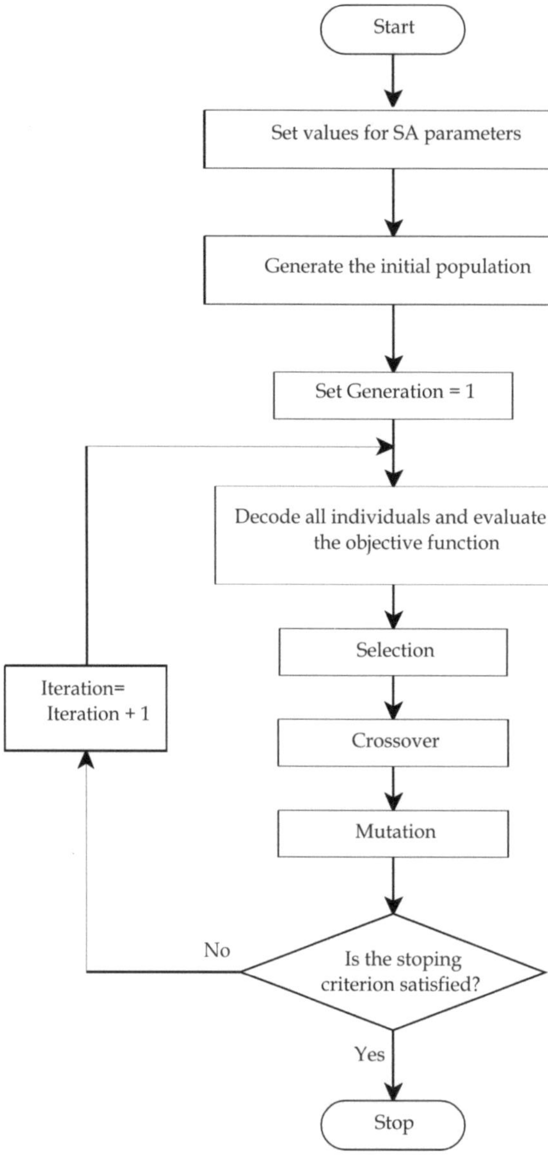

Fig. 5. Flowchart of Genetic Algorithm stochastic optimization method.

The use of harmony memory is important in HS as it is similar to choose the best fit individuals in the genetic algorithms. This will ensure that the best harmonies will be carried over to the new harmony memory. In order to use this memory more effectively, we can assign a parameter $r_{accept} \in [0,1]$, called harmony memory accepting or considering rate. If this rate is too low, only few best harmonies are selected and it may converge too slowly. If this rate is extremely high (i.e., near to 1), almost all the harmonies are used in the harmony memory, then other harmonies are not explored well, leading to potential local solutions. Therefore, typically, $r_{accept} = 0.7$~0.95 is used in the context of global optimization (Yang, 2008).

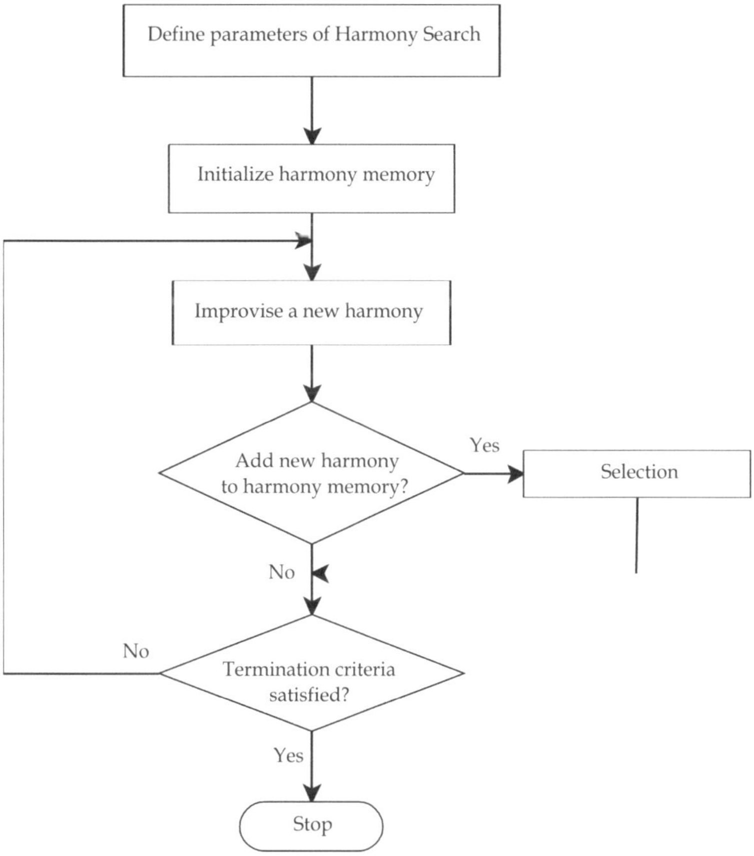

Fig. 6. Flowchart of Harmony Search stochastic optimization method.

Several authors also recommend to adjust the pitch slightly in the second component. In theory, the pitch can be adjusted linearly or non-linearly, but in practice, linear adjustment is used. So, we have

$$x_{new} = x_{lower\ \lim it} \pm x_{range} * rand \tag{2}$$

where x_{range}=$x_{upper\ limit}$ - $x_{lower\ limit}$ and *rand* is a random number generator in the range of 0 a 1. Pitch adjustment is similar to the mutation operator in genetic algorithms. We can assign a pitch-adjusting rate (r_{pa}) to control the degree of the adjustment. For example, if r_{pa} is too low, then there is rarely any change. If it is too high, the algorithm may not converge at all. Thus, it is usually recommended to use r_{pa}=0.1~0.5. In this work, r_{accept}=0.8 and r_{pa}=0.4 have been used.

The third component is the randomization, which is used to increase the diversity of the solutions. Although adjusting pitch has a similar role, but it is limited to certain local pitch adjustment and thus corresponds to a local search. The use of randomization can drive the system further to explore various diverse solutions so as to find the global optimum. The three components in harmony search can be summarized in the flowchart shown in Figure 6. Note that the probability of randomization is p_{random}=1-p_{accept}, and the actual probability of pitch-adjusting is p_{pitch}=r_{accept}*r_{pa}. We have used a HS subroutine implemented in MATLAB®.

3. Optimization strategy

In order to optimize the complex distillation sequences described in the introduction, we used SA, GA and HS coupled to Aspen ONE Aspen Plus. Specifically, for process design of complex separation schemes, the optimization of heat duty of the column is the optimization target. This design problem is a challenging global optimization problem with continuous and discontinuous decision variables. The formulation of optimization problems for the design of separation schemes is given below.

For the multicomponent distillation column used in the hydrodesulfurization (HDS) process, the optimization of the heat duty of the column can be stated as

$$\begin{aligned}&\text{Min}\ (Q) = f(R, P_0, T_F, N_F, N_T)\\&\text{subject to}\\&\vec{y}_m \geq \vec{x}_m\end{aligned} \tag{3}$$

where R is the reflux ratio, P_0 is the column pressure, T_F is the feed temperature, NF is the number of the feed stage and N_T is the number of stages of column. Note that y_m and x_m are vectors of obtained and required purities for the m components, respectively.

In the thermally coupled reactive distillation (TCRDS-SS), the global optimization problem for the minimization of the heat duty of the sequence is defined as

$$\begin{aligned}&\text{Min}\ (Q) = f(R, P_0, F_D, F_S, F_L, N_{F1}, N_{F2}, N_{0\text{Re}}, N_{f\text{Re}}, N_{FL}, N_{FV}, N_{T1}, N_{T2})\\&\text{subject to}\\&\vec{y}_m \geq \vec{x}_m\end{aligned} \tag{4}$$

where R is the reflux ratio, P_0 is the main column pressure, F_D and F_S are the distillate and side fluxes, F_L and N_{FL} are the value and location of the interconnection flow, N_{F1} and N_{F2} are the number of the feed stages, N_{FV} is the stream vapor tray location, N_{0Re} and N_{fRe} are the first and last reaction tray location, N_{T1} and N_{T2} are the number of stages of the main column and stripper, y_m and x_m are vectors of obtained and required purities for the m components, respectively.

In DWC, the global optimization problem is given by

$$\begin{aligned}&\text{Min}\ (Q) = f(R, P_0, F_D, F_{S1}, F_{S2}, F_{L1}, F_{V2}, N_F, N_{P0}, N_p, N_{S1}, N_{S2}, N_T)\\&\text{subject to}\\&\vec{y}_m \geq \vec{x}_m\end{aligned} \tag{5}$$

where R is the reflux ratio, P_0 is the main column pressure, F_D is the distillate flux, F_{S1} and F_{S2} are the side fluxes, F_{L1} and F_{V2} are the values of liquid and vapor interconnection flows, N_F is the feed stage, N_{P0} and N_p are the first and last prefractioner tray location, N_{S1} and N_{S2} are the side stream tray location, y_m and x_m are vectors of obtained and required purities for the m components, respectively. In summary, these global optimization problems have been used for comparing the performance of SA, GA and HS in the design of complex distillation sequences.

4. Case of study

To compare the performance of stochastic optimization methods, we have analyzed three case studies. First, we analyze the design of the multicomponent distillation column used in

the hydrodesulfurization (HDS) process. The feed composition is showed in the Table 1. Note that this composition of the diesel is reported by Viveros-García et al. (2005). The design objective is to obtain in the top of the column thiophene and benzothiophene with 2.13% and 1.29% in mole composition, respectively, and in the bottom dibenzothiophene and 4,6-dimethyldebenzothiphene with 16.0% and 3.2% mole composition, respectively. For this class of systems, thermodynamic model such as Peng-Robinson EoS can be used to calculate the vapor-liquid equilibrium.
Then, we analyze the design of a TCRDS-SS to obtain biodiesel (i.e., the esterification of methanol and lauric acid). The systems include two feed streams; the first is lauric acid with a flow of 45.4 kmol/h as saturated liquid at 1.5 bar, and the second is methanol with a flow of 54.48 kmol/h as saturated vapor at 1.5 bar.

Component	*Mole Fraction*
Thiophene	0.008
Benzothiophene	0.008
n-Undecane	0.489
n-Dodecane	0.316
n-Tridecane	0.008
n-Tetradecane	0.001
n-Hexadecane	0.05
Dibenzothiophene	0.1
4,6-dimethyldibenzothiophene	0.02

Table 1. Feed composition in distillation column of the HDS process used as case of study.

The design objective is a process for high-purity fatty ester, over 99.9% mass fraction, which is suitable for biodiesel application. It is important to highlight that this equilibrium reaction is usually catalyzed using sulfuric acid or p-toluensulfonic acid. The kinetic model (see Table 2) reported in Steinigeweg & Gmehling (2003) was used. For this class of reactive systems, thermodynamic model such as UNIFAC can be used to calculate the vapor-liquid or vapor-liquid-liquid equilibrium.

	Kinetic parameters	
Reaction	K_i (mol/g s)	$E_{A,i}$ (kJ/mol)
Esterification	9.1164×10^5	68.71
Hydrolysis	1.4998×10^4	64.66

Table 2. Kinetic parameters for the pseudo-homogeneous kinetic model of the esterification reaction.

Finally, we have studied the design of a DWC for purification of a mixture of alcohols: n-butanol, 1-pentanol, 1-hexanol, and 1-heptanol. The feed flowrate is 100 kmol/h and the feed is introduced in the column as saturated liquid. The composition in the feed flowrate is 40, 10, 10, 40 in mole percent. The design objective is to obtain each alcohol with high purity (98.6, 98, 98, 98.5 in mole composition percent). For this class of systems, thermodynamic model such as NRTL can be used to calculate the vapor-liquid equilibrium.
Both the tuning process parameters for each one and boundary variables searched were tuned using several short tests for improve the efficiency in the methods. Table 3 shows the limits of the search variables that have been established. The parameter tuning and search

Schemes	*Boundaries*
HDS	R=[0.1 10]
	P_O=[1 10] atm
	T_F=[298 478] K
	N_F=[2 99]
	N_T=[3 100]
TCRDS-SS	R=[10 20]
	P_O=[1 5] atm
	F_D=[8.89 9.53] kmol/h
	F_S=[44.90 45.81] kmol/h
	F_L=[49.89 56.70] kmol/h
	N_{F1}=[2 98]
	N_{F2}=[3 99]
	N_{ORe}=[2 99]
	N_{fRe}=[3 100]
	N_{FL}=[6 98]
	N_{FV}=[7 99]
	N_{T1}=[5 100]
	N_{T2}=[2 50]
DWC	R=[55 75]
	P_O=[1 5] atm
	F_D=[39 41] kmol/h
	F_{S1}=[9 10] kmol/h
	F_{S2}=[9 10] kmol/h
	F_{L1}=[100 300] kmol/h
	F_{V2}=[200 600] kmol/h
	N_F= [26 147]
	N_{PO}=[21 144]
	N_P=[25 148]
	N_{S1}=[33 146]
	N_{S2}=[34 147]
	N_T=[30 150]

Table 3. Values of boundary limits.

limits improve the convergence of stochastic methods. Our study established an initial temperature of 100 and linear temperature profile during the cooling stage for SA. We use default values for the parameters of the genetic algorithm as proposed in the Toolbox of MatLab. To improve the solution, we used populations with 100 individual in each iteration. We have used a harmony memory of 10 individuals (see Table 4).

5. Results

Table 5 shows the results obtained for the design of complex distillation sequences using stochastic optimization methods and different values of function evaluations (NFE). Specifically, in Table 5 we report the average and standard deviation of the heat duty of each sequence. For all stochastic methods, the mean value of objective function (i.e., heat duty) decreased as the NFE increased and, as expected, the performance of stochastic

Stochastic Method	*GA*	*HS*	*SA*
Parameters	Population size: 100 Fitness scaling: Rank Selection: Stochastic uniform Crossover: Scattered Crossover fraction= 0.8 Mutation: Uniform	Harmony memory= 10 harmony accepting =0.8 Pitch adjusting =0.4	Annealing function: Boltzman Reannealing interval= 100 Temperature update: linear Initial temperature= 100

Table 4. Values of parameters used in stochastic methods

		Mean heat duty of the sequence ± standard deviation (kW)		
Scheme	*NFE*	*GA*	*HS*	*SA*
HDS	1,000	884.98±118.59	845.69 ± 56.39	**793.67±55.13**
	10,000	750.83±14.20	746.43±24.01	**739.86 ±13.38**
TCRDS-SS	10,000	1,981.28±128.90	1,916.42±79.39	**1,851.71±77.38**
	20,000	1,702.37±85.79	1,691.83±37.27	**1,641.95±66.32**
DWC	10,000	31,311.01±867.72	**26,887.38±9,010.13**	28,852.35±1,080.74
	20,000	29,284.32±1,561.35	**24,735.58±8,277.29**	27,194.80±1,134.84

Table 5. Mean and standard deviation of heat duty of distillation sequences using stochastic optimization methods

methods increases as NFE increases. Note that SA outperformed the HS and GA in solving global optimization for the design of HSD and TCRDS-SS, while HS is better in the design of DWC, see results reported in Table 5. Overall, GA showed the worst solutions for the design of all distillation sequences.

On the other hand, Table 6 shows that the design parameters (e.g., pressure, reflux ratio, number of stages) are consistent with the design heuristics applied for this type of distillation sequence. In other words, the optimum designs obtained by using these optimization techniques, for complex distillation columns, are likely to be implemented at industrial level. In general, the results show that for the optimization of this type of complex distillation columns, SA is the best alternative. The CPU time needed to solve distillation systems using Aspen ONE Aspen Plus are 10800 seconds for 1000 NFE in multicomponent distillation process, and 345000 seconds for 20000 NFE in thermally coupled reactive distillation in a 2.5 GHz Intel (R) Core (TM)2 Quad computer. In particular, significant CPU time is expended on finding feasible points from random initial estimates and the convergence time of the simulator Aspen ONE Aspen Plus for each calculation in the function evaluated. In general, the CPU time of SA is faster than GA and HS in design problems of complex distillation sequences.

6. Conclusion

In this study, the performance of SA, GA, and HS has been tested and compared in the design of complex distillation columns. To our knowledge, reports on a comparative study about the use of these methods in complex distillation scheme optimization have not been reported. The performance of the stochastic optimization methods tested varies significantly

	Design variables		
Schemes	*GA*	*HS*	*SA*
HDS	R=2.29	R=2.29	R=2.29
	P_0=2.29atm	P_0=1.00atm	P_0=1.00atm
	T_F=478K	T_F=478K	T_F=477.84K
	N_F=60	N_F=87	N_F=88
	N_T=67	N_T=93	N_T=94
	Q_T=752.52kW	Q_T=725.02kW	Q_T=727.06kW
TCRDS-SS	R=21.24	R=15.00	R=12.02
	P_0=3.78atm	P_0=1.31atm	P_0=1.08atm
	F_D=9.39kmol/h	F_D=8.48kmol/h	F_D=8.89kmol/h
	F_S=45.32kmol/h	F_S=45.80kmol/h	F_S=45.39kmol/h
	F_L=50.05kmol/h	F_L=56.42kmol/h	F_L=56.31kmol/h
	N_{F1}=5	N_{F1}=31	N_{F1}=34
	N_{F2}=45	N_{F2}=47	N_{F2}=74
	N_{0Re}=48	N_{0Re}=34	N_{0Re}=4
	N_{fRe}=50	N_{fRe}=47	N_{fRe}=83
	N_{FL}=20	N_{FL}=30	N_{FL}=10
	N_{FV}=20	N_{FV}=22	N_{FV}=37
	N_{T1}=50	N_{T1}=47	N_{T1}=94
	N_{T2}=22	N_{T2}=19	N_{T2}=20
	Q_T=1,583.84kW	Q_T=1,645.27kW	Q_T=1,531.25kW
DWC	R=61.39	R=56.88	R=56.40
	P_0=3.77atm	P_0=3.68atm	P_0=3.14atm
	F_D=40.16kmol/h	F_D=39.93kmol/h	F_D=39.87kmol/h
	F_{S1}=9.89kmol/h	F_{S1}=9.96kmol/h	F_{S1}=9.98kmol/h
	F_{S2}=10.00kmol/h	F_{S2}=9.94kmol/h	F_{S2}=9.95kmol/h
	F_{L1}=225.39kmol/h	F_{L1}=145.73kmol/h	F_{L1}=240.48kmol/h
	F_{V2}=306.02kmol/h	F_{V2}=246.73kmol/h	F_{V2}=258.37kmol/h
	N_F=43	N_F=44	N_F=62
	N_{P0}=24	N_{P0}=35	N_{P0}=27
	N_P=135	N_P=95	N_P=101
	N_{S1}=28	N_{S1}=59	N_{S1}=44
	N_{S2}=31	N_{S2}=70	N_{S2}=63
	N_T=141	N_T=119	N_T=105
	Q_T=25,999.58kW	Q_T=24,658.87kW	Q_T=24,338.40kW

Table 6. Best scheme identified in the design of complex distillation sequences using stochastic optimization methods.

between different problems and is dependent on the problem dimensionality and difficulty. Our results show that SA is a good alternative and offers comparable or better performance than HS and GA methods for this application. In summary, results of this study show the potential of stochastic global optimization methods for solving global optimization problems involved in the design of distillation processes.

7. Notation

This notation corresponds to the optimized parameters for the schemes described in this chapter (see Figures 1 to 3).

B= bottom stream
D= distillate stream
F_D, F_{S1}, F_{S2}= distillate and side (1 and 2) fluxes.
F_L= flux liquid
FL1, FL2= liquid interconnection stream
F_V=flux vapor
FV1, FV2= vapor interconnection stream
N_{0Re}= first reaction tray location
N_F, N_{F1} , N_{F2} =feed tray location
N_{FL}=stream liquid tray location
N_{fRe}=last reaction tray location
N_{FV}=stream vapor tray location
N_P=last prefractioner tray location
N_{P0}=first prefractioner tray location
NS1,NS2= sidestream tray location
N_T, N_{T1} , N_{T2} = total trays
P_0= dome pressure (first stage)
R= reflux ratio
S1, S2= sides streams
T_F= feed temperature

8. References

Aggarwal, A.; & Floudas, C.A. (1990), Synthesis of General Distillation Sequencess Nonsharp Separations, *Comput. Chem. Eng.*, 14, 6, 631-653, 0098-1354.

Andrecovich, M.J.; & Westerberg, A.W. (1985). An MILP Formulation for Heat-Integrated Distillation Sequence Synthesis, *AIChE J.*, 31, 9, 1461-1474, 1547-5905.

Bauer, M.H.; & Stichlmair, J. (1998). Design and Economic Optimization of Azeotropic Distillation Processes Using Mixed-Integer Nonlinear Programming, *Comput. Chem. Eng.*, 22, 9, 1271-1286, 0098-1354.

Bonilla-Petriciolet, A.; Vazquez-Roman, R.; Iglesias-Silva, G.; & Hall, K. (2006). Performance of Stochastic Global Optimization in the Calculation of Phase Stability Analyses for Nonreactive and Reactive Mixtures, *Ind. Eng. Chem. Res.*, 45, 13, 4764-4772, 0888-5885.

Costa, A.L.H.; da Silva, F.P.T.; & Pessoa, F.L.P. (2000). Parameter Estimation of Thermodynamic Models for High-Pressure Systems Employing a Stochastic Method of Global Optimization. *Braz. J. Chem. Eng.*, 17, 3, 349-353, 0104-6632.

Caballero, J.A.; & Grossmann, I.E. (1999). Aggregated Models for Integrated Distillation Systems, *Ind. Eng. Chem. Res*, 38, 6, 2330-2344, 0888-5885.

Corana A.; Marchesi M.; Martini C.; & Ridella S. (1987). Minimizing multimodal functions of continuous variables with the 'Simulated Annealing' Algorithm, *ACM Trans. Math. Softw.*, 13, 3, 262-280, 0098-3500.

Dunnebier, G.; & Pantelides, C.C. (1999) Optimal Design of Thermally Coupled Distillation Columns, *Ind. Eng. Chem. Res.*, 38, 1, 162-176, 0888-5885.

Geem, Z.W. (2009). *Music-inspired harmony search algorithm theory and applications*, Springer, ISBN: 978-3-642-00184-0, United Sates.

Geem Z.W.; Kim J. H.; & Loganathan G.V. (2001). A New Heuristic Optimization Algorithm: Harmony Search, Simulation, 76, 2, 60-68, 0037-5497.

Goffe, B.; Ferrier, G.; & Rogers, J. (1994). Global optimization of statistical functions with simulated annealing. *J. Econom.*, 60, 1-2, 65-99, 0304-4076.

Hernández, S.; & Jiménez, A. (1996) Design of Optimal Thermally-Coupled Distillation Systems Using a Dynamic Model, *Chem. Eng. Res. Des.*, 74, 4, 357-362, 0263-8762.

Holland J. (1975). *Adaptation in Natural and Artificial Systems*, The University of Michigan Press, Ann Arbor, 978-0262581110.

Kim, J.K.; & Wanakat, P.C. (2004). Quaternary Distillation Systems with Less than N - 1 Columns, *Ind. Eng. Chem. Res.*, 43,14, 3838-3846,.

Kirkpatrick, S.; Gelatt, C. D. Jr.; & Vecchi, M. (1983). Optimization by Simulated Annealing, *Science*, 220, 4598, 671-680, 0036-8075.

Kiss, A.; Pragt, J.J.; & van Strien, G.J.G. (2009). Reactive Dividing-Wall Columns - How to Get More with Less Resources?, *Chem. Eng. Comm.*, 196, 11, 1366-1374, 0098-6445.

Martínez-Iranzo, M.; Herrero, J.M.; Sanchis, J.; Blasco, X.; & García-Nieto, S. (2009). Applied Pareto Multi-Objective Optimization by Stochastic Solvers, *Eng. Appl. Artif Int.*, 22, 3, 455-465, 0952-1976.

Metropolis N.; Rosenbluth A.; Rosenbluth M.; Teller A.; & Teller E. (1953). Equation of State Calculations by Fast Computation Machines, *J. Chem. Phys.*, 21, 6, 1087–1092, 0021-9606.

Papalexandri, K.P.; & Pistikopoulos, E.N. (1996). Generalized Modular Representation Framework for Process Synthesis, *AIChE J.*, 42, 4, 1010-1032, 1547-5905.

Paules, G.E., IV.; & Floudas, C.A. (1988). A Mixed-Integer Nonlinear Programming Formulation for the Synthesis of Heat-Integrated Distillation Sequences, *Comput. Chem. Eng.*, 12, 6, 531-546, 0098-1354.

Rangaiah G. (2001). Evaluation of Genetic Algorithms and Simulated Annealing for Phase Equilibrium and Stability Problems, *Fluid Phase Eq.*, 187–188, 1, 83-109, 0378-3812.

Smith, E.M.B.; & Pantelides, C.C. (1995). Design of Reaction/Separation Networks using Detailed Models, *Comput. Chem. Eng*, 19, S1, S83-S88, 0098-1354.

Steinigeweg, S.; & Gmehling, J., (2003). Esterification of a Fatty Acid by Reactive Distillation, *Ind. Eng. Chem. Res.*, 42, 15, 3612-3619, 0888-5885.

Triantafyllou, C.; & Smith, R. (1992). The Design and Optimization of Fully Thermally Coupled Distillation Columns, *Chem. Eng. Res. Des*, 70, 2, 118-132, 0263-8762.

Vázquez - Castillo, J.A.; Venegas - Sánchez, J.A.; Segovia - Hernández, J.G.; Hernández - Escoto, H.; Hernández, S.; Gutiérrez - Antonio, C.; & Briones - Ramírez, A. (2009) Design and Optimization, using Genetic Algorithms, of Intensified Distillation Systems for a Class of Quaternary Mixtures, *Comput. Chem. Eng.*, 33, 11, 1841-1850, 0098-1354.

Viswanathan, J.; & Grossmann, I.E. (1993). Optimal Feed Locations and Number of Trays for Distillation Columns with Multiple Feeds, *Ind. Eng. Chem. Res.*, 32, 11, 2942-2949, 0888-5885.

Viveros-García, T.; Ochoa-Tapia, J.A.; Lobo-Oehmichen, R.; de los Reyes-Heredia, J.A.; & Pérez-Cisneros, E.S. (2005). Conceptual Design of a Reactive Distillation Process for Ultra-Low Sulfur Diesel Production, *Chem. Eng J.*, 106, 2, 119-131, 1385-8947.

Wei-Zhong, A.; & Xi-Gang, Y. (2009). A simulated Annealing-Based Approach to the Optimal Synthesis of Heat-Integrated Distillation Sequences, *Comput. Chem. Eng.*, 33, 1, 199-212, 0098-1354.

Yang, X-S. (2008). Nature-Inspired Metaheuristic Algorithms. 71-74, Luniver Press, 978-1-905986-10-1, United Kingdom.

Yeomans, H.; & Grossmann, I.E. (2002). Disjunctive Programming Models for the Optimal Design of Distillation Columns and Separation Sequences, *Ind. Eng. Chem. Res.*, 39, 6, 1637-1648, 0888-5885.

Phase Equilibrium Modeling in Non-Reactive Systems Using Harmony Search

Adrián Bonilla-Petriciolet[1], Didilia I. Mendoza-Castillo[1], Juan Gabriel Segovia-Hernández[2] and Juan Carlos Tapia-Picazo[1]
Department of Chemical Engineering
[1]Instituto Tecnológico de Aguascalientes,
[2]Universidad de Guanajuato
México

1. Introduction

In recent years, a significant work has been performed in the area of software development for solving global optimization problems in science and engineering applications (Floudas et al., 1999). In particular, global optimization has and continues to play a major role in the design, operation, scheduling and managing of chemical industrial processes and, according to several authors; it will remain as a major challenge for future research efforts (Floudas et al., 1999; Biegler & Grossmann, 2004; Grossmann & Biegler, 2004; Rangaiah, 2010). In the context of chemical engineering, several algorithmic and computational contributions of global optimization have been used for process optimization. As expected, finding the global optimum is more challenging than finding a local optimum and, in some applications such as the phase equilibrium modeling, the location of this global optimum is crucial because it corresponds to the correct and desirable solution (Floudas et al., 1999; Teh & Rangaiah, 2002; Wakeham & Stateva, 2004; Rangaiah, 2010).

Specifically, the modeling of phase equilibrium in multicomponent systems is essential in the design, operation, optimization and control of separation schemes. The phase behavior of multicomponent systems has a significant impact in several issues of process design including the determination of the equipment and energy costs of separation and purification strategies (Wakeham & Stateva, 2004). Note that phase equilibrium calculations (PEC) are usually executed thousands of times in process simulators and, as a consequence, these calculations must be performed, reliably and efficiently, to avoid design uncertainties and erroneous conclusions about process performance. However, literature indicates that the development of reliable methods for PEC has long been a challenge and is still a research topic of continual interest in the chemical engineering community (Teh & Rangaiah, 2002; Wakeham & Stateva, 2004).

Basically, PEC involve two main problems: a) phase stability analysis is used to determine if a tested system under specified operating conditions is stable or not, and b) phase split calculations are performed to establish the number and identity (i.e., composition and type) of phases existing at the equilibrium (Wakeham & Stateva, 2004). These thermodynamic calculations can be formulated as global optimization problems where the tangent plane distance function (*TPDF*) is used as optimization criterion for stability analysis and the Gibbs free energy function (*G*) is minimized for phase split computations. Formally, both optimization problems can be stated as follows: minimize $f(u)$ subject to $u \in \Omega$ where u is a continuous variable vector with domain $\Omega \in \Re^n$, and $f(u):\Omega \Rightarrow \Re$ is a real-valued function. The major challenge of solving global optimization problems for phase equilibrium modeling is that both $f(u)$ = *TPDF* and *G* are generally non-convex, highly non-linear with many decision variables, and often have unfavourable attributes such as discontinuity and non-differentiability. In fact, these objective functions may have several local optimums including trivial and nonphysical solutions especially for multicomponent and multiphase systems. Therefore, traditional optimization methods are not suitable for solving phase equilibrium problems under these conditions (Teh & Rangaiah, 2002; Wakeham & Stateva, 2004).

In view of the above, there has been a significant and increasing interest in the development of deterministic and stochastic global optimization strategies for reliably performing PEC (Wakeham & Stateva, 2004). For example, global optimization studies using deterministic strategies have been focused on the application of homotopy continuation methods (Sun & Seider, 1995; Jalali et al., 2008), branch and bound global optimization (McDonald & Floudas, 1996; Harding & Floudas, 2000), and interval mathematics (Hua et al., 1998; Xu et al., 2005). Although deterministic methods have proven to be promising, several of them are model dependent, may require problem reformulations or significant computational time especially for multicomponent systems (Nichita et al., 2002a; 2002b). On the other hand, stochastic optimization techniques have often been found to be as reliable and effective as deterministic methods but may offer advantages for PEC. These methods are robust numerical tools that present a reasonable computational effort in the optimization of multivariable functions (generally less time than deterministic approaches); they are applicable to ill-structure or unknown structure problems, require only calculations of the objective function and can be used with all thermodynamic models (Henderson et al., 2001). The study of stochastic optimization methods for PEC has become an active research area in the field of chemical engineering because various problems that are very challenging to solve by conventional techniques can be solved by meta-heuristics. To date, a number of stochastic global optimization methods have been studied and tested for PEC in non-reactive mixtures. These methods include: the Random Search method (Lee et al., 1999), Simulated Annealing (Zhu & Xu, 1999; Zhu et al., 2000; Henderson et al., 2001; Rangaiah, 2001; Bonilla-Petriciolet et al., 2006), Genetic Algorithms (Rangaiah, 2001; Teh & Rangaiah, 2003), Tabu Search (Teh & Rangaiah, 2003; Srinivas & Rangaiah, 2007a), Tunnelling method (Nichita et al., 2002a; 2002b; Srinivas & Rangaiah, 2006), Clustering method with stochastic sampling (Balogh et al., 2003), Differential Evolution (Srinivas & Rangaiah, 2007a; 2007b), and Particle Swarm Optimization (Rahman et al., 2009; Bonilla-Petriciolet & Segovia-Hernández, 2010). These meta-heuristics usually show a robust performance in PEC but, in some difficult problems, they may fail to locate the global optimum. Thus, alternative optimization strategies should be studied to identify a better approach for solving phase equilibrium problems.

In particular, Harmony Search (HS) is a novel meta-heuristic algorithm, which has been conceptualized using the musical process of searching for a perfect state of harmony (Geem et al., 2001). This optimization method is based on the analogy with music improvisation process where music players improvise the pitches of their instruments to obtain a better harmony. In the optimization context, each musician is replaced with a decision variable, and the possible notes in the musical instruments correspond to the possible values for the decision variables. So, the harmony in music is analogous to the vector of decision variables, and the musician's improvisations are analogous to local and global search schemes in optimization techniques (Lee & Geem, 2005). This novel optimization method is simpler, both in formulation and computer implementation, than other stochastic optimization methods such as Genetic Algorithms or Particle Swarm Optimization (Lee & Geem, 2005). Until now, HS has been successfully applied to solve various engineering and optimization problems such as water network design, vehicle routing, soil stability analysis, heat exchanger design, and transportation energy modeling (Lee & Geem, 2005; Geem, 2009). In the field of chemical engineering, there are few studies concerning the application of this stochastic method and, to the best of our knowledge, the performance of HS for PEC in non-reactive systems has not yet been reported.

This chapter introduces the application of HS-based algorithms to solve phase stability and equilibrium problems in multicomponent non-reactive systems. Particularly, the performance and capabilities of HS in the modeling of phase equilibrium is studied and discussed. The remainder of this chapter is organized as follows. In Section 2, we briefly introduce HS and the common approaches for its modification or adaptation. The formulation of global optimization problems for phase equilibrium modeling (i.e., phase stability and phase split calculations) is presented in Section 3. Results of PEC using HS-based algorithms are reported in Section 4. Finally, in Section 5, we provide some remarks and conclusions about the application of HS for PEC in non-reactive systems.

2. Harmony Search optimization method

Harmony Search is a music-inspired meta-heuristic algorithm, which has been introduced by Geem et al. (2001). This stochastic optimization method is based on the underlying principles of the musician improvisation of the harmony. Specifically, when musicians improvise they may perform the following steps: playing an existing score from memory, performing variations on an existing piece, or creating an entirely new composition. In the optimization context, HS combines heuristic rules and randomness to imitate this music improvisation process. A comprehensive explanation of HS is provided by Geem et al. (2001) and a flow chart describing its principal stages is given in Figure 1.

In summary, HS involves the following parameters: the harmony memory size (HMS), the harmony memory considering rate (HMCR), the pitch adjusting rate (PAR), the bandwidth or step size for variable perturbation during pitch adjustment (bw), and the number of improvisations (NI). The harmony memory is a memory location where a set of solution vectors for decision variables is stored. The parameters HMCR and PAR are used to improve the solution vector and to increase the diversity of the search process (Geem et al., 2001; Lee & Geem, 2005). In HS, a new harmony (i.e., a new solution vector) is generated using these parameters and the following procedures: a) memory consideration, b) pitch adjustment, and c) random selection. To illustrate the concepts of HS, consider the following unconstrained global optimization problem: minimize $f(u)$ such that $lb_i \leq u_i \leq ub_i$ where u is a solution vector of n_{opt} continuous decision variables with lower (lb_i) and upper (ub_i) bounds for each decision variable (i.e., u_i). To solve this optimization problem, HS performs the following steps (Geem et al., 2001; Omran & Mahdavi, 2008):

1. *Initialize a harmony memory*. First, the parameters of HS (e.g., HMS, HMCR, PAR, bw) are defined and the harmony memory is initialized. This harmony memory preserves the

history of optimization sequence and is useful to identify promising areas for global optimization because good harmonies can be considered as elements of new solution vectors. Usually, the initial values of harmony memory are generated from a uniform distribution in the bounds of decision variables: $u_i = lb_i + rand\ (ub_i - lb_i)$ where $rand \in (0, 1)$ is a random number.

2. *Improvise a new harmony*. As stated, a new harmony vector (v_i) is obtained using the following stages: memory consideration, pitch adjustment and random selection. These stages can be summarized using the following pseudo-code (Omran & Mahdavi, 2008):

   for $i = 1$ to n_{opt} do
   if $rand \in (0, 1) \leq$ HMCR **then** perform *memory consideration*
   begin
   $v_i = u_{ij}$ where $j \in (1,\ldots,\text{HMS})$
   if $rand \in (0, 1) \leq$ PAR **then** perform *pitch adjustment*
   begin
   $v_i = v_i + (0.5 - rand) \cdot bw_i$ where bw_i is the bandwidth (i.e., step size)
   end if
   else perform *random selection*
   $v_i = lb_i + rand\ (ub_i - lb_i)$
   end if
   end for

   These stochastic operators are used to perform both diversification and intensification stages in HS. The diversification is controlled by the pitch adjustment and random selection operators, while memory consideration is generally associated to the intensification. In particular, HMCR is used to determine the degree of contribution of harmony memory (i.e., promising solutions) during random search. On the other hand, PAR and bw are used to control the additional random perturbation of decision variables when memory consideration is applied. In addition, the random selection is useful to explore different regions of objective function and also contributes to increase the diversity of solution vectors. Note that the proper combination of these operators is important to favor the performance of HS in global optimization. The generation of a new harmony (i.e., new solution vector) is called improvisation.

3. *Update harmony memory*. In this stage, a new harmony (v) replaces the worst harmony in harmony memory only if its value of objective function is lower than that of the worst harmony. The decision vectors stored in harmony memory are useful to exploit the history and experience of the search process, being an intensification mechanism of HS method.

4. *Check the stopping condition*. This iterative procedure is repeated until satisfying a proper convergence criterion. Similar to other stochastic methods, the choice of stopping condition can significantly affect the performance of HS. In the literature, the stopping criterions commonly used in HS are based on the number of function evaluations (NFE) or improvisations (NI). The best solution found by HS, which is stored in harmony memory, is expected to be a near global optimum solution.

It is convenient to remark that a boundary violation check must be implemented, principally during pitch adjustment, to verify the feasibility of v; if v is infeasible, a new harmony is randomly generated inside lower and upper bounds of decision variables. A local optimization technique can be used at the end of global search for efficiently improving the accuracy of the best solution obtained by HS. Note that stochastic optimization methods may require a significant computational effort to improve the accuracy of global solution because they explore the search space of decision variables by creating random movements instead of determining a logical optimization trajectory. Thus, this additional intensification step is required for rapid convergence in the final stage of HS.

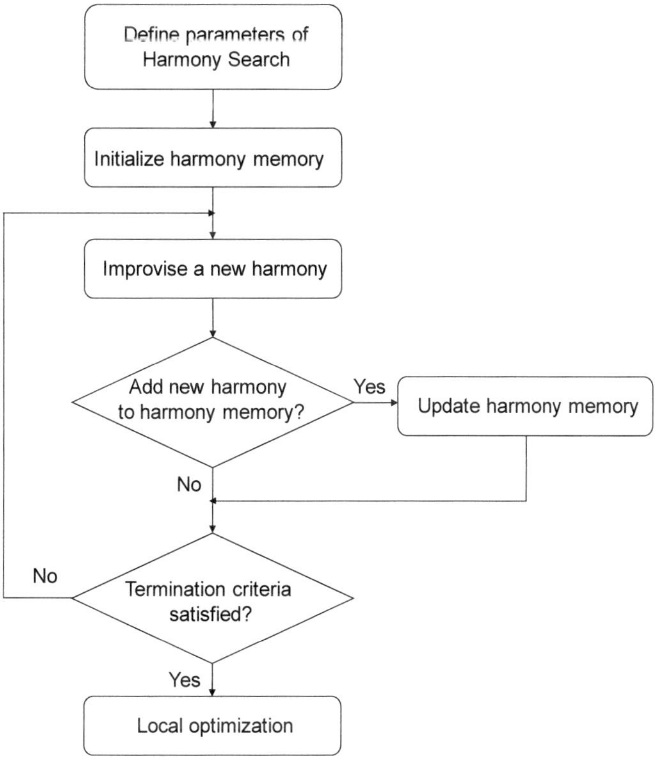

Fig. 1. Flowchart of Harmony Search (HS) stochastic optimization method

As indicated, the parameters HMS, HMCR, PAR and *bw* are important to determine the performance (i.e., reliability and efficiency) of HS in global optimization. For example, some authors have suggested that small values of HMS may lead to the HS to be trapped in local solutions (Mahdavi et al., 2007). However, increasing HMS generally provides better solution vectors but at the expense of more function evaluations. Therefore, the fine tuning of these parameters is very crucial for solving global optimization problems (Mahdavi et al., 2007; Omran & Mahdavi, 2008). Traditionally, fixed values for HS parameters, which can not be changed during new improvisations, are used in global optimization (Geem et al., 2001; Geem, 2009). So, this standard version of HS algorithm is referred as HSC in this chapter.

In the literature, some modifications have been proposed to improve the convergence performance of the original HS. According to Geem (2009), the variations proposed for HS may involve: a) mechanisms for the proper initialization of HS parameters, b) mechanisms for the dynamic adaptation of HS parameters during optimization sequence, and c) the application of new or modified HS operators, which includes hybrid methods using other meta-heuristics such as Simulated Annealing or Differential Evolution. Below, two typical variants of HS are briefly discussed, which has been used in the present study.

Particularly, the dynamic adaptation of HS parameters is the most common approach to overcome the drawbacks of original HS. Results reported by Mahdavi et al. (2007) indicated that small PAR values with large *bw* values may affect the performance of HS and increase the calculations needed to find the global optimum. Although, small *bw* values in final iterations (i.e., improvisations) increase the fine-tuning of solution vectors but, in early iterations, *bw* should take a bigger value to diversify the solution vectors. Furthermore, large PAR values with small *bw* values may cause the improvement of best solutions in final improvisations. Based on this fact, Mahdavi et al. (2007) introduced the Improved Harmony Search (IHS), which uses dynamic values of both parameters PAR and *bw*. Specifically, PAR dynamically changes with improvisation number as follow

$$PAR_{k+1} = PAR_{\min} + \frac{(PAR_{\max} - PAR_{\min})}{NI} * k \tag{1}$$

where PAR_{min} and PAR_{max} are the minimum and maximum pitch adjusting rates, and k is an improvisation counter. On the other hand, the bandwidth for each improvisation is given by

$$bw_{k+1} = bw_{\max} \exp\left((k / NI)\ln(bw_{\min} / bw_{\max})\right) \tag{2}$$

being bw_{min} and bw_{max} the minimum and maximum values for bandwidth, respectively. Note that PAR_{min}, PAR_{max}, bw_{min} and bw_{max} are defined by the user and are problem dependent. Mahdavi et al. (2007) showed that this variant of HS has proven to be competitive with respect to other HS algorithms for solving benchmark and some engineering optimization problems. Therefore, we have considered IHS for solving global optimization problems in phase equilibrium modeling.

Recently, Omran & Mahdavi (2008) proposed an alternative version of HS called Global-Best Harmony Search (GHS), which is inspired by the concept of swarm intelligence used in Particle Swarm Optimization. This method modifies the pitch-adjustment step of HS to encourage that a new harmony can mimic the best harmony stored in the harmony memory. Results reported for several benchmark optimization problems showed that GHS may offer a better performance than those reported for HSC and IHS (Omran & Mahdavi, 2008). In general, GHS has the same structure as IHS with the exception of pitch adjustment step used in the improvisation of a new harmony. Specifically, the pseudo-code to improvise a new harmony in GHS is defined as follows (Omran & Mahdavi, 2008):

for $i = 1$ to n_{opt} do
  if $rand \in (0, 1) \leq$ HMCR **then** perform *memory consideration*
   begin
   $v_i = u_{ij}$ where $j \in (1,\ldots,\text{HMS})$
   if $rand \in (0, 1) \leq$ PAR **then** perform *pitch adjustment*
    begin
    $v_i = u_{i,best}$ where *best* is the index of the best harmony in the harmony memory
   end if
  else perform *random selection*
   $v_i = lb_i + rand\,(ub_i - lb_i)$
  end if
end for

With respect to the parameters of GHS, Omran & Mahdavi (2008) have suggested that using a constant value of PAR improves its performance and this scheme is even better than GHS using a dynamical value of PAR. So, this approach has been adopted in the present study for GHS.
Although these modern optimization methods have been successfully applied in different science and engineering fields, their capabilities have not yet been studied in the modeling of phase equilibrium. Therefore, these HS-based optimization methods have been used in this study for performing PEC in non-reactive systems. All methods have been implemented in Fortran subroutines that can be applied for solving global optimization problems with continuous variables. These codes are available to interested readers upon request to the corresponding author. Finally, with respect to the stopping condition, the following criteria can be applied for global optimization using HS: 1) a maximum number of successive improvisations (SNI_{max}) without improvement in the best function value, or 2) a maximum number of improvisations (NI). Both criteria have been applied in this study and implemented for all HS algorithms.

3. Formulation of global optimization problems for phase stability and equilibrium calculations in non-reactive systems

3.1 Phase stability

Phase stability analysis is a fundamental stage in PEC and allows identification of the thermodynamic state that corresponds to the global minimum of Gibbs free energy (Michelsen, 1982; Wakeham & Stateva, 2004). A mixture at a fixed temperature T, pressure P and overall composition z is stable if and only if the Gibbs free energy surface is at no point below the tangent plane to the surface at the given mixture composition (Michelsen, 1982). This statement is a necessary and sufficient condition for global phase stability. As mentioned in the introduction, this stability analysis can be performed using the Tangent Plane Distance Function (*TPDF*). This function is geometrically defined as the distance between the Gibbs free energy surface at a trial composition y and the tangent plane constructed to this surface at composition z. Properly, phase stability of a non-reactive systems with c components and a global composition $z(z_1,\ldots,z_c)$ in mole fraction units, at constant P and T, is analyzed by the global minimization of *TPDF* (Michelsen, 1982)

$$TPDF = \sum_{i=1}^{c} y_i \left(\mu_i\big|_y - \mu_i\big|_z \right) \tag{3}$$

where $\mu_i\big|_y$ and $\mu_i\big|_z$ are the chemical potentials of component i calculated at compositions y and z, respectively. To perform a stability analysis, *TPDF* must be globally minimized with respect to composition of a trial phase y, which is subject to an equality constraint. This constrained global optimization problem can be written as

$$\begin{aligned} &\min_{y} \; TPDF(y) \\ &\text{subject to } \sum_{i=1}^{c} y_i = 1 \\ &0 \le y_i \le 1 \quad i = 1,\ldots,c \end{aligned} \tag{4}$$

where the decision variables in phase stability problems are the mole fractions y_i. If the global minimum of $TPDF(y) < 0$, the mixture under analysis is considered unstable; otherwise it is a globally stable system. The global minimization of *TPDF* is difficult and requires robust numerical methods since this function is multivariable, non-convex and highly non-linear. To date, several deterministic and stochastic global optimization methods have been reported for performing phase stability calculations (e.g., Sun & Seider, 1995; McDonald & Floudas, 1996; Hua et al., 1998; Harding & Floudas, 2000; Henderson et al., 2001; Rangaiah, 2001; Teh & Rangaiah, 2002; Nichita et al., 2002a; Balogh et al., 2003; Xu et al., 2005; Bonilla-Petriciolet et al., 2006; Srinivas & Rangaiah, 2007a; 2007b; Bonilla-Petriciolet & Segovia-Hernández, 2010).

To simplify this global optimization problem, the constrained problem given by Equation (4) can be transformed into an unconstrained problem by using new decision variables β_i instead of y_i as decision vector (Rangaiah, 2001; Srinivas & Rangaiah, 2007a; 2007b). These new decision variables $\beta_i \in (0, 1)$ are related to composition variables y_i as follows

$$n_{iy} = \beta_i z_i n_F \quad i = 1,\ldots,c \tag{5}$$

$$y_i = n_{iy} \Big/ \sum_{j=1}^{c} n_{jy} \quad i = 1,\ldots,c \tag{6}$$

where $n_F = \sum_{i=1}^{c} n_{iF}$ is the total amount of conventional moles in the feed composition used for stability analysis, and n_{iy} is the conventional mole number of component i in the trial phase y, respectively. Note that the feed mole fractions z_i are obtained from $z_i = n_{iF} / n_F$. Then, we state the unconstrained global optimization problem for phase stability analysis

$$\begin{gathered} \min_{\beta} \ TPDF(\beta) \\ 0 \le \beta_i \le 1 \quad i = 1,\ldots,c \end{gathered} \tag{7}$$

For phase stability calculations, the number of decision variables is c for non-reactive systems of c components. In summary, this unconstrained formulation has been used for all phase stability calculations performed in this study using HS optimization methods.

3.2 Phase equilibrium calculations

After identifying an unstable system in phase stability analysis, the subsequent stage corresponds to a phase split calculation. In this thermodynamic problem, the main objectives are to correctly establish the number and types of phases existing at equilibrium as well as the composition and quantity of each phase such that the Gibbs free energy of the system is a minimum (Wakeham & Stateva, 2004). At constant T and P, a c multicomponent and π multiphase non-reactive system achieves equilibrium when its molar Gibbs free energy of mixing (g) is at the global minimum. Properly, the objective function for Gibbs free energy minimization using activity or fugacity coefficients is given by

$$g = \sum_{j=1}^{\pi} \sum_{i=1}^{c} n_{ij} \ln(x_{ij}\gamma_{ij}) = \sum_{j=1}^{\pi} \sum_{i=1}^{c} n_{ij} \ln\left(\frac{x_{ij}\hat{\phi}_{ij}}{\varphi_i}\right) \tag{8}$$

where n_{ij} is the mole number of component i in phase j, γ_{ij} is the activity coefficient of component i in phase j, $\hat{\varphi}_{ij}$ is the fugacity coefficient of component i in phase j, and φ_i is the fugacity coefficient of pure component i, respectively. Here, the Gibbs free energy of mixing (g) is used to avoid the calculation of pure component free energies, which do not influence equilibrium and stability results.

In a non-reactive system, g must be globally minimized with respect to the set of n_{ij} subject to the mass balance constraints. Thus, the constrained global optimization problem for Gibbs free energy minimization is

$$\min_{n} g(n)$$

$$\text{subject to } \sum_{j=1}^{\pi} n_{ij} = z_i n_F \quad i = 1,\ldots,c \tag{9}$$

$$0 \leq n_{ij} \leq z_i n_F \quad i = 1,\ldots,c \quad j = 1,\ldots,\pi$$

where z_i is the mole fraction of component i in the feed used for phase-split calculations. This objective function is generally multivariable and non-convex due to the non-linear nature of thermodynamic models. Both stochastic and deterministic methods are available for Gibbs free energy minimization (Teh & Rangaiah, 2002; Wakeham & Stateva, 2004). In particular, the methods: Simulated Annealing (Rangaiah, 2001; Henderson et al., 2001), Genetic Algorithms (Rangaiah, 2001; Teh & Rangaiah, 2003), Tabu Search (Teh & Rangaiah, 2003), Tunnelling method (Nichita et al., 2002b; Srinivas & Rangaiah, 2006), Differential Evolution (Srinivas & Rangaiah, 2007a; 2007b), and Particle Swarm Optimization (Rahman et al., 2009; Bonilla-Petriciolet & Segovia-Hernández, 2010) have been applied for Gibbs free energy minimization in non-reactive systems.

To perform an unconstrained minimization of g, we can use again alternative variables instead of n_{ij} as optimization targets. The use of these variables eliminates the restrictions imposed by material balances, reduces problem dimensionality, and the optimization problem is transformed to an unconstrained one (Rangaiah, 2001). For multi-phase non-reactive systems, real variables $\beta_{ij} \in (0, 1)$ are defined and employed as decision vector by using the following expressions

$$n_{i1} = \beta_{i1} z_i n_F \quad i = 1,\ldots,c \tag{10}$$

$$n_{ij} = \beta_{ij}\left(z_i n_F - \sum_{m=1}^{\pi-1} n_{im} \right) \quad i = 1,\ldots,c \quad j = 2,\ldots,\pi - 1 \tag{11}$$

$$n_{i\pi} = z_i n_F - \sum_{j=1}^{\pi-1} n_{ij} \quad i = 1,\ldots,c \tag{12}$$

Using Equations (10)-(12), all trial compositions will satisfy the material balances allowing the easy application of optimization strategies. Thus, the unconstrained global minimization problem is defined as

$$\min_{\beta} \; g(\beta)$$
$$0 \le \beta_{ij} \le 1 \quad i = 1,\ldots,c \quad j = 1,\ldots,\pi - 1 \tag{13}$$

For Gibbs free energy minimization, the number of phases existing at the equilibrium is assumed to be known *a priori* and the number of decision variables is $c\pi - c$ for non-reactive systems of c components with π phases. So, the problem formulation given by Equation (13) has been adopted in the present study for phase-split calculations in non-reactive systems.

4. Results of phase equilibrium calculations using HS-based optimization methods

4.1 Description of phase equilibrium problems

In our study, various phase equilibrium problems from the literature have been used to assess the performance of HS-based optimization algorithms. These problems include multicomponent systems with vapor-liquid and liquid-liquid equilibrium. Feed composition, operating conditions, thermodynamic models, and global optimum of these problems are reported in Tables 1 and 2. It is convenient to note that these problems have

No.	*System*	*Temperature and pressure*	*Model*
1	*n*-butyl acetate + water	298 K and 101.325 KPa	NRTL
2	toluene + water + aniline	298 K and 101.325 KPa	NRTL
3	$N_2 + C_1 + C_2$	270 K and 7600 KPa	SRK EoS
4	$H_2S + C_1$	190 K and 4053 KPa	SRK EoS
5	$H_2O + CO_2$ + 2-propanol + ethanol	350 K and 2250 KPa	SRK EoS
6	$C_2 + C_3 + C_4 + C_5 + C_6$	390 K and 5583 KPa	SRK EoS
7	$C_1 + C_2 + C_3 + C_4 + C_5 + C_6 + C_{7\text{-}16} + C_{17+}$	353 K and 38500 KPa	SRK EoS
8	$C_1 + C_2 + C_3 + iC_4 + C_4 + iC_5 + C_5 + C_6 + iC_{15}$	314 K and 2010.288 KPa	SRK EoS
9	$C_1 + C_2 + C_3 + C_4 + C_5 + C_6 + C_7 + C_8 + C_9 + C_{10}$	435.35 K and 19150 KPa	SRK EoS

Table 1. Examples selected for phase stability and equilibrium calculations in non-reactive systems using Harmony Search-based optimization methods.

		Global optimum	
No.	*Feed composition, z*	*TPDF*	*g*
1	Z (0.5, 0.5)	-0.0324662	-0.0201983
2	Z (0.29989, 0.20006, 0.50005)	-0.2945401	-0.3529567
3	Z (0.3, 0.1, 0.6)	-0.0157670	-0.5477911
4	Z (0.0187, 0.9813)	-0.0039320	-0.0198922
5	Z (0.99758, 0.00003, 0.00013, 0.00226)	-0.0126500	-0.0048272
6	Z (0.401, 0.293, 0.199, 0.0707, 0.0363)	-0.0000021	-1.1836525
7	Z (0.7212, 0.09205, 0.04455, 0.03123, 0.01273, 0.01361, 0.07215, 0.01248)	-0.0026876	-0.8387826
8	Z (0.614, 0.10259, 0.04985, 0.008989, 0.02116, 0.00722, 0.01187, 0.01435, 0.16998)	-1.4862053	-0.7697724
9	Z (0.6436, 0.0752, 0.0474, 0.0412, 0.0297, 0.0138, 0.0303, 0.0371, 0.0415, 0.0402)	-0.0000205	-1.1211758

Table 2. Global minimum of selected phase stability and equilibrium problems.

considered for testing the performance of other stochastic optimization methods such as Simulated Annealing, Genetic Algorithms, Tabu Search, Differential Evolution and Particle Swarm Optimization (e.g., Rangaiah, 2001; Teh & Rangaiah, 2003; Bonilla-Petriciolet et al., 2006; Srinivas & Rangaiah, 2007a; 2007b; Bonilla-Petriciolet & Segovia-Hernández, 2010). The objective functions (i.e., *TPDF* and g) have at least one local minimum, which corresponds to a trivial solution, for all tested conditions. Therefore, these optimization problems have different degrees of difficulty and features, so that the performance of HS methods can be tested systematically.

4.2 Parameter tuning of HSC, IHS and GHS

The key parameters of HSC, IHS and GHS have been tuned by finding the global minimum of some phase stability and equilibrium problems. Following previous studies (e.g., Bonilla-Petriciolet et al., 2006; Bonilla-Petriciolet & Segovia-Hernandez, 2010), the parameters of HS-based methods were tuned using examples No. 4 and 5, which were found to be challenging in preliminary trials. Specifically, parameter tuning was performed by varying one parameter at a time while the rest are fixed at nominal values, which were established using values reported in the literature and results of preliminary calculations (not reported in this chapter). For parameter tuning, all HS methods were run 100 times, with random initial values for decision variables (i.e., β_i and β_{ij}) and random number seed, on each of the selected problems using different conditions for HS parameters. The suggested values for parameters of HSC, IHS and GHS are reported in Table 3. For all calculations performed in this study, we set HMS = $10n_{opt}$ (i.e., harmony memory) in HSC, GHS and IHS. Overall, our preliminary calculations indicate that values given in Table 3 are a reasonable compromise between numerical effort and reliability of HS-based optimization methods for performing PEC.

Method	*Parameter*	*Suggested value*
HSC	HMCR	0.5
	PAR	0.75
	bw	$ub_i - lb_i$
GHS	HMCR	0.5
	PAR	0.75
	bw	$ub_i - lb_i$
IHS	HMCR	0.5
	PAR_{min}	0.5
	PAR_{max}	0.95
	bw_{min}	0.001
	bw_{max}	$ub_i - lb_i$

Table 3. Suggested values of parameters in HSC, IHS and GHS for solving global optimization problems in phase equilibrium modeling.

4.3 Performance of HSC, IHS and GHS in phase stability and equilibrium calculations

In this section, we compare the performance of HSC, IHS and GHS for both phase stability and equilibrium calculations in non-reactive systems. These methods are evaluated based on both reliability and computational efficiency in locating the global minimum of these thermodynamic problems. Each test problem is solved 100 times using HS methods, each time with a different random number seed such that the initial values of decision variables and random operators are different in each trial.

With illustrative purposes, Tables 4 and 5 summarize the mean value of the objective function (i.e., *TPDF* and *g*) calculated by HS methods over 100 runs performed on some selected examples at different levels of computational efficiency, which are obtained by changing the stopping conditions NI and SNI_{max}. As stated, the stopping conditions NI and

			NI/HMS					
f(u)	*No.*	*Method*	25	50	100	500	1000	1500
TPDF	1	HSC	-0.032121	-0.032450	**-0.032466**	-0.032466	-0.032466	-0.032466
		GHS	-0.031792	-0.032297	-0.032455	-0.032466	-0.032466	-0.032466
		IHS	**-0.032460**	**-0.032466**	**-0.032466**	-0.032466	-0.032466	-0.032466
	2	HSC	-0.119234	-0.175243	-0.230080	-0.290298	-0.293195	-0.293929
		GHS	**-0.235608**	**-0.271328**	-0.286175	-0.293712	-0.294317	-0.294416
		IHS	-0.130544	-0.242552	**-0.293399**	**-0.294533**	**-0.294537**	**-0.294538**
	8	HSC	-1.393909	-1.419570	-1.435958	-1.459419	-1.465537	-1.468035
		GHS	**-1.463179**	**-1.473019**	**-1.477031**	**-1.483464**	**-1.484407**	**-1.484719**
		IHS	-1.441306	-1.459395	-1.469119	-1.481068	-1.483426	-1.484304
g	1	HSC	-0.019942	-0.020110	-0.020140	-0.020193	-0.020196	-0.020197
		GHS	-0.019815	-0.019975	-0.020081	-0.020191	-0.020196	-0.020197
		IHS	**-0.020052**	**-0.020189**	**-0.020197**	**-0.020198**	**-0.020198**	**-0.020198**
	2	HSC	-0.332641	-0.335935	-0.339952	-0.351137	-0.352288	-0.352559
		GHS	**-0.338794**	**-0.345940**	**-0.350732**	-0.352721	-0.352873	-0.352910
		IHS	-0.332065	-0.336039	-0.349790	**-0.352946**	**-0.352952**	**-0.352953**
	8	HSC	-0.734627	-0.743442	-0.749865	-0.761014	-0.764000	-0.764984
		GHS	**-0.762602**	**-0.765662**	**-0.767486**	**-0.768955**	**-0.769369**	**-0.769361**
		IHS	-0.748691	-0.758576	-0.764873	-0.768615	-0.769123	-0.769332

Table 4. Mean values of *TPDF* and *g* calculated by HS-based methods at different levels of computational efficiency, using NI alone as stopping condition, for phase stability and equilibrium calculations of non-reactive systems.

		$SNI_{max}/(n_{opt} \cdot HMS)$					
		TPDF			*G*		
No.	*Method*	5	10	15	5	10	15
1	HSC	**- 0.031404**	**-0.032419**	**- 0.032463**	**-0.019697**	**-0.020010**	**-0.020128**
	GHS	- 0.030894	-0.032082	- 0.032339	-0.019623	-0.019879	-0.019949
	IHS	- 0.031358	-0.032364	- 0.032406	-0.019657	-0.019937	-0.020060
2	HSC	- 0.119623	-0.191368	- 0.224470	-0.332387	-0.335297	-0.339812
	GHS	**- 0.266324**	**-0.279203**	**- 0.287641**	**-0.346430**	**-0.350512**	**-0.351517**
	IHS	- 0.118653	-0.195152	- 0.217033	-0.333279	-0.336683	-0.338551
8	HSC	- 1.435201	-1.447226	- 1.452705	-0.748590	-0.754997	-0.758230
	GHS	**- 1.480936**	**-1.482794**	**- 1.484031**	**-0.768323**	**-0.768881**	**-0.769098**
	IHS	- 1.419238	-1.438575	- 1.453591	-0.745669	-0.749071	-0.754977

Table 5. Mean values of *TPDF* and *g* calculated by HS-based methods at different levels of computational efficiency, using SNI_{max} alone as stopping condition, for phase stability and equilibrium calculations of non-reactive systems.

SNI_{max} also contribute to the trade-off between efficiency and reliability of HS. Therefore, the performance of all HS methods is illustrated by changing these stopping conditions. This approach is adopted in the present study because generally no correlation can be established *a priori* between an optimization problem and the required numerical effort for finding the global optimum. So, the proper stopping condition has to be determined by a sensitivity analysis.

Our results indicate that the performance of HS, GHS and IHS varies with the type of stopping condition and, as a consequence, the numerical effort. In general, these results show that increasing the value of both stopping conditions (i.e., NI or SNI_{max}) improves the performance of all HS methods for PEC. But, results indicate that the reliability of HSC, GHS and IHS is generally better using stopping condition NI compared to SNI_{max}. Particularly, GHS and IHS can find solution vectors very close to the global minimum solution and their performance is usually better than that of HSC using either NI or SNI_{max} as convergence criterion. For example, Figures 2 and 3 provide the convergence histories of the norm of $\hat{f}^{cal} - f^*$ for all HS methods in the global minimization of *TPDF* and *g* of examples No. 2 and 8. This norm is based on the average (over 100 runs) of the best objective function $\hat{f}^{cal}$ recorded in the harmony memory at different improvisations (i.e., NFE). Note that the mean value of best harmony (i.e., solution vector) obtained by GHS and IHS is usually lower than that achieved by HSC in both phase stability and equilibrium calculations. Moreover, it appears that the convergence curves of GHS and IHS are faster than that of HSC. These results are in agreement with the observations reported by Mahdavi et al. (2007) and Omran & Mahdavi (2008). Specifically, these authors have indicated that the modifications of traditional HS may allow performing global optimization, efficiently and reliably.

Following our previous study (Bonilla-Petriciolet & Segovia-Hernández, 2010) and, in order to facilitate understanding and to make the performance difference between HSC, GHS and IHS more explicit, we have employed the performance profile reported by Dolan & More (2002). Performance profiles (PP) are an alternative tool for evaluating and comparing the performance of several solvers on a set of test problems. The results of PP allow us to identify the expected performance differences among several solvers and to compare the quality of their solutions by eliminating the bias of failures obtained in a small number or problems. A brief overview of PP is provided in this chapter, and a detailed description of this mathematical approach is given by Dolan & More (2002).

Suppose that a set of N_{prob} problems and a set of S solvers are considered for applying performance profiles. In our study, this problem set corresponds to the collection of phase stability and equilibrium problems reported in Table 1, while the solver set is given by HSC, IHS and GHS. For these conditions, we establish a performance metric $t_{ij} \geq 0$ for every solver $i \in S$ and problem $j \in N_{prob}$. For example, this performance metric should give information on solver reliability, efficiency or another performance measure useful to characterize the capabilities of the solver under evaluation. For each problem $j \in N_{prob}$, we calculate

$$t_j^* = \min\left\{ t_{ij} \mid solver\ i \in S \right\} \tag{14}$$

where t_j^* is the best possible performance for problem j among all the solvers tested. For a particular solver i, the set of performance ratios σ_{ij} is determined by

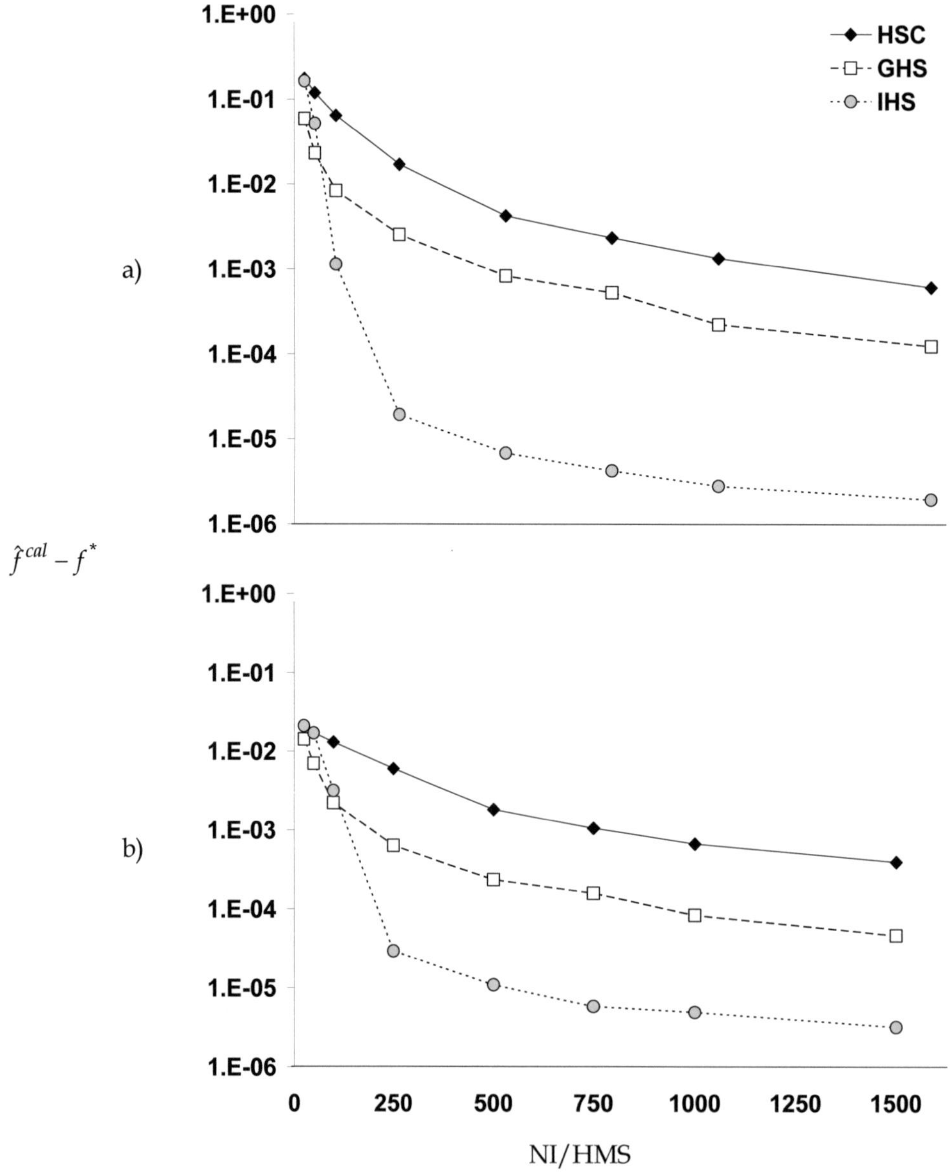

Fig. 2. Convergence profiles for solving phase equilibrium example No. 2 by HSC, GHS and IHS. Objective function: a) *TPDF* and b) *g*

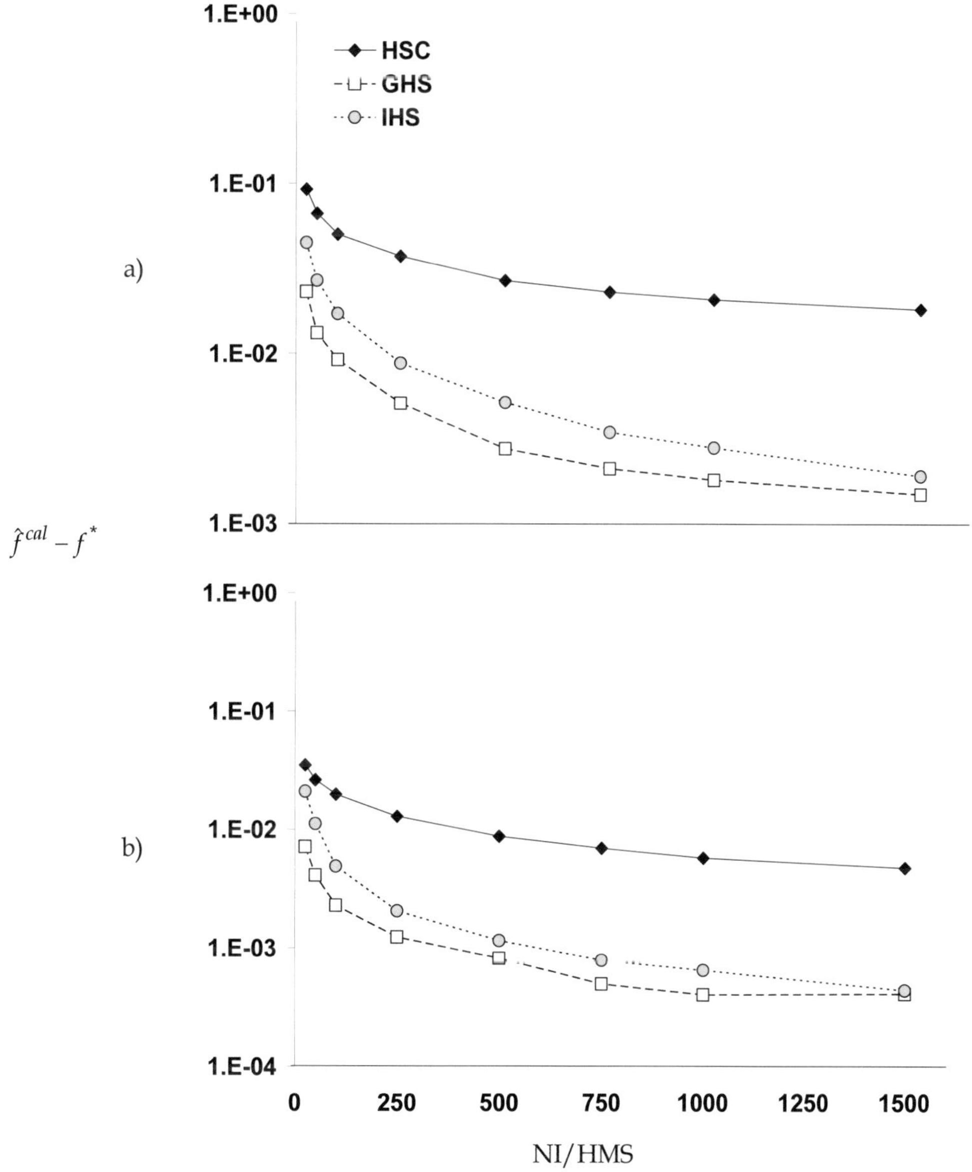

Fig. 3. Convergence profiles for solving phase equilibrium example No. 8 by HSC, GHS and IHS. Objective function: a) *TPDF* and b) *g*

$$\sigma_{ij} = t_{ij} / t_j^* \qquad j \in N_{prob} \tag{15}$$

where the performance ratio σ_{ij} of method i for problem j is defined as the ratio of the method's performance to the best performance value over all solvers for the same problem (Dolan & More, 2002). The value of this performance ratio is equal to unity for the solver i that performs best on a specific problem j. For every solver $i \in S$, let $\rho_i(\xi)$ be the fraction of problems for which $\sigma_{ij} \leq \xi$ where $\xi \geq 1$. Then, we have

$$\rho_i(\xi) = \frac{1}{N_{prob}} size\left\{ j \in N_{prob} : \sigma_{ij} \leq \xi \right\} \tag{16}$$

where the "size" is the number of problems such that the performance ratio σ_{ij} is less than or equal to ξ for solver i. The parameter $\rho_i(\xi)$ indicates the fraction of problems for which solver i is within a factor of ξ of the best solver (according to the performance metric used for solver comparison). In summary, the performance profile of a solver represents the cumulative distribution function of its performance ratios and is a plot of $\rho_i(\xi)$ *versus* ξ. It is convenient to note that $\rho_i(1)$ is the probability (i.e., fraction of problems tested) for which solver i was the best solver overall. Therefore, to identify the best solver using PP, it is only necessary to compare the values of $\rho_i(1)$ for all solvers and to select the highest one.
Base on the fact that, our study compares how well the HS methods can estimate the global optimum relative to another in phase equilibrium problems, we have used the following performance metric for a systematic assessment of HSC, GHS and HIS:

$$t_{ij} = \hat{f}_{ij}^{cal} - f_j^* \tag{17}$$

where f_j^* is the known global optimum of the objective function for problem j, which are reported in Table 2, and $\hat{f}_{ij}^{cal}$ is the mean value of the objective function calculated by the stochastic method i over 100 runs performed with random initial values for decision variables of problem j. This performance metric is useful to identify the algorithm that provides the most accurate value of the global minimum in phase stability and equilibrium problems. In fact, our group has successfully used this performance metric and performance profiles for comparison of several stochastic optimization methods in the context of phase equilibrium modeling (e.g., Bonilla-Petriciolet & Segovia-Hernández, 2010).
Figure 4 shows the results of $\rho_i(1)$ *versus* NI for HSC, IHS and GHS in phase stability and equilibrium calculations using Equation (17) as performance metric. Our results confirm that both GHS and IHS offer the best performance and show the highest probability for finding the best solutions in the collection of phase equilibrium problems used in this study. Figure 4 shows that the probability $\rho_i(1)$ of GHS is better than that obtained for IHS and HSC especially in early NI. However, this probability decreases as NI increased while IHS outperformed HSC and GHS in solving phase equilibrium problems if a larger NI is permitted. Note that HSC showed the worst performance for solving the global optimization problems analyzed in this chapter. Overall, PP indicate that the best solutions found by HSC are worse than the best solution found by both GHS and IHS in the global optimization of *TPDF* and *g*. In summary, GHS and IHS are the best from the standpoint of algorithm reliability and appear to be suitable for solving phase stability and equilibrium problems in non-reactive systems.

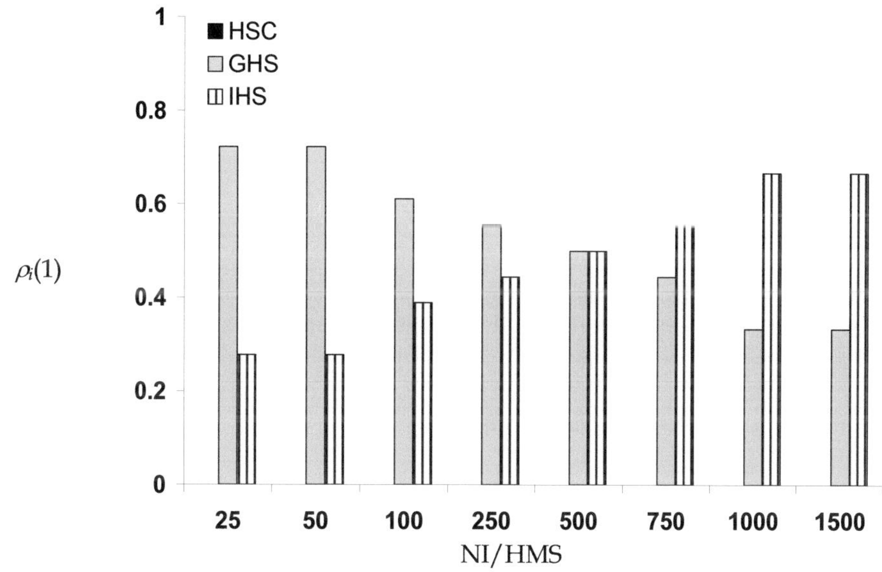

Fig. 4. Results of performance profiles for the comparison of HSC, GHS and IHS in phase stability and equilibrium calculations of non-reactive systems. Performance metric: $t_{ij} = \hat{f}_{ij}^{cal} - f_j^*$. Stopping condition is the maximum number of improvisations and HMS = $10n_{opt}$. The missing bars indicate that the probability $\rho_i(1)$ for solver i is 0.0.

Finally, we have compared the reliability of GHS and IHS in combination of a quasi-Newton method for solving these thermodynamic calculations accurately and efficiently. Specifically, the best harmony stored in harmony memory of both GHS and IHS is used as initial guess for a local optimization technique. This local optimization method corresponds to the subroutine DBCONF from IMSL library, where the default values of DBCONF parameters in IMSL library have been used in these calculations. Under these conditions, GHS and IHS are evaluated based on the reliability in locating the global minimum, which is measured in terms global success rate (GSR). This performance metric is defined as the number of times the algorithm located the global minimum to the specified accuracy out of all trials performed in the collection of phase equilibrium problems. Properly, in these calculations a trial is considered successful if the global optimum is obtained with an absolute error of 10^{-5} or lower in the objective function value, i.e. $\left| f^* - f^{cal} \right| \leq 10^{-5}$ where f^* is the known global optimum and f^{cal} is the solution provided by GHS or IHS method. In some examples, an absolute error of 10^{-7} in the objective function was used to avoid counting local minima as the global optimum.

In general, the GSR ranged from 70.8 to 73.8 % for GHS and from 70.1 to 70.7 % for IHS throughout the tested range of NI. Results of individual problems indicate that both GHS and HIS, each followed by the local optimization method, show high reliability for examples No. 1 - 4 and 8 in phase stability analysis, and examples No. 1 - 4 and 7 - 9 in Gibbs free energy minimization. Both methods failed several times to find the global optimum in phase stability examples No. 5-7 and 9, while phase equilibrium examples No. 5 and 6 are difficult global optimization problems for both HS-based methods.

5. Conclusion

This chapter introduces the application of Harmony Search-based methods for solving global optimization in phase equilibrium modeling of non-reactive systems. Specifically, we have compared the performance of classical HS and some of its variants for performing phase stability and equilibrium calculations. Our results indicate that HS-based optimization algorithms are capable of handling the difficult characteristics of global optimization problems in PEC. In particular, the Global-Best Harmony Search offers the best performance from the standpoint of algorithm reliability, whereas the classical Harmony Search method is the worst for performing the global optimization of objective functions involved in phase equilibrium modeling. In summary, our results indicate that GHS is a suitable and alternative global optimization strategy for phase equilibrium calculations in non-reactive systems. Further research will be focused on the application of this stochastic method in other thermodynamic calculations.

6. References

Balogh, J.; Csendes, T. & Stateva, R.P. (2003). Application of a stochastic method to the solution of the phase stability problem: cubic equations of state. *Fluid Phase Equilibria*, Vol. 212, No. 1-2, 257-267.

Biegler, L.T. & Grossmann, I.E. (2004). Retrospective on optimization. *Computers and Chemical Engineering*, Vol. 28, No. 8, 1169-1192.

Bonilla-Petriciolet, A. & Segovia-Hernández, J.G. (2010). A comparative study of particle swarm optimization and its variants for phase stability and equilibrium calculations in multicomponent reactive and non-reactive systems. *Fluid Phase Equilibria*, Vol. 289, No. 2, 110-121.

Bonilla-Petriciolet, A.; Vázquez-Román, R.; Iglesias-Silva, G.A. & Hall, K.R. (2006). Performance of stochastic optimization methods in the calculation of phase stability analyzes for nonreactive and reactive mixtures. *Industrial Engineering Chemistry Research*, Vol. 45, No. 13, 4764-4772.

Dolan, E.D. & More, J.J. (2002). Benchmarking optimization software with performance profiles. *Mathematical Programming Series A*, Vol. 91, No. 2, 201-213.

Floudas, C.A.; Pardalos, P.M.; Adjiman, C.S.; Esposito, W.R.; Gumus, Z.H.; Harding, S.T.; Klepeis, J.L.; Meyer, C.A. & Schweiger, C.A. (1999). *Handbook of test problems in local and global optimization*, Kluwer Academic Publishers, ISBN: 0-7923-5801-5, Netherlands.

Geem, Z.W. (2009). *Music-inspired harmony search algorithm theory and applications*, Springer, ISBN: 978-3-642-00184-0, United Sates.

Geem, Z.W.; Kim, J.H. & Loganathan, G.V. (2001). A new heuristic optimization algorithm: harmony search. *Simulation*, Vol. 76, No. 2, 60-68.

Grossmann, I.E. & Biegler, L.T. (2004). Part II. Future perspective on optimization. *Computers and Chemical Engineering*, Vol. 28, No. 8, 1193-1218.

Harding, S.T. & Floudas, C.A. (2000). Phase stability with cubic equations of state: Global optimization approach. *AIChE Journal*, Vol. 46, No. 7, 1422-1440.

Henderson, N.; de Oliveira, J.R.; Amaral Souto, H.P. & Pitanga, R. (2001). Modeling and analysis of the isothermal flash problem and its calculation with the simulated annealing algorithm. *Industrial Engineering Chemistry Research*, Vol. 40, No. 25, 6028-6038.

Hua, J.Z.; Brennecke, J.F. & Stadtherr, M.A. (1998). Reliable computation of phase stability using interval analysis: cubic equation of state models. *Computers and Chemical Engineering*, Vol. 22, No. 9, 1207-1214.

Jalali, F.; Seader, J.D. & Khaleghi, S. (2008). Global solution approaches in equilibrium and stability analysis using homotopy continuation in the complex domain. *Computers and Chemical Engineering*, Vol. 32, No. 10, 2333-2345.

Lee, K.S. & Geem, Z.W. (2005). A new meta-heuristic algorithm for continuous engineering optimization: harmony search theory and practice. *Computer Methods in Applied Mechanics and Engineering*, Vol. 194, No. 36-38, 3902-3933.

Lee, Y.P.; Rangaiah, G.P. & Luus, R. (1999). Phase and chemical equilibrium calculations by direct search optimization. *Computers and Chemical Engineering*, Vol. 23, No. 9, 1183-1191.

Mahdavi, M.; Fesanghary, M. & Damangir, E. (2007). An improved harmony search algorithm for solving optimization problems. *Applied Mathematics and Computation*, Vol. 188, No. 2, 1567-1579.

McDonald, C.M. & Floudas, C.A. (1996). GLOPEQ: A new computational tool for the phase and chemical equilibrium problem. *Computers and Chemical Engineering*, Vol. 21, No. 1, 1-23.

Michelsen, M.L. (1982). The isothermal flash problem. Part I. Stability. *Fluid Phase Equilibria*, Vol. 9, No. 1, 1-19.

Nichita, D.V.; Gomez, S. & Luna, E. (2002a). Phase stability analysis with cubic equations of state by using a global optimization method. *Fluid Phase Equilibria*, Vol. 194-197, No. 1, 411-437.

Nichita, D.V.; Gomez, S. & Luna, E. (2002b). Multiphase equilibria calculation by direct minimization of Gibbs free energy with a global optimization method. *Computers and Chemical Engineering*, Vol. 26, No. 12, 1703-1724.

Omran, M.G.H. & Mahdavi, M. (2008). Global-best harmony search. *Applied Mathematics and Computation*, Vol. 198, No. 2, 643-656.

Rahman, I.; Das, A.Kr.; Mankar, R.B. & Kulkarni, B.D. (2009). Evaluation of repulsive particle swarm method for phase equilibrium and phase stability problems. *Fluid Phase Equilibria*, Vol. 282, No. 2, 65-67.

Srinivas, M. & Rangaiah, G.P. (2006). Implementation and evaluation of random tunnelling algorithm for chemical engineering applications. *Computers Chemical Engineering*, Vol. 30, No. 9, 1400-1415.

Srinivas, M. & Rangaiah, G.P. (2007a). A study of differential evolution and tabu search for benchmark, phase equilibrium and phase stability problems. *Computers Chemical Engineering*, Vol. 31, No. 7, 760-772.

Srinivas, M. & Rangaiah, G.P. (2007b). Differential evolution with tabu list for global optimization and its application to phase equilibrium and parameter estimation problems. *Industrial Engineering Chemistry Research*, Vol. 46, No. 10, 3410-3421.

Sun, A.C. & Seider, W.D. (1995). Homotopy-continuation method for stability analysis in the global minimization of the Gibbs free energy. *Fluid Phase Equilibria*, Vol. 103, No. 2, 213-249.

Teh, Y.S. & Rangaiah, G.P. (2002). A study of equation-solving and Gibbs free energy minimization methods for phase equilibrium calculations. *Chemical Engineering Research and Design*, Vol. 80, No. 7, 745-759.

Teh, Y.S. & Rangaiah, G.P. (2003). Tabu search for global optimization of continuous functions with application to phase equilibrium calculations. *Computers Chemical Engineering*, Vol. 27, No. 11, 1665-1679.

Rangaiah, G.P. (2001). Evaluation of genetic algorithms and simulated annealing for phase equilibrium and stability problems. *Fluid Phase Equilibria*, Vol. 187-188, No. 1, 83-109.

Rangaiah, G.P. (2010). *Stochastic Global Optimization: Techniques and Applications in Chemical Engineering*, World Scientific Publishing Co., ISBN: 978-981-4299-20-6, Singapore.

Wakeham, W.A. & Stateva, R.P. (2004). Numerical solution of the isothermal, isobaric phase equilibrium problem. *Reviews in Chemical Engineering*, Vol. 20, No. 1-2, 1-56.

Xu, G.; Haynes, W.D. & Stadtherr, M.A. (2005). Reliable phase stability analysis for asymmetric models. *Fluid Phase Equilibria*, Vol. 235, No. 2, 152-165.

Zhu, Y. & Xu, Z. (1999). A reliable prediction of the global phase stability for liquid-liquid equilibrium through the simulated annealing algorithm: application to NRTL and UNIQUAC equations. *Fluid Phase Equilibria*, Vol. 154, No. 1, 55-69.

Zhu, Y.; Wen, H. & Xu, Z. (2000). Global stability analysis and phase equilibrium calculations at high pressures using the enhanced simulated annealing algorithm. *Chemical Engineering Science*, Vol. 55, No. 17, 3451-3459.